Mother Emanuel

Mother Emanuel

Two Centuries of Race, Resistance, and Forgiveness in One Charleston Church

❖ ❖ ❖

Kevin Sack

CROWN
NEW YORK

CROWN
An imprint of the Crown Publishing Group
A division of Penguin Random House LLC
1745 Broadway
New York, NY 10019
crownpublishing.com

Scripture quotations marked (KJV) are taken from the King James Version.
Scripture quotations marked (NIV) are taken from the Holy Bible, New International Version®, NIV®. Copyright © 1973, 1978, 1984, 2011 by Biblica Inc.™ Used by permission of Zondervan. All rights reserved worldwide. (www.zondervan.com). The "NIV" and "New International Version" are trademarks registered in the United States Patent and Trademark Office by Biblica Inc.®
Scripture quotations marked (ESV) are taken from the ESV® Bible (The Holy Bible, English Standard Version®), copyright © 2001 by Crossway, a publishing ministry of Good News Publishers. Used by permission. All rights reserved.

Copyright © 2025 by Kevin Sack

Penguin Random House values and supports copyright. Copyright fuels creativity, encourages diverse voices, promotes free speech, and creates a vibrant culture. Thank you for buying an authorized edition of this book and for complying with copyright laws by not reproducing, scanning, or distributing any part of it in any form without permission. You are supporting writers and allowing Penguin Random House to continue to publish books for every reader. Please note that no part of this book may be used or reproduced in any manner for the purpose of training artificial intelligence technologies or systems.

CROWN and the Crown colophon are registered trademarks of Penguin Random House LLC.

Library of Congress Cataloging-in-Publication Data is on file with the publisher.

Hardcover ISBN 978-1-5247-6130-1
Ebook ISBN 978-1-5247-6132-5

Editor: Kevin Doughten
Associate editor: Amy Li
Editorial assistant: Jessica Jean Scott
Production editors: Terry Deal and Craig Adams
Text designer: Aubrey Khan
Production: Heather Williamson
Copy editor: Rachelle Mandik
Proofreaders: Tracy Lynch and Chris Jerome
Indexer: J S Editorial, LLC
Publicist: Tammy Blake
Marketer: Mason Eng

Manufactured the United States of America

9 8 7 6 5 4 3 2 1

First Edition

Title page photograph: Shutterstock.com/Al Munroe
Page xi map illustration: David Lindroth Inc.

The authorized representative in the EU for product safety and compliance is Penguin Random House Ireland, Morrison Chambers, 32 Nassau Street, Dublin D02 YH68, Ireland, https://eu-contact.penguin.ie.

To the Emanuel Nine,

to the five survivors,

and to my three—Carol, Dina, and Laura Sack.

*Forgiveness is not an occasional act;
it is a permanent attitude.
This was what Jesus taught his disciples.*

—DR. MARTIN LUTHER KING, JR.
("Love in Action" sermon, 1962–1963)

Contents

	Map of Charleston	xi
I.	The Open Door	1
II.	The Tragedy	18
III.	Charleston's African Diaspora, Free and Enslaved	32
IV.	Church and State	44
V.	Richard Allen and the Insurgency of African Methodism	63
VI.	The African Church	85
VII.	Hot Bed: The Insurrection Plot	102
VIII.	Crackdown: The Vesey Aftermath	120
IX.	Revival: African Methodism Returns South	137
X.	Resurrection: A New Church Rises	160
XI.	Mother Church, and the Daddy of Reconstruction	180
XII.	The Long and Stormy Night	204
XIII.	B. J. Glover and the Gospel of Resistance	228
XIV.	The Movement Church	249

XV.	Clementa Pinckney and the Paradox of Black Power	273
XVI.	Judgment Day	295
XVII.	The Healing	310
	Epilogue: On Forgiveness and Grace	337
	Acknowledgments	355
	Pastors of Emanuel African Methodist Church	361
	A Note on Sources	363
	Interviews	367
	Notes	369
	Bibliography	431
	Index	447

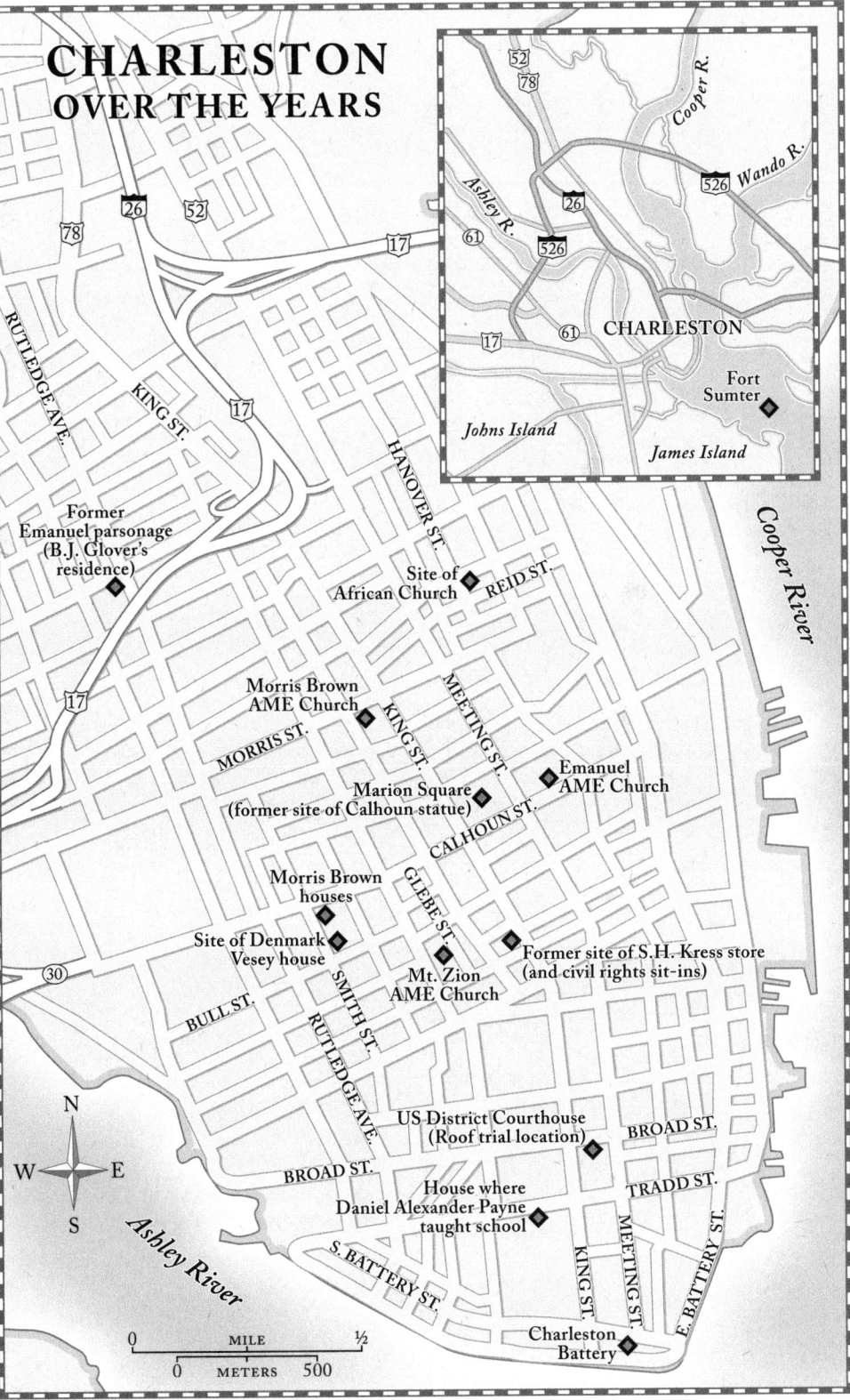

Mother Emanuel

I.

The Open Door

For in the day of trouble he will keep me safe
in his dwelling; he will hide me in the shelter of
his sacred tent and set me high upon a rock.

—PSALM 27:5 (NIV)

Preachers like to proclaim from the pulpit that the doors of the church are always open. As with so much that preachers proclaim, this can intend more than one meaning. It is on the one hand a spiritual invitation, a welcome, an insistence that there is but one body of Christ, and that all are encouraged to join it, the faithful and fallen alike, the well-heeled alongside the unwashed. Christian belief holds that it is never too late to walk the path of righteousness, or to pass through the gates of salvation. And while the physical church may keep office hours, the succor provided by faith and the embrace of fellow adherents is available at all times, or at least is supposed to be.

In the African American church, the open-doors metaphor conveys something extra, an assertion of defiance, and resilience. It is meant to affirm the place of the church as a refuge, both physically and spiritually, not just from the universal stresses of life but from the particular ones born of four hundred years of enslavement, repression, and state-sanctioned discrimination. In these sanctuaries, it is a vow that the people of God will not be cleaved from their faith or their hope, not by centuries of subjugation or the basest attempts at dehumanization, not by dynamite secreted beneath church stairwells or Molotov cocktails hurled through stained glass.

At the most historic Black church in the South's most historic city—Emanuel African Methodist Episcopal Church in Charleston, South Carolina—the gospel of the open door was not merely figurative. In the summer of 2015, it was not uncommon to find the weighty, wood-paneled double doors leading from the parking lot into the ground-level fellowship hall unlatched. They could be locked, of course, and a motion-activated security camera had been mounted recently above the doorway on a white stucco buttress. The imposing Gothic Revival edifice, built in the early 1890s, sat near the intersection of two busy downtown thoroughfares and a stone's throw from Marion Square, the city's central plaza. T-shirted tourists and College of Charleston students sometimes stumbled unwittingly into Bible studies and board meetings, and there had been concerns about homeless men seen wandering about. Nonetheless, the incessant activity in Emanuel's fellowship hall, the coming and going of members to seniors' luncheons and stewards' meetings and choir rehearsals, dictated that the doors be kept open much of the time. So it was on the unholy night of June 17, 2015, when hate walked in without knocking.

WHAT HAPPENED THAT NIGHT—the mass murder of nine innocent worshippers in one of the most horrific racist attacks in American history—catapulted "Mother Emanuel" to global prominence, its brilliant white façade and witch's-hat steeple recognizable around the world. What happened two days later, when victims' family members volunteered public expressions of forgiveness for the unrepentant killer, and two days after that, when ten thousand people of varied hues linked hands across the two-and-a-half-mile arc of the Ravenel Bridge, and five days after that, when the first Black president of the United States delivered a eulogy unlike any in the country's experience, made for defining markers in America's ongoing struggle with the psychosis of race. Once again, history had been made in Charleston, the slave port where nearly half of all captive Africans disembarked in North America and where the Civil War began at Fort Sumter.

Yet, unbeknownst to many, the oldest African Methodist Episcopal congregation in the South already had a backstory as remarkable as any of the nearly four hundred thousand church bodies in the United States, a captivating saga of resistance through faith that dated back two centuries. Charleston's African Methodists had been pummeled time and again by man and by nature and still they rose, ever resurrected. Whether the killer fully appreciated it—and the limited evidence is that he did not—it very much mattered that he had selected this church as his target. Without provocation, he had attacked a historically sacred space, not while people were protesting but while they were praying. It was an assault not merely on the nine faithful who died and the five survivors and their families, but on an entire community, an entire people, a symbolic genocide, at least in intent. Although the authorities would not formally label it as such, it was an act of domestic terrorism with few parallels in the nation's history.

By assailing a church, the killer connected his act to a long line of such desecrations, including the fatal bombing of Birmingham's Sixteenth Street Baptist Church in 1963 and arson attacks against dozens of Black churches in the mid-1990s. The shooter's target had been what Barack Obama, in his eulogy for Emanuel's slain pastor, would call "our beating heart, the place where our dignity as a people is inviolate." And yet, it had been violated, with premeditated deliberateness, a sickening rebuke to the fantasy of a "post-racial" America that briefly accompanied Obama's election. Even before the white suspect's identity and noxious rantings were discovered, it was clear that he had at least a surface understanding of the centrality of the Black church in the timeline of African American survival and self-determination. At some level, his purpose had been not simply to assail whichever Black people he happened to find inside. Rather, he took aim at the audacity of Black resistance to white supremacy, and the still-unrealized promise that 50 million African Americans might live without fear that their skin tone could cost them their lives. That threat had been real enough across nearly four centuries, in Charleston as elsewhere. Recent news of fatal shootings of unarmed Black men by white police officers, including that of Walter Scott two months earlier in neighboring North Charleston, had reinforced its durability.

As I came to learn about Emanuel AME while covering the aftermath of the massacre for *The New York Times*, it occurred to me that the journey that brought the church to that moment provided a unique vantage point, simultaneously microcosmic and panoramic, for surveying two centuries of African American life in Charleston and, by extension, across my native South. The church's very founding had been an act of insurgency. But its culture of defiance had fluctuated over time, the crosscurrents exposing how the struggle for racial dignity competed in dynamic tension with the instinct for racial self-preservation. Emanuel had been an incubator and an agitator over a continuum long enough to show the connectedness of eras and movements across a vast expanse of African American history, from enslavement and Reconstruction to Jim Crow and the Civil Rights Movement to the Obama presidency and the Black Lives Matter summer of 2020. In tracing the congregation's journey to June 2015 in the most caste-conscious of Southern cities—the center of the slave trade, the cauldron of nullification and secession, the birthplace of the Civil War—the epic tale of the Black church's role in America's uneven racial progress seemed to unfold all under one metaphorical roof.

It also seemed that by studying the church's historical and theological origins, and those of its denomination, one might better understand the grace summoned by those who so quickly voiced mercy for the twenty-one-year-old racist who had just slaughtered their loved ones. Many found it almost impossible to process, including devout Christians. What did it really mean in the context of the Black church and of Black suffering? Was it a show of radical Black love or of regressive Black accommodation? For those unable to grasp it, President Obama made clear in his eulogy—before awing the crowd with an a cappella rendition of "Amazing Grace"—that the watchwords of African American faith were best translated through the prism of four hundred years of struggle.

Nearly two centuries earlier, African Methodism had been established in Charleston in an unthinkably audacious act of mass subversion. The year was 1817, when Charleston was America's fifth largest city and, thanks to an abundance of captive labor, among its most prosperous. Charleston also was home to more than a thousand free persons of color. One of them, a mixed-race shoemaker named Morris Brown, led thousands of free and enslaved Black Carolinians in a walkout from white-controlled churches to protest indignities in governance and worship. They formed their own "African Church" and became the first congregation in the Deep South to affiliate with the nascent African Methodist Episcopal denomination, which had just formed in Philadelphia after a three-decade gestation.

Their gatherings came under immediate harassment from white authorities, and the church was destroyed after being linked to the plotting of an ambitious slave insurrection. Thirty-five of those arrested had ties of some kind to the church, and seventeen of them were executed, including the now-celebrated free Black man who was singled out as the ringleader, Denmark Vesey. The foiled uprising prompted a crackdown by white authorities that shaped the remainder of South Carolina's antebellum politics, producing early strains of the state's tendencies toward secessionism and vigilantism.

As soon as the Civil War receded, the congregation reconstituted during the spiritual land rush for nearly 4 million souls that followed emancipation. As the mother church of African Methodism in the South, Emanuel then seeded other congregations that transformed a barren region into the denomination's most fruitful terrain. Within fifty years, African Methodists had established nearly 650 churches in South Carolina alone, powering their spectacular growth into the nation's second largest Black denomination (behind only the Black Baptists). Today it claims more than 2.5 million adherents and 7,000 churches worldwide, and South Carolina—with more than 500 congregations—still boasts the densest concentration.

Those early churches, brick fortresses in city centers and clapboard chapels down backwoods lanes, became epicenters of African American life, creating rare spaces for leadership development, economic collectivity, and social cohesion in an otherwise disorienting world. They also played a leading role in the conversion of liberation theology into Black power, the jiu-jitsu by which Black Christians appropriated the faith of their oppressors to effect their own freedom. In AME thought, a believer's spiritual release from ignorance and sin went hand-in-hand with physical emancipation from enslavement and second-class citizenship. Through the church-based freedom movement of the 1950s and 1960s and beyond, AME congregations stood as exemplars of self-reliance, self-determination, and self-conscious striving. To critics who saw in the Black church an acquiescence to slave religion, African Methodists countered that the rapid expansion of a self-governing Black denomination in the American South was itself a revolutionary act.

Over the years, Charleston emerged as the regional capital of African Methodism, and Mother Emanuel rose as its cathedral. Through a series of dramatic episodes and larger-than-life leaders, the sturdy old congregation came to embody the perseverance of the Black church, and the underappreciated role played by the AME denomination, lauded by no less than W.E.B. Du Bois as "the greatest voluntary organization of Negroes in the world." There were few better models than Emanuel's first postbellum pastor, Rev. Richard Harvey Cain, who used the pulpit he built as a springboard into publishing, real estate, and politics, becoming one of the sixteen Black Southern Republicans elected to Congress during Reconstruction. The church's civil rights–era pastor, Rev. Benjamin J. Glover, simultaneously led the Charleston branch of the NAACP, helped integrate the city's schools, and made Emanuel a staging ground for mass meetings and marches.

"A sacred place, this church," Barack Obama said of Emanuel. "Not just for Blacks, not just for Christians, but for every American who cares about the steady expansion of human rights and human dignity in this country; a foundation stone for liberty and justice for all."

AND YET, AS MOTHER EMANUEL neared the bicentennial of her storied antebellum beginnings, the church's legacy alone could not overcome the forces draining its membership. With its congregation aging and its neighborhood gentrifying beyond affordability, it had been decades since the vast main floor and wraparound galleries had filled regularly on Sundays. Membership had dropped well below one thousand, and the Sunday tithers were far fewer. The physical manifestations were visible in the form of peeling paint, water stains, and burned-out bulbs, while a more insidious threat loomed in the attic and beneath the flooring: the church's thick wooden trusses had been so eaten away by termites and moisture that it was no longer particularly safe to occupy the organ loft.

The day of "The Tragedy," as Emanuel members can only bring themselves to call it, could not otherwise have been more typical. The door to the fellowship hall swung open over and again late that scorching June afternoon. First, members arrived for back-to-back meetings of committees overseeing fundraising and construction for the elevator being installed in the narthex. More showed up before 6:00 p.m. for the summer Quarterly Conference, a status meeting convened by the church's denominational supervisor, the presiding elder. That session would delay by two hours the start of the weekly Wednesday-night Bible study class.

Emanuel's pastor of the last five years, Rev. Clementa Carlos Pinckney, saw the installation of the elevator as central to unifying the congregation and filling the red-cushioned pews. He already had consolidated Emanuel's two Sunday services, at 7:30 a.m. and 11:00 a.m., into a single gathering that started at 9:30 a.m. That, naturally, had prompted grumbling from congregants who preferred the old times to the new one, or who simply could not tolerate change without having a say. As it was, the second-floor sanctuary could be reached only by climbing two steep flights or chancing a ride in a rickety motorized chairlift that ascended behind the altar, beneath a mural of a rising Christ. Every Sunday, dozens of elderly and infirm parishioners chose to watch on a closed-circuit monitor in the basement fellowship hall rather than with family and lifelong friends in the majestic space above. They would often be joined by a trickle of latecomers seeking to avoid notice.

The lack of an elevator caused special strains during funerals and wakes, leaving pallbearers to haul caskets up Emanuel's twenty-three concrete steps like crates of ore from a mine. Before ordering the new elevator, church leaders consulted with local undertakers to make sure it would accommodate the widest coffins they stocked. Finding the money for the project had taken two and a half years, but the $333,000 goal had finally been met. Amid some giddy self-congratulation, the fundraising committee decided that evening that it could dissolve after planning a "First Ride Party," with the honors taken by Pastor Pinckney and the church's nonagenarian members.

AS THE COMMITTEE MEETING WOUND DOWN, Myra Thompson hustled through the door right at 5:00 p.m. The images captured by Emanuel's surveillance cameras show her wearing a black suit and sunglasses, her shoulder-length hair streaked with gray. It was to be a big night for the former middle school English teacher and guidance counselor. Her license to preach in the AME Church was being renewed, an important step toward her goal of full ordination as a minister. Then she would lead Bible study for the first time, a responsibility she took so seriously she had barely left home during two weeks of preparation. Rev. DePayne Middleton, a Baptist minister who also was being licensed that night, walked in at 5:42 p.m., followed a minute later by seventy-year-old Polly Sheppard, a retired nurse and longtime trustee. Dressed in a gray tunic and flip-flops, Sheppard waved to the presiding elder, Rev. Norvel Goff, Sr., still seated in the black Cadillac he had pulled into the spot nearest the door.

Five minutes after that, Rev. Daniel Lee Simmons, Sr.—who had branded himself "Super Simmons" during several unsuccessful campaigns for bishop—stepped out of his silver Mercedes and grabbed an armload of books and papers from the backseat. The church had hired the seventy-four-year-old minister out of retirement as a part-time substitute for Pastor Pinckney, and he usually led Bible study on Wednesday nights. Simmons was the son of a preacher, a Vietnam veteran, and one of Greyhound's first Black bus drivers. He was licensed to carry a handgun and did almost everywhere, including to church, but left his weapon this evening on the front seat. Ever dapper in his trademark black fedora, he clicked the car door locked with an electronic key and strode toward the basement entrance. Others had been hanging out at the church for much of the afternoon, including Susie Jackson, the beloved eighty-seven-year-old matriarch of Emanuel's largest extended family, and Rev. Sharonda Coleman-Singleton, a promising young minister who doubled as a speech pathologist and girls' track coach at Goose Creek High School.

About sixty people attended the Quarterly Conference at 6:00 p.m. Pastor Pinckney and the conference secretary, Carlotta Dennis, who had been born into Emanuel sixty-two years earlier, joined Elder Goff at a rectangular table set before rows of seated members in the west half of the room. Four round plastic tables, the kind that could be collapsed and rolled into storage, awaited the start of Bible study in the east half. A bulletin board still celebrated the previous month's high school graduations, boasting senior pictures of three young women and three young men in caps, gowns, and tuxedos. The unremarkable fellowship hall had been the site of classes and club and board meetings for decades, even before being finished with linoleum flooring, thin paneling, and foam ceiling tiles. During the roiling Charleston summers of 1962 and 1963, it had served as the starting point for demonstrations by Black students seeking to desegregate downtown movie theaters, lunch counters, and clothing stores.

On one end of the hall sat a simple wooden altar, just before the pastor's office and the building's only ladies' room. On the other could be found a men's lavatory, so cramped it was difficult to sidle past the urinals, and an industrial-strength kitchen, where a committee of cooks turned out sumptuous bins of fried chicken, shrimp and grits, red rice, and collards. Steps away, in the base of the steeple, a pocket door slid open to reveal a closet-sized room holding a white marble crypt. In it lay the remains of Rev. Lewis Ruffin Nichols and his wife, Anna Elizabeth Nichols, Emanuel's pastor and first lady in the 1880s and 1890s, when the current edifice was built. Reverend and Mrs. Nichols had not rested in much peace since being reinterred there in 1952, as generations of impish children had made sport of shoving unsuspecting friends into the vault, flicking off the light, slamming shut the door, and waiting for the shrieks of abject terror.

The elder presiding over the Quarterly Conference, Norvel Goff, was new to his job of overseeing thirty-one African Methodist Episcopal churches in the marshy, briny, mystical swath of Carolina coastline known as the Lowcountry. Per AME practice, he would impose a precise order on the meeting, a method, as it were, that had been memorialized for nearly two centuries in the denomination's rule book, *The Doctrines and Discipline*. After an opening devotional and the approval of minutes, Elder Goff asked a prescribed series of questions, more than thirty in all. How many persons had been received into full membership in the last three months? How many members had died? How many marriages had been performed? How many baptisms? There were questions about budgeting and debt and Bible school attendance. Then the church treasurer read a financial report and Carlotta Dennis offered updates from some of Emanuel's manifold auxiliaries and clubs—the eight distinct choirs, the Women's Missionary Society and Young People's Division, the Lay Organization. There were four boards of stewardesses and three of ushers. The reports went on.

Eventually, the presiding elder opened the floor for comments and concerns. Under the hierarchical and authoritarian structure of the AME discipline, this was one of the few sanctioned vehicles for communicating pleasure or displeasure with church leadership. AME pastors were not called or chosen by their congregations, and technically did not answer to them. Rather, they were assigned to churches by the all-powerful presiding bishops in their districts, who enjoyed long tenure after winning costly, competitive campaigns. Once appointed by the bishop, pastors were endowed with substantial authority over congregations that had played little role in their selection, a recipe for tension from the outset. But they also received only annual renewable contracts from the bishops and so could be shuffled virtually at will. That gave disaffected congregants a pressure point to seek a pastor's reassignment. Those who had been around long enough, and plenty at Emanuel had, knew they might influence a bishop by opening their mouths and closing their wallets. The presiding elder served as the bishop's forward scout.

More often than not, the open comment period at a Quarterly Conference was used by the pastor's "amen corner" as an opportunity to flatter and fawn. But in a church as hidebound as Emanuel, with a congregation that had grown static and entitled over nearly two centuries, there were occasional airings of discontent. Emanuel's pulpit was about as prestigious a platform as existed in African Methodism. The church and its precursor had produced 5 of the 132 AME bishops elected to that point, and numerous contenders. Visiting speakers had included Booker T. Washington in 1909, W.E.B. Du Bois in 1921, and Martin Luther King, Jr., in 1962. But the church also had a reputation as a "pastor-killer," a place so immobilized by tradition that it eschewed modernization even as the congregation shrunk toward irrelevance. As the movement for racial equity moved away from the streets, Emanuel's identity had morphed into a stodgy conservatism. Sixty years after the evolution of church music into rock 'n' roll, electric guitars remained as unwelcome in the sanctuary as short pants. No matter the heat, dark suits and frilly hats remained in fashion. It was the old-timey hymns, like "My Hope Is Built on Nothing Less," that still roused this congregation from its seats. The members punctuated their singing with a syncopated "Charleston clap" (two soft beats, one louder one) that harked back to slavery-era ring shouts on the coastal islands and, before that, to the ceremonial rhythms of West Africa. Even the church's business calendar seemed preserved in amber, as Pastor William Smith discovered when he arrived in 1996 and proposed moving a monthly board meeting from Monday night to Tuesday.

"If Monday night was good enough for L. Ruffin Nichols," one member harrumphed, "why not for you?"

Because, the incredulous Rev. Smith pointed out, Rev. Nichols had been dead for nearly sixty years, and had not been pastor for more than a century.

"It's one of those churches," explained Rev. Joseph Darby, a longtime AME pastor and former presiding elder in the Lowcountry, "where drums came in late, where 'Amens' were welcomed but not overly encouraged. It's the age, the tradition. You have people who are third or fourth generation. And that's good, but it's also challenging because there's an atmosphere where there's devotion to the word of God, but also devotion to that congregation. They say, 'We've been doing it this long, it must be right.'"

Across two centuries, the average tenure for an Emanuel pastor had been only five years. "If we don't like a minister, we know how to get rid of them," acknowledged William Dudley Gregorie, a fifth-generation member and Charleston city councilman. Battered by relentless waves of church politics, Pastor Pinckney's predecessor, Rev. Stephen Singleton, had surrendered after five years and fled African Methodism altogether to start a nondenominational congregation. The pastor before him, Rev. Lavern Witherspoon, requested a transfer after less than two years, pleading exhaustion. He had been warned by his presiding elder, Rev. John H. Gillison, a former Emanuel pastor, that "you have to be on your Ps and Qs—make sure you're grammatically correct on Sundays or we will hear about it." That advice did not suffice. Before Witherspoon's departure, congregational leaders itemized their complaints in an eleven-page letter to the bishop, with forty-four bullet points. When the newly appointed Clementa Pinckney sought his counsel, Witherspoon cautioned that Emanuel could be a snake pit. Many of its people were wonderful, but the new pastor would soon discover a small but vocal cabal of committed dissenters. "When they talk it will be like they want to cut your head off," Witherspoon warned. "They're going to question everything you do."

ON THIS NIGHT, when Elder Goff opened the conference floor, sixty-two-year-old Theodora Watson rose from her seat holding handwritten remarks. Watson had joined Emanuel in third grade. After introducing herself as a member of the board of stewards and the director of Christian education, she moved to her point. "I am very passionate when it comes to the well-being of the children of this church," she told the presiding elder, "and I have not had the full cooperation of our pastor since he has been here. And it is time that you and members of this church know what is happening." She catalogued her complaints against Pinckney. The pastor had not preached at the baccalaureate service for high school seniors or dropped in on Vacation Bible School. Church programs always seemed to be scheduled in conflict with youth events. Then there had been her shouting match with the church secretary, whom Pinckney had hired.

If Watson's concerns sounded narrow, they were stoked by a broader frustration that had spread through the congregation like parking-lot gossip. The forty-one-year-old Rev. Pinckney simply wasn't around enough, many felt. Some considered him a part-time preacher pulling full-time pay. He preached on Sundays and met with parishioners by appointment but did not show up much during the week. Indeed, he did not typically attend Bible study on Wednesdays and had come this night, with his wife and the younger of their daughters, only because it would be unthinkable for a pastor to skip a Quarterly Conference with the presiding elder present.

There was good reason for all this. In addition to pastoring the mother church of African Methodism in the South, Clementa Pinckney also was serving his fourth four-year term in the state senate, following two two-year terms in the house. He had long been a prodigy, called to preach at thirteen, ordained at eighteen, and elected to the house at twenty-three, the youngest African American lawmaker ever seated in the South Carolina General Assembly. In both the pulpit and the well, he mesmerized listeners with a luxurious baritone that evoked both James Earl Jones and Barry White, a paternal trait that stretched back five generations. Fellow AME pastors considered him a surefire candidate for bishop down the road. Sometimes his name floated on lists of prospective candidates for Congress or even a statewide post, although the odds for a Black Democrat in conservative South Carolina could not have seemed longer.

The folks at Emanuel rather liked having a pastor who was so visible and connected, of course. But Pinckney's absenteeism chafed them as unbefitting a congregation of its standing. During legislative sessions, his responsibilities kept him at the Capitol in Columbia, a nearly two-hour drive northwest of Charleston. When in recess, he had to tend to the state's largest and most sparsely populated senate district, which sprawled two hours in the opposite direction from the church. His packed days and various responsibilities sent him ping-ponging across the state, often arriving late, sometimes barely before the end of a meeting he had called himself.

This day was no different. He rose well before dawn at his family home seventeen miles west of Columbia and drove to Emanuel for a 7:00 a.m. meeting about the church's property insurance renewal. The early start enabled him to speed back to Columbia to catch a morning Senate Finance Committee hearing in the Gressette Building, a blocky legislative office named for a late segregationist lawmaker. Although both houses were controlled by Republicans, the legislature had failed to adopt a budget on time and a special session had been called to circumvent a looming government shutdown. Pinckney planted himself on the top row of a horseshoe-shaped desk, five seats from the powerful chairman, and—as was his habit—listened to the largely technical discussion with little comment. Only twice did he ask to be recognized, once on a procedural question and once to remark that the $400 million appropriated to road building was "not going to be enough to do anything."

After lunch with fellow senate Democrats, Pinckney sat quietly through another half-hour committee meeting and a floor session that started at 2:00 p.m. He texted his wife, Jennifer, to warn that he might not have time to fetch her and their six-year-old daughter, Malana, for the drive back to Charleston, as planned. He knew, however, that they were counting on spending some quality time with him, even if while hurtling down Interstate 26 in his Toyota Highlander. So after informing the committee staff that he would miss a final session, Pinckney picked up his family and then headed toward Charleston, aiming to beat the presiding elder to Mother Emanuel. He promised Malana, the rambunctious daughter he called his "grasshopper," that they would stop by McDonald's for ice cream afterward as a reward for her forbearance.

From the road, Pastor Pinckney called Althea Richardson-Latham, the church secretary, whose shift was about to end. "You're late," she informed him, "and I don't have the agenda for the Quarterly Conference. Can you shoot it to me so at least I can get it ready?"

"I don't have one, it's in my head," the pastor explained. "Will you please stay until we get there so we can do it? I'll make it up to you." She rolled her eyes at the familiarity of it all and, as usual, agreed to stay.

Pinckney followed in a storied AME tradition of bi-vocational ministers who led in both the spiritual and political realms, seeing the roles as complementary. When he found time, which was not often enough, he had been researching a doctoral dissertation on that very topic—the "pastor/public servant" model of leadership—for a degree from Wesley Theological Seminary in Washington, D.C. Over the years, Pinckney had learned that AME politics could be as rough-and-tumble as those in Columbia. In the Capitol, at least, your enemies had the good grace to attack you behind your back. At Emanuel, your own people might do it to your face, in front of a crowd, while you sat next to your supervisor.

As Theodora Watson concluded her complaint at the Quarterly Conference about Pinckney's absenteeism, the pastor kept his head down and jotted on a sheet.

Carlotta Dennis could see that he had been blindsided. She reached for his hand. "Are you okay?" she whispered. "Everything all right?"

"No, Sister Dennis, I'm just taking notes," Pinckney replied, maintaining a cool façade. Elder Goff sensed the awkwardness and counseled the gathering that Watson had been within her rights. "Now, I don't want anybody talking about her," Goff said. "I didn't have to go in Piggly Wiggly or Walmart to hear it. I heard it right here."

The meeting broke near 7:30 p.m., and the Pinckneys escorted Elder Goff and his wife to their car. The pastor, who stood six-foot-one with broad shoulders, looked distinguished in a dark suit, a crisp, almost luminescent white shirt, and blue plaid socks—as put-together as some in his flock had ever seen him. He wore rimless glasses, a wispy mustache, and a dark wedge of beard on his chin. Pinckney guided his family back inside, then lingered on the step to chat with those leaving and others just arriving for Bible study. At 7:35 p.m., Cynthia Graham Hurd, another lifelong member, left her car wearing a lime-tinted sweater. A revered county librarian, she lugged a tri-panel display board, like the ones students used for science fairs. Pinckney stopped her at the door with a comforting smile. He wanted to see what she had.

The presentation was destined for an upcoming history fair at Magnolia Plantation & Gardens. That former slave labor camp, just north of Charleston along the Ashley River, had once generated immense wealth for the Drayton family through the cultivation of rice by captive Africans and their descendants. Over the last century, it had become a popular destination for nostalgic tourists, nature-lovers, and moss-draped weddings. Like other plantations in the area—Boone Hall, McLeod Plantation, Middleton Place—Magnolia had been working of late to interpret the stories of its enslaved people along with those of its enslavers, and so had invited Emanuel and other Black institutions to attend the fair.

As Hurd unfolded the display for Pinckney, he could see that it outlined the rich heritage of the place where they now stood. On the left and right sides were timelines showing the parallel evolutions of Emanuel and the African Methodist Episcopal denomination. Between them was a collage of dramatic photographs. One captured Emanuel's bleached exterior on a crystalline day, its steep brick buttresses etched against a cloudless sky. Another peered up at the arched stained-glass window that soared behind the altar, bookended by fading murals depicting the crucifixion and ascension of a distinctly pale Christ. Three of the sixteen window panels were lighter in hue than the others, as they had blown out during Hurricane Hugo in 1989 and been replaced with mismatched glass.

There was a picture of the golden-piped organ, "Big Bertha" as some called it, the envy of Charleston when installed in the choir loft in 1908. Wide-angle shots captured the chocolate richness of the oaken pews and pine floorboards beneath a barn-like tin ceiling. The interior was accented with loud swaths of pomegranate red—the well-worn carpet, trod each Sunday by those kneeling at the chancel rail; the pew cushions added in the 1980s to make three-hour services less punishing; the velvet curtain stretched behind the balcony balustrade to protect the modesty of the sisters above from the unwanted glances of the brethren below. Gas lamps remained mounted on columns above the pews, long retired but never removed. The seating capacity—635 on the main floor, and another 400 or so between the gallery and the fellowship hall—made it one of the most spacious churches in downtown Charleston.

Pastor Pinckney took in the display with a smile as the door continued to open. More folks were leaving than staying for Bible study. The Quarterly Conference had delayed things long enough that older members had grown weary or hungry, or wanted to make the drive back to North Charleston or West Ashley before nightfall. On an evening radiating with heat, Rev. Brenda Nelson, a member of the ministerial staff, sped to her house to meet an air-conditioner repairman. Seventy-four-year-old Willi Glee felt his stomach growling and left with his longtime girlfriend, Lois Gethers, to grab a bite at Ruby Tuesday on Savannah Highway. Pinckney propped the door open with his left hip. There was a farewell hug for Ruth Buck, a pat on the shoulder for Jean Ortiz, a wave to Carlotta Dennis, who was heading home to pack for a trip.

"Sister Dennis, I'll see you on Sunday," Pinckney said.

"Oh, no you won't see me on Sunday," she corrected. "I'm going to Chicago."

Pinckney lent a hand to eighty-three-year-old Ruby Martin, a retired principal, as she approached the step down to the parking lot. An Emanuel stalwart, she had devoted more hours to meetings like these than she cared to count but had reached her limit for one day.

"Sister Martin, go home and get out of this heat and get something to eat," Rev. Pinckney said in that booming voice.

She nodded at his colorful socks. "You are very sporty tonight," she teased.

He looked down. "Yes, I have on my happy socks. My kids bought these for me, so I have to wear them."

Few enough people remained that some wondered aloud whether Bible study should be scrapped altogether. Not many would have complained. But the occasion meant too much to Myra Thompson, who had set her mind on teaching from the book of Mark as her very first act of ministry. Her topic would be the Parable of the Sower, Christ's allegory about the nature of faith and humanity's receptiveness to the word of God. Thompson was known as a get-things-done perfectionist, particularly in managing the church's physical plant as the lay leader of the board of trustees. Although few institutions were more patriarchal than the African Methodist Episcopal Church, Emanuel had depended throughout its history on a legion of capable and devoted women like her. Thompson could be strong-willed—some might say bossy—and long-winded, the kind of talker who held you thirty minutes as you tried to escape her front door and then another thirty on the porch. After all her study and planning, Thompson wanted an audience, and wasn't above browbeating friends to make sure she'd have one.

Polly Sheppard made the mistake of going to the ladies' room at the same time as Thompson. They were close friends, so no words were minced.

"I know you're staying," Thompson said. "I would stay for you."

"No, I'm not staying," Sheppard answered. "I'm going home." Sheppard had stopped attending Bible study regularly after Rev. Simmons took over, chafing, like some, at his autocratic, table-thumping style. A diabetic, she had been at Emanuel for meetings since early that morning and had eaten only a few bites of someone else's sandwich for lunch. But she could feel Thompson's eyes follow her as she left the restroom, and grudgingly took a seat at the table closest to the door. She figured she'd slip out when Myra wasn't looking.

Cynthia Hurd, who juggled librarian jobs for the county and the College of Charleston, had planned to drop off her history display and depart. Instead, she bumped into her friend Felicia Sanders, who urged her to stay. The fifty-seven-year-old Sanders, a fourth-generation Emanuel member who presided over one of the usher boards, shared a pew with Hurd every Sunday morning. A hair stylist by trade, she was a Bible study regular, and had been joined of late by her high-spirited younger son, Tywanza Sanders, a recent college graduate. She'd also brought her granddaughter, Ka'mya Manigault, the daughter of her elder son. That child was one of roughly twenty kids—only some of them biologically connected—that Felicia and Tyrone Sanders had helped raise over the years.

Hurd apologized to Sanders for not being able to stay but got a glare in response. "I love you, Felicia Sanders," she offered meekly, hoping it might suffice.

"If you love me, you'll stay in Bible study," Sanders chided. The weary librarian took a seat and reached for a Bible.

Finally, near 8:00 p.m., Rev. Simmons opened with a hymn and a prayer for the twelve faithful who had stayed—eleven adults, ranging from twenty-six-year-old Tywanza Sanders to eighty-seven-year-old Susie Jackson, as well as eleven-year-old Ka'mya. Jennifer Pinckney did not think her fidgety child could sit still through the class, so they retired to the pastor's study. Those who remained were, as a prosecutor later observed, not the "Easter Sunday people" or even "the every-other-Sunday people," but rather "the every-Sunday-and-every-Wednesday people . . . the pillars of that church and the pillars of the community." Three were on the ministerial staff, while two others were working to become AME preachers. Another, Ethel Lance, the church sexton, took pride in keeping the leaky old building as clean and orderly as the scant budget allowed. Others were longtime church members who had held every imaginable leadership position. That didn't make them saints or mean they had lived uncomplicated lives. Among them could be tallied teen pregnancies, divorces, family estrangements, financial struggles, and all manner of heartbreak. But it did make them people who strove to live their faith, with humility, and who felt as sheltered and at ease in Emanuel's fellowship hall as they did in their living rooms.

Myra Thompson was sufficiently devoted to Emanuel that she had refused to abandon it during sixteen years of marriage to Rev. Anthony Thompson, the vicar of a Reformed Episcopal church just a few blocks away. She had been baptized into Emanuel at age ten, and it remained the anchor of her life at fifty-nine. After handing out copies of the study guide she had typed, Thompson led the group in opening their Bibles to Mark and began reading the first verse of Chapter 4. In the familiar parable, Jesus sits in a boat on the water and tells the crowd gathered on the shore about a farmer who ventured out to scatter seeds. Some fell by the wayside and were devoured by birds. Some fell on stony ground, where they germinated but withered in the sun. Some landed among thorns that choked the young plants. "But other seed," Thompson read, "fell on good ground and yielded a crop that sprang up, increased and produced: some thirtyfold, some sixty, and some a hundred."

What was Jesus trying to convey to his followers? After all her study, Thompson felt certain she knew. The soil "represents the human heart, the way we respond to the Word," meaning Scripture, she explained to her brothers and sisters in Christ. "The seed," she said, "represents the Word of God."

II.

The Tragedy

I was a stranger and you invited me in.

—MATTHEW 25:35 (NIV)

As Myra Thompson and her Bible students dissected the meaning of the Parable of the Sower, a black Hyundai Elantra pulled into the parking spot that had been vacated by Elder Goff's Cadillac. The nose of the car bore a decorative plate for the "Confederate States of America."

It was 8:16 p.m., but there still was plenty of daylight as the summer solstice approached. A scrawny young white man, 120 pounds slouched on a five-foot, nine-inch frame, stepped out of the car in scuffed boots. He had turned twenty-one two months earlier but looked no older than eighteen. He wore a gray long-sleeved shirt bunched over an untucked white tee, an odd choice given the heat and humidity. A bulky black tactical pouch flopped over the crotch of his dark jeans. He could have been any kid at the mall, distinguished only by an awkward mushroom-cap haircut and almond-colored bangs that hung to his eyebrows, obscuring his forehead. With little hesitation, Dylann Storm Roof unclicked his seat belt and stepped out of his car, pulling his pants up from the back as he walked to the unlocked door. He tested the right door handle and, when it didn't budge, pulled the left door open and strolled into Emanuel's fellowship hall.

Sharonda Coleman-Singleton, one of the assistant ministers, noticed him first. "Pastor, we have a visitor," she announced.

Clementa Pinckney met the stranger halfway to the tables. "Are you here for Bible study?" he asked gently.

The young man nodded, and Rev. Pinckney offered him the chair next to his, as well as a Bible and a copy of Thompson's study guide. For roughly forty-five minutes, the visitor sat in silence as Thompson paraphrased chapter and verse. "There are people whose eyes are opened but don't see a thing," she said. "Their ears are opened but don't understand a word. They avoid making an about-face to be forgiven." She paused: "The only way we can be forgiven is to accept Jesus as our Lord and Savior." The stranger mostly looked down, his eyes dark and empty, as if deliberating. At some point, Tywanza Sanders posted a snippet of smartphone video to his Snapchat page. It captured a frame of the white man's head before panning to the group's leader, Rev. Daniel Simmons. "Bible study knowledge planter," Sanders typed in white script against a ribbon of black.

Myra Thompson finally finished up around 9:00 p.m., and Rev. Simmons asked the group to stand for the benediction. They held hands around the tables and clenched their eyes as Simmons moved toward the group's traditional closing, the invocation from Genesis known as the Mizpah: "The Lord watch between me and thee when we are absent one from another." He was about to begin when the white man, still seated in a plastic-backed folding chair, unzipped his waist pack and removed a Glock .45 caliber semiautomatic handgun. He had purchased it two months earlier after receiving an IOU from his father on his twenty-first birthday for money toward a pistol. It held a thirteen-round magazine that had been loaded with eleven hollow-point bullets, and the pack also concealed seven other clips bearing eleven rounds each. That amounted to eighty-eight rounds in all, a figure with significance in white-supremacist numerology (the eighth letter of the alphabet being *H*, eighty-eight stood for "Heil Hitler"). Dylann Roof extended his right arm, just as he had practiced in the backyard of his mother's boyfriend's house in Eastover, near Columbia. He watched the red sighting laser dance across Clementa Pinckney's suitcoat and fired. As the pastor reeled, Roof fired again and again and again and again, the barrel recoiling with each touch of the trigger. The fatal round hit Pinckney in the back, piercing his lungs, aorta, and esophagus.

Eyes still shut, Polly Sheppard and Felicia Sanders both assumed the detonations must have been electrical explosions related to faulty wiring or the elevator installation. The building was 123 years old, after all. But as Sanders's eyes popped open, she saw the black object in the stranger's hand.

"He has a gun!" she screamed. "Everybody get under the table."

The Bible-study attendees scrambled to the ground, vainly seeking protection under cloth-draped tables. Daniel Simmons, the old army veteran, saw blood pooling beneath Clementa Pinckney and rose to his aid. "Let me check on my pastor," he said. "I need to check on my pastor." Roof was startled by his approach. He shot Simmons six times, ejected the magazine, and palmed in another. Then he methodically assassinated one helpless church lady after the next, striking each with at least five rounds. The shots reverberated continuously, as if fired from a machine gun, with only the slightest break as Roof reloaded six times. He fired the most hollow-points—at least ten—into the oldest victim, Susie Jackson, an usher and choir member who had walked in with a cane. Two others were at least seventy years old, and four were ministers. At one point, the gun jammed and Roof tossed the partly emptied magazine onto a tabletop next to a Bible, still opened to Mark 4.

The killer worked dispassionately but grew agitated at times. "See what you made me do," he chided Daniel Simmons as he lay dying, "see what you made me do? I didn't intend to shoot women and children."

Polly Sheppard lay on her stomach under a table, her head facing outward, and watched the killer's boots clomp from table to table. The shoes stopped in front of her, and she glanced upward. She saw the barrel pointed at her head and relaxed to await her deliverance. Ever the positive thinker, it occurred to her that at least she would not have to undergo chemotherapy for the cancer diagnosis she faced. She didn't realize it, but she was praying aloud.

"Shut up," the killer demanded. "Did I shoot you yet?"

"No," Sheppard trembled, her voice high-pitched and squeaky.

Roof seemed unnerved by her eye contact. "I'm not going to," he said, turning away. "I'm going to leave you here to tell the story."

Felicia Sanders, still thinking clearly somehow, had pulled her granddaughter down beside her under the third table. On one side, her aunt, Susie Jackson, lay motionless in blood-soaked white pants. On the other sprawled her wounded son, Tywanza.

"Granny, I'm so scared," the girl whimpered.

Sanders clutched the child so tightly she feared she might suffocate her instead of muzzling her. "Just play dead," she whispered. Her legs felt the sting of hot brass casings as they skittered across the linoleum, and she sensed a warm ooze to each side. Surreptitiously, she dragged her feet through the sticky pools, smearing the blood of her loved ones on her legs so the killer might think she had already been shot. She awaited her turn.

Tywanza Sanders knew that his mother and Polly Sheppard were still alive. Although bleeding, he propped himself up on one elbow, momentarily distracting Roof.

"Man, why are you doing this?" he asked.

"I have to do this," the killer explained matter-of-factly, "because you are raping our women and taking over the world."

"You do not have to do this," Tywanza pleaded. "We mean you no harm."

Roof would later confess that he knew his victims were innocents who had done nothing to merit their fates. They were merely collateral damage in the racial conflict he hoped to incite. But after months spent absorbing racist propaganda on supremacist websites, Roof had concluded that some white person needed to send a message. He shot Sanders repeatedly and walked away.

In his final minutes, Tywanza Sanders pulled himself across the floor, as if swimming against a current, grasping to reach the mortally wounded Susie Jackson. "Aunt Susie, Aunt Susie," he called. "I've got to get to Aunt Susie." He kept moving.

His mother tried to keep him calm. A few years earlier, after helping her through breast-cancer treatments, Tywanza had tattooed Felicia's name and the breast-cancer ribbon across his chest. He had ignored her warning that no woman would marry a man so indelibly inked to his mother. That, he had told her, would be the woman's loss.

"I love you, Mama," Tywanza managed.

"I love you, Tywanza," his mother sobbed.

"Aunt Susie," Tywanza continued. "I need some water. I can't breathe." He grasped for his great-aunt's gray hair and expired with a heave.

As Roof's boots moved away, Polly Sheppard reached for the cell phone that had fallen at her side. It was Ethel Lance's. After fumbling with the buttons, she managed to punch 9-1-1.

"Please answer, oh God," she whimpered, hyperventilating as the connection was made.

"9-1-1. What's the address of the emergency?" The operator was a young white woman.

"Please, Emanuel Church," Sheppard said. "There's plenty people shot down here. Please send somebody right away."

"Emanuel Church?"

"Emanuel AME. 110 Calhoun."

"And there's people shot?"

"Yes, he shot the pastor, he shot all the men in the church. Please come right away."

"Okay, my partner's going to be getting some help on the way while I get a little bit more information from you, okay? Stay on the line with me. Are you safe?"

"He's still in here. I'm afraid. He's still in here." Sheppard saw the boots moving back her way. "He's coming, he's coming, he's coming. Please . . . He's reloading." She kept praying. "Oh God, please. Help us, Lord. Please, Jesus, help us."

The man seemed to be muttering to himself. "My life has ended at twenty-one," he said.

In the pastor's study, Jennifer Pinckney and her daughter, Malana, could hear the executions being carried out on the other side of the wall. A school librarian, Pinckney had her laptop open, preparing for the next academic year, when the pop-pop-popping began. She cracked open the side door into the fellowship hall, realized there was gunfire, and closed and locked it without looking.

Malana stood up from watching cartoons. "Mama, what was that?"

Jennifer hushed her, grabbed her by the arm like a rag doll, pulled her into the adjoining secretary's office, and shoved her under the desk. After locking the door to the vestibule, she knelt in front of her. The child wouldn't stop talking.

"You have to be quiet," Jennifer told Malana. "Those are gunshots."

"Mama, what do you mean?"

"Shut up!" Jennifer Pinckney told her daughter with unaccustomed firmness. "Don't say anything. You've got to be quiet." Through the wall, she heard a groan and wondered if it was her husband of fifteen years.

Pinckney had left her cell phone in the other office. She reached for her daughter's hands. "If I hear the gunshots at a distance, I'm going to make a run for it," she said. "If I get out the door, lock it and hide. I love you, and tell your sister that I love her. I've got to make a run for it. I've got to get help."

But the gunfire only grew louder, closer. One round whizzed through the wall, near enough for Jennifer to feel the air move, and she scrambled to join Malana under the desk.

"Mama, is Daddy going to die?" the girl asked.

"Malana, be quiet. Don't say anything."

She put her hand over her daughter's mouth, and Malana did the same to her. The doorknob rattled, just feet away, and Jennifer Pinckney felt a chill streak down her body. This is it for us, she thought. But the lock did not give, and the killer chose not to waste a bullet on it. Pinckney heard the entry door to the parking lot click open. She crawled into the adjoining office, found her phone, slid back under the desk, and tapped 9-1-1.

There had already been an abundance of stupid luck working in Dylann Roof's favor. He had cased the church on six trips from his home near Columbia over the previous six months, but never on a Wednesday evening like this one. On one scouting visit, he would later tell the FBI, a woman outside had provided the start time for Bible study. Yet he did not even set out from Columbia—nearly two hours away—until 6:13 p.m. for a class that normally would have started at 6:00 p.m. and ended an hour later. Had it not been for the delay caused by the Quarterly Conference, which Roof could not have suspected, he likely would have found the church locked and empty. As it was, he happened upon a compact assemblage of trusting people, large enough but not too large, sitting distant from the exits. How did he bumble his way into such fortune? "There is always 'divine intervention,'" he wrote in a letter from death row in 2020. "Not that I believe in it."

The killer's luck continued as he left the fellowship hall. Assuming he would find the parking lot pulsing with blue lights, he had saved one magazine of bullets to take his own life before being captured or killed. He had posted a long note online to explain his purpose and knew the police would find it soon enough. Instead, at 9:06 p.m., fifty minutes after he had arrived, Dylann Roof pushed open the heavy church door, tentatively at first, then swinging it wide. He glanced right and left into the darkness, holding the superheated murder weapon at his right side. To his astonishment, there was not a cop in sight. Roof reached into his left pocket for his keys, slid into his car, and flicked on the headlights. He backed out in no particular hurry, cruised past the parked vehicles of his victims, and paused long enough to look both ways before taking a left onto Henrietta Street. One minute later, the first squad car arrived. After searching fruitlessly for the killer, and tending to Dan Simmons, who was still breathing, the officers called for body bags. Once Polly Sheppard and Felicia Sanders told their stories, the police issued an alert for a twenty-one-year-old white male with sandy blond hair. They also labeled the shootings a hate crime, although South Carolina was then one of five states (and one of only two as of 2024) without a law that augmented penalties for such offenses.

IN THE MONTHS BEFORE HIS ATTACK, Dylann Roof had done cursory internet searches for names and addresses of prominent Black churches across South Carolina. He scribbled a dozen on lined sheets of paper, places like Charleston's Morris Brown AME, Calvary Episcopal, and Central Baptist. He would later tell the FBI that he liked visiting Charleston and felt that its association with slavery would amplify the statement he hoped to make. Another page of jottings included the name "Denmark Vessey," a misspelled reference to the African Church member who died on the gallows after being convicted of plotting the 1822 slave revolt. A friend of Roof's would later inform investigators that Roof said one drunken night that he planned to shoot up a church that Martin Luther King, Jr., had visited.

But there is little evidence that Roof, who had been raised a Lutheran, had any deeper sense of Emanuel's history. After his arrest the next day in North Carolina, the remorseless killer explained to two FBI agents that he had read online that Emanuel "was a historic AME church," but he could not say what made it so. He told the agents he thought that AME stood for African Methodist Episcopal but wasn't completely sure. Roof, a high school dropout of considerable innate intelligence, eagerly acknowledged his white-supremacist beliefs and explained his purpose: to commit a retaliatory attack that would awaken Caucasians to the scourge he imagined of Black-on-white crime. White people had become second-class citizens in their own country, he told them, a country with a Black president. Only by agitating racial animosities and awakening the white population to its plight was there any hope of returning African Americans to their separate and properly subordinate place.

"What I did is so minuscule to what they're doing to white people every day," Roof told the agents.

They asked why he had chosen Emanuel. "I wasn't going to go to another church, you know, because there could have been white people there," he explained. Beyond that, the selection seemed just shy of random.

THE SHOOTINGS TOOK PLACE one day after the real estate mogul and reality television star Donald Trump descended the escalator in his eponymous Manhattan tower to announce that he was running for president of the United States. But it was the Obama era that the aftermath in Charleston would help define. The massacre inspired a Black president who had stepped gingerly around race to deliver his most pointed and meditative remarks on the subject. Its impact on the country's politics and hyperpolarized debates over race and guns has reverberated ever since.

Roof's trial in 2016 and 2017 produced the first federal death-penalty conviction in American history for offenses related to hate crimes. Two of the survivors, Felicia Sanders and Polly Sheppard, spoke at the 2016 Democratic National Convention to spotlight the party's position on gun control. In January 2024, Joseph R. Biden, Jr., became the first sitting president to speak at Emanuel when he delivered a campaign speech there about the "poison" of white supremacy. Four years earlier, at a critical juncture in his 2020 campaign, Biden had engaged in a poignant televised exchange about faith with Anthony Thompson, Myra Thompson's widower, helping him win the South Carolina Democratic primary and ultimately the presidency. That same year, the legendary civil-rights leader and congressman, Rep. John Lewis of Georgia, penned a deathbed essay that defined the murders of the Emanuel Nine as a cultural turning point. Along with the May 2020 police killing of George Floyd, an unarmed Black man in Minneapolis, the carnage in Charleston had revived the nation's awareness that racism remained vicious, virulent, and violent in a post–civil rights age. "If we are to survive as one unified nation," Lewis wrote, "we must discover what so readily takes root in our hearts that could rob Mother Emanuel Church in South Carolina of her brightest and best."

The killer's self-identification with Confederate symbols shamed South Carolina's Republican leadership into lowering the battle flag that had flown at the Capitol in Columbia for fifty-four years as an affront to the more than 25 percent of the state's population that is African American. That sparked a wildfire movement across the South to rid public spaces of memorials to the Lost Cause, prompting the toppling of statues from New Orleans to Richmond and the renaming of streets and schools. For a time, it seemed only slightly hyperbolic to suggest that the final shots of the Civil War had been fired in Emanuel's fellowship hall, four miles from Fort Sumter, 150 years after Appomattox.

And yet, perhaps the most searing legacy of the massacre came in the spiritual realm. On the night after the shootings, Chris and Camryn Singleton, the now motherless teenage children of forty-five-year-old Sharonda Coleman-Singleton, attended a tearful vigil in her memory at Goose Creek High School, where she had worked and coached. On their way out of the gymnasium, a

British television reporter, one of the scores of journalists who had descended on Charleston, thrust a microphone toward them and asked what they were feeling. Chris, a college baseball player as strikingly handsome as his mother, responded with unearthly poise. "We already forgive him for what he's done," he said, as Camryn nodded, "and there's nothing but love from our side of the family." To this day, Singleton cannot explain how those words came out of his mouth. Although he had attended Emanuel regularly as a child, he had spent more time in the pews scrolling through his phone than reflecting on the great theological questions. It was almost innate, a true "out-of-body" sensation, as if centuries of Black religious teaching had been distilled through spiritual experience, and he, an eighteen-year-old believer, had merely been designated the vessel. "It just happened," he said several years later, "zero premeditation. I wish I had a feeling that I was compelled to do it, but I didn't. I didn't have any of that. I wasn't thinking about the community. I wasn't thinking about anything. It just came out, which is unreal. There is no way in a million years someone could tell me I would forgive the person who murdered my mom. The reason I know it was God was because if it was fake there is no way I would still feel this way."

Two DAYS AFTER THE KILLINGS, as Charleston officials braced for the possibility of civil unrest, Roof made his first appearance at a state court bond hearing on murder counts for each of nine victims—Rev. Sharonda Coleman-Singleton, Cynthia Hurd, Susie Jackson, Ethel Lance, Rev. DePayne Middleton, Rev. Clementa C. Pinckney, Tywanza Sanders, Rev. Daniel L. Simmons, Sr., and Myra Thompson. Family members of the victims were invited to attend but received no warning that the judge would ask if they wished to be heard. Nor had it sunk in that the hearing would be televised worldwide. The slender defendant, swallowed by his striped prison jumpsuit, could be seen on a closed-circuit monitor from a holding cell, his hands cuffed behind him. Folded paperwork had been stuffed into his breast pocket. Two guards, one white, one Black, stood behind him wearing bulletproof vests and wary expressions. None of the nine bodies had been buried. A devastated nation watched on live television, desperate to understand how such hatred and heartlessness could reside in someone so callow and slight. But rather than condemn Roof to hell, the children and spouses of the dead rose one by one to offer a measure of forgiveness and mercy. They had not seen the Chris Singleton interview, nor consulted with one another, but they seemed to have been moved by the same ethereal force.

First came Nadine Collier, one of the daughters of Ethel Lance, the church sexton, wearing a scoop-necked green dress. Known for speaking her mind, Collier worried as she walked to the podium that any words she might summon would prove unfit for a courtroom. The emptiness she felt, and the fury, were indescribable. She really wanted to give this punk a piece of her mind. But she knew her mother would not countenance that, not today. She had only seconds to pull herself together, but it was enough for a power she can only identify as divine to take control.

Collier looked at the boyish face of evil on the screen. "I just want everybody to know, to you, I forgive you," she began, her calm giving way to soft sobbing. "You took something very precious away from me. I will never talk to her ever again. I will never be able to hold her again." She was wailing now. "But I forgive you. And have mercy on your soul. You've hurt me. You hurt a lot of people. But God forgive you and I forgive you." Roof looked ahead impassively, his eyelids sagging as if he might nod off.

Next up was Anthony Thompson, Myra's heartbroken widower, wearing his clerical collar. He had come to court after instructing his family that they would observe the proceedings but not speak, not to reporters, not to anyone. "I don't want y'all to open y'all's mouths and say the wrong thing," he had told them. "Can't take it back once you've said it." But when the judge asked if the Thompsons wanted to speak, he too felt overtaken. He detected a whisper, like the one he had heard as a child, calling him to preach. God, he felt, had something to say. He glanced at Roof and stood up as his children watched in amazement.

"I forgive you and my family forgive you," Thompson began, "but we would like you to take this opportunity to repent. Repent. Confess. Give your life to the one who matters the most, Christ, so that he can change it and change your ways no matter what happens to you and you'll be okay. Do that and you'll be better off than what you are right now."

He was followed by Felicia Sanders ("May God have mercy on you") and Alana Simmons, Daniel Simmons's granddaughter ("Their legacies will live in love, so hate won't win") and Bethane Middleton-Brown, DePayne Middleton's sister ("We have no room for hate, so we have to forgive and I pray God on your soul"). They did not speak for everyone, not within the church, not even within their families. Some detected in their leap to forgive the kind of shuffling accommodation at times associated with Charleston's Black community. Many could not find anything to absolve in Roof's hellish act, or any conceivable godly purpose in the taking of nine innocent believers. But it was nonetheless a breathtaking exercise of grace, a reflection of a Christianity so seemingly pure that few had ever witnessed it, much less experienced it. Many hearts softened, not just in Charleston but across the world, and anyone inclined to fan the embers of retribution found them quickly snuffed, even as outrage smoldered.

Some of the emotion on the streets was redirected into Sunday evening's walk across the Arthur Ravenel, Jr., Bridge, where an estimated ten to fifteen thousand people formed a "unity chain" in a pedestrian lane reserved for sightseers and joggers. The cable-stayed bridge, a Charleston landmark known for its diamond-shaped supports and dramatic views, is named for a former congressman and state legislator who advocated flying the Confederate flag and once referred to the NAACP as "the National Association for Retarded People." On this day, however, Black and white Charlestonians in gym shorts and running shoes embraced across Arthur Ravenel's bridge and held hands aloft through nine minutes of silence for the Emanuel victims. Drivers honked in solidarity as they cruised past. Boats bobbing in the Cooper River flew pennants declaring "Charleston Strong." At least temporarily, an act meant to divide had instead brought together a city whose history had been one of separation and subordination. The storyline of the Emanuel massacre was shifting from one of hate to one of love.

Future historians will debate whether that transcendent moment led to any meaningful narrowing of the Lowcountry's notorious racial inequities in education, housing, economic opportunity, and criminal justice. But by the time President Obama finished his melodic eulogy for Rev. Pinckney, a forgiveness narrative had been etched in stone. Mother Emanuel had become the forgiveness church, and Charleston a model for reconciliation, or so it was perceived.

Pinckney's service was held in the College of Charleston's TD Arena, around the corner from the church, to accommodate the expected throng of mourners and dignitaries. Its more than five thousand seats did not begin to fill the demand, and almost that many more watched outside on screens set up around town. Onstage, President Obama was backed by rows of AME bishops, resplendent in their purple vestments. Just beneath him rested Clementa Pinckney's brown wooden casket, polished to a gleam and blanketed in red roses. In the front row, scanning from left to right, Obama could see former Secretary of State Hillary Rodham Clinton, Rep. James E. Clyburn, United States Sens. Tim Scott and Lindsey Graham, Gov. Nikki Haley, Mayor Joseph P. Riley, Jr., Second Lady Dr. Jill Biden, Vice President Joe Biden, and First Lady Michelle Obama. Across the center aisle, six-year-old Malana Pinckney sat wrapped in her mother's arms, her bubblegum-pink sandals dangling just above the floor.

Obama had often struggled to find the proper balance of timing, setting, and message to address America's racial divisions. Intent on being perceived as a president for all and confronted with an urgent economic crisis, he approached racially charged matters with caution in his first term. He was less constrained after winning reelection in 2012, and could not help but take the Emanuel attack somewhat personally. It drove home what he and his wife had long sensed, that their ascension was itself a provocation that contributed, in Michelle Obama's words, to "a reactionary sense of fear and resentment" among extremists willing to use violence. "The hatred was as old and deep and dangerous as ever," she later wrote. Consequently, the president shed his reticence in Charleston and spoke with unusual—even acerbic—directness.

The words were all his. The night before Pinckney's service, Obama had taken his speechwriter's draft and drawn long diagonal lines through the last two pages before rewriting them in black ink on a yellow legal pad. In just a few hours, he rebuilt the scaffolding of the eulogy around one of his favorite hymns, "Amazing Grace," and the assertion of its English composer, the slave-trader-turned-clergyman John Newton, that "I once was lost but now am found, was blind but now I see."

Obama had been raised in Hawaii and Indonesia by a white mother who, although spiritual by nature, harbored a healthy skepticism of organized religion. He did not come to the Black church until he was well into his twenties, while working as a community organizer in Chicago. There, however, he learned the rhythm and idiom of the Black pulpit and came to appreciate the political, cultural, and theological import of African American congregations. Looking trim in a dark suit and steel-blue tie, he began by acknowledging that "our pain cuts that much deeper" because the murders were committed in church—"a place to call our own in a too often hostile world." Historically, he said, Black churches had served as "hush harbors where slaves could worship in safety, praise houses where their free descendants could gather and shout hallelujah, rest stops for the weary along the Underground Railroad, bunkers for foot soldiers of the Civil Rights Movement." Today they were "community centers where we organize for jobs and justice, places of scholarship and network, places where children are loved and fed and kept out of harm's way and told that they are beautiful and smart and taught that they matter." The mourners nodded and applauded in recognition.

It could not be known, the president said, how much of this the young killer understood. "But he surely sensed the meaning of his violent act," he said, lips pursed. "It was an act that drew on a long history of bombs and arson and shots fired at churches, not random, but as a means of control, a way to terrorize and oppress. An act that he imagined would incite fear and recrimination, violence and suspicion. An act that he presumed would deepen divisions that trace back to our nation's original sin."

Obama paused for effect.

"Ohhh, but God works in mysterious ways. God has different ideas. He didn't know he was being used by God." Blinded by hatred, Obama said, the killer could not see "the light of love that shone as they opened the church doors and invited a stranger to join in their prayer circle." He could not have imagined the response of the families or the people of Charleston. A placard placed near the podium punctuated the message: "Wrong church! Wrong people! Wrong day!"

Obama pivoted to his reflections on grace. Christian tradition, he explained, held that grace was not earned but rather was "the free and benevolent favor of God as manifested in the salvation of sinners and the bestowal of blessings." Through the tragedy at Emanuel, God had visited that grace upon the nation, he continued, "for He has allowed us to see where we've been blind. He has given us the chance, where we've been lost, to find our best selves. We may not have earned it, this grace, with our rancor and complacency, and shortsightedness and fear of each other—but we got it all the same."

It was now up to the nation to prove worthy of God's gift by awakening to racial injustices it had been too blind to see, including the pain caused by Confederate symbols and "the unique mayhem" inflicted by gun violence. It would be an expression of God's grace, Obama said, to take down the flag, to treat every child as important regardless of skin color, to remove bias from the criminal justice system, and to make "the moral choice" to change gun laws. This was a Black president giving validation to experiences that Black Americans understood too well. "Maybe we now realize the way racial bias can infect us even when we don't realize it," he said, "so that we're guarding against not just racial slurs, but we're also guarding against the subtle impulse to call Johnny back for a job interview, but not Jamal."

He quoted his regular pen pal, Marilynne Robinson, the Pulitzer-winning author of *Gilead* and other contemplative novels about faith, in defining grace as "that reservoir of goodness" that enabled humans to treat each other with extraordinary generosity. "If we can find that grace," he said, "anything is possible. If we can tap that grace, everything can change." He paused, shaking his head slightly, a preacher absorbing the Spirit. "Amazing grace," he intoned. "Amazing grace." Then he fell mute, holding the crowd captive to his silence as thirteen seconds ticked away. One of the bishops behind him, Vashti Murphy McKenzie, figured that Obama had lost his place on the teleprompter. But reaching for a soulful E flat, the president began to sing, almost imperceptibly at first. "*A-maaaa-ziiing grace* . . . " It took but a moment for the bishops behind him to catch on and for the organist to catch up. "Hah-hah," exulted Bishop Julius Harrison McAllister, Sr., waving his right hand to the heavens as he lifted himself to his feet. Most every mourner in the arena rose to join the president in warbling "*how swe-eet the sou-ou-ound.*"

Steeped in the theology and traditions of the Black church, Obama recognized that the grace volunteered at the bond hearing had grown organically from the fiber of African Methodism, a denomination two centuries old. The families' words may have sounded like a grant of absolution, or an earnest prayer for the soul of an unrepentant sinner. But they were more precisely heard as an iteration of a timeworn survival mechanism, a tactic that had helped African Americans withstand enslavement, forced migration, captivity, indentured servitude, segregation, discrimination, denial of citizenship, and the constant threat of racial and sexual violence with their souls still, somehow, intact. This, after all, had been the story of African people and their descendants in the South Carolina Lowcountry for nearly five hundred years.

III.

Charleston's African Diaspora, Free and Enslaved

Slaves, obey your earthly masters with respect and fear, and with sincerity of heart, just as you would obey Christ.

—EPHESIANS 6:5 (NIV)

A feat as improbable as the planting of an independent Black church in antebellum Charleston could only have been cultivated under the most fertile conditions. It was no coincidence that when African Methodism first took root in the South in the early nineteenth century, it did so in a majority-Black city in one of only two states where Black people outnumbered white ones. Nor was it accidental that the congregation materialized in the looser confines of an urbane seaport rather than on an isolated and tightly policed plantation. It also proved pivotal that Charleston was one of several Southern cities with three distinct castes—a dominant class of free white people, a subordinated one of enslaved Black people, and a legal and social purgatory occupied by people of color who had, by hook or crook, managed to escape bondage. These free Black people were the founding forebears of Mother Emanuel.

It was in 1526 that enslaved West Africans were first brought to the lush estuarine marshland that would become South Carolina, with perhaps as many as a hundred serving a Spanish exploratory expedition from the West Indies. They found the shoreline indented with bays and natural harbors, and a coastal plain thick with loblolly pines, spiny palmettos, and meandering oaks, their limbs bearded with Spanish moss. Stymied by inclement weather, inadequate supplies, disease, and the death of its commander, the mission lasted only a few months before the survivors retreated to Santo Domingo. That was long enough for the Spaniards' servants to mount the first act of Black resistance on Carolina soil, the torching of a hut housing the party's imperious leaders.

Not until 1670 did the first English settlers moor in the harbor they would name Charles Town in flattery of Charles II. The restored king had awarded a virtually unlimited grant for the exploration of lands between Virginia and Florida to eight politically connected investors who styled themselves the Lords Proprietors. The first of their ships to complete the voyage, a two-hundred-ton frigate christened the *Carolina*, arrived in April at the confluence of two rivers that would be named for one of the Proprietors, Lord Anthony Ashley Cooper. Between the Ashley and Cooper Rivers they found a low-lying foot-shaped peninsula of about eight square miles. A decade after settling on the west bank of the Ashley, they moved to the peninsula's strategically advantageous tip (today's Battery), which they named Oyster Point because of the mounds of bleached shells discarded there by Native Americans. Soon they plotted a grid of cross-stitched streets, contained within brick and earthen fortifications.

The settlers began importing a steady stream of Black laborers from islands like Barbados, which supplied Carolina with many of its early colonizers and became a model for its brutal plantation culture. Enslaved men and women also were traded from colonies in the North and then directly from Angola, Senegambia, the Gold and Windward Coasts, and elsewhere in West Africa.

With the introduction of rice cultivation in the Lowcountry at the end of the seventeenth century, shipments accelerated to supply the labor needed to clear swamps, build dikes, hoe fields, and thresh and husk the harvested grain. The development of indigo as a cash crop in the 1740s further stoked demand, as did the construction of the grand Georgian mansions rising south of Broad Street, a reflection of Charleston's immense early prosperity. What began as a relative trickle of imported captives grew to more than 1,000 a year by the mid-1720s, and to about 9,000 annually shortly before the American Revolution. Roughly 1 in 7 did not survive the nightmarish transatlantic crossing, which lasted more than a month, and many of those who made it to South Carolina perished soon after from smallpox and other diseases. But by the time the federal prohibition on foreign slave trading took effect in 1808, about 46 percent of the more than 350,000 Africans known to have been shipped to North America had entered through Charleston. In the final four years before the ban, South Carolina stood alone among states in continuing to import enslaved Africans and did so at record rates. After being quarantined, the captives were auctioned from ships moored at wharves jutting into Charleston Harbor, fetching thousands in today's dollars.

South Carolina reported having a Black plurality as early as 1708, the highest proportion in the thirteen colonies, with a census of 4,100 enslaved people of African descent, 4,080 white people of European descent, and 1,400 enslaved Native Americans. The first United States census, in 1790, found that Black people comprised 44 percent of South Carolina's population, still the highest proportion in any state, and 51 percent in Charleston. Charleston had far more Black residents—7,684 enslaved and 586 free—than New York, Philadelphia, and Boston combined. They became a majority in South Carolina by 1820 and remained so for another century, until Jim Crow drove thousands to points north during the Great Migration. Although some returned, African Americans made up only a quarter of the state's population in 2020 and less than a fifth of Charleston's.

As the racial imbalance widened in colonial Carolina, the fear of insurrection lodged in the white psyche like a fencepost. Starting with its first slave laws in 1690, the colonial assembly responded by designing an ever-tightening architecture of control, adding layers of repression, year after year, like a hardening callus. The rationale provided in its 1714 version could not have been more explicit: "The number of negroes do extremely increase in this Province, and through the afflicting providence of God, the white persons do not proportionably multiply, by reason whereof, the safety of the said province is greatly endangered." A later amendment to the slave law stereotyped Black people as "barbarous, wild and savage" and called for policing to "restrain the disorders, rapines and inhumanities to which they are naturally prone." It did so through a ticketing system that required the enslaved, when away from their owners, to present signed passes on request, and that permitted white people to assault and even kill them upon any show of resistance. It also regulated the pursuit of runaways, established a process for prosecuting and executing insurrectionists, and authorized regular searches of slave quarters for weapons. Even by the ethos of the day, Carolina's culture of forced labor and control struck visitors as particularly inhumane, with the murder and assault of enslaved servants all but sanctioned by law. "A poor Slavewoman was barbarously burnt alive near my door without any positive proof of the Crime she was accused of, which was, the burning of her Master's House," Francis Le Jau, an early Anglican missionary to South Carolina, wrote to superiors in 1709. The woman "protested her innocence even to my self to the last," he wrote.

Over time, new provisions extinguished any flickers of autonomy by limiting the ability of enslaved people to hire themselves out and by requisitioning their cattle and crops. Few activities were beyond the scope of white regulation. Enslaved people could not be sold alcohol or taught to write (although reading, seen as necessary for studying the Bible, was left unaddressed until the 1830s). They were prohibited from dressing "above the condition of slaves" and could not play drums or horns or possess horses, boats, or canoes. Charleston's slave ordinances banned public gatherings of more than seven (except for funerals), the smoking of pipes or cigars in public, walking with a cane unless necessitated by blindness or infirmity, and assembling for "dancing or other meriment [sic]." Any "negro or person of colour" found guilty "of whooping or hallooing any where in the city, or of making a clamorous noise or of singing aloud any indecent song" could receive up to twenty lashes.

To preclude any scheming that idleness might accommodate, the legislature curtailed the granting of Saturday afternoons off and encouraged constables to break up social gatherings on the Sabbath. In 1739, the assembly mandated that white churchgoers carry guns in case Black residents were tempted to mount a sneak attack on a Sunday. Visitors from Europe and the North frequently commented on the city's militaristic mood, particularly at nightfall, when drumming and bell-ringing announced a curfew for enslaved Charlestonians.

Capital punishment was sanctioned for a broad array of offenses, including a fourth conviction for petty larceny, a common enough crime in a stark world of haves and have-nots. Other crimes carried penalties designed to leave an imprint, like face-branding, nose-slitting, emasculation, ear removal, and, most utilized of all, barebacked whipping. Slaveholders who lost human property to execution or maiming typically were compensated by the government. The killing of an enslaved person carried no jail time, only a fine based on whether the act was willful or merely the result of "sudden heat or passion, or . . . undue correction." For those without the stomach for such "correction," the task could be outsourced to Charleston's infamous Work-House on Magazine Street. Wryly nicknamed the "Sugar House," the chamber of horrors featured a dungeon whipping room stocked with knotted lashes and a treadmill where chained inmates were made to grind corn for hours on end.

The paranoia of white South Carolinians about the prospects for Black rebellion was not without cause. Across the lifespan of American slavery there were more than 250 such uprisings and plots, all of them, of course, ultimately unsuccessful, according to historian Herbert Aptheker's 1943 book, *American Negro Slave Revolts*. Another historian, Peter H. Wood, argued in *Black Majority* in 1974 that Black resistance in antebellum South Carolina also took numerous other forms: verbal insolence, work slowdowns, malingering, crop destruction, theft, poisoning, arson, assault, self-mutilation, suicide, and, of course, escape. Advertisements offering rewards for runaways, who numbered in the thousands in South Carolina, spackled the front pages of Charleston's newspapers throughout the slavery years.

In the Lowcountry, the threat of insurrection became real with the emergence of a number of plots during the first half of the eighteenth century. The most robust happened on Sunday, September 9, 1739, when a band of twenty enslaved people assembled near the Stono River, twenty miles southwest of Charleston. They began by stealing weapons and ammunition from a shop and killing the two keepers. Then they marched south toward Florida, where the Spanish governor had promised freedom to escapees. They looted stores, set fire to homes, and murdered most any white person they encountered before being defeated in a firefight with a planters' militia. More than a dozen of the insurgents were killed and dozens more were captured and executed. But the Stono Rebellion also resulted in the deaths of more than twenty white people, and accounts of the terror spread breathlessly through South Carolina and up the seaboard. Such moments gave Black Carolinians a glimpse of the potential power of their overwhelming numbers, as well as of the ruthlessness with which white authorities responded to any threat. They would later turn to a less violent brand of revolt by leaving white churches en masse to form a congregation of their own.

IN MANIFOLD WAYS, the steepled cityscape of Charleston was uniquely suited to the founding of an autonomous Black church. Unlike the countryside, the city was home to a sizable population of free people of color who had been manumitted from bondage for either financial or benevolent reasons. Those enslaved in cities like Charleston, meanwhile, were allowed modest privileges typically not known on the plantations. In almost every aspect—severity of labor, ease of movement, financial wherewithal, exposure to ideas, quality of housing, clothing, and food—they tended to have advantages over their country neighbors. This does not suggest that anything about their lives was desirable, or that even free Black elites did not face considerable mistreatment, only that it might pale compared to the backbreaking toil, suffocating heat, and debasing conditions endured on plantations upriver.

Among the distinctions, of course, were the numbers. While a Lowcountry planter might enslave scores or even hundreds of laborers, city dwellers were more likely to have but a few. Yet slaveholding was pervasive in Charleston. In the 1820 census, more than three-quarters of the city's white heads of families listed at least one enslaved person in their households. By 1830, that figure approached 90 percent. Large holdings were not unknown, with 1 of every 7 white families enslaving at least ten people. Because males were sometimes sent to work on a family's farm, or sold or leased to a planter, the city's enslaved population skewed female.

They cooked and cleaned, laundered and sewed, polished and shopped, served as wet nurses and minded white children. The men landscaped and gardened, cared for horses and carriages, and served as coachmen and butlers. Children were used for tasks like shooing flies from the dinner table with peacock feathers or palmetto fronds. Others were bestowed upon teenage masters and mistresses as gifts, like prized hunting dogs. Unlike those who toiled under plantation overseers, city dwellers often were given broad responsibilities and a measure of independence. If they had a marketable skill, some were allowed to be hired out as carpenters, painters, porters, dressmakers, housemaids, mechanics, wheelwrights, brick masons, even fishermen, and might keep a share of their earnings. Some mastered the artisanry of ironworking, forging a legacy of ornate fencing and curlicued gates that remains central to Charleston's architectural mystique. Enslaved Black tradespeople in Charleston were required to wear copper badges stamped with their registration number and occupation—porter, fruiterer, servant, mechanic.

Those enslaved in the city typically lived in a room or two in airless outbuildings within walled compounds, separated from the main house by a yard or garden. They often were served from the same pantry, if not in the same quantities, as those in the manor house. The proximity and communal nature of housing kept these servants under close observation while at home, perhaps more so than on farms where slave quarters might be distant from the big house. But when hired out or tasked with an errand, they enjoyed a degree of self-reliance and could successfully disappear into a grog shop or grocery. That mobility, along with the availability of teachers, churches, newspapers, and books made literacy possible for some city residents.

By the time Charleston incorporated in 1783, it had become an impressively cosmopolitan city, afloat with commerce in goods, news, and ideas from across the seafaring world. Black Charlestonians could not be sequestered from either the hum of activity or the loudening calls for slavery's abolition. Not only was Charleston then the young nation's fourth most populous city, behind only New York, Philadelphia, and Boston, it also served as the region's capital of culture and trade. Like most seaports, Charleston was a polyglot place, settled by Anglicans and Scottish Presbyterians but also by French Huguenots, Quakers, German Palatines, and Sephardic Jews, along with Africans and Native Americans. The trade in cotton, rice, indigo, and humans had made it the most affluent city in colonial America, and home to some of its most aristocratic families. On the eve of the Revolution, 9 of the 10 richest men in British North America came from Charleston or its surrounding parishes. Its free citizens enjoyed an average net worth that was nearly six times that of Philadelphians, seven times that of Bostonians, and eight times that of New Yorkers. On both sides of the Atlantic, the city earned a reputation for its opulence, frivolity, and European tastes. Even at the onset of the Civil War, the per capita wealth of Charleston's free people—boosted by the value of their unfree people—was still three times that in Massachusetts, New York, and Pennsylvania.

The fortunes of the city's leading families grew not only through commerce but also through intermarriage, and an insular and exclusive social elite formed to protect its own interests. Over the centuries, that insularity—and an intense resistance to racial and economic change—would stifle Charleston's growth and leave it lagging behind upstart competitors, including other cities in South Carolina.

Antebellum Charleston could be at once elegant and roughhewn. Some of the finest homes in America rose south of Broad Street, including Charleston's distinctive multistoried "single houses" with their breeze-catching piazzas. But elsewhere tenements teemed with working-class white and free Black people, and the poorhouse was oversubscribed with paupers. The climate could only be described as pestilent, and the city combatted repeated outbreaks of yellow fever, smallpox, malaria, influenza, cholera, and other plagues well into the twentieth century. At times, childhood mortality ran as high as 80 percent.

Hurricanes and fires regularly flattened the landscape, as would a catastrophic earthquake in 1886. The suffering almost always landed hardest on the enslaved and the poor, broadening the receptivity of Black Charlestonians to the balms of Christianity.

From the start, the life of the city was inseparable from its churches, and steeples and bell towers remain Charleston's most recognizable landmarks. In the 1680s, the Anglicans built a modest structure of black cypress—St. Philip's—at the southeast corner of what are now Broad and Meeting Streets. By 1700, the Congregationalists, Huguenots, Baptists, and Quakers each had established congregations as well. After outgrowing its space, the St. Philip's congregation moved in 1723 to the site it still inhabits on Church Street, between Cumberland and Queen, and built a domineering brick cruciform that was later plastered in sand-colored stucco. In 1761, the diocese opened a grand new church, St. Michael's, on the former site of St. Philip's. Its white wedding-cake bell tower and steeple served as a beacon for harbor navigators and as a watchtower in wartime. The church today anchors Charleston's "Four Corners of Law," with the other quadrants of Broad and Meeting occupied by city hall, the Charleston County courthouse, and the U.S. courthouse and post office (which shares its architect, John Henry Devereux, with Mother Emanuel).

As a colony and into its early statehood, South Carolina would be known for its religious diversity and comparative religious liberty. Among those found in the churches of its various denominations were Charleston's free people of color, who would eventually tire of accepting second-class citizenship in white-governed places of worship.

IT IS NOT CLEAR when the first free people of color appeared in colonial South Carolina, but records suggest their presence by at least the turn of the eighteenth century. One of the colony's earliest slave codes, enacted by the assembly in 1712, explicitly exempted from its proscriptions those "negroes, mulatoes, mustizoes or Indians" who had been "made and declared free," a stance that would change soon enough. Their numbers remained small through the American Revolution, with the 1790 census finding 1,801 free persons of color among South Carolina's 249,073 residents, or seven-tenths of 1 percent. More than half lived in the Lowcountry, with most in Charleston proper, where 586 free men and women accounted for 3.6 percent of the city's 16,359 residents and 7 percent of its Black population.

Virginia, Maryland, and North Carolina had much larger numbers of free people of color. But those in Charleston, like those in New Orleans, played outsized roles in the city's antebellum life. Their interests—and actions—did not always align with those of their enslaved countrymen. Indeed, they at times distanced themselves from their social underlings in seeking the privilege and safety of white association, and in emulating white norms. But it was their independence, resources, and gumption that ultimately made possible the development of many of the first Black institutions in the South, including an independent and self-governing African Methodist Episcopal church in Charleston.

Charleston's free people of color became so in a variety of ways. Some were born free or had gained their freedom in England or the West Indies before seeking a fresh start in America, including refugees from the slave revolution in Saint-Domingue. Others had been enslaved but were permitted to hire themselves out and, after paying owners a negotiated share of their earnings, accumulated enough savings to bargain for their freedom. The prospects for manumitting a full family dimmed when members were enslaved by different owners, as was often the case. Some enslaved people were granted liberty as a reward for faithful service, perhaps after they had aged past utility or when their enslavers died. On occasion, they were freed by the government after providing an essential or heroic service, like extinguishing a fire or fighting Spanish or Native American raiders. Their owners were reimbursed from the public treasury.

But the largest component of Charleston's free people of color consisted, of course, of the sexual victims and consorts of white Carolinians and the generational offspring of their miscegenation. As many as one-third of recorded manumissions in colonial South Carolina may have been mixed-race children, and three-quarters of all adults who were freed were female. By 1860, 3 of every 4 free persons of color in the Charleston district were classified by the government as "mulatto," compared to fewer than 1 in 10 slaves.

South Carolina's colonial government recognized early on that free people of color posed complications of both logic and security for a caste system based on pigmentation. It soon began using its frequent enactments "for the better ordering and governing of Negroes and other slaves" to regulate free Carolinians of color along with enslaved ones. South Carolina's colonial assembly started trying to control the growth of the free Black population as early as 1722, when it ordered newly manumitted slaves to leave the state within a year. The state restricted private manumission in 1800, and all but suspended it in 1820 by requiring legislative approval on a case-by-case basis. It also banned free persons of color from crossing into South Carolina. A humane exception was allowed for those unfortunate enough to wash up on Carolina's shores after a shipwreck, with the understanding that they would make their way out within a month.

Unlike their captive countrymen, free Black Carolinians could work for their own wages, wander Charleston's muddy streets without a pass, and purchase real property, including fellow humans. Indeed, there were at least three dozen free people of color who enslaved other Black people in Charleston in 1790 and more than 250 in 1830. By the 1740s, however, Carolina's lawmakers had started to delineate the rights of free Black people from those of their free white counterparts. Over time, they constructed a Byzantine netherworld in which these purportedly free citizens were denied the ability to vote, hold office, sit on juries, testify in court, or bear arms. They eventually would be required to have white guardians and be barred from schooling and worship without white supervision. Onerous "capitation taxes" were purposed to drive them from the state. Although not constitutionally devalued to three-fifths of a human, these "slaves without masters," in the coinage of historian Ira Berlin, nonetheless embodied the essential contradiction of their young nation, that its fight for independence had only translated into full freedom for some.

Despite this unequal treatment, Charleston's free Black community expanded after the Revolution at a substantially faster rate than either its white or enslaved populations. The city had 3,237 free persons of color on the eve of the Civil War, a nearly sixfold increase over a seventy-year span, making them 8 percent of the population. They supplied the Lowcountry with many of its skilled tradesmen—carpenters, tailors, seamstresses, shoemakers, draymen, cooks, butchers, barbers—presenting walking contradictions to white myths about Black indolence and ineptitude. Naturally, the community's self-identification grew along with its numbers. For many in its moneyed classes, it seemed more important, or perhaps just more realistic, to maintain their status above the enslaved than to aspire to full citizenship. "Status differences continually eroded the bonds of racial unity and turned free Negroes and slaves against each other," Berlin wrote. "In the eyes of some free Negroes, the degradation of the slave elevated their status just as the degradation of all blacks elevated the status of all whites."

Accustomed to rejection, and fearful of white backlash, Charleston's free people of color kept a low profile and moderated their demands, at least initially. In 1809, for instance, a group of twenty-nine prominent free Black Charlestonians, including hotelier Jehu Jones and carpenter Richard Holloway, asked the legislature to exempt them from paying the annual $2 "capitation tax" levied on free persons of color. Among the signatories were a shoemaker named Morris Brown and a tailor named Charles Corr, who would soon be central to establishing the "African Church," Mother Emanuel's predecessor. The petitioners did not take the opportunity, however, to argue that the tax was inherently discriminatory. Rather, they only complained that it resulted in double taxation for those free people of color like themselves who happened to also own taxable property. Predictably, their request was summarily rejected and the tax remained a burden until the end of the Civil War.

There was a degree of social striving as well, with skin tone often the determinant of status. In 1790, five free Charlestonians of color formed the Brown Fellowship Society, the first and most prestigious of an array of philanthropic clubs for the mixed-race elite. All were congregants at St. Philip's Episcopal Church, which allowed them to be baptized and married but not to be buried in the oak-shaded cemetery (where John C. Calhoun and founding fathers like Edward Rutledge and Charles Pinckney would later repose). Conceived as a burial and benevolent society for widows and orphans, the group modeled itself self-consciously after similar white clubs in Charleston, seeking members of both financial and moral standing. Among them would be Charles Corr and Malcolm Brown, Morris Brown's son.

The society's formation institutionalized the color-based classism that long remained a stubborn fixture in Charleston's Black community. Although its bylaws did not specifically reference complexion, its members were almost always of mixed race. Other organizations would follow, including the Friendly Moralist Society and the Humane Brotherhood, which catered to darker-hued freemen not welcomed by the Brown Fellowship Society. Over the years, Charleston's Black churches would not prove immune to the toxicity of caste, as the Baptists, Catholics, Congregationalists, Episcopalians, Methodists, Presbyterians, and African Methodists each established discrete congregations for their lighter-skinned elites.

The benevolent societies founded by Charleston's free people of color served as precursors of sorts to the development of the city's first Black church. They set a precedent for collectivity and tested the limits of white permissiveness toward Black assembly and solidarity. If the church's free Black founders expected, however, that the same permissiveness would be extended to an autonomous Black religious congregation, a congregation that would serve the enslaved along with the free and disseminate the gospel of God's love for all men and women, they badly miscalculated. Many white Carolinians had long been wary of introducing their enslaved people to their faith. Despite its civilizing intent, they feared that Christianity could prove exceedingly dangerous in the wrong hands.

IV.

Church and State

*My doctrine shall drop as the rain,
my speech shall distil as the dew;
as the small rain upon the tender herb,
and as the showers upon the grass.*

—DEUTERONOMY 32:2 (KJV)

From the earliest days of permanent European settlement in South Carolina, a century and a half before Mother Emanuel's origins, the religious instruction of enslaved Africans posed an absurdist—and consequential—predicament for its white colonists. Despite their lengthy cohabitation, Christianity and slavery had always made for uncomfortable bedfellows. For all the scriptural references to slaveholding, for all the assurances of religion's sedative effects, the owners of America's chattel recognized that Christianity, left unchecked, could encourage a subversive egalitarianism. In colonial America, it was well understood that religion's power for good also threatened the white supremacist underpinnings of the developing nation's farm-based economy and caste-based social structure.

Central to evangelical Christianity's mass appeal was the assertion of its holy texts that God was no respecter of persons, that the faithful were as equivalent in the eyes of the divine as paper dolls in a chain. Think what you might about the prophetic curse of Ham. There was no bar to eternal salvation beyond belief, not on the basis of color or class or even past sin. That God was the master of both enslaver and enslaved suggested a fundamental equality, at least in the next life if not on Earth. If little else, the church acknowledged the essential humanity of those in bondage, and recognized that their degraded condition did not render them soulless. That made it perplexing that an omnipresent and benevolent deity would countenance the oppression of one race by another in God's kingdom on Earth.

This was a dangerous reckoning in a colony where the enslaved so outnumbered the white population. But as organized religion found revival through the Great Awakening and beyond, that wariness among white Carolinians coexisted in tension with the scriptural imperative to cast God's word broadly. And so until slavery's dying days, South Carolina's leading white churchmen reinterpreted the Gospel to reaffirm the racial status quo. The conversion and cultivation of "heathens" became a perverse justification for slavery, and Southern preachers willfully misrepresented human bondage as a natural state that benefitted the captive as well as the slaveholder. It was, in its own convoluted way, diabolically cunning as a means of enforcing lines of caste and power and wealth. In the American South, the Christian ministry, as moral arbiters of the prevailing class, blessed white supremacy by insisting that the Bible of the exodus and the resurrection demanded subordination rather than liberation. For those in bondage, it seemed a dissonant takeaway from the hopeful origin stories of an anointed people's miraculous escape from captivity and the supernatural resurrection of the crucified Christ.

As the white church prostituted the Gospel, legal strictures were devised to control the means by which Black Americans received it, so that worship services and camp meetings would not become pretenses for insurrectionist scheming. Among the most concerning aspects of slave religion to white Southerners was its association with literacy, which posed obvious risks. As it happened, three of the most fearsome slave insurrection plots on American soil would be associated with literate men who drew inspiration from Scripture—Gabriel Prosser near Richmond in 1800; Denmark Vesey in Charleston in 1822; and Nat Turner in Southampton County, Virginia, in 1831. By 1850, every slaveholding state had erected barriers to the free practice of religion by enslaved people, with many banning assemblies altogether or requiring white supervision. In South Carolina, a statute enacted in 1800 made it illegal for "slaves, free negroes, mulattoes or mestizoes, even in company with white persons, to meet together and assemble for the purpose of mental instruction or religious worship" between sundown and sunrise. Daytime gatherings could not be held behind locked doors, even with white overseers in attendance. Those provisions would be relaxed at times at the urging of white ministers, and laxly enforced at others. But they effectively restricted Black South Carolinians to worshipping in churches that were under white control and supervision.

Even before the *Carolina* arrived from England in 1670, Charles II and the

Lords Proprietors had prescribed the religious character of the new province, including for enslaved and indentured laborers. In the first of two charters, the king charged the overseas venture with promoting "the propagation of the Christian faith, and the enlargement of our empire and dominions." Among the vast powers he conveyed to the proprietors was the licensing of churches.

The proprietors themselves addressed slave religion in a draft governance document, authored by John Locke, known as the Fundamental Constitutions. Although never ratified by the colonial populace, it served as a statement of values and guidance on all manner of legal and political matters during South Carolina's pre-constitutional period. Its provisions required an acknowledgment of the existence of God and established the Church of England as the colony's official tax-supported denomination. It also conveyed an unusual level of religious tolerance so as not to discourage immigration by dissenters.

The Fundamental Constitutions explicitly granted freedom of religious choice to enslaved men and women who otherwise enjoyed little personal agency. The document made it equally explicit that those rights did not extend beyond the meetinghouse door. Until Virginia closed a loophole in 1667, slaves there had occasionally sued for their freedom after converting to Christianity. In Carolina, there would be no such misunderstanding. The constitutions and later statutes specified that baptism might convey freedom from sin, but not from captivity. "It shall be Lawful for slaves and all others to enter themselves and be of what church any of them shall think fit and best and thereof be as fully members as any freeman," the proprietors decreed. "But yet no Slave shall hereby be exempted from that civil dominion his master has over him but be in all other things in the same state & condition he was in before."

Carolina's early planters tended to be more concerned with the productivity of their enslaved people than with their piety. Some feared that schooling of any kind, and particularly in Old Testament concepts of justice, would inspire their servants to become "proud and Undutifull," as Francis Le Jau, the Anglican missionary, put it, encouraging fantasies of manumission, desertion, and revolt. They also questioned whether Africans had the capacity to learn or appreciate the Gospel. "Many Masters can't be persuaded that Negroes and Indians are otherwise than Beasts, and use them like such," Le Jau wrote to superiors in 1709. Le Jau, who was posted in Goose Creek, north of Charleston, complained about hostile planters who denied him access to slave cabins.

Rather than challenge them on moral grounds, he promised to not baptize enslaved men and women without first requiring them to swear to their understanding that it would not bring them freedom. It was an early manifestation of competing Christian prerogatives. The missionaries could only fulfill the calling of slave conversion with the acquiescence of white enslavers. But white trust could only be gained through the corruption of Christian values. In the slave states, the churchmen realized, proselytization would have to be sold as a mechanism for profitability and control.

By the dawn of the eighteenth century, church leaders in England were growing concerned that resistance from white planters in the colonies was impeding the Christianization of the slave population. In 1701, they founded a missionary wing, the Society for the Propagation of the Gospel in Foreign Parts (SPG), with the charge of converting Native Americans and enslaved Africans in the colonies. If success was measured by the number of souls saved, the SPG had little to show after three decades. In a trove of letters, the missionaries complained of their struggles against sin, disinterest, and disease. In 1727, the Anglican bishop of London, Edmund Gibson, acknowledged his frustration about "how small a Progress has been made in a Christian Country, towards the delivering those poor Creatures from the Pagan Darkness and Superstition in which they were bred." Although he encouraged compassionate treatment of the enslaved, he noted that any corporal punishment that might be inflicted would pale "compar'd to the Cruelty of keeping them in the State of Heathenism."

Eight years later, and still facing dismal prospects, the SPG assigned a pair of Oxford-educated brothers to the thankless task of ministering to the colony being settled by the British social reformer James Oglethorpe, at Savannah, eighty-five miles south of Charleston. Envisioned as a fresh-start refuge for imprisoned debtors and persecuted sects, Georgia was to be the first new British colony in North America in fifty years, and the last. It also would be the only colony that prohibited slavery, at least until Parliament lifted that ban in 1751.

The sibling ministers joined Oglethorpe, a family friend, on his second voyage to Savannah, which began in October 1735. The elder, at age thirty-two, would serve as the colony's chaplain, and his twenty-seven-year-old brother as Oglethorpe's private secretary and "Secretary of Indian Affairs." Their names were John and Charles Wesley, and despite a markedly unsuccessful mission to the South they would later build on their experience to forge the Methodist movement into the most popular American Protestant denomination of the nineteenth century. By midcentury, Methodism would claim more than a third of the country's church membership. Nearly 15 percent of its members were Black at that point, with about double that proportion in the South, most of them enslaved.

JOHN AND CHARLES WESLEY were the fifteenth and eighteenth of the nineteen children of Samuel Wesley, the Anglican rector of Epworth, a town in Lincolnshire, and his wife, Susanna. Ten of the children survived infancy. Slightly built, John Wesley had dark, wavy hair that fell to his shoulders. He wore it parted down the middle to frame an expansive forehead and aquiline nose. Charles shared his brother's nose and bulbous chin but had a blockier face and slightly shorter hair. In 1729, while at Oxford, the Wesleys and two friends formed a religious society that met several nights a week to study Scripture and the Christian philosophers. Seeking to emulate the primitive faith of the antiquities, they complemented their studies with fasting, intensive prayer, and a commitment to Christian deeds, like preaching to inmates. They did not abandon Anglican ritual. But they did ascribe free will to those who, through acts of self-sanctification, might gain an understanding of God and a true, liberating faith. The self-consciousness of their piousness drew mockery. Fellow students derided the Wesleys' band as "The Holy Club," "The Sacramentarians," "The Enthusiasts," and, finally, "The Methodists," a commentary on the rigid and abstemious discipline they practiced, religiously and personally.

Upon arriving in Savannah with Oglethorpe in February 1736, the Wesleys began ministering to five hundred colonists who were at the work of transforming a dense coastal forest into a grid of stately residential squares. By April, John Wesley had convened a society of twenty to thirty white worshippers who met at his home several times a week "to reprove, instruct, and exhort one another." Charles, meanwhile, was stationed in the nearby settlement of Frederica. The regular meetings they held presaged the Methodist class system, with adherents assigned to small groups, headed by lay leaders, for weekly prayer and mutual support. When attendance was negligible in Savannah, as it often was, John traveled by foot, horseback, and piragua through frost-rimed swamps, preaching wherever he found open ears. Such itinerant evangelism also became a hallmark of the Methodist brand.

In a frontier colony populated by ruffians and dissenters, both brothers faced stiff resistance to their heavy-handed evangelizing. It did not help that they came off as insufferable scolds, and were perceived as meddlesome and self-important. The Wesleys also found few opportunities to fulfill their assigned mission to convert Native Americans and enslaved Africans. Before landing in America, John and Charles had little direct exposure to the slave trade, and abolitionist thinking was rare on either side of the Atlantic. Because slavery was temporarily banned in Georgia, their only meaningful exposure while in the colonies came during trips to Charleston. They were not fully prepared for the barbarity they encountered, but their firsthand witness would profoundly influence Methodism's early stands on slavery and race.

In his journal, Charles Wesley wrote that he had learned of an endless number of "shocking instances of diabolical cruelty which these men (as they call themselves) daily practise upon their fellow-creatures, and that on the most trivial occasions." He shuddered at seeing white children who possessed slaves their own age "to tyrannize over, to beat and abuse out of sport," as if in apprenticeship. He related that slaves were nailed up by the ear to be whipped and scalded, and that others had legs amputated and teeth extracted as punishment. In one incident related to him, an enslaved woman was horsewhipped to the edge of death and then doused with hot sealing wax. "Her crime," Wesley wrote, "was over filling a tea-cup."

The brothers' first visit to Charleston was in the summer of 1736, when they sailed north so that an ailing and despondent Charles might seek passage back to London. The day after their arrival, John Wesley preached to a crowd of three hundred at St. Philip's at the invitation of Rev. Alexander Garden, the Anglican bishop's representative in the Carolinas. Wesley noted with pleasure that the worshippers included "several negroes," one of them a woman who related that she had been instructed in Christianity by her late mistress. But upon deeper examination, Wesley found her training unacceptably thin. He asked the woman if she understood what religion was, or a soul. She said she did not.

"Do not you know there is something in you different from your body?" the preacher prodded. "Something you cannot see or feel?"

"I never heard so much before," she said.

"Do you think, then, a man dies altogether as a horse dies?" Wesley asked.

"Yes, to be sure," the woman responded.

Wesley took the exchange as a distressing indicator. "Oh God, where are Thy tender mercies?" he pleaded in his journal. "Are they not over all Thy works? When shall the Sun of Righteousness arise on these outcasts of men, with healing in His wings!"

Wesley had a similar experience when he returned to Charleston in April 1737. Then he encountered an enslaved woman named Nanny, the property of a fellow minister, who told him she had regularly escorted her mistress's children to church but had been taught little while there. Wesley tried to convey the basics of the Christian contract, offering the hope of an unshackled afterlife, no doubt an enticing prospect. "If you are good," he told Nanny, "when your body dies your soul will go up, and want nothing, and have whatever you can desire. No one will beat or hurt you there. You will never be sick. You will never be sorry any more, nor afraid of anything."

John Wesley's final trip to Charleston marked his departure from America after twenty-two months. He left Savannah with his fledgling ministry in disarray, skipping town half a step ahead of the law. He had denied Holy Communion to a woman whose affections he had lost to another man, and she and her husband had pursued his indictment for defamation. A grand jury tacked on charges for a series of ecclesiastical innovations, like reordering the Anglican liturgy, dipping infants for baptism, and preaching to wives and enslaved people without regard for the "commands of their respective husbands and masters." Clearly, Wesley had outstayed his welcome, and on December 2 he secreted himself out of Savannah against a court's clear instructions. Three weeks later he had made his way to Charleston and found a berth home.

On the transatlantic voyage, a fast-tracking storm tossed the ship violently and Wesley, like others on board, found himself fearful for his life. The experience crystallized that his faith was not yet absolute. "Let death look me in the face, and my spirit is troubled," he realized. "Nor can I say, 'To die is gain'!" Five months after John's return to London, however, he experienced the light of conversion that had escaped him in America. While listening to a reading from Martin Luther at a prayer meeting on Aldersgate Street, he found himself suddenly overcome by rapture. "I felt my heart strangely warmed," he wrote of his Aldersgate experience. "I felt I did trust in Christ, Christ alone for salvation; and an assurance was given me that He had taken away my sins."

In the decades that followed, the Wesleys refined the raw material mined from their adventures in the American South into a new alloy of Christian practice. Their most fundamental theological difference with the Anglicans and prior reformers like Luther and Calvin grew from their skepticism about predestination, and their conviction that God's salvation and grace were available to all believers. Other key components of Wesleyan heterodoxy included a palpable conversion experience, infant baptism, and a direct relationship with God. Liturgical innovations encouraged extemporaneous preaching, emotional, even ecstatic, forms of worship, and prayer through song, eschewing the gilded rituals and rational sermonizing of the high church. Methodism, it was said, was Christianity in earnest. The Methodists insisted on strict order in governance, subdividing congregations, or societies, into twelve-member classes, which doubled as collection agencies for weekly offerings. Despite the challenges posed by eighteenth-century travel and communications, the Wesleys devoted themselves to global evangelism (John famously said he looked "upon all the world as my parish") and enforced discipline through regular connectional gatherings. They published prolifically. And in clear counterpoint to the Anglican church of kings and queens, they stirred the oppressed and laboring classes through tireless itinerant preaching and fiery, plainspoken language. They baptized slaves, elevated women as exhorters and lay preachers, and became early and ardent abolitionists.

ONCE METHODIST CIRCUIT RIDERS began disseminating Wesleyan thinking in the second half of the eighteenth century, their empathy for the dispossessed and uncompromising stance against slavery endeared them to both free and enslaved African Americans. Methodism's imposition of order on a deeply disordered world carried great appeal. But as slavery took firmer hold in the South, dividing the emerging American confederation, the Methodists found that their antagonism toward it stymied their growth in regions where they otherwise enjoyed bright prospects. The retreats they fashioned, along with other insults directed at Black members, eventually repulsed African American Methodists into creating an independent church.

Unlike the Calvinists, who held that individuals were predestined to salvation or damnation as the price for original sin, the Methodists suggested that the oppressed bore no responsibility for their condition. Even more promising, those in chains enjoyed the free will to gain deliverance in the afterlife through absolute faith and Christian acts. If the promise of ultimate justice centered more on heaven than earth, it at least provided a lifeline to be grasped. "I ask you if dere ain't a heaven, what's colored folks got to look forward to?" a formerly enslaved South Carolinian named Anne Bell once asked (in dialect as transcribed by her interviewer with the Federal Writers' Project). "I 'umbles myself here to be 'zalted up yonder."

The Wesleys' searing experiences in South Carolina clearly shaped the Methodists' early positioning on race. In *Thoughts Upon Slavery*, an unsparing abolitionist essay published in 1774, John Wesley recounted the castrations and immolations, the whippings and wound-salting, and contrasted it to the palliative effects of Christianity on plantations where the enslaved had been indoctrinated. Unusually for the times, he did not simply take the position that conversion made for a more dutiful servant. He instead drew a moral line, not only against the slave trade, which he labeled "that execrable sum of all villanies," but also against white supremacy. Both, he argued, violated not only concepts of justice inherent in natural law but also the clear intent of Jesus Christ concerning the treatment of "the least of these."

"Arise and help these that have no helper, whose blood is spilt upon the ground like water!" Wesley prayed at the close of his essay. "Are not these also the work of thine own hands, the purchase of thy Son's blood?" He may not have fully appreciated the implications, but the democratization of Christianity that he advocated would inspire new liberationist interpretations of the Gospel.

Wesley spoke truths to white power that landed like heresy. "Certainly the *African* is in no respect inferior to the *European*," he contended. "You first acted the villain in making them slaves, (whether you stole them or bought them.) You kept them stupid and wicked, by cutting them off from all opportunities of improving either in Knowledge or Virtue: And now you assign their want of Wisdom and Goodness as the reason for using them worse than brute beasts!"

"Liberty," Wesley concluded, "is the right of every human creature, as soon as he breathes the vital air."

For all their evangelistic spirit and outrage over slavery, the Wesleys never ventured back across the Atlantic. The task of translating their beliefs and practices for the American frontier therefore fell to protégés. The most significant was a fellow Holy Clubber named George Whitefield, who had been mentored at Oxford by the Wesleys. A theatrical orator, Whitefield made seven wide-ranging trips to the colonies between 1738 and 1770, including several eventful visits to Charleston. He became America's most celebrated evangelist, preaching variants of the reformist Methodist message hundreds of times to massive crowds. That included African American listeners, who delighted in the animation and emotion of the evolving Methodist pulpit style. One of Whitefield's earliest Black converts, a freeman named John Marrant, later told of happening upon a packed Charleston church one evening when Whitefield was preaching. "I enquired what it meant, and was answered by my companion, that a crazy man was hallooing there," said Marrant, who was thirteen at the time. Undeterred, Marrant pushed his way inside and shortly found himself so thunderstruck by the power of Whitefield's sermon that he collapsed, "speechless and senseless near half an hour," revived only by smelling salts and a splash of water. "Jesus Christ has got thee at last," Whitefield assured Marrant after the service.

Whitefield, who became a central figure in America's first Great Awakening, had an ambiguous history with African Americans that vexes his biographers. He sought them out on his peripatetic journeys, negotiating with slaveholders to preach in their quarters, and they flocked to his revivals. He became convinced that the enslaved, once properly instructed, would become devout Christians, and dreamed of opening schools for Black children in South Carolina and Pennsylvania. In 1740, Whitefield penned a pamphlet, printed and distributed by his friend Benjamin Franklin, that chastised slaveholders for working their humans harder than horses and treating them worse than dogs. "I think God has a Quarrel with you," he wrote in an open letter to the South, "for your Abuse of and Cruelty to the poor Negroes."

But unlike Wesley, Whitefield did not critique the morality of slavery. He later argued for legalizing it in Georgia, where he used slave labor to operate an orphanage, thereby becoming a slaveholder himself. Whitefield saved his severest criticism not for the abuse of the enslaved but for the failure to Christianize them. "Enslaving or misusing their Bodies would, comparatively speaking, be an inconsiderable Evil, was proper Care taken of their Souls," he wrote in 1740. He appealed not to the conscience of white planters but to their self-interest, predicting that continued mistreatment would incite revolt. "I have wondered," he wrote, "that we have not more Instances of Self-Murder among the Negroes, or that they have not more frequently rose up in Arms against their Owners. *Virginia* has once, and *Charlestown* more than once been threatened in this Way."

LIKE THE VIBRANT FAITHS of their African homeland, Methodism offered the enslaved a religion of dignity and hope rather than of judgment and wrath. Theologians will long debate whether Christianity grafted like a hybrid onto

African roots or filled a void left by the evisceration of African culture. Views still vary about whether conversion was primarily spiritual or tactical for the enslaved. But clearly, the Africans who came to Christianity did more than simply submit to it. They molded and integrated it with traditional tenets and rituals to form a uniquely vital Afro-Christian culture that still thrives in its separateness.

It remains one of the great curiosities of American religious development that enslaved Africans and their descendants so readily embraced the faith of their oppressors, and then so adeptly reshaped it into a liberation theology. They compartmentalized the white ministry's directives on obedience and docility, and learned to receive skeptically the white Christian portrayal of America as a new Israel, exceptional among nations for its goodness and godliness. Instead, they took hope from the Bible's fantastical stories of divine deliverance and redemption, identifying with both the exodus of enslaved Israelites from Pharaoh's Egypt and the unjust persecution and suffering of the subversive preacher from Nazareth. They rejoiced in his resurrection, and despite their mistreatment found evidence of God's sovereignty in their own survival. Contrary to the assertions of the dominant culture, they construed a way to find God in themselves. And from both the pulpit and the choir loft, they developed a distinctive idiom of praise.

"Wherever one stands in the great debate over the origins and character of African American worship, there is no denying that slaves found solace in the creed of their captors," wrote Stanford University historian James T. Campbell. "In the Old Testament particularly, they encountered a God who was immanent in the world, who loved justice and cherished the lowly." Yet Christianity also provided a matrix for asking the most incriminating questions, Campbell observed, like how a just and loving God could allow the subjugation of millions. "How," he asked, "could black Christians reconcile the joy they felt in their new faith with their horror at the means of its acquisition?" The late African American historian Vincent Harding, who wrote extensively about the Black freedom struggle, spoke of "the doubleness" of black religious experience. On the one hand, he found Marx's assessment of religion as "the opium of the people" to be unassailable in the context of American slavery. Yet Harding also surveyed the history of attempted slave revolts and successful escapes, including those of Frederick Douglass and Harriet Tubman, and concluded that Black resistance and protest almost always had roots in Black Christianity.

The disorienting brutality of the Middle Passage did not fully cleave enslaved Africans and their descendants from their beliefs in a supreme being and constellations of lesser gods, or in an active spirit world, or the veneration of ancestors, or priestly powers of divination and healing. They held fast to rituals of marriage and death, and to dancing, drumming, singing, and costuming as manifestations of faith. In the process, they remade the ethos and practice of Christianity into an authentic form that leapt the bounds of religion, infusing American music, dance, literature, art, theatre, oratory, education, commerce, and politics for generations to come. In their 1998 study, historians Sylvia R. Frey and Betty Wood asserted that "the passage from traditional religions to Christianity was arguably the single most significant event in African American history."

The influence of Africa diluted over time, naturally, but vestiges lingered on the plantations of South Carolina's barrier islands, where the isolation of large communities of enslaved people, refreshed by waves of imports, slowed the rate of assimilation. It was there, after all, that they developed their own dialect, Gullah, a creole mélange of European and African tongues that is still spoken on the Sea Islands and bleeds into Charleston's distinctive patois. In 2005, the American Bible Society published the first Gullah Bible, "De Nyew Testament," translating John 3:16 as "Cause God lob all de people een da wol sommuch dat e gii wi e onliest Son."

Attempts to force a transition from African religions to the staid worship style, inaccessible language, and complex doctrine of Anglicanism did not deliver immediate results. Over time, however, evangelical Protestantism made inroads with its repetitive messaging, pledges of eventual spiritual equality, and emphasis on oral teaching and emotional, improvisational performance. "Perhaps the religious heritage of American Protestants and the African religious background were not completely antithetical," Albert J. Raboteau posited in 1978 in *Slave Religion*. "Culture contact was not in every case culture conflict with either Africa or Europe emerging victorious." Some elements of African religions, like the worship of a hierarchy of gods, withered within a few generations. But Raboteau argued that others, notably ecstatic behavior and spirit possession, blended like stirred paint with the practices of the Methodists and other early evangelicals. For evidence, he pointed to the rituals of ring shouting and dancing, singsong rhythmic preaching, call-and-response chanting, and frenzied movement during open-air revivals.

Slave religion, and the Black Christianity that developed from it, bolstered notions of self-worth and collective identity despite conditions that sapped the soul. For a people starving for hope, it cracked the door on free thought. One could aspire to spiritual liberation even while physically bound. "Out of black religious life emerged a conception of black national identity," the scholar Eddie S. Glaude, Jr., has written. "It also enabled them to view themselves as bound together, as in communion with one another." Designed to serve uniquely Black needs, Black Christianity became culturally distinct from white Christianity even when theologically parallel. It was, and is, in the construct of Eugene D. Genovese, the eminent historian of American slavery, "a religion within a religion in a nation within a nation."

Genovese also argued, however, that the embrace by African Americans of a faith that encouraged spiritual resistance, but within the bounds of European institutions, regulated their revolutionary potential. "The synthesis that became black Christianity," he wrote, "offered profound spiritual strength to a people at bay; but it also imparted a political weakness, which dictated, however necessarily and realistically, acceptance of the hegemony of the oppressor. It enabled slaves to do battle against the slaveholders' ideology, but defensively within the system it opposed." At times, that would place the church on the establishment end of debates that animated Black liberation politics through the Civil Rights Movement and beyond, first pitting Booker T. Washington against W.E.B. Du Bois and later Martin Luther King, Jr., against Malcolm X. And yet the growth of Christianity among African Americans did establish a clear moral standard for measuring the contradictory behaviors of slaveholders. It did not take much churchgoing for the enslaved to comprehend the hypocrisy of white Christians who committed wicked crimes while donning the cloak of piety. Take the experience of Cureton Milling, who belonged as a child to a blacksmith named Levi M. Bolick in Fairfield County, South Carolina. By 1860, Bolick owned a plantation of about five hundred acres and eighteen slaves, as well as a reputation for hotheaded heartlessness. According to Milling, his master bred people for sale, separated siblings for auction, and raped with impunity. On Sundays, he went to church.

"He take 'vantage of de young gal slaves," Milling said, as reported by his Federal Writers' Project interviewer. " 'You go yonder and shell corn in de crib,' he said to one of them. He's de marster so she have to go. Then he send de others to work some other place, then he go to the crib. He did dis to my very aunt and she had a mulatto boy dat took his name and live right in dis town after freedom. Marster was doin' dis devilment all de time and gwine to Presbyterian Church at Salem every Sunday; dat make it look worse to me."

THE METHODIST MOVEMENT began to institutionalize as Wesleyan disciples from England, Ireland, and Wales immigrated into American cities and formed their own societies. As lifelong Anglicans, the Wesleys had little stomach for separating from the Church of England, the literal faith of their father. They viewed their mission instead as reforming and revitalizing a moribund and decadent church from within. But starting in 1769, John Wesley finally acceded to the breakaway that would lead to Methodism's emergence as an independent denomination. He dispatched his own ministers to the colonies, including Francis Asbury and, later, Thomas Coke, who roamed widely to preach and start new societies. Wesley's lieutenants bided their time during the American Revolution, when the Methodists came under suspicion for Tory sympathies and, in some quarters, for abolitionism. But their survival presented opportunities after the war with the gradual disestablishment of the Church of England and the departure of many Anglican ministers. Methodism, according to Dee E. Andrews, a historian of the early church, now less resembled the "rebellious if righteous child" of Anglicanism than its "potentially devouring offspring."

Late in December 1784, some sixty preachers held a landmark convention at Baltimore's Lovely Lane Chapel to unite the country's disparate Wesleyan societies into the Methodist Episcopal Church in America. Asbury and Coke became co-superintendents, effectively making them the country's first Methodist bishops. Although the documentary evidence is scant and circumstantial, some church historians argue that among those likely attending were two talented but un-ordained Black preachers, Richard Allen and Harry Hosier.

In one of the notable acts of the so-called Christmas Conference, the Methodists spelled out an absolutist stance against slavery in language that melded the foundational concepts of Christianity and American independence. "We view [slavery] as contrary to the Golden Law of God on which hang all the Law and the Prophets, and the unalienable Rights of Mankind, as well as every Principle of the Revolution," the conference proclaimed. In states where manumission was legal, slaveholding members would be denied communion and expelled if they did not emancipate their bondmen. Anyone buying or selling enslaved people would be ousted immediately, unless the purpose was to free them. The American Methodists backed up their rhetoric by approving the ordination of Black ministers in 1800 (Asbury had already unilaterally ordained Richard Allen the previous year). Three decades later, they pioneered a program of dispatching missionaries onto South Carolina's plantations. Only the Quakers rivaled them in abolitionist zeal and concern for the souls of the enslaved.

Newspapers in Britain and America depicted the early Methodists as holy-roller crackpots. But their views on universal salvation, personal holiness, moderation in lifestyle, and communal uplift proved wildly popular with the American masses. Numbers nearly doubled to almost 15,000 in the five years preceding the denomination's formal organization, and then quintupled in the next seven, to 76,000 in 1791, the year Wesley died in London at age eighty-seven. Black membership in the United States grew sevenfold in the final fifteen years of the century as language barriers fell and Northern states made their first moves toward abolition. By 1790, African Americans accounted for 1 of every 5 American Methodists, many of them women. The growth continued unabated in the nineteenth century, with membership reaching 580,000 in 1840, shortly before the denomination split over slavery into Northern and Southern branches.

Bishop Asbury, who traversed the seaboard to plant new churches, founded Charleston's first congregation early in 1785, two months after the Christmas Conference. Construction began the next year on a two-story clapboard building on Cumberland Street, between Meeting and Church. Known as the Blue Meeting House, it was outfitted with plain pine benches on a floor of clean white sand. As was typical, Black members were relegated to back pews and a gallery upstairs. By 1800, two other Methodist congregations had been founded—Trinity and Bethel—each with an overwhelmingly Black membership. Within the Methodist churches, Black members typically were segregated into their own classes under the charge of white preachers or lay leaders. That white churchgoers arranged for their servants to worship with them reflected their fear of Black autonomy more than any belief in spiritual brotherhood.

The Methodists' unconventional practices and abhorrence of slavery at first made for some lonely Sundays in Charleston. A decade after the denomination's founding, there were but 345 adherents among the city's roughly 15,000 residents, and 80 percent were either free persons of color or the slaves of white members. The city's first Methodist congregations were ridiculed as "negro churches" and their ministers as "negro preachers" and incendiaries. When South Carolina's Methodists met in Charleston as a statewide conference for the first time in 1787, they resolved "to leave nothing undone for the spiritual benefit and salvation" of both free and enslaved people of color. Eight years later, twenty-three ministers petitioned that year's conference to defrock colleagues who refused to emancipate their slaves. The churchmen wrote that they were "deeply sensible of the impropriety and evil of slavery in itself and its baneful consequences, on Religious Society."

Despite their modest numbers, Charleston's Methodists made the city's white establishment deeply insecure, racially as well as theologically. Presentments issued by grand juries in the Lowcountry during the 1790s complained that "large bodies of negroes" were assembling to conduct worship services and celebrate weddings. Less than two years after the Cumberland church opened, with Asbury back in town, a mob hurled brickbats and stones through the windows, with one missile crashing near the pulpit while the bishop delivered his sermon.

In 1800, American Methodist leaders resolved at their quadrennial gathering in Baltimore that regional officials would appeal to their states' legislatures for the gradual abolition of "the great national evil of Negro-Slavery." Signed by Bishops Asbury and Coke among others, the statement characterized slaveholding as "repugnant to the unalienable rights of mankind, and to the very essence of civil liberty, but more especially to the spirit of the Christian religion." Such hypocrisy in the purported land of the free, the Methodists charged, was "an inconsistency which is scarcely to be paralleled in the history of mankind!" In South Carolina, such a full-throated assault made the document both blasphemous and seditious, so much so that U.S. Sen. Jacob Read warned Gov. John Drayton that allowing its circulation would "lay the firebrand to our houses and the dagger to our throats."

Later that year, word spread that a Methodist preacher in Charleston, John Harper, had been shipped copies of the offending tract for distribution in the Lowcountry. After being tipped off, the city's intendant, or mayor, seized the pamphlets and burned them. Soon, two hundred angry men besieged Harper's house, "with a lawyer of note at their head, who uttered great threats." The following Sunday, a gang surrounded Harper as he departed the Cumberland Street church, and a brawl ensued before he could be led to safety. The posse returned the next evening to search for him but found another minister, George Dougherty, instead. They dragged the sickly, half-blind minister to a public tap on a wintry night and, while chanting "pump him, pump him," held his head under the gushing spigot until he nearly drowned. He was only rescued by the timely appearance of an ardent Methodist churchwoman "who boldly rushed into the midst of this infuriated mob, and stuffed her shawl into the spout." A man then stepped forward with an unsheathed saber and led the shivering parson to safety.

Harper's friends suggested that he leave town along with his family. Instead, he sought to pacify his antagonists by distancing himself from the antislavery positions imposed by Methodist leaders in the North. "I have ever thought it my duty in my intercourse with slaves to inculcate humility, submission, diligence, and faithfulness, as duties becoming their station, and calculated to render them safe and happy," he swore in a public deposition. But only when the congregation stationed a burly bouncer at the church door did the anti-Methodist disturbances quiet for a while. When the guard made an example of one agitator by administering a "necessary dressing" and tossing him out, "it got out that the Methodists had begun to fight for their rights."

Eager to dodge further conflict, Black Methodists began migrating from the Cumberland church to Bethel, about nine blocks north, but trouble followed them there soon enough. One Sunday in 1807, an armed and uniformed contingent of the city guard surrounded the church during an afternoon prayer service. The captain swaggered in with his sword raised and ordered the crowd to disperse, offering no explanation. Black members in the gallery hustled toward the exits, some scampering through windows only to be captured outside and then marched en masse to the "Sugar House." Not until 1818, when an appellate court reinforced that police could not disrupt daytime services if white observers were present, would there be any protection against such random harassment.

Asbury, deeply invested in the Charleston church he had started himself, found it troubling that Methodism would not take root there as readily as elsewhere. He tired of being openly insulted on the streets during visits and remarked in his journals about the "gross immoralities" and "desperate wickedness" of the place. The bishop, who had traveled so widely, considered the city to be "the seat of Satan, dissipation, and folly," observing that Charlestonians occupied themselves with "playing, dancing, swearing, racing" and were "intolerably ignorant of God." But Asbury also recognized that the racial imbalance in Methodist churches and the denomination's positioning on slavery held back its growth. "I doubt if in Charleston we have joined more than one hundred and seventy-eight members of the fair skin in twenty years; and seldom are there more than fifty or sixty annually returned," he lamented. "Death, desertion, backsliding: poor fickle souls, unstable as water, light as air, bodies and minds!" Asbury understood that with such resistance from white Charlestonians in the city, few plantation owners nearby would consider allowing missionaries to preach to their enslaved laborers.

Over time, frustration gave way to resignation and accommodation. Less than a year after the Christmas Conference, opposition from planters in Virginia and the Carolinas prompted the Methodists to suspend their nationwide ban on slaveholding. Adapting American federalism to their own needs, they maintained official repugnance for "the great evil of slavery" while gradually delegating decisions about slaveholding to the local and regional organizations known as "annual conferences." A major capitulation came in 1804, when the quadrennial nationwide "general conference" explicitly exempted members in the Carolinas, Georgia, and Tennessee from all rules against slaveholding and trading, and soon allowed them to set their own. The conference also withdrew its prior call for states to enact gradual emancipation plans and sent a clear signal that John Wesley's principled stance against slavery had outlived its utility. "Let our preachers from time to time as occasion serves, admonish and exhort all slaves to render due respect and obedience to the commands and interests of their respective masters," the Methodists resolved at the Baltimore session. They soon began printing separate Northern and Southern versions of their denominational rule book, *The Doctrines and Discipline*. Asbury all but issued a formal surrender, conceding that he was "called upon to suffer *for Christ's sake*, not for slavery." Membership in South Carolina took off immediately, exploding from 4,682 in 1800 to 25,990 a decade later, to 54,604 in 1840, and to 76,820 in 1860. South Carolina's district contained more Methodists at that point than any other, 55 percent of them Black and the vast majority enslaved.

As the years passed, the white Southern church collaborated ever more closely with the dominant caste to move the theory and mechanics of slavery away from coercion and toward paternalism. That shift grew out of market changes produced by the ban on transatlantic slave trading and the need to buffer the institution from Northern abolitionist attacks. Eventually, the church's refusal to oppose slavery evolved into a vigorous defense of it, at least by its Southern branches. "We denounce the principles and opinions of the abolitionists *in toto*," the South Carolina Methodist Conference declared in 1836. "We consider and believe that the Holy Scriptures, so far from giving any countenance to this delusion, do unequivocally authorize the relation of master and slave."

Along with similar stands taken by other denominations, Methodism's backsliding heralded the formation of a defiantly pro-slavery wing of Christendom in the South, and foreshadowed the coming schisms of Baptists, Methodists, and Presbyterians into Northern and Southern branches. It also signaled to Black Southerners that they would not find the refuge or autonomy they craved within white-governed denominations, even those they found most appealing. To experience true equality in the sight of the Lord, they would need to sit under their own vine and fig tree.

V.

Richard Allen and the Insurgency of African Methodism

*Everyone will sit under their own vine
and under their own fig tree,
and no one will make them afraid,
for the Lord Almighty has spoken.*

—MICAH 4:4 (NIV)

The yearning by African Americans to control their practice of faith resonated as strongly up North as down South, and it was in Philadelphia, more than 550 miles distant, that Mother Emanuel's story largely began. It was there, in the cradle of freedom, that a formerly enslaved man named Richard Allen, arguably America's least acclaimed founding father, defiantly established the country's first broad-based Black denomination. As a preacher, organizer, businessman, strategist, and social activist, and as a pioneering, boundary-breaking innovator, Allen has few peers in early American life. His exodus from slavery, recounted in a slim posthumously published autobiography, is a parable of man's spiritual journey from darkness toward revelation. Because Allen molded African Methodism in his own image, it is also quite literally the origin story of America's Black church, one that fuses divine prophecy with human intervention.

By leading a nonviolent exodus from the white-controlled Methodist church, Allen created a radical model for direct action that would be replicated in Charleston three decades later and emulated by generations of Black clergy who marched in his footsteps. He achieved unusual prominence for an African American in his day and was lionized within the Black church, then as now (a Richard Allen postage stamp was issued in 2016). "Already he has become an ideal character," Frederick Douglass wrote with a flourish in the nineteenth century, "and his name has been invested with a sanctity seldom accorded to that of any other man this side of the Apostolic age."

Little is known of Allen's upbringing other than that he was born on February 14, 1760, as the son of a mixed-race mother and an African father, and as the property of Benjamin Chew, a prominent Philadelphia lawyer. Chew, who became both attorney general and chief justice of the Pennsylvania colony, owned a manor in the city, working plantations in Delaware, and a bevy of enslaved people to service them. It is not clear which might have been the boy's childhood home. But when young Richard (his only known name at the time) was roughly eight years old, Chew's financial prospects dimmed and he opted to unload some of his human holdings. In a transaction that led first to heartbreak but ultimately to freedom, Chew sold Richard, his parents, and three siblings to a neighboring Delaware farmer named Stokely Sturgis.

In his memoir, which he dictated to his son before dying in 1831, Allen remembered Sturgis somewhat wryly as "what the world called a good master." He described the old farmer as tender and humane, "more like a father to his slaves than anything else." Read today, it seems a curious depiction given that Sturgis soon addressed his own financial troubles by disposing of Richard's mother and three of her children. Richard, his oldest brother, and a sister stayed with Sturgis, tending his corn, wheat, and flax. The days were long, the labor monotonous and grueling. Even with an owner who did not resort to the lash, the young man found that "slavery is a bitter pill." His already splintered family lived with the fear that they would be sold to the highest bidder as soon as Sturgis died, if not before. Enslavement seemed their settled lot, any fantasy of freedom a gauzy daydream. When Methodist circuit-riders crisscrossed the area dangling the promise of spiritual liberation, the message likely held considerable appeal for a restless teenager robbed of his parents and destined for a life of toil.

At about seventeen, Richard Allen experienced a mystical conversion not unlike John Wesley's at Aldersgate. He told of feeling unmoored before being rescued by a revelatory spirit: "I was awakened and brought to see myself, poor, wretched and undone, and without the mercy of God must be lost. Shortly after, I obtained mercy through the blood of Christ, and was constrained to exhort my old companions to seek the Lord." As Allen proselytized, he questioned the authenticity of his rebirth, and renewed his spiritual search. "One night I thought hell would be my portion," he remembered. "I cried unto Him who delighteth to hear the prayers of a poor sinner, and all of a sudden my dungeon shook, my chains flew off, and, glory to God, I cried. My soul was filled."

Convinced that his sins had been pardoned, Richard began attending Methodist class meetings every other Thursday at a clearing on a nearby farm. He and his siblings, also converted, soon became the subject of idle gossip from wary neighbors who thought Sturgis too lenient for allowing the gatherings. To quiet the talk, they redoubled their work habits, "so that it should not be said that religion made us worse servants." If they were behind in their tasks, they skipped the Methodist meetings even though Sturgis, who was not himself religious, encouraged their attendance. "At length," Richard recalled, "our master said he was convinced that religion made slaves better and not worse, and often boasted of his slaves for their honesty and industry." Eventually, Richard persuaded Sturgis to invite a Methodist class leader to preach regularly at the farm. That paved the way for a celebrity visit by Francis Asbury himself in August 1779, and another to the area by one of Asbury's most charismatic protégés, Freeborn Garrettson.

Acclaimed as the "Paul Revere of American Methodism," Garrettson traveled thousands of miles by horseback to spread the doctrine of John Wesley's new movement. He had inherited his family's Maryland plantation and enslaved laborers but after his conversion felt divinely called to liberate them and became an ardent abolitionist and pacifist. In his sermon to Sturgis's family and bondsmen, likely delivered on November 19, 1779, Garrettson took his text from Daniel to decry the immorality of slavery. "Thou art weighed in the balance, and art found wanting," he thundered at Sturgis. The old farmer found himself so affected that he renounced slaveholding. Sturgis's finances may have been a contributing factor, as he was not so moved that he manumitted Richard and his siblings on the spot without compensation. Rather, he proposed a five-year installment plan that would allow Richard and his brother to buy their freedom for $2,000 in Continental currency. To make that possible, Sturgis allowed Richard to hire himself out. Richard chopped wood until his hands blistered, worked in a brickyard for $50 a month, and, in the closing years of the Revolutionary War, hauled wagonloads of salt to port from the Delaware shore. In 1783, more than a year ahead of schedule, he paid Sturgis in full and threw in eighteen bushels of salt as a gratuity.

On September 3, the day the British recognized American independence by signing the Treaty of Paris, twenty-three-year-old Richard walked away from his own captivity. The coincidence must have felt profound, as the colonists' more than seven-year battle for liberty and democracy held inescapable applications to the plight of the enslaved. Just as the freedom narratives of the Bible made it harder to rationalize human bondage, so America's Revolution and ensuing constitutional debates posed questions about whether the new confederation would be born in hypocrisy. The Revolution established "liberty as the American lingua franca," wrote one of Allen's biographers, Richard S. Newman. It also unleashed a surge of both secular and evangelical attacks on slavery that led to the enactment of at least gradual abolition in every Northern state by 1804, bifurcating the nation. John Wesley's Methodist itinerants, who were by then trekking across the mid-Atlantic of Richard Allen's youth, helped lead the charge.

The newly liberated Allen marked the occasion by taking a surname, the birthright of all free men. He never identified his namesake (although one possibility is Benjamin Chew's close friend, William Allen, a successful merchant and jurist). But he self-consciously rejected any association with either of his enslavers. Going forward, he would be his own man.

As he contemplated the reversal in his fortunes, Allen connected the transformation of his physical circumstances to that of his spiritual circumstances. The Methodist message, after all, had been directly responsible for the unanticipated freeing of both his body and his prospects. "I have had reason to bless my dear Lord that a door was opened unexpectedly for me," he realized. It seemed natural, therefore, to dedicate his own freedom to pursuing the liberation of others.

Relying on his wit and determination, and the kindness of fellow Methodists, Allen spent the next three years as a self-appointed itinerant-in-training, trekking across Delaware, New Jersey, Pennsylvania, and Maryland. He traveled until his clothes went threadbare, then stopped and worked until he could afford a new set. He'd chop wood by day so he could preach at night and on Sundays, moving on to another village after a few weeks or months. Exhaustion and the elements took their toll on his health. In Radnor Township, west of Philadelphia, his feet became so sore from walking that he could not even limp to his hosts' table for tea. They brought the table to him, and the wife bathed his feet with warm water and bran. Allen preached for several more days, including on Sunday to "a large congregation of different persuasions." He must have impressed, for word spread of his performance and parish officials convinced him to delay his departure. Allen reported that his farewell sermon created a sensation among the mostly white members. "Seldom did I ever experience such a time of mourning and lamentation among a people," he recalled. "Some said, 'This man must be a man of God; I never heard such preaching before.'" One congregant offered Allen a wiry horse to ease his travels, a debt the preacher repaid years later.

Others did not always share Allen's view of his own pulpit skills, and his level of literacy is unclear. The abolitionist minister and orator Henry Highland Garnet wrote that Allen, although wise, "was not what men call an eloquent preacher, neither was he distinguished for his literary, scientific, nor theological acquirements." But across his life, Allen proved to be a lightning-quick study and a natural leader of broad interests and multifarious involvements, in the life of his city and of the nation. He became a serial entrepreneur, both as a churchman and a businessman, accumulating considerable property and means. He was among the first to integrate the egalitarian Christian ideal with a nascent Black consciousness and spoke trenchantly on matters as varied as the Fugitive Slave Act, African colonization, and the "Colored Conventions Movement." Time and again, and against stacked odds, he outwitted and outlasted his antagonists through resourcefulness, stubbornness, and resolute faith—in his own abilities as well as in God.

Allen stood of medium build, with sinewy arms and legs that testified to his labor and travels. He wore his close-cropped hair with the sideburns long and a pronounced widow's peak that gave his face the shape of an elongated heart. Paintings cast his skin in peanut-shell tones (although Garnet described him as dark brown), with full lips and the droopy eyes of a basset hound. When Allen was preaching or engaged in conversation, however, those eyes "seemed to blaze with a fire that attracted the attention of all who beheld them," Garnet wrote. In his portraits, Allen is dressed in a black coat with a white cravat knotted tightly against his neck. His expression is invariably one of insouciant self-confidence.

With Allen gaining favor in Methodist circles, Bishop Asbury asked him in 1785 to join him on a mission into the slaveholding South. There would be conditions, Asbury explained. Because the Methodists were viewed as abolitionist instigators, Allen would not be allowed to mingle with enslaved people. There might be nights that Allen would have to sleep in a carriage, since hosts might not offer a bed to a Black guest. Additionally, Asbury could not afford to compensate Allen beyond food and clothing for the trip. Somewhat unthinkably, given Asbury's status as a bishop, a white man, and a mentor, Allen declined, not once but twice. "I told him I would not travel with him on these conditions," he said. Afflicted with rheumatoid arthritis, Allen told Asbury that he worried there would be no one to care for him if he took ill. More to the point, having struggled so long to gain his freedom, he could not tolerate the prospect of racial regression, even if it advanced the evangelical cause.

Although not yet ordained, Allen received an invitation in early 1786 to preach to a small band of Black congregants at St. George's, the dirt-floored Methodist church on Fourth Street in central Philadelphia. He absorbed the insult of being relegated to a 5:00 a.m. slot, so that white worshippers would not be inconvenienced, and gamely won several converts. Allen saw that the end of the Revolution and the gradual abolition of slavery in Pennsylvania, enacted six years earlier, had created a critical mass of unschooled freedmen in the city who were ripe for religion. He could read the trend lines. In the 1790 census, Philadelphia recorded 1,630 Black residents, more than 80 percent of them free, among its 28,522 inhabitants. Within ten years, the city's population had exploded to 41,220, and the Black population had more than doubled to 4,265, only 55 of them enslaved. "I soon saw a large field open in seeking and instructing my African brethren, who had been a long forgotten people," Allen said. "And few of them attended public worship." He began preaching all about town, sometimes four or five times a day, and by the end of the year had attracted forty-two adherents to his society of Black Methodists. One of them was fellow preacher Absalom Jones, another formerly enslaved man from Delaware, thirteen years his senior. Jones shared Allen's passions for both Scripture and Black autonomy and had been chafing under the yoke of the local Episcopal church.

Allen and Jones agreed on the need to establish a church solely for Black worshippers, but they began incrementally by forming a nondenominational benevolent society. Founded in 1787 as one of the country's first mutual aid collectives devoted to Black welfare, Philadelphia's Free African Society met monthly, sometimes at Allen's house, with members making regular contributions to support the needy. The preamble to its bylaws explained that Allen and Jones had created the group "from a love to the people of their complexion whom they beheld with sorrow, because of their irreligious and uncivilized state." They had decided that "a society should be formed, without regard to religious tenets, provided, the persons lived an orderly and sober life, in order to support one another in sickness, and for the benefit of their widows and fatherless children."

The Free African Society did not wall itself off from religion altogether. Like the Quakers, its meetings began with silent meditation. But that did not satisfy Allen's craving for a real church, an independent African Methodist church. Mindful meditation might be fine for the Friends, but his people preferred "an unconstrained outburst" of religious ardor. Allen's inflexibility on the issue quickly rubbed up against the founding spirit of the society, and he was effectively drummed out in 1789 for "attempting to sow division among us."

Allen continued to preach, but white officials at St. George's perceived his growing influence with Black worshippers as a threat and ordered him to stop. As a result, an ever-expanding pool of Black congregants began squeezing into the cramped church for its regular Sunday services. The church's Black members, Allen complained, "were considered as a nuisance." With seating limited, a predictable clash over race and status ensued, with white churchmen insisting that Black members sit along the walls, and eventually in a segregated section. One Sunday, over the course of a few minutes, that tension erupted into a formative moment for the Black church in America, one that echoed centuries later when Rosa Parks refused to cede her bus seat to a white man and when students sat in at whites-only lunch counters. Yet despite the event's import, there is no settled understanding of when it took place, with a baffling gap of five years between the alternate dates.

Whenever it happened, in 1787 as Allen himself asserted, or in 1792 as later research suggests is possible, the drama unfolded shortly after Allen arrived to worship at St. George's one Sunday. In Allen's telling in his autobiography, an usher explained that church leaders had decided that Black congregants would now be seated in "the gallery," and directed him and others to go there. They assumed they could take seats near the front, directly above their old ones, and did so. White officials had other ideas. "Meeting had begun," Allen recalled, "and they were nearly done singing, and just as we got to the seats, the elder said, 'Let us pray.' We had not been long upon our knees before I heard considerable scuffling and low talking. I raised my head and saw one of the trustees, H-M- [Henry Manley], having hold of the Rev. Absalom Jones, pulling him up off of his knees, and saying, 'You must get up—you must not kneel here.'"

Jones asked Manley to wait for the end of the prayer.

"No, you must get up now, or I will call for aid and force you away," the white trustee barked.

Jones pleaded once more. "Wait until prayer is over, and I will get up and trouble you no more."

With that, Manley summoned another white churchman, who began to lift a second Black parishioner from his knees. Allen had seen enough. Black congregants had dutifully contributed money toward building the church, and now were being told they could not sit or pray where they wished. He lifted his head, rose from his knees, and led his fellow freemen out of St. George's, never to return. "We all went out of the church in a body," Allen said, "and they were no more plagued with us in the church. This raised a great excitement and inquiry among the citizens, in so much that I believe they were ashamed of their conduct. But my dear Lord was with us, and we were filled with fresh vigour to get a house erected to worship God in."

Allen does not date the walkout in his autobiography. But in a historical note introducing the first AME guidebook, *The Doctrines and Discipline*, co-published by Allen in 1817, the year is given as 1787. Black congregants, responding to various "acts of unchristian conduct," started meeting that year "to devise a plan in order to build a house of our own, to worship God under our own vine and fig tree," the authors wrote. That date went unquestioned until the 1970s, when historian Milton C. Sernett sifted through the archives at St. George's. He found architectural records showing that the second-story gallery was not completed until 1792. Sernett also determined that church officials referenced by Allen were not in place until after 1787. Advocates for the earlier date, including AME historians, argue that Allen's semantics may have been imprecise and that too much import can be given to the date of the gallery's construction. Yes, they acknowledge, Allen remembered in his autobiography that Black members were told "to go in the gallery" and that they expected to take seats "over the ones we formerly occupied below." But there is no mention of a gallery in the earlier reconstruction of events in *The Doctrines and Discipline*. There it was written instead that white churchmen pulled Black worshippers from their knees "and ordered them to the back seats." Perhaps, some researchers suggest, the rear of the church held raised, tiered seating in the 1780s before the second-story gallery was built.

No dispute has emerged about Allen's depiction of the walkout itself. The significance of its date, therefore, lies in whether it directly precipitated the separatist movement that followed, or merely reinforced one already under way. One version is more theatrical than the other, but both make it clear that Richard Allen, Absalom Jones, and the other free Black congregants of

St. George's resented their treatment by their white brothers and sisters in Christ and had concluded that the white church could not be reformed from within. Systemic change and an entirely new structure would be needed. Their conviction that "the evil of racism in the white church was beyond redemption" made Allen and Jones revolutionaries as much as any insurrectionist, the late theologian James H. Cone argued.

The Free African Society, meanwhile, became ever more churchlike. It played moral arbiter by taking stands against drunken or disorderly conduct and cohabitation outside of marriage. It frowned on the pleasures of gaming and feasting and dancing, arguing that "it is this practice of ours that enables our enemies to declare that we are not fit for freedom." In 1791, the society began staging a monthly worship service. Simultaneously, Jones and Allen renewed their commitment to the creation of a Black church and began searching for a site. The city's ranking Methodist minister, known as the elder, visited Allen and others to warn that they would be excommunicated if they persisted.

"We told him we were dragged off of our knees in St. George's Church, and treated worse than heathens; and we were determined to seek out for ourselves, the Lord being our helper," Allen said. "He told us we were not Methodists, and left us." The elder changed tactics in a second meeting, hoping the Black dissidents might respond to friendly persuasion. They didn't, as Allen had not forgotten the man's earlier posture. "If you deny us your name," Allen told him, "you cannot seal up the scripture from us, and deny us a name in heaven. We believe heaven is free for all who worship in spirit and truth."

Allen and Jones helped their cause by winning the moral and financial backing of several white Philadelphians of high standing, notably Dr. Benjamin Rush, a signer of the Declaration of Independence, and Robert Ralston, a prosperous merchant. Among those solicited by Rush for contributions were President George Washington and his secretary of state, Thomas Jefferson. On the first day that Allen and Jones made the rounds of white Philadelphia, they returned with a substantial $360. In September 1791, Jones and others published a letter in various newspapers to promote the fundraising campaign for an "African Church." They stressed two rationales for self-governance, each of which strategically soft-pedaled the role of racism. First, they wrote, men were more likely to be influenced on subjects of morality "by their equals, than by their superiors" and were "more easily governed by persons chosen by themselves for that purpose, than by persons who are placed over them by accidental circumstances." Secondly, they said, a separate church made sense for a people united not only by race but by a "general deficiency of education, by total ignorance, or only humble attainments in religion, and by the line drawn by custom as well as nature, between them and the white people."

In 1792, with little dissent, the Free African Society formally transitioned into its new corporate existence as the African Church. Two lots had been purchased as possible building sites, one of them by Allen himself, and a schoolhouse was leased as a temporary worship space. A meeting was held to approve a form of governance and adopt articles of faith and practice. Despite their friction with Philadelphia's Methodists, Absalom Jones and Richard Allen proposed remaining within the denomination. "I was confident that there was no religious sect or denomination [that] would suit the capacity of the coloured people as well as the Methodist," Allen recalled, lauding the Wesleyans for their "plain doctrine" and "good discipline." He still credited the Methodists for his own emancipation and believed in the capacity of Methodist virtues like industriousness, temperance, self-reliance, and thrift to liberate his people from both slavery and sin. It was the rare denomination that seemed concerned with the souls of the enslaved. "The Methodists were the first people that brought glad tidings to the coloured people," Allen remembered. "We are beholden to the Methodists, under God, for the light of the Gospel we enjoy; for all other denominations preached so high-flown that we were not able to comprehend their doctrine."

Allen and Jones stood alone. The rest of the emerging congregation, still smarting from the treatment at St. George's, voted to join the Episcopalians, giving rise to what became the African Episcopal Church of St. Thomas. The group asked Allen to be its minister in 1793—"for there was no colored preacher in Philadelphia but myself"—but he declined on grounds that he would forever be a Methodist. Instead, the job went to Jones, who accepted "after some deliberation" and was later ordained as the first African American Episcopal priest. Allen told St. Thomas's organizers he would not compete with their fundraising efforts but planned to found his own African Methodist congregation. Having accumulated some wealth as a shoe merchant and chimney sweep (his company cleaned President Washington's flues in what was then the nation's capital), he bought the frame of a former blacksmith shop and had it hauled to the lot he had purchased on Sixth Street, near Lombard. Allen had carpenters retrofit the building into a modest sanctuary, and he built a crude wooden pulpit and several benches with his own hands. In tribute, today's AME emblem intertwines a crucifix with a blacksmith's anvil.

On June 29, 1794, Richard Allen opened the doors to his African Methodist church. Bishop Asbury, Allen's longtime mentor, signaled his blessing by preaching the inaugural sermon. When one of the day's other speakers read from Genesis about Bethel, the "gate of heaven" imagined by Jacob in a dream, the name took hold—Bethel African Methodist Episcopal Church. Today the church goes by "Mother Bethel," and its fourth incarnation, a Romanesque colossus of red brick and gray stone, sits on the same tract. Deeded by Allen to the church's trustees shortly after its opening, the parcel has been continuously held by African Americans longer than any property in the United States.

Allen put forth the rationale for a Black church in a public declaration of independence. "Whereas from time to time many inconveniences have arisen from white people and people of color mixing together in public assemblys, more particularly in places of public worship, we have thought it necessary to provide for ourselves a convenient house to assemble in separate from our white brethren," his statement read. The African Methodists, he said, hoped "to obviate any offence our mixing with our white brethren might give them." The document explicitly subjected Bethel to the regulations and governance of the Methodist Episcopal Church, while asserting certain autonomous rights. Among the distinctions, Allen and his fellow trustees specified that membership and leadership positions were intended for "descendants of the African race." Regarding the all-important matter of ordination, Allen insisted that Bethel's members would have the right to present their own candidates for full ministry, and that the congregation could, by a majority vote, call anyone it wished to preach and exhort. Because Allen was not yet ordained, the charter allowed the Methodist elder in Philadelphia to officiate marriages and administer sacraments like baptism and communion.

But Richard Allen fully intended to pastor Bethel African Methodist Episcopal Church whether the Methodist Episcopal Church had ordained him to do so or not. In his view, Black control, at least at the local level, would be imperative. That inevitably ran up against his desire to remain within the Methodist Episcopal tent. The very Wesleyan "discipline" that Allen so admired vested the bishop and local elders with absolute authority to appoint ministers and manage congregations, and with the ownership of church property. Allen acknowledged that his congregation, by being racially separatist, had "in some measure discriminated ourselves." But he argued that the discord of the past left African Methodists with few options if they were to remain Methodists at all.

EVEN BEFORE RICHARD ALLEN and Absalom Jones founded their congregations, each envisioned the Black church as a vehicle for social welfare and activism. In rebuttal to the white church's insistence that deliverance awaited them in the next life, their churches would intervene for Black believers in this world as well. Years later, African Methodism would reinforce the point in its motto: "God Our Father, Christ Our Redeemer, Man Our Brother." As the Wesleys had instructed, the true faith could not be separated from Christian acts. Indeed, it demanded that Christ's example be followed in caring for the poor and sick and in denouncing injustice.

The opportunity for both presented itself in 1793, when Philadelphia fell victim to one of the deadliest epidemics in U.S. history, a ravaging outbreak of yellow fever. An estimated five thousand people died of the virus from August through November, roughly a tenth of the population of the city and its suburbs. Many suffered excruciating ends accompanied by temperature spikes, dehydration, organ failure, bleeding, vomiting, and delirium. Scientists would not confirm for more than a century that the virus was transmitted between people and mosquitoes, and not by human contact. Those who could afford to leave the city did. Those who stayed feared that every interaction, even with family members, might prove fatal. Spouses abandoned one another on death-beds, and old friends crossed streets to avoid contact. As hospital wards reached capacity, the sick and dying often suffered alone, or tended by helpless children. Their corpses might go days without collection and disposal. Few people—particularly white people—were willing or well enough to take on such grotesque and perilous work.

In the epidemic's early weeks, Dr. Benjamin Rush, Allen's revered patron, observed that the fever did not seem to plague Black people as it did white people. He hypothesized, incorrectly of course, that the descendants of Africa had developed resistance, and suggested to Allen in a letter that Black Philadelphians therefore bore "an obligation to offer your services to attend the sick who are [afflicted] with this malady." Appealing to Allen's religiosity, Rush argued that such selflessness would be "pleasing in the light of that god who will see every act of kindness done to creatures whom he calls his brethren, as if done to himself." Richard Allen and Absalom Jones surely agreed with Rush on that point, while remaining clear-eyed that a white man was asking his Black neighbors to risk their lives based on an unproven theory. They soon learned the fallacy of the doctor's prognosis, as Allen contracted the fever himself and spent weeks recovering. But the Black churchmen also sensed that a Christian crusade by Black Philadelphia to rescue white Philadelphia from further catastrophe bore public-relations value at a critical time for their independent church movement. That is why it hurt so deeply, and prompted such a powerful response, when they found that their good deeds had not gone unpunished.

At a time when few would take such risks, Allen, Jones, and the Black troops they marshaled nursed and buried the fever's victims by the hundreds. Among the tasks they carried out for Rush—who it must be said in retrospect did not have a good epidemic—was the bleeding of more than eight hundred people, to mixed results. They hired gravediggers and fronted payments for hearses and coffins, often at a loss. They prayed with the dying, burned bedding and belongings, and arranged for the care of newly orphaned children. When the epidemic finally retreated into winter, they expected a measure of appreciation, and received some. But it was tainted by accusations by newspaper publisher Mathew Carey that "some of the vilest of the blacks" had engaged in price-gouging and plundering. In a bestselling pamphlet, Carey gave credit where it was due, praising Allen and Jones by name and acknowledging that the misdeeds of a few should not lessen the city's gratitude. But he also claimed that some nurses had charged up to $5 a night for a $1 job. "Some of them were even detected in plundering the houses of the sick," Carey alleged.

Jones and Allen could not let such slanders stand and published their own scathing "refutation." Even then, they understood the importance of controlling a narrative. When a Philadelphia printer released their pamphlet in February 1794, it became the first publication by African American authors to gain a United States copyright. The ministers took readers along on their dreadful rounds, calling for the dead from the streets, and provided a full accounting of the losses they incurred on coffins and labor. They also reported that despite assertions of racial herd immunity, any number of African Americans had become infected and died. They allowed that there had been "some few black people guilty of plundering the distressed"—five at most, they estimated—but observed that the Black miscreants paled in comparison to those who were paler. "Is it a greater crime for a black to pilfer, than for a white to privateer?" Jones and Allen asked. "We wish not to offend, but when an unprovoked attempt is made, to make us blacker than we are, it becomes less necessary to be over cautious on that account." They called out white offenders, like the caretaker who was found senselessly drunk with her dead patient's ring on her finger. It was discriminatory treatment, and the stigmatization by race, that most drew their ire.

They appended a letter of commendation from Philadelphia's mayor, as well as several shorter essays on slavery that reveal an early emphasis by Allen and Jones on self-help and on forgiveness. They chastised white Americans for holding unreasonable expectations of Black people after generations of servitude. But they also encouraged their own people to express resistance through faith. God would make the final judgment, and it would be the same for "those of all colours that love him." The supremacy of white over Black would end at heaven's gate, where "the power of the most cruel master ends, and all sorrow and tears are wiped away." Until then, however, Jones and Allen urged their Black countrymen to prove themselves worthy of white respect. "If we are lazy and idle, the enemies of freedom plead it as a cause why we ought not to be free," they wrote. "By such conduct we strengthen the bands of oppression."

Jones and Allen nonetheless granted broad absolution for white mistreatment, modeling the grace that came to define the Black church and that still found expression two centuries later at Dylann Roof's bond hearing. "Let no rancour or ill-will lodge in your breasts for any bad treatment you may have received," they counseled their formerly enslaved readers. "If you do, you transgress against God, who will not hold you guiltless." They cited both Testaments in urging African Americans to turn the other cheek. Christ, they wrote, "hath commanded to love our enemies, to do good to them that hate and despitefully use us." Forgiveness should be offered as one wishes to receive it, they said, less for the benefit of the forgiven than for the serenity of the forgiver. "We think it a great mercy to have all anger and bitterness removed from our minds," Jones and Allen wrote. "We appeal to your own feelings, if it is not very disquieting to feel yourselves under the dominion of a wrathful disposition." True to their word, the two men did not allow the epidemic's aftertaste to poison their patriotism, or their activism. During the War of 1812, they helped organize a battalion of twenty-five hundred African Americans to fortify Philadelphia's defenses against the British.

Richard Allen's Bethel Church began with thirty-two members, split into two classes. The first included Allen; his brother, John; his first wife, Flora, the pious helpmate he married in 1790; and Sarah Bass, the widow who became his second wife shortly after Flora died in 1801, and who bore his six children. In its first decade, Bethel's membership grew more than tenfold, to 457, and after a second decade, when a brick building replaced the frame blacksmith shop, it had nearly tripled, to 1,272. It accommodated more than 3,000 when Allen died in 1831. The congregation's rapid expansion alarmed its white overseers, and the ecstatic nature of its worship raised eyebrows as well. The Russian artist and writer Pavel Svin'in, after visiting around 1812, depicted Philadelphia's Black Methodists as comically enraptured. He told of a croaky-voiced preacher whose warnings of God's wrath accelerated into a booming crescendo. "Here from all sides came the moans of the repentant, the screams and laments of the possessed," Svin'in wrote.

Bethel's "warfare and troubles" with white Methodism "began afresh," in Allen's words, with the writing of its articles of incorporation in 1796. Crafted by a white deacon at St. George's, the document established the church as racially distinct and erected checks and balances with the white denominational leadership. But only years later would Allen come to understand that it nonetheless placed the congregation and its property under the control of the Methodist Episcopal Church. As a national entity, the MEC had started to retreat from its unqualified opposition to slavery, alienating Black Methodists who had been enticed by its initial commitment to abolition. Seeing his breakaway church as a vehicle for Black liberation, Allen found fewer and fewer advantages to aligning with the white-led denomination, even as he maintained his enthusiasm for Methodist tenets, values, and practices. When a new Methodist elder sought to assert control in 1805 by demanding Bethel's keys and books, and prohibiting meetings without prior approval, Allen balked: "We told him the house was ours. We had bought it, and paid for it."

Bethel's attorneys warned Allen that his bluster might not hold up under judicial scrutiny. Their remedy called for amending the charter by a vote of the members, and in 1807 Allen reclaimed the right of self-determination for African Methodism with a new set of bylaws. Under the African Supplement, as the amendments came to be known, Bethel's trustees, and not Philadelphia's Methodist elder, would control decisions regarding church property, membership, disciplinary expulsions, and the assignment of preachers and exhorters. Indeed, it specifically authorized Bethel's Black trustees to veto ministerial appointments made by the white Methodist elder, and empowered them to appoint their own officiant if the elder declined to administer communion or baptisms. Mutiny had been declared, and rather overtly, as the African Supplement usurped Methodist authority and disregarded Methodist policy on multiple fronts. "This raised a considerable rumpus," Allen reported drily.

Allen specified in a letter to Bishop Asbury that Philadelphia's Black Methodists did not wish to separate from the denomination, just as John Wesley had not wished to leave the Church of England. But he also insisted that their autonomy would be nonnegotiable. "Our only design," Allen wrote, "is to secure to our selves our rights and privileges, to regulate our affairs, temporal and spiritual, the same as if we were white people." Desperate to keep his longtime friend within the fold, Asbury accepted Bethel's conditions in the hope that "our African brethren will evince their unshaken stability and firmness as Methodists." The bishop's underlings, however, continued to treat Black Bethel as an adjunct of white St. George's. The elder in Philadelphia declared the African Supplement unenforceable, and new squabbles soon erupted over how much Bethel would pay for the occasional services of white ministers from St. George's. Methodist officials in Philadelphia excluded the Black church from denominational meetings and, in the ultimate affront, put Bethel up for sale at a sheriff's auction in June 1815. Ever industrious, Allen presented the winning bid, an eye-popping $10,125. That gave the African Methodists clean title to their property, but denominational officials continued their attempts to control its operations. On at least two occasions, elders from St. George's showed up without invitation to preach at Bethel and found themselves physically blocked from the pulpit. It was a fair-play turnabout of the treatment Richard Allen and Absalom Jones had received at St. George's.

The power struggle eventually wound up in court, in a case filed by the white Methodist elder seeking nullification of the African Supplement and restoration of his control over Bethel. Allen retained savvy lawyers, and they argued that the congregation's ownership of the property and its enactment of the African Supplement made it unassailable. In January 1816, the Pennsylvania Supreme Court ruled in Bethel's favor, securing its independence forever. "By the Providence of God we were delivered," Allen exulted. The victory demonstrated the potential potency of American jurisprudence when combined with peaceful mass resistance, a lesson absorbed by future generations of civil rights leaders. It left one final step to complete Bethel's evolution into a national African American denomination.

THE PENNSYLVANIA COURT ruling did not make Bethel the first independent Black congregation in America. There had been a handful of others, including in the South. Free and enslaved Black Baptists formed the Silver Bluff Church near Augusta, Georgia, and the First African Baptist Church of Savannah around the time of the Revolutionary War. Similar congregations sprouted in Virginia. Within Methodism, Black congregants unwilling to tolerate segregated worship and white control had, like Allen, formed their own churches in the great denominational centers of Baltimore, New York, and Wilmington (Peter Spencer's congregation in Wilmington grew into the breakaway Union Church of Africans in 1813, while New York's Methodists created the African Methodist Episcopal Zion denomination).

What separated Allen from other founders of early Black congregations was the intensity and immediacy of his drive to leap Bethel's bounds and create a nationwide "connection," the term adopted for a network of churches and regional organizations. In April 1816, fewer than four months after the Bethel court victory, Allen invited Black Methodist leaders from the mid-Atlantic states to an organizational conference in Philadelphia. Four Philadelphians joined Allen. Daniel Coker, the leader of the Baltimore church, brought five others. Peter Spencer came from Wilmington, along with three preachers from Attleborough, Pennsylvania, and one from Salem, New Jersey, making sixteen in all. Each had revolted against a Methodist Episcopal church that had itself formed in revolt against the Church of England. Meeting at Bethel, the men resolved "that the people of Philadelphia, Baltimore, and all other places, who should unite with them, shall become one body under the name and style of the African Methodist Episcopal Church." The only known news coverage of the session, a four-paragraph article in a Baltimore newspaper, gushed that "on no similar occasion, since the Apostolical aera of the church, has more Christian love and unanimity been manifested than by this Convention." With little notice, and few witnesses, a freedom church had been born.

In *The Doctrines and Discipline of The African Methodist Episcopal Church*, the denominational guidebook published the next year, Allen, Coker, and a third coauthor, James Champion of Philadelphia, spelled out their purpose: "We have deemed it expedient to have a form of Discipline, whereby we may guide our people in the fear of God, in the unity of the Spirit, and in the bonds of peace, and preserve us from that spiritual despotism which we have so recently experienced." They emphasized not only the religious nature of their enterprise, but the communal aspect as well, pledging that the church's adherents would "bear each other's burthens" through "our mutual striving together." That preamble provided all the rationale the African Methodists felt they needed for separating from the Methodist Episcopal Church. By adhering to Methodism, they made clear that they had not left the faith, only the church. More precisely, the church had left them, or at least left them little choice. The considered inclusion of "African" in the name of the new denomination affirmed that this would be a church for free and enslaved Black people, with autonomous governance and a proudly Afro-Christian culture. But unlike Bethel's founding documents, *The Doctrines and Discipline* stood silent on any racial requirement (or prohibition) regarding membership or leadership.

At 192 pages, the book methodically dictated everything from the manner of ordination to the order of funeral prayers and the assignment of choral parts. It also laid down a conservative moral code, frowning on the use of "spirituous liquors" and of "superfluous ornaments" in Sunday attire. Theologically, Allen's church strayed little from either the dogma or structures of the Methodist Episcopal Church. Theirs had been a schism over race and control, not belief or practice. Despite two decades of strife, Allen remained a proud Methodist. He resisted any temptation to shed the label and adopted the Methodist Episcopal Church's *Discipline* virtually intact. If African Methodism's first act, its breakaway from the MEC, had been boldly political, its next one, the adhesion to the Methodist name and ethos, marked it as a church of forgiveness.

The African Methodists made sure to distinguish themselves from the Methodist Episcopal Church on one important score: slavery. Allen and his co-founders knew the Methodists had abandoned their moral high ground to accommodate Southern churches. They also knew there were current and prospective African Methodists who might themselves be slaveholders. Nonetheless, they adopted an absolutist stance. "We will not receive any person into our society, as a member, who is a slave-holder," *The Doctrines and Discipline* declared in its first edition. "And any who are now members, that have slaves, and refuse to emancipate them . . . shall be excluded."

Allen also held steady in his regard for the episcopal form of governance and the enforcement of church discipline through a hierarchy topped by all-powerful bishops. Given the momentum of his court victory, and his initiative in staging the founding conference, it might have seemed natural for the delegates to elevate Allen as the first AME bishop. And eventually they did. But with the largest voting bloc hailing from Baltimore, the group initially anointed Coker, "on account of his superior education and talents," according to Daniel Alexander Payne, the eminent nineteenth century AME historian. As no extant minutes or first-person accounts have been found, the details of what happened next are lost. But the following day, Coker abdicated the AME crown and was quickly supplanted by Allen. Consecrated by the laying-on of hands of five ordained ministers, including his longtime friend, Absalom Jones, the formerly enslaved fifty-six-year-old Richard Allen became America's first AME bishop.

Whether accurate or not, it is revealing that Payne and other early AME historians attribute Coker's indignant resignation to concerns about his pale skin tone. Darker-skinned members argued it would be awkward to have a man who could pass for a white person serve as the inaugural figurehead of an unapologetically African American denomination. In this early test of the young church's political culture, race-consciousness seems to have prevailed. Coker, deeply wounded, stepped down to make way for Allen's election on a second ballot.

ALLEN INVITED ONLY MEN to the inaugural conference in Philadelphia, establishing an AME patriarchy that would persist through 1960, when the church finally countenanced the ordination of women as elders with full ministerial powers after repeatedly rejecting it. (In 2000, the 46th General Conference elected Baltimore native Vashti Murphy McKenzie as the first female bishop; five others had followed her as of 2024.) But Allen also understood that women, then as now, in congregations large and small and of every faith, would form the backbone of his new denomination and of the freedom movement it presaged. He knew, of course, that women had walked out of St. George's "in a body" along with men and had helped crowd the aisles to block the Methodist elder from preaching at Bethel. Although women could not serve as Bethel trustees, Allen noted in his autobiography that the vote of the membership for the African Supplement had been "unanimously agreed to, by both male and female." In the yellow-fever pamphlet, he repeatedly cited the work of Black nurses and other female Samaritans who, in tending to the sick and dying, established a model for his denomination's social-welfare mission. He made a point of praising one of them by name, Sarah Bass, "a poor black widow [who] gave all the assistance she could, in several families, for which she did not receive any thing," and who later became his wife and the first lady of African Methodism. Sarah Allen, who outlived her husband by nearly two decades, is still celebrated in AME circles as a fierce advocate for her husband's church. She coordinated the care and feeding of visiting preachers, including darning their threadbare clothes, and provided counsel and cash to those who had escaped bondage. Today, the wives—and now husbands—of AME bishops play similar roles as designated assistants to their spouses, and it is the AME Women's Missionary Society that leads the denomination's outreach to those in need, at home and abroad.

The denomination's early struggles to define the role of women are revealed in the saga of Jarena Lee, who was born free in New Jersey in 1783 and became a devoted member of Allen's Bethel AME Church. A woman with a deep and mystical faith, Lee felt summoned by God to preach and approached Allen about doing so. He responded legalistically at first: *The Doctrines and Discipline* said nothing about allowing women in the pulpit. But Lee, who was prone to biblical visions and dreams (as well as occasional suicidal ideation) maintained supreme confidence in her calling. "Why should it be thought impossible, heterodox, or improper, for a woman to preach? seeing the Savior died for the woman as well as the man," she asked in one of two autobiographies.

Lee kept after Allen, and after eight years he allowed her to hold prayer meetings in her rented house, and serve as a lay exhorter, the lowest rung on the Methodist clerical ladder. Then one Sunday at Bethel, a preacher named Richard Williams lost either his inspiration or his train of thought while expounding on Jonah 2:9. Jarena Lee sprang from her seat—"as by altogether supernatural impulse"—and finished the sermon for the startled minister. She preached powerfully enough, she said, "to show the world that I was called to labor according to my ability." Lee worried as she took her seat that she was about to be expelled. Instead, Bishop Allen rose from his spot in the church and acknowledged that he had been wrong to rebuff her eight years earlier. He declared her as capable as any minister in the house, and soon licensed her as the African Methodists' first female itinerant lay preacher. Although full ordination remained beyond her reach, she spent several decades spreading the AME gospel across the Northeast, Mid-Atlantic, and Canada.

Allen served as the sole AME bishop for the first twelve years of the denomination's life, when his age and the church's growth finally dictated that his duties be divided. He died three years later, in 1831, at seventy-one, with a remarkable compilation of firsts. He had founded the first Black mutual-aid society in Pennsylvania and the first independent Black church of national reach. He had been ordained the first Black Methodist deacon and consecrated the first AME bishop. He had published the first uniquely African Methodist hymnbook. He and Absalom Jones (who died in 1818) had been the first African Americans granted a copyright. The incorporations of their respective churches, months apart in 1796, created the first corporate entities controlled by Black Americans. The year before his death, Allen organized the first countrywide gathering of African American abolitionists and reformers, held at Bethel, a signal event that inspired the four-decade-long national Colored Conventions Movement. He also accumulated considerable wealth as one of Philadelphia's most successful Black businessmen and landlords, enough to support his sizable family while bankrolling the early operations of his church.

And yet, that still understates the legacy of Richard Allen, who is entombed at Mother Bethel along with Sarah. Others had been earlier in breaking away from white churches and building freestanding Black congregations. But Allen had given form and name to an independent Black denomination that claimed the entirety of the young country as its territory, including the South, and soon would aim its evangelism at Africa and the Caribbean. He firmly associated that church with the cause of American Black nationalism. After a lengthy flirtation with the African colonization movement—which advocated the migration of free Black people across the Atlantic—Allen declared in an 1827 letter that America now belonged as much to the descendants of Africa as to those of Europe. His unflinching rhetoric still echoes in Sunday sermons and stump speeches. "This land which we have watered with our *tears* and our *blood*, is now our *mother country* and we are well satisfied to stay where wisdom abounds, and the gospel is free," Allen declared. Writing sixty years after Allen's death, Daniel Payne asserted that "history regards him, not only as the founder, but also as the master-spirit of the African Methodist Episcopal Church."

Allen's denomination grew quickly. By the time AME preachers reconvened in Philadelphia in May 1818, this time at Allen's house, it had expanded from six congregations to sixteen in only two years. Those congregations reported having 6,748 members. Notably, although born of the Revolutionary ethos in the emancipated North, the African Methodists had by then extended their reach into the slaveholding South, indeed to the very capital of American slavery. For when Bishop Allen tallied the membership rolls at the 1818 conference, he recorded the second largest cohort—1,848 washed-in-the-blood African Methodists—as being from Charleston, South Carolina. That placed Charleston ahead of Baltimore and behind only Allen's burgeoning operation in Philadelphia, which claimed nearly half of all AME members.

No one from Charleston had even attended the initial conference in 1816. Now, after only two years, the conference was joined by two preachers who had journeyed all the way from the Lowcountry to consult with Allen and seek ordination in his new connection. One was the mixed-race shoemaker Morris Brown, the other a formerly enslaved man named Henry Drayton. The saga they recounted of their own travails so closely paralleled those of the Black Methodists in Philadelphia and Baltimore that the conference seated the Charlestonians with the stature of original members. Although not in attendance in 1816, they had been "known to be present in *sympathy, desire* and *purpose*," according to Payne. And yet, despite that solidarity, there was an important difference. For in challenging the racial architecture of organized religion in the South, Charleston's African Methodists would be breaking not only social mechanisms of white control but also the law, and placing their lives and tenuous freedoms at grave risk.

VI.

The African Church

Turn again our captivity, O Lord, as the streams in the south.
They that sow in tears shall reap in joy.

—PSALM 126: 4–5 (KJV)

In 1815, the year before Richard Allen first convened his AME brethren in Philadelphia, a new Methodist sheriff rode into Charleston. Rev. Anthony Senter, a native North Carolinian, was but thirty years old when he arrived. He had trained as a blacksmith, and prospered at it, but at age twenty-one had undergone a conversion experience at a Methodist society meeting. His newfound faith was rewarded while riding home that very night when he took a hard fall from his horse and was unexpectedly rescued after praying for mercy. He joined the church, became the leader of one of its twelve-member classes, and then entered the ministry. In true Methodist fashion, Senter had been stationed in six different Carolina circuits in six years before his assignment to supervise the churches in Charleston. It would be among his last postings, as the young preacher died of consumption only two years later.

Why Senter, during his yearlong stay in Charleston, felt it necessary to upset the working accommodation that had developed between Black and white Methodists is a matter of conjecture. He was, of course, a native Southerner who had joined the Methodist connection just as its intolerance of slavery was starting to wilt. While it is not known whether he owned servants while in Charleston, he apparently did by the time of his death in nearby Georgetown (they may have come from a recent marriage). Furthermore, Senter was known to be "a strict disciplinarian," a by-the-book Methodist. That may have been reason enough for him to demolish the hybrid structure that had evolved to address the realpolitik of Methodism in Charleston: an overwhelmingly Black membership under the control of a very small white minority. Even the mission-driven itinerants who helped contrive the system acknowledged that it likely skirted not only Methodist rules but also state laws that restricted the rights of Black South Carolinians to assemble and worship.

When Senter got to Charleston, the city's Methodist churches counted 3,793 Black members and only 282 white ones—a ratio of more than 13 to 1. Indeed, there were then more Black Methodists residing in Charleston than in any American city. At both the Blue Meeting House on Cumberland Street and its newer offshoot, Bethel Methodist Church at the corner of Pitt and Boundary Streets, there simply were not enough white leaders to supervise so many Black congregants in accordance with laws prohibiting Black assembly without oversight. William Capers, a white Methodist preacher assigned to Charleston four years earlier, wrote that it had been fortunate therefore—"as if raised up for the exigences of the time"—that the congregations included "some extraordinary colored men." By this he meant free people of color who had gained the respect of white Charleston through their industriousness and devotion. They included the carpenter Richard Holloway, an early member of the Brown Fellowship Society, and Castile Selby, a teamster and hauler with a reputation for devotion to the church. Capers, who went on to become a Methodist bishop, mentioned six others: Harry Bull, Alexander Harleston, Smart Simpson, Peter Simpson, Amos Baxter, and Tom Smith. These, he said, were "men of intelligence and piety, who read the Scriptures and understood them, and were zealous for religion among the negroes."

Over time, white Methodist preachers in Charleston had granted a rare degree of autonomy to these lay leaders. Black congregants admitted their own members and organized them into classes. They conducted their own church trials for violations of moral or ecclesiastical codes, like adultery, drunkenness, or breaking the Sabbath, and ran their own "quarterly conferences" to debate matters of church polity and governance. They flocked to Methodist revivals and camp meetings, the rock festivals of their day, where celebrity preachers showcased the fire of salvation to enraptured mass audiences. Black leaders even took in offerings and disbursed the proceeds to church projects and good works. Each Monday, these free Black "agents" of the white ministry reported back in detail on Sunday's activities and collections. "They were the only persons who for Christ's sake were zealous enough to undertake such a service," Capers wrote. "I am satisfied that we did right to encourage them to the degree we did, notwithstanding we could not exactly square it either by the statutes on one hand, or the rules of Discipline on the other. We knew them to be good men; the work was one of the most sacred obligation to be done; and this was our only alternative."

The system also proved useful in opening the surrounding countryside to Methodist missionary work. To many plantation owners, free Black Methodists from the Lowcountry were more familiar—and trusted—than the interloping white circuit riders who came and went, often bearing a faint scent of abolitionism. They were recognized by the white elites in Goose Creek and Wando, in the parishes of St. Paul and St. James and St. John, on Wadmalaw Island and in Pon Pon. "In all these parts," Capers wrote, "some one of them was known and approved by some several of the planters, for whom they had been accustomed to do work, (one as a millwright, another as a carpenter or shoemaker,) or out of whose estates they had been liberated." White ministers, he noted, even slave-owning ones, got run off plantations simply because they were Methodists, "as if by some sentence of outlawry." But free Black preachers were permitted "to hold meetings with the negroes pretty freely."

The racial permissiveness of Methodist practices did not escape notice in white Charleston, nor could clapboard church walls contain the raucousness of unsupervised Black worship, at all hours. "That the meeting of a numerous assembly of black people to hear the scripture expounded by an ignorant and (too frequently) vicious person of their own color, can be of no benefit to either themselves or the community, is certain," began a letter to a Charleston newspaper in July 1816. "That it may be attended with many evils, is, I presume, obvious to every reflecting mind." The writer, identified only as "H.T.F.," implored city authorities to break up church services that created disturbances well past midnight. "Almost every night there is a meeting of these frantic, noisy worshippers," he complained. "I say noisy, for their assent to any part of the doctrine preached to them, is attended with groans, clapping of hands, hysterical laughter, together with violent distortions of the body, and apparently with mania. This is an evil; it requires *immediate* and *decided* suppression. Passion, like a hidden fire, needs but a small breeze to bid it blaze: let the sparks, therefore, be thoroughly extinguished, lest per adventure they become too formidable, and lay waste the structure of security, and the seat of power."

His sensitivities already heightened, Rev. Senter then picked up intelligence that Black church leaders had used Sunday offerings "to buy slaves out of serfdom to set them free." While no document has been found to prove the claim, there are reasons to consider it credible. State archival records confirm that several of the city's leading Black Methodist freemen had purchased enslaved people, both before and after Senter's tenure, and that at least some were then emancipated. Because most of South Carolina's manumission records have been lost or destroyed, it is difficult to document any organized connection to the Methodist churches or know whether any particular person was purchased in order to be freed.

But whatever precisely Preacher-in-Charge Senter discovered, he found it deeply disturbing. With white membership so dismally low, Senter had no higher priority than converting Charleston's many white Methodist dabblers into tithing members, the kind who might underwrite church operations and donate to building projects. What prevented many of those curiosity-seekers from leaving other churches was the Methodists' hostility to slavery. Nothing, therefore, could have been more antithetical to the image that Senter was hoping to market than news that his churches had financed an ongoing manumission operation. In response, he quickly snuffed out every flicker of Black self-determination. All monies collected would now be delivered immediately into the hands of white stewards. Church trials would take place only in the presence of the preacher-in-charge. Most offensive of all to Black congregants, Senter abolished their separate quarterly conferences, their only claim to self-governance. This "soon awakened quite an agitation among the colored membership," Methodist historian Francis Asbury Mood observed.

If there is a likely chief instigator of Senter's ire, it would be Morris Brown, the future leader of the breakaway African Methodist church that preceded Mother Emanuel. Brown, who had been born free of mixed parentage in 1770, purchased at least fourteen enslaved countrymen in nine different sales between 1810 and 1819. He freed many, and it can be assumed all, but the scarcity of records prevents an absolute conclusion. Although Brown earned a comfortable living as a shoemaker, real estate investor, and lay preacher, it would have been difficult for him to accumulate the more than $5,000 spent on those purchases without communal effort. It makes sense, therefore, that Brown may have served as a purchasing agent for what had become, in essence, a Black Methodist benevolent society.

In Brown's first known transaction, on August 16, 1810, he spent £650 to buy "a mulatto woman slave named Bella and her five children named Malcolm, Charlotte, Mary, Samuel and Sarah," in the wording of the bill of sale. This was Morris Brown's family, with Bella possibly a nickname for the first of his two wives, Elizabeth. The seller was Hannah Lesesne, the Philadelphia-born widow of a Huguenot planter and Revolutionary War veteran who lived on East Bay Street. Four years later, Brown arranged to legally free Bella and their children. By waiting until their eldest son, Malcolm, had just turned twenty, he may have been navigating the state's 1800 law that allowed emancipation only for those who could demonstrate "their ability to gain a livelihood in an honest way," as judged by a court.

Senter's edicts may have stifled the overt use of church funds for manumissions, but Brown continued to purchase enslaved people for several more years. Other free Black Methodist leaders in Charleston also bought and freed them on occasion, at least until 1820, when the state legislature began requiring its stingy approval for manumission. But there also were free people of color associated with the Methodist churches who bought humans, held them as property—either by choice or because the law made emancipation all but impossible—and traded in them as commodities just as white enslavers did.

MORRIS BROWN AND CHARLESTON's other Black Methodists seethed quietly for a while about Anthony Senter's reassertion of authority. In the recounting of Methodist historians, Black leaders took "considerable umbrage" and began denigrating the white ministry in whispered conversations. They portrayed white preachers, "whom they had hitherto regarded as their best friends," as "their oppressors, who had not only injured them, but designed to rob them and their poor, to enrich themselves," wrote Rev. James O. Andrew, a white minister who served Charleston's Methodist circuit the year after Senter. "These things were gradually and artfully insinuated into the minds of the people." Then white church officials in Charleston found a way to so offend their Black brethren, with a gesture of such searing symbolism, that it brought their fury to full boil.

Perhaps inevitably, given the dearth of available land on the narrow Charleston peninsula and the cultural resonance of funeral practices, the clash arose over a "burying ground." Demand regularly outpaced the supply of dry earth for the dead in antebellum Charleston, where malaria, yellow fever, childhood disease, and infant mortality kept undertakers fully subscribed. The search by churches and benevolent groups for new plots was incessant, and by the turn of the century the crowding of graveyards had been cited as a public health threat by the district grand jury. Six years earlier, the small Methodist cemetery attached to the Blue Meeting House on Cumberland Street had approached capacity, along with seating in the sanctuary itself. The white

Methodist leadership set out to find property for a second burial ground, with plans to eventually build a new church—Bethel—on part of the plot. When fundraising efforts flagged, Methodist leaders persuaded Thomas Bennett, the father of a future governor of the same name, to donate his parcel at the corner of Pitt and Boundary Streets. Located today in the heart of downtown, where Boundary has been renamed Calhoun, the site was then considered the exurbs.

The Methodists designed a wooden two-story church for the site, forty feet wide by sixty feet long, topped by a simple pediment inlaid with a glass rosette. As with the Blue Meeting House, there would be no steeple to draw the eyes heavenward, and no ornaments of grandeur. The church would include upstairs galleries for the enslaved and benches at the rear for free persons of color. Framing and carpentry work began when half of the expected construction cost of £600 had been raised. Although it would take another eleven years to plaster the interior and replace the primitive preacher's platform with a formal pulpit, the church opened in 1798 and quickly filled on Sundays, mostly with Black worshippers. Three years later the congregation added a parsonage on the lot, and by 1806 it had accumulated sufficient reserves to give Bethel its first coat of paint. White church leaders also decided that year to search for yet another burial ground, as the one at Bethel, which had been subdivided between white graves on the north and Black plots on the south, was filling fast.

The final insult for Charleston's Black Methodists came in 1817 when Bethel's white trustees announced their decision to build a garage for the church's horse-drawn hearse atop the Black half of the burial ground. Black members voiced their opposition to the desecration of their ancestors' resting places, and the white trustees swatted them away like gnats. Yes, Black members may have contributed substantially to Bethel's finances, but they had no authority over the land, the trustees explained. They had only been granted its use by the white leadership's benevolence, and now it was being reclaimed. The dismissive tone proved a critical miscalculation, as it provided precisely the accelerant needed by the Black Methodist leadership to transform dissent into action. "Great excitement ensued," Mood wrote.

Clearly there must have been considerable cohesion and coordination, led by men of charisma and organizational acuity, most notably the lay preacher and moral leader Morris Brown. For at some point that year, likely in the fall of 1817, nearly every Black class leader tendered his resignation to the Bethel trustees "at one fell swoop," and a sizable share of the city's Black Methodist membership, totaling 4,367 people, withdrew at once. The walkout mirrored the one led by Richard Allen and Absalom Jones in Philadelphia, except of course that the bulk of those who resigned their Bethel memberships were enslaved. Not since the Stono uprising eight decades earlier had Black Carolinians carried out such a daring and overtly political rebellion, defying not only years of established practice but also foundational theories of inherent Black inferiority and ineptitude.

The next Sunday found Bethel's balcony "almost completely deserted, and it was a vacancy that could be *felt*," Mood reported. "The absence of their responses and hearty songs was really felt to be a loss to those so long accustomed to hear them." The Black exodus depleted not only the church's spiritual fervor but also its collection plate. Between 1817 and 1818, the membership of the Methodist Episcopal Church in Charleston plummeted from 6,049 to 1,677. Only 1,323 of 5,699 Black members remained. In the context of the Southern racial hierarchy, such individual and communal acts of secession were as unthinkable as spitting in a white man's face. What happened next proved even more so.

The Methodist schism reinforced the fear that many white Charlestonians had harbored all along about the racial democratization of religion. Methodist minister Solomon Bryan found it so alarming that he wrote the city council in November 1817 that he was "apprehensive of sinister designs" by the Black Methodists. Bryan's letter has not survived to explain his suspicions. But his choice to flag an internal church controversy for city officials suggests he anticipated the formation of an autonomous Black congregation, a novel legal entity that would test state and city restrictions on Black assembly. His entreaty may have found a receptive audience, for on December 28 the city guard apprehended and briefly jailed 469 "black & colored persons" who had been conducting worship services "in a manner contrary to the law of the state" and "in a way calculated to be a nuisance to the neighbors." *The Times* reported the following day that the unmonitored assemblies had "been held for some time past" but had only recently come to official notice. "We trust the reprimand they received will induce them to act with more discretion in future," the newspaper suggested.

Despite such ongoing harassment, Morris Brown dreamed of leading his people to a new Zion, an independent African Methodist church modeled on Richard Allen's Bethel. Although Brown would become the second bishop of the African Methodist Episcopal Church and the namesake of a college in Atlanta and of churches in Charleston, Philadelphia, New York, and New Orleans, surprisingly little is known about his early life. His parents and the circumstances of his birth and free status have never been identified beyond the assertion of AME historian Daniel Payne that he "was a man of mixed blood, and on the father's side of Scotch descent." State law had established since 1740 that a child's slave status "shall follow the condition of the mother," so either Brown's mother also was free or his father succeeded in manumitting him at birth. He was said to be sweet-tempered and reverent toward authority as both a child and an adult. But unlike Richard Allen, Brown left no account of his conversion or his evolution as a lay preacher. He apparently received no formal schooling, and the learned Payne, who later served as his private secretary, labeled him an "illiterate." Payne wrote that Brown had at some point learned to read the Bible—likely taught "by some white person, who was paid for his trouble with baked sweet potatoes"—and in his will Brown bequeathed books on religion and history to his sons. But he could not write beyond affixing his name to documents, and like Richard Allen employed an amanuensis to write his sermons and letters. "As a preacher he was behind many of his brethren," Payne observed.

However, Brown excelled in other ways that mattered more for his time. He commanded with a firm hand, carried himself with dignity, and lived with unquestioned rectitude. "He was seldom eloquent, but there was a deep tone of piety running through his entire discourse," Payne wrote. "Notwithstanding all the literary disadvantages under which he labored, he was, in spirit, abreast of the age, and to the utmost of his knowledge and power encouraged the education of his people." Brown stood an imposing six feet tall and was "well proportioned, with a slight tendency to corpulency." His large head rose to a Yosemite-esque dome above a ridge of shaggy eyebrows. He wore his sideburns long, and combed a crinkly mane behind his ears. "His complexion was yellow, his forehead lofty, and intellectual, and a glow of benevolence radiated his whole countenance," wrote Rev. Henry Highland Garnet. "He possessed in a very high degree, those fine manners, which are peculiar to the refined and well-bred classes of South Carolina."

Brown had established a shoemaking shop at 50 King Street by at least 1802, when he was thirty-two. He became a man of some means, building a two-story Charleston single house with a double-tiered piazza on a lot he bought on Smith Street in 1814 and then buying the house next door four years later. He purchased a third tract, on Anson Street, for $1,300 in 1821, and sold it for $100 profit less than two years later. When not running the shop, Brown dedicated himself to his ministry and was among those free Black missionaries dispatched by the Methodists to nearby plantations. Later in life, he reflected on that work in a sermon about Moses's devotion to God. "I knew a man in Charleston, S.C., who, if he is alive, is about eighty years of age," Brown began. "He was a slave, but he was also a man of prayer, and he used to go with me on a Saturday night to preach the Gospel to the slaves on the plantations in South Carolina." Brown went on to explain that his companion had pledged to devote half of his time to God's work if he ever gained his freedom, but then did not do so when it happened. "I only tell this," Brown told his listeners, "to show how few will give up the world for God like Moses."

The departure of thousands of African Methodists from Bethel, high-minded as it might have been, presented Morris Brown and his collaborators with immediate challenges, none more urgent than finding a house of worship and renewing the search for burial space. They considered making a legal claim for Bethel itself, given that Black members had contributed so generously toward its construction, but abandoned that approach as politically far-fetched. Instead, they found two adjoining lots on Judith Street in the Wraggborough neighborhood that could be stitched into a cemetery of 80 feet by 128 feet. Because the properties fell just outside the city limit, they would need the legislature's approval to establish a burying ground there. Brown used the occasion to assemble a leadership cadre, hoping there would be force and protection in numbers.

On November 24, 1817, he and twenty-two other free persons of color petitioned the state house of representatives: "Your petitioners, who are free persons of color, on behalf of themselves and others, of the religious sect or denomination called Methodists, in the City of Charleston, are desirous of purchasing two lots of land to be appropriated as a place of interment for themselves and their descendants; the present burial ground being inadequate for that purpose," they pleaded. Morris Brown signed first, followed by Henry Drayton, Charles Corr, and William Eden. Next came Morris Brown's eldest son, Malcolm, Abraham Ash, and Marcus Brown, a liberated slave who had taken Morris Brown's surname after being bought and manumitted by him. The list also included Amos Cruckshanks, Smart Simpson, and the four Mathewes brothers—Peter, John, Henry, and Isaac. Following the Richard Allen playbook, Brown recruited six upstanding white Charlestonians to endorse the request, including postmaster Thomas W. Bacot, former city councilman Simon Magwood, and Charles Cotesworth Pinckney, a signer of the Constitution. The petition received a positive recommendation from the Committee on Religion in the house of representatives, and initially won approval from the full chamber. It was disapproved, however, by the state senate, where the Committee on Incorporations had rejected it without explanation. Property records suggest the final purchase of the two lots never took place.

THERE IS NO KNOWN RECORD of how long or how regularly Morris Brown and Richard Allen had been in contact. But it was sufficient for Brown to learn that a second AME conference would be held in Philadelphia in May 1818. He and his chief lieutenant, Henry Drayton, journeyed there, presumably by schooner, and arrived in time for the praying and singing that opened the session at Allen's house that May 9. By the end of the eleven-day meeting, the Charleston preachers had been fully indoctrinated into the practice and policy of African Methodism. Bishop Allen ordained each of them, making Drayton a deacon and Brown a higher-ranking elder, a recognition that Charleston had ascended as the young denomination's Southern stronghold. The leaders of the Black separatist movement in slaveholding South Carolina had formally associated themselves with the Northern liberationist and abolitionist ethos of Richard Allen's AME church, a decidedly subversive and radical act.

Some early Methodist histories, seeking to assign conspiratorial intent, assert that Brown and Drayton had secreted themselves to Philadelphia well before the Black walkout in Charleston in 1817. Those accounts contend that once trained and ordained by Allen the two men came home to await a pretext that could be cleaved into a schism. "With these additional powers, they returned to Charleston, and waited a favourable opportunity to blow up to a flame the slumbering embers of discontent," James O. Andrew wrote in 1830. Three decades later, Francis Mood argued that "a regular scheme had been devised for the formal secession of the disaffected ones from the church" and that "for two years their plans were being matured." Although it is likely that Brown or Drayton had been in communication with Allen, there is, in fact, no evidence known that anyone from South Carolina met with the AME bishop until the 1818 conference they attended. Indeed, Daniel Payne pointedly noted their absence from the inaugural meeting in 1816. "At that time there were thousands in Charleston, S.C., holding the same sentiment," Payne wrote. "But the representatives of this latter city were not present, in person, because the difficulties in the mode of traveling, with many legal obstacles, prevented them."

The trip in 1818 must have been fortifying. Almost immediately after returning to Charleston that spring, Brown and Drayton took $1,500 from an account fed by Sunday offerings and purchased the land on which they would build Charleston's landmark African Church. They settled on a lot near the northeast corner of Hanover and Reid Streets in the Hampstead Village neighborhood on Charleston's East Side. It was situated in a diverse and somewhat unruly stretch of the Charleston peninsula known as the Neck, which was unincorporated and thus less heavily policed than the high-society neighborhoods at the southern tip of the peninsula. The property ran 200 feet down Hanover and 80 feet along Reid. The seller, Susannah Cart, the wife of lumber merchant John Cart, had inherited the land in trust four years earlier from a prosperous planter named Christopher Williman, whose relationship to her is unclear (Cart was the only heir who was not one of Williman's children or grandchildren). Morris Brown had done business with Susannah Cart before, having bought one of his properties on Smith Street from her in 1814.

Brown and his fellow Black Methodists had organized themselves at this point into an entity they called the "African Society," and the land in Hampstead was purchased in its name by seven trustees. Morris Brown, as always, listed his name first in the five-page deed, followed by Henry Drayton, Amos Cruckshanks, Malcolm Brown, John Mathewes, Peter Mathewes, and Smart Simpson. As with the burial ground, this would by legal necessity be an initiative of free persons of color with property rights, not their enslaved brethren. Dated June 4, the deed specified a process for replacing trustees who stepped down or were found unacceptable by three-fourths of the membership.

Like the secession of the prior year, the planting of a flag for a physical church, a place where freedom might be preached and plots might be hatched, was viewed by white Charlestonians as a hostile provocation. It was seen as a glaring emblem of the dangers of allowing even limited rights to persons of color. The rapid, forceful, and multifaceted response by the police and the legislature became part and parcel of the concerted campaign to rid South Carolina of its free Black community.

On June 7, the first Sunday after the deed had been recorded, the city guard busted up a crowded afternoon service in a house in the suburbs and hauled 140 Black worshippers to jail. They were charged with violating statutes against Black assembly without white supervision, and there was no discrimination between the free and the enslaved. The next morning, the city council sentenced five of the leaders, presumably including Brown and Drayton, to a month in jail, unless they preferred to be exiled from the state. Eight other ministers were given a choice between ten lashes or a five-dollar fine. Various newspaper accounts maintained that the five jailed leaders included "some blacks constituted as Bishops and Preachers in one of the Northern cities." This may have been a confused reference to Brown and Drayton, as there is no indication that Richard Allen—the only AME bishop—or other denominational leaders traveled to Charleston in what would have been a legally foolhardy venture.

It wasn't like Brown and Drayton and the others hadn't been warned. There had been prior rounds of arrests at prayer meetings in the private homes that served as worship spaces while a church was being built. At first, the offenders received slaps on the wrist, released by city magistrates after a stern lecture and an uncomfortable night in the lockup. The church's leaders sought relief from the city council, asking for official backing for their meetings, but the aldermen "decided that it would be both unlawful and inexpedient to permit the formation of a distinct independent congregation of blacks."

Northern editorial writers reacted with revulsion to news of the arrests of free people at prayer. "We have rarely recorded a deed that excited emotions so unpleasant," wrote the editors of the *Boston Recorder*, a religious newspaper with abolitionist leanings. "In this case, not only slaves, but blacks *as free as any man in the country*, are taken up on the Sabbath, and committed to prison, and sentenced to continued confinement, to the whipping-post or a heavy fine, and to banishment from the state—for what? Because they assemble quietly to worship 'the God of love and peace' on the day which he has expressly set apart, and required to be devoted to his worship!" The writer warned of the wrathful consequences of such repression—"when assemblages of Negroes will be formed for less holy purposes than to serve Jehovah; and those men who deny them a privilege to which God has entitled the black and the white alike, will fall victims to *other* passions than those encouraged in the temples of the Lord."

That earned a scolding from a Charlestonian, identified only as "L," whose response was published in the Boston newspaper the following month. He explained that the African Methodists had repeatedly flouted the law, leaving authorities little choice, and sought to dispel the notion that Black Charlestonians had been blocked from practicing their faith. There were seventeen churches in the city and all accommodated Black worshippers, more than six thousand in all, he said. In some of those churches, Black congregants had their own lay preachers, exhorters, and class leaders who worked hand-in-glove with white pastors. They held hundreds of prayer meetings around the city every week. "Yes, Mr. Editor, of these people who are represented as the objects of stern and cruel persecution, six thousand constantly sit down at the table of the Lord with those who are held up to view as their religious oppressors," the writer parried. "I believe it would be difficult to point out any community, equally numerous, in the Christian world, in the enjoyment of greater religious freedom, or more frequent opportunities of hearing the Gospel, or of which a larger proportion professedly embrace the offers of salvation." Furthermore, the man argued, an independent Black church would be susceptible to manipulation by outside agitators and corruption by ne'er-do-wells. "Is it not easily supposable," he asked, "that one of the numerous villains who crowd the State Prisons of the Middle States, might come and announce himself to them as a Bishop, and kindle a flame, which would overwhelm them with ruin?"

Even after a month in jail, Morris Brown's fealty to African Methodism remained strong, as did his desire to shape its national presence, and in April 1819 he again risked an out-of-state trip to an AME conference in Baltimore. Seventeen men attended. As the standard-bearer for the country's second largest concentration of African Methodists, Brown found his stature rising. Surely he reported to Allen and the others about his congregation's confrontations with authorities, and the ongoing construction of the church at Hanover and Reid. It was being built of lumber atop a brick foundation—many members had carpentry and masonry skills—and likely resembled the Quaker style of the city's two-story Methodist churches. One AME historian described the building as "a commodious but modest house of worship." Francis Mood referred to it as "a neat church building" that was erected "after great exertion." The congregation reserved part of the churchyard for yet another burial ground. Members also met at two auxiliary sites, one on Anson Street and one in the short and secluded lane known as Cow Alley (today's enchanting brick-walled Philadelphia Alley). Oral tradition has it that the three branches came to be known as the Bethel Circuit. There is no known contemporaneous documentation for that, nor is it known whether Bethel referenced the AME church in Philadelphia that the Charlestonians hoped to emulate or the Methodist Episcopal church on Pitt Street that they had abandoned.

WHITE CHARLESTON, NATURALLY, kept a close watch. "Would it not be well if the attention of the community were directed towards some of its members, at present engaged in building a place of Public Worship, in Hampstead, intended to be known as an 'African Church!'" one writer asked in a Charleston newspaper in April 1820. "Do those things appear right and compatible with the Constitution?" Six months later, a petition from nearly 150 leading citizens alerted the legislature "that a spacious Building has lately been erected in the immediate neighborhood of Charleston for the exclusive worship of Negroes and coloured people, from means supplied them by the Abolition Societies in the Eastern and Northern States, as your petitioners are credibly informed." The lobbyists from Charleston paired their alarm about the church with calls to strangle the flow of free persons of color into the state and to prohibit the teaching of reading to enslaved people. In a letter to a Boston journal, a Charleston clergyman wrote that South Carolina's governor, John Geddes, a devoted Presbyterian, had recently withdrawn his backing for the African Church and that construction had been suspended. "You will not be surprised at the jealousy of people against religious meetings, consisting entirely of blacks, and particularly where the worship is to be conducted by them, when you are informed, that most of the incipient schemes of insurrection, &c., that have been detected, have taken place at *professedly religious meetings*," the Charlestonian wrote.

Sensing that his church was about to be shuttered before it could open, Morris Brown sought to outmaneuver his antagonists by filing his own petition to the legislature. Given his failure to win approval for the burial ground three years earlier, he understood it would be an even longer shot to gain the legislature's blessing for an independent church. This time he persuaded twenty-five other free persons of color to sign, along with thirty-two white supporters, including merchants and planters and some of the most influential religious leaders in the city. Rev. Benjamin M. Palmer, pastor of Circular Congregational Church, topped the list, along with the region's leading Presbyterian ministers—Rev. George Reid from First Scots, Rev. Artemas Boies, newly ensconced at Second Presbyterian, Rev. John Buchan of St. Andrew's, and Rev. A. W. Leland from nearby James Island. They were among the area's most ardent paternalists, believing that slavery could best be morally justified—and defended against abolitionist condemnation—if the enslaved were Christianized and nurtured like the helpless children of benevolent parents. The city's Methodist ministers, of course, did not sign.

To give the African Church its best odds in South Carolina's General Assembly, Brown larded the petition with commitments to best behavior and directly addressed each of the white citizenry's misgivings about a Black church. He pledged that the doors would stay open to allow inspection. Services would not be held after dark. Decorum would be maintained. Local white ministers would be welcome. Northern Black ones would not. He invited the lawmakers to tack on their own restrictions. With Morris Brown's name affixed first, followed by top lieutenants like Henry Drayton, Charles Corr, Amos Cruckshanks, John and Peter Mathewes, and Malcolm and Marcus Brown, the filing landed in the house of representatives in Columbia on November 28, 1820.

"Your petitioners are free persons of color, attached to the African Methodist Episcopal Church, in Charleston, called Zion, and have recently erected a house of worship, at Hampstead, on Charleston Neck, at the corner of Hanover and Reid Streets," the request began. This is the only known use of "Zion" to name what was otherwise identified, certainly by white scribes, as the African Church. The men asked "to open the said building for the purpose of Divine worship from the rising of the sun, until the going down of the same" provided that "the door of the said building shall always remain open, and that all white ministers of the Gospel of every denomination shall be respectfully invited to officiate in the said Church, whenever disposed so to do, and that separate seats shall be provided for such Citizens as may honor the congregation with their presence, either for religious instruction or to inspect their morals and deportment." They went on to promise that "no minister of color, who does not reside in this State shall officiate for the said congregation nor shall any slave be admitted a member thereof, without the approbation of his or her owner." They pleaded that their motives had been misrepresented, and pledged that their only design was "to worship the omnipotent ruler of the Universe 'in spirit, and in truth.'"

Those prostrations proved insufficient, as sentiment in the statehouse had only intensified against the free Black population. One day before the African Church petition arrived in the house, Gov. Geddes had alleged in a message to the legislature that free persons of color were sneaking into the state. He proposed the permanent exile of newly emancipated people. "The policy of our country forbids the increase of this class of persons amongst us," Geddes wrote, "and under existing circumstances imperiously calls for the adoption of the strongest measures to prevent it." The governor emphasized that his concern, like that of many Carolinians in 1820, was animated by the congressional battle over slavery that had just produced the Missouri Compromise. That agreement simultaneously admitted Missouri to the union as a slaveholding state and Maine as a free state, while prohibiting slavery above the 36°30' latitude line in states subsequently carved out of the Louisiana Purchase territories. Despite the victory in Missouri, the South shuddered at the precedent established for Washington's authority to dictate slavery policy to the states. As abolitionist sentiment grew in the North, the region found itself increasingly isolated and wary. As always, that defensive stance was more pronounced in South Carolina because of the state's widening racial imbalance. Between 1800 and 1820, the number of enslaved South Carolinians grew by 77 percent and the Black population exploded past the white population into a 53 percent majority.

In that charged atmosphere, the Charleston delegation in the state house of representatives, which took up the African Church petition, needed only four days to announce its opposition. The lawmakers acknowledged that the request to open the church had been "couched in humble & respectful terms" and they stressed the legislature's "every desire to extend all the benefits and comforts of religion to people of this class." But the delegation was otherwise unmoved. Free persons of color did not need their own congregation because they could find "sufficient room" in the city's existing churches. "Your Committee think the petitioners would be better instructed by well educated and pious Divines in the Churches in that city than by ignorant and fanatical preachers of their own Colour," the delegation advised. Five days later, the measure had been "ordered to lie on the table," in the parlance of the House Journal, never to be revived. In the state senate, it never emerged from committee.

Offering the state's imprimatur to the African Church would have been an invitation to free persons of color to migrate to South Carolina, hardly the deterrent being sought by Gov. Geddes. Instead, the lawmakers turned their attention to crafting an "Act to restrain the emancipation of Slaves, and to prevent Free persons of Color from entering into this State." The law, which passed five days before Christmas 1820, ended the practice of private manumission through deed or self-purchase by requiring legislative approval on a case-by-case basis. It also threatened any free person of color who crossed into South Carolina after March 1, 1821, with heavy fines and, if unable to pay, with sale into slavery for up to five years. The city government, meanwhile, cracked down on free Black lay ministers like Morris Brown and sympathetic white pastors who, in their enthusiasm to impart the Scriptures, might be teaching unschooled Black people to read. In January 1821, the city council instructed the marshal "to inform the Ministers of the Gospel and others, who keep *Night and Sunday Schools for slaves*, that the *Education of such persons is prohibited by law*, and that the City Council feel imperiously bound to enforce the penalty." Simply put, white Charleston increasingly perceived free persons of color, and their church, to be an odious threat. "An excrescence of the body politic," one Charleston newspaper called them, "depriving the general system of its health and vigour, and corrupting its vital functions . . . It is from this quarter we are to apprehend danger."

But for Charleston's early African Methodist leaders, the pull to represent the South in the creation of an independent Black denomination proved stronger than any risk of punishment. Morris Brown attended an AME conference in Baltimore in April 1822, where Marcus Brown and Amos Cruckshanks were made deacons. Charles Corr and Henry Drayton attended the inaugural New York AME conference two months later. That same year, with the church outgrowing Richard Allen's ability to manage it, a vote was held to elect a first assistant to the bishop and Morris Brown finished second among three contenders. By the early summer of 1822, Charleston had developed a solid AME infrastructure, led by Elder Brown and ten other licensed preachers—Marcus Brown, Harry Bull, Charles Corr, Amos Cruckshanks, Henry Drayton, James Eden, Alexander Harleston, John B. Mathewes, Smart Simpson, and London Turpin.

Daniel Payne wrote that members of the young African Church were repeatedly arrested and "driven like a flock of sheep before the civil authorities" to be fined and flogged. "This little band of Christians had to suffer great persecutions on account of their *independent spirit, their opposition to colorphobia,* and *their desire to worship God in their own house consecrated to His service*," Payne wrote. Eventually, he said, "they were allowed to worship God in their own house, but under the most humiliating restrictions." Francis Mood, the Methodist historian, wrote on the other hand that the African Methodists "were never permitted to worship in their own building." Rather, he said, they "dragged out a miserable existence until the year 1822."

That year would unfold unlike any other in Charleston's history.

VII.

Hot Bed: The Insurrection Plot

And they utterly destroyed all that was in the city, both man and woman, young and old, and ox, and sheep, and ass, with the edge of the sword.

—JOSHUA 6:21 (KJV)

On a pleasant May Saturday in 1822, just before the summer swelter made Charleston all but uninhabitable, a house servant named Peter finished his shopping at the fish market and ambled down to a wharf along the Cooper River. As Peter enjoyed the soft breezes and surveyed the panorama of fishing skiffs and tall-masted vessels, another enslaved man of his acquaintance, named William, engaged him in small talk about a curious flag flying atop one of the ships. After a minute of banter, William's tone turned ominous, seemingly out of the blue.

"Do you know that something serious is about to take place?" he whispered.

Peter said he did not.

"Well, there is," William said, "and many of us are determined to right ourselves!"

Peter asked William to explain himself.

"Why, we are determined to shake off our bondage, and for this purpose we stand on a good foundation. Many have joined, and if you will go with me, I will show you the man, who has the list of names who will take yours down."

As whispers of a mass uprising had begun to spread furtively through Black Charleston, enslaved men like William had been cautioned to be scrupulous about who they approached. "Take care and don't mention it to those waiting men who receive presents of old coats from their masters," one organizer warned. "They'll betray us." But William, who was later depicted as "an over-zealous convert, whose discretion was shorter than his tongue," did not take that directive to heart. For in Peter, who was of mixed race, he had targeted just such a dutiful servant, a miscalculation that would carry grave implications for Black South Carolinians for decades to come.

The consequences for Charleston's nascent African Church would be severe. As the plotting unraveled, starting on the waterfront that day, white authorities became convinced that it had incubated within the already nettlesome Black congregation. By summer's end, Charleston's brief experiment with Black religious autonomy would be brutally repressed, with many of its leaders executed or exiled. Historians have reinterpreted the unsettling events of 1822 over the years, and will continue to do so. But what has come to be known as the Denmark Vesey affair, named for the man prosecuted as the ringleader, remains central to the aura of resistance surrounding Mother Emanuel's origin story and essential to the church's sense of itself.

THAT DAY ON THE WHARF, Peter recoiled at being asked to join what he disparaged as "this business." He was satisfied with his condition and grateful to his master "for his kindness," he told William before hurrying away. That, at least, is the self-serving account Peter provided to authorities on May 30 after first unburdening himself to his owner, John Cordes Prioleau, a wealthy planter with a grand house on Meeting Street. Prioleau immediately alerted the city's intendant (or mayor), James Hamilton, Jr. The dashing and ambitious Hamilton took the threat seriously enough that he convened the city council two hours later and summoned Gov. Thomas Bennett, Jr., so they could hear directly from Peter.

The authorities quickly rounded up William, who was enslaved by a merchant named John Paul. He first denied Peter's story. But after a week in the "black hole" of the city's dreaded Work-House, where he was repeatedly interrogated and presumably tortured, William confessed that Black people across the Lowcountry were plotting the indiscriminate murder of their white overseers. He named names, and two alleged conspirators were brought in for questioning and their belongings searched. Investigators failed at first to confirm the initial reports, and began to have doubts. But on the evening of Friday, June 14, Intendant Hamilton received a frantic 8:00 p.m. visit from John Wilson, the state engineer. Wilson's enslaved man, George, had confirmed to him not only the existence of a widespread plot but also the appointed hour of attack, midnight on Sunday, June 16, only two days hence.

The Charleston peninsula was placed on high alert, with guards stationed at strategic positions. The quartermaster general stocked the armory with three hundred muskets and twenty thousand ball cartridges. "Although there was necessarily great excitement, and among the female part of our community much alarm, yet the night passed off without any thing like commotion or disturbance," Intendant Hamilton wrote in an after-action report. "The conspirators finding the whole town encompassed at 10 o'clock, by the most vigilant patrols, did not dare to show themselves, whatever might have been their plans." Within two weeks, a dragnet had pulled in dozens of suspects, Hamilton had constituted a court of prominent citizens, and investigators had zeroed in on a purported mastermind, a formerly enslaved man named Denmark Vesey. Vesey had a reputation as both a skilled carpenter and a bold rabble-rouser. He was also, if one can believe the remarkable trial record generated by the case, a Scripture-quoting member of Morris Brown's African Church, the forerunner of Mother Emanuel.

By the time a pair of courts finished their work in August, a narrative had been constructed—concocted, in the view of some historians—of a plot at once far-reaching and fantastical. The judges concluded that the conspirators had been actively scheming for six months, since near Christmas 1821, and that the plot had been "in agitation" for four years, coinciding with the formation of the African Church. They took from the testimony of alleged conspirators and self-interested witnesses, albeit not all demonstrably credible, that a guerilla army of thousands of Black desperadoes stood ready to muster on June 16. As midnight passed, the rebels allegedly planned to empty house cabinets of muskets and bayonets and then raid an unguarded militia storehouse and the poorly secured arsenal. Enslaved laborers from the countryside would help themselves to axes, hatchets, spades, and hoes, and paddle across the marshes in dugout canoes. A blacksmith had been enlisted to forge crude bayonets and pike heads that could be affixed to long poles. Draymen and stableboys would make off with horses to mobilize the force. A hairdresser had been lined up to manufacture wigs and whiskers to disguise rebel leaders as white men.

All but 10 of the 130 Black Charlestonians initially implicated and all but 3 of the 69 ultimately convicted were enslaved. But as city dwellers, many had been allowed by their owners to hire out their services as carters and porters and the like, enabling a certain freedom of movement and association. Monday Gell, a trusted African-born man who purportedly was central to the planning, ran a successful harness-making shop that he made available for clandestine meetings. In choosing the men later identified as his lieutenants, Vesey shunned his fellow freedmen and surrounded himself instead with enslaved men who may have made for less likely suspects. Among the accused were the servants of some of the most prominent families in South Carolina, with four belonging to Gov. Bennett and others to men like Elias Horry, a former intendant; Thomas Blackwood, the president of Planters' & Mechanics' Bank; and Job Palmer, the father of noted Congregationalist minister Benjamin Morgan Palmer. Like slaveholders across the South, these men had deluded themselves as to the contentment of their captives and could not fathom the professed bloodlust of their designs.

"Tell me, are you guilty," Horry, a rice planter, is said to have demanded of his imprisoned coachman, John, during the trial, "for I cannot believe unless I hear you say so."

"Yes," John reportedly answered.

"What were your intentions?" the horrified Horry asked.

"To kill you, rip open your belly & throw your guts in your face," John explained.

The testimony, as recorded, raised the specter of a merciless onslaught, intending nothing short of the violent overthrow of the Lowcountry's white minority. The insurgents had counted on the element of surprise, and on a tepid response from a white population depleted by seasonal migration to cooler climes. The throats of slave owners and overseers would be slit, the governor and intendant executed in their sleep. Selected buildings would be torched, and when fire bells drew unarmed men into the streets they would be slaughtered with clubs and axes. Little sympathy was to be shown to white women and children. "What was the use of killing the louse and leaving the nit?" Vesey was said to have asked. Vesey personally planned to march a company of men to the Guard House and unchain its prisoners. Bank vaults would be emptied, stores looted, and the South's most elegant mansions plundered. The entire city would eventually be put to the torch. Black onlookers who declined to join the marauding army would be treated little differently than white people. Amid the chaos, rebels would commandeer ships in Charleston Harbor and set sail for Haiti, home to the recent slave revolt against the French that had inspired their own.

In his mid-fifties, Vesey (pronounced VEE-See) was far older than the others arrested. Some modern historians question whether he was the essential instigator that the trial record makes him out to be and suggest that the leadership structure may have been more coalitional. They favor a recasting of "the rising" as less a military operation than a social movement. But whether truthful or trumped-up, the evidence gathered by the court pointed it toward a central organizer. Like other accused conspirators, William Paul testified that Vesey was "the Chiefest man & more concerned than anyone else." Such avowals helped persuade Lionel H. Kennedy and Thomas Parker, the magistrates who oversaw most of the trials, to open their "Official Report" with the assertion that "at the head of the conspiracy stood Denmark Vesey" and that "with him the idea undoubtedly originated." After a three-day search, a captain in the city guard located Vesey at the house of his enslaved first wife and hauled him out during a drenching downpour on the night of June 22. Six days later he was condemned to hang, a sentence carried out a mere four days after that, on July 2, when Vesey and five others were executed.

That was just the beginning of the gruesomeness. Although not a drop of white blood had been shed, thirty-five Black men were hauled to the gallows over five weeks—twenty-two on a single morning—in what historian Michael P. Johnson calculates to be "the deadliest civilian judicial proceedings in American history." It could have been worse. Another seventeen condemned men were spared by the court and governor, either as an act of mercy or a reward for incriminating testimony. The owners of executed men received compensation from the state, and informants like Peter Prioleau and George Wilson won manumission and lifetime stipends, thus incentivizing future betrayals. The Black bodies only stopped swinging once city officials grew convinced that their message had been conveyed. "There can be no harm," Intendant Hamilton wrote later that year, "in the salutary inculcation of one lesson, among a certain portion of our population, that there is nothing they are bad enough to do, that we are not powerful enough to punish."

HAD THE PLOT REVEALED in the court documents come to fruition, it would have been the most ambitious and sophisticated ever attempted by African Americans in the antebellum South. As it is, the Vesey affair is increasingly regarded as a consequential episode in the annals of antebellum resistance and in South Carolina history, perhaps *the* signal event in the half century before the bombardment of Fort Sumter. There is an argument for linking the two, as news from the summer trials hardened the commitment of white Carolinians to state sovereignty and helped set the state on its path toward nullification and secession. The revitalization of age-old fears of a slave uprising shattered paternalistic myths of a satisfied and simple-minded underclass and a divinely bestowed social order. It rearmed those who were wary of evangelizing to the enslaved and prompted a legislative crackdown that cinched the noose of white control over Black South Carolinians until the close of the Civil War.

The Charleston uprising also has become the focus of one of the most enduring and vituperative debates ever to animate the study of American history. For a quarter century, scholars have jousted about whether a plan for an insurrection actually existed, and whether the record demonstrates Vesey to be a selfless freedom fighter or merely a patsy for white politicians seeking a pretext for retribution. Not far beneath the surface lurk sensitive questions about the forms and ferocity of Black resistance to American slavery.

The argument among scholars grows out of conflicting takeaways from the same handwritten trial documents. The record includes a report from Intendant Hamilton, a narrative reconstruction by magistrates Kennedy and Parker, a message to the legislature by Gov. Bennett, and a partial transcript of the proceedings that he appended, providing rich depictions of antebellum Charleston. But it also is maddeningly incomplete, with the transcript far from the verbatim stenography that later became standard. That means the records are unmistakably political documents, tailored for public consumption to enhance the roles played by their authors and to contextualize the threat of danger according to their positions and ambitions.

The special court appointed by the intendant and council consisted of the two presiding magistrates—Kennedy and Parker—and five white freeholders, a jury of non-peers. The council also stood up a special "committee of vigilance and safety," staffed by wardens and guards, to conduct searches and chase down fugitive suspects. The trials began out of public view on June 19 within the city's fortress-like Work-House and proceeded at a galloping pace before ending on August 8 (the court adjourned on July 26, having disposed of the lead suspects, but further arrests led to formation of a second panel). As in today's criminal courts, some of the accused offered dubious professions of ignorance and testified against friends to obtain leniency. Given the size of the alleged conspiracy, a relatively small number of key witnesses provided the most damning testimony. Irregularities by future judicial norms were rife. George W. Cross, the lawyer who represented Vesey, also served as a witness, testifying to the credibility of his own slave, Yorrick, who presented evidence against several defendants. Another lawyer, Jacob Axson, Jr., became a jurist on the second court after representing enslaved defendants before the first one. Almost no physical evidence was presented. Although witnesses testified about plans to purchase and manufacture weapons, few were reported discovered beyond a crude dagger in Rolla Bennett's trunk, some musket balls concealed under a dock, and about a dozen ten-foot poles that might have been forged into spears. The court found many defendants guilty largely by association, based on testimony about chance meetings and ambiguous comments.

On one point, however, there seemed little ambiguity: from the vantage of white Charlestonians, the plot and the African Church were coiled together like blades of bulrush in a Sea Island basket. Those who pressed the cases on behalf of the white citizenry seemed intent on prosecuting the African Church—and Black religion more broadly—as pointedly as any of the accused. Church membership was itself viewed as circumstantial evidence of guilt, and witnesses were interrogated about it just as they were about clandestine meetings and incriminating conversations. The surviving transcript of witness testimony includes more than twenty mantra-like repetitions or approximations of the phrase "He belongs to the African Church," presumably prompted by prosecutorial questioning. Yorrick Cross testified that when one of Vesey's chief recruiters asked him "to join," he at first mistakenly assumed the man meant the congregation, not an uprising. Another witness testified that he was led to a planning session at Vesey's house on Bull Street under the guise of it being a class meeting. Collections were taken, just as at church, to help pay for arms and horses. On the barrier island plantations, prayer meetings were said to double as organizational strategy sessions.

There are suggestions in letters and trial testimony that it was the mass arrests of African Church members in June 1818 that first set the plotters to plotting, and that Vesey and his collaborators whipped up support by spotlighting white harassment of the congregation. "He said, we were deprived of our rights and privileges by the white people, and that our Church was shut up, so that we could not use it, and that it was high time for us to seek for our rights," one of the accused, Jesse Blackwood, said in a confession ascribed to him.

The trial records and other documents include assertions and inferences that 35 of the 130 free and enslaved men initially arrested had a current or prior connection to the African Church. Eight, including several enslaved men, were identified as class leaders or other church officials, although only one accused conspirator—Quash Harleston—had signed the 1820 petition to the legislature seeking to open an AME church in Charleston. Among those convicted at trial, connections to the church were even more prevalent, as at least 30 of 69 had ostensible ties to the congregation. That included Vesey and four of the men identified by the court as his closest confidants—Ned Bennett, Monday Gell, Peter Poyas, and "Gullah Jack" Pritchard.

Suspects connected to the church were more than twice as likely to be convicted, to be sentenced to death, and to be executed without a pardon than those who were not. The correlation may not have been directly causal, as the judges said they assigned the death penalty to those who "exhibited peculiar energy and activity" in their participation. But it also was true that nearly half of those who were hanged were reported to be current or former members of the African Church, and that nearly half of the church members who were tried took their last breaths on the gallows. Those not executed were sentenced to deportation, and in some cases even those acquitted were recommended for "transportation," as it was called. Several, including at least two church members, died in the city's pestilent Work-House before their owners could arrange their exiles. By contrast, nearly 60 percent of those not affiliated with the church either were acquitted or discharged before trial for lack of evidence, escaping punishment four times more often than church members.

The court elicited testimony from key witnesses that the church played a critical role, and that its unsupervised meetings, often at night, were used to strategize and communicate plans. "This business originates altogether with the *African Congregation*," one enslaved witness reportedly said. Another was recorded as testifying he had been told that "*all the African Church were engaged in it*," the words italicized by Magistrates Kennedy and Parker for emphasis. The judges needed little convincing, concluding—with only slight exaggeration—that it had been a "characteristic of this plot . . . that a decided majority of the Insurgents, either did or had belonged to the African Congregation; amongst whom the inlistments were principally and successfully carried on." They took direct aim at the preaching of "inflamatory and insurrectionary doctrines" by ministers and class leaders who exerted a mesmerizing influence "over the minds of the ignorant blacks."

To white Charlestonians, the African Church's very existence seemed insurrectionary. Although the church was not indicted as a corporate entity, the political establishment rendered a verdict just the same. "Religious fanaticism has not been without its effect on this project," observed Intendant Hamilton.

"The secession of a large body of blacks from the white Methodist church, with feelings of irritation and disappointment, formed a hot bed, in which the germ might well be expected to spring into life and vigour."

Surely there were those in the congregation who took courage and inspiration from the liberationist ethos of African Methodism. The Charleston church's laborious birthing pains, following years of mistreatment by Methodist and municipal authorities, may have primed some for an escalation.

But the trial record also highlights early political divisions within the African Church, of the kind that would afflict Black churches like Emanuel across the centuries. Among the church's ministers and lay leaders were strong institutionalists who had committed themselves, above all, to preserving Charleston's only independent vehicle for Black Christian worship and communion. They viewed the daily life of the church as an ongoing act of resistance, and believed that protecting it merited occasional accommodation. That kind of incrementalism likely bore more appeal for free persons of color than for the enslaved, who might be subjected on any random day to public flogging or the separation of their families. None of the church's early leaders—all free men of mixed race—were arrested or implicated in the conspiracy. Indeed, the trial included evidence that the plotters schemed to keep the church's ministers and deacons in the dark. "Morris Brown, Harry Drayton, and Charles Corr, and other influential leaders of the African Church, were never consulted on this subject, for fear they would betray us to the whites," church member Monday Gell was quoted saying in a post-conviction confession.

And yet there also was evidence that church leaders knew things they were not supposed to know, and that they sympathized with the insurrectionists' cause and even their methods. Morris Brown, Henry Drayton, and other church founders conveniently left Charleston that spring to travel to African Methodist Episcopal conferences in the North, distancing themselves from the plot as it took shape. But third-hand testimony suggested that "Gullah Jack" Pritchard had made Brown aware of the uprising before he left and that Brown had offered a nod of approval: "Father Morris said he was going to the North—but if you can get men you can try this business, but don't call my name." In another thirdhand account, Morris Brown was said to have discussed the plans with potential conspirators and "swore them on the Bible never to divulge the secret, even if they suffered death." One defendant, meanwhile, recounted coming upon Henry Drayton on a Sunday afternoon and being told by him *"that the whites wanted nothing but a good spanking with the sword."*

The uncertainty about the role of church leaders extends to Vesey, and whether he held the standing within the congregation that he has been assigned over the centuries. Numerous histories have declared or suggested that he was a "founding member" of the African Church and a "class leader." While each is possible, neither has been documented. There was direct trial testimony from seven witnesses—each a defendant himself—that some two dozen others were members. Those reported members included Denmark Vesey's son, Sandy. But no witness was recorded as saying as much about Denmark, and no records have been found that establish his membership. The only assertion of Vesey's membership came from the magistrates, Kennedy and Parker, in their summary narrative. Although they characterized him that way, they also stated that he was not a class leader and distinguished him from those who were. Any comments Vesey made were not transcribed, but one secondhand account reported that when the judges asked what church he belonged to, he answered "with a very firm decisive tone 'None.'" That, of course, may have been a subterfuge designed to protect the African Church.

Further complicating the question of his affiliation, Vesey had joined a predominantly white congregation—Second Presbyterian—only a few months before Morris Brown orchestrated the walkout of thousands of Black members from Charleston's Methodist churches. On Sunday, April 13, 1817, at roughly fifty years of age, Vesey became a communicant at the imposing new church on Wragg Square after a rigorous process of Christian education and self-reflection. That does not mean that Vesey, as a freeman, could not have then moved his membership to the African Church once that option became available. It makes sense that an autonomous Black church would have appealed to a man with a revolutionary mindset. It does demonstrate, however, that Vesey had not recently arrived at Christianity after some revelatory seizure. Indeed, he presumably had been baptized even before becoming a communicant at Second Presbyterian. Although it is not known where he received his religious training, his adeptness at rattling off Scripture suggests a sophisticated understanding. Coursing throughout the trial record is one suggestion after another that Vesey relied on the Holy Bible, and especially the Old Testament, for moral justification for the bloody overthrow of white oppression. Biblical precedent, he argued, showed that God not only countenanced it but commanded it. His favorite texts warned of a wrathful omnipotent's unrelenting vengeance upon the unjust, as in Joshua 6:21 (quoted at the top of this chapter) and Zechariah 14:2 ("For I will gather all nations against Jerusalem to battle; and the city shall be taken, and the houses rifled, and the women ravished.").

Naturally, the epic of the Exodus carried particular resonance for Vesey. Rolla Bennett testified that at one organizational meeting the rebel leader rallied his troops by reading to them about "how the *Children of Israel were delivered out of Egypt from bondage.*" He was known to preach from Exodus 21:16, which ordered the death penalty for those that "stealeth a man, and selleth him." It would have been a nimble selection by Vesey, given that much of the chapter is devoted to establishing a strict judicial code for the purchase and handling of enslaved servants. Yet Vesey had little patience for those who fell back on Scripture to justify their refusal to enlist. When Smart Anderson lamented that it would be a sin to kill women and children, Vesey called him "a friend to the Buckra," meaning the white overlord. Magistrates Kennedy and Parker concluded that Vesey "rendered himself perfectly familiar with all those parts of the Scriptures, which he thought he could pervert to his purpose." They seemed oblivious to the irony that white churchmen had long perverted the same holy text to justify slavery.

The religious practices of Africa also played a part, primarily through the involvement of "Gullah Jack," the enslaved man of shipbuilder Paul Pritchard. Born in East Africa, Jack arrived in chains in Charleston as a teenager in 1806 with his reputation as a sorcerer already established. Slight of build, and known for his bushy, dark whiskers, Jack encouraged Black Charlestonians to believe "that he could neither be killed nor taken," and that his charms could convey the same powers to others. Over time, he integrated his conjuring with Christian practices and, like Vesey, joined the African Church, according to the report by Kennedy and Parker. Never, however, did he abandon his reliance on mysticism. "He gave me some dry food, consisting of parched corn and ground nuts, and said eat that and nothing else on the morning it breaks out," Yorrick Cross was quoted as telling the court. "And when you join us as we pass put into your mouth this crab-claw and you can't then be wounded." Vesey would have understood the value in having such a man by his side, and some witnesses testified that it was as much Gullah Jack Pritchard as Vesey who "stood at the front of all." In sentencing him, the court noted that Pritchard's sorcery had proven powerless against white Christian might. "Your

Altars and your Gods have sunk together in the dust," the court said in condemning Pritchard. "The airy spectres, conjured by you, have been chased away by the superior light of Truth, and you stand exposed, the miserable and deluded victim of offended Justice."

WHATEVER DENMARK VESEY'S actual agency of the plot, he is depicted in the trial record as a fearsome firebrand who spoke his mind at every opportunity—in grog shops, in alleyways—about the grotesqueness of slavery and the repugnance of white supremacy. "If his companion bowed to a white person," Kennedy and Parker wrote, "he would rebuke him, and observe that all men were born equal, and that he was surprised that any one would degrade himself by such conduct, that he would never cringe to whites, nor ought any one who had the feelings of a man. When answered, We are slaves, he would sarcastically and indignantly reply, 'You deserve to remain slaves.'"

It was only by a stunning bit of fortune—with measurable odds of 3,300 to 1—that Vesey had not himself remained enslaved. On November 8, 1799, at about thirty-two years of age, Denmark Vesey hit the lottery. With $6 saved from his outsourced work as a carpenter, he had purchased ticket number 1844 for a drawing devised by the city to pay for the long-deferred extension of East Bay Street. When the city treasurer drew that number, Vesey won the grand prize of $1,500. Almost immediately, he negotiated his bargain-basement purchase for $600 from the wife of Joseph Vesey, the Bermuda-born slave-trading ship captain who had owned him since childhood. On December 7, 1799, by luck of the draw, Denmark Vesey became one of South Carolina's roughly 3,200 free persons of color.

As an enslaved Carolinian, it had been an adventurous and picaresque life. Vesey's given name and parentage are not known, nor is whether he was born in West Africa or the West Indies. But in 1781, when he was about fourteen, he became one of a cargo of 390 captives whom Capt. Vesey loaded aboard the *Prospect* in the Danish sugar colony of Saint Thomas for conveyance to Saint-Domingue (present-day Haiti). During the voyage, the captain and his crew found themselves taken with "the beauty, alertness and intelligence" of the dark-skinned teen and "made a pet" of him by using him as a cabin boy. They dubbed him Telemaque, after Telemachus of Greek myth, the son of Odysseus and Penelope. Over time, the name corrupted into Denmark. Any temporary affection for Telemaque did not dissuade Capt. Vesey from selling the boy along with the others in the ship's hold. But when Vesey made a return trip months later, he found that Telemaque's purchaser had buyer's remorse. It seemed that any time the boy was ordered into the fields he would be felled by epileptic seizures, a condition some historians attribute more to clever malingering than misfiring neurons. A physician confirmed the boy's unfitness and, following the business etiquette of the day, Capt. Vesey took back the defective product and issued a refund. Knowing he would not be able to offload such certifiably damaged goods, Vesey decided to keep the boy as his own possession. For nearly twenty years, the multilingual Telemaque served the captain at sea and in Charleston, where Vesey settled in the early 1780s to work as a merchant of both dry goods and enslaved Africans. It can only be presumed that Vesey treated his servant relatively well, as "Denmark" kept his former enslaver's surname after his manumission.

It was, of course, the fact of Vesey's freedom that most bewildered his white adjudicators, and transformed him into an icon of Black resistance. On the one hand, they recognized that Vesey's emancipated status afforded him the time, resources, and mobility to conceive and construct a vast conspiracy. But the judges could muster no rationale for a freeman of Vesey's age and means taking a leading role in a scheme that could only end on the gallows. "It is difficult to imagine what *infatuation* could have prompted you to attempt an enterprize so wild and visionary," the court said in sentencing Vesey. "A moments reflection must have convinced you, that the ruin of *your race*, would have been the probable result, and that years would have rolled away, before they could have recovered that confidence, which, they once enjoyed in this community."

What the judges may not have fully appreciated was that Vesey had not been able to buy the freedom of his several enslaved wives and children. Having exceeded the average lifespan of African Americans by more than twenty years, Vesey may have figured he therefore had little to lose. "Vesey said he was satisfied with his own condition, being free, but as all his children were slaves, he wished to see what could be done for them," Monday Gell was recorded as testifying. Another witness said that after gaining his freedom Vesey had considered immigrating to Africa, but *"wanted to stay and see what he could do* for his fellow-creatures."

At sentencing, the judges acted as an ecclesiastical court in convicting Vesey not only of attempted insurrection but also of "the grossest impiety." Their verdict sought to return the Scriptures to the ark of paternalism. Vesey had sought "to pervert the sacred words of God into a sanction for crimes of the blackest hue," they said. He clearly did not understand that the Gospel had been imparted "to reconcile us to our destinies on earth." The judges cited Saint Paul's admonition to the Ephesians that servants obey their masters, as if it were a code section rather than a verse.

Like most of the accused, Vesey had pleaded not guilty. He sat during his trial with arms folded and eyes fixed on the floor as he listened to the court's questioning and cross-examination by his attorney. Then he asked to directly address the half dozen witnesses who presented either confessions or testimony against him, most of them his accused fellow collaborators. "He at first questioned them in the dictatorial, despotic manner, in which he was probably accustomed to address them," the magistrates wrote. When that proved ineffective, they said, "he questioned them with affected surprise and concern" about their betrayals and "still failing in his purpose, he then examined them strictly as to dates, but could not make them contradict themselves." Vesey argued to the court that a freeman of his means had little motive to take such a desperate risk. Although Kennedy and Parker credited him for defending himself "with great art and plausibility," they could not be convinced.

"Your professed design was to trample on all laws, human and divine," the magistrates told Vesey at sentencing, "to riot in blood, outrage, rapine and conflagration, and to introduce anarchy and confusion in their most horrid forms. Your life has become, therefore, a just and necessary sacrifice." Tears streaked down the defendant's cheeks.

Vesey is said to have awaited the hangman in "a very hardened state," aggrieved at what he considered an unfair trial but convinced that "it was a Glorious cause he was to die in." The only freeman among the condemned, he made no confession and sought no blessing from the several white ministers who visited the ringleaders in their cells. When Rev. Benjamin Morgan Palmer pleaded with the men to repent of their sins before dying, one of them, perhaps his congregant Rolla Bennett, took the opportunity to deliver a lecture on America's founding contradiction. "Sin? What sin?" the imprisoned man asked. "You applaud the leaders of the American revolution, who resisted a small tax on tea; and rather than pay it killed tens of thousands, but what was that tax to our sufferings? Washington was a white man and you idolized him; but I, alas, am a black man, and you hang me for the very act you applauded in him." Eyewitnesses recalled that some of the condemned shouted as they ascended the scaffold so that their enslavers could hear them: "Now we are going to have *freedom*, the glorious liberty of the children of God, and you can no more deprive us of that." When a trapdoor malfunctioned, Bacchus Hammet served as his own executioner by hurling himself forward. "*As he swung back,*" his former owner recalled, "*he lifted his feet, so that his knees might not touch the Board!*"

Large numbers of Black and white Charlestonians gathered on July 2 to witness the first hangings, of Vesey and five others. The precise location is disputed—it was once rumored to be an oak tree that divided Ashley Avenue but is now thought to have been the municipal gallows at Blake's Lands, just two blocks north of the African Church on the Neck. An even larger crowd, seemingly everyone in town, turned out three weeks later at a makeshift gallows nearby for the ghoulish final procession of twenty-two men, each seated in a wagon atop the coffin he would soon occupy. John Bailey Adger, who would later become a Presbyterian minister, remembered watching as a child from the third-floor window of his family's house on King Street as nooses were looped over each man's head. The line of hanging beams stretched toward the horizon. "This was certainly a sight calculated to strike terror into the heart of every slave," he wrote years later. To reinforce the point, the bodies were buried with such disrespect—near fortifications from the War of 1812 known as the Lines (modern-day Line Street)—that residents complained of the "alarming nuisance occasioned by the slight and offensive manner in which many of the Culprits lately executed have been interred."

EVEN BEFORE VESEY'S EXECUTION, there had been warnings about the prospects for a macabre rush to judgment, and from two of the most prominent men in the state. On June 21, with the trials just starting, William Johnson, Jr., a Charleston native and Jeffersonian appointee to the United States Supreme Court, published an allegorical column in *The Charleston Courier* about an innocent enslaved man named Billy who had been lynched in an absurd miscarriage of justice more than a decade earlier. Johnson, who was married to the sister of Gov. Bennett, never mentioned the insurrection or ongoing trials. But with the headline "Melancholy Effect of Popular Excitement," his message landed as intended and prompted immediate recriminations. "Billy was hung amidst crowds of execrating spectators," Justice Johnson wrote, obviously urging caution, "and such appeared to be the popular demand for a victim, that it is not certain a pardon could have saved him."

Charleston's leaders, already fierce advocates for states' rights, could not let such an insult stand, not even for twenty-four hours. Who did this federal appointee think he was to meddle in the affairs of a local court, comprising men of the highest caliber and charged with protecting the South's most important city from savage attack? The next day, Intendant Hamilton responded with a letter to a competing newspaper that accused Justice Johnson of an "unjust libel." The insurrection court submitted its own defense, pronouncing itself "injured and defamed." Justice Johnson parried rather hyperbolically that the judges had levied "one of the most groundless and unprovoked attacks ever made upon the feelings of an individual."

Ten days later, Gov. Bennett, whose enslaved men Batteau, Ned, and Rolla were to be hung the next morning along with Vesey, voiced his own concerns about secrecy and due process in a letter to state Attorney General Robert Y. Hayne. The state's chief legal officer responded that the law made it clear that enslaved South Carolinians enjoyed only limited rights. "Magna Charta [sic] and Habeas Corpus and indeed all the provisions of our Constitution in favor of Liberty, are intended for *freemen* only," Hayne wrote. The governor, nearing the end of his two-year legislative appointment, remained disturbed by the public's exclusion from the trials and the inability of some defendants to confront their accusers. In a message to the General Assembly, he charged that the court had been "illegally constituted" by local rather than state authorities and said he "deeply lamented" the convictions in closed court based on uncontested and self-interested testimony—"the offspring of treachery or revenge, and the hope of immunity." He also questioned the maturity of the plot, pointing out that no cache of arms had been found and that the conspirators seemed more a loose confederation than a rebel army.

Despite such contemporaneous skepticism, the so-called heroic interpretation of Denmark Vesey's saga went largely unchallenged for more than a century, upheld as strong proof that enslaved Americans mounted a determined, varied, and ambitious resistance to their captivity. Those who took inspiration from it included Frederick Douglass, Harriet Beecher Stowe, and Henry Highland Garnet, the abolitionist preacher who referenced Vesey in a famous 1843 speech that urged Black Southerners, "Let your motto be resistance!" Over the last quarter century, however, scholars have waged an impassioned battle over whether the records really show Vesey to have been a freedom-fighting subversive or merely a suitable fall guy, with loose talk of an uprising inflated into a doomsday threat by scheming politicians.

Not surprisingly, the battle to define Vesey's legacy also has remained bitterly contested within Charleston. In the mid-1970s, as African Americans gained a political foothold in the Lowcountry for the first time since Reconstruction, Black community leaders proposed various ways to honor Vesey as a martyred icon of Black resistance. They hoped it would jump-start the process of balancing Charleston's many memorials to slaveholders and segregationists. After suggestions to rename a school or erect a statue went nowhere, the city council in 1976 commissioned a painting by a local African American artist that depicted a broad-shouldered Vesey from behind, preaching to the crowded pews of the African Church. The hostile reaction of white Charlestonians to displaying the portrait in the lobby of the municipal auditorium revealed a great deal about the city's racial progress in the century and a half since Vesey's execution.

"If black leaders in Charleston had searched for a thousand years, they could not have found a local black whose portrait would have been more offensive to many white people," began a column in *The News and Courier*. A white letter writer suggested that if Vesey qualified for such veneration so did "Hitler, Attila the Hun, Herod the murderer of babies, and the PLO murderers of the Israeli athletes in Munich."

Commemoration matters in Charleston, and so Black Charlestonians rightly viewed the moment as a turning point. Vesey to them was the progenitor of a long struggle that had recently borne fruit in the election of African Americans to the city council and legislature. At the painting's unveiling, Bishop Frank Madison Reid, Jr., then the presiding African Methodist Episcopal prelate in South Carolina, sought to reclaim Vesey as a Moses-like figure. "This is a creative moment for it recognizes that Vesey was no wild-eyed, monster-minded racist," he said. "He was a liberator who God had sent to set the people free from oppression." About six weeks later, a stealthy vandal ripped the painting from its mount and made off with it in the dark.

History repeated four decades later when the city finally erected a statue of Vesey, the culmination of a nearly twenty-year campaign by Black educators and activists. They had hoped to locate the monument centrally in Marion Square, where a twelve-foot bronze figure of slavery defender John C. Calhoun had peered down upon Black pedestrians since 1896. The private group that owns the square denied the request. Eventually, in 2014, the sculpture of Vesey, imagined clutching a carpenter's satchel in one hand and a Bible in the other, was tucked away in a hard-to-find grove in Hampton Park, well off Charleston's tourist paths.

The statue's remoteness has not protected it from defacement. On May 29 or 30, 2021, one or more vandals slinked into the park, which is named for a slaveholding Confederate general, and hammered at the pedestal until the etching of Vesey's name was obliterated from the black granite. It seemed a transparent counterpunch to an ongoing campaign to rid public spaces of the names and images of Confederate leaders. That cause had gained momentum after the 2015 massacre at Mother Emanuel because of Dylann Roof's self-identification with the Confederate battle flag. The day after the vandalism was discovered, Mother Emanuel's pastor, Rev. Eric S. C. Manning, visited Hampton Park to bear witness. The level of destruction convinced him that the attack had not been some teenage amusement. "It's almost as if they're trying to remove the entire name of Denmark Vesey from history," Manning said in a post on Facebook Live. "We are living in a day and age where there are so many attacks on our history as a people."

"We must always remember," he incanted. "We must remember, we must remember. We must never forget."

VIII.

Crackdown: The Vesey Aftermath

Blessed are they which are persecuted for righteousness' sake; for theirs is the kingdom of heaven.

—MATTHEW 5:10 (KJV)

The auctioneer's advertisements began appearing on August 14, 1822, only six days after the close of the insurrection trials. They ran for three days in each of Charleston's leading newspapers. Surrounding them were classifieds hawking elixirs and spirits and linens and books, all newly offloaded at Charleston's bustling port. There were ads for flour from Baltimore and sperm oil from New Bedford, announcements of meetings of the prestigious St. Cecilia Society and the South Carolina Agricultural Society, timetables for schooners sailing for Boston and Providence and Havana, and come-ons for the Grand National Lottery, with its eye-popping jackpot of $100,000. One seller sought bids for "a prime fellow" that he vouched to be an excellent carpenter. Another advertiser offered to hire out "a Negro wench" for washing and ironing, at moderate wages since she would be accompanied by a young child. The *City Gazette and Commercial Daily Advertiser* carried three separate reward offers for fugitives—$50 for Isaac, recognizable by the scald on his chest; $100 for Charlotte, missing more than a year; and $200 for Hyacinthe, easily identified by a deformed toe.

This vendue master's ads, however, had been placed by William A. Caldwell, who traded in goods ranging from fresh figs and wagon parts to bedroom furniture and house servants. The page-three notices summoned all interested buyers to the corner of Hanover and Reid Streets on August 16, where they would find the stacked remains of the African Church.

> On FRIDAY AFTERNOON, at 4 o'clock, will be sold by order of the Trustees of the African Church, on their Lot in Hampstead,
>
> *All The LUMBER,*
>
> Which comprised the said Church, in lots to suit purchasers.
>
> Conditions cash, and the Lumber, to be taken charge of immediately after the sale, and removed the next day.

This is what is known of the fate of the African Church. For most of Mother Emanuel's existence, oral tradition has held—and countless chroniclers have repeated—that the first stage of its life ended in an inferno, set by white authorities in a dramatic reassertion of control. Barack Obama said so in his eulogy for Clementa Pinckney. The web page listing Emanuel on the National Register of Historic Places makes the same assertion. Both, of course, merely echoed a claim that had thickened into legend over the years, like okra soup left to simmer on the stove. The recent discovery of Caldwell's advertisements suggests it was sinew and not flame that brought down the African Church. Having built the simple structure with their own hands only a few years earlier, the men of the congregation apparently dismantled it board by board until only piles of scrap remained. If not as apocalyptic, the clawing of each nail head must nonetheless have been despairing work, like digging one's own grave at gunpoint.

There is no known record of an edict to destroy the building, but nineteenth-century histories claim it was "demolished" by the order of "the civil authorities of the city and state." It can only be presumed, based on the preservation of the timbers, that the actual work fell to the congregation and not to city workers or a white mob. Perhaps the ministers and trustees negotiated with city hall to protect the structure from the torch so the lumber could be sold, a small but pragmatic consolation. The only known record of the disposition of the wood comes from an AME journal written nearly seventy years later, which reported that the planks were "sent over to Ashepoo," likely a reference to a plantation northwest of Charleston. Intendant Hamilton later wrote that the African Church had "voluntarily dissolved," but there seemed to have been little voluntary about it. According to AME historian Daniel Alexander Payne, the civil authorities "ordered their organization to be suppressed." In one blow, African Methodism lost three thousand of its nearly ten thousand members as Charleston's Black church was "blotted from the pages of Ecclesiastical History."

The city fathers also moved to destroy the church's leadership, despite the dearth of evidence of its involvement in the insurrection plot. As if prosecuting Al Capone for tax evasion, they found ways to ensure that ministers like Morris Brown and Henry Drayton would not be available to reconstitute their displaced and disbanded congregation. Their mechanism was the legislature's 1820 law prohibiting free persons of color from traveling into the state. Violators could be fined $20 and, if unable to pay, sold at auction for an indenture of up to five years.

Even as the specially appointed Court of Magistrates and Freeholders wrapped up the insurrection trials, another legal body—the Court of Common Pleas and General Sessions—tried Brown and Drayton on charges they had traveled to AME conferences up North and then returned to South Carolina in disregard of the new prohibitions. Technically, it would seem there had been no violation. Drayton had even consulted an attorney before departing and been assured that the effective dates made his travels legal. The statute provided a two-year window for free Black South Carolinians to return if they had been abroad when the law took effect. But it left unaddressed those who might choose to leave the state temporarily and return within that two-year period, the circumstance that applied to Brown and Drayton. They had ventured North in early April 1822, more than eight months before the expiration of the grace period. Brown had returned from the conference in Baltimore before the end of the month, while Drayton traveled to sessions in Philadelphia and New York and then back to Charleston in late June.

The justice of the peace appointed to consider the trumped-up charges, attorney John B. White, convicted the preachers anyway, essentially for violating the spirit of the law. "They were here at the passing of the act, they knew of the law, they departed of their own free will and accord, and have now returned within the limits of this State, contrary to what I consider the intention, as collected from the context, and even the letter of the act," he ruled. White ordered Brown and Drayton to leave the state within fifteen days. A week later, a different jurist, Elihu Hall Bay, rejected an appeal by Drayton. That likely came as little surprise since Bay was among the 148 prominent Charlestonians who had petitioned the legislature to pass the very law being used to prosecute Brown and Drayton. That entreaty had complained about the "existing evil" of the African Church. If ever the fix was in, it would seem to have been here.

Brown and Drayton made hasty arrangements to flee to Philadelphia, worried that vigilantes might impose harsher punishment. Brown sensed they were being watched closely. "All that was needed for his arrest and death was the shadow of a proof," wrote Payne, later a trusted aide to Brown. The pastor eventually sought protection from Intendant Hamilton, who had steadfastly defended the African Church's leaders even while sourcing the plot to their congregation. Brown trusted the intendant enough that he signed documents shortly before leaving town that gave Hamilton power of attorney to sell his property. Hamilton viewed the threat to the minister as real enough that he briefly hid him in his own house before helping ensure his safe passage to Philadelphia. According to Payne, Hamilton was "well acquainted with the lamb-like temper of Brown, and his profound respect for law and authority" and therefore "could not indulge the suspicion that he was in any manner connected with the contemplated insurrection." The ambitious young intendant's full motives can only be supposed. But with Hamilton eager to restore his city to calm and avoid further damage to its reputation in the North, the exile of the church's leaders without mob violence did not count as a bad outcome.

The younger of Morris Brown's children eventually joined him in Philadelphia. But the heartbreaking day in August 1822 when he left Charleston may have been the last time he saw his wife, Elizabeth, and eldest son, Malcolm, who had by then married and established his own shoemaking business. It seems unlikely that Elizabeth ever ventured North, knowing it might have meant abandoning South Carolina and her family there forever. Records place her in Charleston both in March 1823 and December 1829, when she signed releases for sales of Morris Brown's properties on Anson Street ($1,400) and Smith Street ($875). When Brown died in Philadelphia on May 9, 1849, five years after suffering a stroke, he was married to a woman named Maria, who inherited most of his property. At that point, he had served for twenty-one years as Richard Allen's successor, the second elected and consecrated bishop of the African Methodist Episcopal Church. Bishop Brown, who also served as the fourth pastor of Mother Bethel AME Church in Philadelphia, is credited with extending the denomination beyond the Alleghenies and into western Pennsylvania, Ohio, Indiana, Illinois, Missouri, Kentucky, and Canada, despite its proscription in his native South. Other leaders of

Charleston's African Church, like Marcus Brown, Charles Corr, and Amos Cruckshanks, followed Brown and Drayton to Philadelphia and remained trusted confidants.

The African Church's thousands of members, most of them enslaved, dispersed like dandelion fluff in the wind. A number drifted back to the city's Methodist churches, some signed on with Rev. Benjamin Morgan Palmer at Circular Congregational, and still others, including Rev. James Eden, one of Morris Brown's early lieutenants, joined First Scots Presbyterian. So many African Church refugees applied for membership at Second Presbyterian that their requests consumed much of an elders' meeting there on October 10. Some of the former faithful never gravitated back to church at all and, in the words of one Methodist chronicler, "became identified with the ungodly world."

Mother Emanuel's oral tradition holds that the congregation operated underground until allowed to surface after the Civil War. There is no postwar memoir or interview to validate that. But the AME Church's ability to reconstitute so quickly in Charleston after the war suggests an enduring nostalgia, and perhaps the dry bones of an organization. Certainly, groups small enough to evade detection practiced their faith as they could in the candlelit parlors of Charleston single houses and the hush harbors of nearby plantations. They gathered after dark to sing and pray, led by lay preachers who huffed and stomped through sermons that rose to screeching crescendos.

Any number of steps might be taken for security. A kettle or wash pot could be turned upside down to capture and muffle the echoes of ring-shouts and spirituals. Sand was swept to cover footprints left by ecstatic dancing. "While we read the book we had a watchman, and if any one was approaching the watchman whistled and the singing was stopped," remembered Emanuel Gibson, a free Black man who joined Charleston's Trinity Methodist Church in 1838. He recalled forging passes for enslaved friends so they could attend clandestine sessions of a prayer group known as the Cross. As a young man, Moses B. Salter, who would later become pastor at Emanuel and then an AME bishop, served as a sentry at illicit religious gatherings. "I used to put my ear to the ground to hear the tramp of the horse," he said. If he detected any vibration he whispered an urgent alarm: "The buckra coming." Plantation overseers were sometimes bribed to look the other way. "It was death for three to five negroes to meet to pray in private," Salter said.

The trustees of the African Church, who had been so determined to recoup their losses on building materials, never sold the land at Hanover and Reid Streets. Perhaps they imagined a day when a new church would rise there. Instead, the property sat fallow for decades, used only as a burial ground, which eventually expanded into the church's footprint and filled time and again. An analysis of death records by the Chicora Foundation, a preservation group, found that an astonishing 7,145 bodies—8 per possible gravesite—had been interred in the "African Burial Ground" between 1819 and 1910. That is when city health officials declared the untended cemetery a health hazard and suspended its use.

The cemetery was managed for some time by original trustees of the African Church who stayed in Charleston rather than follow Morris Brown into permanent exile. But after the last of them, Peter Mathewes, died and was buried there, no successor came forward. The church, after all, no longer existed as a corporate entity. Mathewes's descendants kept up the property as best they could. But at some point in the late nineteenth century, a Black Presbyterian congregation that had been granted use of the cemetery claimed possession. Unable to afford the cleanup demanded by the city, that church then sold off a parcel to a man who, according to a subsequent lawsuit, dug up graves and discarded their contents into the street. In 1922, the oldest lineal descendant of Peter Mathewes—Peter Mathewes Frost—agreed to a settlement to the suit that restored control of the unsold portion of the cemetery to him and several other successor trustees. Two decades later, in 1940, the property came full circle when those trustees sold it to another AME congregation. The African Methodists built a brick church atop the graveyard, a common practice over the years on the land-starved Charleston peninsula.

THE DECONSTRUCTION OF THE AFRICAN CHURCH, and with it the extinction of Black religious autonomy in Charleston for the next forty-three years, would be the most visible aftershock of the foiled insurrection plot. In visceral ways, the events of the summer of 1822 underscored to white Carolinians the fundamental security threat posed by the Christianization of the enslaved, exposing quicksand beneath a firmament of Southern faith. By no means, however, was religion the only realm of concern. In the Venn diagram of white Charleston's existential angst, the insurrection scare intersected with all of the dominant caste's deepest sensitivities—the widening racial imbalance in the Lowcountry, the threat embodied by free people of color, the relative independence of enslaved people in the city, the indulgences of paternalism, the spread of abolitionist messaging, the example set by the Haitian slave revolt, the states' rights implications of the Missouri Compromise. Bogeymen were everywhere, scaring up a sense of siege.

As a consequence, the campaign of repression that followed targeted virtually every liberty available to African Americans, further hobbling their already limited capacity to travel, assemble, work, learn, and, of course, worship. South Carolina found new ways to repress people of color and invigorated the enforcement of old ones, giving rise to a tradition of extralegal policing. In Charleston, militias redoubled their patrols to address public complaints about loitering, gambling, and drinking by Black residents. Even the physical landscape was transformed for defensive purposes, as the state appropriated money for a central garrison to protect the peninsula against domestic attack: The Citadel.

Until 1822, paternalism's appeal had been driven by the need of a Christian people to justify their rather unchristian behavior, and to rebut the ever-loudening condemnation of Northern abolitionists. In order to defend the institution against abolitionist assault, and preserve a regional way of life in an expanding federation, a transformation in perception was needed. Better that slaveholding be viewed as benevolence toward childlike wards than the brutal and oppressive regime it was. Paternalism's goal, argued Lacy K. Ford in his insightful study, *Deliver Us from Evil*, was "to render slaveholding consistent with existing republican and emerging humanitarian ideals while accepting the inevitability of the region's dependence on slave labor." It called for slaveholders "to attend to their slaves' spiritual welfare as well as their physical needs, most often by devotedly inculcating Christian doctrine and morality, or at least the masters' version of them." But after the rumored insurrection of 1822 those who had supported literacy and religious autonomy as tools for indoctrinating the enslaved found those permissive positions no longer tenable. Mary Lamboll Beach, a Charleston widow, spoke for others when she lamented to her sister that the trust built between white masters and Black servants was now "forever at an end." Naturally, there were concerns about financial repercussions as well. "I fear this kind of property is fast losing its value on the Sea Coast," Charleston attorney Henry William DeSaussure wrote to a fellow slaveholder.

With the South Carolina General Assembly preparing to convene in November, there was no shortage of demands to turn the legislative screws. "Far be it from me to recommend despotic laws," began a letter to the *Southern*

Patriot from Alexander Garden, Jr. (written under the pseudonym Rusticus). "But I certainly do think that after our *late warning* we should not suffer *this class*... We may be kind and indulgent masters without *assimilating them* to us." DeSaussure, who had been both intendant of Charleston and director of the U.S. Mint, proposed that Black people be barred from receiving an education, worshipping in independent churches, or working as mechanics or artisans. Slavery might be "an evil," he conceded in his own treatise, but the cost of compensating property owners for a general emancipation—which he estimated at more than $450 million, roughly thirty times the federal budget—made it inconceivable. Newspaper editor Edwin C. Holland called for the state to banish free persons of color—"the '*Jacobins*' of the country"—or encourage their departure through usurious taxation. One group of concerned Charlestonians suggested reviving restrictions on how people of color could dress. "Every distinction should be created between the whites and negroes, calculated to make the latter feel the superiority of the former," they urged in a petition. State policy, they wrote, should "extinguish at once every gleam of hope which the slaves may indulge of ever being free." That meant proceeding on "the only principle that can maintain slavery, the 'principle of fear.'"

The two politicians who most shaped the contours of Charleston's insurrection summer—Gov. Thomas Bennett, Jr., and Intendant James Hamilton, Jr.—continued to cast events in distinctly different lights. Gov. Bennett, surely embarrassed by the executions of three servants convicted of plotting under his nose, held fast to his view that "the scheme has not been general nor alarmingly extensive." He argued there would be no need for reactionary laws that "may produce excessive coercion" if only the city's notoriously inattentive patrols enforced those already on the books. Bennett encouraged lawmakers to assign enforcement of the slave codes to a professional state police force and to empower local boards to conduct random inspections of slave dwellings. Intendant Hamilton, by contrast, maintained that the plot would have matured into a full-fledged catastrophe had he not acted so decisively to suppress it. He called for the state legislature to exile any free person of color who had arrived in the last ten years. Without proposing exactly how, he also suggested thinning the population of enslaved males in Charleston. Days later, the South Carolina General Assembly rewarded Hamilton's vigilance by appointing him to a vacant seat in Congress.

The legislature did not adopt each of the harshest proposals. But for free persons of color, in particular, South Carolina became a markedly more hostile place by the end of the session in December 1822. An omnibus law prohibited them from returning to the state once they left, levied a $50 annual tax on most free males who had lived in South Carolina fewer than five years, and obliged free males older than fifteen to enlist white guardians who could attest to their "good character and correct habits." The lawmakers ended the practice of contract labor by prohibiting enslaved males from being hired out. They also appropriated $100,000 toward the construction of The Citadel, which was to be manned with a well-armed force of 150 men. The next year, they further addressed the state's racial imbalance by banning free Black people from entering the state under any circumstances and ending slave importation from Northern states, Europe, the West Indies, and Latin America. The same law denied free persons of color their constitutional right to carry firearms. In 1834, the legislature prohibited the hiring of Blacks as clerks or salespersons and banned the sale of liquor to enslaved persons.

The enactment that left the deepest impression, however, was South Carolina's landmark Negro Seamen Act of 1822, which required the jailing of free Black sailors while their ships were moored in Charleston Harbor. Even foreign nationals could be rounded up, and ship captains had to pay fines and cover the cost of their sailors' imprisonments. If they did not, their crewmen could be sold into slavery. Ever conscious that Denmark Vesey had been a mariner, and had disseminated news of the Haitian revolt, the lawmakers designed the measure to stymie the spread of poisonous ideas and "moral contagion." Seven other Southern states adopted their own versions over the ensuing four decades.

In Charleston, more than 150 free Black seamen were taken into custody in the first ten months, many with the help of a newly formed extralegal policing group known as the South Carolina Association. But the law's obvious impediments to interstate and transatlantic commerce soon provoked constitutional and diplomatic challenges that foreshadowed fiercer debates to come over state sovereignty.

The initial federal test case, which landed before Supreme Court Justice William Johnson, sitting in Charleston as a circuit judge, concerned a mixed-race Jamaican crewman named Henry Elkison, a British citizen who had been carted off a Liverpool-based ship in contravention of trade agreements between the two countries. Lawyers defending the act argued that the spread of pestilential ideas by free Black sailors was just as threatening to public safety as the arrival of diseased immigrants without quarantine. "In South-Carolina,"

Benjamin F. Hunt told Johnson, "we think the presence of a free negro, fresh from the lectures of an Abolition Society, equally dangerous; and we require his stay in a particular enclosure." A state had the duty to act proactively, Hunt insisted, before "her citizens behold their habitations in flames."

Justice Johnson concluded that as a federal judge he could not free Elkison from state custody. But in a sensational opinion he ruled nonetheless that the Negro Seamen Act "implies a direct attack upon the sovereignty of the United States." Although a slaveholder himself, Johnson took a strikingly progressive stand on race for South Carolina in 1823, not unlike his civil rights–era successor on Charleston's federal bench, J. Waties Waring. He mocked the statute for criminalizing skin color and warned that the union would dissolve like "a mere rope of sand" if states could subvert the Constitution whenever they wished. It was the first time in the young nation's history that a federal judge applied the Commerce Clause to restrain state power. The next year, Johnson helped affirm that interpretation in *Gibbons v. Ogden*, the landmark Supreme Court decision that first established broad federal powers to regulate interstate commerce.

Because Johnson's ruling carried only the force of a circuit court opinion, it did not generate a national precedent regarding the Negro Seamen laws. And as it conflicted with state court rulings, South Carolina officials largely ignored it over the next four decades, nullifying it for all intents and purposes.

NATURALLY, THE HEIGHTENED FEAR of insurrection spurred a rethinking of the relationship between enslavement, Christianity, and morality, a debate that preoccupied the Lowcountry until settled by the Civil War. If the South's pendulum had been arcing toward paternalism, and in some corners even a grudging concession that slavery must eventually end, its momentum now swung backward with force. Charleston's foremost white preachers of the Gospel, the Gospel that Denmark Vesey had mined for inspiration, found themselves squarely on the defensive. One after the next, they struck devil's bargains by enlisting the Bible to justify slavery, seeing it as the only way to preserve the tatters of the paternalist ethos. Regardless of the pulpit, they offered full-throated endorsements of the peculiar institution, often publishing their sermons for those who could not be present on Sundays. In doing so, these Southern churchmen became complicit in sanctioning both slavery and white supremacy and provided a counterpoint to Northern moralizing about immediate emancipation. Many, of course, were slaveholders themselves.

In interviews conducted for the Depression-era Slave Narrative Project, formerly enslaved men and women from across South Carolina recalled that church life almost always centered on white congregations, since laws against assembling without supervision were now stringently enforced. They sat apart at the rear of the sanctuary or in upstairs galleries. The preachers relied on white financial backing and fulfilled their part of the Faustian bargain. "I member when a preacher say, 'Honor your missus an' mossa dat your days may be long for dey is your only God,'" recalled Dave White, who had been enslaved in Congaree, South Carolina, his dialect as transcribed by his interviewer. John Andrew Jackson, who wrote an autobiography after escaping a plantation north of Charleston, remembered that Methodist preachers reinforced Black inferiority and compliance even in administering communion. "It was the custom among them when conducting the Lord's Supper," Jackson wrote, "to have the white people partake first, and then say to the negroes—'Now all you n----rs that are humble and obedient servants to your masters, can come and partake.'"

Above all, white pastors were eager to distance their congregations and denominations from the incubation of the plot. If that required the tarring of their African Methodist brethren, so be it. Yes, acknowledged the influential Baptist preacher Richard Furman, many of those executed "laid claim to a religious character." But "very few" had been members of mainline churches like his. "Several of these," he charged, "were grossly immoral, and, in general, they were members of an irregular body, which called itself the African Church." Similarly, Frederick Dalcho, a priest at St. Michael's in Charleston, attested in writing that "*None of the Negroes belonging to the Protestant Episcopal Church were concerned in the late conspiracy.*"

Furman, the president of the state Baptist convention, understood that the post-scare crackdown, which was broadly supported by white congregants, could not be justified if there was any moral ambiguity about slavery itself. And so he declared that "the right of holding slaves is clearly established in the Holy Scriptures," and posited that the Apostles would not have tolerated human bondage had God frowned upon it. The Lord, he said, had ordered his universe with slavery as a component.

Dalcho maintained that the enslaved merited Christian instruction but joined Furman in declaring their captivity to be divinely sanctioned. They might be God's creation, but enslaved people were "ignorant and indolent by nature, improvident and depraved by habit, and destitute of the moral principle," he wrote. They should not be trusted to hold unsupervised worship services or to be tutored in religion by men of their own color, he added. Similarly, the tireless Presbyterian missionary Charles Colcock Jones explained in a lengthy pamphlet that the obligation to bring God's Word to Black people did not undermine the coequal truth that "there is superiority on the one hand and inferiority on the other." His 1842 treatise suggested that the indoctrination of enslaved persons should only be entrusted to native Southerners or those who embraced Southern values.

Some Carolinians found the white clergy to be hopelessly naïve for continuing to support the religious training of Black Christians at all, particularly after an enslaved preacher named Nat Turner led a bloody revolt in Southampton County, Virginia, in 1831. "In general, our religious instructors are comparatively deficient in the practical knowledge of mankind," Whitemarsh B. Seabrook, a South Carolina planter, state senator, and future governor observed in 1834. In the pursuit of order and control, Seabrook said in an address, the religious education of the enslaved should begin and end with obedience and salvation. There was no need to preach on more subversive scriptural imperatives like freedom or justice: "Is it advisable to make them acquainted with the whole Bible, or to teach them every doctrine which that holy book inculcates? In a word, do considerations, predicated on the spiritual welfare of the Blacks, demand, that their religious knowledge should be co-extensive with that of their owners. I answer unhesitatingly, No!"

The same year, after several failed attempts, Seabrook and other fire-eaters in the legislature helped enact a law that forbade teaching enslaved people to read, a loophole left open since 1740. Conscious that leading plotters like Denmark Vesey and Monday Gell had been literate, officials in Charleston had been lobbying for such a measure for years. Under the new statute, the most draconian since the immediate post-Vesey crackdown, white violators could be sentenced to six months in jail and a $100 fine, while Black ones might receive fifty lashes. The same section ordered the closure of schools operated by free persons of color for either free or enslaved Black students. Black educators and white sympathizers found ways to circumvent the ban, and some churchmen depicted it as anti-Christian and unconstitutional because it inhibited the free exercise of religion. But the law nonetheless made it dangerous to teach literacy as a path to the Scriptures. Any overt religious instruction would have to be oral.

By the mid-1840s, the disagreement over slavery between Southern and Northern churchmen became so irreconcilable that America's white Methodists and Baptists formally split, with those in slaveholding states forming the Methodist Episcopal Church, South, and the Southern Baptist Convention. The Presbyterians had already divided along sectional lines in 1837, although not explicitly over slavery, and would do so again at the start of the Civil War. The Methodist schism opened at the denomination's general conference in New York in 1844, when delegates learned that a Georgia-born bishop, James O. Andrew, had inherited enslaved servants through bequest and marriage. Eight years earlier, as a sop to the South, the Methodists had formally abandoned their antislavery roots by declaring that they were "decidedly opposed to modern abolitionism" and would not interfere in a civil and political matter like slavery. But breaking the precedent against slaveholding bishops proved a step too far for the church's abolitionist wing. After days of agitation from the Northerners, the conference voted to remove Andrew from office. A year later, Southern Methodists gathered in Louisville to secede and form a new entity, just as the Confederate States would in Montgomery in 1861.

LIKE THE REGIONAL SCHISMS within Methodism and the Baptist Convention, paternalism and missionary outreach were means to the end of sustaining slavery for as many years as possible. Not long after the denominational splits in May 1845, leading clergymen, planters, and politicians gathered in Charleston to assess efforts to evangelize to enslaved people on Lowcountry plantations, long considered a risky proposition. They met at the Bible Depository on Chalmers Street, the cobblestone lane where only that week the notorious slave trader Thomas Ryan had offered twenty-nine "Negroes at private sale," starting at age six. Before the conference opened, the organizers had surveyed ministers and civic leaders in nine states to collect evidence of the salutary effects of Black churchgoing. As their testimonials were read, the meeting evolved into a celebration of paternalism's resilience after its near-death in the 1820s. "We look upon the religious instruction of the negroes, as THE GREAT DUTY, and in the truest and best sense, THE FIXED, THE SETTLED POLICY OF THE SOUTH," the group declared in a position paper.

The survey found that many white churches had for years tailored separate services, hymnal selections, and Bible school classes for Black members. Although some Black churchgoers could read, preachers relied heavily on oral catechisms that imprinted the rudiments of Christianity through call-and-response repetition, a ritual with African roots. The author of one such catechism, Methodist missionary William Capers, questioned whether an enslaved and illiterate people could master the complex theology, history, and mysticism of Christianity. "We have . . . discarded all hard words," he explained in his preamble, "and aimed to present truth in a guise so simple as to suit their capacities."

"What is a servant's duty to his master and mistress?" Capers's catechism asked.

"To serve them with a good will heartily, and not with eye-service," the enslaved person was to respond.

The religion shaped by white Christians for Black Christians emphasized marriage, fidelity, temperance, and Sabbath-keeping. Enslaved congregants were exhorted against stealing, lying, malingering, disloyalty, and sloth. Preachers to Black audiences expounded on the Golden Rule at their own peril, according to Henry McNeal Turner, a free Black South Carolinian who became an AME minister in 1858. "You could not preach the pure gospel," he recalled. "God's word had to be frittered smeared and smattered to please the politics of slavery."

Regardless of denomination, white preachers found it difficult to innovate a hybrid style capable of engaging both free and educated white Southerners and enslaved and unschooled Black worshippers. To address that concern and others, several leaders of Charleston's Presbyterian and Episcopal congregations dared the next step in the late 1840s and proposed branch churches for Black members. The congregations would remain under strict white supervision and control. And proponents argued that separate buildings and services would enable preachers to cater to their distinct audiences and relieve crowding in the stifling galleries of white churches.

Seating for Black congregants in white churches had again become a point of contention after the destruction of the African Church. Nowhere were tensions more acute than in Charleston's three Methodist churches, where Black members outnumbered white ones by roughly 7 to 1. By the early 1830s, Cumberland Street, Trinity, and Bethel could shoehorn only half of their more than three thousand Black members into their galleries. When white attendance was sparse, elderly Black congregants began testing white tolerance by taking seats on the main floor. More joined in the civil disobedience each week, until "what was conceded as a privilege, was finally claimed by them as a right," according to Methodist historian Francis Mood. Some white worshippers, finding their usual seats occupied, made a show of storming out in a huff. Complaints to the presiding elder led to the stationing of sergeants-at-arms at each church. Two Sabbaths in a row, the bouncers at Bethel forcibly ejected Black members who refused to give up their places. This "produced quite a sensation" that evolved into a full-fledged schism, replete with "criminations and recriminations, rejoinders and surrejoinders." A fusillade of angry letters led to church trials, expulsions, and ultimately a walkout by 165 white members.

It chafed Charleston's white ministers that thousands of potential Black supplicants went untrained because their churches could not hold them. "What becomes of the unconverted?" asked Presbyterian minister John L. Girardeau. "Are they to be excluded from hearing the Gospel, from lack of room in our church edifices?" Girardeau and others suggested that if white churches did not find a way to provide Black Charlestonians with spiritual sustenance, the preachers of a more nefarious gospel would. "Separate congregations . . . they *will* have," the *Southern Presbyterian Review* warned in 1847. "If our laws and the public sentiment of the community tolerate them, they will be open, public, responsible. If our laws prohibit them, they will be secret, fanatical, dangerous."

Thus began an era of segregated churchgoing that continues today. On a May Sunday in 1847, Rev. John Bailey Adger rose to the pulpit at Second Presbyterian and asked for his congregation's blessings—and contributions—to open a separate chapel for Black members. The Charleston native took his sermon from Matthew 11:5—"and the poor have the gospel preached to them"—and used it to redirect the rationale for proselytizing the enslaved. Christians had a fundamental duty to impart God's Word to "the least of them," he said, and enslaved Southerners inarguably fit that description. "Nowhere are the poor more distinctly marked out than our poor," Adger observed, "and, yet, strange to say, nowhere are the poor so closely and intimately connected with higher classes as our poor with us. *They belong to us*. We, also, *belong* to them."

Adger's proposal struck some as radical. But he won denominational support by pitching it as a way to redeem the South's image. Northern abolitionists could caricature Southern slavery as blasphemous and uncaring if they wished, but "here was a church built by Christian slaveholders for the religious benefit of the slaves." The presbytery of Charleston granted its backing after concluding that branch churches would provide "the most effectual answer which can be given to the calumnies of Abolitionists and misguided Philanthropists."

A brick chapel with seating for several hundred was soon built on Anson Street at a cost of $7,500. The congregation outgrew the space within a decade and by 1859 an imposing new Black church, Zion Presbyterian, had been erected near the southeast corner of Calhoun and Meeting Streets. White donors covered most of the $25,000 cost. Zion gradually came to operate semi-independently, but always under the control of a white minister and with regular white attendance. In what must have been a satisfying turn, the church's Black congregants occupied the main floor on Sunday mornings, while a sprinkling of white observers took seats in the galleries. The church, which sat opposite the current site of Mother Emanuel, remained Charleston's largest place of assembly for African Americans until its demolition in 1960.

In the Episcopal denomination, Father Paul Trapier, the former rector at St. Michael's, won approval to stand up his own Black branch in 1848. So long as the group of about 130 worshippers met inconspicuously in borrowed space with white observers in attendance, Charleston officials seemed satisfied with the Episcopalians' assurances that the assemblies were closely monitored. But when the diocese began construction of a stand-alone building at the corner of Wilson and Beaufain, to be called Calvary Church, the town erupted. "If such things as these are permitted," one scribe wrote in the *Mercury*, "will not our blacks soon be taught to consider themselves our equals in other respects?" One Saturday night in July 1849, a mob gathered at the construction site prepared to destroy the unfinished building. The city was already on edge because a court that day had condemned the ringleader of a thwarted rebellion at the Work-House, and testimony had indicated he held strong religious beliefs. Only a promise by Mayor T. Leger Hutchinson to convene a public hearing persuaded the crowd outside the Calvary site to disperse.

Hutchinson personally presided over the jam-packed hearing and did what politicians do when faced with unpopular choices: formed a commission. After four months of investigation and debate, that commission's majority validated the legality and advantages of branch churches like Calvary. "Nothing could be further from the intention of the founders, than to weaken the safeguards of public peace and order," they wrote. The group found that separate entrances and raised seating for white visitors would impart to Black worshippers "a sensible image of the subordination that is due those to whom, by the course of Providence, they are to look up to as their rulers." So long as a separate Black congregation followed the law—meeting during daylight, with the doors open, and white people present—the legislature had left the field "open to the free exercise of Missionary zeal." A month later, just before Christmas, Trapier's band of Episcopalian pioneers consecrated their new church.

Branch churches in the antebellum South helped normalize a culture of Sunday-morning segregation—first involuntary, then voluntary—that has persisted across America for the better part of two centuries. Once Black and white Christians began worshipping the same God in separate spaces, there was little to bring them back together. Four of five U.S. churchgoers still attend services with congregations that are predominantly one race.

But for reasons of both math and memory, there was no formal movement to create a separate Black church within the denomination with the largest Black membership in Charleston—the Southern Methodists. By the eve of the Civil War, one of every four Black Charlestonians had joined a Methodist church, more than 4,300 in all. There were more Black Methodists in Charleston than anywhere in the South, and they constituted more than 80 percent of the denomination there. Given that racial imbalance, Methodist ministers felt the best structure for engaging—and surveilling—their Black members remained the class system, with trusted Black leaders reporting to white clergy. The only structure resembling a branch Methodist church in Charleston could be found at Bethel, which addressed its crowding problem in 1853 by building a grand new sanctuary in the style of a Doric temple. The existing wood-frame building was moved to the rear of the property and designated for use by Black members, with supervised services held on Sunday nights. Not until a dozen years later, after the Union Army forced the Confederate surrender of the Lowcountry, would Charleston's African Methodists truly worship again in their own church.

IX.

Revival: African Methodism Returns South

*And he said, I seek my brethren:
tell me, I pray thee, where they feed their flocks.*

—GENESIS: 37:16 (KJV)

When South Carolina effectively banned the formal education of Black people in the 1830s, no one took it harder than the free Black schoolmaster Daniel Alexander Payne. Born in Charleston in 1811, seven years before the construction of the African Church, Payne had been a bookish child who attended the best schools available to the city's free people of color. He opened his own academy at only eighteen but was forced to close it after five years when the new prohibitions took effect in 1835. He then fled his lifelong home for the North, expecting never to return, so that he could practice his chosen profession and his Methodist faith without government interference. After joining the AME ministry in Philadelphia, he became a prolific writer, preacher, and poet, the denomination's most ardent advocate for an educated ministry, its first official historian, and its sixth bishop. As the Civil War drew to its bloody close, Payne engineered the triumphant return of African Methodism to the Lowcountry and the reestablishment of a flagship church amid the rubble of Charleston. It would be named Emanuel.

Payne's father, London, who died when Daniel was four, had been a class leader at Charleston's Cumberland Street Methodist Episcopal Church, and the boy's earliest memories were of being awakened each morning by his hymns and prayers. London Payne had been born free in Virginia, but as a boy was lured by traffickers onto a ship that made off for Charleston. There he was sold to a house painter and remained a servant until adulthood, when he managed to buy his freedom with $1,000 he had saved from being hired out. Payne described his mother, Martha, a descendant of both Africans and Native Americans, as a woman of "amiable disposition, gentle manners, and fervent piety." Both parents were brown-complected and slightly built, as was their son. As an adult, Daniel Payne had an almost tubercular appearance, his face bony and thin, his cheeks drawn beneath egg-shaped spectacles. A Lincolnesque beard began not on his chin, but behind it, and his hair swept across his head from left to right like a cresting wave. He was invariably swallowed by a heavy dark overcoat.

Payne was "naturally of a weak constitution," according to his friend Rev. Francis J. Grimke, and compensated by living in a "thoroughly systematic" fashion. Like his Wesleyan forebears, he rose each day before dawn for study, and guided his activities by the principle that there was "a time for every thing and every thing in its time," Grimke wrote. He could be impatient with those who led a less ordered life, and proper to the point of eccentricity. When a longtime acquaintance visited his home and tossed his hat on a chair, Payne sat on it and remained in place until his guest got up to leave. He then returned the crumpled fedora along with enough money to replace it, explaining that hats were to be placed on racks, not on chairs.

Orphaned at age nine, Payne became the educational ward first of the Minors' Moralist Society, a club of free Black Charlestonians that supported the schooling of indigent children, and then of Thomas Bonneau, the city's most prominent free Black teacher. An insatiable student with a religious bent, he took particular delight in subjects like history and spelling. As a teen, he was apprenticed to a shoe merchant, then to a carpenter, and finally to a tailor. But while deep in prayer one day he sensed an internal voice: "*I have set thee apart to educate thyself in order that thou mayest be an educator to thy people.*" From then on, Payne gave himself to the study of most any book he could afford, and soon mastered subjects as varied as philosophy, geography, arithmetic, English grammar, Greek, Latin, French, botany, chemistry, and astronomy. His interest in the latter led him to observe the solar eclipse of 1832 with his naked eyes, causing damage that compromised his sight for the rest of his life.

Payne began his teaching career in 1829 by tutoring three children and three enslaved adults in a house on Tradd Street for 50 cents per student per month. He gradually attracted nearly sixty free Black students, so many that he outgrew the room and moved to a larger one built for him in a yard on Anson Street. Demand for his services grew enough that he could charge between $3 and $6 each quarter. Payne fancied himself a pedagogical showman, teaching in a pink robe and adopting a preacher's cadences. On Saturdays, he led his students into the woods to search for insects, reptiles, and plants for the taxidermic menagerie that populated his classroom. He once bought a live alligator, goaded a student into making it snap, and then shot it through its gaping jaws with a pistol. "As soon as he was stunned," Payne wrote in his autobiography, "I threw him on his back, cut his throat, ripped open his chest, hung him up and studied his viscera till they ceased to move." He later cooked and ate the meat, a conservationist practice he followed with all such specimens, save snakes and toads, which he simply could not stomach.

Payne observed that it may have been his fascination with zoology that led to his downfall in Charleston, at least indirectly. In the summer of 1834, he sent three students to fetch a water moccasin that had been captured by an enslaved man on a nearby plantation. They were to bring it back alive in a large jar. The plantation's owner happened to be Lionel Kennedy, the influential lawyer who had presided over the Vesey insurrection trials with fellow magistrate Thomas Parker. When the youngsters arrived, Kennedy and his son, a physician, interrogated them about their purpose, and then inquired more broadly about Payne's school. They were horrified by what the students revealed about the extensive curriculum being taught to people of color. "Why, Pa," the younger Kennedy said, "Payne is playing hell in Charleston." The Kennedys raised their own hell, and by year's end the legislature had outlawed the teaching of reading and writing to enslaved people and ordered the closure of schools operated by free people of color. The law subjected violators to up to fifty lashes and a $50 fine.

Payne was traumatized by the stranglehold on his livelihood. He tossed and turned for nights on end, praying for God to grant him sleep. "Sometimes it seemed as though some wild beast had plunged his fangs into my heart, and was squeezing out its life-blood," he wrote. He began to question whether God was just, or even existed. "If so, why does he suffer one race to oppress and enslave another, to rob them by unrighteous enactments of rights, which they hold most dear and sacred?" Payne raged. He told himself that if South Carolina's lawmakers had but one neck, he "would be the man to sever the head from its shoulders." Then he remembered the instruction from Peter's second epistle, that with the Lord one day is as a thousand years and a thousand years as one day. The verse soothed his soul. "Trust in him," Payne told himself, "and he will bring slavery and all its outrages to an end."

That did not mean Payne was willing to wait it out in Charleston without means of support. He collected letters of introduction from the city's most prominent white clergymen—Methodist minister William Capers, Episcopalian rector Christopher Gadsden, Congregationalist leader Benjamin Morgan Palmer, and Lutheran pastor John Bachman, the latter a noted naturalist with whom Payne shared a scientific friendship. Bachman, who had long supported the religious instruction of enslaved Carolinians, made clear his ambivalence about the crackdown on teaching but suggested in a letter to Payne that he accept his fate. "Yield submissively to the laws of the land," he advised his friend. "Do your duty and trust in God, and all will most assuredly be overruled for your future good."

Payne wasn't particularly submissive when it came to matters of white supremacy, but he took the rest of the prophecy to heart. The young tutor administered his final round of examinations, and on May 9, 1835, bade a mournful farewell to friends as he boarded a steamer for the five-day voyage to New York. Payne watched St. Michael's spire fade into a sinking sun as the ship chugged out of Charleston's harbor, his eyes "almost blind with tears." On his very first night in New York, he attended a meeting of the American Anti-Slavery Society, co-founded by the unyielding abolitionist editor William Lloyd Garrison.

Bachman's letter of introduction led to Payne's admission to the Lutheran seminary at Gettysburg. After two years of study, he considered seeking ordination as an African Methodist, but was warned by a friend about the denomination's anti-intellectualism. AME preachers, the friend said, started their sermons with the common-touch boast that they had "not rubbed their heads against college-walls," and were rewarded with shouts of "Glory to God!" when they declared they had never studied Greek, Latin, or Hebrew. Payne took ordination as a Lutheran instead, but unable to find work accepted a position at the head of a small integrated Presbyterian church in East Troy, New York. He also became an outspoken abolitionist, declaring in one essay that slavery "subverts *the moral government of God*" by restricting the ability of Black Christians to worship freely. Payne eventually moved to Philadelphia and opened a school on Spruce Street in 1840, bringing him into regular contact with Bishop Morris Brown and other AME leaders. They convinced him to begin the two-year process for becoming a licensed AME minister.

Soon after his appointment to a church in Washington, D.C., Payne began writing and speaking in support of educational requirements for the African

Methodist clergy. Unapologetically high-hatted, he took the attitude that the unschooled pioneers of the Black church had done their part but needed to make way for a second generation of Christian soldiers who were trained in theology, philosophy, and homiletics. Although a master rhetorician, Payne could be indelicate when it came to his benighted elders. "While we acknowledge that your advanced life and domestic cares may present insurmountable barriers to your improvement, we hail you as the pioneers of the Church," he wrote in 1845. Then he warned that the lions of the church should not block progress on their way to the grave, lest their legacies be tarnished: "Let it never be said that you were opposed to the cause of sacred learning, or that you hindered the car of improvement."

Payne's disregard for the emotionalism he found in some AME congregations—the spirituals and ring shouts and pulpit-thumping sermons—rivaled his distaste for illiterate ministers. He readily linked the two and scoffed at those who believed "that he who hallooes the loudest and speaks the longest is the best preacher." His puritan's crusade to "modify some of the extravagances in worship" cost him at least one job. Payne wrote that the stewards of a Baltimore church rejected his appointment because "they said . . . that I had too fine a carpet on my floor." He was too proud to take tea with congregants, they thought, and derided their songs of praise as "cornfield ditties." Payne's scolding approach was informed by his politics as well as his faith. Not until Black Americans demonstrated their capacity for full citizenship and proved themselves the peers of their white counterparts would their demands for equal treatment be taken seriously, he believed. His would be a church that urged its followers to be punctual, pious, and abstemious, and to shun the kind of "slovenly and ragged appearance" that perpetuated "the malignity of prejudice."

"Then, as water rises to its natural level, so will we rise to the position destined by reason and heaven," Payne wrote. He later boasted that "the African Methodist Episcopal Church has done more to *demonstrate the manhood* (his emphasis) of the Anglo-Africans than any other ecclesiastical organization in the great Republic." Indeed, the redemption of racial manhood from the emasculating effects of slavery and second-class citizenship was central to the African Methodist ethos, so central that the struggle of Black women was often sacrificed on its altar, some historians have observed. "What is African Methodism," AME minister Benjamin T. Tanner wondered in 1867, "but an outburst of all that is manly in the Negro—manly political, manly ecclesiastical."

At the 1844 AME General Conference in Pittsburgh, presided over by Bishop Morris Brown, Payne introduced a resolution to establish rigorous educational requirements for AME clergy for the first time: four years of study for ministers and two for exhorters. He was so confident the measure would pass that he did not speak on its behalf. Instead, the proposal generated intense opposition from elders—as when "a fire-brand is cast into a magazine of powder"—and the delegates voted it down. Overnight, however, Payne's resolution gained powerful allies after a group of pro-education ministers threatened to secede and form their own branch. Upon reconsideration the next day, the curriculum passed unanimously. Education has since been central to AME culture. Payne later helped found Wilberforce University as an AME institution and became its president. Named for the famed British abolitionist, the Ohio school was the first of what are now seven freestanding AME colleges and universities, along with several seminaries.

Payne was elected an AME bishop in 1852, assigned to oversee the northeastern states, and devoted the next dozen years to the administrative responsibilities of his ever-expanding church. While subsequently headquartered in Washington, he became an occasional wartime counselor to President Abraham Lincoln, urging him at a meeting in 1862 to sign the District of Columbia emancipation bill. Three decades after being banned from his Charleston schoolhouse, Payne was now welcomed at the White House and treated cordially by the president of the United States. "President Lincoln received and conversed with me as though I had been one of his intimate acquaintances or one of his friendly neighbors," Payne wrote. Surely, they discussed Payne's dream of reviving the denomination he now led in the region that had once been his home.

The first opportunity emerged in the spring of 1863 when Bishop Payne, while presiding over an AME conference in Baltimore, received a visit from a white New York merchant named Charles C. Leigh. Leigh was a former state legislator, a lay preacher of the northern branch of the Methodist Episcopal Church, and the chairman of the New York National Freedman's Relief Association. That abolitionist group had been founded a year earlier to aid formerly enslaved Civil War refugees who were flooding into the North, as well as those abandoned on coastal plantations confiscated by advancing Union troops. A philanthropic forerunner of the government's Freedmen's Bureau, its mission was to bring work, sustenance, schooling—and Christianity—to newly emancipated Americans. Leigh impressed upon Payne that while a growing number of formerly enslaved people on South Carolina's barrier islands might now be physically free, they remained spiritually adrift, "like sheep without a shepherd." He asked that Payne provide two AME missionaries to the Lowcountry.

The bishop was intrigued. "How soon do you want them?" he asked.

"Within ten days," Leigh answered.

Payne explained the history of African Methodism in his home state of South Carolina, how against all odds it had established a beachhead only to be exiled after the insurrection summer of 1822. The church had been ruthlessly suppressed, Payne said, because it had dared to promote "personal freedom and responsibility for the Negro."

Leigh found himself stirred. Nothing, he felt, would be more fitting than for the AME Church to lead the religious reoccupation of a soon-to-be-conquered South. "The field is yours," he encouraged Bishop Payne. "Go and occupy it."

IN NO OTHER STATE would the four-decade run-up to the Civil War be as tumultuous as in South Carolina. That is because in no other state was slaveholding as pervasive, and nowhere else was the planter aristocracy as fixed on preserving its plantation economy in the face of prevailing winds. Competition and evolving markets had sapped South Carolina's commercial prospects while overcultivation depleted its soil, shifting the South's population and wealth to more fertile plains and deltas to the west. Abolitionism was gaining momentum in the North and abroad. Yet the Lowcountry elite held fast to the delusion that their historic advantages would predominate, even in an altered economic and political landscape, securing for generations the traditions and opulence to which they had grown accustomed.

South Carolina's path to secession began a decade after the foiled insurrection plot in Charleston, not with a direct confrontation over slavery but with a proxy battle over tariffs. With slavery as its long-term imperative, South Carolina acted—alone—on the novel theory that states could nullify federal laws if they decided the national government had exceeded its delegated powers. After years of resentment, South Carolina's leaders called a special convention in November 1832 that declared a series of tariffs imposed by Congress to be null and void. Determined to defend the union against treason, President Andrew Jackson threatened to collect the duties by military force. The standoff was resolved and a more serious constitutional crisis averted through a compromise that lowered the tariffs and allowed South Carolina a face-saving escape.

Three years later, in 1835, another defining state-federal conflict exploded in South Carolina, this time involving the delivery of the U.S. mail. On July 29, the steam packet *Columbia* arrived in Charleston on its usual circuit from New York with bundles from that city's post office. As the first envelopes were opened and their contents revealed, the city erupted in fury. The ship, according to one news account, was "literally overburthened" with abolitionist tracts mailed by the American Anti-Slavery Society. It was the first propaganda bombardment of the South by the two-year-old group, and Charleston was the port of entry for pamphlets and newspapers posted to towns across the region. Some had been addressed to clergymen in the hope they might find sympathetic eyes.

The city offered a $1,000 reward for the apprehension of anyone distributing the incendiary publications. On the night after the offending mail's arrival, townspeople jimmied a post office window in the Exchange building and seized a bag of confiscated pamphlets. The next evening, as several thousand Charlestonians cheered on the Citadel square, the purloined papers fueled a bonfire that also consumed effigies of William Lloyd Garrison and his abolitionist allies.

Bloodshed was averted in the nullification and post office crises, but South Carolina's defiant course had been set, awaiting only a pretext for disunion. In 1837, the state's most prominent politician, Sen. John C. Calhoun, declared in a notorious floor speech that the enslavement of Black people was "instead of an evil, a good—a positive good." Separatist sentiment nearly came to a boil in 1851, when radicals in the state legislature mounted an unsuccessful campaign for secession, and finally did, of course, a decade later in response to the election of President Abraham Lincoln. Six weeks after Lincoln's victory in 1860, delegates from across South Carolina met in Charleston to make the state the first to adopt and sign an Ordinance of Secession from the Union. They did not mask their rationale. "An increasing hostility on the part of the non-slaveholding States to the institution of slavery, has led to a disregard of their obligations," the secessionists declared, "and the laws of the General Government have ceased to effect the objects of the Constitution." When federal troops refused the Confederate demand to abandon Fort Sumter, the Civil War opened on April 12, 1861, with a predawn barrage from batteries positioned around Charleston Harbor. The next afternoon, Maj. Robert Anderson surrendered the federal government's harbor redoubt. Lincoln immediately ordered a blockade of Charleston and other Southern ports.

Charleston would not be occupied by Union forces until February 1865, following a withering siege and nearly twenty months of intermittent shelling. But early in the conflict, in November 1861, a Union fleet swept into Port Royal Sound, fifty miles to the south, hoping to establish a deep-water base to support the blockade of the South Carolina coast. With little resistance, the blue-coated forces took control of Beaufort, Port Royal, and Hilton Head Island. White families fled inland, leaving nearly ten thousand of their enslaved workers on plantations and farms. The white ministers who had pastored the area's churches followed their patrons in flight.

In the first reconstructionist experiment of its kind, the federal government, along with philanthropic and religious groups like Charles Leigh's New York National Freedman's Relief Association, stepped in to keep farms in production and provide laborers with wages, schooling, and medical care. On January 1, 1863, thousands of formerly enslaved Sea Islanders, many now clad in the uniform of the United States Army, assembled near a grove of live oaks in Beaufort to hear the oration of Lincoln's Emancipation Proclamation. It was to that swath of the Lowcountry below Charleston, thick with scrub oak and palmetto, that Bishop Daniel Alexander Payne was asked to send AME missionaries to tend to the spiritual needs of the newly liberated.

ALTHOUGH FOUNDED IN RACIAL PROTEST, the AME denomination devoted more energy in its early decades to organizing and expanding than to waging a frontal war on the immorality of slavery. The institution was then, as now, socially conservative, politically mainstream, committed to order, and consumed with church-building and self-preservation. By way of example, its patriarchy had overwhelmingly rejected the ministerial licensing of women at the General Conference of 1852, after being scolded by Daniel Payne for even considering it. Not only was the ordination of women not biblically sanctioned, Payne had charged, it threatened to "break up the sacred relations which women bear to their husbands and children, by sending them forth as itinerant preachers, wandering from place to place, to the utter neglect of their household duties and obligations." That social conservatism predominated nearly two centuries later, as delegates to the General Conferences of 2021 and 2024 voted to continue the church's prohibition against conducting same-sex marriages.

Given the tension between liberation and preservation, perhaps it was not so surprising, then, that the AME approach to slavery at times seemed more emancipationist than abolitionist. Yes, denominational assemblies passed resolutions calling for fasting and prayer in support of abolitionist leaders or declaring opposition to African colonization or the Fugitive Slave Law. But rarely did they go substantially further. The New England Conference, meeting in Providence in 1854 with Bishop Payne presiding, resolved to "wage a life-long and sleepless warfare with the principles of slavery," but specified no action beyond presenting the resolution to the governor of Rhode Island. The church did make minor incursions into border and slaveholding states between the mid-1840s and early 1860s, but they qualified as little more than toe-dipping. When the Missouri Conference was formed in 1855 it tallied but 1,698 members in the seven states of Missouri, Illinois, Kentucky, Tennessee, Mississippi, Louisiana, and Alabama, less than a tenth of the nationwide AME membership of nearly 20,000.

Only in 1856, on the eve of the Civil War, did the issue come front and center. Meeting in Cincinnati that year, delegates to the General Conference were asked to decide how quickly current or aspiring church members should be required to emancipate any enslaved persons they owned. *The Doctrines and Discipline* had always prohibited slaveholding by free AME members, of course, but it only called for expulsion if a churchman refused to emancipate his property "after due notice has been given by the preacher in charge." Those with more abolitionist leanings felt that language left wiggle room and condemned it as "pro-slavery." They feared the rule might allow negotiation in circumstances where church members obtained slaves to manumit them, but perhaps only after they worked off their purchase price. There had been occasional reports that applicants for AME membership had sold their human property before joining, which rather defeated the purpose. A seven-man committee was formed to consider alternatives, and the deliberations left them so divided that they presented dueling recommendations.

Hardline abolitionists called for automatic expulsion for anyone who did not immediately liberate their property, arguing that slavery "is a sin of the first magnitude, and should not for one moment be allowed in the holy communion of the church of God." But the church's powerful institutionalists worried that African Methodism would gain a reputation as an abolitionist front. That could provoke white officials whose grace was needed to operate in slaveholding states like Louisiana, putting itinerant preachers at risk. Many

LEFT: Emanuel African Methodist Episcopal Church. *Courtesy of Emanuel African Methodist Episcopal Church*

BELOW: Interior of Emanuel African Methodist Episcopal Church. *Courtesy of Emanuel African Methodist Episcopal Church*

Bishop Richard Allen, founder of African Methodism (by Peter S. Duval, ca. 1840). *National Portrait Gallery, Smithsonian Institution*

Rev. John Wesley, founder of Methodism (engraving by J. Thomas after J. Jackson). *Wellcome Collection* ©

Bishop Francis Asbury, Methodism's first American leader (by John Paradise, 1813). *National Portrait Gallery, Smithsonian Institution*

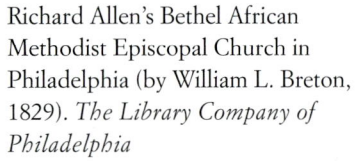

Richard Allen's Bethel African Methodist Episcopal Church in Philadelphia (by William L. Breton, 1829). *The Library Company of Philadelphia*

Jarena Lee, first female African Methodist preacher (by Alfred Hoffy, ca. 1849). *The New York Public Library*

Bishop Morris Brown, founder of Charleston's African Church and second bishop of the AME denomination (by Albert Newsam, 1844). *National Portrait Gallery, Smithsonian Institution*

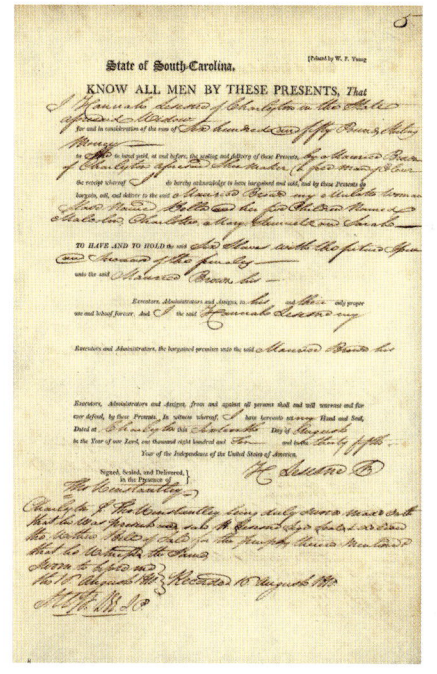

Bill of sale for Morris Brown's family members by Hannah Lesesne to Maurice (Morris) Brown, for £650, August 16, 1810. *South Carolina Department of Archives and History*

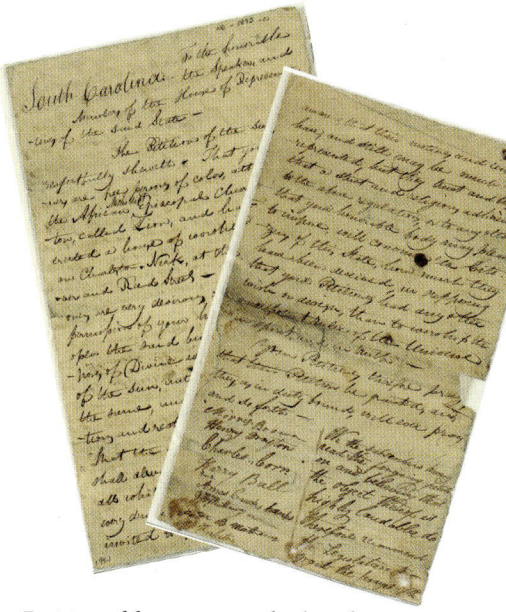

Petition of free persons of color of Charleston to the General Assembly of South Carolina to open an African Methodist Episcopal Church, November 24, 1817. *South Carolina Department of Archives and History*

Deed for purchase of the lot at Hanover and Reid Streets, site of the African Church, June 1818. *Charleston County Register of Deeds*

Statue of Denmark Vesey, Hampton Park, Charleston, SC (Vesey's physical appearance has never been documented). *Tony Cenicola/The New York Times/Redux*

ABOVE: Advertisement in Charleston's *City Gazette* of August 14, 1822, for the upcoming sale of lumber from the African Church, which had been dismantled after that summer's insurrection trials.

RIGHT: Bishop Daniel Alexander Payne, who oversaw the return of African Methodism to his native Charleston (by Frederick Gutekunst, ca. 1888). *National Portrait Gallery, Smithsonian Institution; acquired through the generosity of Nik and Melissa Apostolides*

George A. Trenholm, secretary of the Confederate treasury and seller of the Calhoun Street property to Emanuel church trustees in 1865. *The American Civil War Museum, Richmond, VA*

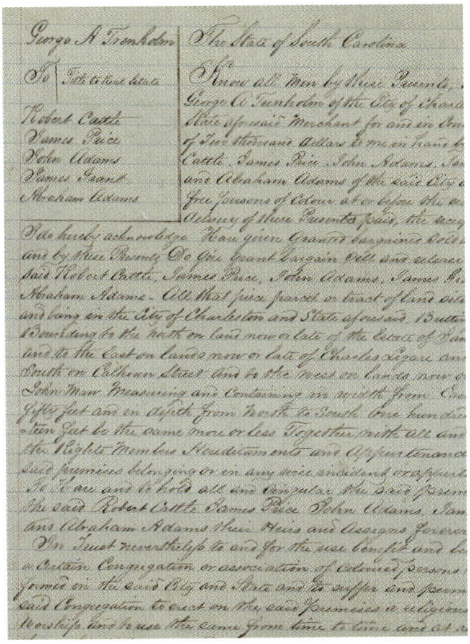

Deed for the purchase of land on Calhoun Street for the future Emanuel African Methodist Episcopal Church, September 6, 1865. *Charleston County Register of Deeds*

The original wood-frame Emanuel AME survived the devastating earthquake of 1886, as demonstrated by this photo taken in May 1890 during the Quarto-Centennial Conference of the African Methodist Episcopal Church of South Carolina. *Courtesy of Emanuel African Methodist Episcopal Church*

Bishop Richard Harvey Cain, first postwar pastor of Emanuel AME and two-term member of Congress, undated. *Avery photograph collection, AMN 1112, Avery Research Center for African American History and Culture, College of Charleston, Charleston, SC, USA*

Bishops of the AME Church, including Richard Allen, Morris Brown, and Daniel Payne, 1876. *The Library Company of Philadelphia*

ABOVE LEFT: Rev. Norman Bascom Sterrett, Emanuel AME pastor and founder of Mt. Zion AME Church, undated. *Sterrett-Hodge Family Papers, AMN 1060, Avery Research Center for African American History and Culture, College of Charleston, Charleston, SC, USA*

ABOVE RIGHT: Rev. Lewis Ruffin Nichols, pastor of Emanuel AME during the current building's construction. Photo taken between February 1901 and December 1903. *C.M. Bell Studio Collection, Library of Congress*

RIGHT: Emanuel AME Church under repair, ca. 1909. *Historic Charleston Foundation, gift of Darlene and John Zacharias, great-nephew of Henry T. Zacharias*

Trustees, Stewards, and Stewardesses of Emanuel AME Church, ca. 1916.
Richard R. Wright, Jr., Centennial Encyclopaedia of the African Methodist Episcopal Church, 1916, Courtesy of HathiTrust

W. E. B. Du Bois, center, with sightseeing party during March 1917 visit to Charleston.
Avery photograph collection, AMN 1112, Avery Research Center for African American History and Culture, College of Charleston, Charleston, SC, USA

The Emanuel AME congregation, undated.
Courtesy of Emanuel African Methodist Episcopal Church

took the position that keeping African Methodism solvent and vibrant was itself a liberationist act of the first order. Besides, they shrugged, what were they really supposed to do about slavery?

"We have neither civil nor political power; hence, no civil or political influence, and, therefore, the responsibility does not rest upon us," asserted Rev. Alexander W. Wayman of Baltimore, a secretary of the General Conference and future bishop. "But there are many things wanted to be done in our Church which we can do. We want more vital piety, more holiness, more intelligence, more sinlessness. These we can have, and these will greatly aid in lifting us out of the dust of degradation and elevating us to respectability in the land." He supported a resolution that called for fasting and prayer to "hasten the day when all oppression shall come to an end." By a landslide of 40 to 12, his colleagues agreed that would suffice. The delegates to the next AME General Conference, on the eve of the Civil War, resolved that they "identified" with the enslaved and "do deeply sympathize with them in their tears and blood." Beyond that, they offered "our constant prayers" and "good wishes."

Militancy was one thing, but membership was another. And so even as African Methodism muted its protest against the enslavement of Black Southerners, it prepared diligently for the day when nearly 4 million of them would gain the wherewithal to worship as they pleased. Those preparations took on urgency once Lincoln freed the enslaved of the District of Columbia in April 1862 and then warned in September that he would issue a general proclamation of emancipation on January 1, 1863. The week that Lincoln signed the D.C. emancipation bill, which compensated slaveholders for manumission, Bishop Payne preached a sermon of invitation in Georgetown to those now free to look for their own church home. Titled "Welcome to the Ransomed," it reflected the conviction of African Methodist leaders that church membership, like American liberty itself, carried expectations of moral citizenship. Ransomed from physical bondage by Congress, freed men and women now could pursue spiritual deliverance through the example of Christ. Payne encouraged his listeners to work hard and sacrifice, to avoid fine clothing and strong drink, and to save for the betterment of their children. "Enter the great family of Holy Freedom," Payne instructed, "not to *lounge in sinful indolence*, not to *degrade yourselves by vice*, nor to *corrupt society by licentiousness*, neither to *offend the laws by crime*, but to the *enjoyment of a well regulated liberty*."

IN CONSIDERING CHARLES LEIGH'S REQUEST to send AME missionaries into the Lowcountry, Bishop Payne understood that it would be perilous to place free Black men so deep behind enemy lines. But he also found the prospect tantalizing in its possibilities, an opportunity to plant the AME flag ahead of other denominations that would soon be competing for the allegiances and tithes of millions of emancipated African Americans. Payne received assurances that his missionaries would be afforded military protection in South Carolina, and with that he quickly won the denomination's approval to dispatch Rev. James Lynch of Baltimore and Rev. James D. S. Hall of New York.

Born free in Baltimore, the son of a merchant and part-time preacher who had bought his wife out of slavery, Lynch was but twenty-four when selected for this most sensitive of missions. Distinguished in appearance, with piercing eyes and a rectangular goatee, he was clearly a young man on the make in AME circles. Admired for his "almost matchless eloquence" and manifold involvements in church affairs, Lynch evangelized tirelessly and wrote fearlessly, wielding sarcasm like a stone-sharpened saber. He could not have been more earnest, however, about the Christian work to be done in the South. Only a few weeks before being dispatched by Payne, Lynch proposed in *The Christian Recorder*, the AME newspaper founded in 1852, that every church form a missionary society to raise funds for the recruitment of newly emancipated Southerners. "Christian colored men and women must rush to these our brethren," he wrote, "standing on the sea shore of freedom, saved from the wreck of slavery, but shivering with the cold blast of prejudice; naked with ignorance, and hungry for the bread of life." Hall, an AME minister and organizer since 1852, had most recently been pastoring a church on New York's Sullivan Street, where he had proved himself a compelling orator. Like Lynch, he was leaving his wife behind in order to satisfy the bishop's command.

At twelve minutes before noon on May 20, 1863, Bishop Payne stood on a Manhattan wharf to watch Lynch and Hall depart on the *Arago*, a wood-hulled, double-masted sidewheeler that transported Union troops to Hilton Head. He was joined by Rev. Richard Harvey Cain, an AME pastor in Brooklyn who would soon leave his own long mark on South Carolina. It felt like they were sending sons off to war, and as Payne watched the *Arago* disappear into the Atlantic he could not help but remember his own journey in the opposite direction. In 1835, a repressive new law had forced him to close his school and abandon his home with little hope of seeing it again. Now in a matter of days his own ministers would be teaching Lowcountry freedmen to read and write and cipher and study the Bible and the Constitution of the United States. "Only the sword of the Lord and of Gideon could, within the life of a single generation, bring to pass such wonderful changes!" the bishop exulted.

Cain shared in Payne's delight. Like his bishop, he saw biblical prophecy in the return of African Methodism to the South. "Heaven has graciously opened the way for the spreading of our beloved Zion in that land," Cain reported to *The Christian Recorder*. "It is there we have the best right to plant our standard; there above all other places on this continent, should be preached the Gospel of Christ; and there, more than elsewhere, the people will welcome our church which looks after their welfare—their social, moral, and spiritual elevation . . . It is an era for the church to spread her curtains, and lengthen her cords, and gather in her long neglected children."

Cain predicted, correctly as it turned out, that few institutions would have such a natural claim on the hearts and loyalties of South Carolina's freedmen. The extinction of African Methodism in Charleston in 1822 had been part of their shared history, and centuries of common experience bound them in ways that white ministers simply could not simulate. They were of one blood, bone of their bones and flesh of their flesh. "None are so eminently qualified for this work as our ministry," Cain declared. "We can feel and enter into all the sympathies of our poor down-trodden brethren. Other teachers and preachers have feelings, but not as we fell [sic] for our kindred."

Lynch and Hall were in fact received with great enthusiasm in the Lowcountry. For many of the newly emancipated, the choice of a faith and a church represented their very first assertions of free will, before they could buy property or vote, before they could read a newspaper or sign their name, perhaps even before they had selected that name. Emancipation had not automatically conveyed political rights, which would accrue gradually, at least for men, through the ratification of the Fifteenth Amendment in 1870. Nor had it invalidated the Supreme Court's 1857 holding in *Dred Scott v. Sandford* that even free descendants of enslaved Africans were not citizens. In that continuing netherworld, the choice to leave a former enslaver's church for an autonomous Black one served as a declaration of personhood and an assertion of racial solidarity. The Black church replaced the disintegrating communal structure of the plantation, an anchor yet again in a roiling sea of social disruption. "The church was one of the few areas in which Blacks were relatively free to define an aspect of freedom in ways that made sense to them," historian Reginald F. Hildebrand wrote in his 1995 study of African Methodism after emancipation. Secular freedpeople, Hildebrand observed, were in no mood to remain religious slaves.

The AME missionaries set to the task of establishing Methodist societies within the Port Royal occupied zone, south of Charleston, with Hall working in Beaufort and Lynch focusing on Hilton Head. Their reports back to the *Recorder* rejoiced in the thirst of free Carolinians for self-improvement and old-fashioned Methodist structure. By the end of 1864 they also had planted AME congregations in Lady's Island, Port Royal, and St. Helena. In the last, Lynch found about eight hundred Black residents sharing an abandoned Episcopal church. Lacking direction and leadership, Black Methodists, Presbyterians, Baptists, and Episcopalians were all "worshipping together, or what is nearer the truth, quarreling together." Lynch began preaching there and soon claimed the congregation for the African Methodists. "To this they all readily assented, with the exception of a few Baptists," he wrote. The following Sunday, the sanctuary filled two hours before the service, and Lynch baptized 25 adults and received 153 new members. A week later he added 20 more. He soon started both a day school and a Sunday school that each attracted about 150 students.

"Ignorant though they be, on account of long years of oppression, they exhibit a desire to hear and to learn, that I never imagined," Lynch wrote a month after arriving. "Every word you say while preaching, they drink down and respond to, with an earnestness that sets your heart all on fire, and you feel that it is indeed God's work to minister to them."

Wherever they trekked, Lynch and Hall worked their way through a backlog of weddings, baptisms, and christenings. Soon after landing in Beaufort, Hall buried the sixteen-month-old son of the daring Robert Smalls, the formerly enslaved man who, a year earlier, had hijacked a Confederate ship, the *Planter*, sailed it out of Charleston Harbor, and delivered it, and his family, to the U.S. Navy. The missionaries licensed local ministers and exhorters to help with the workload. They raised money for church construction and hawked subscriptions to *The Christian Recorder*, which arrived in bundles on ships each week, dense with both war news and the Good News. Lynch preached in the countryside and in military camps, serving as an unofficial chaplain to the 54th Massachusetts Volunteer Infantry, the all-Black regiment immortalized in the 1989 film *Glory*. He visited the unit's wounded in hospitals—"I never saw men so cheerful in suffering in my life"—and catalogued its casualties and injuries for the *Recorder*. One of the dead was Bishop Payne's nephew. To foster patriotism and unity, Lynch planned Independence Day and Emancipation Day celebrations for the freedmen, with speeches and feasts of roasted oxen. The missionaries also served as de facto monitors of the Union Army's treatment of its African American charges. When Lynch discovered that Black soldiers, and civilians like himself, were banned from the airy upper decks of government steamers sailing between Beaufort and Hilton Head, he dashed off a letter of complaint to the commanding general. The general responded immediately by granting Lynch "the same privileges on transports as are given to white persons of his profession."

By the fall of 1863, Lynch and Hall faced determined competition from a white minister who had been sent to Beaufort by the Northern branch of the Methodist Episcopal Church, Rev. T. Willard Lewis. The well-funded Northern Methodists hoped to retake ground lost in the great slavery schism of the mid-1840s, which had split American Methodism into separate regional denominations. In a scenario that became commonplace as Union troops reclaimed Confederate territory, the battle for souls soon devolved into a racial conflict over church property. Lewis arrived in Beaufort from Massachusetts with the understanding from his bishop that the War Department had authorized him to claim any Methodist church not under the control of a loyal white minister. Things got complicated when he found the church in Beaufort already confiscated by the African Methodists. They were neither white nor loyal to the Methodist Episcopal Church, North, as the Northern branch was called. They also felt they had a legitimate property claim based on the contributions made by Black members to build and maintain the church.

Lewis learned in a heated conversation with Hall that his Black Methodist brothers would not be ceding their congregation to him and had little interest in sharing space. He argued in response that the postbellum church needed to be multiracial and charged that African Methodism, by its very name, was exclusionary.

"You call us Africans, why should we not call ourselves so?" Hall countered.

"But we receive colored members into our church," Lewis answered, "and you don't receive whites into yours. There's the great difference."

"We receive all the white members that offer themselves," Hall quipped. The actual difference, he said, was that the African Methodists were self-governing and neither Northern nor Southern white Methodists were prepared to submit to their rule.

Despite Hall's vigorous defense, the AME denomination did understand that the inclusion of the word "African" in its name, while perhaps alluring to freedmen as an expression of common oppression, might at some point hold back its expansion. Indeed, at the very time that the African Methodists were fending off the Northern Methodists, Lynch was mounting a determined campaign to strike the reference from the church's title. In one of several essays published in the *Recorder*, he warned that African Methodism would become "a waning power" if it engaged in the very race prejudice it had been founded to fight. As a political pragmatist, Lynch believed that white Southerners, even after a devastating military defeat, wielded too much power over Black interests to be held at a distance. "I find that *all intelligent colored men of the South* believe it best to cultivate the sympathy and regard of the whites," Lynch wrote. "Nay, more, conciliate them whenever it can be done without sacrificing their manhood."

As disputes multiplied over the control of abandoned churches in the South, the Lincoln administration eventually clarified that it was not in the business of favoring one denomination over another. New and extant congregations would decide for themselves how to affiliate, with property rights to be litigated after the war. That, Lynch believed, gave the African Methodists all the advantage they needed. "Notwithstanding the strong effort that has been made to divide the Methodist people," he wrote from Hilton Head, "it is a well known fact here, that the A.M.E. Church is *the* Methodist Church here."

THE UNION SIEGE AND BOMBARDMENT of the Charleston peninsula, which began in the summer of 1863 and lasted 587 days, reduced to rubble sections of a city that had already been devasted by fire in late 1861. The war claimed roughly a third of South Carolina's white men of military age, a stunning loss compared even to other Confederate states. By the time Gen. William Tecumseh Sherman mounted his blitz through the Carolinas in early 1865, he no longer considered Charleston worth burning, despite its symbolic value as the birthplace of secession and rebellion. He recommended to Gen. Ulysses S. Grant that they bypass it for Columbia. "Charleston," he wrote his superior, "is now a mere desolated wreck and is hardly worth the time it would take to starve it out." He was right. The city surrendered on February 18, 1865, as Sherman's forces overran the state capital. Initial Union control of Charleston fell to units of Black soldiers.

James Lynch had been among twenty Black ministers and church leaders who attended a landmark meeting with Sherman and Secretary of War Edwin M. Stanton a month earlier in Savannah, where Sherman was headquartered after his march to the sea. The ministers used the opportunity to lobby for a radical plan of land redistribution, arguing it would be the best way to help the newly emancipated achieve self-reliance. Four days later, Sherman issued his famously short-lived Field Order No. 15, which confiscated four hundred thousand acres of coastal land between Charleston and north Florida and allocated it in forty-acre parcels to families liberated from Lowcountry servitude (the award of surplus army mules came later). Lynch made an initial foray into Charleston—"this nest of treason"—within a week of its fall. He could not have been more upbeat about AME prospects there. "The colored population of Charleston may be counted in the thousands; and it has been greatly augmented by the defeat of the rebels," he wrote in a February 27 update to the *Recorder*. "The Methodists are in the majority; and the initiatory steps for the organization of an African M.E. Church, have already been taken, and I expect to succeed." His recruitment efforts had started the previous day with Sabbath preaching at both Zion Church, the Black Presbyterian fortress on Calhoun Street, and Old Bethel, the Black Methodist branch five blocks to the west.

In mid-March, Alexander Wayman, who had become an AME bishop the previous year, gained government permission to make the voyage from New York to Hilton Head, accompanied by Elisha Weaver, the editor of *The Christian Recorder*. They toured that village and then headed to Savannah, where they visited a school for Black children that had been converted from a former slave market. Wayman pulled open a desk drawer and was shocked to find "a bill of sale for human beings." A few days later the men sailed for "the once haughty but now humbled city of Charleston," where Wayman and Weaver witnessed mind-blowing reversals: Black soldiers checking the papers of white men and Black churchgoers staking out front-row pews. They visited one of Morris Brown's sons, presumably Malcolm, whose dialect they found deeply redolent of his father's. The men also paid a visit to John C. Calhoun's tomb in the St. Philip's graveyard and left with a souvenir: a shard of the top-stone that had been smashed by vandals. They preached to packed houses at Old Bethel and Zion, where Wayman delivered a sermon that would be appropriated by other Southern missionaries over the years. He took it from Genesis 37:16, in which Jacob instructs his chosen son, Joseph, to search distant grazing lands for his shepherding brothers. Like Joseph, Wayman said, he had come to South Carolina "to seek my brethren," his Black Methodist brethren, his brethren in affliction, bonded by their persecution and a common love of humankind.

The brethren responded, as did the sistren. At a meeting at Zion in April, Bishop Wayman and Rev. Lewis of the Northern Methodists each made presentations about why the city's Black Methodists should sign on with his denomination. A heavy majority favored the African Methodists, Weaver reported. Lynch told the *Recorder* that the great mass of the three thousand Black Methodists in Charleston were ready to affiliate. In April, twenty-one Black exhorters, class leaders, and stewards from the Bethel, Trinity, and Cumberland Methodist congregations petitioned to be accepted into the AME connection. Rev. Lewis and the Northern Methodists continued to assert a claim to churches like Bethel, but Lynch felt there was little that Lewis could do about it. "Certainly," he wrote, "two thousand Methodist members are not to be forced from their churches because they do not choose to follow Mr. Lewis."

For Black Carolinians, the liberation of Charleston opened a season of jubilee. They thronged to mass meetings at churches with military officials and dignitaries from the North. Hundreds of formerly enslaved plantation families migrated to the city, attracted by wage labor and government schools. Black entrepreneurs opened grocery stores and other markets. "The thrift, energy, industry and perseverance of the colored people, since the emancipation, has astonished the enemies of that measure," *The Christian Recorder* reported from Charleston. "Colored people are seen working every where, and at every thing, and would be engaged in more business if they had the means."

Most everyone in town turned out for a parade in March that featured Black marshals on horseback, Black preachers armed with Bibles and hymnals, a brigade of Black firemen, guilds of Black tradesmen—butchers, painters, blacksmiths—and hundreds of jubilant Black schoolchildren. One student carried a banner proclaiming "We know no masters but ourselves." On April 14, 1865, a grand celebration was held amid the ruins of Fort Sumter as Maj. Gen. Robert Anderson, who had abandoned the installation precisely four years earlier, presented the tattered flag he had taken with him that day. It was raised once again to the salute of one hundred guns and a rousing rendition of "The Star-Spangled Banner." News of the surrender of the Army of Northern Virginia had just arrived, stoking the jubilation. The crowd sparkled with luminaries—commodores and generals, a senator and a Supreme Court justice, famed abolitionists William Lloyd Garrison and Henry Ward Beecher, Maj. Martin R. Delany, the country's highest-ranking Black soldier, Robert Vesey, the son of the Charleston martyr of 1822. War hero Robert Smalls sailed up in the *Planter*, her deck teeming with newly emancipated men, women, and children. President Lincoln stayed in Washington but sent his private secretary. It turned out to a be star-crossed choice, as Lincoln instead took in a comedy that night at Ford's Theatre, where he was assassinated by a pro-slavery fanatic named John Wilkes Booth.

The grand culmination of the AME reoccupation of South Carolina came on the afternoon of May 13, 1865, when the church's fifty-four-year-old bishop, Daniel Alexander Payne, sailed into Charleston Harbor almost thirty years to the day after his coerced departure. Payne felt the weight of the moment as he entered the broad seaway aboard the *Arago*, the same ship that had carried Lynch and Hall away from Manhattan two years earlier. First Folly Island came into view, then Morris Island and James Island and Sullivan's Island, and finally Forts Wagner and Sumter and Moultrie, each now flying the standard of the United States of America. "The first sight of my native State was followed by indescribable feelings," Payne recalled, "that of my native city by pleasurable and sad emotions rapidly interchanging."

Payne and his young companions would never forget their first glimpses of the destruction in Charleston that Saturday evening. The bishop noted the scorched and crumbled walls of the Circular Congregational and Cumberland Methodist Churches, and the pockmarked façades of the city's finest mansions. One fellow minister, Rev. Theophilus G. Steward, wrote that "houses on every hand had been perforated by huge shot and shell from [the Union] fleet; great fires had swept through the city leaving a vast army of sullen-looking, solitary chimneys; business was generally suspended." Rev. James H. A. Johnson found the city in a forlorn state. "Pastures were forming in the foundations of demolished houses," he remembered. "There was no necessity for cows to betake themselves to the meadows." Richard Harvey Cain, who arrived a few days before Payne, saw continued evidence of God's judgment and indignation. "Here has been offered more bloody sacrifices to the Moloch of slavery than in any other spot on this continent," he wrote. "And here are the marks of a most terrible retribution."

Bishop Payne saw in the devastation "a prophecy of the future, that New England ideas, sentiments, and principles will eventually rule the entire South." Having already secured financial support from the American Missionary Association, he hoped to move quickly in establishing an institutional structure for the services and class and organizational meetings already occurring in homes and other gathering spots, like James D. Price's saddle shop. He opened his second day in Charleston with an early prayer meeting at Circular, then preached to a packed house at Zion, and finished with an evening sermon at Old Bethel. Cain did his part by dispensing the Lord's Supper, the first time many Black congregants had received the sacrament of communion from a minister of their race.

At 10:00 a.m. the next morning, Monday, May 15, Payne returned to Zion and opened the eight-day session that organized the South Carolina Conference of the African Methodist Episcopal Church, encompassing the Carolinas, Georgia, and Florida. The bishop was joined that week by seven other AME ministers from the North who would be tasked with cultivating the Southern field. They included Lynch, who would soon rotate to Philadelphia and become editor of *The Christian Recorder*, and Richard Harvey Cain, the dynamic leader assigned to succeed him in Charleston. On the first day, Payne also admitted nine local African Methodist preachers on trial, giving denominational sanction to the work they had already been performing and setting them on the path to full ministerial privileges. Committees were established, including one on temperance, as were a missionary society, a historic and literary society, and a preachers' aid society. District lines were drawn, ministers were assigned to circuits, and $214.48 was collected for the conference's initial operations.

"Thus equipped, the South Carolina Conference, like an armed ship launched, was sent forth to conquer the lands of the South," Payne later recalled. "Here was a field broad, long and rich in its soil."

The conference pioneers came with a deep appreciation for the dawn of a new era. Their rhetoric pealed with the joy of deliverance and, as it ended up, with the naïve conviction that equity would flow naturally from emancipation. "God's Providence had leveled the barriers, and rolled away tyranny's mountain," Cain told his fellow ministers. "The pathway was cleared, lit up by the sunlight of liberty, and the presence of God." The people, he said, were prepared to fulfill the prophecy from Psalm 68: "Ethiopia shall soon stretch out her hands to God." In something of a celebrity keynote, which packed the church, Martin Delany, who was a physician and journalist as well as a soldier, reinforced the hopeful tone by lecturing on "The Unity of the Races."

The conference proceedings drew considerable interest from Charleston's Black Methodist laity, particularly the "old mothers" as Cain described them. Bent like willows from age and hard labor, they made their way to their pews each morning and "listened with rapturous delight" to the most mundane of deliberations. At any reference to God's delivering mercies they "would lift up their voices in fervent thanksgiving." When each day's session ended, they begged to kiss the hands of the missionaries.

If much of the conference's work was dry and administrative (as it still is today), those attending that first session in Charleston could not help but be inspired by the church's return to the place of its banishment. Cain wrote movingly at the time about the legacy of the Vesey revolt and of Morris Brown's exile, when "our Church was demolished and blotted out of existence." Ever since, he wrote, "our people have had to wear the accursed yoke of religious bondage; paying for all the church property belonging to the Methodists, and supporting the bloody-handed ministers, who have administered unholy doctrines." He analogized Bishop Payne's return to the reunion of Joseph with his brothers.

On the conference's fourth day, Payne and Cain chose to directly address the challenge posed by Rev. Lewis and the Northern Methodists. That meant publicly clarifying that neither the denomination's name nor its doctrine was meant to be exclusionary. The conference approved a resolution, sponsored by Cain, stating that "we hail all men as our brothers, whatever be their complexions, and we have ever maintained that ours is a Church without distinction of color." Payne added that he looked forward to the day when prejudice might disappear and Black and white Methodists could worship at a common altar under common multiracial authority. But until that day arrived, he said, racial separation in American churches would be the rule. Cain argued that any freedman who consented to sit in a segregated gallery, as was still the practice in Rev. Lewis's churches, "ignored half his own manhood."

Lewis confronted a political thicket as he struggled to maintain some hold on Charleston's Black Methodists. He did not want to appear too hostile to AME interests, and so sent formal greetings to the AME conference and allowed

AME services to be held in Methodist churches. But when he saw the size of the crowd that Payne attracted to Trinity for the conference's ordination service, Lewis decided he had made a self-defeating mistake. After the benediction, he summoned Black worshippers to the church basement and "harangued them with a tirade of abuse against the African M.E. Church," according to Cain, urging them to reject it on the grounds of its racial exclusivity. He threatened, not unlike Richard Allen's white Methodist antagonists, that those who left Methodism for African Methodism would forsake any legal claim they had to church property.

The strongarm tactics backfired. By the end of May, Black members of Charleston's three Southern Methodist congregations—Cumberland, Bethel, and Trinity—had held a pair of meetings at Zion and resolved to depart for a new AME Church. Their ties to the Methodist Episcopal Church, they agreed, had come about only "by force of circumstances" and amounted to "religious bondage, with no rights but to obey orders." Now that the white Methodists had been stripped of their power in the South, Charleston's Black Methodists could choose for themselves. Many opted for self-governance. For the time being, Sunday services would be held at Zion, which was made available by the trustees of the Presbyterian church, first at 4:00 p.m. and again at 7:30 p.m.

The denomination's growth in South Carolina, as across much of the former Confederacy, would be nothing short of spectacular, "truly one of the marvels of the age," in Theophilus Steward's estimation. A year after the founding of the four-state South Carolina Conference, it claimed 22,338 members and had ministers riding seventeen circuits, two of them in Charleston. A year later, membership had grown by 126 percent, to 50,441 adherents across 101 circuits in five states. Forty percent came from Charleston and environs, which by 1867 had more than 20,000 members and probationers in nineteen congregations. Although there were 450 AME preachers and exhorters in the South, denominational leaders believed they needed 100 more to supply the demand. They soon split Florida and Georgia into their own conferences to better manage the expansion.

Thanks to the voracious appetite for African Methodism in the South, AME membership nationwide increased eightfold in less than two decades, from roughly 50,000 members and probationers in 1864 to more than 400,000 in 1881. As it did, the church's power base shifted markedly southward. Barely a decade after the war's end, three-fourths of AME membership and half of the church's financial support came from the eleven original states of the former Confederacy, a region where the church barely existed before 1863. South Carolina led the way, supplying 1 of every 4 members and 1 of every 8 dollars. After a second decade, Southerners accounted for nearly two-thirds of church receipts. "Everywhere the cry is, send us the Gospel through the heralds of the A.M.E. Church," the South Carolina Conference's Committee on Missions and Education proclaimed in 1867. The source of the flood was no mystery. A year after the war's end, Southern Methodist churches had lost nearly two-thirds of their Black membership. The number of Black Southern Methodists in South Carolina dropped from 42,853 in 1861 to 15,718 in 1866. Charleston's Methodist churches, which counted 4,034 Black members in 1861, reported none in 1866.

As they transitioned to African Methodist governance, Charleston's Black Methodists did not formally relinquish their property claims to the denomination's churches. But Richard Cain, now the lead pastor in Charleston, was in no mood to wait out a court fight with the deep-pocketed Northern Methodists. He also felt he had enough momentum to raise the money needed to build a standalone church, with Black ownership that could never be challenged. Cain's timetable accelerated in July, when the new pastor at Zion Presbyterian withdrew permission for the African Methodists to hold services there. Cain now had thousands of eager supplicants with no place to worship. The solution seemed clear. In a letter to the *Recorder* dated July 22, he announced that he and his congregation "are now seeking a piece of ground on which to erect a church for the A.M.E. Connection."

X.

Resurrection: A New Church Rises

The glory of this latter house shall be greater than of the former, saith the Lord of hosts: and in this place will I give peace.

—HAGGAI 2:9 (KJV)

As the Civil War drew to its close in the spring of 1865, the highest-ranking South Carolinian in the Confederate government was fifty-eight-year-old George Alfred Trenholm, the secretary of the treasury. Trenholm had succeeded his friend and fellow Charlestonian, Christopher G. Memminger, in Jefferson Davis's cabinet the previous July (although his image had not replaced Memminger's on the $5 CSA banknote). Before the war, the dashing, self-made Trenholm had been one of the wealthiest men in the South, a cotton broker, merchant, and financier with interests in shipping, hotels, wharves, real estate, plantations, and enslaved laborers, of which he owned nearly one thousand. Admired for his financial acumen and genteel manners, he had been made a director of both the Bank of Charleston and the South Carolina Railroad. He also had served several terms in the legislature. Once war broke out, Trenholm's firm—Fraser, Trenholm & Co.—financed the construction of Confederate gunboats, and its Liverpool office acted as European financial agent for the secessionist government. His company's vessels proved to be among the most adept at running the Union blockade of Southern ports, hauling cotton, tobacco, and turpentine to England and returning with guns, ammunition, and gunpowder (as well as textiles and Bibles, which were no longer obtainable from Northern publishers). Although never proven, literary sleuths have speculated that Trenholm may have been Margaret Mitchell's inspiration for Rhett Butler, the swashbuckling blockade-runner in *Gone with the Wind*.

When the Confederate government evacuated Richmond in early April

1865, an ailing Trenholm fled to South Carolina, where he was arrested and imprisoned, first in Charleston and then in a damp cell at Fort Pulaski, near Savannah. It was while there, with time to dwell on his collapsing finances and his firm's looming bankruptcy, that Trenholm chose to generate cash by selling a piece of land on Calhoun Street. It is not clear whether he communicated his desires to his wife, Anna, when she visited Fort Pulaski, or by letter to Theodore D. Wagner, an executive at the firm who served as his power of attorney. But on September 6, 1865, Wagner closed a deal to sell the parcel for $2,000 to Charleston's still unnamed African Methodist Episcopal congregation.

Five original church trustees—Abraham Adams, John Adams, Robert Cattle, James Grant, and James D. Price—paid Trenholm $300 at closing and borrowed the remaining $1,700 from him through a mortgage (which was satisfied, with interest, six years later). They had been free persons of color before the war, and the deed reflexively described them in that anachronistic manner even though all persons of color were now free persons of color. Four of the five signed their own names on the mortgage, suggesting some level of literacy, while only one left an X as his mark. Trenholm, who was soon paroled and later pardoned by a sympathetic President Andrew Johnson, had purchased the land two years earlier for $6,600, likely in Confederate dollars, from the estate of a free person of color named Charles Legare. Few moments in that topsy-turvy year of 1865 could have been as emblematic as the desperate sale of property by the imprisoned treasurer of the former Confederacy to the unshackled leaders of Charleston's new African Methodist Episcopal congregation.

The lot ran 50 feet along the north side of Calhoun between Meeting and Elizabeth Streets and 114 feet deep, barely a tenth of an acre. Fifteen years earlier, the site would have abutted the city's northern boundary, at the gateway to the rough-and-rowdy district known as Charleston Neck. But the City of Charleston had annexed the area in 1850 and renamed "Boundary Street" after the state's pro-slavery favorite son, Calhoun, who had died earlier that year and been buried eight blocks south. The deed specified that the buyers represented "a certain Congregation or association of coloured persons recently formed" who planned "to erect on the said premises a religious house of worship." The building was to be of yellow pine, and at 95 feet long and 45 feet wide it would consume almost the entire property. The arched ceiling, braced with heavy oak timbers, would stand 18 feet high, and galleries would overhang three sides, bringing seating capacity to an impressive 2,500. The pulpit was to occupy a recess in the rear of the building. The aisles would be wide, and rows of tall windows, upstairs and down, would provide light and ventilation against Charleston's tropical heat.

It seemed fitting that the man selected by Pastor Richard H. Cain as "architect" of the new church was Robert Vesey, the son of the martyred insurrectionist whose alleged designs had prompted the destruction of the old church. Shortly before the building's completion, a local journalist stopped by and apparently spoke with Vesey. "In a conversation with a portly and venerable looking freedman, we learned that he was a native carpenter, the contractor of the building, and had himself 'architected' it, as he expressed it," the reporter wrote. It would have asked too much of the white correspondent to offer undiluted praise for Black proficiency, so the self-appointed critic led with sarcasm and qualifiers. "It is not quite equal to the Cathedral at Cologne, or the Minster at Strasburg," he sniffed, "but, nevertheless, is highly creditable to the native artist."

Rev. Cain presided over an afternoon cornerstone-laying ceremony on September 25, 1865, that, by his estimate, attracted more than three thousand people. A platform had been erected on the site, decorated by the women of the congregation with evergreens and flowers. After an opening prayer and choral hymn, Cain took his sermon from the Book of Kings. "Consecrating this house which thou art building," he told the throng, "if thou wilt walk in my statutes and execute my judgments, and keep all my commandments to walk in them, then will I perform my word with thee." A large collection was taken up, and the cornerstone placed atop a widemouthed jar that served as a time capsule. It contained a history of the AME denomination, the names of the bishops and members of the inaugural South Carolina Conference, a Bible, a hymnal, and a copy of *The Doctrines and Discipline*, the AME rule book. Children tossed in silver coins and slips of paper bearing their names (only the coins would survive). "Never has there been such a sight in Charleston," Cain reported to *The Christian Recorder*. "Houses, fences, porches, wagons, and every means of getting a good view was resorted to by the people." Construction progressed steadily, with members providing much of the labor. Church women traipsed to a lumber mill on the Ashley River, where they hitched up their dresses, waded into the water, and dragged out boards to be hauled back to the site. The men of the church, many trained as carpenters and bricklayers, hammered and sawed with purpose. "Every man who is working on it is a colored man," Cain boasted.

The pastor estimated the cost of construction at $10,000 and set an optimistic timetable, believing he might dedicate the church by mid-November. Both projections missed the mark. When the church actually was dedicated in May 1866, the published price tag had risen to "nearly $15,000," and work continued well into the summer. A later report, from 1881, placed the final cost at $22,000. Cain proved a capable and incessant fundraiser. About $1,500 was collected in the first three months and nearly $6,000 in the first nine months, mostly from congregants, many of whom were earning wages for the first time. Eventually, the trustees opened an account at the Freedman's Bank in order to pay off the church's debts.

Until the Calhoun Street site could be occupied, Sunday worship services and class meetings were held most anywhere available—at Bonum's Hall on John Street, under a shade tree in a nearby yard, even in a forest clearing outside of town. A pair of Sunday schools attracted nearly 350 students. Cain pleaded to churches in the North to send boxes of hymnals and Bible worksheets. In October, he won approval from Charleston's Southern Methodists to use one of that denomination's buildings—Trinity Methodist Church on Hasell Street—as a temporary home.

The Southern Methodist denomination was in disarray immediately after the war, with churches abandoned by pastors in flight. Any "Christian kindness" it showed likely was influenced by its ongoing antagonism with the Northern Methodists. Better, the Southern Methodists felt, that Black Methodists worship as a separate denomination, and not elbow-to-elbow with white congregants. "These persons prefer to be separate in their religious organization, worship and ministerial appointments," wrote E. J. Meynardie, one of the remaining Southern Methodist ministers in Charleston. "We say, be it so."

Although still under construction, Cain's new building in Charleston was used for Sunday services as early as mid-February 1866, with "rough seats and a rough pulpit having been extemporized for the occasion." The vibrance and dynamism of the congregation showed itself from the start. In early April, the women of the church held a "grand fair" aimed at raising money to finish and furnish the building. Led by Cain's wife, Laura, the organizing committee sold tickets for 15 cents a day, or $1 for the entire ten-day run of the event. The ladies promised that "no pains will be spared to make this one of the most pleasant and agreeable entertainments ever given in this city." In one fundraising spectacle, costumed congregants staged a series of tableaux that reenacted the discovery of Moses amid the bulrushes, the sale of Joseph into captivity, and the pilgrimage of the Magi to Bethlehem. The event, which cost $18 to mount, cleared $118 for the building fund. Cain and other church leaders also began raising $7,500 to repurpose a former plantation a few miles outside of Charleston into a home for paupers, orphans, and the aged. In May 1866, the church sponsored a two-week camp meeting about fifteen miles outside of town, and in June a Sunday-school picnic on a nearby farm. The picnic began with a procession that seemed to stratify the congregation by mode of transport, with light-skinned elites arriving in handsome carriages, the middle classes following in horse-drawn carts, and those less fortunate trailing on foot.

Missionaries' dispatches from Charleston conveyed both the urgency of the freedmen's needs and an unassailable optimism that a brighter day had arrived. Black worshippers "who were cramped in their privileges in bygone days, are now in a state of religious prosperity and progress," exulted Rev. E. J. Adams, a Black Presbyterian from the North, in a letter to *The Christian Recorder*. The speed with which the AME congregation took traditional shape was striking, as if making up for lost time. Clubs and committees and auxiliaries formed, many headed by women exerting leadership outside of their households for the first time. The church organized street parades of Sunday-school students, hosted concerts of touring songstresses, and welcomed the New Year with Emancipation Day celebrations. Weddings and funerals were held. In July 1866, the celebrated Black poet and antislavery orator Frances Ellen Watkins Harper delivered a series of lectures at Cain's invitation. Such addresses—on topics like "State Education" (Francis J. Grimke) and "Commercial Advantages and Wealth of Africa" (Martin Delany)—became common during the church's early years. Throngs packed the building for weeklong revivals that grew so feverish that worshippers passed out of consciousness. "It is a regular thing for two, three and sometimes more females to be carried home through the streets in a state of real or apparent insensibility," *The News and Courier* reported. "The invariable response to the inquiries of the curious, is that the subject has been 'converted.' To all appearances, the converts are dead, as they are rigid and perfectly passive in the arms of their friends."

As finishing touches were applied, the building became an expression of racial pride by Charleston's freed men and women. Its pine frame rose as a manifestation of the unbridled hope that briefly accompanied the start of Reconstruction, before the promise of forty acres and a mule became a betrayal. God had delivered His people, as prophesied, and the erection of His temple would proclaim not only His glory but the arrival of Black autonomy. The *South Carolina Leader*, a new Unionist and Republican newspaper, glorified the structure as "evidence of the indomitable energy of the religious class of our citizens." The editors suggested that "any of the friends of slavery who think the colored people cannot take care of themselves ... are free to pay a visit to the A.M.E. church, in this city, upon any evening when their concerts are being held, and listen to the children sing and declaim."

Bishop Payne returned to his native South in mid-May, first to lead the second session of the South Carolina Annual Conference, which met this time in Savannah, and then to dedicate the new church in Charleston. He did so at the 10:30 a.m. service on May 27, 1866, the first of three held in the yet-to-be-completed building that day. The pulpit had been adorned with roses and ferns. One devoted churchwoman, Charlotte S. Riley, gathered some of the unused blossoms as a souvenir and pressed them between the pages of her Bible, where they remained for twenty years. Serving as the guest preacher, Bishop Payne opened the claret-covered Bible on the lectern and delivered a forward-looking sermon from Philippians 1 about the components of power in a successful church: "Intelligent love, correctness of judgment, and persistent holiness." In recognition of what could only be interpreted as their divine rescue and resurrection, the congregants agreed to call the church Emanuel, from the Hebrew name meaning "God with us."

THE RAPID GROWTH OF Charleston's African Methodist Episcopal congregation served as a harbinger of the grand transformation to come in American churchgoing. It would, by the end of Reconstruction, see most practicing Black Christians self-segregate into churches under their own control and governance, establishing the Black church as the central institutional force in African American life.

As at Black churches across the South, Emanuel quickly became both a physical and spiritual incubator for the development of Black leadership, the fostering of Black economic cooperation, the realization of Black community, and the expression of Black joy. In these churches, Daniel Payne said, the formerly enslaved "found an Asylum from the blasphemous and degrading spirit of caste." Scores of new members joined Emanuel every Sunday, abandoning virtually every denomination—Presbyterians, Lutherans, Episcopalians, Catholics, Congregationalists, Baptists. By the spring of 1866, the Charleston church had two thousand communicants and Cain had planted sister congregations in Georgetown and Columbia and organized extensively on Lowcountry plantations. He would soon spend $8,000 to purchase a Lutheran church on Morris Street that would become Charleston's second AME congregation, named for Morris Brown. Even after shedding hundreds of members to Morris Brown AME, "Emanuel Church," as its name was often shorthanded, remained the denominational colossus, "a monument of power" in the description of one church elder. A decade after its founding, the mother church claimed 2,764 members and 372 probationers. They were served not only by the pastor but a staff of fourteen local preachers and seven exhorters. Twenty-five teachers and two superintendents managed a Sunday school that attracted six hundred students. Although the church held three services each Sunday, hundreds were sometimes turned away for lack of seating. With more than twice as many members as Morris Brown AME, its nearest rival, Emanuel accounted for 1 of every 14 congregants among the 268 AME churches in South Carolina, and for nearly one-fifth of the dollars they raised.

Although a Yankee interloper, the indefatigable and endlessly entrepreneurial Cain would become one of Charleston's most conspicuous figures in the decades following the Civil War. His varied involvements—the church, civil rights, publishing, politics, and real estate speculation, each practiced at a high level—made him a man of constant fascination to the city's scribes. Well before ascending to the episcopacy of the AME Church as its fourteenth bishop, he grew famous enough in Charleston to be caricatured in the newspapers as "Daddy Cain." He had been born free in slaveholding Virginia—in Greenbrier County in the future West Virginia—on April 12, 1825. As a child, he moved with his Cherokee mother and Black father to Ohio, a non-slave state where he gained a rudimentary education and attended Sunday school. He converted to Methodism as a teenager and joined the ministry in slaveholding Missouri in 1844 after working as a steamboat hand along the Ohio River. He lasted but a few years before growing frustrated with the Methodist Episcopal Church's segregationist practices, leaving the state for Cincinnati, and transferring into the AME fold. His first assignment was a pulpit in Muscatine, Iowa.

With precisely shaved muttonchops that all but enveloped his face, Cain was not a man to be overlooked. In the late 1850s, his intellect and organizing skills came to the attention of Daniel Payne, who deemed him to be "a young man of great uncultivated talents, but rude and unpolished." Payne became a mentor, arranging for Cain to further his education at Wilberforce University and then moving him east with assignments to a pair of churches in Brooklyn. Although he resided in free states, Cain learned once the Civil War started that discrimination did not respect borders. Stirred to join the Union cause after the shelling of Fort Sumter, he helped muster a volunteer company of 115 Black Wilberforce students who offered themselves for service to the governor of Ohio. The governor, William Dennison, sent the young men away with the confounding rebuke that "this was a white man's war and that the negro had nothing to do with it." (President Lincoln did not officially authorize the use of Black regiments in Union combat forces until issuing the Emancipation Proclamation on January 1, 1863.)

In both the Midwest and in New York, Cain threw himself into the country's Colored Conventions movement, advocating for universal manhood suffrage, land redistribution, and other civil-rights causes. He also took a leadership role in the African Civilization Society, which encouraged the settlement of African Americans to West Africa. As the Civil War progressed, he used New York's churches to raise money and supplies for newly emancipated Southerners. When the hyperkinetic Cain absented himself from Brooklyn for two weeks to help open a freedmen's school in Washington, D.C., some in his congregation found it a relief from his incessant solicitations. "This city will have rest at least two brief weeks," one wrote, "and the community will have time to catch their breath, and stop fair and concert going for a time, and will replenish their pockets again." By the time the thirty-eight-year-old Cain joined Payne at New York's harbor to bid farewell to the initial AME envoys to Carolina, he had tired of dealing with the "small-souled contentionist[s]" in New York's churches and had determined to join the groundbreakers down South. He planned to make it his life's cause to improve the lot of the freedmen. "I felt like a 'lion bound,'" Cain wrote of watching the pioneers, James Lynch and James Hall, sail away. "If it was only my happy lot to be in that noble band, to share their hardships and partake of their joys. Oh! how consoling it would have been to my panting soul." His opportunity would come two years later.

Cain felt he could employ fifty preachers in the Lowcountry if he had the men, and recruited aggressively in the pages of *The Christian Recorder* in February 1866. He acknowledged that there would be minimal financial support and considerable physical hardship. He reported suffering "a few days of prostration from excessive labor" himself, and several early AME missionaries did in fact succumb to fevers or smallpox. Cain also advised that patience would be required to overcome "the ignorance of these liberated masses." But he promised recruits that it would be noble and gratifying work. Their mission would be nothing short of the redemption, reclamation, and renewal of a people. Plus, AME missionaries would find Black Southerners unfailingly generous with the little they had. "We need those who can teach school as well as preach the gospel, those who can point out the duties of social life, and of family responsibilities," Cain pleaded. "The people in the country want to be taught how to live like freemen, and how to guide their children."

Dozens of preachers answered the call from the North and the South, and Payne ordained forty-six elders and deacons at the 1866 South Carolina Annual Conference. With education requirements temporarily relaxed, the number of new ministers more than doubled the next year to ninety-eight. Many of the initiates, like Rev. Augustus T. Carr, who would become Emanuel's third postwar pastor in 1871, and Rev. Richard H. Vanderhorst, who would later become a bishop in a Southern Methodist offshoot known as the Colored Methodist Episcopal Church, had at one point been enslaved. As a teenager, Vanderhorst had been a servant to two white sisters and his responsibilities included carrying their hymnbooks and Bibles to their Southern Methodist church. Carr had managed to buy his freedom and that of his family and establish a successful livery stable before the war.

Rarely one to shun hyperbole, Cain proclaimed "a mighty revolution in this city—an earthquake in churches." Rarely one to shy from confrontation, he goaded his Northern Methodist rivals by flaunting AME successes. The advance of African Methodism, Cain wrote, demonstrated that the freedmen could discern "between true manhood and a spirit of cringing servility to the old spirit of caste." It had given the lie to predictions of calamity by "the shortsighted, the bigots, the self-constituted seers of the color-phobia stamp," by which he transparently meant Rev. T. Willard Lewis of the Methodist Episcopal Church, North, whom Cain detested and happily demonized. "*What object can the M.E. Church North have in opposing the establishing of a church, by black men among black men?*" Cain asked, appealing to racial pride. "What is it which prompts the agents of that *church* to seek to tear down the work of colored men among colored men, the very people whom they profess to come to benefit? . . . Cannot a colored man be just as good a Christian worshipping under a black bishop as under a white one, who has no interest in his race?"

Not all Black Methodists joined AME congregations, of course. Some remained with their former Methodist churches, including those under Lewis's control. But as the pioneering historian Carter G. Woodson pointed out, white congregants showed diminishing interest in sharing their Sundays with Black churchgoers once emancipation mooted the need to control and surveil them. As a result, the local ties to the AME movement, the accessibility and emotionalism of its theology, and the zeal of its missionaries left it with few serious rivals in South Carolina. Before the war, the potential audience for African Methodist evangelism had largely been circumscribed to the 225,000 free people of color in the North and Midwest. Now that universe had grown twentyfold, to include any of the country's 4.4 million African Americans, and the AME Church felt it had a virtual birthright to the 95 percent who resided in the former slave states. "We claim to be the proper administrators [of Methodism] to our wronged and oppressed race," the denomination's *Christian Recorder* declared as the war wound down.

With that charge, AME missionaries blitzed through Southern Methodist territory from Virginia to Texas with the ruthlessness of an invading army. A denomination accustomed to adding a thousand or so new members a year began growing by scores of thousands instead. In the Lowcountry, AME chapels sprouted up and down the coastal byways, where they remain today. On and along the sixty miles of U.S. Highway 17 from Charleston north to Georgetown can be counted sixteen AME churches—Olive Branch and Greater Goodwill in Mt. Pleasant; Greater Zion, Mt. Nebo, and Union in Awendaw; Bethel, St. James, and Tibwin in McClellanville; Singleton Chapel, Bethel, Saint Stephens, Dickerson, Greater St. Stephen, Mt. Olive, Mt. Zion, and St. Michael in Georgetown. Another twenty-two AME churches sit on or near the same highway in the sixty miles south of Charleston.

"Our success has been abundant," AME bishop John Mifflin Brown declared in 1872. "Fourteen *new Conferences* have been organized: more than *two hundred thousand souls* have been added to the church: quite *nine hundred* itinerant preachers have been added to our itinerant ranks; and our church property has been increased to the value of more than $8,000,000 and is still constantly increasing. Even our school property in the South has greatly increased, and parsonages are everywhere being built."

OTHER DENOMINATIONS COMPETED vigorously for Black worshippers, notably the Baptists but also the Presbyterians, Episcopalians, Congregationalists, and Catholics. Many built new churches that became central to Black life in Charleston, like Morris Street Baptist, or converted existing branches, like Zion Presbyterian and Calvary Episcopal, into standalone congregations. Those then quickly spawned others. The demise of slavery in Charleston did not, however, bring with it the evaporation of caste, which was inevitably linked to complexion and the pedigree it suggested. Within virtually every denomination, there was at least one church—Centenary Methodist, Plymouth Congregational, Mission Presbyterian, Central Baptist, Mt. Zion AME (a later offshoot of Emanuel)—that catered to lighter-toned Black congregants. That preference often applied to the pastorate as well. Perhaps the most notoriously elitist of Charleston's Black churches was St. Mark's Episcopal, founded largely by freeborn former members of the city's most class-conscious white congregations—"the flower of the city," as *The Christian Recorder* put it. Over the years, the congregation at the corner of Warren and Thomas Streets developed a reputation (likely neither fully accurate nor deserved) for being unwelcoming to those with skin browner than a paper bag or hair that did not give way to a fine-toothed comb.

That was decidedly not the milieu at Emanuel, a congregation described in 1866 as being "composed mostly of *Freedmen*," meaning those only recently emancipated. Pastor Cain remarked frequently on the challenges of ministering to those still traumatized by the aftershocks of bondage, writing in April 1866 that "they have yet to unlearn much that they have acquired under slavery." Another observer noted that because so many members had been enslaved for most of their lives "they deserve so much the more credit for not only building themselves this *church*, which is paid for as the work advances, but for purchasing another edifice in the upper part of the city," a reference to the future Morris Brown AME. Clearly, Emanuel welcomed believers of all classes and palettes. Those who had been free before the war had resources, connections, and status, and so naturally assumed early leadership roles as stewards and trustees. But those elites gradually "relapsed into secondary men," Cain observed, replaced by leaders who were newly "asserting their manhood."

The dedication and generosity of those laboring people overcame any skepticism that Emanuel could be built. "The reason that the Church is what it is today is because it is made up of the working people," Rev. William M. Thomas, an AME elder, said upon Emanuel's twenty-fifth anniversary, "men who sawed wood and laid bricks, and who followed other industrial pursuits; of women who washed clothes, and of people who were not ashamed of work, nor too stingy to give their money to the Church after they had made it."

Thomas pointed out that Emanuel "was the only Church they could sing and pray in, in accordance with their feelings." In the Episcopal Church, by contrast, "they could not say a word outside of the prescribed form."

As Thomas suggested, the caste distinctions between Charleston's nascent Black churches were not only visible in their makeup but also audible in their worship styles. The elite congregations hewed to the staid and orderly forms seen in the white churches that many Black Episcopalians, Presbyterians, and Congregationalists had deserted. African Methodist and Baptist churches, on the other hand, moved more in the spirit, accommodating the folk traditions that had flowed and mutated on currents from Africa to the Sea Islands and into Charleston. That God had heard their calls and responses, their fervent prayers and tear-stained spirituals, had been affirmed by the Union Army's victory in battle. How could there be any moderation in thanksgiving? The theatricality of Black Southern worship, and the mysticism inherent in ecstatic praise and rapturous conversion, made church services among the most anticipated and entertaining hours (usually plural) of the week. "Conversion from the Negroes' point of view," the historian Alrutheus Ambush Taylor wrote in the 1920s, "was a thunder-peal followed by a deluge of the spirit and a bursting forth of the sun clearing the sky and filling the world with gladness."

Ever covetous of white respectability, Bishop Payne continued to crusade against what he considered anti-intellectual forms of worship, with only occasional success. He found himself dismayed on site visits to Southern churches by practices he considered clownish and undignified, like ring shouts in which coatless congregants "sung, clapped their hands and stamped their feet in a most ridiculous and heathenish way." Payne considered the ring shouters to be "disgraceful to themselves, the race, and the Christian name." It disgusted him that they subordinated prayer to performance, often late into the night, when most vulnerable to Satan's temptations, and yet they deemed their celebrations to be "the essence of religion." On one visit to a "bush meeting" in the late 1870s, the bishop demanded that the group's pastor put a halt to the dancing. The pastor reluctantly followed orders, but he could not stop the singing or rhythmic swaying.

"*Ashes to ashes, dust to dust*," the group chanted. "*If God won't have us, the devil must. I was way over there where the coffin fell; I heard that sinner as he screamed in hell.*"

After fifteen minutes, Payne could bear no more and insisted that everyone sit. The ring finally broke apart, but rather than taking their seats its members "walked sullenly away." Payne confronted the leader of the group but made little headway. "Sinners won't get converted unless there is a ring," the layman lectured the bishop.

"You might sing till you fell down dead," Payne countered, "and you would fail to convert a single sinner, because nothing but the Spirit of God and the word of God can convert sinners."

The man held firm. "The Spirit of God works upon people in different ways," he explained, leaving Payne to wonder whether such "stupid and headstrong" people should not simply be ousted from the church before further disgracing it.

Predictably, early AME missionaries to the Lowcountry found that a degree of reeducation in the fundamentals of dogma and ritual would be necessary. Rev. James H. A. Johnson, who arrived in Hilton Head in 1865, recalled instructing adult congregants—"as you would teach a lesson to a little child"— that they were to take the bread of communion by hand rather than await its delivery to their gaping mouths, like nestlings. Marriages were arranged for longtime couples whose unblessed relationships offended the church. Funeral processions, in which mourners had ridden in carts while seated atop caskets, were injected with a measure of dignity and solemnity. Traditional hymns and choral and instrumental compositions gradually came to supersede the spontaneous eruption of spirituals. "The people had to be trained to sing as they sing in Charleston today," Johnson said, "for then they sang any kind of a composition that came into their minds."

The spiritual demands of a traumatized population were, of course, endless. Families had been ripped apart, parents and children were dead or gone, people had been tortured and raped, the vanquished city smoldered like Sodom and Gomorrah. Answers were needed to unanswerable questions. Yet here, too, in the liberation of millions after centuries of servitude, was evidence of all that Scripture had prophesied in the way of justice and deliverance. It was for the ministry to explain why God had taken so long, and allowed so much suffering. Henry Ward Beecher, the famed Congregational minister and abolitionist, gave it his best during his visit to Charleston in April 1865. "If a pine tree that is to stand for a century, grows so slowly that from day to day you can see no change," he posited while preaching to a mostly Black audience at Zion, "how much more slowly might we expect the kingdom of God to be, that embraces every circumstance that ever happens, and every race and condition of man, and is for eternity. It is this truth of God's design to establish His kingdom upon the earth, and of His overruling everything to that end, that is the foundation of our Faith and Hope."

The church set puritanical moral standards that, in time-honored fashion, its leaders did not always adhere to themselves. Alcohol was an evergreen concern, and AME temperance societies, comprised heavily of women, monitored the relentless advance of "this fearful monster." The habitual use of tobacco, snuff, and cigars was viewed as "a twin sister to drunkenness." Regional and national conferences regularly condemned "popular amusements" like dancing, billiards, checkers, cards, operas, circuses, theatrical performances, and lotteries, calling them a "growing evil among us." Church hardliners called for the excommunication of ministers or members who separated from spouses and then remarried while the first spouse was living.

Simplicity and piety were encouraged. "We wore calicoes and homespun dresses to church," Janie Mitchell, an Emanuel member who was eleven when the war ended, wrote in the memoir she jotted into a worn composition book. "Enjoy the Sermons and live decent and upright. It was lamp oil and kerosene times. It was days of Morality and Virtue."

To men like Bishop Payne and Rev. Cain, it was essential that African Methodism serve as a platform for demonstrating the capacity of a people for full citizenship, even in the wake of a crushing servility. A resolution approved at the 1867 South Carolina Annual Conference pronounced the church to be "an instrument in the hands of God to lift our race up from degradation." AME missionaries were often clear-eyed about the challenges. Cain admitted that he found some freedmen to be idlers, unaccustomed to working for themselves, and others morally bankrupt by the standards of his Northern church. His people were "*emancipated but not free,*" he said, still enslaved to outmoded notions of their personhood and worth. "We know how to serve others, but, have not learned how to serve ourselves. We have always been *directed by others* in all the affairs of life: they have furnished the thoughts while we have been passive instruments, acting as we were acted upon, mere *automatons.*"

Cain and his fellow African Methodist leaders believed the church's emphasis on self-help and self-improvement would erode that pathology. It would disabuse white Southerners of the fallacy that enslavement had been an appropriate disposition for a hopelessly inferior and depraved race. This, they felt, would be the first step in bringing emancipated Southerners into the

American mainstream and gaining the political clout needed to make meaningful improvements in their condition. They preached old-school Methodist virtues like industry, thrift, fidelity, and sobriety and cheered government efforts to establish schools and return Black farmers to work with labor contracts. They could not change their complexion, Cain remarked, but they could improve their intellectual competitiveness and moral character.

He was convinced this was a job best left to an educated Black clergy, not a white one, that the church would uplift its people by example. When Black congregants experienced a Black preacher in full command on a Sunday morning, it "gives an exalted opinion of the race to which they belong, and enables them to feel that they have a claim to equal manhood with others," Cain wrote. His own preaching style made generous use of podium-thumping gestures. "A table tapper," Janie Mitchell remembered. Cain argued that the meticulously ordered and deliberative Methodist way, with its classes and conferences and elections and resolutions, helped prove Black readiness for democratic institutions. "The discussions and preaching, enchaining the attention of multitudes who crowd to our churches, the readiness with which our ministers grasp hold of all the varied subjects relative to government and law, convinces all classes that the black man is destined to hold an important place in the affairs to [sic] the nation."

Emanuel's early lay membership ran the gamut. There were carpenters and cooks, tailors and saddlers, fishermen and butchers, painters and draymen. There was a cadre of amateur preachers who had honed their skills under the cover of hush harbors and class meetings, like James S. Grant, a blacksmith who became a deacon in 1866, and Abraham Adams, a porter and, like Grant, an original Emanuel trustee. Most, of course, performed church duties during time off and weekends. Joseph F. Russel, the superintendent of the Sabbath School, worked as a tailor and his wife, Lydia, a housekeeper. Shadrach Broughton, an early trustee, waited tables at the Pavilion Hotel. William D. Wilkerson, another trustee, worked as a packer and porter for W. L. Webb, the furniture and china retailer on Meeting Street. Elisabeth Nesbit, who helped stage the annual fundraising fair, kept a small shop in the city market. Her helpmates Catherine Provost and Charlotte Gadsden were dressmakers.

Emanuel brought together the formerly enslaved and former enslavers. Moses Vanderhorst, who hosted one of the first organizational meetings at his home on Morris Street, had been sold twice in twelve days back in 1849 and apparently gained his freedom only at war's end. George Garrett, an early class leader, had lost one of his brothers to a slave sale before the war and not seen him since. On the other hand, one trustee, a former free person of color named Robert Cattle, had himself owned six males and four females, ranging in age from four to sixty, as recently as a decade before the war. He made a living as a wagon driver and had profited from the hostilities by hauling rice for the Confederates. Like several of Emanuel's early trustees, he is characterized in public records as "mulatto."

Not surprisingly, a number of church leaders gravitated to postwar politics and became active in benevolent societies and trade guilds. There was a clamoring to belong and to express the communal power and fraternity that had been denied them in antebellum Charleston. Men and women who had been subordinated for life were suddenly in position to lead, and there were jobs to be filled. Henry C. Hammond, who became an Emanuel trustee in the early 1870s, also served as president of the Painters' Charitable Association. Founding Emanuel member Nathaniel Hill, a carpenter who eventually became an AME pastor, was elected treasurer of the newly formed Mechanics' Association. He would be succeeded by William Eden, a millwright whose wife, Maria, was among the church's most tireless volunteers. In 1875, one early trustee, Joseph Russel, won election as a city alderman while another, James Grant, lost his race in a different ward. Other than Pastor Cain, no church member was more consumed with Charleston's emerging Republican politics than James D. Price, another founding trustee. A saddler by trade, Price helped organize the 1865 statewide convention of Black South Carolinians that was called to set a postwar political agenda. He attended state and county Republican conventions as a delegate, served as an election commissioner, and sat on committees that planned celebrations for Emancipation Day and Independence Day.

Like most collections of pioneers, the congregation could be a tough and colorful crowd, starting with the clergy. One original member, Rev. John S. Everett, a local preacher who helped lead members to Emanuel from Charleston's Methodist churches, must have been versed in the chapter of Mosaic law that justifies the killing of a thief at night, while making it a capital crime in daylight (Exodus 22:2–3). For on March 22, 1875, between 1:00 a.m. and 2:00 a.m., Rev. Everett was awakened by a commotion in his henhouse and detected movement in the shadows. After calling out and receiving no answer, he grabbed his gun and fired toward the coop. The shot flushed one man into the street, where he was later nabbed by a policeman. The preacher found a second thief mortally wounded in the henhouse, bleeding from birdshot in his head, just behind the left ear. "Strange to say," *The News and Courier* reported, the surviving accomplice wound up being Rev. Everett's teenage son, Francis, who narrowly avoided death at his father's hand. A coroner's inquest the next day absolved the minister, finding the killing to be justifiable, as per both the Old Testament and the South Carolina criminal code. His son served fifteen days in jail.

As in most churches, family ties mattered. Among the leading women of Emanuel's early years were Eliza Ready, the wife of a seafarer; her sister, Maria Eden; and her sister-in-law, Catherine Fenwick. Many members, including each of the original five trustees listed on the property deed, lived within an easy walk of the Calhoun Street site. Despite its stature, Emanuel drew worshippers largely from the area surrounding its downtown neighborhood and from the extended families who populated it, a pattern that would endure until disrupted by gentrification a century later.

ONE SUCH NEIGHBORHOOD DENIZEN was Susan Hamlin, a formerly enslaved house servant who joined Emanuel five years after its founding and had been a member for sixty-seven years when interviewed in 1937 for the slave narrative archive compiled by the Federal Writers' Project. Her interviewers found her on the doorstep of a two-story clapboard house on Henrietta Street that no longer stands, directly behind the church. After freedom, she sampled several Black churches, often driven by convenience, first Old Bethel Methodist, then Zion Presbyterian, and finally Emanuel AME. "I is near my church and I don't miss service any Sunday, night or morning," she is transcribed as saying. "I kin walk wherever I please."

Hamlin's recollections are among the most riveting of the more than 2,300 narratives of formerly enslaved people that were collected by the Federal Writers' Project, a Depression-era initiative of Franklin Roosevelt's Works Progress Administration (WPA). Because illiteracy was so widespread among the formerly enslaved, her interviews provide a rare firsthand glimpse into the life of a rank-and-file parishioner. They are also unintentionally revealing because Hamlin was visited twice by the project's staff, first by one of the few African American interviewers enlisted for the work, and a month later by a white woman. Furthermore, the white interviewer never revealed to Hamlin her actual purpose. Instead, she allowed Hamlin to believe she worked for the welfare department, which had previously provided Hamlin with relief payments. Rarely has there been a cleaner field to observe the effects of interviewer bias.

The two conversations highlight how formerly enslaved people may have constructed fond recollections for the benefit of their mostly white interrogators. In her conversation with the white woman, Hamlin depicted her enslavers as benevolent and caring; to her Black interviewer, she volunteered grotesque detail of the brutal punishments and gratuitous cruelty she witnessed at their hands. Read side by side, they demonstrate that slavery's pathology gripped its survivors firmly enough, even after sixty years, to reflexively contaminate the expression of memory, or at least make it selective. Three years after the encounters, a WPA evaluator critiqued the white interviewer's methods as "a splendid example of the use of the wrong method of interviewing ex-slaves or anyone else."

Hamlin described herself to her visitors as being of "mix blood," with a white grandfather on one side and a "mulatto" grandmother on the other. "I got both blood, so how I going to quarrel wid either side?" she asked Jessie A. Butler, her white visitor. The woman explained that her maiden name had been Calder and that she had married a man named Hamlin, but she did not discuss him or any children. Her precise age was unknown, but both interviewers commented on her spryness. She told her Black interviewer, Augustus Ladson, that she was 101, but he observed that she had the gait of a forty-year-old. She told Butler that she was 104, but Butler believed it more likely that the "wonderfully well preserved" woman was in her late nineties. The 1870 census reported Hamlin's age as twenty-three and the 1930 census sixty years later recorded it—consistently—as eighty-four, which would place her in her early nineties at the time of the interviews. Whatever the actuality, she had lived through at least the last two decades of slavery, and, as she told Butler, "kin remember some things like it was yesterday."

Hamlin was born not in Charleston but on one of several plantations on nearby Edisto Island belonging to the family of Ephraim Mikell, a planter of indigo and rice. Her father, she told Ladson, had lived on a separate plantation, where he served as coachman for a slaveholder with a particular reputation for volatility. One Sunday, the man whipped her father relentlessly for some perceived misdeed. The next day, on a four-mile drive into the woods, her father made a high-risk decision to reciprocate. He tied the white man to a tree "an' give him de same 'mount of lickin' he wus given on Sunday," Hamlin said. Her father, she said, fled for his life to the waterfront, caught a boat carrying farm produce to Charleston, and somehow found work on a ship that set sail for the North, enabling his escape. Back on Edisto, a search party tracked him to the river with bloodhounds and concluded wrongly that he had drowned.

After Ephraim Mikell's death, Hamlin's family was passed down to one of his daughters, Mary, and eventually to the man she married, Edward N. Fuller, a Princeton-educated native of Charleston. In the late 1850s, with secession looming, Fuller moved his family and a number of his enslaved laborers into Charleston, where he had taken a job with a bank and bought a house on St. Philip Street. Hamlin's mother moved her three sons and three daughters into the slave quarters behind the house, where they were allotted two upstairs rooms and cooked in a communal kitchen. Hamlin was hired out to care for other people's children, earning $7 a month.

"I did not get the money," she told Butler, her white interviewer. "Mausa got it."

"Don't you think that was fair?" Butler asked in a typically leading exchange. "If you were fed and clothed by him, shouldn't he be paid for your work?"

"Course it been fair," Hamlin answered. "I belong to him and he got to get something to take care of me."

There was no such sycophancy in Hamlin's conversation with her Black visitor. In a freeform cascade of dark memories, she bore unflinching witness to slavery's depths. She recounted the disfiguring punishments and the wailing of parents whose children had been abducted for sale. She recalled how new mothers were forced back into the fields within hours of birth and the cruel separations of husbands and wives. "No minister nebber say in readin' de matrimony 'let no man put asunder' 'cause a couple would be married tonight an' tomorrow one would be taken away en be sold," Hamlin said.

As intended, the whippings left the most lasting impressions. "W'en any slave wus whipped all de other slaves wus made to watch," Hamlin said. "I see women hung frum de ceilin' of buildin's an' whipped with only supin tied 'round her lower part of de body, until w'an dey was taken down, dere wusn't breath in de body."

With both interviewers, Hamlin stressed that her faith had sustained her through slavery and would do so through the harsh economic times she now faced. Her conversion experience had unleashed her spiritually even as her body remained bound. It took place one Sunday at Old Bethel. She had walked to the altar and sunk to her knees as a preacher prayed over her. She had felt a dark weight on her back, sagging her shoulders like a pack. She interpreted it to be sin. "I look up and I see de glory," she recalled. "I see a big beautiful light, a great light, and in de middle is de Sabior, hanging so just like he died." She stretched out her arms to mimic the crucifixion. "Den I gone to praying good, and I can feel de sheckles loose up and moving and de pack fall off."

There were times she had strayed, she admitted, especially when she was young. But her years at Emanuel convinced her that it was the Christian's duty to live with purity and righteousness. "Pray an' praise," she said. "Beliebe on de delibrin Sabior. Trus' Him. He lead yuh. He show yuh de way." Every day, she got on her knees when she awakened, again before climbing into bed, and sometimes in between. God had been good to her, had not forsaken her, had kept her healthy and humble as she prepared for her final rest.

"I don't care if I drop in de street, I don't care if I drop in my room," she said. "I don't care where I drop, I ready tuh go."

XI.

Mother Church, and the Daddy of Reconstruction

Restore us, O Lord God of hosts!
Let your face shine, that we may be saved!
—PSALM 80:19 (ESV)

A year before the Civil War ended, with the Union's victory seemingly at hand, Richard Harvey Cain, then an AME pastor in Brooklyn, wrote to *The Christian Recorder* with irrepressible optimism. "A brighter day is dawning for our race," the reverend exulted. "The long prayer for the day of deliverance, from the bondage of centuries of slavery, the devout wishes of our fathers, that their children might be the partakers of a better dispensation, is now, fully at hand." He punctuated his sentences with a preacher's cadences. "We are to bear in mind the fact, that revolutions do not go backwards; and that the ultimate triumph of the Government will be the security of our own liberties, and those of our children."

Cain was not alone among AME preachers in his belief in the providential destiny of his people and the inexorability of progress, what he called "the mighty march of civilization." He would cling for some time to the illusion that revolutions did not regress, as he used his pulpit at Emanuel to springboard into state and national politics and became, himself, the personification of all that was possible during the headiest days of Reconstruction. Cain's ascendant political career—he served as a city alderman, a state senator, and a two-term U.S. congressman all within a decade—put Emanuel's founding pastor at the center of the first state and federal legislative efforts to protect the civil rights of nonwhite Americans. His was among the most robust voices in the state with the country's most energized Black politics. At 59 percent, South Carolina had the largest Black majority of any state at the close of the Civil

War. As a consequence, the Palmetto State placed 316 African Americans into office during Reconstruction, nearly a fourth of the total in the eleven original states of the former Confederacy. It elected six Black men to Congress, twice as many as its closest competitor. It was the only state where African Americans maintained a majority in the state house of representatives throughout the era.

Cain seemed to be present for every significant event during these formative years of Black politics in South Carolina, including the extension of Lincoln's and Grant's Republican Party into the state and the landmark constitutional convention of 1868. He also became an exemplar of Black economic independence. He chaired the advisory committee of the Charleston branch of the Freedman's Bank and helped found companies that laid railroad track and dug canals. He became one of the state's first Black newspaper publishers when he bought a Republican weekly, the *South Carolina Leader*, rebranded it as the *Missionary Record*, and converted it into an organ of the AME church.

Cain's every involvement reflected his confidence in the ultimate realization of the American promise. His articulateness, self-confidence, and aptitude helped put the lie to white depictions of these first-generation Black politicians as naïve, overmatched, coarse, and corrupt. But by the time Reconstruction ended after a dozen years, a counterrevolution had in fact taken hold, one that would maintain its reactionary grip on the South for nearly a century. Deflated by the betrayal, Cain retreated from politics and back into the protective womb of the church.

The story of Cain's fifteen years in South Carolina reveals that the intricate intertwining of the Black church and Black politics began in the South almost immediately after emancipation. As pastor, Cain regularly made Emanuel available for political assemblies, like a mass meeting in February 1867—"crowded to suffocation"—where a chastened Gov. James L. Orr announced his support for giving Black South Carolinians the vote (so long as they were male and literate, or owned $250 in property). His was a civil-rights church, and its pastor assumed the varied roles that civil-rights preachers of the 1950s and 1960s would, as an outspoken advocate and political fixer for his people as well as a spiritual intervenor.

When a Black teenager in Charleston named Jefferson Williams was jailed without a hearing for fighting with a white child, Cain dashed off an angry letter to Maj. Gen. Robert K. Scott, the state director of the Freedmen's Bureau.

He did not limit his protest to the case at hand but cited it as an example of the "gross injustice, and rongs [sic] constantly inflicted upon the helpless colored people of this city." Williams, who likely was one of Cain's parishioners at Emanuel, soon was released on his own recognizance.

When Emanuel developed plans to convert a former plantation into a home for orphans and the elderly poor, Cain aggressively sought a $1,000 federal grant from the Freedmen's Bureau to make the down payment. "Great destitution exists," he wrote, and "many old people and young orphans are flocking into Charleston for rations." Cain's pitch nearly succeeded, winning early support from Gen. Scott before a Washington bureaucrat explained that such funds could be used only to provide direct relief and not to buy property. Cain then redirected his efforts, requesting food, clothing, and cash assistance for residents of the farm.

In short order, the forty-year-old Cain transformed Emanuel into one of the most effective political machines in the city, one that served him well beyond his three-year tenure as pastor. Just as its predecessor, the African Church, became an emblem of resistance because of the 1822 insurrection plot, so would Emanuel be linked to the vibrant Black politics of Reconstruction-era Charleston. Two other ministers who would later serve as Emanuel's pastor—Rev. Bruce H. Williams (1887–1890) and Rev. William Wesley Beckett (1895)—first held seats in the state senate and house of representatives, respectively. Indeed, historian Thomas Holt calculated in *Black over White* that 32 of the 190 Black men who sat in South Carolina's legislature between 1868 and 1876 were ministers, a fourth of those being African Methodists. Across the South, at least 237 of 1,510 Black Reconstruction-era officeholders were ministers, with 53 being AME, according to research by Eric Foner, the preeminent chronicler of the period.

The opportunities and demand for men of such energy and ambition must have seemed boundless. They saw that the most urgent needs of their newly freed parishioners—labor protection, land ownership, and public schooling—would be addressed in the political realm, not the spiritual one. In state after state, Black preachers came to view political organizing as almost obligatory to their responsibilities as pastors and missionaries.

This remains a strong tradition in the Black church, of course. The twenty-first-century heirs to Cain's legacy include Rev. Raphael G. Warnock, who has represented Georgia in the U.S. Senate while serving as pastor of Ebenezer Baptist Church in Atlanta, Dr. King's former pulpit. In Charleston, Rev. Kylon

J. Middleton, the pastor of Mt. Zion AME Church, won election in 2020 to the county council, following the preacher-politician model of his martyred friend Clementa Pinckney. The list of African Methodist leaders who have played prominent roles in Black politics and activism since the Civil War is long. The first Black U.S. senator, Hiram R. Revels of Mississippi (1870–1871), began his career as an AME minister, and Rep. Floyd H. Flake served simultaneously as an AME pastor and a congressman from Queens (1987–1997). The AME rolls also include Rep. James E. Clyburn of South Carolina, the former House Democratic whip, and former Rep. Val Demings of Florida, who made Joe Biden's vice-presidential short list in 2020. Tom Bradley, the first Black mayor of Los Angeles, was AME. Frederick Douglass had important affiliations with both the AME and AME Zion denominations. The NAACP's Rosa Parks, who instigated the Montgomery bus boycott, and Daisy Bates, who oversaw the integration of Little Rock's Central High School, were members. Trade unionist and civil-rights warrior A. Philip Randolph grew up the son of an AME minister. Vernon E. Jordan, Jr., who led the National Urban League and became a consigliere to President Bill Clinton, was a longtime stalwart of the august Metropolitan AME Church in Washington, D.C.

ONCE THE CIVIL WAR ended and Andrew Johnson succeeded the slain Abraham Lincoln, the new Democratic president from Tennessee sought a rapid reintegration of the conquered states. Johnson quickly offered amnesty and restored property rights to secessionists willing to swear fidelity to the national government. In summer 1865, with South Carolina firmly under military control, the president appointed a provisional governor and instructed him to call a constitutional convention of men who would take such a loyalty oath. As in other Confederate states, the convention was tasked with nullifying the Ordinance of Secession, formally abolishing slavery, and setting a path for the restoration of civilian rule—all conditions for rejoining the union. The president did not, however, insist that Black men be given the vote, the reform most vital to ensuring their equal participation and protection and the one most threatening to white hegemony. That put Johnson, a former slaveholder with a documented history of racism, on a collision course with the more "radical" elements of the Republican majority in Congress.

As it happened, South Carolina's two-week constitutional convention in Columbia that September reunited any number of the state's former Confederate leaders, including a senator, a governor, several generals, and a dozen delegates to the secession convention. They all were white males, of course, as Black men would not gain the vote in South Carolina until the issue was forced by the Reconstruction Acts of 1867 and the ratification of the Fifteenth Amendment in 1870. While these white men had accepted military defeat, they did not accept that it meant a total restructuring of the two-tiered political, social, and economic system that their sons had died to defend.

The delegates fulfilled their obligations, providing for new elections for lawmakers and other constitutional officers without contemplating either Black suffrage or Black office-holding. The provisional governor, Benjamin Franklin Perry, conceded in an opening address that slavery was "gone, dead forever, never to be revived." But to extend the franchise to the freedmen "in their present ignorant and degraded condition," he said, "would be little less than folly and madness." Perry insisted that white supremacy remained the law of the land, thanks to the Supreme Court's *Dred Scott* decision, which still held that Black Americans were not citizens. "This is a white man's government, and intended for white men only," the governor decreed. The convention called for Perry to appoint a two-man commission to draft recommendations for codifying the discriminatory treatment of Black South Carolinians in nearly every sphere, particularly labor. They did so under the guise of providing protections for those no longer under the paternalistic rule of their enslavers. But in fact, the Black Codes, as they were accurately labeled, were designed to re-enslave newly emancipated men and women by limiting their employment options and re-creating the plantation structure.

As the intent of South Carolina's all-white government became apparent, Charleston's emerging Black leadership, in its first postwar exertion of power, demanded to be heard. No one voiced more indignation than the freeborn Richard Harvey Cain, who as a South Carolinian for barely four months apparently felt unrestrained by the state's traditions. Three days after the constitutional convention adjourned, *The Christian Recorder* published a letter from Cain, a Black man, that blistered the white governor of South Carolina by name. Cain accused Perry of "*animus*" and charged that the defeated Confederates had been restored to power by an "*unjust policy*" that would "hand us over to the tender mercies of our haters." The policy announced by Perry, he wrote, "ignores our manhood, and denies us a place in the body politic." There was "a law of eternal progression," Cain said, and millions of emancipated Black people would not be satisfied with "the husks of liberty."

Cain and other prominent Black Carolinians understood enough about politics to know that words were made potent by organization. Excluded from the formation of a new state government, they marshaled an assembly of their own, a statewide Colored People's Convention. In late November 1865, shortly before the all-white legislature convened, fifty-two delegates and honorary members met for six days at Zion Presbyterian Church, just across Calhoun Street from the muddy Emanuel construction site. They included Pastor Cain and Emanuel trustee Joseph F. Russel, while fellow trustee James D. Price served as one of two official doorkeepers.

Frustrated that freedom had not translated into power, the delegates concluded, in the words of one organizer, that "agitation is our best weapon." They asked the legislature to repeal all racially discriminatory laws, give Black men the vote, and allow them to serve on juries and testify against white people in court. "In our humble opinion," they offered, "a code of laws for the government of *all*, regardless of color, is all that is necessary for the advancement of the interests and prosperity of the state." The convention delegates reasserted other fundamental rights and privileges, like property ownership, quality education, and judicial due process. Skeptical that their pleas would receive a fair hearing at the statehouse in Columbia, they also asked the Congress in Washington to enforce their equal rights. The petition arrived in the capital accompanied by 3,740 signatures on sheets that unfurled for fifty-four feet.

South Carolina's Colored People's Convention posed no objection to the government's authority to place qualifications on suffrage or office-holding, and made no demand for affirmative action. "We ask for no special privileges or peculiar favors," the delegates said. "We ask only for *even-handed Justice*." The rhetoric and resolutions, which bore Cain's mark, drew from both the Bible and the Declaration of Independence. With so many pastors in attendance, there were expressions of Christian forgiveness for past sins, in the hope that white people might then view power-sharing as less threatening. "As the old institution of slavery has passed away," one resolution read, "we cherish in our hearts no hatred or malice toward those who have held our brethren as slaves." The delegates defended themselves against white perceptions of idleness and improvidence, pledging that Black Carolinians "shall be found ever struggling to elevate ourselves."

On the meeting's third night, Cain addressed the gathering about suffrage and workers' rights. "He has a military way of massing his arguments," the *South Carolina Leader* observed, "and hurling them like an avalanche against the weaker position of the lines of his opponent . . . He uses words to express his ideas, and not to adorn them, and never sacrifices sense to sound. The fruit predominates over the flowers."

To no one's surprise, South Carolina's reconstituted legislature disregarded the Colored People's Convention and made it the second state, after Mississippi, to enact a Black Code. The rest of the former Confederacy soon followed in a foreshadowing of the Jim Crow laws that would subordinate Black Southerners for the next hundred years. South Carolina's version defined people of color as those whose ancestry was more than one-eighth Black. It then enshrined their mistreatment by stipulating that persons of color could not work as artisans, mechanics, or shopkeepers unless they received judicial approval and paid a substantial fee. They could not own a distillery or tavern. Black farmworkers could not leave a plantation or entertain visitors without the owner's permission. The code continued to use terms like "master" and "servant" as if nothing had changed. It required servants to "obey and execute all lawful orders and commands of the family in whose service they are employed," including working from sunrise to sunset, and allowed them to be moderately "corrected," meaning they could be whipped.

The new laws prohibited people of color from migrating into the state without a $1,000 bond to assure their good behavior and self-support. They could own property, make contracts, sue and be sued, and receive standard legal protections, some for the first time. But they could not possess firearms or other weapons without approval, other than to hunt, and could not join a local militia. Interracial marriages were outlawed, as Black people were "not entitled to social or political equality with white persons." Black children who were not being taught "habits of industry and honesty" could be taken as wards of the state and apprenticed until the age of twenty-one, for males, and eighteen, for females. A separate court system was created to handle cases involving Black parties.

But rarely have state governments so misjudged the political mood in Washington. Although the states-rights Democrat in the White House took a largely conciliatory approach, the radicalized Republicans who controlled Congress and their allies in the Northern press exploded in rage at the Black Codes. Less than two weeks after the legislature adjourned, the federal military commander of South Carolina declared the codes invalid and decreed that state law would apply equally to all races. When Congress convened, the Republicans declined to seat Southern members. In April 1866, they overrode President Johnson's veto of a civil-rights bill that prohibited racial discrimination in the states. Next on the agenda was the Fourteenth Amendment, which clarified that all persons born in the United States were citizens and entitled to equal protection under law.

When the congressional elections of 1866 became a referendum on Reconstruction, voters gave the radical Republicans a veto-proof majority. Legislatures across the South, including South Carolina's, responded by refusing to ratify the Fourteenth Amendment. That prompted a determined Congress to revoke Johnson's generous terms for rejoining the union by passing the Reconstruction Acts. The rebel states were remanded to military control with requirements for a new state constitutional convention comprising delegates elected by universal male suffrage, white and Black. If South Carolina wanted to regain its political autonomy and its voice in Congress, its convention would have to ratify the Fourteenth Amendment and ensure the voting rights of African American men.

In electing constitutional convention delegates in November 1867, South Carolinians of color voted for the first time, and in large numbers. White citizens largely stayed home in protest and disgust. When the convention met in January 1868 in a brick mansion on Meeting Street, roughly three-fifths of the elected delegates were Black men. It would be among the country's first experiments in biracial legislative cooperation. At least a fourth of the Black delegates were ministers, a pattern evident in other Southern states as well. One was Richard H. Cain, the pastor of Emanuel African Methodist Episcopal Church and, by then, a luminary within his influential denomination.

Cain's reach was already expanding. He had bought the *South Carolina Leader* in June 1866 and become the newspaper's editor and lightning rod. His associate editors included Alonzo J. Ransier and Robert Brown Elliott, both of whom would later join him in the state legislature, in Congress, and in business ventures (Ransier would be elected South Carolina's first Black lieutenant governor). Cain had affiliated with the nascent Union Republican Party of South Carolina, and he and other AME leaders helped deliver thousands of church members to the Republicans as a bloc. He made Emanuel available for Republican gatherings. "The colored delegates evince a disposition to paddle their own canoe, without white assistance," Charleston's *Daily News* reported after one Republican meeting there, "and the few whites who have insinuated themselves into the association are evidently looked upon with distrust, as in many instances their antecedents are not free from the taint of secession."

Cain played a central role at the 1868 convention, which after fifty-three days guaranteed the vote to all adult men, regardless of race, education, or wealth, and set a minimum level of compulsory public schooling. He called for land redistribution to disentangle Black farmers from the penury of sharecropping and encourage self-sufficiency. Cain railed against a proposal to suspend the collection of debts, feeling it favored white plantation owners who had overextended themselves on purchases of enslaved labor. If allowed to miss payments, he argued, they might hold on to encumbered land that otherwise could be sold to freedmen. He also proposed that the state petition Congress for a loan of $1 million—one-eighth of the budget of the Freedmen's Bureau—to obtain land that could then be sold to the poor of both races. Cain disdained the notion of prolonged dependency on the government. But he believed that giving purchasers five years to pay for plots of ten to one hundred acres would provide housing to 125,000 displaced people. "A man may have rations today and not tomorrow, but when he gets land and a homestead, and is once fixed on that land, he never will want to go to the Commissary again," Cain told the convention.

Given the government's financial limitations after four years of war, some white delegates found the notion laughable and dismissed Cain as a demagogue. He brushed off the charge during three days of feisty debate and saw the measure pass by a vote of 101 to 5. Despite a prospecting trip by Cain to the U.S. Capitol, the loan request gained no traction in Washington. The delegates then called on the legislature to authorize a state land commission, financed by bonds, that would serve a similar purpose.

THAT BLACK MEN were meeting in council with all the parliamentary decorum and oratorical flamboyance of a white legislature, deciding the future contours of their beloved state, was more than many white Carolinians could take. The arch-conservative *Charleston Mercury*, edited by the fire-breathing Robert Barnwell Rhett, Jr., distinguished itself for its petulant tone and unabashed racism in referring to the "Negro Convention" as a gathering of "The Great Ringed-Streaked and Striped." Cain did not escape the paper's buffoonish caricature of Black delegates, which often began with a physical assessment. After all, his apparent intellect, eloquence, and verve undercut the central argument of white supremacy. The pastor from Charleston, the *Mercury* wrote, "although black, ugly, and shabby, or perhaps because of these exceptional qualities, enjoys considerable influence among the darkies." The writer credited Cain for being "a good tactician" and "very successful as a builder of churches" but "less brilliant" as a politician.

At another juncture, the *Mercury* characterized one of Cain's floor speeches as "a violent and blatherskite appeal to the passions and prejudices of the ignorant." The address had "raised a howl of delight within the menagerie which proved but too truly the revengeful and blood-thirsty instincts of some of the animals." *The Charleston Daily News*, in only slightly less inflammatory fashion, depicted Cain as "robust in person, confident in manner, with native shrewdness written in every line of his face, and a ready facility for keeping on the winning side." His oratorical gifts gained him a considerable following, the paper said: "Whenever he says anything of a peculiarly bitter character, he sugar-coats it with a benign smile, such as a Feejee Islander bestows on an uncooked Christian missionary whom he is about to eat." The *Daily News* also disclosed Cain's practice of riding a squat marsh tacky to the convention and leaving it tied to a pump outside, "as if his master was going to dinner." The white newspapers quickly made the image of "Daddy Cain" astride his "pony" a trademark of the pastor's political identity, like Lincoln's stovepipe hat. The *Mercury* chortled for weeks in June 1868 when the sheriff temporarily seized the horse, while Cain was out of town, to assure payment of a $35 debt.

Northern writers found it possible to be more generous. "The colored men in the convention possess by long odds the largest share of mental calibre," an observer from *The New-York Times* reported. "They are the best debaters; some of them are peculiarly apt in raising and sustaining points of order; there is a homely but strong grasp of common sense in what they say, and although the mistakes made are frequent and ludicrous, the South Carolinians are not slow to acknowledge that their destinies really appear to be safer in the hands of these unlettered Ethiopians than they would be if confided to the more unscrupulous care of the white men in the body."

The new state constitution produced by the convention included a preamble asserting that "all men are born free and equal," that "slavery shall never exist in this State," and that South Carolina "shall ever remain a member of the American Union." It effectively undermined the Black Codes by holding that "distinction on account of race or color, in any case whatever, shall be prohibited, and all classes of citizens shall enjoy equally all common, public, legal and political privileges." That had not long before seemed an unimaginable assertion in South Carolina, the epicenter of American slavery. Newly enfranchised Black men registered to vote by the thousands and created a solid Republican majority that ratified the document by a large margin. Congress granted its approval in May and President Johnson followed in July, formally readmitting South Carolina to the union.

Within two weeks of the constitutional convention's adjournment, Cain had been nominated at an all-night meeting of the local Republican committee to run for state senate from Charleston County. Given the party's strength in the district, the nomination all but ensured his election in the balloting a few weeks later, and Cain set off across the state to campaign for the ticket. "His advice was to vote early and late against the Democrats," the press reported after a rally in Columbia, "for he informed his hearers that if the *Dam*ocrats, as he termed them, should succeed in getting into power, the colored man would be put in the condition he occupied before the war." On the strength of the Black vote, the Republicans built overwhelming majorities in both houses of the legislature. In the senate, they won 25 of 31 seats, with 10 held by Black members, including Cain. One Black candidate—Francis L. Cardozo, a Presbyterian minister from Charleston—became the first African American to win statewide office, as secretary of state.

A month after his election to the state senate, Cain won a second political post by being appointed a Charleston city alderman by Maj. Gen. Edward Canby, the federal military commander of the state. Canby had removed 13 of the 18 sitting aldermen on the all-white board, apparently because of prior secessionist leanings, and appointed 7 Black men among their replacements, all of them freeborn. The rapid consolidation of influence by a single Black man—senator, alderman, pastor, publisher—discomfited white Charlestonians, especially once Cain's *Missionary Record* began warning of civil strife if conditions did not improve for the freedmen. "The Whirlwind Cometh—Beware!" the *Record* warned in a column that recalled the French Revolution. The editors of the *Daily News* found such "revolutionary howlings" to be evidence of "incendiarism, riot and wrong," and called for Canby to remove the overextended Cain, whom it described as "a good hater of the entire white race." By July, Canby had done so.

Cain left Emanuel's pulpit shortly after his election to the senate, having been appointed presiding elder over all of Charleston's churches (he would later serve as pastor of Morris Brown and of an AME church in Columbia). He still preached regularly at Emanuel, which would be known as "Cain's church" for years to come, and his militant spirit seemed to have never departed the building. His successor, Rev. William H. Brown, gained notice for reportedly praying, in a Fourth of July sermon, "that God would permit the colored people to continue their feet upon the necks of the whites, and 'lay 'em low in de dust.'"

In the state senate, as at the constitutional convention, Cain did not bow to tradition or to his white colleagues. Among his first proposals was that the senate determine whether white members who voted against the Fourteenth Amendment had violated their oaths. After considerable discussion, the measure was tabled. He also introduced a bill calling for the full repeal of the Black Codes. And yet, when the state's first civil-rights legislation came to the floor, Cain took a position so moderate that it placed him at odds with more radical Black lawmakers. In the 1868 session, Cain spoke persuasively for an amendment that watered down a more sweeping senate bill. The amended proposal prohibited discrimination in contracts and courtrooms and real estate dealings. But sensitive to white fears about "social equality," it limited its scope over public accommodations to railroads and other "common carriers" while omitting licensed businesses like hotels and taverns. With the chamber packed with onlookers, Cain argued that the bill redundantly replicated the federal civil rights law of 1866. But he also testified to the discrimination he had witnessed in the free North, which he said demonstrated that only time and education, not laws, could wring the hatred from men's hearts. Until then, Cain forecast, white Americans would find ways to circumvent statutes that forced them to share space with those they perceived as inferior.

"He said that prejudices could not be legislated away," the *Daily News* reported. "He had his prejudices, and they could not be legislated out of his bosom . . . It was said in Holy Writ that the Ethiopian changes not his skin, nor the leopard his spots. Could they then expect to make Massachusetts men out of South Carolinians in a day? These South Carolinians had their prejudices, the prejudices of two hundred years." With something of a wink, Cain reassured his listeners that Black people were not maneuvering for social equality with their white neighbors. He would never enter another man's parlor without an invitation, he said and, more to the point, nor would another man ever enter his. This, he suggested, was not the cause for which Black lawmakers should provoke a white backlash, warning them "not to risk what they already possessed in the too eager grasping after more." The senate passed the more limited version, but then failed to reach a compromise with the more radical Republicans who controlled the state house of representatives. Civil-rights legislation died for the year.

Whether Cain's stance was primarily principled or political isn't clear. He was acutely aware of his growing depiction in the white press as an "incendiary" and a meddlesome carpetbagger, the slur attached to profiteering interlopers from the North. And for better or worse, Cain had a pragmatic streak, refined perhaps by his decades in church politics, that made him respectful of white power, even at its nadir. He believed that racial progress would occur only once white Americans became comfortable with Black Americans, and that it was in the interest of Black Americans to make that happen. He may well have concluded that he and his constituents would be better served if he were perceived as less bellicose.

If so, his repositioning had the intended effect. Almost overnight, Cain became the darling of white publishers whose ink had barely dried on their prior screeds against him. The *Courier* called Cain's speech "as remarkable for its conservatism and ability, as it was unexpected from such a source." The *Daily News* offered the highest praise it could summon for a Black leader, saying Cain had "displayed an amount of ability, knowledge, foresight, moderation and sound sense, of which no white man need have felt ashamed." In Cain, the paper said, Black Southerners had a friend who would "lead them out of the wilderness of political excitement into the happy Canaan of honest and remunerative labor." Cain's nods toward mollification bled into the pages of his newspaper, and as the *Missionary Record*'s columns started to urge friendship among the races, white newspapers began to reprint them. This vastly expanded Cain's influence and renown since much of his Republican newspaper's natural audience could not yet read. Even the *Mercury* stopped flogging Cain's defenseless pony long enough to flatter him as "a sensible man" whose newspaper "gives sound advice to his people."

The state house of representatives again sent a muscular civil-rights bill to the senate during the 1870 session, and once more there were efforts by white Republicans to temper it. This time, perhaps feeling that disunity had harmed the bill's prospects, Cain joined its supporters in enacting a strikingly progressive law that reconfigured the underpinnings of caste. It imposed a ban on racial discrimination by any public or private entity that required a charter or license, to include railroads, ships, restaurants, hotels, and theaters. The penalties were no slap on the wrist—a $1,000 fine and five years at hard labor in the penitentiary. Managers were held criminally responsible for the misdeeds of underlings and companies could lose charters. When cases made it to court, the burden fell on defendants to demonstrate they had not mistreated the complainant on account of race.

During his single two-year term in the state senate, Cain showed himself to be garrulous, quick-witted, fearless, and confrontational, even in opposing his own party. "When he secures the floor, it is altogether a question of time when he will yield it to any one else," the *Daily News* observed in 1870, Cain's final year. The senator from Charleston was not above employing either Scripture or sarcasm as oratorical bulwarks. When fellow Republicans spoke disparagingly of his city's captains of commerce, the former purveyors of cotton, slaves, and secession, the senator would rise in mock indignation. "Don't abuse those men," he would harrumph, "those are my constituents." It always brought down the house, an affirmation of the surreality that only five years after the demise of slavery a Black man from the North was, in fact, representing the white society of Charleston in the state's highest forum.

Both on the floor of the state senate and in the *Missionary Record*, Cain railed against what he saw as corrupt leadership within South Carolina's factionalized Republican Party, particularly among white carpetbaggers whom he found insufficiently sympathetic to the freedpeople. He questioned why the state land commission had not helped more former slaves buy farms and why more schools had not been built despite increased appropriations. Whenever Cain was perceived to have tacked to the right, or back to the left, it inevitably prompted unsubstantiated smears that he must be on the take. But Cain's dissent seems just as explicable by unvarnished racial politics. Cain felt that Black Republicans, and particularly native Carolinians, should hold government positions—with their salaries and patronage—that had instead been appropriated by white Republicans from the North. In a dynamic not dissimilar to today's Democratic Party, Black voters formed the base of the Republican Party in South Carolina, while white politicians frequently held the highest offices. Because he did not trust white Republicans to represent Black interests, Cain favored proportionality.

"Colored men must place their eyes on every office now filled by men who have leaped into them by the means of fraud and corruption," he wrote. "Remember that none of them have benefitted your race one *sou markee*, and yet you have foisted them into office, and are now walking about the streets, penniless, homeless, and without a prospect of ever attaining anything." Cain was not above direct racial appeals. In publicly recruiting a congressional candidate to challenge a white Republican incumbent in 1870, he asserted that *"the negro proposes to send a true representative of his race, to represent his interests . . . These long, lank, sharp-nosed gents may prepare for defeat . . . The col*ored people have been *sold* often enough, and they have come to the conclusion that *these adventurers with white faces and black hearts shall not any longer belie them and fatten off their stupidity."*

Cain alienated party regulars sufficiently that they did not renominate him to his senate seat in the fall of 1870. Instead, he called his own rump convention and orchestrated his own nomination to retain his seat on an opposition ticket. This did not go over well. That night, a crowd of Republican Party loyalists, many of them Black, marched on Cain's house with an effigy labeled CAIN, THE TRAITOR and torched it. Cain finished a distant third in the three-man race even though the top vote-getter had died a day before the balloting. Two years later, Cain returned to the regular Republican fold in trying to win the party's nomination for lieutenant governor. Instead, he received the nod to run for an at-large seat in Congress and defeated his opponent, Lewis E. Johnson, with 72 percent of the vote, making him the first Black clergyman ever elected to the U.S. House of Representatives. Four of the five Republicans who swept the state's congressional races in the fall of 1872 were Black men: Cain, Robert B. Elliott, Alonzo J. Ransier, and Joseph H. Rainey. Such an occurrence is difficult to imagine in modern-day South Carolina, even though it is again controlled by Republicans.

THE PRACTICE OF POLITICS bore considerable risks for outspoken Black leaders during Reconstruction. As intolerance for Black authority grew rabid, white Southerners regularly expressed their resentment through political violence, often without accountability. Four Republican officials, two of them Black men, were assassinated in South Carolina's upstate during the fall campaign of 1868, when Cain ran for state senate. One of them, a Black senator from Orangeburg named Benjamin Franklin Randolph, had a résumé that virtually duplicated Cain's. A freeborn native of Kentucky, he too had been educated in Ohio and had arrived in Charleston as a Methodist missionary at war's end. He too had edited a newspaper there, had addressed the Colored People's Convention in 1865, and been a delegate to the constitutional convention in 1868. On October 16, 1868, while stumping for Republican candidates as chairman of the state party executive committee, Randolph stepped off a train onto a depot platform in Abbeville County and was shot to death in full view of onlookers. Each of three white assailants fired, striking him in the head, chest, and lower body before riding off on horseback.

It would later be learned that the killing was the work of a terrifying new organization of armed vigilantes that called itself the Ku Klux Klan. Founded in Tennessee with the aim of repressing the Black vote, the Klan had made inroads into the South Carolina upcountry and effectively become an armed wing of local Democratic organizations. Although a Klansman confessed to congressional investigators that he had shot Randolph and named his two accomplices, no one was ever convicted.

Naturally, Randolph's murder created a "profound sensation" in Columbia, Washington, and Charleston, where a crowd of one thousand protesters, most of them Black residents, gathered at White Point Garden on the Battery. Eight days after the killing, Cain wrote to the state's Republican governor, Robert K. Scott, the former Freedmen's Bureau director, to request state police protection for Black leaders in the closing days of the campaign. Scott, a Pennsylvania native, had already offered a $5,000 reward for Randolph's killers and threatened to remove law enforcement officials who did not pursue reports of political violence. But Cain stressed to the governor that the failure to make arrests had "emboldened" white assailants to target several Republicans before Election Day, including the two of them. "The lives of the *leading* men of our party are threatened," Cain wrote. He warned that if the killing continued, Black Charlestonians would not stand by. "I tremble for this city if any unwise step be taken by the [Democrats], to murder any prominent man in this community," Cain wrote. "The people have sworne [sic], to burn this city to ashes and have no mercy on the Democrats." Cain, while careful not to advocate violence, warned of it with some frequency, intending white people to understand that Black Americans no longer felt trapped by the self-protective passivity of slavery.

Cain's family felt shadowed by the prospect of violence when he ran for Congress in 1872. "You can imagine the bitter conflict his candidacy brought on," his adopted daughter, Anna Jane Edwards, recalled more than sixty years later. "A Negro running for public office against a white person in a Southern state that was strong for slavery does not seem the sensible thing for a man to do, but he did and was, of course, successful. From the moment he became [a] delegate to the Constitutional Convention a guard was necessary night and day to watch our home. He was compelled to have a bodyguard wherever he went. We, his family, lived in constant fear at all times. Many times mother pleaded with him to cease his activities, but her pleadings were of no avail."

Edwards, a formerly enslaved woman who was eighty-one when interviewed for the Federal Writers' Project, remembered that white Charlestonians seemed shell-shocked and demoralized immediately after the war, leaving an open field for Black ambitions. They "recovered" soon enough, she said, spurred by the contempt they felt for the elevation of Black men to public office. "As they did, determination to establish order and prosperity developed, and they resented the Negro taking part in public affairs," Edwards said. "On the other side of the cause was the excess and obstinate actions of some ignorant Negroes, acting under ill advice. Father was trying to prevent excesses being done by either side. He realized that the slaves were unfit, at that time, to take their place as dependable citizens, for the want of experience and wisdom, and that there would have to be mental development and wisdom learned by his race, and that such would only come by a gradual process."

The presence of armed guards did not always ward off danger. "Attempts were made to either burn the house or injure some member of the family," Edwards said. "A day or two before election a mob gathered suddenly in front of the house, and we all thought the end had come. Father sent us all upstairs, and said he would, if necessary, give himself up to the mob and let them satisfy their vengeance on him, to save the rest of us." The leader of the pack demanded that Cain come outside. As he did, the sheriff and several deputies appeared just in time to intervene. They appealed to reason more than law, convincing the lynch mob that if harm came to someone of Cain's prominence the Grant administration in Washington would surely reinstate martial law in South Carolina. "The men then dispersed," Edwards said, "after some discussion among themselves."

Cain served two terms in the House, first from 1873 to 1875, and then, after a two-year hiatus, from 1877 to 1879. Throughout his tenure, he maintained the focus on land reform and civil rights that marked his years in Columbia. He arrived in the Capitol as Congress was taking up the bill that would become the Civil Rights Act of 1875, the second major piece of anti-discrimination legislation of the Reconstruction era. The first measure, passed in 1866, had declared all natural-born Americans to be citizens and guaranteed them equal treatment. It had not, however, outlawed barriers in public conveyances and accommodations. As a transplant to the South, Cain considered the daily insult conveyed by separate quarters and second-class seating to be a "relic of barbarism and American slavery." At the 1872 AME General Conference in Nashville, he had authored a resolution supporting the bill and made it personal by disclosing that bishops traveling to the meeting had been forced into second-class rail cars after paying first-class fare.

Cain used the same tactic on the floor of the House, where he delivered a series of searing testimonies that made vivid the ongoing discriminatory treatment of Black Southerners. In January 1874, he told of his own encounter just the previous week, when he sought a meal in a North Carolina train depot while traveling to Washington. "I entered a place of public resort where hungry men are fed, but I did not dare—I could not without trouble—sit down to the table," Cain recounted. To avoid a confrontation, he and his fellow travelers ordered food to be delivered to their cars, and paid for the service, but then found that the railroad staff did not approve. "They said we were putting on airs," Cain said. As in the state senate, Cain sought to ease fears that Black Americans desired social equality. But he argued that if the Constitution guaranteed the same rights to all men, as it now did, it must also afford them the same privileges. That meant not just being able to ride a train, but to do so in the car of one's choosing. "We simply come and plead conscientiously before God that these are our rights," Cain said, "and we want them." To grease the law's passage, Cain and other Republicans sacrificed a clause that would have attacked discrimination in public education. As a result, it would be another eighty years before the Supreme Court required the desegregation of public schools (ruling then in a case with deep South Carolina roots).

Cain appreciated the craft of oratory, excelled at using retrograde opponents as political foils, and orchestrated even his impromptu speeches with a maestro's precision. In his final address on the civil-rights bill, in February 1875, he showcased rhythms and themes that would find their way into Barack Obama's attention-grabbing keynote address to the Democratic National Convention in 2004. Cain prayed for a time "when there shall be no white, no black, no East, no West, no North, no South, but one common brotherhood, and one united people, going forward forever in the progress of nations." One congressional correspondent, while ridiculing Cain's "peculiar appearance," pronounced herself impressed by his skill at facial expression and gesticulation. "He gave full play to his African birth-right of fervid eloquence, to a keen, ready wit and sarcasm, and added these to a display of dramatic power not often found out of the theatrical arena," Marie Le Baron wrote.

Cain's at-large seat was eliminated due to reapportionment, and in 1874 he failed to gain the party's nomination for a district seat in the state's northwest corner. He was not as widely known there as in the Lowcountry, and it did not help that he recently had been indicted on charges related to his real estate speculating.

That troublesome sideline began one day in 1867 when Cain was a passenger on a train that stopped about twenty miles northwest of Charleston to take on wood and water. He was accompanied by six other AME leaders, including Rev. Moses B. Salter and Rev. Lewis Ruffin Nichols, each of whom would later become pastor at Emanuel. During the stop, Cain and the others learned that land nearby was being offered for sale. At Cain's urging, the group formed a consortium and contracted to purchase an initial tract, with $1,000 due in six months. Within a few years, nearly two thousand acres had been accumulated and subdivided for sale to other Black stakeholders at modest prices. Between 1868 and 1876, Cain sold fifty-five parcels within the tight borders of the community, and another nineteen nearby. The state land commission that he helped create had foundered amid corruption. But Cain believed he could replicate its function with private capital, creating a model for Black property ownership. It would be one of the first self-contained communities of freed men and women in the South, anchored by a still-extant AME church. Cain and the others named it in honor of the martyred president who had proclaimed their emancipation: Lincolnville.

It would eventually come to light, however, that Cain started selling off the subdivided plots before paying for and taking title to the land. Ownership disputes, evictions, and decades of litigation ensued, along with foreclosures and the threat of a sheriff's sale. In January 1873, a newly elected prosecutor, Charles W. Buttz, had Cain indicted and arrested for "obtaining money under false pretences." Cain engaged a series of politically connected lawyers who delayed as long as possible before reaching a financial settlement.

As CAIN LEFT THE HOUSE, which shifted to Democratic control in 1875, the grand aspirations of Reconstruction had started to deflate under the pressure of white resistance, terroristic violence, and political repression. No event in South Carolina made the future course more apparent than the massacre of Black militiamen by a white mob in 1876 in the predominantly African American village of Hamburg, near the Georgia line. It began on the Fourth of July, the centennial of the nation's independence and a day of festivity for the freedpeople of the South. As the Black militia paraded on a city street, two white men rode up and insisted that the soldiers break ranks to allow their carriage to pass. Words were exchanged before the troops finally let them through, but the white men did not forget the challenge to their supremacy. Several days later, they pressed charges against the leader of the militia for "obstructing a public highway." On July 8, the day of the first court hearing, hundreds of members of white paramilitary "rifle clubs" inundated the small town. Guided by former Confederate Gen. Matthew C. Butler, the vigilantes demanded that the Black militiamen disarm and, when they refused, laid siege to their armory. Several of the militiamen were captured and six were executed, with some shot after scampering through a field like startled deer.

Although denounced by some white leaders, the massacre sparked outrage among Black people nationwide and further inflamed South Carolina's racial politics. Nine days after the attack, Cain and other Black leaders in Charleston staged an "indignation meeting," a forerunner of the mass meetings of the civil-rights era, to declare that they would not sit by passively. Cain was considered "the leading spirit" of the gathering, which attracted one thousand Black people to Market Hall, and five hundred white listeners to the surrounding sidewalks. "This thing must stop," Cain demanded, according to one newspaper account. "Every wrong done in this State injures its prosperity, injures its commerce, its agriculture and its business, and drives away those people who could best help to build up the common prosperity." Cain told the crowd that "the colored people expected to be law-abiding citizens of the State, but they wanted every man who violated the laws of this State to be brought to justice and to punishment." A statement coauthored by Cain warned that Black Americans would not subject themselves to such treatment forever. "Remember there are 80,000 black men in this State who can bear Winchester rifles, and know how to use them," it read, "and that there are 200,000 women who can light a torch and use the knife, and that there are 100,000 boys and girls who have not known the lash of a white master, who have tasted freedom once and forever . . . There is a point at which forbearance ceases to be a virtue."

The events in Hamburg gave way to the bloody and fraudulent campaign of 1876, when Democrat Wade Hampton and his red-shirted vote-suppressors put an end to Republican rule in South Carolina by seizing the governorship. As with the presidential election that year between Rutherford B. Hayes and Samuel Tilden, which hinged on disputed electoral votes from South Carolina and three other states, the results were close and contested. But they signaled in both Washington and Columbia that the policies of Reconstruction would soon be reversed. In the same election, Richard Cain, back in the news thanks to Hamburg, reclaimed a seat in Congress. He had won the Republican nomination in a far more natural district that included Charleston and Orangeburg, where 65 percent of the population was Black. Cain defeated his white Democratic opponent, Michael P. O'Connor, with 62 percent of the vote.

Cain's second term had to be despairing, a metaphor for the plunge into darkness that marked the waning hours of Reconstruction. Despite his victory margin, he spent much of the next two years defending his election against a legal challenge by O'Connor, who alleged widespread fraud. The House voted to seat Cain anyway, but the battle was all-consuming, a sign of aggressive maneuvering by Democrats to reclaim the South. From his perches in Charleston and Washington, Cain could see as few others the impact of the gradual withdrawal of federal support for full equality for Black Americans. The Freedmen's Bureau had ceased operations in 1872 and the Freedman's Savings Bank had failed two years later, leaving thousands of depositors with losses. The Klan and its impersonators had communicated to Black Carolinians that voting might be a choice not only between candidates but between life and death. Then in April 1877, President Hayes withdrew the last federal troops stationed around the statehouse in Columbia, upholding his end of the bargain with congressional Democrats that had guaranteed his election. It could not have been a surprise to Cain, who had met with Hayes at the White House the previous month, shortly after his inauguration. That day, Cain and six other prominent Black South Carolinians lobbied the president for forty minutes on behalf of the Republican candidate in the state's disputed gubernatorial election. But Hayes made clear "with perfect frankness" that he favored less federal intervention in the South, not more. On the day the last soldiers abandoned the State Capitol, so did the final Republican governor to serve South Carolina for almost a century.

Over the next dozen years, the white Democrats who controlled state government constructed an almost impermeable wall between Black voters and the ballot box. The bricks of disenfranchisement included onerous registration requirements, local discretion over voter eligibility, broadened disqualifications for criminal convictions, gerrymandering to dilute the Black vote, distancing of polling places, and the infamous eight-box law, a literacy test that left voters to determine the properly labeled receptacle for each of eight ballots. Eventually, local Democratic organizations simply denied Black citizens the right to participate in their "tantamount-to-election" conventions and primaries, and the state constitution was revised to include a poll tax, a literacy test, and a requirement that registrants demonstrate understanding of the state constitution. The tactics proved ruthlessly effective. The Republican vote in the state—most of it supplied by Black men—withered from a peak of 91,870 in 1876 to 9,313 in 1896. In 1872, there had been 96 Black members of the South Carolina General Assembly, all Republicans. By 1882, only 15 remained, 3 of them Democrats.

In 1890, the state elected as governor an agrarian populist demagogue, Benjamin Tillman, who characterized his ascension as a "triumph of Democracy and white supremacy over mongrelism and anarchy, of civilization over barbarism." Tillman held that voting was "beyond the capacity of the vast majority of colored men" and reassured the crowd in his inaugural address that South Carolina had been redeemed. "The whites have absolute control of the State Government," he asserted, "and we intend by any and all hazards to retain it." At Tillman's urging, a new state constitution, approved in 1895, mandated the racial segregation of public schools and prohibited (and voided) marriages between white South Carolinians and anyone with at least one Black great-grandparent. The federal Civil Rights Act that Cain helped pass was overturned by the Supreme Court in 1883, and South Carolina and other Southern states began enacting Jim Crow laws that forced the physical separation of Black and white people in every imaginable domain—restaurants, taverns, theaters, hotels, streetcars, railways, steamboats, ferries, textile mills, the jury box. In 1896, the Supreme Court ruled in *Plessy v. Ferguson* that such ostensibly "separate-but-equal" accommodations were constitutional.

Cain's faith in radical Republicanism had started to erode several years into its reign. "Reconstruction, so far as the colored man is concerned, is a failure," he observed in 1870. The withdrawal of federal troops helped him understand that Black advancement would now rely solely on institutions controlled by African Americans, like the AME Church, and not on those controlled by white people, like Congress and the presidency. "The present administration has torn away the props that have supported us ever since the war," Cain told an AME gathering in 1878. "Now we have got to build up a superstructure from the ground. The negro has got to educate the negro ... We have depended too much on other people."

Cain's disillusion was apparent in the legislative agenda of his second term in Congress. Melding his primary policy objectives, he proposed a bill to dedicate the proceeds of public land sales to education spending. He did what he could to portray the bill as beneficial to all, but it never emerged from committee. A second bill he introduced—to establish steamship routes for mail and passengers between the United States and Liberia—further reflected Cain's disenchantment. He had felt the tug of the back-to-Africa impulse before. But along with thousands of other Black Carolinians, his interest revived with the erosion of Reconstruction. Cain reasoned that if Black Southerners could not control their destinies, and must risk their lives to exert political autonomy, perhaps Africa beckoned with its promises of self-government and arable farmland. Only three years earlier, in debating the civil-rights bill, he had famously declared that Black Americans were "not going one foot or one inch from this land." Now, despondent about their prospects at home, he hoped to make it easier for them to sail some five thousand miles away. "There are thousands who are willing and ready to leave," Cain wrote to the American Colonization Society's William Coppinger in 1877. "The Colored people of the South are tired of the constant struggle for life and liberty."

Under the circumstances, Cain felt some ambivalence about running for reelection in 1878. When a Republican district convention in Charleston selected another candidate by acclamation without so much as hearing from the incumbent, he considered the snub a "gross insult" but otherwise took his forced retirement rather philosophically. "I hope that your future will be as bright as has been your past," Cain told the Republican delegates, perhaps tongue in cheek. The Republicans' replacement nominee then lost the general election to Cain's nemesis, Michael P. O'Connor, shifting the state's congressional majority from Republican to Democratic.

Cain's political obligations at times interfered with his church work. In 1879, the board of the denomination's missionary society unceremoniously removed him as its corresponding secretary, charging that his responsibilities in Washington prevented him from fulfilling his duties, for which he was salaried. He previously had been removed as pastor of Metropolitan AME Church in Washington for the same reason. Some in the AME hierarchy, notably Bishop Daniel Payne, felt that Cain had "damaged his usefulness as an ambassador of the Cross" by lowering himself into the grimy worlds of politics and land speculation. Payne, a persistent critic of mixing church and elective politics, wrote that "the only apology which can be made" for Cain and other AME preacher-politicians "is that for intelligence and organizing power their equals could not be found in the laity, hence politics laid hold of them and by a kind of conscription forced them into the army of politicians." Payne clearly believed that his former protégé had been compromised. "While full of energy, tact, and pluck, Richard Harvey Cain was greatly lacking in moral conscience," Bishop Payne wrote toward the end of his life. "He seemed to be perfectly oblivious of the moral significance of a promise—so much so that in financial dealings with his acquaintances and friends he was a miserable failure."

Payne likely was thinking of Cain when, quoting from Titus, he told delegates to the AME General Conference of 1880 that the bishops they were about to elect "must be blameless." But the old lion's denominational influence was shrinking, and the clout of Cain's Southern base was expanding. On the fourth ballot, the conference elected Cain as the last of three new bishops. He was appointed to oversee the Ninth Episcopal District, which included Texas and Louisiana, and made his name there by helping to found Paul Quinn College in Waco. He also served as its president. Cain finished his career as the presiding bishop of the First Episcopal District, which included much of New England and the Atlantic seaboard. When he died in Washington, D.C., on January 18, 1887, the remembrances of his life traced the arc of his achievements as well as their undoing, as if eulogizing the Reconstruction era itself. "He was a zealous man even to over-enthusiasm," Wesley J. Gaines, a fellow AME bishop, wrote in 1890, by which time Reconstruction had fully deflated. "His dreams of the coming greatness of the race caused him to be perhaps too visionary, and, basing too much upon what he conceived to be our present greatness, to plan more largely for the immediate future than we could hope to accomplish, but it was to build up the race."

In South Carolina, however, "R.H. Cain was supreme," remembered AME minister Theophilus G. Steward. Upon his death at age sixty-one after the fullest of lives, the congregation at Emanuel AME in Charleston, the mother church that Daddy Cain built, draped the pulpit and altar rail and galleries in black mourning cloth, darkening the sanctuary in his memory for sixty days.

XII.

The Long and Stormy Night

And the rain descended, and the floods came, and the winds blew, and beat upon that house; and it fell not: for it was founded upon a rock.

—MATTHEW 7:25 (KJV)

If anything, the forced removal of Black Southerners from American politics only made the Black church more vital following the deconstruction of Reconstruction. As other institutions withered under the assault of Jim Crow and his nightriding enforcers, the church still towered over African American life like a Gothic cathedral. Before the departure of some four hundred congregants in 1882 to seed yet another AME church in Charleston—Mt. Zion on Glebe Street—Mother Emanuel was said to have an astonishing four thousand members and another eight hundred probationers, making it the largest body of African Methodists anywhere and the largest of any faith in Charleston. "This one church," exulted Benjamin T. Tanner, the editor of *The A.M.E. Church Review*, "has more members than the New England and New York Conferences combined!"

The numerical strength of Mother Emanuel and her various offspring gave African Methodism a predominance in Charleston that was almost unparalleled in any American city, particularly by a niche denomination that appealed mostly to one race. By 1916, 1 of every 5 churchgoers in Charleston, Black or white, belonged to an AME congregation. Only Chicago, with thirty-seven times the population, had more AME adherents. There were more African Methodists in Charleston than there were Baptists. There were almost as many African Methodists as Episcopalians, Lutherans, and Presbyterians combined. Indeed, although slightly outnumbered by Roman Catholics, the African

Methodist Episcopal Church had become the largest of the city's Protestant denominations. One of every fifty African Methodists in the country lived in Charleston County. One of every six lived in South Carolina. The church's surging popularity there and in Georgia and north Florida continued to drive its phenomenal national expansion. In the quarter century between 1890 and 1916, when the number of AME congregations grew by 167 percent, its planting of new churches outpaced almost every other American faith group. Membership grew by 21 percent, to nearly 550,000 in a country of just more than 100 million people, only 10 million of them African American.

Before the gentrification of downtown Charleston in the second half of the twentieth century, most of Emanuel's members lived on the peninsula, many within a Sunday-morning walk of the church. When new members joined, they were assigned to a class, as in the old days, and filled out an index card listing their favorite Scripture verse and hymn. For Verdelle Green, in class forty-three, it was the 24th Psalm and "Pass Me Not, O Gentle Savior." Marguerite Michel in class twenty-three had trouble narrowing it down, even to two. She listed the 23rd and 139th Psalms and Matthew 5:23–24, along with "I Am Thine, O Lord," "I Will Trust in the Lord," and "Abide with Me." In spite of the denomination's unapologetically chauvinistic leadership, most of the growth was among women, the nurturers and sustainers of the Black church. Records from the early 1900s show that nearly two-thirds of AME members were female.

Emanuel's pastors reported regularly on the mother church's vibrancy and reach, as did visiting dignitaries. In 1873, Rev. Augustus T. Carr wrote that worship services and Sunday school were heavily attended and that an anniversary jubilee had been a triumph. The congregation had retired a debt of $2,500 and purchased a new burial ground. He had baptized 37 adults and 73 children in the past six months alone. Two years later, 75 sinners were won over at an AME camp meeting in nearby Mt. Holly that attracted more than thirteen thousand people, the largest such assemblage since the war. In 1884, the New Year's Eve Watch Night service packed the house long before its 9:00 p.m. start, and police officers had to keep order among the throng left in the cold. It was not just Emanuel's numbers but also the carriage of its people that impressed outsiders. In 1882, Rev. James M. Townsend, a prominent AME leader, observed after a visit that the pastor, Rev. Norman Bascom Sterrett, had been "generous and kind hearted almost to a fault," while the lay leaders were "efficient, gentlemanly and loyal, and the people good and true." Emanuel, he declared, was "one of the largest and I think by far one of the most aristocratic congregations in the entire connection."

Satellite branches soon opened around town, one on Archdale Street and another on Chalmers that was named for Bishop Cain. In 1875, the congregation spent $3,000 for a house on Mary Street to use as a parsonage. That purchase was followed by the addition of several tracts abutting the church property for possible future expansion. By the early 1880s, the congregation had carpeted the pulpit and altar and outfitted the loft with a regal pipe organ to accompany its "choir of sixteen well-trained voices." A vestry room and vestibule had been added, and the building given a fresh coat of paint. A flourishing Sunday school employed thirty teachers in the instruction of more than eight hundred students.

When Emanuel's pastors wanted to make something happen, they had an army at their disposal, and they often characterized their missions in military terms. Once Rev. Sterrett determined in 1882 that Emanuel had grown too large, and that a new AME church was needed, he organized a "Regiment of Willing Workers" to wage a fundraising blitzkrieg. It was divided into forty companies, each with a captain. Many were "female soldiers" who had been "mustered into the service." Rev. Sterrett, himself a Union Army veteran, remarked upon their ferocity in assailing the purses of their victims. "Squads of a dozen able bodied men are put to flight by the appearance of one of these female soldiers," he wrote with jaunty pride. "Grog shops, pedestrians, and young men in the parlor with their lady loves, are alike charged upon, and compelled to retreat in good order, to open fire in return with greenbacks and silver. Many have declared that Egypt never had a plague more infesting than the Willing Workers."

It had fallen to Sterrett to mediate a dispute within Emanuel's congregation about how to solve its crowding problem, which was wearing down the physical plant. Some favored buying land and erecting a colossal new church. Others insisted on staying on Calhoun Street, which they now considered sacred ground. Sterrett suggested they do both—make badly needed repairs to the existing building while also splitting the congregation. He quietly arranged to purchase two lots at the southeast corner of Rutledge Avenue and Montagu Street for $2,100, took a mortgage, made a $700 down payment, and appointed a five-man committee to design a new sanctuary. Once the purchase became public, however, "the aristocratic residents of that vicinity" protested the siting of a Black church in their backyards. As he considered his options, Sterrett received a mysterious visit at the parsonage one night from a messenger. The envoy invited Rev. Sterrett to meet surreptitiously with his principal—"Mr. M."—at his mansion after dark the following evening, instructing him to park his carriage a block away and to rap lightly at the door. The bizarre invitation made the preacher so nervous that he armed himself before setting out.

When Sterrett arrived, "Mr. M" extracted the pastor's "sacred promise" to never reveal his identity, a pledge that Sterrett strove to keep. He left enough clues, however, that when combined with church and real estate records it can be concluded that "Mr. M" was David McPherson, a forty-four-year-old merchant of Scottish heritage, who lived at 24 Rutledge. McPherson inquired about Sterrett's plans to build a few blocks away and then asked if he wouldn't prefer to buy an existing church, namely the forty-year-old classical edifice of Zion Presbyterian. Two Presbyterian congregations, Zion on Glebe Street and Central on Meeting, had decided to merge and sell off one of their two buildings. As the president of Central's board, McPherson figured the best way to ensure the survival of his own church was to arrange a strong bid for the other one. He had inside information. Target prices had been placed on each building. The one that came closest when offered at a same-day auction would be sold, while the other would be removed from the market to house the consolidated congregations.

McPherson informed Sterrett that a bid of $15,000 for the Glebe Street church, with $6,000 paid up front, would win the day. Sensing McPherson's desperation, the preacher countered that he would first need to sell the property he had just bought, and at a profit. McPherson agreed to pay back the $700 down payment and add a bonus of $500, which Sterrett suspected would be raised from neighbors eager to rid themselves of the Black church.

McPherson recommended that Sterrett enlist a white agent to buy the property on his behalf, as Zion Presbyterian's members might balk at selling to a Black congregation. Sterrett took that suggestion to heart. But he could not bring himself to heed McPherson's other request, that he not even inspect the church he was about to buy, in order to avert suspicion. The next Sunday, the light-skinned preacher slipped into the 5:00 p.m. service, taking a seat near the door, and spent the next hour eyeballing every inch of the interior. An after-church conversation with the pastor convinced him that the prearranged price was a bargain. To maintain secrecy, Sterrett ignored AME protocol that required approval of real estate transactions by church trustees. He ordered his white agent to place the winning bid and deceived his trustees into unknowingly granting their approval after the fact, as if pre-dating a check. The next Sunday, Sterrett informed Emanuel's worshippers that they were the first Black congregation in Charleston to own a masonry building, an emblem of immense prestige.

As it was, Sterrett was a bit of a status-conscious dandy, "the most fashionable minister that I have met anywhere South," observed AME Bishop Alexander W. Wayman. He was impeccably groomed, with a distinguished receding hairline and a Teddy Roosevelt mustache. He drove a smart little four-seat buggy about town, drawn by a horse named "Dandy Jim." Before ascending Emanuel's pulpit, he took care to remove his street boots and don a pair of fine black gaiters that he kept with his toiletries in a drawing room to the side. It perhaps came as little surprise, then, that many of the Emanuel members who followed Sterrett to what became Mt. Zion AME Church saw themselves in his image. As a group, they were reputed to be more high-minded and proper than those who stayed. A lawyer for Mt. Zion explained at the time that those who left Emanuel did so specifically "to avoid the noisy and emotional methods of manifesting religious fervour common there." Many of Sterrett's flock also were, like him, of lighter complexion, and Mt. Zion would be known for much of its life as a Black church that attracted fair-skinned members and preferred fair-skinned pastors.

"It was a tonal split, within a race," said Rev. Kylon J. Middleton, who was appointed to Mt. Zion's pastorship in 2015, despite his dark complexion. "I'm the thirty-third pastor and up until the twenty-ninth in the late '70s, they were all fair-skinned. They will remind me that in the older church I would never have been here."

The unchecked expansion of African Methodism in the Lowcountry generated its own adversities, internally and externally. For starts, white Charlestonians had yet to fully accept the exuberance of independent Black churches, the clamor of which now wafted through open windows and into their neighborhoods. In the summer of 1883, a local magistrate ordered the arrests of the pastor, trustees, and sexton of a satellite AME chapel in the center of town and charged them with being public nuisances. Neighbors complained at a hearing that if the boisterous services did not stop, they would be forced to sell their homes at a loss. "The residents in the immediate vicinity find sleep at night impossible," *The News and Courier* reported. "The wild screeching of the women repeatedly alarms and arouses the neighbors, who in their fright imagine murder is being committed." The charges apparently came to nothing after the presiding elder pledged to address the problem. Three years later, one of Charleston's leading Anglican clergymen, Rev. A. Toomer Porter, wrote in a newspaper column that such displays undercut the elevation of African Americans in white eyes. "Do stop these repeated so-called religious scenes, singing and loud praying, and stentorian preaching," Porter demanded of Black ministers. "God is not deaf, and I don't suppose all the congregations are, and need not be 'hollered' at so."

The more serious challenge came from within the denomination, a result of the postwar shift in its power base from the mid-Atlantic to the Deep South. It produced a schism in several Charleston churches that threatened to divide African Methodism into Northern and Southern branches, just as the white Methodist and Baptist churches had before the war. Those splits had been over slavery. This one was over power and control. Specifically, a second generation of Southern-born AME church leaders, better educated than their predecessors, chafed that their congregations were supplying the Philadelphia-based denomination with the lion's share of its money and manpower. Rightly or wrongly, they perceived that those dollars did not bring Southern churches proportional resources or influence in return. They paid the bishops' salaries and supported an expanding infrastructure, but those same bishops then appointed Northern loyalists to the most desirable Southern pulpits, ensuring the continued flow of dollars up the seaboard. The interloping pastors sometimes ruled like autocrats in a strange land, exacerbating regional resentments.

In April 1884, a vicious internecine skirmish erupted at Morris Brown AME, the church that Richard Cain had formed from Emanuel's rib in 1867. A new pastor, Rev. Samuel Washington, had just arrived and nominated a slate of trustees to help run the church at his direction. Washington was a West Indian who had immigrated to Philadelphia—not a Southerner, in other words—and rebellious congregants refused to accept his candidates or turn over church assets. One night in early May, as Washington led a revival, a mob of three hundred people took control of the church, escorted him out, and changed the locks. He had the new locks removed the next day, but the mob returned and threatened to slit his throat. He then summoned the police, and charges were pressed against nineteen of his own parishioners, many of them women. Two days later, the mutineers regrouped and retook the building. They stationed guards in the sanctuary and installed Rev. Joseph E. Hayne as their pastor, relegating Washington to the parsonage. To the considerable embarrassment of denominational officials, the dispute wound up in the courts and in the newspapers, where the parties waged a singularly unchristian battle. When Hayne was quoted as saying during a worship service that his denominational superior, Presiding Elder P. W. Jefferson, had "trailed the sacred robes of his office in the dirt of dishonor," Jefferson responded by referring to the rebels as "bilgewater and scum." After reconsidering for two days, Jefferson clarified in print that he had not meant to refer to all of the rebels as bilgewater and scum, "but only to certain individuals among them."

In late June, AME leaders dispatched Bishop Henry McNeal Turner to Charleston to settle the dispute. Eager to snuff out any secessionist sentiment before it spread, they instructed him to take an unyielding stance with the trespassers. He didn't. Instead, Turner crafted a shrewd compromise, announcing at a crowded meeting at Morris Brown that he was restoring Rev. Washington to his pastoral post, but only for twenty-four hours, after which he would be transferred to a church in Kentucky. Turner's remedy reasserted the authority of the bishops but granted the congregation a pastor of its choosing. Clearly, he hoped to stanch the public relations bleeding before it got worse. "We have become the ridicule of the white race, who use our dissension as an argument to prove that the negro is incapable of self-government," he told the gathering. The Morris Brown church remained within the AME fold, as it does today. A number of disaffected members left and transferred their memberships back to Mother Emanuel.

WHEN BISHOP WAYMAN graced Emanuel on the Sunday morning of September 25, 1881, he chose as his text the verses from the seventh chapter of Matthew about the invincibility of the church. The verses assert that Christ's church was founded upon a rock and could not be dislodged by any array of hostile forces. It was the truth of Christ's Gospel—the immutability of the Golden Rule—that made his church immovable. The apostle made his point metaphorically, depicting a house capable of withstanding the most menacing forces, and Bishop Wayman picked up where Matthew left off. Christ, he preached, stood as "a strong tower of defense" against any "tempest and hurricane" that might confront his believers. "The heavens may be overshadowed with threatening clouds, the thunder may roar, the lightnings flash, the powers of earth and hell combine against them," the bishop said, peering over gold-ribbed spectacles. "But they can stand like the rock of Gibraltar, because their faith is founded on Christ."

The first test of Bishop Wayman's assurance came on August 25, 1885, when a Category 3 hurricane caught a defenseless Charleston by surprise. The relentless storm flooded the peninsula with an immense tidal surge and ripped the tops off buildings with gusts that reached nearly 125 miles per hour. Trees splintered and roofing tiles whipped through the air like razor-edged boomerangs. Homes along the Battery took on six feet of water. The spire of Citadel Square Baptist Church, Emanuel's immediate neighbor, tumbled backward into a three-story house, splitting its piazzas and front wall. Twenty-one people died and the city sustained more than $2 million in property losses. The cyclone badly damaged many Charleston churches, but Emanuel was blessed to have "felt the effects of the storm but slightly."

The church would not be quite so lucky when, a mere 371 days later, a magnitude-seven earthquake leveled much of the Lowcountry. Carolinians would forever refer to that terrifying night simply as "The Shake," but that descriptor does not convey the otherworldliness of the seismic disturbance of August 31, 1886. Striking in the dark at 9:50 p.m. and lasting nearly a minute, the massive quake produced tremors that rattled windows as far away as Chicago and Havana, as well as scores of traumatizing aftershocks. It remains the most destructive U.S. earthquake east of the Appalachians in recorded history. More than 120 people died and nearly every brick building in Charleston was damaged. Photographs document that scores of structures were reduced to rubble, including along Mother Emanuel's Calhoun Street, where houses and churches collapsed into mounds of bricks. The top cupola of St. Philip's landmark belltower appeared to have been hollowed out by a howitzer shell. Miles of telegraph line and railroad track were uprooted, leaving the city isolated in its time of need. Still seeking renewal after the displacement of war, Charleston had again been brought low by a cataclysmic upheaval.

Rev. Sterrett had been seeking the night breeze on his porch in Summerville, near the epicenter, when the rumbling began. The forty-four-year-old preacher found nature's fury more terrifying than any battlefield bombardment he had seen during the Civil War. The ground began to tremble, he wrote a few weeks later, "as though a subterranean cannonading had taken place." Houses imploded, chimneys toppled, sand and water spouted from creases in the earth. Shrieking, disoriented people staggered away from their homes and into flooded streets. Incessant prayers were hurled heavenward—"Oh, Jesus, save me!" and "My God, have mercy!"—and Sterrett took note of the sudden spike in his neighbors' religiosity. "There was a general rush for the chariot wheel of the Almighty," he wrote. "Both saint and sinner conceived it to be their only resort. And there they were bowed in the streets, from the old Christian sire to the inveterate sinner, all pleading to God, with fervent hearts, to sheath the sword of vengeance."

Although Emanuel's lore holds that the earthquake destroyed the wooden church, it did not. It left walls listing, the organ smashed, and the sanctuary coated with plaster, like a dusting of snow in the summer heat. But the building apparently escaped catastrophic damage and was thought structurally sound enough that a funeral for an earthquake victim was held there five days later. An engineering inspection found all four walls in "good" condition and noted only that a stovepipe had shattered a window and that a chimney had fallen from a house located on church property.

The pastors of Charleston's AME churches appealed through *The Christian Recorder* for collections for those whose homes and livelihoods had been demolished. Tent cities sprouted among the ruins, consuming parks and squares, while some homeless found temporary shelter in railroad cars. Rev. Lewis Ruffin Nichols, who became Emanuel's pastor after Sterrett's departure for Mt. Zion, joined with other Black clergy in advertising a particular need for donations to their communities. That earned a scolding from *The News and Courier* for drawing a "color line" at a time when unity was needed.

By mid-October, inspectors had determined that Emanuel, while spared, was not safe for worship. It would take $2,800 in repairs to make it so. Under normal circumstances, "that would be nothing for Emanuel Church to raise," Rev. Nichols wrote, but the quake had caused such widespread destitution that he had no choice but to beg. "The earthquake has left most of the people who own property with their hands full attending to making their property habitable," Nichols explained. "A great number of those who rent are still camping out. We therefore appeal to all lovers of African Methodism and of Christ to help us get our church so that we may safely worship God therein." Among those who responded was Grover Cleveland, the president of the United States, who mailed Nichols his personal donation of $10 (after first sending twice that amount to help repair the Confederate Home, an asylum for white widows and orphans). "I am very glad to contribute something for so worthy a cause," Cleveland wrote Nichols from the White House, "and though the sum is not large, it is accompanied by the wish that through the kindness of those who appreciate the value of such an instrumentality for good, your church may soon resume its career of usefulness."

The church was quickly patched and returned to service. But Nichols soon decided that its now-compromised condition only added to the urgency of building a new Emanuel that would be large and sturdy enough to contain its congregation. The process would take some time—and be interrupted by yet another punishing hurricane in 1893 that caused $3,000 in damage. Fundraising began in the fall of 1887 with concerts and fairs and special Sunday offerings and continued the next year with rallies aimed at raising $5,000 of the expected $20,000 construction cost. Plans initially called for another wooden building with a footprint of 118 feet by 55 feet, about 50 percent larger than the existing church, and a 50-foot bell tower at one corner. Ground was broken ceremonially on May 16, 1890, when Emanuel was thick with black-suited dignitaries attending the "Quarto-Centennial Conference" of the AME Church in South Carolina. A line of bishops, ministers, and congregants, all singing "Children of the Heavenly King," processed out of the church and shoveled clumps of dirt into a barrel, tossing coins into another for good luck.

The old building was razed a year later to make way for the new one, with the cornerstone laid in August 1891. This time, a brass band played as a box containing recent newspapers, a Bible, and a photograph of Bishop Cain was lowered into place. Before construction could start, however, the bishops let it be known that they wanted the new Emanuel to be built of brick and stone, a monument to the resilience of the denomination and its might in Charleston. Befitting its stature, this bulwark of African Methodism would be Gothic in design, with marble trimmings and a "steeple kissing the sky." Designed by a white Charleston architect, John Henry Devereux, it would have a high, vaulted ceiling, banks of pointed-arch windows fitted with stained glass, and ornate chandeliers with domed lamps that drooped like bluebells. The floors would be made of oaken planks that still reverberate when the choir gets to stomping with selections like "Holy Ghost Power." The footprint was expanded once more, to 80 feet by 104 feet, and the height of the spire tripled to 145 feet. The alterations helped double the estimated cost to nearly $50,000. Nichols felt the denomination should absorb some of the burden and asked every AME minister to buy a brick for 25 cents. Nonetheless, most of the money had to be borrowed. "By divine aid we intend to build the grandest AME church in all this south land," Nichols declared. Some of that aid came not from the divine but from the Equitable Building and Loan Association, a bank in Augusta, Georgia.

A share of the $50,000 cost, of course, went to Devereux, among Charleston's most prominent architects of the late nineteenth century. Born in Ireland in 1840, he had immigrated at age three, served as a Confederate calvary captain, and worked as a plasterer before studying as an architect. With Charleston in ruins after the Civil War, and again after the earthquake, there was plenty of work. Devereux designed some of the city's most acclaimed buildings—St. Matthew's Lutheran Church on King Street, which stood for a century as the state's tallest spire; the Masonic Hall at King and Wentworth, now remodeled into luxury condominiums; the imposing granite U.S. post office and courthouse at the Four Corners of Law, which adjoins the addition where Dylann Roof was tried.

The Gothic Revival façade of St. Matthew's, with its buttresses and soaring steeple, clearly served as a model for Emanuel. Devereux's early drawings for the AME church oriented the building differently from his final plan, with the bell tower anchoring the southwest corner, as it does now, but with a triple-arched entryway at ground level on the west side of the rectangular site. Instead, the main entrance to the church was built on the stubbier south side of the property, along Calhoun Street. It was a fortress of rich red brick with dentil work along the peaked roofline and quatrefoil ornamentation over the front doorways. The four-tiered steeple, with its arched windows and hexagonal spire, would be completed in 1907, and a booming pipe organ, shipped from Boston, was introduced the next year with a recital by eight local choirs. Electric lights replaced oil lamps that year as well. A local artist, John H. Green, painted the altar murals of Christ's crucifixion and ascension in 1945, a job that took thirty-five days. Only during a restoration that began in 1949, with the goal of arresting erosion caused by salt air and hurricane winds, was the church plastered with stucco and painted white to affect its current radiant sheen.

By late 1891, enough of the building was completed for the congregation to hold services in the basement, even as construction proceeded above. A temporary ceiling made of felt kept out rainwater and debris and gave Sunday worship the flavor of an old-time tent meeting. Although the main sanctuary was able to be occupied by the summer of 1894, work continued gradually throughout the decade, with much of the carpentry and stonework once again provided by members. The "solid masonry and elegant finish" made the new church a showcase in a region where African Methodism had come of age in wood-plank chapels. A mortgage was burned at a Sunday-morning service in September 1899.

As the new century dawned, Emanuel had become as central to African American life in Charleston as any structure on the peninsula. In addition to worship services and crusades, it hosted performances of sacred dramas like *Heaven Bound* and *The Pilgrim's Journey*, recitals by noted soloists and choirs, poetry readings, art exhibitions, and lectures. The renowned poet Paul Laurence Dunbar appeared on a double bill in 1902 with the tenor Sidney Woodward, self-medicating in advance with an "ample supply" of alcohol to overcome a tubercular cough. There were political meetings and charity benefits, school plays and graduations, oratory competitions, and fraternal gatherings of the Masons and Odd Fellows. Starting in 1909, the church lent itself to a citywide campaign aimed at combating tuberculosis in the Black community. South Carolina's African Methodists regularly held their district conferences and assemblies there, and the sanctuary was, of course, the setting for countless weddings and funerals.

Such celebrations and commemorations were invariably well attended, sometimes perilously so. One stiflingly hot afternoon in July 1902, the rickety 15-foot-high platform outside the main entrance collapsed under the weight of two hundred mourners straining to watch pallbearers load a coffin into a hearse. A number suffered compound fractures. The chaotic scene led some to see more than faulty engineering at work. One woman present told *The News and Courier* she was convinced she had witnessed "the first chapter of Judgment Day."

AS THE MECHANISMS OF DISCRIMINATION and its extralegal enforcement robbed Black Southerners of dignity, the pulpits of their churches served as lonely redoubts of resistance. Once the Supreme Court blessed state-mandated segregation in *Plessy* in 1896, the reach of Jim Crow would be limited only by the imaginations of Southern legislators. After enacting more conventional laws against sharing space in railroad cars, theaters, and schools, South Carolina's legislature chose to require separate entrances at circuses, ban interracial pool halls, and prohibit Black cotton-mill workers from using the same stairways or drinking water as white counterparts. A law passed in 1910 made it illegal for a white child to be placed in the permanent custody of a Black adult. Another in 1934 established Black and white beaches on the Atlantic shoreline. Racial designations on water fountains, waiting rooms, ticket windows, and playgrounds soon followed, and inequities not mandated by law were enforced by custom and manner. Black Charlestonians understood, for instance, that the shady peninsula-tip park along the Battery was not theirs to stroll, unless they were pushing a white baby in a carriage. "Our people are, in the main, without any protection at all in reference to law and citizenship," reported Rev. William David Chappelle, a presiding elder and future bishop from South Carolina (as well as the great-grandfather of comedian Dave Chappelle). "If something in some way is not done for the people of the South, I mean the white people, in the way of Christian civilization, the Negroes must eventually be crushed."

Emanuel soon became a primary venue for the expression of Black indignation and advocacy. In November 1900, some fifteen hundred Black Charlestonians packed the church to call for the firing of a white police officer who had shot and killed a Black suspect. Those in attendance appointed a committee to take their complaint to the mayor and formed a "protective association" to defend Black residents mistreated by the authorities. Four years later, another mass meeting was held at the church to protest a legislative proposal to require separate compartments for Black passengers on steamboats. The group resolved that the bill was "both unjust and uncalled for" and had as its only purpose the "further humiliation and degradation" of a people "already overburdened and outraged by unjust laws." The measure passed anyway.

Naturally, nothing outraged the Black clergy more than the increasingly commonplace murder and lynching of Black men and women and the impunity typically shown to the perpetrators. One of the first such cases to captivate Charleston was the October 2, 1885, killing of a Black livery stable operator named Stephney Riley by a prominent white physician, Dr. Amos N. Bellinger. Just after ten that morning, Bellinger emptied his revolver into Riley in the middle of Bull Street before numerous witnesses. The men were neighbors, and the confrontation had started the previous night when Bellinger chastised Riley for beating a balky horse. There were curses and threats and Riley, who had been emancipated from slavery, told the white man in no uncertain terms to mind his own business: "I am not your servant. I am attending to my business. I am my own boss." The men resumed the argument the next morning, and Bellinger used a racial slur before reaching into his pocket as casually "as if he was going to take a chew of tobacco," according to one witness. He drew his gun at close range and fired at least four shots, two of them to Riley's head. The doctor wiped his pistol clean with his coattail, retrieved the hat that had tumbled from his head, and strode down Bull Street to turn himself in.

Bellinger's trial the next month typified the kind of farcical jurisprudence that Black Charlestonians had come to expect. The doctor testified, without challenge from prosecutors, that he had acted in self-defense. Riley, he said, had brandished an open knife during their initial argument, a claim no witness was recorded as verifying. Bellinger, who had served the Confederacy as a battlefield surgeon, acknowledged that he had armed himself the next morning in case he encountered Riley again. When Riley came after him with that same open knife, he said, he felt his life was in danger. Only one of eight witnesses to the incident—a white man—testified to seeing Riley with a knife, and no blade was entered into evidence. Two other white witnesses said only that they saw Bellinger backing away as he fired. Not one of the five Black witnesses testified to seeing a knife or any provocation by Riley. They recalled consistently, however, that Bellinger fired his final two or three rounds after Riley had fallen and was begging for mercy. Nonetheless, eleven of the twelve jurors contented themselves with Bellinger's explanation, while one held out for a manslaughter conviction, prompting a mistrial. The only real question for the jurors, *The News and Courier* editorialized, had been whether they would believe "a gentleman" with no record of violent behavior or "the dramatic tales of the colored figurantes." When prosecutors retried Bellinger eight months later, he was found not guilty.

A month after the Riley shooting, Black church leaders held a mass meeting at Morris Brown AME. As usual, the pews filled, mostly with women, for a series of orations about the heightening sense of danger and injustice. They included warnings that the cauldron would boil over if the civil rights of Black Americans continued to be disregarded. The first speaker was Emanuel's pastor, Lewis Ruffin Nichols, who urged Black consumers to patronize Black businesses, a reflection of hardening segregation. They needed to understand that they were on their own, Nichols advised, and that it was possible to love their own people without disrespecting the white man. "Every people has a race pride," he began. "The Englishman loves his own race; so with the French, Germans, and so on; then why should we not patronize each other? . . . I say that if we are to attain any prominence on this continent we must help each other even to the exclusion of all other races."

The session produced an elegant manifesto, signed by three AME pastors and two Methodists, that labeled discriminatory courts, sharecropping contracts, and convict leasing as inherently anti-American. With a keen sense of public relations, the pastors amplified their message by coordinating their

Sunday sermons on November 22. Each preached from the seventeenth chapter of Judges—"In those days there was no king in Israel, but every man did that which was right in his own eyes"—a verse about the moral chaos that prevails in a lawless land. At Emanuel, every seat was taken as Pastor Nichols rose to the lectern. He began by asserting that it was human nature to crave orderly government, led by able men who administered justice impartially and protected the rights of all. "Oppression has lifted her wings dripping with human gore, and I am sad," the preacher said, referencing the Riley case. "There is nothing that makes a people so suspicious and uneasy and fires their prejudices as injustice and the feeling that they have lost faith in their rulers, that the Courts are corrupt, that justice is not to be meted out where color is concerned, and that one of them may be shot down like a dog in broad daylight and no one is punished."

Lynching reached its peak in South Carolina in 1898, when there were fourteen such vigilante killings. Between 1877, when federal forces withdrew from the South, and 1950, the state would be the site of 185 racial lynchings, most in the upstate region. That might seem a modest number compared to the 654 in Mississippi or 589 in Georgia (out of roughly 4,100 nationwide) but it was surely enough to make the point. In 1891, South Carolina's legislature refused to pass even a moderate anti-lynching measure that would have allowed the governor to remove any sheriff who let a prisoner come to harm. Four years later, a new state constitution did provide that authority, but the offense was considered a misdemeanor and there were no new penalties for those directly involved.

The victims in the peak year of 1898 included Frazier B. Baker, the forty-two-year-old Black postmaster of tiny Lake City, South Carolina, and his young daughter, Julia. Their executions in the mostly white hamlet, seventy-five miles north of Charleston, followed a prolonged campaign of harassment by residents who could not countenance the sorting of mail by Black hands. It escalated from letters of complaint to an ambush of gunfire and the torching of the post office itself. That prompted the determined postmaster to open shop in a corner of his small house. In one of the more bloodthirsty acts of the era, an armed posse rode up to Baker's residence around 1:00 a.m. on February 22. Without warning, they set the house aflame to flush out the family and began firing indiscriminately into the cabin. The twenty-three-month-old child was shot out of her mother's arms. Baker saw his daughter fall as he opened the door to lead his family in flight, and then was struck himself. Their remains were found in the ashes, charred beyond recognition. Baker's wife, Lavinia, and three of their other five children also were shot but managed to escape into the woods.

Ten weeks later, on May 2, 1898, incensed Black Charlestonians gathered at Emanuel to draft a protest to President William McKinley. The four-page letter, penned by a committee of seven that included five ministers, outlined the particulars of the Baker case while stating the tiresome truth that "this is no new story." As ever, the Black churchmen attempted to hold white Christianity to account for not practicing what it preached. "We think it is time for this savagery to stop," they wrote. "The lawgivers tell us there is a right for every wrong. If so, why does Christian America stand with crimson hand in this scene of human butchery, helpless and without remedy?" The committee asked that Baker's wife be granted a government pension, called for Congress to pass anti-lynching legislation, and requested a federal trial for thirteen perpetrators who had been identified by investigators. "What will you do about it?" they demanded of the president. "Lynching has become a National crime, and the Nation must act or stand disgraced in the eyes of the civilized world." Also lobbying the president was the crusading journalist Ida B. Wells-Barnett, whose anti-lynching crusade took on new vehemence after the Lake City attack.

After state authorities declined to prosecute, the petitioners got the federal trial they requested. They would discover, however, that there was no more protection for Black Southerners from an all-white federal jury in South Carolina than from an all-white state jury. None of the men tried in Charleston the following year were convicted, as two turned state's evidence, three were acquitted by directed verdict, and eight were freed after the jury deadlocked (with seven of twelve members favoring acquittal). Even Charleston's white newspapers deemed the verdict a travesty, albeit a predictable one. The only real surprise, *The News and Courier* editorialized in disgust, had been that five white men could be persuaded to convict. "If the politics and complexion of the actors in the tragedy had been different," the editors wrote, "the jury would have brought in a verdict of guilty without leaving their seats." Frazier Baker's family received no compensation, and the only meager reparation came 120 years later when Congress voted to name the Lake City post office in his memory.

The ever-looming risk of violence, along with the ubiquitous indignities, disenfranchisement, and inferior schooling of the Jim Crow era, helped drive hundreds of thousands of South Carolinians from the state starting in the late nineteenth century. Economic factors played their part, of course, including the ongoing decline of rice and cotton production (which accelerated with the boll weevil's arrival in the 1920s), the allure of Northern wages, and ultimately the disruptions brought by the Great Depression and two world wars. The first waves of migrants tended to settle nearby, sometimes moving from farm to city, from the Lowcountry to upstate, or to adjacent states with more fertile land. By the second decade of the twentieth century, their direction had turned markedly north, as Carolinians joined the Great Migration of more than 6 million Black Southerners to cities like Philadelphia and New York. The 1930 census found that 29 percent of native-born Black South Carolinians lived in other states. Fully 13 percent of Black Philadelphians, 10 percent of Black New Yorkers, and 8 percent of Black Washingtonians had migrated from the Palmetto State. Meanwhile, in Charleston, which lost more than a tenth of its Black population between 1920 and 1930, only 3 percent of those who remained had been born in another state, a smaller share than in any major city. Between 1920 and 1970, South Carolina's Black population dropped by 75,000, or 9 percent, even as the white population grew by 120 percent. By 1930, white South Carolinians had regained their statewide majority for the first time in 120 years. The gap widened throughout the twentieth century, and the white population reached 62 percent in 2020.

The flight of so many Black South Carolinians could not help but drain the state's Black churches of membership and dollars. Between 1916 and 1926, the number of African Methodist Episcopal Church members in South Carolina plunged from 90,469 to 59,372. When the Second World War ended in the mid-1940s, Emanuel's membership had dipped below 2,000 for the first time since its founding.

As in succeeding generations, Black Americans in the early twentieth century differed starkly in their approaches and responses to the repressive conditions of Jim Crow. Across the first decades, Emanuel's members were positioned to hear the full spectrum of argument without leaving their pews. On March 19, 1909, the church welcomed the famed educator Booker T. Washington, hailed by a white Charleston newspaper as "the greatest negro in the world" because of his reputation as "a safe leader" who "teaches good and wholesome lessons." A dozen years later, on February 16, 1921, the same pulpit was occupied by Washington's longtime antagonist, the sociologist and journalist W.E.B. Du Bois, certainly a contender for the "greatest" title even if not bestowed by the white Southern press.

Washington's appearance at a jammed Emanuel capped a weeklong twelve-city expedition through South Carolina that bore all the trappings of a presidential whistle-stop tour. "The Wizard of Tuskegee" was accompanied by an entourage wherever he went, including reporters from Boston, Chicago, and Washington, D.C. They traveled by train in a "well-appointed special car" that spared them some indignities of segregated travel, and were greeted at depots by brass bands and children holding banners inscribed with the great man's adages. Washington spoke from the rear platform to throngs gathered at several stops. At Charleston's Union Station, he was greeted by the famed orphanage founder Rev. Daniel Jenkins, and his renowned band of child musicians, fresh from William Howard Taft's inaugural parade. An arrangements committee, which included Emanuel's pastor of the moment, Rev. H.W.B. Bennett, organized a luncheon in Washington's honor, and then a tour of the city and its famous harbor by trolley. Charleston's white mayor paid tribute to Washington at Emanuel that evening, as white mayors had in other South Carolina cities. Special arrangements were made by the committee "to accommodate all white persons who may wish to hear Dr. Washington," presumably meaning that separate seating would be available. White newspapers published Washington's every word. A sumptuous banquet in Emanuel's fellowship hall followed his lecture, and the toasts—led by a prominent Black physician—drew on so long that Washington and his party did not depart the city until 3:20 a.m.

Washington's South Carolina tour, which drew an estimated fifty thousand listeners over the week, found the great educator at the acme of his influence. Washington had made such cross-state trips before, most notably through Mississippi the previous year, and it was not his first visit to the Lowcountry. But with the establishment of the National Association for the Advancement of Colored People only a month earlier, his stature as America's leading Black spokesman would soon be challenged. As on prior tours, he hoped to assess the condition of Black life on the ground and urge his people toward self-improvement through education and the mastery of skilled trades. But he also hoped to lay down a marker, some fourteen years after his groundbreaking "Atlanta Compromise" address and eight years after the publication of *Up from Slavery*. The ongoing violence and harassment aimed at African Americans compelled him to argue that his measured approach to reconciliation remained relevant in a less patient age. "The timely trip through South Carolina provided Washington with the forum he needed to show blacks and whites alike that he reigned as the most important black leader in America," wrote historian David H. Jackson, Jr. "The Tuskegean calculated how to maintain his national power and prestige, and tours such as this one became a vehicle for doing so, guaranteeing that his ideas, philosophy, and solutions to the race problem would be plastered time and again in newspapers all around the United States."

The speech at Emanuel was vintage Washington, a methodical sermon on the virtues of self-help built upon a framework of accommodationist conservatism. In his 1895 speech to the Cotton States and International Exposition in Atlanta, the first of its kind by a Black man to a racially mixed audience in the post-Reconstruction South, Washington had posited that Black Americans would gladly cede any claim to "social equality" with white people in exchange for support for Black self-improvement. "In all things that are purely social we can be as separate as the fingers," he famously said then, "yet one as the hand in all things essential to mutual progress." Similarly, in Charleston, his approach implicitly accepted segregation while focusing on the "equal" component of the separate-but-equal doctrine. Tailoring his message to white listeners, Washington assured his audience that Black Americans did not desire to share restaurant tables or railway cars (or bedrooms or marriages) with white people; they simply wanted equal accommodations in their separate spaces. "Let me say as emphatically as I am able, that judging by my observation and experience, nowhere in this country is the negro race seeking to obtrude itself upon the white race," Washington said. "I think you will find that the more the negro is educated, the more he gets to understand himself and the world, the more he finds satisfaction in the company of his own people, the less he desires to force himself in any place that he is not wanted."

If blame was to be placed for the state of twentieth-century race relations, Washington suggested, it fell partly on his own people. "All races have had their silly periods, and the negro race is no exception," he said. "It was natural enough, coming out of slavery as we did, entering into a life that was new to us in so many respects, that we should do a great many foolish things, that we should have a great many absurd and impractical notions, that we should frequently grasp the shadow when we were seeking for the substance." That was now changing, he said, and white Southerners could accelerate the process by improving living and working conditions on their farms and providing adequate schooling to Black children. That would give meaningful work to "the idle and vicious class of loafers who are to be found in too large numbers around the street corners without steady, reliable, productive employment."

Washington's Charleston speech highlighted how deeply his thinking was shaped by the quest for acceptance from white people, not for its own sake but because experience convinced him that Black Americans could not advance without their acquiescence. "In all that concerns the welfare of the negro in the South, there is no person in the world who can be so helpful to him as his white neighbor," Washington said at Emanuel. Perhaps, as some historians suggest, he was a crafty pragmatist. In an era when white politics was fueled by racist caricatures of Black vagrancy and fiendishness, Washington felt that counter-messaging was needed.

But his words read today as strikingly out of touch with the lives of those whose condition he had come to assess. Washington posited at Emanuel that Southerners should congratulate themselves that relations between the races were not any worse. Nowhere on the globe, he contended, had such dissimilar races "succeeded in getting on better in all the affairs of life than the black man and the white man have done and are doing at the present time in the Southern States." The question that captivated him was less whether Blacks should expect equal treatment than whether their labor would be exploited to its fullest potential. That required proper training for Black men and women in the skills and dignity of work. "We must awaken their ambition," Washington said. "We must give them something to work for."

Washington enjoyed considerable popularity in AME circles across the country, as his philosophy dovetailed in many ways with Richard Allen's founding ethos of Black self-reliance and Daniel Payne's quest for respectability. He spoke regularly from AME pulpits, received warm applause at General Conferences, corresponded with African Methodist leaders, and contributed articles to the *A.M.E. Church Review*. In an essay for that quarterly journal in 1894, he wrote that "it is my firm conviction that every right of which we are now deprived can be secured through business development, coupled with education and character." Tuskegean thinking continued to grip Emanuel for a while. A year after Washington's appearance, the church hosted a mass meeting to promote industrial education that included an address by Charleston's white mayor pro tem, titled "How the Colored People May Help Themselves in Seeing the Wisdom of Confiding in Their White Neighbors." Another white speaker at the nearly four-hour session, Rev. Alexander Sprunt, the pastor of

First Presbyterian Church, analogized the schooling of Black workers for particular trades to the raising of livestock. "We train some horses for speed, some for driving and some as draught horses," the pastor explained.

When Du Bois showed up at Emanuel in 1921, the South depicted by Washington likely seemed largely unfamiliar to most Black Charlestonians. Two years earlier, on a Saturday night in May 1919, the city had been the scene of a rampaging race riot that left three African Americans dead and many more injured. The precise origins are murky, but it took place as servicemen wound their way back to the port city and its Charleston Navy Yard after World War I. They included Black soldiers and sailors who had fought to make the world "safe for democracy" but then returned to a South that was neither safe nor democratic. The confrontation apparently started when a young Black man failed to pay proper deference to two white sailors on a sidewalk, jostling them as they passed (other accounts have it starting as a pool hall argument). A chase gave way to gunshots and false rumors that a sailor had been killed, inciting a night of looting, marauding, and brutality by bluejacketed gangs that all but hunted down their Black prey. It was among the first eruptions of random violence in what came to be known as the "Red Summer" of 1919, a nationwide outbreak of more than two dozen racially motivated disturbances that left hundreds dead. The clashes ignited spontaneously in major cities like Washington, D.C., and Chicago, and in hamlets like Elaine, Arkansas, site of the single deadliest rampage. Each started in its own way. But the unrest coincided with the return of victorious soldiers and the tensions created by unmet Black expectations for improved treatment and white fears about Black assertiveness and competition for jobs.

Charleston's night of terror made indelible the kind of devaluation that Black residents lived with every day. In 1910, when Black and white numbers were comparable in the city, infant mortality among Black babies exceeded that of white ones by more than three to one. Black death rates in South Carolina far outpaced those of white people for most major ailments. Thanks to rampant tuberculosis, influenza, and heart disease, Charleston had the highest death rate among Black residents of any U.S. city that compiled data, more than double the white rate. Per capita spending on Black schoolchildren was one-tenth of that for white students, and pay for Black teachers was barely a third of that for white ones (only Louisiana had a larger differential). The determination of white people to exert iron-fisted rule had supplied the state's chain gangs with Black convicts, depleted its rolls of Black voters, excluded Black Carolinians from the professions, and successfully relegated Black farmers to hopeless tenancy. As a social scientist, editor, and orator, Du Bois found it delusional to think that industrial education alone—a nationwide flowering of Tuskegees—could narrow such fundamental inequities, prevent the lynching of Black men without trial, and reverse the re-institutionalization of discrimination by racial caste.

Although Washington and Du Bois had once been respectful co-admirers, by the time Du Bois got to Emanuel, a week before his fifty-third birthday, their bitter rivalry had been long established. In his most acclaimed work, *The Souls of Black Folk* (1903), Du Bois devoted a chapter to eviscerating Washington for urging Black Southerners to lower their sights. That chapter, observed Du Bois's biographer, David Levering Lewis, served as "the manifesto of the Talented Tenth," the assertion by Du Bois that "the Negro race, like all races, is going to be saved by its exceptional men."

By assailing Washington in print, Du Bois dared go where few other Black writers had. Without voting rights, civil rights, and a liberal higher education, he wrote, it was foolhardy to think, as Washington did, that a demonstration of uprightness would bring a better day for Black Americans. "Mr. Washington's programme practically accepts the alleged inferiority of the Negro races," Du Bois charged. He argued unsparingly that Washington's focus on work and material accumulation was myopic, noting its departure from the "attitude of revolt and revenge" that had been modeled by Denmark Vesey and other antebellum resistance leaders. "In the history of nearly all other races and peoples the doctrine preached ... has been that manly self-respect is worth more than lands and houses," Du Bois wrote from his desk at Atlanta University. Rather than lifting Black Americans up from slavery, Washington was leading them back into it, Du Bois charged. Even if the goal was economic advancement, white racism had to be resisted, not accommodated. Washington, he said, left the impression that the victim should be blamed for his degradation and was solely responsible for his reclamation.

In the decade and a half before his Emanuel speech, Du Bois had helped initiate the Niagara Movement, create its successor in the NAACP, and become the founding editor of its crusading monthly magazine, *The Crisis*, which he would lead for twenty-four years. He first spoke in Charleston in 1917, appearing at Centenary Methodist Episcopal Church in a twenty-five-cents-per-head fundraiser for the Colored YWCA. Only four days earlier, as if to herald Du Bois's arrival, his former student at Atlanta University, Edwin Augustus Harleston, a gifted painter and the son of a prominent Emanuel member, had led a band of twenty-nine Black Charlestonians in forming a local branch of the NAACP. Du Bois wrote afterward in *The Crisis* of visiting several Black churches, perhaps including Emanuel. "Mighty are the churches of colored Charleston," he observed. "I did them in rhythm on a great blue day. In the first, the tall black preacher beat upon his audience with skillful repetitions, which alone meant little, but his hearers surged and bowed, as swept by an unseen wind, and one slim black woman whirled and screamed, with outstretched arms."

At the point Du Bois returned four years later to speak at Emanuel, the Charleston NAACP had scored an early victory by petitioning the city to reverse its requirement that Black students in segregated schools be taught by white teachers. Going forward, they would be taught only by Black teachers, a result that produced Black jobs and loosened white control even as it reinforced segregation. Du Bois considered the change an improvement, but it did not alter his view of Charleston as a place of "poignant beauty side by side with crass ugliness—the blatant and naïve exploitation, the difference between the 'People' and 'Negroes', the continued imminence of the mob."

Du Bois's interests, meanwhile, had expanded to encompass a fervent devotion to Pan-Africanism, which sought to unify African people and the diaspora in a global campaign against racial discrimination and colonial exploitation. His appearance at the church was part of a Southern speaking tour with several aims: to aid the NAACP in its new goal of signing up 250,000 members, to collect material for articles for *The Crisis*, and to raise funds to send delegates to the upcoming Second Pan-African Congress in London, Brussels, and Paris (the first had been held in Paris in 1919). Du Bois had calculated that steamship passage alone might cost up to $400 and had been seeking contributions through *The Crisis*. Tickets for his Emanuel lecture about the congress cost 35 cents.

There is no known record of Du Bois's speech that night, but a local NAACP official depicted it as a "historical and wonderfully inspiring lecture" that was "greeted by a large, appreciative and enthusiastic audience." Du Bois's three-day stay in the city, Edward C. Mickey wrote, had been "an event in literary and social circles." If his remarks in Charleston resembled those made at other stops, he would have reviewed the work of the first Pan-African Congress and outlined his hopes for the grand reconvening scheduled for August and September. He also would have led his listeners through a survey of the discriminatory treatment of African peoples in Liberia, in Haiti, in Jamaica, and in the French and British colonies in Africa. Black soldiers serving the British military in Africa could not become officers, he told an audience in Kansas a month later. In some European countries, it was still taboo for Black people to practice medicine or law. Although American racism might be uniquely despicable, it had to be viewed in global context. "He spoke of the way the European countries treat the colored people, how they are governed, and the recognition the colored race gets from the white leaders," a newspaper in Topeka reported. "Mr. Du Bois believes that the white people should begin to realize that the Negro question must be settled now and cannot wait until all the other world questions are settled."

Surely, Du Bois also made a pitch for his beloved NAACP and its young chapter in Charleston. Perhaps he updated the audience on his recent war of words with Marcus Garvey, the militant editor who dreamed of liberating the African continent by force and installing himself at its head. Just perhaps, in the church that made resistance its watchword during the days of Denmark Vesey, he auditioned the material he would weave into a Pan-Africanist manifesto: "We who resent the attempt to treat civilized men as uncivilized, and who bring in our hearts grievance upon grievance against those who lynch the untried, disfranchise the intelligent, deny self-government to educated men, and insult the helpless, we complain; but not simply or primarily for ourselves—more especially for the millions of our fellows, blood of our blood, and flesh of our flesh, who have not even what we have—the power to complain against monstrous wrong, the power to see and to know the source of our oppression."

XIII.

B. J. Glover and the Gospel of Resistance

Who shall separate us from the love of Christ?
Shall tribulation, or distress, or persecution, or famine,
or nakedness, or peril, or sword?

—ROMANS 8:35 (KJV)

Rev. Benjamin James Glover, the fearlessly militant preacher who would propel both Mother Emanuel and the Charleston NAACP through the Civil Rights Movement, was born in 1915 in Promised Land. That was the aspirational name given to a small Black enclave in rural Abbeville County, South Carolina, that was settled by freedpeople five years after the Civil War. As the son of an AME minister and his strong-willed wife, and the son-in-law of the first statewide president of the NAACP, Glover came honestly by his intolerance for racial disrespect and his audacity in resisting it at any cost. By age twenty-six, he had watched white vigilantes burn down his family's barn and been arrested and severely beaten for showing insufficient respect to a white officer. None of that, nor the terroristic harassment that he and his family faced across decades of activism, dampened Glover's enthusiasm for confrontation in the name of a righteous cause.

B. J. Glover, as he was universally known, did not bow to either white mayors or Black bishops and left a legacy that included the desegregation of Charleston's public schools—by his daughter, Oveta, among others—and the end of discriminatory treatment by the city's retailers, restaurants, and hotels. Tall and slender with a laconic voice, a faint mustache, and a stern gaze, Glover was omnipresent on Charleston's streets during the city's direct-action summers of 1962 and 1963. He helped organize what came to be known as "The Charleston Movement," marching, boycotting, preaching, demanding, filling the jails. He broke barriers with both his will and his wit. Glover anchored all of these efforts from the church, his church, Emanuel African Methodist Episcopal Church, which he helmed longer than any pastor, from 1953 to 1965, a dozen of the most vital years in the African American journey. His activism posed real risks for Mother Emanuel, and not all of his congregants approved.

Glover's blending of his roles as pastor and activist reflected the moment when the Black church matured to make the Civil Rights Movement possible. Melding biblical and Gandhian thinking into an audacious approach to nonviolent protest, these men and women of faith brought their congregations out of their sanctuaries and into the uncontrollable streets. There, over the course of two explosive decades, they successfully shamed their country into abandoning its four-century-long tradition of legalized discrimination, establishing at least a stated national goal of equalizing treatment across races. They infused their indignation with the certainty that all men and women were children of God and goaded their followers to liberate themselves from the internal effects of oppression along with the external ones. By redeeming the dignity of their race, they hoped to restore the nation's democratic experiment.

Although not a purely religious movement, the battle to desegregate America in the 1950s and 1960s could never have succeeded in the stirring way it did without the stature and structure of the Black church, without the intense Christian faith of its adherents, and without the women and men, like Glover, that it elevated to leadership. Like other civil-rights pastors, Glover not only rejected the perversity of white supremacy but directly confronted it, mocking it into eventual submission. He used his pulpit to convey God's condemnation of inequality, offered his sanctuary for rallies stoked by spirit and song, gave over his fellowship hall to weary teenage marchers. Along with a few other downtown churches, notably Morris Brown AME and Morris Street Baptist, Mother Emanuel became the movement's spiritual home in Charleston, a staging ground as well as a revivalist refuge. In her packed pews, young men and women in starched white shirts crossed arms to join hands and sway metronomically to the rhythms of "We Shall Overcome." Heated meetings about the course of downtown boycotts took place in the basement, exposing rifts between brash young demonstrators and older, less militant strategists. When Martin Luther King, Jr., made his first significant foray into Charleston, it was to speak at Emanuel. When he was assassinated six years later, and rioting erupted across the country, Emanuel hosted a peaceful citywide memorial service that welcomed mourners with a voter registration booth. For a time, at least, Emanuel was Charleston's movement church, and Glover its prime mover.

As a tactician, Glover utilized the federal courts as well as the power of protest to petition for change. He was a party to the case that desegregated Charleston's schools and another that led the U.S. Supreme Court to validate the right of demonstrators to protest peacefully. "B. J. Glover was the ultimate agitator," remembered U.S. Rep. James E. Clyburn, who was jailed with Glover in the march that led to that ruling. "And the folks at Emanuel church, maybe it was because of B. J. Glover, they were the people who were doing things around town."

It is no accident, of course, that so many titans of the civil-rights era emerged from the ministry. Pastors with a passion for protest brought advantages to the task that few aspiring organizers could muster: a sanctified and bully pulpit, community respect, leadership experience, established networks, and—as with undertakers, insurers, doctors, lawyers, and entertainers with primarily Black clientele—a measure of financial independence from white power.

Even though South Carolina was decidedly an NAACP state, with a secondary role played by King and his Southern Christian Leadership Conference, the pattern of pastoral leadership persisted. Black churches were essential to NAACP organizing and fundraising in the state. Along with Glover, the clergy provided tacticians like Rev. Joseph A. De Laine, the AME minister and NAACP leader from Clarendon County who instigated South Carolina's seminal school desegregation lawsuit, and Rev. Isaiah DeQuincey Newman, a United Methodist who served as the state's longtime NAACP field director. Another United Methodist, Rev. Alonzo W. Wright, became the first statewide NAACP president in 1939, a dozen years before his daughter, Lydia, married B. J. Glover. James G. Blake, the NAACP youth leader at the forefront of Charleston's demonstrations, would become an AME pastor after graduating, like King, from Morehouse College and Boston University's seminary. They would be joined, of course, by leading civil-rights figures from other sectors: J. Arthur Brown (real estate); Harold R. Boulware, Sr. (law); Septima Poinsette Clark (education); Harvey Gantt (student activism); Esau Jenkins (community organizing); James M. Hinton, Sr. (insurance); John Henry McCray (media); Mary Moultrie (healthcare); Matthew J. Perry, Jr. (law); William Saunders (community organizing); Cleveland Sellers (student activism); Modjeska Monteith Simkins (public health); and Emanuel AME trustee John H. Wrighten III (law), to name a few.

GLOVER'S NARRATIVE ASCENDS from the depths of Jim Crow into the dawn of a new era. He was named for his paternal grandfather, a formerly enslaved man who, like many in his line, enjoyed remarkable longevity and died at 105. The roughhewn region where Glover grew up, Abbeville County, had never been known for racial moderation. Tucked into South Carolina's upstate corner, it was the birthplace of John C. Calhoun and an early hotbed of secessionist fury. Five days before B. J.'s first birthday, the county was the site of one of the state's most notorious lynchings, of a prosperous farmer named Anthony Crawford.

Crawford presented an appealing target for those who found Black success an affront to the white-supremacist paradigm. At fifty-one, he had accumulated 427 acres of land and possessed both "a good bank account and a family of thirteen children." Crawford was dapper and dignified with a high forehead, untamed sideburns, and a mustache that escaped the bounds of his face. He had served as an officer of Cypress Chapel AME Church for two decades.

The day Crawford was killed, October 21, 1916, began with an argument at a general store about the price the proprietor had offered him for cotton seed he was bringing to market. When Crawford cursed the shopkeeper for trying to cheat him, word of his insolence galloped down the street. He was arrested for disorderly conduct but quickly bailed himself out, and as he headed toward the town cotton gin he was pursued by a posse of liquored-up ruffians. He retreated into a boiler room, armed himself with a hammer, and managed to strike a blow as the mob rushed in. But he was soon overtaken, and his white assailants pummeled away with fists, boots, and knives until the sheriff rescued the gravely injured Crawford and locked him in an upstairs cell. The lawman offered little resistance, however, when the mob raided the jail and removed the helpless Black farmer. "They dragged by either arm his broken body down three flights of stairs and threw it to the howling horde at the door," NAACP secretary Roy Nash reported after the agency conducted an investigation. "While a hair rope was being knotted, the gentlemen of Abbeville took turns in digging both heels with a running jump into the Negro's upturned, quivering face." The vigilantes hauled Crawford through the city to the fairgrounds, strung him from a pine, and shot up his body. Some carved bullets out of the tree for souvenirs. Although there were scores of witnesses, a coroner reported that Crawford had died "at the hands of parties unknown."

The governor and leading newspapers voiced outrage, but with townspeople unwilling to testify, no one was prosecuted. Instead, Crawford's family members were pressured to leave the state. Thousands of Black neighbors took the hint and joined them over the years, accelerating the exodus from South Carolina's Piedmont to the North.

One family that refused to flee was that of Rev. Charles G. Glover and his wife, Queen Ester, who at that point had birthed all twelve of their children, with B. J. the youngest. As an African Methodist leader in the county, Charles Glover must have known Anthony Crawford and his extended family and undoubtedly understood the risk in remaining after his fellow churchman's murder and mutilation. He chose, however, to continue serving the small country churches that dotted the area, while also farming a family plot.

Violence found the Glover homestead soon enough. While B. J. was too young to recall the murder of Anthony Crawford, his earliest memories included the torching of the family's barn in Abbeville County. The Glovers had extended the shed's roof to provide cover for a Model T that Rev. Glover drove across his sprawling circuit and a Model A owned by one of B. J.'s brothers. These were rare possessions for a Black family in that time and place, and apparently attracted unwanted notice. "We just assumed that this was too much for the community," B. J. Glover later recounted, "and the Ku Klux Klan came one night and set the house afire. They burned the barn, the two cars, and all the food we had." The child watched the white men drive off as cinders popped and flames leapt into a midnight sky. His mother, weeping for the first time in his experience, reached down to stroke his head. "Someday this won't happen," she told him, "and you will play a part in it."

B. J. Glover inherited from his mother his habit of speaking plainly to and about white folks. The indignities she confronted, like being called "Auntie" in her own home by a white door-to-door salesman, stuck with him for years. So did Ester Glover's steely response to the disrespectful salesman: "I didn't know I had any white nieces and nephews. My name is Mrs. Glover." As an insular Black community, Promised Land afforded some level of protection from such insults. But there were, nonetheless, regular reminders of a Black boy's subordinate status—the two-mile treks to and from school as the white bus passed him by; the mistreatment at clothing stores, with their whites-only dressing rooms; the expectation that he tip his hat to white passersby (which only persuaded him to stop wearing hats). B. J.'s parents could not shield him—no parent could—but they tutored him that God made everyone in His image, and that God's justice would come. "I was never given an idea that I was less than anybody else," Glover told an interviewer late in life.

Despite the size of his family, Charles Glover had accumulated enough wealth by the time B. J. was a teenager to send him away for schooling. He knew the opportunities would be limited at home and saw potential for his son to escape the farm, perhaps by becoming a full-time minister. He shipped B. J. off to Gastonia, North Carolina, and then to Cincinnati, Ohio, where the young man lived with relatives and attended night school. B. J. later worked his way through Wilberforce University, the AME flagship, and its Payne Theological Seminary.

A rougher education commenced when Glover returned to South Carolina, where he was appointed in late 1940 to pastor Mt. Lebanon AME Church in Due West, about twenty miles from Promised Land. Not long after he started, on September 29, 1941, he visited a state highway patrol office in nearby Greenwood to apply for a South Carolina driver's license. The office shared space with a Chevrolet dealership in the Moore's Incorporated Building on Maxwell Avenue, just down from the bus terminal. An officer reportedly asked to see Glover's current license and, noting that it was from Ohio, asked Glover why he was in South Carolina and how long he planned to stay. According to a subsequent report in *The Pittsburgh Courier*, a leading African American newspaper of the day, Glover was perceived as answering "in a manly way" and not showing proper deference.

"You must take your hat off when talking to a white man in the South," the patrolman instructed, according to the newspaper. Others in uniform gathered around. "Let's teach that D . . . N. . . . . a lesson," one suggested before slugging Glover, according to the *Courier*. The skinny young preacher—six feet tall and only 164 pounds—tried in vain to defend himself but four or five others jumped him and "beat him into a bloody mass," the newspaper reported. The troopers then took Glover to the police station, and a magistrate sentenced him to spend thirty days on a chain gang or pay a fine of $100 on each of three charges—resisting arrest, assault and battery, and disorderly conduct. "On arrival at the chain gang stockade the minister was again beaten and although badly bleeding and spitting blood was forced to do some work from which he fell exhausted to the ground," the *Courier* reported. When Glover's father learned of the detention he hurried to the police station, paid the $300 in fines, and secured his son's release. The article said that even a month later Glover remained at home under a physician's care.

The *Courier* characterized Glover's beating as a near-lynching, "one of the most brutal instances of police terrorism as widely practiced in the South." It did not disclose the source of its "reliable information" but datelined its article from Due West, suggesting that its correspondent had been there and had spoken to the Glovers. Neither the *Courier* nor *The Chicago Defender*, which published a similar report, printed any response from the state patrol. A short article in Greenwood's newspaper one day after the incident confirms that Glover was charged after a scuffle that "grew out of an attack by Glover on State Highway Patrolman C.H. Trotti when the negro applied for a driver's license." Glover's injuries were severe enough that he could not preach for the next five Sundays at Mt. Lebanon and had to enlist substitutes. A photograph of him from that era, peering out the window of his convalescent bedroom, depicts a haunted man with seething eyes. He suffered thereafter from recurring back problems, and his day book, scribbled with entries about each Sunday's attendance and collections, noted that he started missing church regularly because of illness. Simply making it through worship became cause for exultation. "Another Sunday is gone, and God is still with me," he wrote after a service in January 1943.

Although Glover was a keen and gifted storyteller, he did not make the police beating a regular part of the biographical narrative that he conveyed to his family, friends, and congregants. He did, on the other hand, often tell of an even more vicious attack, this one ostensibly perpetrated by Klansmen or the like, that shared elements with the state patrol incident but also differed in substantial ways. Beyond Glover's own recollection of his trauma, which he summoned in interviews, conversations, and sermons, no contemporaneous reports have been found.

While Glover's alleged offense with the state patrol amounted to racial insolence, he portrayed the Klan attack as retribution for his attempts to register to vote in South Carolina. Glover variously dated the incident to 1937 or 1939, but neither year jibes with what can be documented of his whereabouts, which have him living in Ohio through most of 1940 before relocating to the Palmetto State. Glover's fullest surviving descriptions of the assault come from oral history interviews he gave in 1979 and 2005. But he is recorded speaking about it at least as early as 1959 and repeated the story often to family members and friends. His children, who grew up in the 1950s and 1960s, remember the accounts vividly.

In those tellings, Glover said his troubles began when he showed up one day at the Abbeville County courthouse and dared to register to vote. To qualify, he knew he would have to read and interpret portions of the Constitution and show proof that he owned property and had paid the poll tax. He came with his paperwork in order. "I read the Constitution—at that time I could have read it in three languages besides English," Glover recalled in the 1979 interview. His ease with the literacy test prompted the registrar to make a phone call, and Glover said he overheard snippets of conversation about having "a smart n----r in here." The man returned to tell Glover that he had been rejected. Glover asked if there had been a problem with his reading. The man smiled: "I just can't register you." The young preacher left without a voting card, but with a newfound reputation as a troublemaker. He only enhanced it, he said, by preaching from Mt. Lebanon's pulpit about the importance of registering and the injustice he had faced at the courthouse.

Shortly thereafter, Glover said in 1979, he took the bus one afternoon from Due West to Greenwood. As with the state patrol incident, his purpose, he said, was to renew his driver's license. Someone must have been tracking his movements, he said, because after he got off the bus and began walking down Maxwell Avenue he was accosted by a gang of five white toughs. They asked him to identify himself. "I told them my name, but I didn't say 'Yes, sir' or 'No, sir,'" Glover recalled. "They took me from there in a car, blindfolded, out in the country. I fought until I couldn't fight any more. They did every kind of thing you could imagine." Glover said the ordeal lasted five hours, and that the men made him strip and taunted him sexually. Shortly before his death in 2010, he told his son Shawn Glover that the men "did some unmentionables to him," without being more specific.

As they assaulted Glover, the men made clear why they had targeted him. "Why don't you leave things like they are?" Glover said they demanded as they beat him. "They said they had come to make an example of me. I was an uppity, smart n----r from the North. I had come back with Northern ideas."

Glover said that only bizarre fortune saved him that day, perhaps with longer odds than Denmark Vesey's lottery ticket. There was a prostitute—"a no-good woman," his parents called her—who plied her trade in those same woods, as the town could not support a no-tell motel. Glover said he had never been a customer, but occasionally offered the woman a kind word and so she recognized him when she came across his near-lifeless body. "She found me and ran two or three miles back to my home and fell on my steps and cried out, 'They killed B. J. They killed B. J.,'" Glover said. His father collected his son in his car, brought him home, and called for Greenwood's Black doctor. B. J. revived later that night but faced a lengthy recuperation. In conversations with his children, the story of his rescue by the woman became a Christian parable. "Be kind to everybody," Glover would counsel, "because you never know who's going to save your life."

Regardless of whether the two beating stories are separate or somehow conflated, the psychological effects seem to have lingered for years. For a time, Glover said, the mere sight of a white person—or even of a light-skinned Black friend—triggered violent hallucinations. "I had a severe psychosis about white people and I had to work very hard and pray very hard to overcome it," he said later in life. "It was a madness, and it would come up often." Once physically capable, he returned to the North and his refuge in Ohio, where he continued his schooling at Antioch, a multiracial campus. He also had the opportunity to study in Europe, with white classmates. Through introspection and prayer, he said, he finally resolved his bitterness and came to feel pity and sorrow for white racists rather than hatred. That epiphany had not come easily, but was spiritually necessary. "You see," he explained, "we believe that there is a heaven and a hell, and that you cannot be admitted to the kingdom if you feel hatred. I had to overcome my psychosis in order to be able to be admitted." Glover may as well have been speaking for those who expressed forgiveness for Dylann Roof after his murderous rampage at Emanuel in 2015.

BY THE TIME GLOVER was assigned to Emanuel on November 8, 1953, he had already held ministerial posts in Wilmington, Ohio; Columbia, South Carolina; and Charleston at Morris Brown, where he served three years. At Emanuel, he found a congregation that was culturally conservative, that dressed for church, that minded its children, that loved its pipe organ, that preferred hymns to spirituals, that did not smile upon excessive fervor or showy demonstrations of faith. For African Methodists, it was high church, with the millinery to show for it. Tradition mattered and did not die easily. Even though the congregation was now highly literate, preachers still engaged in the antebellum practice of "lining out" hymns, first reciting the verses in a singsong prompt before overlaying the melody. To sanctify the arrival of the pastor's sermon, ushers hooked velvet ropes across the aisles to announce that any moving about, including trips to the downstairs bathrooms, was henceforth suspended. Those practices endure to this day.

And yet, there was a spirit to the place, born of common experience and shared purpose, that Glover believed he could harness. Even with two thousand members, Emanuel felt like a family. Those who grew up in the church under Glover recall walking to Calhoun Street each Sunday morning and staying much of the day. If an unattended child detoured into a corner shop to buy candy with his Sunday-school offering, his parents would likely hear about it before the service ended. This is not to say that limits weren't tested. Girls played patty-cake in their seats until they were shushed or bribed with a peppermint. Two particularly rambunctious boys had a habit of scampering under the pews during worship, prompting Pastor Glover, who happened to be their father, to stop in midsentence, call them by name—"Shawn! Bruce!"—and order them back to their seats.

The church was usually packed on Sundays, especially the first one of the month, when congregants came to the altar rail to kneel for communion. Large extended families might fill one pew and part of the next. "We were a massive body of Christ at that time," remembered Sharon Coakley, a second-generation member who walked to Emanuel from a house down Calhoun Street. "Of course, church was all day. We started with Sunday school. We'd go home to eat breakfast, whatever my mom would make, and then we would come back. There was no conversation about going to church or to the Easter program."

Inside Emanuel's walls, men and women could be simply that, men and women, unsubordinated by the whim of the dominant caste. They could lead and hold positions of authority in ways that the public and private sectors did not yet allow. A Black South Carolinian in the 1930s could not aspire to become so much as a notary public, much less a bank president or state senator. At Emanuel, however, men and women could be elected trustees and stewards, appointed as committee chairs and class leaders, and showcased as choir soloists and dramatic leads. "During the week you may drive a bus or something," said Emanuel member Harold Washington, a retired transportation supervisor for a utility company who spent five years on the trustee board. "But on Sunday you got your shirt and tie on and you can stand up. You have value." All week, Emanuel's members were at the mercy and direction of white people, but in church they displayed their gifts and commanded respect. Unburdened, at least for the Sabbath, they floated freely. "I recall as a child that it was a safe place," said Ruby Nesbitt Martin, a retired educator and Emanuel stalwart, "a place where we were all accepted, people embraced us, protected us, and taught us. It was a happy place ... There were not too many other places you could go except for the Boys & Girls Club. That and the church was what was available to us."

As Martin suggests, this sense of community prevailed largely as a matter of necessity. Traditional housing patterns dictated by the compactness of the Charleston peninsula and the architecture of slavery kept the city from being as residentially segregated as others in the South. Indeed, one study found that housing patterns in Charleston in 1940 were less segregated than in any major U.S. city. But separation and subordination were nonetheless white policy priorities in any setting that might bring the races together: restaurants, hotels, theaters, schools, buses, trains, ships, restrooms, parks, playgrounds, swimming pools. "We'd be on the Blacks-only side of the beach and I'd think how do they keep that water from coming over and becoming part of this water," Sharon Coakley remembered of her family's trips to segregated Riverside Beach on the Wando River. Even the prospect of an enemy air raid could not dislodge white Charleston from its commitment to apartheid. In February 1942, two and a half months after the attack on Pearl Harbor, *The News and Courier* published a useful guide to nineteen civilian emergency shelters in case the city, with its Navy Yard, became the next target for Axis bombers. Like everything else, the shelters were designated by race—eleven white and eight "colored," some only a block apart, as was the case with those at "colored" Emanuel AME and white Citadel Square Baptist.

If there was a personification of Mother Emanuel during this period, it was her beloved "Mama Hilda," as the church's first female assistant minister, Hilda Blanche Scott, was known to all. Born in Charleston in 1914, Scott had no biological children but effectively adopted every youngster who passed through Emanuel's Sunday school for the better part of fifty years. Scott saw it as her God-driven mission to instill confidence in Black children who had few opportunities to prove themselves. She set an example for the church's many strong-willed women in the process, as well as for their daughters.

"She knew everybody and was in everybody's business," remembered Dorothy Jenkins, a third-generation member who grew up in the 1950s and 1960s. "She would spurt out words of encouragement and wisdom to keep us motivated and along the path. She made sure I knew how to conduct myself as a young lady, in and out of the church. There were things I could and couldn't do, expectations that were required of me. Girls had to sit a certain way, you don't have your legs open, have them crossed at the ankle, make sure your dress was below the knee, you had to have your hat and gloves and pocketbooks and stockings. So just old, traditional-type things to make sure you had the right kind of character, that you had respect for yourself as well as others, that you transferred the love that God gave you to others, that you treated others the way you wanted to be treated."

It was during Glover's pastorship that Hilda Scott broke Emanuel's stained-glass ceiling. As a General Conference delegate, she supported the resolution that finally authorized the full ordination of women, and then became one of the first to take advantage of it. Although unsalaried, she was everywhere in the church at once, a tireless dervish, not only superintending the Sunday school but also the children's Sunbeam Choir, the Jubilaires Chorus, and the Willing Workers Club. When there were leftovers from church dinners, it was Scott who packed them up and delivered them to shut-ins and others who needed a helping hand. She took preaching duties on occasion when the pastor was elsewhere and was authorized to administer the sacraments. But her singular focus was Emanuel's children. Despite her diminutive stature, Mama Hilda meted out tough love one earlobe twist at a time; the mere wag of her index finger set teenagers atremble. She made a practice of requiring recalcitrant children to sing, recite, pray, and perform in public, often with little notice, taking only "Yes, Ma'am" for an answer. A lifelong non-driver, she walked through the city's toughest neighborhoods to get to Emanuel and to members' homes, but never had to worry about being disrespected. When she retired in 1994, two bishops showed up to pay tribute (Scott died in late 2002).

"She just taught us, bullied us, pushed us out to do things," Ruby Martin said. Scott insisted that every child participate in youth services, and Martin remembered the Easter Sunday when Mama Hilda realized she had neglected to save a speaking part for Martin's young niece.

"Well," she told the child, "you're going to play the piano.'"

"I can't play the piano," the girl explained.

"Well, you're going to play," Mama Hilda explained back.

"And so she just went up there and plunked away," Martin said, "the same thing over and over again. My husband looked at me and said, 'Did Debbie take music?' And I said, 'No.'"

After the service, the Martins asked their niece what made her think she could play the piano in front of the whole church. "Because Rev. Hilda said I could," she explained.

The team of Scott and Glover provided Emanuel with stable, self-assured leadership for an uncommonly long period that was otherwise marked by external unrest. It helped that Glover preached with command, that he knew where he stood, that he spoke his mind. "Dad would slap the back of his hand in the other and people would know he was meaning business," Oveta Glover recalled. Glover carried himself with dignity, feeling that first impressions meant more for a Black man in the South. He wore a suit and tie to church, of course, but also to the feed store. "Straight off the pages of *GQ* magazine," remembered his nephew Gean Glover. "I remember him going to Europe, and they came to stay for a couple of days before they left from New York, and he had this huge steamer chest, a suit for every day of the week and shoes to match, ties. I've never seen a man with a wardrobe like that."

Congregants did not always approve of Glover's activism, but they admired his carriage, courage, and forthrightness. Glover had no problem chastising a congregation for inadequate piety, even if it was not his own. When guest-preaching at Bethel AME in Columbia in 1966, he interrupted his sermon to call out his listeners for their indifference. "I've been sitting here joining in, but some of you, I've watched you ever since you came into church, you haven't said a thing," he scolded. "You haven't bowed your head when they were praying, you didn't join in the singing, you didn't take the Scripture to read the Scripture... If you believe it, I want you to voice it." Glover signed letters to his congregants with a stern instruction: "Pray every day and attend Church each week."

Glover's pulpit style comes through in a sermon he delivered about the Parable of the Sower, the same text chosen by Myra Thompson for Bible study on the night of the 2015 massacre. In Glover's treatment, the four types of soil—wayside, stony, thorny, good—represented four types of churchgoers. "Whether one is helped by going to church depends not so much on the church or the preacher but upon himself," he began. There was a place, he said, for "stony soil people" whose spirit for religion was loud but shallow. "We sometimes refer to certain people as 'religious fanatics,'" Glover said, "but I'd rather try to restrain a fanatic than to resurrect a corpse." He analogized the seed that fell among thorns to those who received God's word but then lost it in their busy-ness. "Gradually God is choked out," he said. Glover mused that his deepest challenges often came from within his own church. "Every preacher is a prisoner of his congregation," he said. "In my denomination the bishop moves the preacher. I think sometimes he ought to move the congregation and let the preacher stay."

Glover preached theatrically, with his whole body. He was not above hurdling the altar rail if the congregation needed a jolt. "I still have an appreciation for preachers who preach like him," said Sonya Fordham, a history teacher whose family has attended Emanuel since the nineteenth century. "All that jumping up and down. He did do a lot of movement, but it was to evoke a feeling. He really made you feel like you had been to church." Another lifelong member, Melvin L. Graham, Jr., remembered that his mother stayed inspired by a Glover sermon long after leaving the sanctuary. "My Mom would just get in the spirit, because she loved the way he preached," said Graham, whose sister, Cynthia Hurd, was among the victims of the 2015 attack. "She'd say, 'He tore the church up this morning.'"

GLOVER'S DISPOSITION TOWARD CONFRONTATION, spurred by the trauma of his youth, ran headlong at times into the preservationist instincts of his denomination and his congregation. He surely felt pulled one way by the urgency of civil-rights activism and another by the institutionalist culture of African Methodism and its bishops. As at many AME churches, Emanuel included, the spirit of resistance waxed and waned across time among the denomination's national leadership. By the height of the civil-rights era, there certainly were bishops who had earned reputations as key strategists, negotiators, and firebrands. But until then, the global AME church rarely seemed in the vanguard, its voice often fainter than it might have been for a body of its size and potential strength (membership exceeded 1 million by 1950, in a nation of 151 million people). Its fixation on survival remained paramount. And so as essential as the Black church would become to the protest movement, it often exerted a conservative influence in the decades preceding it. The church of Jesus Christ, the uncompromising radical, at times held militancy in check.

That could be particularly true in a place like South Carolina, where the inclination toward gradualism was nourished by a prolonged and subjugating experience with slavery and the economic constraints of Jim Crow. Only in Mississippi and Arkansas did Black Americans have a lower median income in 1950. In no state was the racial income gap wider, with the median for white people ($1,684) more than three times that for nonwhite people ($525). There was not much cushion to absorb economic reprisal, or many routes to escape the pathologies of poverty. Under those circumstances, Black preachers often "found it easier to denounce black sin than white racism and were readier to save souls than to face the social and economic problems of their community," observed Idus A. Newby in his 1973 history of Black Carolinians in the twentieth century. "They engaged Satan in the fiercest kind of combat, but the white man was too menacing to challenge."

Every four years, the AME bishops collaborated on a published address to the General Conference that served as a denominational state of the union. Only occasionally in the span from 1892 to 1952 did they use that platform to directly confront the policies and practices that subjugated every African American in the church's most populous region, or to propose direct action against them. As Black Americans were forced to defend themselves against charges of moral degradation, the denomination focused on "uplifting the race" through imperatives like temperance, marital fidelity, and the Methodist work ethic. In their attention to the wages of sin and the heavenly reward, the bishops at times barely mentioned race at all. At others, they wrote with blinders willfully affixed. "We have great reason to rejoice that we live in this wonderful age which furnishes us with so many opportunities to do good and to work for the elevation of our race and the salvation of mankind," they proclaimed in 1896. The only consideration of race that year was a defensive one, a rejection of those who accused African Americans of "ignorance, immorality, indifference and disregard for the marriage vow." In 1900, a year when at least eighty-nine Black Americans were lynched, the bishops pronounced the condition of the race only to be "not the most satisfying."

The AME bishops gradually grew more vocal about lynching, voter disenfranchisement, and obnoxious Jim Crow laws (particularly those that segregated itinerant Black preachers into second-class railroad cars). They did so, however, while warning against antagonizing white people. "We would caution against attempts at revenge or retaliation, because such a course would be unchristian and because, for us, it would be suicidal," they wrote in 1940. "We would remind our group of the fact that it is as much a sin for a black man to hate a white man as it is for the latter to hate the former." They encouraged their followers to obey the law and to "refrain from doing or saying such things as might be provocative of ill feeling or might be used as incitements to prejudice and violence."

The pressure to be more aggressive accelerated as Black servicemen returned from World War II—and families mourned those who didn't—only to find that the freedoms they fought and died for did not apply to them. In 1952, the bishops' tone grew less patient: "Racial inequalities and injustices cannot be tolerated in a country which calls itself democratic, for Democracy can become a corpse when its living spirit is not renewed and nourished." By 1964, with the makeup of the leadership changed by three elections, they were cloaking themselves in the militancy of the day. "We are in revolt against the prejudiced power structure all over the world," they wrote. "Theorizing is no longer appreciated and gradualism has lost the war. Direct action, even where personally costly for individuals and institutions, is the order of the day." That was true enough, but direct action had already been the order of the day for quite some time, as this was nine years after Rosa Parks and the Montgomery bus boycott, four years after the Greensboro sit-ins, and three years after the Freedom Rides. The church, the bishops wrote self-referentially that year, had been "hesitant, at first" but "has now become an integral part of the movement." They declared themselves "strong supporters" of the NAACP.

The NAACP considered Black churches natural allies in organizing and fundraising, and Mother Emanuel's ties to the Charleston branch date almost to its origins. Although Emanuel members do not seem to have been among Edwin A. Harleston's band of pioneers in 1917, the local branch began meeting at the church as early as June 1919, when it announced an ambitious goal to sign up two thousand members. The following year, on September 15, 1920, an NAACP mass meeting at Emanuel featured a talk by William Pickens, the South Carolina–born assistant national field secretary. Robert W. Bagnall, the national director of branches and an AME preacher, addressed an assembly at Emanuel on November 3, 1921. In addition to B. J. Glover, four of the church's pastors held significant NAACP titles at points in their careers—Jesse E. Beard (Charleston branch president), R. E. Brogdon (state conference second vice president), H. B. Butler (Charleston branch first vice president) and Alonzo W. Holman (state conference president). When Glover was pastor, the church hosted the association's Southeastern regional conference in February 1956, its statewide convention in October 1958, and the kickoff for a major membership drive in 1962. He made the church a life member of the NAACP at a not insubstantial cost of $500. Walter White, the NAACP's executive secretary, spoke at Emanuel in 1954 on the eve of the *Brown v. Board of Education* decision, and his successor, Roy Wilkins, ascended the pulpit several times in the latter 1950s and 1960s. At the 1958 conference at Emanuel, Ruby Hurley, the Southeast regional secretary, suggested that every branch have a committee devoted to church relations. "NAACP needs the church and the church needs the NAACP," Hurley said. "Let us remember that we are Christians. We will come out on top if we put on the whole Armor of God, and tell the truth. Let us put on the 'Breast Plate' of righteousness."

Within a few years of its founding, the Charleston branch of the NAACP racked up several credibility-boosting victories. It pushed successfully for repeal of the law requiring white teachers in Black schools, pressured the Charleston Navy Yard to hire Black women in its clothing factory, and spotlighted racial crimes in which Black people had been victimized or unfairly prosecuted. In 1946, the group brought national attention to the brutal beating and blinding of a newly discharged but still uniformed and decorated Black serviceman, Sgt. Isaac Woodard, Jr., by a white police chief in Batesburg, South Carolina. And yet, between the fear of reprisal and the migration of potential members to the North, maintaining an active membership proved a recurring challenge. Infighting and unfocused leadership also played a role, and Charleston's NAACP branch was all but dormant for stretches. In the mid-1930s, South Carolina ranked dead last in branch payments sent to the national organization—a pathetic one one-hundredth of the total. After touring Charleston's segregated parks and schools in 1932, Bagnall, the national director of branches, wrote that the city's Black residents were noted "for their complacent satisfaction with their 'good race relations.'" Seven years later, W. H. Miller, the Charleston branch president, complained to national officials that the members he had been able to muster tended to be "dilatory, lethargic and non-committal." Black Charleston, he wrote, was "obsessed with unmitigated fear of the dominant group and in consequence moves with the greatest caution."

Boosted by a series of successful court fights in the 1940s, the NAACP strengthened its presence in South Carolina by the early 1950s. Although South Carolina was the smallest of seven Deep South states, and fifth in the number of Black residents, it by then had the most NAACP members—just more than seven thousand in 1952. Under pressure from the white Citizens' Councils, which formed to resist implementation of the *Brown v. Board* decision, the state legislature responded in 1956 by enacting a series of measures aimed at prolonging segregation. One of the most egregious barred NAACP members from employment by state or local governments, including in schools, and required the signing of an oath. After the NAACP challenged the measure, the state softened the law to require only a listing of an employee's affiliations. But the tactic remained ruthlessly effective. Dozens of educators lost their jobs, including Septima Poinsette Clark and Lydia Glover, Rev. Glover's wife, who had been teaching in the Charleston schools. To help support her family, she left South Carolina in 1960 to teach home economics at a historically Black college—Kentucky State in Frankfort—while her children were still young and her husband was pastoring at Emanuel. Relatives helped care for the kids. The impact of the fear campaign was measurable: NAACP membership in South Carolina plummeted from 8,266 in 1955 to 1,418 in 1958.

Until the late 1950s, the NAACP's greatest achievements in South Carolina stemmed from its role as a civil-rights law firm. The group litigated landmark federal lawsuits that led to the equalization of pay in Charleston for Black and white teachers (*Duvall v. J. F. Seignous*, 1944); the elimination of South Carolina's whites-only Democratic primary (*Elmore v. Rice*, 1947); the opening of a law school for Black students at South Carolina State College in Orangeburg (*Wrighten v. Board of Trustees*, 1947); and the desegregation of purportedly "separate but equal" schools (*Briggs v. Elliott*, 1951). Each of those cases placed the NAACP's legal mastermind, Thurgood Marshall, before one of the most intriguing Charlestonians of his generation, the renegade federal judge J. Waties Waring. Judge Waring—Waties was his mother's maiden name—also presided over the trial of Isaac Woodard's attacker, and had been sickened by the police chief's acquittal by an all-white jury.

Waring made for the unlikeliest of civil-rights groundbreakers. An eighth-generation white Charlestonian and the scion of former slaveholding Confederates, he enjoyed impeccable credentials among the city's bluebloods, with a respected law practice, a house south of Broad, and all the right social, political, and church connections. The town was scandalized, therefore, when the sixty-four-year-old judge split with his wife of nearly thirty-two years and immediately married an opinionated, racially progressive, twice-divorced woman from the North. White Charlestonians grew even more appalled by the judge's increasingly anti-segregationist rulings and their provocative language.

Few cases would be more important in the careers of Waring and Marshall than *Briggs,* which was later consolidated with appeals from Kansas, Virginia, and Delaware into the *Brown v. Board* challenge. It was the first of the *Brown* cases to be filed, decided, and appealed, and the one from deepest in the South. It was in *Briggs* that Marshall, with Waring's explicit prodding and strategic counsel, shifted tactics to directly challenge the constitutionality of school segregation rather than seeking equity in separate facilities. As expected, a three-judge panel sitting in Charleston rejected Marshall's argument in a 2-to-1 decision that required the equalization of separate Black and white schools. But the approach taken by Waring in his bold dissent, that separate facilities constituted "per se inequality," provided the blueprint for the Warren court's ruling in *Brown* that segregated schools were "inherently unequal" and thus unconstitutional.

The *Briggs* litigation challenged school segregation in Clarendon County, the Blackest county in South Carolina and one of the poorest and most virulently racist. Situated north of Charleston, Clarendon spent four times more on each white student than on each Black one, paid white teachers two-thirds more than their Black counterparts, and transported white schoolchildren on buses while Black students walked for miles along muddy roads. The plaintiffs had been organized by Rev. Joseph A. De Laine, an AME minister, educator, and local NAACP leader. Like others involved in the case, De Laine encountered significant retaliation. He lost his teaching job and dodged the bullets of nightriders, only to face assault and battery charges for firing back with a shotgun. His house was burned, his church was vandalized. When the denomination transferred him to a church in Lake City, anonymous letters threatened that he would suffer the same fate as Frazier Baker, the Black postmaster lynched there in 1898. Eventually De Laine was spirited out of South Carolina for New York, where he was shielded from extradition (South Carolina officials symbolically dropped the shooting charges at a ceremony in 2000, twenty-six years after De Laine's death).

When Judge Waring retired in 1952 at age seventy-one, six months after the *Briggs* decision, he and his wife, Elizabeth, decamped immediately for New York. They felt socially and politically ostracized, and until being buried in Charleston in 1968 Waring returned to his hometown only once, in 1954, to attend an NAACP dinner in his honor. It wasn't that Waring had not received other invitations. B. J. Glover extended one in May 1961, when he was both pastor of Emanuel and president of Charleston's NAACP. It is not clear which hat Glover was wearing, or whether Waring's appearance was to be at the church. But Glover was a longtime admirer of Waring. Two days after the *Briggs* ruling, he had written the judge with his compliments. "It is quite evident as shown in the Clarendon county school segregation case that you are still aware of the fact that this is not a true democracy and that you believe in the Fatherhood of God and the Brotherhood of Man," Glover wrote. "Your dissenting vote . . . places one more mile, in an indirect manner, on the road to progress." Waring responded immediately that it was heartening to hear from someone "who does not have to be told of the injustice and sufferings caused by the false doctrines of racial supremacy."

Glover may have been stunned, therefore, when he received a blistering response from Waring to his invitation to visit Charleston. The retired judge had spent his exile brooding about what he saw as the reluctance of Black Carolinians to take full advantage of rulings he felt he had presented on a silver platter. It was fully seven years after *Brown*, but white-controlled state governments across the South had largely succeeded in their campaign of "massive resistance" to school desegregation. No Black student had yet shared a classroom with a white one in Charleston and none would for another two years. To Waring, South Carolina in the early 1960s did not seem so different from South Carolina in 1948, when its Dixiecrat governor, Strom Thurmond, swore that "there's not enough troops in the Army to force the Southern people to break down segregation and admit the Negro race into our theaters, into our swimming pools, into our homes, and into our churches." From the perch of his small apartment on Fifth Avenue, the former judge blamed the NAACP for not keeping legal heat on the states and blamed Black Carolinians for not using the voting strength he had granted in *Elmore*.

Waring began by explaining to Glover that Elizabeth was too ill to travel, and he would not leave her, so they could not make it to Charleston. But he did not leave it at that.

"There is another and more potent reason," he began, laying out his post-*Brown* critique. "The Negroes (represented by the N.A.A.C.P.) in South Carolina sat on their hands and the Clarendon Case died. It is impossible for Courts to help people when they abandon cases which have been won for them." Waring's fingers seemed to type more furiously with each sentence. It was not for him, now an outsider, to return to Charleston to "urge the Colored people of South Carolina to do that which they are unwilling to do for themselves." Movement leaders in other states had been marching and sitting in, putting their lives and livelihoods at risk, he said. He did not acknowledge that some, including Glover, had already been doing so in South Carolina. "I hope that some day in the future the Colored citizens of South Carolina will awaken to the fact that the locks on the door leading to freedom have been broken; but that the people living in semi-slavery must themselves be willing to walk through the door and not wait to be carried . . . One who accepts tyranny does not deserve freedom."

B. J. Glover, of all people, did not need the sermon. He may have taken it to heart, however, as the next few years would be tumultuous ones in Charleston, and Emanuel's pastor would soon place himself, his family, and his church in the midst of the maelstrom.

XIV.

The Movement Church

*The law of the Spirit of life in Christ Jesus hath
made me free from the law of sin and death.*

—ROMANS 8:2 (KJV)

B. J. Glover had been thinking since at least the late 1940s about how to weaponize Black economic power to wage a guerilla war against segregation. Yes, the NAACP had won important victories in the courts, and notably in South Carolina, generating a sense of building momentum. But cases slogged through the judicial system. Months might be spent searching for plaintiffs who had to be both fearless and faultless. Then came the filings and discovery periods and battles over standing. Eventually there might be a trial, followed by rounds of appeals. It took years to get favorable rulings and years more and additional litigation to force adherence in states that were hell-bent on circumventing them. Constitutionalism was by no means an accommodationist approach to seeking equal rights, but it was undeniably a deliberate one, with its indignation robed in the civilities of the courtroom.

Meanwhile, Black residents of postwar America had grown less patient, B. J. Glover included. Black soldiers had returned to the South from the front lines, or not returned at all, and found that their sacrifices had not earned them basic respect, much less equal treatment. In cities like Charleston, the inequities bequeathed by segregation had become so glaring by 1950 that Black residents increasingly felt they had little to lose by speaking out. The Lowcountry offered almost no way out of economic subjugation. Of the 11,769 Black working men in metropolitan Charleston, only 257 were considered professionals, and almost all of them were preachers or teachers. There were nine doctors, six dentists, a single lawyer, one pharmacist. The city had no Black engineers, architects, or accountants. Among Black women, more than 60 percent worked as housekeepers, cooks, waitresses, beauticians, and the like. Unemployment in Charleston for Black workers stood at 13 percent, more than triple the white rate. There were few hospital beds for Black patients, and Black schools were so crowded that they had to conduct multiple sessions each day. The median number of grades completed by nonwhite students was five, roughly half the figure for white students. Nearly half of Black residences in Charleston did not have running water and 6 in 10 did not have indoor toilets.

By the time Glover arrived at Emanuel in 1953, he felt firmly that passivity was no longer an option in the face of such conditions. He also believed that Black Carolinians did not need a Howard University law degree like Thurgood Marshall's to have an impact. The men and women who toiled all week as mill workers and housekeepers, who shopped on King Street on Saturday and prayed at Emanuel on Sunday, had the power of their pocketbooks at hand. Glover believed it might prevail where moral suasion had not. Why should Black Carolinians continue to patronize establishments that made a policy of disrespecting them? "If Negroes would organize their buying power," Glover wrote in 1949, "it would improve job opportunities and give employment to more of our own group . . . We could lift ourselves above the 'have to take it or leave it' stage in buying and living, fight for fair employment practices, establish cooperatives and reduce costs."

It would be another decade—several years past the groundbreaking Montgomery, Alabama, bus boycott—before Glover and others could test that theory in South Carolina. On February 1, 1960, the sit-in movement catalyzed when four freshmen from North Carolina A&T State College occupied a Woolworth's lunch counter in Greensboro. Within two weeks, their innovation in passive resistance spread to Black college towns throughout that state and then across the border to a department store in Rock Hill, South Carolina. It advanced quickly to Columbia, Florence, Sumter, Orangeburg, and Greenville, where seven Black teenagers were arrested for walking into a public library designated for white users. By early April, Black students from Charleston's Burke High School—there was no Black college in town—had orchestrated the city's first protest at the S. H. Kress department store on King Street, known for its sand-colored Art Deco façade. Some were as young as sixteen. Without the knowledge of their parents, they had prepared by role-playing nonviolent responses to being cursed at, shoved in the back, and spat upon.

On the morning of April 1, sixteen boys and eight girls, dressed as if for church, took seats side by side at the lunch counter and asked to be served. The manager directed them to leave, and a waitress doused the counter with pungent ammonia to encourage their departure. When they refused and instead began reciting the Lord's Prayer and Psalm 23, the manager summoned the chief of police, William F. Kelly, who ordered the students' arrests after a six-hour standoff. The teenagers were bonded out that evening for $10 apiece by J. Arthur Brown, president of the local branch of the NAACP. They included his daughter, Minerva, and a pair of intrepid young agitators from Burke High School named James Blake and Harvey Gantt.

Gantt, who was both an outstanding student and the football team's quarterback, remembered attending a meeting soon after in Mother Emanuel's basement. Matthew J. Perry, Jr., who was fast becoming the state's leading civil-rights lawyer (and later won appointment as its first Black federal judge), spoke to the students about the legal implications of what they had done. He assured them that the trespassing charges they faced were minor and would not leave a lasting stain on their records (indeed, the U.S. Supreme Court eventually reversed their convictions). He also said that the NAACP, which had called for national boycotts of discriminatory department stores, would back them wholeheartedly. "He said, 'You guys are going to be okay, you're going to be able to go to college,'" Gantt recalled. "Most of us were seniors in high school and that's what our parents were concerned about, that it would keep us from going to college." Perry encouraged the students to keep at it and aim even higher, a message that stuck with Gantt. "You guys did a very brave thing," Perry said, "and there is a lot of ground to plow to get us to first-class status. Perhaps one of these days one of you folks will step forward and go even further. You might even go to Clemson or the University of South Carolina." It had never occurred to Gantt that he as a Black student might enroll at one of the state's segregated flagship universities. But two years later Perry filed the lawsuit that led to Gantt's admission as the first Black student at Clemson. He married the second Black student there, Lucinda Brawley, graduated with honors in architecture, continued his training at the Massachusetts Institute of Technology, set up an urban design practice in Charlotte, North Carolina, and in 1983 won the first of his two terms as that city's first Black mayor.

Five days after the initial Charleston sit-in, the NAACP's local leadership called a mass meeting at Ebenezer AME Church that attracted five hundred people, including several of the student demonstrators. Pastor Glover, then first vice president of the Charleston branch, called for Black shoppers to boycott three King Street department stores with segregated lunch counters—W. T. Grant, S. H. Kress, and F. W. Woolworth. "We don't feel we should spend money where we can't get equal service," he said. J. Arthur Brown told the students in the crowd that "the NAACP didn't send you, but we'll stand behind you now."

Regular picketing of the stores began, with Mother Emanuel serving as a staging ground. Glover used the announcements section of the church bulletin to advertise mass meetings and encourage discipline during the boycott, particularly once the holiday season arrived. "NO CHRISTMAS GIFT BUYING," the program urged one Sunday in December 1960. "'Abhor That Which Is Evil', We Know That discriminations And Injustice Are Evil—WOOLWORTH, KRESS, GRANTS Are Known To Practice Discrimination And Injustice, We Must Show Our Resentment To Merchants Who Continue To Treat Individuals As Second Class Citizens. God Gave His Son, The Son Gave His Life—To All—For All—The Human Family." The sit-ins continued into the next year, and the police regularly hauled demonstrators off to jail, with Chief Kelly on the scene to ensure proper handling. In contrast to other Southern cities, the students were not beaten or taunted in front of news cameras, a reflection perhaps of Charleston's gentility and of the shrewdness of its mercantile and political classes. "The white power structure in South Carolina has been smart and diplomatic," Glover observed a few years later. "Conditions here are the same as in Alabama and Mississippi—only they don't throw tear gas bombs at you."

Nonetheless, the accelerating movement for civil rights had taken a turn in Charleston as it did elsewhere, moving urgently into the streets with students as its foot soldiers. B. J. Glover's own daughter, Oveta, would become one of them.

In the wake of the *Brown v. Board* ruling, South Carolina, like other states of the former Confederacy, had devoted itself to massive resistance to school integration. But anticipating that the federal courts would, at the least, require some equalization of resources for Black and white schools (as they had in *Briggs*), the state legislature passed a $75 million school construction program in 1951, financed by a three-cent sales tax. For the first time in decades, new schools for Black students were built in Charleston and grudging improvements were made at existing ones, including at Burke High. At the same time, however, the legislature established a "segregation committee" tasked with finding legal, if circuitous, means of preserving the racial status quo. South Carolina's schools also continued to indoctrinate students from a white supremacist framework. In the mid-1960s, the cover of the standard state history text still featured a statue of Confederate general Wade Hampton on horseback. The book depicted Reconstruction as the work of carpetbaggers and scalawags and asserted that South Carolina had been governed then by "a ruthless band of thieves" who "managed to break up the old feeling of friendship and confidence" between Black and white people. The Ku Klux Klan, in the view of the author, Mary C. Simms Oliphant, was at first "intended only as a means of maintaining order" and of imposing justice in cases "when the courts did not punish Negroes who were supposed to have committed crimes."

Not surprisingly, B. J. Glover and other NAACP leaders took little satisfaction from the state's efforts to shore up the "equal" component of separate-but-equal. The Glovers lived in Emanuel's two-story parsonage at 529 Rutledge Avenue, directly across the street from an inviting playground and, beyond it, Julian Mitchell Elementary School. It was a signpost of segregation that the playground and the school, both so tantalizingly close, were reserved for white families only. This was naturally bewildering to young Black children, and B. J. and Lydia Glover's stern instructions to their daughters to avoid the park only made the temptation more irresistible. "We used to run across the street and swing real fast and run back home before we got caught," Oveta Glover remembered. Her parents offered little explanation when Oveta asked why she could not swing and slide like the white children she watched through a front window. "One day, baby, one day you'll be able to play there," her father assured her.

That made it all the more amazing to six-year-old Oveta when her father took her by the hand on the morning of October 10, 1960, and walked her across the verboten terrain to enroll at Mitchell Elementary. She had been outfitted that morning in her gray Sunday dress with puffy white sleeves. Once through the park, Glover led his tiny first grader up the stone steps and past the towering Ionic columns guarding the entrance to the school. She felt him squeeze her hand. "Baby, just hold on to me," he told her. "I got you." As they walked down the hallway, a chubby white boy jabbed her in the hip with a pencil. "Go home, N-word," Oveta Glover said the boy ordered. She lunged to go after him but her father tightened his grip. "Don't lose your dignity," he instructed. In the school office, the principal studied Oveta's transfer paperwork and explained that she could not be admitted because of an oversight—the principal of her former school had failed to write in the name of the new school. Six decades later, Oveta could still recall her father's crestfallen response. "The sadness on his face, it was like I had died or something," she said. "He turned around, and as we were leaving he said, 'We're going to do it one day.'"

The Glovers were not alone that October morning in an effort that had been loosely coordinated among activist parents. J. Arthur Brown, who had recently ascended to the state presidency of the NAACP, also was rebuffed in his attempt to enroll his daughter, Minerva, and another Burke student, Ralph Dawson, at the all-white High School of Charleston. White Charleston was, of course, outraged by the audacity of the Black parents in seeking to carry out a six-year-old Supreme Court mandate. In reporting on it the next day, Charleston's reactionary newspapers published the street addresses of the Glovers and Dawsons, just in case anyone needed to find them. Several weeks later, the city school board formally rejected applications for the transfers, finding that they had been filed late. That decision helped trigger a boycott in which Black parents kept 8,513 children—94 percent of the total—out of school for a day in a protest against crowded classrooms. For an untested community, and one reputed for its meekness, Black Charlestonians showed impressive solidarity. At one elementary school, so crowded that it ran three sessions a day, only 3 students out of 1,002 showed up for class. The day ended with a mass meeting at Emanuel, where Glover, now president of the Charleston NAACP, orchestrated the unanimous and thunderous approval of a resolution urging Black parents to seek enrollment at the schools closest to their homes, regardless of their racial designation. Community leaders said they hoped to avoid the kind of sensational ugliness that accompanied school integration in Charlotte and Little Rock. They pleaded with white Charlestonians to accept the inevitable.

It would take another three years and further federal intervention. But in August 1963, the Browns, Glovers, and five other families that had sued Charleston's school system after the failed enrollment attempts won an unassailable desegregation order from a United States District Court judge. The Black students and parents were represented by the NAACP's Matthew J. Perry, Jr., from Columbia, and Constance Baker Motley, from New York. At a hearing, school officials acknowledged that per capita spending on white students far outpaced that for Black students—$267 versus $170. Judge J. Robert Martin rejected the arguments of school officials that Black children were intellectually inferior based on genetic differences and that the segregation of Charleston's schools served "the best interest of both races." It was the state's first desegregation order affecting elementary and secondary schools. Minerva Brown had graduated and moved on to Lincoln University, but her younger sister, Millicent, replaced her as lead plaintiff. Named second was Oveta Glover, still in elementary school.

Because the ruling came down just weeks before fall classes began, Judge Martin did not subject the city to the chaos of an immediate system-wide desegregation. Instead, he ordered that the named plaintiffs be enrolled the next month and that the entire system of nine Black and six white schools desegregate the following academic year. This gave white parents time to move their children to private "segregation academies" if they desired, and many did. From 1963 to 1967, the white share of the city's public school population dropped from 25 percent to 14 percent.

On September 3, nine-year-old Oveta, accompanied once again by her father, entered the fourth grade at James Simons Elementary (Julian Mitchell Elementary had closed). There were no incidents that day and few reports of overt hostility in the classroom throughout the fall. But at the Glover home, the mere ring of the telephone invoked terror. "We're going to kill your daddy," a man threatened when Oveta answered. "Tell your daddy don't walk out the door." She summoned her mother, who told her to hang up. Eventually, her parents prohibited her from answering. Living with fear put strains on the family and on the marriage. "They're going to kill you, B. J.," Lydia Glover would wail. "And you're going to get my baby killed." But her father was resolute and convinced of his calling, Oveta Glover remembered. "A train couldn't have knocked him off the tracks back then," she said.

AS THE DIRECT-ACTION CAMPAIGN took shape in South Carolina, Rev. Glover seemed to spend as much time in the streets as he did in the pulpit. The most consequential demonstration took place on March 2, 1961, in Columbia, when Glover joined the state NAACP field director, I. DeQuincey Newman, in leading scores of high school and college students in a march on the copper-domed State Capitol Building. With the legislature in session, police officers allowed the protesters to walk through the grounds for about forty-five minutes, carrying placards with slogans like "Down with segregation." But when a large crowd of onlookers assembled, the officers gave the group a deadline to disperse. The protesters responded by singing hymns and

"The Star-Spangled Banner," leading the authorities to detain 190 of them, including Glover and Newman, in one of the largest mass arrests of the era. Without enough police wagons, officers paraded scores of youngsters on foot to the city and county jails. Bond was set at $50 for each person charged with breaching the peace, an offense that carried a possible sentence of up to thirty days or a $100 fine. Glover spent about five hours in jail. At trial before a city magistrate two weeks later, he testified that he had "no intention of being arrested" but "felt there was no better time nor place to demonstrate than on the Capitol grounds which is the seat of our policymaking."

Almost all of the accused were found guilty, including Glover, Newman, and future congressman James Clyburn, who was twenty at the time. After South Carolina's Supreme Court upheld the convictions, the case of *Edwards v. South Carolina*—named for one of the student protesters—landed before the U.S. Supreme Court. In a landmark opinion in 1963, the Warren court vacated the convictions and ruled that the First and Fourteenth Amendments guaranteed rights of free speech, assembly, and petition to demonstrators, so long as they were lawful and peaceful. Writing for the 8-to-1 majority, Justice Potter Stewart explained that the demonstrators at the Capitol had been exercising their First Amendment freedoms "in their most pristine and classic form." The Constitution, he wrote, "does not permit a State to make criminal the peaceful expression of unpopular views." It was a seminal legal and strategic victory for a movement that had come to rely on nonviolent protest to communicate its message in a newly televised age.

Glover's arrest in Columbia did not deter him for long. Dressed in a dark suit and shoes so shiny they glistened, he picketed stores on King Street with torso-sized sandwich boards slung over his shoulders. DISCRIMINATION BECAUSE OF COLOR IS UNAMERICAN, one read in block letters. He encouraged church members to cancel credit card accounts at department stores that did not allow Black customers to use dressing rooms and declined to hire Black clerks. After collecting the cards in a shoebox, he presented them to managers at King Street stores like Condon's and Edward's. "That challenged the establishment," Glover said. After five weeks of relentless picketing in the spring of 1962, leading up to Easter Sunday, Glover was asked by a reporter how long the disruption might persist. "When lunch counter service is integrated and when merit is the basis for employment and not color, if it takes until Easter 1972," he said. The picketers kept track of who crossed their lines, keeping a "Judas list" that they illustrated with Polaroid snapshots. Glover boasted of filling a water pistol with black liquid shoe polish and squirting it at the backs of Black shoppers who crossed his lines, branding them as traitors to the race.

Glover detested the daily inequities of Jim Crow life, and relished tweaking white power. It grated on him, for instance, that when living in Emanuel's parsonage on Rutledge Avenue his family had to haul their laden laundry baskets past a "whites-only" launderette to reach a dingier Black facility further away. One day, Glover asked his wife to load their dirty sheets and linens into a pillowcase. He grabbed a box of Duz detergent ("For white, white washes, without red hands") and strode, alone, to the white launderette. Glover walked in like a regular and began loading tumblers and feeding coins into slots. As expected, he drew scowls from other patrons, and a quick visit from the manager, who immediately summoned the police. Glover was still stuffing in bedsheets when the patrolman arrived and threatened to arrest him.

"Where am I violating the law?" the Black preacher inquired. He nodded at the placard on the wall: "White Only." He showed the policeman the washer's contents. "Officer, I only have whites," he said. The policeman looked in the tub, glanced at the manager, and shook his head. For whatever reason, on that day, he did not want the hassle. "Leave that damn n----r preacher alone," the officer muttered, according to Glover's retelling in 2005. Glover said the launderette effectively desegregated as neighbors and friends heard his story and followed his lead.

IN APRIL 1962, Charleston's accelerating protest movement received a morale boost from the emerging national leader of the American civil-rights cause. The visit by Dr. Martin Luther King, Jr., on April 12 came at a soul-searching moment for the Baptist preacher from Atlanta, a welcome respite from the arduous public-accommodations campaign being waged in Albany, Georgia. King and other leaders of his Southern Christian Leadership Conference had been jailed there while leading a march the previous December, and the city's business and political leaders had managed to withstand ongoing boycotts. To retake the offensive, the SCLC was mounting a series of "People-to-People" tours aimed at registering thousands of Black voters and recruiting volunteers for a nonviolent protest campaign. King had already led such tours of the Mississippi Delta and central Virginia. Charleston would be the first of three stops in South Carolina, with King and SCLC leaders like Wyatt Tee Walker walking door-to-door in Black communities to urge people to register.

As the most spacious Black church in town, Emanuel drew the honor of hosting King's featured appearance. Every seat was taken that evening, main floor and gallery alike, with more than fifteen hundred in attendance. Lifelong Emanuel member Sharon Coakley, who was ten at the time, remembers her parents bringing all eight children, even the five-year-old twins, and explaining about Martin Luther King, Jr., on the way. "We all got dressed up and there were so many people," Coakley said. "I remember us not getting upstairs and her trying to get us up the side steps." The Coakley children wound up in the damp and dreary basement, where they could hear King's voice reverberate down the rear stairwell. They caught a glimpse of him, but little more.

King's appearance at Emanuel was sponsored by the Citizens Committee of Charleston County, founded by Esau Jenkins, the venerable civil-rights warrior from nearby Johns Island. A vase of white gladiolus adorned the pulpit, obscuring the view of King's seat on the podium. He was flanked to his right by Rev. Glover, sporting a necktie as thin as a ribbon, and on his left by a white man, Myles Horton, founder of the Highlander Folk School in Tennessee. Like the Penn Center on nearby St. Helena Island, Highlander had trained hundreds of activists in nonviolence and provided King and his SCLC cohorts with a refuge for planning and revitalization. In a stemwinding introduction, Jenkins encouraged the crowd to be like the agitators in washing machines. "We've got a lot of cleaning up to do in Charleston County," Jenkins said in his gravelly Sea Island accent. "And we've got one of the best agitators in the country coming here to give us some instructions." Although it was King's first trip to Charleston for the SCLC, he seemed familiar with the Lowcountry's reputation for white paternalism and Black passivity. "We must make the American dream a reality," King urged his audience at Emanuel. "We must challenge the system of segregation and make it clear we don't like it." He chided South Carolina for having only 57,000 registered voters among its more than 370,000 qualified Black residents. "Our two-year goal is to double registration in the South," King said. "If it rose from 1.3 million to four million, don't you know the governor of South Carolina would talk in different terms."

Other than to visit Penn Center, King did not venture regularly into South Carolina, seeming to recognize the NAACP's dominion in the state. His next trip of consequence to Charleston came more than five years later, in July 1967, nine months before his assassination. "Martin Luther King had less of a presence in South Carolina because the NAACP was very strong," said Andrew Young, the King lieutenant who went on to become mayor of Atlanta and ambassador to the United Nations. The NAACP's leaders in the state tended to be older and more measured than their counterparts in the SCLC and Stokely Carmichael's Student Nonviolent Coordinating Committee (SNCC), which had emerged from the sit-ins. "Because of that, I think they dealt with their problems more diplomatically than other places," Young said. "It was more rational and less emotional. After a certain age, you don't want unnecessary risk. You're not looking to be a martyr."

Two months after King's 1962 visit, the NAACP countered by sending a luminary of its own to Emanuel—the executive secretary, Roy Wilkins. A thousand people streamed into the church on a Sunday afternoon in June, their cardboard fans flapping like horsefly wings. Wilkins did not disappoint. He began by crediting Charleston for desegregating the library it had recently opened on King Street. "Real progress is being made," Wilkins said. "I have heard of no riots. Neither have I heard of any interracial marriages resulting from the fact that both whites and Negroes read the same books. Another thing that I have heard nothing about is a rise in the number of stolen books." That the region had not followed suit by desegregating its schools was disgraceful, Wilkins said. "People are going into outer space and are even ready to land on the moon," he thundered, "and you can't even get into an integrated school . . . You should not have to fight for freedoms guaranteed in the Constitution and guaranteed to us by God himself. But if we are forced to earn these freedoms, then earn them we will." When he returned to Emanuel the following year, Wilkins offered an assessment of South Carolina's distinct approach to Jim Crow. "It's a peaceful and graceful segregation," he said. "They're firm but not rough." He closed by asserting that equality was worth fighting for with any weapon except violence. "Remember, we are not fighting white people," he said. "Rather, we are fighting for an idea. You don't need guns. You only need this dynamite-like idea of freedom."

The move from the courtroom to the streets may not have been natural for the NAACP, but the group felt prodded by competition from the SCLC, SNCC, and CORE, James Farmer's Congress of Racial Equality. With the threat of violence ever present, the choice to march was not always an easy one. "It took a lot of courage to pick up a picket sign and join the other brave souls fighting for the basic freedoms guaranteed by the Constitution of this country," recounted Harvey Jones, one of Rev. Glover's youthful soldiers.

"For me, it also took anger. I was determined to live like a human being or die trying!" In what came to be known as "The Charleston Movement"—effectively a subsidiary of the NAACP—pickets and boycotts grew in intensity and size throughout the spring and summer of 1963. In addition to department stores, the list of targets expanded to include the Gloria and Riviera movie theaters, the Chow Mein Inn restaurant, Robertson's Cafeteria, Felder's Luncheonette, the Heart of Charleston Hotel, the Hampton Park playground, the George D. Burges Memorial Swimming Pool, even the briny waters off Folly Beach, where eight young Black men conducted a "wade-in."

Marches to and from those sites often began or ended at Emanuel, with tutoring in nonviolence offered in advance by Glover and other adults. "He taught us how to be humble, how to turn the other cheek," remembered Ellen Jackson, who grew up in Emanuel. "He would always tell us, 'If you're not ready to turn that other cheek don't go out there.' We would practice what to do if someone hits you. He was there to tell us from the spiritual part, how it's going to hurt where you want to give in, and he would quote Scripture, always tell us the Ten Commandments and turn the other cheek." With Glover in the lead, the students would march out of the church, two by two, dressed in crisp, white shirts, taking a right on Calhoun Street, past Marion Square, and on to King Street. For anyone paying attention, there was clear subtext in the disregard for skin tone. Black men and women of all hues marched side by side and shared in leadership roles, eroding the effects of centuries of caste and class disunity. "Ain't Gonna Let Nobody Turn Me Around," they vowed in soulful unison.

"Emanuel was very well placed because it was so central," said Millicent Brown, one of Charleston's school desegregation pioneers. "We could pop over quickly before they saw us coming. Students would sit in and then when it was time to relieve them you would come to the basement of Emanuel to get bologna sandwiches." The basement was largely unfinished then, with a concrete slab floor and unpainted walls. Charles (Bud) Ferillo, a rare white high school student who served on the bologna brigade, remembered it being outfitted with folding tables and chairs and a ratty old refrigerator. "We used several other churches but this was the base church," Ellen Jackson said. "Every time we would finish picketing, we had to come back here and then we would have lunch and then we would have another session and then our mass meetings at night and then would go home. It was just like a job." The meetings served dual purposes—to inform activists of future events and to fortify their spirits. The excitement was infectious, bringing students back night after night. "We were involved in something," Jackson said.

There were many reasons that America's Civil Rights Movement found its natural habitat in Black churches like Mother Emanuel. Since the time of Richard Allen and Absalom Jones, those institutions had embraced a liberation theology inspired by mystical accounts of both physical and spiritual release. The Christian ethos meshed seamlessly with the principles of nonviolence that informed the sit-ins and Freedom Rides. That tradition had matured over two centuries such that church leaders like B. J. Glover were by then fully clothed in it. Those ministers also were among the few community leaders with the financial and professional independence to speak truth to power. Indeed, their stature with at least some constituents grew with their willingness to say what their parishioners could not. Black churches also afforded a prefabricated organizational structure and the physical space needed for meetings and refuge.

Culturally, the church and the movement often seemed inseparable. Spirituals transformed seamlessly into freedom songs. Pulpit oratory provided melody and motif, punctuated by choruses of amens. "There was so much singing in the movement and comfort with people being emotional," Millicent Brown said. "They weren't afraid of us in the churches." Clearly, the movement also benefitted from an aura of divine blessing. The backbones of countless marchers were stiffened by the conviction that their cause was favored by a just and active God. That the movement was so unavoidably Christian, in both its makeup and its approach, surely gave pause to some white Americans of faith.

There was an additional factor at work in the Lowcountry, where the lingering culture of enslavement could feel so intractable. From long experience, Black church leaders there understood that the battle against white supremacy must first be a battle for Black minds, and that the church was singularly positioned to be the point of that spear. The movement only came to fruition once a critical mass became convinced of its urgency and found the courage and unity to break free of generations of conditioning. Laying that groundwork had always been the church's domain.

And yet, as Emanuel's experience demonstrated, the Black church writ large and AME congregations in particular tended to be conservative by nature, theologically and socially, and preservationist in their internal politics.

Pastors like Glover who felt compelled by the civil-rights cause often found themselves well out in front of their congregations. They rotated mass meetings among their churches so as not to make any single one a disproportionate focus of white resentment. Molotov cocktails and crude explosives were mainstays of the white supremacist arsenal, and the targeting of churches became gruesomely real with the deadly bombing of Birmingham's Sixteenth Street Baptist Church in 1963.

During the summer of 1962, when Glover was organizing boycotts of department stores like Edward's on King Street, he received an anonymous letter from an Emanuel member who chastised him for his aggressiveness. "Rev. Glover, you are doing the wrong thing to stop people to go in Edward store on Saturday because if they work for they money they can spend it any way," the writer contended. "The white people was taking care of us a long time and they treat us nice . . . You better mind because you is a sick man. They keep you down if you don't stop it."

Emanuel member Daniel Martin, Sr., remembered that Glover would picket in front of Piggly Wiggly on Saturday, and then scold his own congregants on Sunday morning for crossing his line. "He blasted them," Martin said. "He'd say, 'You have no self-respect. We're out trying to change the conditions for you and you, of all people, come and cross the picket line and go into the store.' He would call the store owners by name and say, 'He doesn't even have a black janitor in the store and you're going in there.' A lot of the officers and members were afraid. They didn't want anyone trying to burn down the church . . . But he was the type that said that's what the church is for. The church is to be used for the benefit of the members and this is an avenue we have to travel."

Some Emanuel members could not be convinced that their investments, financially and spiritually, should be put at risk. On occasion, they withheld their tithes to voice their discomfort. "Some people didn't like it," Ruby Martin said. "You were just drawing in all these people that you didn't know. The older people thought the church was going to hell in a handbasket. Just too much going on. They felt their property was going away." Doris Coaxum Sanders, another lifelong member, said, "They thought he was putting the church in danger, but he stood up for the rights of people and what he believed in and what the Bible said about how we are to live and treat other people."

Ruby Martin said she did not participate in the demonstrations because she could not afford to lose her new job as a public schoolteacher. Similarly, Emanuel member Sonya Fordham remembered that she could not march "because my mother was a teacher and she would get fired and we needed her cash." Melvin Graham, who grew up in the church, said his family proceeded with caution because his mother's livelihood as a housekeeper depended on the benevolence of white matrons. "My mom worked for some very excellent people," he said, "but I can remember her saying you have to be careful what you say because you can be fired." Elnora Taylor, a teenager during the 1960s, said many parents forbade children from marching because they worried about brutality in the jails and the creation of criminal records. "Fathers and mothers back in those days didn't want to see us involved," she said, "because they wanted us to better ourselves and they wanted us to be safe." Yet, she said, the congregation grudgingly accepted that Rev. Glover "was going to do what he was going to do."

As a veteran jail-goer, Glover recognized the perils and accepted that not all Black Charlestonians could afford to join him. "Every time we go into the streets, we are potential jailbirds," he said. "Many people with families to support cannot take the risk." That is where the leadership of the Black church came in, bolstered by a faith born of centuries of oppression and resistance. "A whole lot of people criticized us," Glover reflected later in life. "They wouldn't even stand up to talk to us because they were afraid they'd get in trouble. But we had enough people who believed what was right."

ONE NIGHT IN JUNE 1963, more than three hundred protesters showed up for a 10:00 p.m. rally in front of police headquarters. A week later, twice that number marched down King Street. With white businesses suffering from the disruption, Mayor J. Palmer Gaillard, Jr., won a temporary restraining order that prohibited Black leaders from organizing "mass demonstrations and-or processions" in Charleston. The city's complaint named Glover as one of fourteen defendants. The order had little effect, as Black leaders had already demonstrated their readiness to go to jail. On the night after a hearing in the case, some five hundred demonstrators descended on the building at King and Columbus that housed Charleston's two newspapers, *The News and Courier* and *Charleston Evening Post*, to protest the unapologetically segregationist slant of their coverage. A skirmish began—it was never determined exactly how—and five police officers and a fireman suffered lacerations and other injuries from hurled bricks and stones. It was the first outbreak of violence during the

Charleston protests, and the police arrested 95 people. *The News and Courier* depicted it as a "near riot," and the governor deployed 130 state troopers and placed the National Guard on alert. Defiantly, more than 100 protesters left Emanuel at noon the next day and marched on city hall.

The incident put pressure on organizers like Glover, who helped lead the movement's Charleston steering committee, to maintain nonviolent discipline in the ranks while keeping white politicians on defense. Any shift in the debate from civil rights to civil unrest would cede the movement's high ground and jeopardize support from Northern benefactors. Rev. Glover, whose two-year term as NAACP branch president had ended, told a mass meeting the next night that he regretted the violence and had hoped that Charleston's movement would not succumb to it. But he scoffed at assertions that demonstrators had attacked the police. Rather, he said, the police had handled demonstrators roughly, swinging nightsticks and frog-marching suspects, inciting a response from an undisciplined few. He vowed that a single unfortunate night would not discourage his ground troops. "If they think this business is going to stop," Glover announced, "they've got another thought coming." Ending the demonstrations, he said, would reinforce white thinking that the protesters were nothing but rabble-rousers. He kept his dudgeon high. "If I want to go to a restaurant for a decent meal I'm going to go there," Glover said. "If that's a violation of the law they might as well open some more jails. My wife has the same right as Mrs. Glover that Mrs. Gaillard has as Mrs. Gaillard."

The arrests outside the newspaper building brought the six-week total to more than six hundred, with charges typically for minor offenses like trespassing or obstructing traffic. Youthful Emanuel members remember being loaded into police wagons and taken to the county's derelict jail near the foot of the Cooper River Bridge. The midsummer heat afforded little choice but to strip to their underwear for relief. The menu rarely diverged from pork and beans and cold biscuits, and the cells ran rampant with mutant-sized palmetto bugs. Inmates archly referred to their lodgings as the Seabreeze Hotel. Those not jailed were tasked with the job of bonding the others out, and over the course of the summer the community generated more than $1.4 million in bail through contributions and collateral. The process could take several days, sometimes more than a week. "We sang a lot," remembered Minerva Brown King, who spent four days in a cell after the newspaper protest. "We were just filled with the spirit of the thing."

Rev. Glover found himself arrested once again in late June when he and four other Black community leaders strolled into the whites-only lobby of the Hotel Fort Sumter, a luxury high-rise along the Battery, and asked to be seated for supper. The disappointed diners, a group that included J. Arthur Brown and Esau Jenkins, were sentenced to spend ten days in jail or pay a $100 fine. Glover returned to the hotel two weeks later to be arrested again. On July 20, he scored his third arrest in less than a month when he and three others were cited for disregarding a traffic signal while leading a march just outside Emanuel. Also jailed in Charleston that month was AME Bishop Decatur Ward Nichols, the son of Emanuel's builder, Rev. Lewis Ruffin Nichols, as he sought service in a hotel cafeteria.

Eventually, the economic pressure generated by pickets and boycotts began to produce results. In the late spring and early summer of 1963, more than a dozen King Street stores agreed to hire Black clerks, cashiers, and bookkeepers and the Kress and Grant department stores quietly began serving Black customers at integrated lunch counters, according to an NAACP report that Glover coauthored. Glover made a point of publicly commending establishments that desegregated, but refused to be satisfied with half a loaf. Token desegregation, he said repeatedly, was not enough. "We shall pray, we shall fight, we shall march until the doors of City Hall are open to us, until the seats of every restaurant are open to us, until every school is open to us," Glover said during a march after church one Sunday in June. Shortly thereafter, Mayor Gaillard began holding closed-door talks with a delegation of four Black leaders, including Glover.

In July, Charleston's movement leaders issued a list of ten demands that included the desegregation of all schools, hospitals, parks, playgrounds, pools, public buildings, restaurants, hotels, drinking fountains, and restrooms. They insisted on equal employment by retailers, the appointment of Black citizens to city committees and jobs, promotions for Black police officers, the establishment of a biracial committee, and the withdrawal of charges against demonstrators. Later that month, another sixty-two merchants signed a statement agreeing to employ Black clerks, extend the use of courtesy titles like Mr. and Mrs. to Black customers, and desegregate restrooms and water fountains.

Some organizers were ready to end the marches. But at a meeting one evening at Emanuel, youth leaders like James Blake insisted that they not relent. Charleston's response to street demonstrations might have been gentler than elsewhere, Blake maintained, but its commitment to segregation was just as firm. Glover agreed with his young comrade. When a reporter asked if the demonstrations might be suspended, he responded: "On the contrary, they will be intensified." Marchers left from Emanuel almost every day until August 1, when another eighty-seven small businesses agreed to the desegregation demands. With the momentum now irreversible, and summer's end approaching, Glover and other movement leaders then suspended the protests, while reserving the right to selectively picket establishments that were slow to get on board.

Some theaters, restaurants, hotels, and public facilities would not remove their whites-only policies until the federal Civil Rights Act forced them to a year later. But the backbone of segregation had been broken in Charleston, America's capital of racial subjugation. With that victory in hand, B. J. Glover, I. DeQuincey Newman, and J. Arthur Brown set off by rail to attend the August 28 March on Washington, where Martin Luther King, Jr., spoke of his dream that Black Americans would one day be judged by the content of their character.

"That summer certainly produced the kind of change and surprise to the white community that had not been expected from 'our Charleston Black folk,'" said retired municipal judge Arthur C. McFarland, a former Emanuel member who marched with Glover as a teenager. "There was always this effort to maintain control by being 'Charleston nice,' of not having the kind of violence you had in Birmingham and Montgomery and other places, that if we aren't as heavy-handed as some of these other communities we can maintain the control we've had for three hundred years."

Even though the color barrier was fracturing, Glover's reputation for uncompromising resistance did not leave him popular with white Charlestonians. In July 1964, on the day after President Lyndon B. Johnson signed the Civil Rights Act, Glover returned to the Hotel Fort Sumter, where he had twice been arrested the previous summer. He was again accompanied by J. Arthur Brown as well as Herbert U. Fielding, a funeral-home owner and community leader. Unlike the prior year, the white hotel manager did not summarily banish the entire group. Rather, he offered to seat two of the three—Brown and Fielding. "Reverend Glover, I am refusing you service not because you are colored," explained the manager, Wesley W. Graves. "Rather I do not feel you a fit person to eat in our dining room." Glover threatened legal action and the men left for the Charleston Inn, where they were served without incident. Over the next year, Glover continued to monitor Charleston's public facilities for signs of nonadherence to the new law. In January 1965, he wrote to the president of the city's Medical College Hospital, Dr. William McCord, to report that he had visited and found its waiting rooms still segregated. He demanded the immediate removal of whites-only signage.

With Jim Crow limping toward the grave, Glover turned his attention to Black self-improvement. He established programs to combat Charleston's school dropout rate, organized voter registration drives, and encouraged Black youngsters to dress and act with dignity. Glover left Emanuel in mid-1965 after being named president of Allen University, the AME college in Columbia, for the first of two terms. Shortly after taking office, he addressed the twenty-fifth annual convention of the South Carolina NAACP. A shift in strategy was needed, the veteran street fighter announced. "The time has come to replace mass demonstrations with mass intelligence and mass voting," Glover said. "By using the ballot, we can further our march to freedom. And through education we will be able to get green power—and that's money—to give us better places in society."

EMANUEL DID NOT LOSE its activist bent with Glover's departure. He was succeeded by another NAACP firebrand, Rev. Henry B. Butler, Jr., a goateed growler who preached regularly about the church's civil-rights legacy. "We think of those that were hanged, those that were persecuted, those that were killed, those that have had hose and water poured on them, those that have had bloodhounds on their trail, those that have been mistreated," Butler rumbled from the pulpit one Sunday in 1968. "And in the midst of it all, somehow, they stood up, because they had a spiritual backbone that caused them to look beyond the temporary things of life. If we are to move in this new day, we cannot have backbones like a jellyfish." In 1966, Butler had welcomed the young Black activist Julian Bond to a voter registration rally at Emanuel. Bond had at that point twice been denied his duly elected seat in Georgia's house of representatives because of his opposition to the Vietnam War. Lanky and self-confident, with the silken delivery of a soul station DJ, he spoke about the emerging Black Power movement and the importance of Black unity. "It is not enough to make the world safe for democracy," Bond said. "You have to make democracy safe for the United States." Black power begat Black pride. Like other African American churches that had reclaimed their iconography, Emanuel hung a large pair of brown praying hands in front of the pulpit window, a counterpoint to the adjacent figures of a Caucasian Christ that had been painted into the wall murals.

The demand for social and economic empowerment met its full realization in Charleston in 1969 in one of that decade's final expressions of mass discontent. The vehicle would be a prolonged labor strike by more than four hundred licensed practical nurses and "nonprofessional" hospital workers, almost all of them low-income Black women. In a city where street activism had largely been the province of churches and students and their minders in the NAACP, the hospital workers' strike flowered as a grassroots uprising against inequities that stubbornly survived the demise of legalized segregation. In the view of historian Stephen O'Neill, it "exploded, once and for all, the myth of black satisfaction that had been so powerful in governing the actions of white Charlestonians." It also established the city's African American minority as a political force that could no longer be coopted or ignored. Along with churches like Morris Brown AME, Central Baptist, and Zion-Olivet Presbyterian, Mother Emanuel again found herself in the vanguard of resistance.

The more-than-one-hundred-day strike initially targeted the hospital at the state-controlled Medical College of South Carolina, one of the city's proudest institutions. Emblematic of Charleston itself, it was run exclusively by white officials, with no Black doctors on staff and no Black nursing students. By contrast, Black workers filled most of the lowest-paying positions, with licensed practical nurses, nursing aides, orderlies, cooks, and janitors making less than the federal minimum wage. The organizational flow-chart placed experienced Black staffers under the authority of less-tenured white ones and allowed supervisors to dismiss subordinates with little recourse.

The dispute began in December 1967 when five Black workers—practical nurses and nursing aides—walked off the job after a white supervisor refused to provide them with case reports on their patients. Under pressure from federal regulators, who had been monitoring the Medical College's compliance with civil-rights laws since 1965, the hospital reinstated the workers the next year. But community activists Mary Moultrie, a nurse's aide at the hospital, and William Saunders, a veteran organizer, were already forging an alliance between Charleston's disgruntled hospital workers and a powerful New York healthcare union. They soon spun off their own branch, Local 1199B of the National Organizing Committee of Hospital and Nursing Home Employees, and elected Moultrie as president.

Although not recognized by the hospital in right-to-work South Carolina, the union began picketing in late 1968. After twelve members, including

Moultrie, were fired in March 1969, the workers voted to strike. The police made more than eight hundred arrests during the massive street demonstrations that followed. To broaden economic pressure for concessions, the strikers picketed not only the hospital but also King Street retailers and government offices. There were instances of rock-throwing and firebombing, and city officials won an injunction against mass protests. The governor declared a dusk-to-dawn curfew and stationed nearly one thousand armed and helmeted National Guardsmen on the streets, their bayonets fixed. The tension was real, as just the previous year, seventy miles up the road in Orangeburg, state troopers had fired on unarmed Black demonstrators from South Carolina State College, killing three and wounding twenty-eight. The strike drew national media attention as outsiders came to appreciate the boldness of poor Black women confronting armed white power in staunchly anti-union South Carolina. "I cut hooky from school and remember trying to hide from the cameras because we didn't want our parents to see us," remembered Emanuel member Theodora Watson.

Seeking revival in the aftermath of King's assassination, the SCLC dispatched Rev. Ralph David Abernathy, its forty-three-year-old president, and Andrew Young, its thirty-seven-year-old executive vice president, to Charleston throughout the spring of 1969. Black churches would be central to the organizing efforts. One union official, Henry Nicholas, recalled asking at an early meeting with hospital workers how many belonged to a church. "Everybody raised their hand, and then I knew we had something going," he told author Claudia Smith Brinson. Any number of downtown churches lent their sanctuaries to mass meetings organized by the SCLC and local strike leaders. Protests drew huge numbers, with an estimated ten thousand joining Abernathy, Moultrie, and United Automobile Workers president Walter Reuther in a Mother's Day parade. "Just a massive amount of people," remembered Emanuel member Lee Bennett, Jr. "It felt a little bit surreal."

Few gatherings were as electric as the four-hour rally at Emanuel on April 29 that featured a stoic address by Coretta Scott King. Barely a year earlier, her husband had been slain while supporting an eerily similar strike in Memphis. The striking sanitation workers in Memphis, almost all male, had carried placards asserting I AM A MAN. The striking hospital workers in Charleston, almost all female, adopted the slogan "I Am Somebody." Mrs. King arrived at Emanuel to find more than three thousand people crammed inside and thousands more outside. The forty-two-year-old widow was joined on the pulpit by her father-in-law, Rev. Martin Luther King, Sr., and her brother-in-law, Rev. A. D. King. She wore a pale blue dress, accented with strings of beads and the blue-and-white cap of Local 1199.

King told the crowd that she planned to join them in marching the next morning. "I am ashamed to admit it," she said, "but I have never had the privilege of going to jail." Her husband had always insisted she remain free so that at least one of them could care for their small children. But with his death, she said, she felt obligated to follow him into the streets and behind bars if needed. "If my husband were alive today, he would be right here with you tonight," she assured the crowd. "This unity was my husband's dream and the dream of all decent people throughout the world." Mrs. King railed about conditions at the hospitals. "Hospital workers have been working full-time jobs at part-time pay," she said. "After all, $1.30 an hour is not a wage. It is an insult. I also have another interest for being here and that is many of the hospital workers throughout our nation are women, Black women, many of whom are the main supporters of their families. I feel that the Black woman in our nation, the Black working woman, is perhaps the most discriminated against of all of the working women." She made it personal by asking why Charleston's political and business leaders had "learned nothing from the hard story of Memphis." But she told the workers she was confident they would win. "I believe you mean business," she said to a boisterous ovation. "The only question is how much blood and tears must be shed before the victory is won."

And then from the pulpit of the oldest AME church in the South, Martin Luther King's widow reflected on the tragic year she had just lived, and the centuries of trauma that her people had survived, with only their faith to uplift them. "The greatest power we have," she said, "is the power of our souls to endure, suffer and sacrifice. We have been doing it for many years and we will have to continue if we want to be first-class citizens in this great country of ours."

The strike resolved only when the Nixon administration, fearful of escalating violence and nationalized labor strife, forced the hospital's hand by threatening to withhold federal funding as a penalty for its discriminatory practices. The feds insisted that the hospital reinstate the twelve fired workers and establish policies for recruiting, hiring, paying, and promoting Black employees equitably. Finally, in late June, an agreement was reached. The minimum wage for hospital employees was raised to $1.60 an hour, with some making $2.10.

A credit union was formed and a grievance process established. The union, however, would not be recognized, leaving workers with only a temporary resolution.

That the victory was partial and that Local 1199B collapsed within a few years does not diminish the strike's enduring impact on Black empowerment in Charleston. In the prior two decades, Black Charlestonians had failed to exert their newfound political power in proportion to their 45 percent share of the voting-age population. Although no longer disenfranchised, many remained reluctant to register to vote. Black power brokers were regularly coopted with patronage and other handouts from the Democratic "Broad Street machine," which ran the city through the seven mayoral terms of William M. Morrison (1947–1959) and J. Palmer Gaillard, Jr. (1959–1975). The white vote, meanwhile, had expanded through the annexation of suburban precincts off of the peninsula. But registering Black voters had been a major focus of the hospital workers' strike. At least partly as a result, the number of Black registered voters in Charleston County more than doubled in the decade between 1965 and 1974. Their share of the voting pool grew from 22 percent to 32 percent even as the Black proportion of the county's population remained roughly static.

The impact was felt immediately. Businessman St. Julian Devine broke the color bar on the city council in 1967, and the council appointed Richard E. Fields as the first Black municipal judge two years later. In 1970, Herbert Fielding became the first Black Charlestonian elected to the South Carolina house in the twentieth century. A pair of Emanuel members—Daniel E. Martin, Sr. (1983–1992) and Floyd Breeland (1993–2008)—would be among those to follow him. Lonnie Hamilton III, a jazz saxophonist and high school band director, broke ground with his election to the county council, also in 1970. In the next year's municipal election, Black voters delivered their support to challengers of incumbent Mayor Gaillard, first in the Democratic primary and then in the general election, nearly costing him both contests. A significant political shift was under way. There was talk of running a Black candidate for mayor in 1975. Instead, a young, white state representative named Joseph P. Riley, Jr., who had both a South of Broad pedigree and a liberal record on race, forged a biracial coalition to win the first of a transformative ten terms as mayor.

Riley campaigned on pledges to place more minorities in city positions and to bring jobs, affordable housing, and greater police presence to blighted

Black neighborhoods. He won an estimated 75 percent of the Black vote. The city council elected alongside him consisted of six white and six Black members. At his inauguration, Riley arranged for the invocation to be delivered by AME bishop Decatur Ward Nichols. The musical selections included the African American anthem "Lift Every Voice and Sing."

"Fundamentally," Riley stressed in his address, "we are but one people."

The new mayor made good on his promise to integrate his cabinet and city agencies, and in his second term appointed as Charleston's police chief a no-nonsense newcomer named Reuben Morris Greenberg, who was both African American and an observant Jew. It had taken more than three hundred years, a century beyond the reversal of Reconstruction. But through the courage and determination of civil-rights warriors like B. J. Glover, the descendants of those brought to Charleston in chains had finally gained a voice in the regulation of their own lives.

XV.

Clementa Pinckney and the Paradox of Black Power

*You are a chosen people, a royal priesthood, a holy nation,
God's special possession, that you may declare the praises of him
who called you out of darkness into his wonderful light.*

—I PETER 2:9 (NIV)

The morning worship had ended at St. John AME, a modest brick chapel at the intersection of two country lanes in Ridgeland, South Carolina, population roughly 1,100. As Clementa Pinckney walked through the church with its ten rows of pews, he was startled to hear a disembodied voice. It was soft, almost whispery, yet clearly audible. *Preach*, it said, *I have called you to preach the Gospel.*

It was the mid-1980s and Pinckney was but thirteen. But in his frequent telling of the story, that was not too young to discern the voice of God and to take the instruction accordingly. The youngster had already started down a rather precocious path, toting his Bible and briefcase to Jasper Primary School at age nine and sitting his parents down a year later to inform them, "I've got work to do for God." When his grandmother Gracie Stevenson Broome telephoned from New York, he told her, "Grandma, I believe I'm called to preach," just as assuredly as another kid might forecast his future in the NBA. If a teacher asked Clementa how he was doing, he tended to answer with an exclamation: "I'm doing fine in the name of the Lord!"

Pinckney came from a line of politically active AME preachers, most notably his maternal great-uncle, Rev. Levern Stevenson, a presiding elder in South Carolina and an NAACP branch president whose mentorship young Clementa sought at every turn. But no one in the family had experienced anything quite like this. "I loved him to death but, whooo, I found him kind of weird," remembered his sister, Johnette Pinckney Martinez, who was four years and four days younger. His father, John Pinckney, a self-trained auto mechanic, at times sensed the supernatural at work in his son, almost like seeing a haunt. "It scared me for a while," he said. "It wasn't just his doing. It was something God did to touch him."

Within months of his calling that morning at St. John, thirteen-year-old Clementa Pinckney stood before hundreds of African Methodist Episcopal preachers at an Annual Conference to present himself as a candidate for ministerial training. Bishop Frederick Calhoun James, the most powerful AME figure in the state, asked the tall and lanky teen what he aspired to become. Clementa did not hesitate. "A humble bishop of the AME church," he answered, no hint of a smile. The audience began to titter. Even a thirteen-year-old who had spent any time in AME churches likely understood that bishops were not known for their humility. More to the point, many of the denomination's most determined pastors had been maneuvering for decades to reach the episcopacy, some running four or more times without success. This child's preternatural audacity and ambition took them aback. "Those who knew the power of the bishop were trying to keep a straight face, but the laughter could not be restrained," remembered Rev. John Paul Brown, Pinckney's former pastor at St. John. "Even the bishop laughed, but he commended him for his fortitude and willingness and encouraged him to study." After several years of training, and a trial sermon that packed his home church, Pinckney was ordained at eighteen. The bishop quickly assigned him to fill in for an ailing pastor at a small church in Green Pond, South Carolina, ministering to folks four times his age.

Child-prodigy preachers were not unknown in the African Methodist tradition, a vestige perhaps of bygone days when Spirit possession was considered more important than formal schooling in demonstrating fitness for ministry. Born on July 30, 1973, in Beaufort, South Carolina, Clementa (Cle-MEN-tay) Carlos Pinckney was the eldest of the three children of John and Theopia Pinckney. Roberto Clemente, the Pittsburgh Pirates All-Star and global humanitarian, had died in a plane crash seven months earlier and Theopia suggested adapting his name in tribute. Clementa's surname was among the most aristocratic in South Carolina. Two Pinckney cousins, Charles and Charles Cotesworth, had been among South Carolina's four signatories to the Constitution, and Clementa's great-great-great grandparents, Plenty and Sallie

Pinckney, and their son, Benjamin, likely were captives on a Pinckney plantation near Hilton Head. Clementa's parents split when he was young. He saw both regularly, but lived with his mother, who ran a daycare center in her home until her death in 2005 from pancreatic cancer. From her, he inherited a persistent concern for the welfare of others, a thirst for education, an unflappable demeanor, and an abiding African Methodist faith.

Even as a preteen, Clementa seemed a grown man trapped in the body of a gangly boy. The unmistakable resonance of his voice could silence most any room. He set himself apart by wearing a suit, tie, and polished shoes to a high school where T-shirts and Nikes were de rigueur. He stayed in the library at lunchtime and fell asleep at home with a Bible or sci-fi novel (or Spider-Man comic) on his chest. He occasionally introduced himself at church youth functions as "Reverend" Clementa Pinckney, well before he had earned the title.

Pinckney preferred 4-H debate competitions to Little League, eschewed the outdoors, could not dribble a basketball, hammer a nail, or bait a hook. He played the saxophone in the school band but posed no threat to Coltrane. Yet, he maintained the respect of cooler peers, offsetting his old-soul nerdiness with a charismatic presence and unassuming confidence that would serve him well in both preaching and politics. "His mindset was already that he was going to be professional and profound," remembered Roslyn Fulton-Warren, a classmate. "He led by example, pretty much. When he spoke, you just, 'Hey, stop'—you had to pay attention. We never questioned him. We wore our jeans and our T-shirts and he had his suit and tie. It was fine by us."

Situated along Interstate 95 between Charleston and Savannah, Ridgeland was, like most Southern towns, still heavily segregated in the 1970s and 1980s. The hallmarks of Pinckney's childhood were his Black neighborhood, his Black school, his Black church, and its Black youth groups. He presided over the student government at school and the Young People's Division at church. As a high school junior, he participated in a summer jobs program that assigned him to the Jasper County administrator's office, where he was expected to fetch coffee and empty trash cans. On his first day, he asked the administrator, Henry Moss, Jr., for a copy of the budget, explaining that he planned to look for inefficiencies.

"What part of the budget do you want?" the amused administrator inquired.

"I'll start with the overall budget," Pinckney said, "and then go department to department."

The teenager soon keyed in on several line items. "Darn if he didn't find a few things to fix," Moss told friends.

At twenty-three, Rev. Pinckney became the youngest African American ever elected to South Carolina's General Assembly, winning a house seat in a district that traversed three counties. He had been a page while in college for the seat's previous occupant, nine-term incumbent Juanita White, and she handpicked him to succeed her upon retiring in 1996. His youth became an issue in the campaign, but he reminded skeptics about other precocious high achievers: Martin Luther King, Jr.; Nelson Mandela; Ludwig van Beethoven; Wolfgang Amadeus Mozart; Jesus Christ. After two terms in the house, he broadened his constituency by winning a race for the state senate in South Carolina's largest geographic district. By the time his life was taken, forty-three days shy of his forty-second birthday, the Democrat had been reelected three times, twice without Republican opposition and once with two-thirds of the vote. He had obtained a bachelor's degree from Allen University (where he was a proud member of Alpha Phi Alpha fraternity), then a master's in divinity from Lutheran Theological Southern Seminary, another master's in public administration from the University of South Carolina, and was working toward a doctorate from Wesley Theological Seminary in Washington, D.C. There he was writing a dissertation on "Bi-vocational Pastor-Public Servants in the African American Community." He had pastored five AME churches, including the state's most prestigious pulpit in Mother Emanuel, and had been named a presiding elder at age thirty-three. That post, with oversight of twenty-two churches, typically fell to ministers far more senior.

That Pinckney had accomplished so much at such an age made his murder all the more devastating. He had lived a life of breathtaking achievement, and then, in an instant, joined the pantheon of African American luminaries cut down before fulfilling their promise. Like other regressions, his assassination set back any notion of a peaceful advance toward Black empowerment following the Civil Rights Movement. Although legalized discrimination had been proscribed, there was, of course, no way to legislate or litigate an end to white supremacist thinking. If anything, the growing prominence of African Americans in public life, with a Black man elected president in 2008 and reelected in 2012, had only incited reactionary forces. It seemed far from coincidental that Dylann Roof, before finishing his bloody work in Emanuel's fellowship hall, had told his victims that he felt compelled to act because Black people were "taking over the world."

✦ ✦ ✦

THE MOTHER EMANUEL that Clementa Pinckney inherited in 2010 was much changed from the packed-to-the-rafters cathedral that hosted the mass meetings of the civil-rights era. The stucco façade looked largely the same, although a cataclysmic Category 4 hurricane, named Hugo, had toppled the steeple and blown out stained glass when it devastated Charleston in September 1989. The damage required more than $200,000 in repairs. The more lasting harm, however, came from a demographic upheaval in Charleston that had placed the congregation, like many Black churches downtown, under considerable strain.

During Joe Riley's four decades as mayor (1975–2016), a city that spent nearly a century in recovery from the Civil War (and segregation and economic passivity) blossomed into one of the nation's most desirable tourist destinations and hottest real estate markets. There were varied forces at work: a robust preservation movement; geographic and zoning restrictions on growth; the development of top-tier culinary, hospitality, and cultural institutions; the construction of parks, museums, and performance spaces; and, of course, the bottomless nostalgia of tourists for a magnolia-scented past. As a rejuvenation project, it was hard to argue with the intoxicating results. The compact, pedestrian-friendly seaside city, with its endless maze of meticulously tended antebellum homes and gardens, soon topped list after list of "best places" to visit and live.

The cost, however, was the rampant gentrification of the Charleston peninsula, also at a nation-leading pace. After three decades of suburban flight to escape school desegregation, the peninsula's white population started to stabilize in the 1980s as wealthy out-of-towners and retirees discovered its charms. Enrollment growth on the College of Charleston's moss-draped campus added to the demand for affordable housing downtown. Swaths of units in predominantly Black neighborhoods had already been bulldozed to make way for a crosstown expressway and a complex of municipal buildings. Real estate prices and taxes began to soar as deep-pocketed white investors displaced poorer Black residents who could not keep pace.

The city of Charleston lost nearly a fifth of its Black population between 1960 and 2020 even as the total number of residents more than doubled. The exodus from intown neighborhoods near Emanuel was severe, and continued well into the new century. In 2022, the last Black homeowners in Ansonborough, a historic neighborhood abutting the church, finally acquiesced and sold the house their family had purchased in 1944 for $14,000. It went for $862,000. Nine months later, without making significant improvements, the investors who bought it flipped it for $1.655 million. By 2020, Black residents comprised less than one-fifth of the city's population, compared to half in 1960. Many Black families moved to suburbs west of the Ashley River or up the neck of the peninsula to North Charleston. The mass migration there drove a fivefold increase in population between 1960 and 2020, making North Charleston the state's third largest city, after Charleston and Columbia.

In Emanuel's heyday, virtually every family lived close enough to walk to Calhoun Street on Sunday mornings or to get there with a short bus ride. That ensured a certain generational continuity. As the Black population shifted away from downtown, fewer and fewer were willing or able to make the trek. As they dispersed, some former members found churches closer to their new homes. Younger ones stopped going altogether or gravitated to hipper megachurches that welcomed them with electric guitars, shorter services, digestible sermons, and diverse ministries, including for LGBTQ members (AME doctrine, based on scriptural interpretation, "strictly prohibits and forbids" ministers from marrying people of the same gender, under threat of defrocking; Mother Emanuel, according to parishioners and pastors, has had no openly gay members). By 2016, among the very few worshippers who could still walk to Emanuel were the church's only white members—married empty-nesters from Boston who had retired to Charleston, purchased a two-bedroom condo in Ansonborough, and joined the church after being moved by its response to the massacre.

Emanuel's congregation was shrinking and aging all at once. More were being buried than baptized. "On a couple of occasions, I had five funerals in one week, two on the same day, twice in the week," remembered Lavern Witherspoon, the pastor from 2004 to 2006. "People styled me the Charleston eulogist. I think the first year it was forty-nine deaths, the second year it was sixty-seven. I just stopped counting." When Clementa Pinckney arrived, the reported membership had dropped below 1,000, with the actual number assumed to be lower. By 2024, the count was down to 576, and Sunday altar calls for new initiates often went unanswered. A succession of other Black churches downtown could not withstand the fiscal stress brought on by declining membership and crumbling infrastructure. Shiloh AME, Greater Macedonia AME, and Plymouth Congregational each abandoned their downtown sites for new ones in the West Ashley area, while Zion-Olivet Presbyterian, Eastside Missionary Baptist, and St. Matthew Baptist relocated to North Charleston. Several of the abandoned church buildings were demolished and replaced with condominiums or apartments. Greater Macedonia's sanctuary, three blocks from Emanuel, was converted in 2023 into a cycling studio.

As Emanuel's membership dwindled, its physical plant necessarily suffered from benign neglect. Peeling paint and water stains marred the ceilings and walls. The air conditioner leaked and occasionally wouldn't cool, prompting pastors to declare "dress-down Sundays" during summer months. An engineering firm hired during Pinckney's tenure found that water had seeped repeatedly through the roof into the masonry and trusses, creating "a perfect environment for termites." The firm's nightmarish report, presented in 2015, concluded that the termite damage was so severe, the brickwork so eroded, the support columns so out of plumb that the building should "*never* be occupied during any period of high winds." The rickety choir loft was deemed sufficiently unstable that the pipe organ was mothballed and the singers moved downstairs. The church budget of roughly $500,000 a year had become so tight that altar boys no longer lit all the candles for Sunday worship.

But for better or worse, the centrality of Emanuel's site to African Methodist history made it unthinkable that the congregation would ever be uprooted. The building had been included in the National Register of Historic Places as part of a larger district in 1978 (and gained its own listing in 2018, following the shootings). That meant that Pinckney and his successors would be burdened with gargantuan fundraising challenges. "Emanuel's not moving except for an act of God," said AME bishop Samuel L. Green, Sr., whose term as overseer of South Carolina's churches ran from 2016 to 2024. Yet Green readily acknowledged that Emanuel's devotion to its past could not but impede its path to a more vibrant future. "In the historical churches," he said, "I think vision is impaired by memory, the memory of how it used to be, the significance of what they did yesterday and how it impacted and moved them spiritually."

It fell to Pinckney, therefore, to revitalize Mother Emanuel by luring young, new members even as longtime congregants insisted on having their old-time religion. He also was charged with reviving the activism of a congregation that had settled into a redundant complacency, with the same programs and celebrations year after year—the oyster roast fundraisers, the Founder's Day and Emanuel Day commemorations, Men's Day, then Women's Day, the health fair, the blessing of the school backpacks, the Watch Night service on New

Year's Eve. The balance of power between pastor and congregation had started to shift from the pulpit to the pews. Rev. Alonzo W. Holman, considered the most successful pastor of the post–civil rights era, or at least the most popular, had come to understand this during his tenure from 1978 to 1988. "I just figured out where they wanted to go," he once explained, "and got out front." It was during Holman's tenure that the church paneled and tiled its unfinished basement to create a utilitarian fellowship hall with space for offices, classrooms, and a kitchen.

As time drew on, the church's clergy put less energy behind addressing the ills that plagued Black Charleston. Pinckney found that disconcerting as he started the job at Emanuel. His approach to pastoring had always reflected the social gospel of his AME forerunners. "I believe in heaven on Earth," he said shortly after first being elected to the state senate. "Life ought to be prosperous. You aren't just waiting to die. We are charged with making the world a better place than we found it."

In that striving, Pinckney recognized that he stood on the shoulders of the ancestors, whether Richard Allen or Morris Brown or Denmark Vesey or Daniel Alexander Payne or Richard Harvey Cain or B. J. Glover. Those warriors often had little choice but to fight for equality from the outside, as the system would not allow them in and countered any resistance with reprisal. Two years before Pinckney was born, his great-uncle Levern Stevenson's house had been burned to the ground by white nightriders, forcing Stevenson and his wife and six children to escape in their bedclothes. It happened just days after he had organized a well-publicized boycott of Ridgeland's schools to protest the inequitable treatment of Black students. Stevenson would not be intimidated, however. The next year, he filed a federal lawsuit that challenged South Carolina's at-large system of electing legislators from countywide districts, which had diluted Black voting strength. After the U.S. Supreme Court ruled in his favor, and required single-member districts, the number of African Americans elected to the South Carolina General Assembly jumped from three in 1970 to thirteen in 1974. Stevenson could not have imagined that his own great-nephew would benefit from that ruling down the road. By the time Clementa Pinckney joined the legislature in 1997, striding through doors forced open by his forebears, African Americans held 26 of 124 seats in the state house of representatives and 8 of 46 in the senate.

Pinckney would do his civil-rights work from within the halls of power, lending his distinctive baritone to some of the state's most marginalized citizens. Although he viewed himself first as a pastor, he considered his dual roles as complementary, particularly given that many of his constituents qualified as "the least of these." His 45th District, anchoring the southernmost corner of South Carolina's triangle, ranked among the poorest in a state that itself ranked forty-fourth in median income. African Americans comprised half of the district's population, and more than a fifth of its residents lived in poverty. A classic gerrymander in the shape of a wing-flapping raptor, the 45th covered 2,373 square miles, nearly the size of Delaware. It curved like a boomerang around wealthy coastal enclaves like Hilton Head Island but did not include them. Bypassed during South Carolina's surges in automobile manufacturing and tourism, the area suffered from such dim prospects and cash-starved schools that it had been written off as part of the state's "Corridor of Shame." In his two decades in the legislature, Pinckney fought to bring skilled jobs, improved education funding, and expanded healthcare to his neglected district, just as he provided spiritual nourishment to his parishioners. Emanuel's pulpit and the well of the state senate were separated by 115 miles of highway, but Pinckney felt little distance.

"We don't see ourselves . . . as just a place where we come and worship, but as a beacon and as a bearer of the culture and a bearer of what makes us a people," Pinckney told a group of visiting college students at Emanuel in 2013. "But I like to say that this is not necessarily unique to us. It's really what America is all about. Could we not argue that America is about freedom, whether we live it out or not, but it really is about freedom, equality, and the pursuit of happiness? And that is what church is all about, freedom to worship and freedom from sin, freedom to be full what God intends us to be and to have equality in the sight of God." Heard later, his words seemed to foreshadow his martyrdom. "Sometimes you've got to make noise to do that," Pinckney continued. "Sometimes you may have to die like Denmark Vesey to do that. Sometimes you have to march, struggle, and be unpopular to do that . . . There are many people who say why would you as a preacher, why would you as a pastor be involved in public life. I've said it but I'll say it again: our calling is not just within the walls of the congregation, but we are part of the life and the community in which our congregation resides."

With Black political representation secured, Pinckney believed the next great civil-rights struggle was for equal opportunity. "To just have the vote without any economic power or stability or influence, it's almost like an empty road," he once said. "To be educated but yet not be able to control your destiny by having the opportunities for jobs or to be seen as equals . . . and not be able to pursue dreams is still an imbalance." As a Democrat, Pinckney never served in the majority in either chamber and so had limited influence over legislation and pork-barrel spending. That did not stop him from advocating diligently, albeit fruitlessly, for economic development projects that would have made a difference for workers in his district. As a senator, he pushed for state tax incentives for an upscale shopping outlet in Jasper County and for appropriations to build an oceangoing port facility there. Despite any ministerial misgivings about gambling, he got behind a casino and hotel project that a Native American group pitched for Hardeeville. As a house member in 2000, he supported an education lottery for South Carolina because he knew that people in his district regularly crossed the Georgia line to buy tickets that benefitted schools there. "He said we cannot stop the gambling; it's like breathing," recalled Helen Pittman, a longtime legislative aide. "But we need good-paying jobs for our citizens." Governor Nikki Haley's opposition killed the casino's prospects. Haley and Republican leaders in the General Assembly also doomed other Pinckney priorities, like a state minimum wage, public campaign financing, and expanded Medicaid eligibility.

Like Richard Allen and Richard Harvey Cain before him, Pinckney believed that Black Americans, once vested with the franchise, still needed to control their destinies by voting and mastering the political arts. He understood, colleagues said, that decisions to pave roads and provide clean water were not made in churches.

"We are in an American system," Pinckney said in a 2012 interview with Harvard scholar Henry Louis Gates, Jr., "where politics and money and the power that it generates controls and impacts our life, not every aspect but many aspects, from the eyedrops that goes into a baby's eyes to how a death certificate reads . . . So, we need to be a part, if we want a say in our own life, if we want to be independent, if we want to influence what's happening around us. Or the reverse is to let everybody else control and influence and then we just sort of take whatever comes. That's what slaves did. But, you know, we're not slaves. We're Americans so we have a responsibility to look at ourselves, self-help if you will."

PINCKNEY DID NOT SHARE the audacious ambition of Barack Obama, or his exotic multiracial childhood or Ivy League education. But they came of political age in the same era, at a time of hope and possibility for Black aspirations. The men met briefly by chance on the night before South Carolina's presidential primary in January 2008, which Obama won handily over Hillary Rodham Clinton. The U.S. senator from Illinois made his final appearance that evening at the Pink Ice Ball, an annual gala in Columbia for the Alpha Kappa Alpha sorority. Pinckney and his wife, Jennifer, happened to be standing at the back door when an exhausted Obama and his wife, Michelle, left for their campaign bus. The couples spoke only long enough for Obama to thank Pinckney for his support and shake hands. But the chance encounter left an impression, and Pinckney took immense inspiration from Obama's victory. "There was an overwhelming sense of pride and vicarious accomplishment that here an intelligent, sharp, captivating African American was able to rise to the highest office of the land and the world," he told Gates in their interview. "As a young man, I could see myself in him. I could see my nephews, my cousins in him." Those younger family members, he said, would now have something his generation had not, a role model who looked like them and had realized the ultimate American aspiration. Pinckney told Gates about Mother Emanuel's oldest member, Marguerite Michel, who was 101 at the time. One Sunday after Obama's victory she stood before the congregation to testify that she never thought she would see the day. "But praise God, look what the Lord can do," Pinckney quoted her as saying. "If I were to close my eyes today, I know that the Lord is good."

As both a pastor and a legislator, Pinckney had a reputation for valuing the views of others, or at least appearing to by employing an empathetic nod or reassuring touch. "He would say, 'Mmm-hmm, I understand, I appreciate it,'" said Rev. Joseph Darby, "and then would go and do what he was going to do anyway. He would listen to the most cockamamie stuff and be kind and pleasant about it." James L. Gilliard, a member of Campbell Chapel AME Church in Bluffton, where Pinckney served before Emanuel, said the pastor "could tell you to go to hell and the way he would tell you, you would say, 'Well, how do I get there?'"

It was much the same way in the General Assembly. Pinckney made a point of greeting colleagues on the floor, asking about family members by name. Rep. Bill Herbkersman, a Republican whose district overlapped with Pinckney's, remembered fighting it out with him on a bill one day and sharing breakfast with him the next. "You could have a battle with Clem," Herbkersman said, "but when you punched out he was your friend." Democratic Rep. William Bowers agreed. "The most irritating thing about Sen. Pinckney," he said, "is that when you had a debate he would just come over and pat you on the back and say, 'Maybe tomorrow you'll be thinking right.' He was full of love and full of respect."

Pinckney was a deliberative legislator who studied his way through positions and picked his spots. In the house in 2000, he joined other Black Democrats in opposing the compromise that finally removed the Confederate battle flag from its perch atop the State Capitol, where it had flown defiantly and offensively to many for thirty-nine years. The bill, which passed anyway, allowed the flag to be raised instead at a Confederate memorial on the Capitol grounds, a move that opponents viewed as merely extending the life of the insult (the flag only came down fifteen years later in response to the murders of Pinckney and the others at Emanuel). But Pinckney didn't care much about credit and tended to leave the flamethrowing on racial issues to more excitable members of the Legislative Black Caucus. As a result, when he did rise to speak, standing six-foot-one but looming even taller, people tended to stop chattering on the floor and listen.

Never was that more the case than during the April 2015 debate preceding a bipartisan vote to expand the use of police body cameras. The bill, which required departments to formulate policies for using the devices, gained momentum after the killing of Walter Scott, an unarmed Black man who was shot repeatedly by a white North Charleston policeman as he fled a traffic stop. A bystander with a cell phone captured video of the shooting, which took place barely two months before Pinckney would himself die by gunfire.

In a floor speech on April 14, ten days after Scott's death, Pinckney dug into Scripture for the story of Doubting Thomas, the apostle who refused to believe reports of Christ's resurrection until he could see and touch the wounds from his crucifixion. The initial reaction had been similar, Pinckney said, to the first reports of Walter Scott's death at the hands of Officer Michael Slager. "There were many who said there is no way that a police officer would ever shoot somebody in the back six, seven, eight times," Pinckney said, pounding his fist in the air as if striking an anvil. "But like Thomas, when we were able to see the video, and we were able to see the gunshots, and when we saw him fall to the ground, and when we saw the police officer come and handcuff him on the ground, without even trying to resuscitate him, without even seeing if he was really alive, without calling an ambulance, without calling for help, and to see him die face down in the ground as if he were gunned down like game, I believe we all were like Thomas, and said, 'I believe.'"

The centuries of aggregated suffering, the years of undetected police abuse, seeped into the timbre of Pinckney's voice. But he did not harp on the racial component of the incident. Rather, he implored his colleagues to use the attention brought by the Scott killing to demonstrate that South Carolina could live up to its stated values. "We have a great opportunity to allow sunshine into this process," he said, gesturing as if gripping a weighted apple, "to at least give us new eyes for seeing so that we are able to make sure that our proud and great law enforcement officers and every citizen that we represent is able to at least know that they will be seen and heard and that their rights will be protected." The preacher closed his legislative sermon by modeling the Christian ethos, summoned from the source later tapped by those who would forgive his killer. "Our hearts go out to the Scott family, our hearts go out to the Slager family, because the Lord teaches us to love all," he said, "and we pray that over time, that justice be done."

Any "amens" were whispered. But former Sen. Marlon Kimpson, a prime sponsor of the legislation, said the moral force of Pinckney's speech proved invaluable. "We thought we had the votes going in but if there was any reluctance to be overly confident it was alleviated after Clem took the podium," he said. "We've got a lot of self-professed evangelicals in the state senate and none of them challenged Clem ever on his interpretation of Scripture."

Pinckney's collegiality made him well liked on both sides of the aisle. When a coveted seat came open on the senate finance committee, he persuaded a Democratic colleague, Sen. Darrell Jackson, who represented parts of Columbia, to cede it even though Jackson outranked him in seniority. The position was valued because of the committee's influence in directing appropriations. "He said, 'Darrell, I don't ask for much, but you're from an area with a lot of people fighting for it, and it would mean so much for my part of the state to be on finance,'" Jackson remembered. "'It would help the poorest part of South Carolina unlike you could imagine.' I was like, 'Clem, you're asking me to give up the right to go up to the finance committee.' He said, 'Think about it. I want to fight for family clinics and health money.' And he made such a compelling argument that I gave up my chance to go up . . . He was very grateful and never forgot it."

After the 2010 census, Pinckney won a measure of protection from his Republican colleagues in the decennial redrawing of legislative districts. Shifts in population made it possible for the Republican majority to redesign Pinckney's district so that he would be forced into a difficult reelection against another incumbent. Instead, the Republican president pro tem, Sen. Glenn F. McConnell, supported keeping Pinckney's district largely intact, with a Black and Democratic majority among registered voters. The senators had established redistricting guidelines that discouraged pitting incumbents against one another, regardless of party. But McConnell, a Charlestonian who once owned a Confederate memorabilia shop, also acknowledged his fondness for his Democratic colleague. "He was just such a nice, polite person that people wouldn't have an ax to grind against him," McConnell said. "He was well spoken and stood up for what he believed in, but he respected the collegiality of the institution . . . He made friends rather than enemies and if people could help him, they'd help him if it didn't cost them politically."

Pinckney's reputation as the "conscience of the senate" did not always preclude him from testing boundaries. He occasionally asked legislative aides to do church work, and vice versa. It could be hard to tell whether he lived in Jasper County or Aiken County or Lexington County, and he fought off a residency challenge in his final reelection campaign. Like other lawmakers, he steered staff and page positions to relatives, family friends, and parishioners. In each of his last eight years in the state senate, he left required state ethics disclosure forms all but blank, without details about his church salary, assets, and any gifts from interest groups. He collected $45,000 in a state worker's compensation settlement in 2011 from a claim related to his senate employment (his lawyers, including fellow state Sen. Gerald Malloy, a longtime friend, took 25 percent).

In 2013, Pinckney ignored a possible conflict of interest, not to mention the separation of church and state, to arrange a grant from the state legislature for the elevator project at Mother Emanuel. That spring, with the General Assembly in session, the senator broached the topic with Mike Shealy, the influential director of the finance committee, on which Pinckney sat. Shealy was a longtime staffer who knew how to get things done, often through the surreptitious insertion of a line item here or there. "He came to me and he said, 'Mike, I've got to find some money for my church because we've got a bunch of little old ladies and they can't get up and down the steps,' " Shealy recalled. "I looked at him and sort of tilted my head and said, 'You know that's against the establishment clause of the Constitution,' and he kind of smiled. I said, 'But let me give it a little thought and see if I can find a way to get you to your goal.' "

Shealy did some research and came to appreciate the historic stature of Pinckney's church. He also learned that Emanuel's sanctuary sometimes served as a venue for events and performances mounted by the Avery Research Center for African American History and Culture, an archive operated by the College of Charleston. The college was a state-funded institution, and that was all the connection that Shealy needed. "I helped him redesign the request so that money went to Avery and then they contracted back with Emanuel so the money went back to Emanuel," Shealy explained. The sum was wrapped into a $300,000 appropriation to Avery, and in March 2014 the college cut a check for $135,000 to the church. It came with the understanding that Emanuel would continue to be available for Avery functions. "It's just the sausage-making process," Shealy said. "I wasn't going to allow him to do anything that was blatantly illegal."

Although willing to use his legislative position to benefit his church, Pinckney shied from bringing politics directly into the pulpit. He encouraged congregants to register and to vote and allowed candidates to drop by and be recognized on Sunday mornings. But Congress in 1954 had prohibited tax-exempt nonprofits like churches from engaging in direct campaigning, and so he did not make explicit endorsements. That held true even for William Dudley Gregorie, an Emanuel member on the city council. "He might say, 'We don't endorse any particular person,'" Gregorie said, "'but one of our own happens to be running.'" If members felt Pinckney inched too close to the line, as some did one Sunday in 2010 when he encouraged them to attend a Democratic Party gathering, he directed them back to their Bibles. "Brothers and sisters," he said that morning, "I want to remind all of us that Jesus was a rabble-rouser, that Jesus was a man who asked all of us to look at the conditions of our fellow men and women. We live in a country that believes in democracy which means that we have a voice in all that happens . . . And it is a tradition in the African American community that ministers and church members are involved in all of these issues. So, I'm not asking anybody to vote for anyone. I'm not endorsing a candidate. But I invite all to come so we can be about the people's business. Amen?"

Politics within the AME Church was renowned for being at least as grubby as its secular counterpart, and as a lifelong participant and aspiring bishop Pinckney felt at home in that world as well. Although born in revolt, the governance of the AME Church in the new millennium often seemed lodged in the past. Its upper echelons were rife with nepotism (three of six bishops elected in 2024 are the sons of former bishops). Women still struggled to find a voice in the ministry, and those who identified as LGBTQ often found the denomination unwelcoming.

More pointedly, like other denominations, the AME Church had been tainted over the years by recurring scandals involving financial or sexual impropriety by pastors, presiding elders, and bishops. In 1999, for example, a female pastor in Kansas City won a large settlement—originally $6 million but reduced on appeal to $1 million—after alleging sexual harassment by the presiding elder in her district and retribution for blowing the whistle. In 2009, the denomination agreed to another large settlement with a man who claimed he had been molested as a minor by a Los Angeles pastor. In 2021, a retired bishop and presiding elder agreed in a settlement with the New York attorney general to repay a combined $800,000 they had collected in "finder's fees" and kickbacks from the sale of church properties to a developer.

The church began to confront the worst outrage in its more than two-hundred-year history in 2021 when it was discovered that tens of millions of dollars in pension-fund valuation was illusory. Ministers expecting to retire with the money learned that two-thirds of the AME pension fund's stated worth was based on inflated or nonexistent returns from sketchy investments. The victimized ministers filed a class-action lawsuit against the denomination and the denomination in turn sued its former director of retirement services, alleging fraud and embezzlement. John Thomas III, the reform-minded editor of the official AME organ, *The Christian Recorder*, saw the money's disappearance as a predictable outgrowth of decades of unchecked graft. "There is something very wrong with an AME Church culture that has clearly privileged personal gain over the uplift of our community," he wrote in an editorial.

The base salary for the twenty-one all-powerful active bishops, who rotate among geographic districts, usually every eight years, has been deceptively low—$63,000 in 2024 (not including benefits and expenses). But AME bishops often lived and traveled sumptuously, certainly by comparison to their parishioners, and some retired to palatial homes or luxury condos. It was assumed within AME circles that their true intake, including cash offerings from ministers and congregations, could amount to hundreds of thousands of dollars a year (depending on a bishop's interest and adroitness in monetizing the job, and the wealth of his or her district). On occasion, the means by which church leaders accumulated wealth had prompted investigations. But more insidiously, it simply had become an ingrained assumption that a share of the millions that churches passed up the denominational chain wound up in the service of something other than needy AME missions and colleges. The laity, conditioned against challenging religious authority, had largely declined to rebel.

Despite the financial strains on their churches, some bishops took in scores of thousands of dollars each year in what amounted to tribute from pastors and congregations in their districts. In Pinckney's day, they might expect $1,000 or more as a "love offering" for each of the several times a week they showed up at a church to preach a sermon, cut a ribbon, or consecrate a new wing. In the late summer and fall, bishops made the rounds of district conferences where pastors who were beholden to them for jobs and postings lined up to offer their financial respects. Despite the availability of smartphone vending apps, collection plates stacked up with cash, the transparency of the process normalizing it.

Following the opening worship service of the 2019 South Carolina Annual Conference, the district that includes Mother Emanuel, Bishop Samuel L. Green, Sr., called for a $20 offering for the conference. He first asked the roughly eight hundred people gathered in a convention center ballroom to wave their bills and checks in the air, and they did. Dressed in a white and purple robe, the prelate then invited a parade of pastors to his tall leather chair, with the ministers placing their offerings in his palm as he acknowledged each by name. Bishop Green passed the payments to a team of assistants, cloaked in white, who counted the collection at a table, thumbing bills like bank tellers. The process lasted thirty minutes as an organist played hymns.

Subsequently, Bishop Green invited each church's pastor to provide a brief public report about their accomplishments of the past year. One by one, they stood before him to tell about the purchase of an air conditioner, repairs to the bathrooms, the sponsorship of a health fair, a new Boy Scout troop. Like others, Rev. Clinton Hall of New Hope AME Church in St. George approached the podium backed by a posse of congregants, bolstering his case for reappointment by the bishop to another one-year term. To reinforce the point, Hall told Bishop Green that his congregation so valued him that it had rewarded him with a Mercedes-Benz. This prompted a wry smile. "I'm going to move him and assign myself there," the bishop joked. "And I like mine in silver." As the crowd chuckled, the bishop continued to riff. "I'll send *him* back," he told the congregants, "if you park a Mercedes-Benz outside the bishop's residence."

The perceived value of becoming a bishop could be quantified by the millions spent every quadrennium by dozens of candidates vying for the positions (the jobs came open when prelates died or reached mandatory retirement in their mid-seventies, and through periodic expansions). Their operations resembled national political campaigns, with placards and buttons, newspaper advertising, years of travel to churches and conferences on several continents, fundraising solicitations, battles for endorsements, and easily abandoned pledges of reform. Retired bishop Preston Warren Williams II, among other past candidates, said the cost of successful campaigns often ran well into six figures. "You have to go to the bank and borrow money, mortgage the house and whatever you've got," said Williams, who was elected in 2000. "Then the congregations have people raise money with fish dinners and barbecues." At some General Conferences, the elections became multi-ballot spectacles that stretched on for hours, with winners determined through horse-trading and, it is persistently rumored, financial arrangements among candidates and power-brokering bishops. Rarely did failure on a first attempt dissuade hopefuls from trying again. The late Bishop Zedekiah L. Grady, the longtime former pastor of Morris Brown AME Church in Charleston, ran at every quadrennial General Conference from 1972 to 1992, finally winning on his sixth attempt. Starting with Richard Allen in 1816, the church had elected 148 bishops through 2024, including six women beginning in 2000.

Every AME district was expected to submit a defined dollar amount each year to the worldwide "connectional church" organization headquartered in Nashville, Tennessee. Each congregation had an enumerated obligation to contribute to that payment as well as to the programs and operations of its local district, including the financial support of the presiding elder and bishop. Depending on the size, location, and makeup of the congregation, a church's commitment could amount to between 10 percent and 20 percent of its annual income. Hard times or competing needs were not considered acceptable excuses for a shortfall. Pastors and presiding elders might pay a heavy price if they missed their marks, including possible demotion by the bishop to less desirable postings. To avoid such a fate, they regularly tapped their own resources to fill gaps in their payments. That, of course, only incentivized the clerics to find creative ways to repay themselves.

"You find the money, in some way," said Rev. Joseph Darby, who has served as both a pastor and presiding elder for many years. "At my first church, I had twelve members, and it was five hundred or six hundred bucks a couple of times a year. I called and said, 'Elder, I don't have the money from Piney Grove yet.' And he said, 'I figured you didn't have the money *from* Piney Grove, but do you have the money *for* Piney Grove?' And I understood exactly what he meant. I had to put my hands on six hundred dollars, and the church reimbursed me by the end of the year. If you're a decent pastor, you plan how to do it at the beginning of the year and you make the numbers . . . If you don't pay your budget you're pretty much up the creek."

In 2024, the AME churches of South Carolina—the Seventh Episcopal District—were slated to contribute 9 percent of the international AME connection's $14 million annual budget. The amounts contributed by congregations helped explain why aging churches could not keep up with maintenance needs. "At some churches, it's a matter of paying the district budget or putting on a new roof," one AME pastor said. In Clementa Pinckney's first full year at Emanuel, the church devoted $79,132, or 16 percent of its $482,235 budget, to various district, state, and national AME accounts. That left less than $20,000 for maintenance and capital improvements. Pinckney was salaried at $45,000, and received roughly $35,000 in housing and health insurance benefits. Like most AME ministers, he worked a second job, although his legislative pay brought in only $10,400 in salary, plus per diems.

Pinckney's route to Emanuel had been circuitous, in the careening way that AME politics could sometimes direct a minister's career. After postings at churches in Irmo, Beaufort, and Yonges Island, he was elevated in 2006 to presiding elder of a district between Charleston and Columbia that was speckled with country churches. He was proud to be following in the footsteps of his revered great-uncle, leaving his own mark on the family calling. It should have positioned him for future promotion to a more prestigious presiding elder district and set the stage for a run for bishop. Instead, after three years, the same bishop who had elevated Pinckney effectively busted him by assigning him to fill an unanticipated opening in the pastor's office at Campbell Chapel AME in Bluffton. The since-retired bishop, Preston Williams, declined in an interview to explain his thinking beyond that he, like all bishops, had followed his godly judgment in matching a talented young preacher with a church in need of help. But friends of Pinckney believe one factor may have been his struggle to submit the full amount owed to denominational officials by his district's churches. "The talk was that he couldn't make his budgets," said Pinckney's friend and AME colleague, Rev. Kylon J. Middleton. "It was a smaller district with small churches, not a district that could generate enough revenue. He was not in a position financially to do it himself and he couldn't borrow the money. He told me he was stressed out. He was under a lot of pressure."

To a young man in a hurry, with little experience of failure, the move from presiding elder back to pastor felt very much like a demotion. "He was hurt," Pinckney's widow, Jennifer, said, "but was told he would eventually be made an elder again, which never happened."

Pinckney initially resisted when Bishop Williams first disclosed that he wanted to transfer him to Mother Emanuel. He had hoped to regain the rank of presiding elder, preferably within his senate district so he might spend less time on the road. He knew of Emanuel's reputation for being difficult to manage. "He almost had a heart attack," Williams recalled. "He said, 'Oh, my Lord, oh, my bishop, please, please don't do it to me.'" But Williams was convinced of the fit. "Anytime you deal with the Holy Mother you've got to have the right person with the right temperament, who is very understanding of where you are and what you're about," he said. "Not just any preacher can go there and take over the helm of that church. I said, 'Look, you have the right stature. I need somebody like you. The Lord needs you.'" As a company man who could cite chapter and verse of the AME *Doctrines and Discipline*, Pinckney honored the vow of obedience that he had taken when ordained. "Frankly, for me, I'm not feeling it," he told Williams. "But you're my bishop. I respect you and I'll go. It's sure not what I had in mind."

Middleton said that Pinckney was "definitely a product of the system," in church politics as in state politics. "He walked their walk, talked their talk, played their games, and it did not work for him in the end," he said. "He wanted to be a presiding elder, and he got it through that paradigm and it was taken away from him through that paradigm. It was a big blow."

Another Pinckney friend, Kay Taylor Hightower, who happens to be the great-granddaughter of Emanuel's builder, Rev. Lewis Ruffin Nichols, said he "went to Emanuel with very mixed feelings."

"Emanuel is unique in African Methodism," she said. "There are only two churches in the denomination where your predecessor is in his grave looking over you to make sure you do it right"—meaning Mother Emanuel, where her great-grandfather is entombed, and Mother Bethel in Philadelphia, burial site for Richard Allen and Morris Brown. "It's a denominational appointment. It's more work and less money than being a presiding elder, a lot more work and a lot less money. But it had this kind of prestige, and that's the rationalization he made."

Pinckney did quickly make peace with his new assignment and grew to wear his title—Senior Pastor of Mother Emanuel African Methodist Episcopal Church—with great pride. It was, after all, the oldest AME church in the South, and one of the most storied Black congregations in America. Its pulpit had been occupied by Bishops Morris Brown and Richard Harvey Cain, by Booker T. Washington and W.E.B. DuBois and Martin Luther King, Jr. And now by Clementa Carlos Pinckney, at only thirty-seven years of age. If he could not be a presiding elder, there were worse fates.

Pinckney soon learned, of course, that the warnings he'd received were true. He could not slay Emanuel's dragons, as his predecessor Lavern Witherspoon had referred to the congregation's relentless second-guessers. Nor could he singlehandedly arrest the demographic forces aligned against the church. But he did feel as time went by that he was gaining respect among older members—the elevator campaign had helped—and that he could use that accumulated capital to reenergize worship services in ways that might attract younger ones. He was doing what he could, at the pace the congregation would allow, using the political judgment he had honed in each of his careers. "It's turning, but it's like a large ship," Pinckney told Bishop Williams on one of their monthly calls. "It takes a while for the captain to turn, but it's turning, it's coming."

As the Sundays passed, Pinckney developed a profound appreciation for the history that had been made where he stood, and he employed it to enliven the faith of his congregation. In a New Year's Day sermon in 2012, he transported his people back to the days of their ancestors' enslavement and marveled at their unwavering trust in redemption by a Christian God. The story of the Black church, he believed, taught today's African Methodists "to remember where God has brought us from" while challenging them to hope for a better future.

"In the midst of their darkness, in the midst of being whipped, in the midst of being rebuked and scorned, in the midst of making other people rich at our own expense, they believed that somehow, some way, God would deliver us," Pinckney preached, cradling his red-bound Bible in his palm. "They believed that in spite of all that had happened, in spite of nearly two hundred years of slavery and being bonded, they believed they would arise and shine because of the light of the covenant." Draped in a white robe embroidered with gold crosses, he recounted the martyrdom of Denmark Vesey and the triumphant return of African Methodism to Charleston under Daniel Alexander Payne. Payne had prayed and rejoiced, he said, upon disembarking on native soil in 1865. "He knew that Jesus had lifted the darkness and that we could open our doors and worship the Lord one more time," Pinckney said. "Arise and shine. Our light has come." The same was true, he told his flock, as they passed out of a year marked by economic hardship. The flipping of the calendar would not automatically bring recovery, he said. "Brothers and sisters, the Scriptures don't say that the troubles have gone away," Pinckney explained. "The Scriptures say that in the midst of your darkness a light has come . . . In other words, in the midst of your heavy burden, Jesus is going to be right there . . . God will move in our lives. In the midst of the hopelessness that the world wants us to feel, God says don't be hopeless because I'm not dead."

In late April 2015, fifty-two days before his death, Pinckney served as host for a "Requiem on Racism" program held at Emanuel and sponsored by the local YWCA. Standing tall in his pulpit, one floor above where he would be murdered, he offered an opening prayer that invited God to fill Emanuel with His love. "We know only love can conquer hate, that only love can bring all together in your name," he said. "Irregardless of our faiths, our ethnicities, where we are from, together we come in love, together we come to bury racism, to bury bigotry, and to resurrect and to revive love, compassion, and tenderness."

It was a hopeful prayer, the right prayer for the moment. But it was an invocation that would go unanswered.

XVI.

Judgment Day

For the wages of sin is death; but the gift of God is eternal life through Jesus Christ our Lord.

—ROMANS 6:23 (KJV)

Dylann Roof's federal death penalty trial could not have been less satisfying in revealing how a directionless twenty-one-year-old devolves from a reclusive consumer of internet bile into a ruthless lone-wolf jihadist (his word). Observers were left with only the unsettling realization that 150 years after the Civil War and five decades after the Civil Rights Act, despite the ascendancy of leaders like Barack Obama and Clementa Pinckney, delusions of racial superiority could still drive white Americans to commit unthinkable acts of terror. Most white supremacists did not, of course, view their cause as one worth dying for, or spending a life in prison for, and did not make Roof's leap to act on violent impulses. That was something Roof emphasized in the most pointed explanation he provided for his decision to pull the trigger seventy-seven times. "We have no skinheads, no real KKK, no one doing anything but talking on the internet," he complained in the manifesto he posted to his website before leaving for Charleston. "Well someone has to have the bravery to take it to the real world, and I guess that has to be me."

Few can compete with Dylann Roof as an emblem of the sickening persistence of racial violence in the post–civil rights age. His radicalization online and the video-game detachment of his savagery marked his descent as particular to his times. But in his choice to attack Mother Emanuel there also seemed a distillation of the serial efforts over two centuries to suppress the first AME congregation in the South, starting with the destruction of its church and exile of its leaders in 1822. That the cosmos inflicted such a desecration, at the hands of someone so trifling, upon a people already steeped in such suffering, felt like the cruelest of twists. Did this church among all those Roof might have targeted really need another test of its durability and devotion? Could this congregation not already appreciate the fragility of life and liberty for African Americans in the South? How were a God-fearing people to interpret the visitation of such a bolt of evil? Roof's trial offered his victims and a confounded nation some small chance to wring sense from it all, and to plumb for signs of humanity in a killer who refused to reciprocate any of the grace that had been granted to him.

But in his bizarre and disquieting trial, which began in December 2016, Roof hijacked his own defense to ensure that his martyrdom for the white nationalist cause would not be misconstrued, particularly by any suggestion that he was unstable. If that meant he would die for his actions, so be it. Death, he certainly felt, would be better than leaving his neo-Nazi compatriots with any misimpression that he had not fully premeditated his attack on Mother Emanuel. Nor did he wish to be seen as a mental "defective," a label that might target him for elimination along with Black people, Jews, and homosexuals in the post-revolutionary world he imagined. Roof considered himself a zealot, not a lunatic, and did not want the worldwide coverage of his trial to muddy that distinction or discredit his intent. Given the assault that he perceived on whiteness by Blackness, it seemed to him the opposite of crazy to try to "agitate race relations," his stated goal. His remorse when confronted by grieving, furious survivors and his shattered, bewildered family was less than zero. Even his own lawyer, the veteran death-penalty antagonist David I. Bruck, acknowledged that without deeper insight into his inscrutable client it would be "the most natural thing in the world for people to say this is simply the face of evil."

With considerable cunning, Roof made sure that his jury of nine white and three Black citizens would see no other face. Deeply self-conscious about his appearance, Roof had designed his trademark bowl haircut to obscure a forehead that he believed to be grossly misshapen. Acquaintances observed that he wore a hoodie like a cocoon. In similar fashion, in the glare of a sensational trial, he did anything he could to prevent the world from glimpsing the fullness of his dysfunction.

Rather than hearing of Roof's broken family and undiagnosed autism, jurors saw video of his confession to the FBI that he "had to do it because somebody had to do something, because, you know, Black people are killing white people every day." They were read the jailhouse journal in which he made it "crystal clear" that he had no regrets and had "not shed a tear for the innocent people I killed." They heard the young killer emphasize his own free will in the rambling opening and closing statements he made to the jury after sidelining his legal team in the trial's penalty phase. "You might remember in my confession to the FBI that I told them that I had to do it," Roof said in a soft monotone, "and obviously that is not really true, because I didn't have to do it. I didn't have to do anything, and no one made me do it. But what I meant when I said that was that I felt like I had to do it, and I still feel like I had to do it."

To preserve his chosen narrative, Roof willfully undermined the only defense that stood any chance of persuading even a single juror to spare him. As his trial date approached, he realized that his court-appointed lawyers were fixated on saving his life with a psychiatric defense and did not share his objectives. After the trial's initial guilt-or-innocence phase, he won U.S. District Judge Richard M. Gergel's permission to suspend his defense team and represent himself in order to block the disclosure of evidence about his mental health. That evidence, which had been presented at a pair of closed-door competency hearings and was unsealed after Roof's convictions, did not show him to be psychopathic. But it did provide a more multidimensional portrait than the jury saw of a withdrawn yet strikingly intelligent misfit who plunged down a toxic internet rabbit hole, found perverse meaning in its racist distortions, and never climbed back out.

Roof's shrewdness became apparent in the plot he hatched to sabotage Bruck and his defense team. In early November, a month before trial, he handwrote a jailhouse letter to prosecutors that accused his own lawyers—"the sneakiest group of people I have ever met"—of lying to him about their trial strategy. He predicted they would try to deceive the jury as well. "Because I have no real defense," he wrote, "my lawyers have been forced to grasp at straws and to present a pathetic, fraudulent excuse for a defense in my name." Roof knew the prosecutors would have to turn the document over to Judge Gergel, who called a closed-door hearing. "I don't want anybody to think that I did it because I have some kind of mental problem," Roof told the judge matter-of-factly. "I wanted to increase racial tension." Bruck countered that Roof's letter demonstrated his instability.

Gergel, an Obama appointee, was himself a learned student of his native state's civil-rights history. The judge and his historian wife, Belinda, had co-written a book about the early Jewish settlers of Columbia. He had been working for years on a manuscript about the racist attack that blinded Sgt. Isaac

Woodard in 1946 and the case's impact on his judicial hero, J. Waties Waring. Gergel was sixty-two, with a helmet of white hair, a twangy drawl, and a disarmingly broad smile that he used to great effect in managing Roof's trial. The Jewish jurist calmly warned his avowedly racist and anti-Semitic defendant about the likely consequences of representing himself during the penalty phase. But he ultimately concluded there was not sufficient evidence of incapacity under Supreme Court precedent to prevent Roof from presenting his case as he wished, even if it felt like suicide by jury.

The competency assessments revealed that Roof had exhibited social anxiety and detached behavior from an early age. His parents had divorced three years before his birth, and he was conceived during a short-lived reconciliation. They split for good when he was five. Dylann moved from house to house and school to school as his mother gained and lost boyfriends. As a child, he played alone and rarely initiated conversation. As a teen, he had few friends and no apparent romantic involvements.

He developed a daily marijuana habit, dabbled with prescription drugs and alcohol, dropped out of school after repeatedly failing ninth grade, and secluded himself in his bedroom, interacting almost exclusively with his computer. He worked briefly for a landscaping company owned by a family friend but distanced himself from coworkers and eventually lost the job due to absenteeism. Roof's only encounter with the mental-health system came when he was fourteen and made three visits to a county clinic after telling his mother he wanted to run away and kill himself. He declined to take anti-anxiety medication or continue therapy, and his tendencies toward depression, delusional thinking, and grandiosity otherwise went unaddressed until his arrest.

Those who examined Roof at that point consistently described him as childlike and socially stunted, yet he placed in the 95th percentile on an IQ test. He listened to National Public Radio and opera and read Goethe and Dostoevsky and Machiavelli. Bruck compared his client to "a precocious ten-year-old" whose "geyser of autistic symptoms" had been masked by innate intelligence and verbal adeptness.

As evidence, Bruck presented disturbing videos of Roof's jailhouse visits with his parents and other relatives. In spite of their devotion under wrenching circumstances, Roof entertained himself during their limited time together like a cat toying with a stuffed mouse. Appearing via closed circuit from a booth inside the Charleston County detention center, he could not have seemed more disinterested in his parents' worries or more eager to stoke their exasperation. His father, Franklin Bennett (Benn) Roof, could not take it anymore when Dylann taunted that he planned to do something before his trial to "make it even worse."

"What is wrong with you, son?" the father snapped.

"Nothing."

"What is wrong with you? You have got to be kidding me. Please don't do anything stupid. I mean, you've already done enough. God dang, man." He had to leave the room to regain his composure.

Roof's unnerving disengagement also was apparent in a series of forty-seven telephone calls that he placed to his mother and grandparents from the jail. The young killer and his relatives were aware that their calls were being monitored, and so avoided any discussion of his crimes and motivation. But in ten hours of conversation over an eighteen-month span, Roof displayed a breathtaking void of regret and concern, even for his own family and personal circumstances.

In a call with his grandfather two months after the murders, Roof expressed amazement that family members were being subjected to regular interrogation by investigators and lawyers. "Dylann, I'm not fussing at you," Carl Joseph (Joe) Roof, a prominent lawyer in Columbia, tried to explain, "but you don't seem to understand what all we've been going through . . . It has affected everybody's life in more ways than we can ever count. And, again, I'm not fussing at you. You know enough that I don't need to fuss at you. That's not my intent. But I'll just tell you that your Papa, at least, and your Grandmama have been through pure hell."

Roof chuckled. "Are you serious?" he asked.

"I am deadly serious," Joe Roof said solemnly. Dylann changed the subject.

That is as confrontational as the conversations got, as Roof's mother and grandparents handled him as gently as a wounded bird. What they presumably intended as unconditional love came across as abject appeasement, as if any disapproval or demand for accountability might have shattered him. They indulged his various obsessions, dedicating fifteen-minute calls to his queries about the health of the family cats and the color of the sweaters his mother had bought. He was full of requests—for a book on medieval knights, for an encyclopedia entry on German literature, for money to replenish his commissary account—and they jumped to fulfill them. At one point, to his mother's disbelief, he asked for a French language primer.

In a pair of letters written from death row in 2020, Roof sounded very much like the disconnected, petulant young man who had tormented his family from jail. He largely ignored pointed questions I had asked about his motivation and timing and choice of targets. His primary interest seemed to be establishing dominance in a new relationship. Roof did take a few paragraphs to explain that his view of himself and the world had not changed from the confines of his cell. "What I will say is that I'm not the bad guy," he wrote. "I'd like to think I'm not even a bad person. There are at least 10,000 reasons a person might have done what I did, none of which you are interested in considering, much less writing about."

He continued, "I am a member of a group targeted for genocide. What complicates things is that many of the people doing the targeting are also part of this group. But they don't see themselves as part of the group because they only identify as individuals, and so they target themselves without fully understanding what they're doing." There was no further explanation.

After scores of hours of interviews and testing, defense experts diagnosed Roof with mild to moderate autism, debilitating social anxiety, and precursor symptoms of psychosis. Those belated determinations did not in any way explain his rampage. Plenty of similarly situated young men did not buy a handgun, stake out a historic Black church, then set out to murder innocents in prayer. But Rachel Loftin, an autism expert who assessed Roof for the defense, suggested that his condition likely encouraged his fixation on white-supremacist thinking. "The clarity and rigidity of these racial categories allows Dylann, a person with limited social insight who often does not perceive or understand high level social behaviors, to organize people and make sense of the world," she wrote. "This is a system that simplifies human interaction and renders it comprehensible." Roof's isolation, at an age when others were starting college or careers, left him with few influences to counter the torrent of racial grievance he confronted online. As a result, Loftin wrote, "Dylann pursued his preoccupation with racism with an autistic intensity. It pervaded all aspects of his life."

ALTHOUGH ROOF'S FATHER, a construction contractor, could be coarse and derogatory toward people of color at times, virulent bigotry did not seem to have been an organizing principle in Roof's various households. Dylann told the FBI he had not personally suffered any injury or mistreatment at the hands of Black people.

Rather, Roof consistently attributed his indoctrination to the dark corners of the World Wide Web, notably a site sponsored by the white supremacist Council of Conservative Citizens. "It sounds lame, you know . . . but it's pretty much just the internet," he told his FBI interviewers. "All the information's there for you." His spiral began as early as 2008 and accelerated in 2012 after the fatal shooting of Trayvon Martin, the unarmed Black teenager gunned down in Florida by a white neighborhood-watch volunteer. Upon learning of it, Roof typed "black on white crime" into the Google search bar and came upon misleading statistics that he distorted into evidence of an epidemic. Everything changed, he told investigators and evaluators, and he began a journey toward becoming "completely racially aware." David Bruck compared his young client's online awakening to "a magic decoder ring" that enabled him to sort out his disordered thinking. Roof had been going nowhere fast. Now he saw purpose and a path to relevance. "He felt suddenly better because it offered him an explanation for his uncomfortable feelings," wrote Dr. Donna Maddox, a defense psychiatrist. "He stated that he had always known something was wrong but he did not know what it was." Roof evolved into an equal-opportunity bigot—Black people, Hispanics, Jews, Muslims, and homosexuals all came in for vilification in his writings.

Roof explained in his FBI interview that he considered various options to avenge the crimes of Black people against white people, including a mass shooting at a predominantly Black gathering, like a festival or picnic. He settled on attacking a Black church because it provided a soft target and would be the very "caricature of a racist act," calculated to generate a response that might spin into full-fledged conflict. He had expected resistance from the Bible-study parishioners when he entered, and could only think to take a seat when they welcomed him instead. He deliberated throughout the class— "going back and forth in my mind"—knowing he could walk away. Then, "like a jerk reaction," he decided that if he did not act then he never would.

Roof's living situation had deteriorated in the weeks prior to the shootings. His parents, displeased with his idleness and isolation, had hassled him about getting a job, threatening eviction unless he found a way to pay rent. His mother cut off internet service to force him off the computer. He slept some nights in the log house in exurban Eastover that she shared with her boyfriend, Danny Beard, and others on the sofa of his father's bungalow in Columbia. Sometimes he just stayed in his car or on the floor of a friend's two-bedroom trailer in Red Bank. That friend, Joey Meek, a rare skateboarding pal from middle school with whom he had recently reconnected on Facebook, reported that Roof openly advertised his racism on those visits, speaking admiringly of segregation, Hitler, and Rhodesian apartheid.

Investigators would later learn through the global positioning technology in Roof's car that he made six scouting trips to Charleston over six months. Clad in black, he used the visits to tour historical sites associated with slavery and the Confederacy, like the beach at Sullivan's Island, where thousands of captive Africans came ashore, and the slave cabins at Boone Hall Plantation. Roof left a photographic record that included selfies taken on those trips and in his bedroom and backyard, where he posed menacingly with his gun and a Confederate flag. In his most chilling bit of cinematography, he set his phone to video and recorded his target practice sessions in the expanse behind Danny Beard's house. Wearing blue tartan pajama pants and an ill-fitting Gold's Gym tank top, he took aim at water jugs and phone books, blowing them to shards. At one point, he fired directly toward the camera, meaning that viewers in the courtroom, including survivors and family members, felt the red glare of his laser jiggle between their eyes before he stilled his right hand and fired, the same sensation their loved ones may have felt in their final seconds.

Roof bought his weapon for $695.49 at Shooter's Choice, a gun store in West Columbia, two weeks after he turned twenty-one and two months before he used it at Emanuel. His father had given him a birthday card with an adorable otter pictured on the front and an IOU scribbled inside for $400 toward the purchase of a pistol, contingent on Roof getting a job. "I love you buddy!" Benn Roof wrote. After a mandatory waiting period of three business days, Roof picked up his shiny black .45 caliber Glock on April 16, 2015, and began buying hollow-point bullets. It never should have happened. Roof had been arrested at a Columbia mall six weeks earlier on a drug charge and admitted possessing an unprescribed controlled substance, Suboxone. By the rules, that admission should have triggered a denial by the FBI firearms background checker. But confusion by the examiner over jurisdiction and delayed responses by local agencies led to the expiration of the waiting period. That allowed Shooter's Choice to legally close the sale. By the time the FBI examiner issued her denial, the Emanuel Nine had been dead for twelve days.

The dreadful screw-up later prompted an internal review by a contrite FBI. It revealed that hundreds of thousands of background checks were not completed within the three-day window each year, typically around 3 percent. In 2017 alone, that had enabled 4,864 improper weapon sales. The review prompted renewed efforts by the bureau to expand the use of databases and to streamline contacts with local agencies. But Democrats in Congress failed through 2024 to gain needed Republican support to close the so-called Charleston Loophole by lengthening the background-check period. A bill to extend it to ten days passed several times in the House, where it was sponsored by Rep. James Clyburn, whose district included parts of Charleston. Staunchly opposed by the National Rifle Association, the measure failed to gain sufficient bipartisan support in the Senate, where sixty votes are needed. Similar legislation stayed bottled up in South Carolina's Republican-dominated General Assembly, where mourning senators once draped Clementa Pinckney's desk in black. Instead, the legislature passed a law in 2021 allowing those twenty-one or older to openly carry handguns with a permit and one in 2024 that lowered the age to eighteen and eliminated requirements for permits and training.

The ease with which Roof obtained his weapon thrust Emanuel and its people squarely into the gun-control debate. "Once again, innocent people were killed in part because someone who wanted to inflict harm had no trouble getting their hand on a gun," Barack Obama said from the White House the day after the shootings. In 2018, Pastor Eric S. C. Manning called for stronger background checks in testimony to a state legislative panel. The following year, Rep. Clyburn staged a press conference in Emanuel's sanctuary to promote his federal bill. Survivors of the 2015 attack—Felicia Sanders, Polly Sheppard, Jennifer and Malana Pinckney—and relatives of the victims became outspoken lobbyists for gun restrictions, appearing at White House press conferences and the Democratic National Convention and in presidential campaign ads. They also sued the federal government for its negligence. After five years of pretrial proceedings, Joe Biden's Justice Department agreed in October 2021 to a landmark $88 million settlement, with each Emanuel victim's family receiving between $6 million and $7.5 million and each survivor getting $5 million.

It was an acquaintance of Roof who first called a police tip line and identified him at 6:20 a.m. the day after the shootings, once a wanted poster began circulating. The next caller to name the figure captured by Emanuel's security camera was Roof's older sister, Amber, who would soon be cancelling the wedding she had planned for that weekend.

The news from Charleston saturated the morning shows, and Debbie Dills, a fifty-one-year-old florist from Gastonia, North Carolina, found herself fixated on the *Fox & Friends* reports about the nationwide dragnet for the church shooter. As the music minister at her church, she felt a real affinity for the Bible-study worshippers, never mind that they were African Methodists and she was a white Southern Baptist. In her car, running late to the shop, she whispered a little prayer for them. Not long after, she noticed a black car in the adjacent lane of U.S. 74. It seemed oddly familiar, and her mind flitted back to the Hyundai on the wanted poster she had seen on TV. "Nah, that's not his car," she told herself. She glanced again and saw that it had South Carolina plates. When she steered close enough to see the driver's haircut she freaked. Dills called her boss at the florist shop. He told her to trail the car while he called the police, who quickly confirmed that the license plate—LGF330— belonged to Roof. Dills caught back up with the Hyundai in Shelby, some 250 miles northwest of Charleston, and watched with relief as white police cruisers zipped by her.

At 10:52 a.m., Shelby officers pulled Roof over on a busy four-lane road and approached the car with guns rather casually drawn. Roof complied when they commanded him to place his hands on the steering wheel, turn off the engine, step slowly out of the car, and stretch his arms across the driver's side door. They asked his name and he answered truthfully and volunteered that there was a gun in the backseat. As one officer frisked and cuffed him, another found the Glock under a white pillow. When a sergeant asked Roof if he had been involved in the incident in Charleston, he answered, "Yes." A fuller confession came several hours later at Shelby's police headquarters, once FBI agents Michael Stansbury and Craig Januchowski arrived. Hungry after a long night in flight, Roof had been provided a Whopper from Burger King, a kindness many doubted would have been afforded a Black mass murderer. He waived extradition and was flown that afternoon to Charleston on the state's executive airplane, which Governor Nikki Haley dispatched to bring him home. Roof took the seat that Haley usually occupied on her industrial recruitment trips and speaking tours of the state. On landing, he was held without bond on nine counts of murder.

A month later, Loretta Lynch, the first Black woman to serve as Attorney General of the United States, announced a thirty-three-count federal indictment on weapons, hate crimes, and other charges related to Roof's targeted selection of African Americans who were exercising their faith. Fittingly, it was his use of the internet, both in choosing his target and in posting his manifesto, that provided the link to interstate commerce needed to assert federal jurisdiction. Lynch also noted that the Justice Department had gotten involved because South Carolina was one of the few states without hate-crimes provisions of any kind. Racially motivated violence, she declared, qualified as "the original domestic terrorism." Ten months later, Lynch announced that for the first time the federal government would seek the death penalty in a case related to hate crimes, on eighteen of the counts. She did so over the objection of her subordinate, William N. Nettles, the U.S. attorney for South Carolina, who argued that a federal prosecution would needlessly replicate the state's case.

The survivors and family members of the victims were divided over that call, as were members of Mother Emanuel. Some, like Cynthia Hurd's husband, Arthur S. Hurd, and her brother, Malcolm Graham, a former North Carolina state senator, left the impression they would gladly depress the lethal injection plunger themselves. Roof's form of hatred had no right to endure even "in America's smallest jail," said Graham. "If there's any case in America where the death penalty is deserved, it is this one." Tyrone Sanders, Felicia's husband and Tywanza's father, said he fantasized during Roof's trial about hurdling the courtroom bar to seek his own vengeance. "My thoughts were if I could get to him, what would I do," Sanders said after Roof's conviction, adding that only God prevented him from carrying out "medieval" justice. But others felt tugged by the command to forgive and morally conflicted about the Old Testament's endorsement of an eye for an eye. The African Methodist Episcopal denomination opposed the death penalty as a matter of policy. So did a hefty majority of Black South Carolinians, both on moral grounds and because of the penalty's disproportionate use against African American defendants. Roof's lawyers had said he would plead guilty in exchange for a life sentence. Many of those already traumatized hoped to be spared the recurring nightmare of a prolonged trial and a two-decade slog through capital appeals. "Don't you think he's a misguided soul?" shooting survivor Polly Sheppard asked, explaining her opposition to executing Roof. "I kind of feel sorry for the young man. I mean he hadn't had a chance to live yet, you know, at twenty-one."

The feds won the race to the courthouse, and Roof's trial opened in December 2016 in the stately stone building near the Four Corners of Law. There was never any question about his guilt, but that did not alleviate the anxiousness in Charleston's Black community. After all, in the county courthouse across Broad Street, the prosecution of North Charleston policeman Michael Slager for shooting unarmed Black motorist Walter Scott had just ended in a mistrial. Those concerns diminished as lead prosecutors Julius Ness (Jay) Richardson and Nathan S. Williams guided jurors through the overwhelming evidence—Roof's pre-assault manifesto, his taped confession to the FBI, his remorseless jail-cell writings, the bloody crime-scene photos, the gruesome testimony of ballistics experts and medical examiners, the GPS tracing of Roof's travels, the racist imagery taken from his camera and computer, the notebook pages listing Mother Emanuel and other possible targets, the records showing Roof had called the church, the pictures of him buying the gun, and, of course, the security-camera video of his entering the lower-level door on the night of June 17. To counter David Bruck's suggestion that Roof was detached from reality—"on a different planet from the rest of us"—the prosecutors argued that there were such things as hatred and evil in the world, at times beyond human understanding. Roof's preparation and premeditation demonstrated it, they said. The jurors heard the stunned voices of the first responding officers as they attempted an initial count of the dead, their tally captured by a body camera. "We've got one, two, three, four, five, six, seven, eight, make that eight," one officer said, falling a body short of the final toll.

The lead FBI agent, Joseph Hamski, outlined the bureau's meticulous investigation: 530 pieces of evidence, 215 interviews, 65 subpoenas, 13 searches, all involving at least 50 agents. After Richardson outlined Roof's misdeeds in his opening argument, Roof's mother, Amelia Cowles Roof, collapsed from what his lawyers said had been a heart attack. Roof's father did not attend the proceedings, which were not televised, but his paternal grandparents occasionally sat behind him in the courtroom, their heartbreak palpable. The other side of Courtroom Six filled each day with relatives and friends of the deceased, AME dignitaries, and members of Mother Emanuel. Felicia and Tyrone Sanders watched from the first of six rows of wooden benches, while Pastor Manning sat one row back. Rev. Anthony Thompson, whose late wife, Myra, led the Bible study that night, took his place in the fifth row, along with John Pinckney, the former pastor's father, in a wheelchair. It was the first time many had laid eyes on Roof, and their revulsion alternated with astonishment at how insubstantial he appeared. "He looks so frail," observed Sharon Risher, one of victim Ethel Lance's daughters, "like you could snap him like a twig."

The adult survivors served as heartrending star witnesses, with Felicia Sanders opening the government's case and Polly Sheppard closing it. Appearing purposeful and composed in a violet jacket, Sanders introduced the

Rev. Benjamin J. Glover during recuperation from racist beating. *Courtesy of daughter Gail A. Glover*

Rev. Benjamin J. Glover. *Courtesy of daughter Gail A. Glover*

Rev. Benjamin J. Glover (holding poster) leading demonstrators during a 1963 civil rights march in Charleston. *AP Photo/J. Spencer Jones*

First African American students to desegregate Charleston's schools in 1963, including Oveta Glover (seated, far right) and Millicent Brown (standing, second from right). *Isaiah DeQuincey Newman Papers, South Carolina Political Collections, University of South Carolina*

Civil rights mass meeting at Emanuel AME Church, undated. *Courtesy of Rev. Benjamin J. Glover's family*

Dr. Martin Luther King, Jr., speaking at Emanuel AME Church, April 12, 1962. *Avery photograph collection, AMN 1112, Avery Research Center for African American History and Culture, College of Charleston, Charleston, SC, USA*

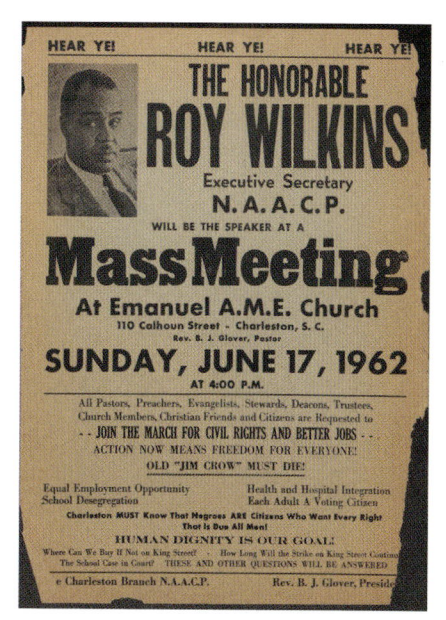

Advertisement for civil rights mass meeting at Emanuel AME featuring NAACP executive secretary Roy Wilkins, June 17, 1962. *Courtesy of Rev. Benjamin J. Glover's family*

Coretta Scott King and union leader Mary Moultrie, to her left, singing at the podium of Emanuel AME during the Charleston hopital workers' strike, April 19, 1969. *Avery photograph collection, AMN 1112, Avery Research Center for African American History and Culture, College of Charleston, Charleston, SC, USA*

Rev. Clementa C. Pinckney, shortly after his appointment in 2010 as pastor of Emanuel AME Church. *Grace Beahm Alford/The Post and Courier*

Security camera screenshot capturing Dylann Roof entering Emanuel AME Church on the night of June 17, 2015. *United States District Court for the District of South Carolina, United States of America v. Dylann Storm Roof, Government Exhibit 104*

Sharonda Coleman-Singleton

Cynthia Hurd

Susie Jackson

Ethel Lance

DePayne Middleton

Clementa C. Pinckney

Tywanza Sanders

Daniel L. Simmons, Sr.

Myra Thompson

The Emanuel Nine, killed during Bible study on June 17, 2015. *United States District Court for the District of South Carolina, United States of America v. Dylann Storm Roof, Government Exhibits 13–19, 687); Grace Beahm Alford/The Post and Courier*

Tyrone, Tywanza, and Felicia Sanders at Tywanza's graduation from Allen University, 2014. *Courtesy of Tyrone and Felicia Sanders*

Tywanza Sanders, seen here with his mother, Felicia, had her name tattooed across his chest during her battle against breast cancer. *Courtesy of Tyrone and Felicia Sanders*

Shooting survivors Polly Sheppard (center) and Jennifer Pinckney (right) with Rev. Clementa Pinckney inside Emanuel AME Church. *Emanuel African Methodist Episcopal Church Archives*

Presiding Elder Norvel Goff, Sr., who became interim pastor of Emanuel AME after the shootings, preached on the first Sunday after the massacre, June 21, 2015. *Paul Zoeller/The Post and Courier*

President Barack Obama sang "Amazing Grace" at the memorial service for Rev. Clementa Pinckney, June 26, 2015. *Stephen Crowley/The New York Times/Redux*

Malana Pinckney eyed President Barack Obama at the memorial service for her father, Rev. Clementa Pinckney, June 26, 2015. *Stephen Crowley/The New York Times/Redux*

Rev. Betty Deas Clark became Emanuel AME's first female pastor in January 2016 but kept the job for only six months. *Leroy Burnell/The Post and Courier*

Rev. Eric S. C. Manning, who was named Emanuel AME's pastor in June 2016. *Courtesy Eric S. C. Manning*

Shooting survivor Polly Sheppard and family members of the victims, including Rev. Leroy Middleton (rear), met with President Joe Biden after his speech at Emanuel AME on January 8, 2024. *Courtesy of Polly Sheppard*

Joe Biden became the first president to speak from Emanuel AME's pulpit during a campaign event on January 8, 2024. He is flanked by Rep. James E. Clyburn of South Carolina (left); Bishop Samuel L. Green, Sr. (center); and Pastor Eric S. C. Manning (right). *AP Photo/Mic Smith*

jury to the nine beloved victims and described the Bible study, Roof's eruption, and Tywanza's heroic last moments. "I watched my son come in this world and I watched my son leave this world," she told the jury in her Lowcountry lilt. Seeking any entry to plant questions about his client's sanity, Bruck asked Sanders in a brief cross-examination if she remembered Roof saying he was only twenty-one. She said she did. What did he say next, Bruck asked, miscalculating Sanders's response. "He say he was going to kill himself, and I was counting on that," she answered icily. "He's evil. There's no place on Earth for him except the pit of hell." Bruck tried once more, repeating his prompt about Roof's suicidality. Sanders would have none of it: "Send himself back to the pit of hell, I say." After Polly Sheppard testified about staring down the barrel of Roof's gun, Bruck opted not to take the same gamble. "Miss Sheppard, I am so sorry," he said. "I have no questions for you." The jury deliberated only two hours before convicting Roof on all counts.

AFTER A HOLIDAY BREAK, the trial recommenced on January 4, 2017, so the jury could take the steps required to render a death sentence that seemed as inevitable as it did inadequate. Dressed in a charcoal cable-knit sweater and gray slacks, the now-convicted mass murderer addressed the jury directly in an opening statement that lasted only three minutes. He did not, as some feared, use the opportunity for white-supremacist flag-waving. Rather, he defended his sanity, imploring jurors to forget anything his lawyers had said. "You may or may not have heard," he said, "that the reason I chose to represent myself in this phase of the trial was to prevent my lawyers from presenting mental-health mitigation, and that's absolutely true. But it isn't because I have a mental illness that I don't want you to know about, and it isn't because I'm trying to keep a secret from you . . . The point is that I'm not going to lie to you either by myself or through anyone else."

Jurors then sat through a four-day procession of grief as spouses, children, grandchildren, and best friends gave flesh-and-blood dimension to the loss of each victim. They heard of Anthony Thompson's enchantment with his wife Myra's smile. "I mean, she got anything from me when she smiled," he said, "and I think that's why she smiled all the time." They heard about the seventieth birthday party that Susie Jackson's family had arranged secretly in Emanuel's fellowship hall, knowing it would be easiest to surprise her in "the place that she's always at." They learned of librarian Cynthia Hurd's life motto—"Be kinder than necessary"—and that church sexton Ethel Lance sang "One Day at a Time" while scrubbing Emanuel's bathrooms. The jurors also heard the voices of the dead—recordings of Rev. Clementa Pinckney lecturing proudly about Mother Emanuel's history, of Rev. DePayne Middleton booming an a cappella solo, of Rev. Sharonda Coleman-Singleton praying to a crescendo at a friend's funeral. Roof called no witnesses and presented no evidence to counteract the government's case.

The trial's most dramatic moments, however, came on the day after the jurors returned their death sentence, taking little more than three hours. The decision had been obvious enough that they sent out for a late lunch before notifying the judge so as not to appear too hasty in dispatching a young man to death row. Before Judge Gergel formally sentenced Roof, those victimized by his actions were given a chance to address the killer face-to-face. Thirty-six Black men and women went to the microphone, one after the next, some striding with anger, others sagging under incalculable weight. They demanded, often with voices raised, that Roof turn to look at them, that he connect with them through eye contact if nothing else. He refused to give them even that, sitting as if in a trance, expressionless, staring ahead. "I wish you would look at me, boy, but I know you hear me," insisted Janet Scott, Tywanza Sanders's self-described favorite aunt. Some speakers forgave Roof with Christian grace. Others damned him to hell. Dan Simmons, Jr., pleaded with Roof to repent and "feel the awesome power of the Holy Spirit." He counseled his father's killer that forgiveness was "the heartbeat that pulls us to another level." Emanuel member Marsha Spencer, on the other hand, called Roof a "subhuman miscreant." DePayne Middleton's sister, Bethane Middleton-Brown, predicted that his soul would become "Satan's playground." Many were still searching for God's reason. But almost all proclaimed that Roof had failed in his mission to sow racial conflict. "The hatred that you possess is beyond human comprehension," said Melvin Graham, Jr., Cynthia Hurd's brother. "You wanted to start a race war. You wanted people to kill each other. But instead of starting a race war, you started a love war. What you did pulled people together in a way that I did not know could happen." Graham listed off the honors granted and good deeds performed in memory of his sister, a devoted librarian. He finished by reminding Roof that his actions had been instrumental in removing the Confederate flag from the State Capitol grounds in Columbia.

If not closure—and it certainly wasn't that—the hearing provided the nearest thing to catharsis that Roof would allow his victims. Felicia Sanders clutched her bloodstained Bible, which a police lieutenant had retrieved from a bin of hazardous waste. She told Roof of the trauma that still reverberated from his gunshots, the way she jumped at the pop of a balloon or thwack of a fallen acorn. "Most importantly, I cannot shut my eyes to pray," she said. "Even when I try I cannot because I have to keep my eye on everyone that is around me." Although she had wished God's mercy on Roof at his bond hearing, she was unsparing now: "When I think of you, I just see somebody cold who is lost, who the devil has come back to reclaim." Her husband, Tyrone, told Roof he hoped he would lose a limb each time he filed an appeal at taxpayer expense. The final speaker, Emanuel's pastor, Rev. Manning, spoke of the challenges of healing his devastated congregation. He quoted from Psalm 27—"The Lord is the stronghold of my life. Of whom shall I be afraid?"—and said that even when he led Bible study in the fellowship hall he somehow found hope. "If we are quiet, we can hear the echoes of the Holy Spirit throughout that lower level because what Satan may have meant for evil, God has meant it for good."

Judge Gergel did not tarry in pronouncing Roof's sentence. "This trial has produced no winners, only losers," he began. "The families have lost their beloved and irreplaceable loved ones, and the defendant will now pay for his crimes with his life. But the trial has not been a futile act because the jury, acting as the conscience of this community, has stated clearly and unequivocally that this hate, this viciousness, this moral depravity, will not go unanswered." Although not required to be there that day, most of the jurors attended to show solidarity with the families. A month later, they paid their respects as a group by visiting Emanuel for Sunday worship. Rev. Manning maintained their anonymity by introducing them simply as "civic servants."

In late March 2017, Roof reached an agreement with state prosecutors to plead guilty to their separate murder charges in exchange for life sentences. Both the Fourth Circuit Court of Appeals and the U.S. Supreme Court upheld his federal convictions. In the final month of his presidency, Joe Biden commuted the death sentences of thirty-seven of the forty inmates awaiting execution on federal convictions, reducing their terms to life in prison. Dylann Roof was one of the three not spared, along with Pittsburgh synagogue assailant Robert Bowers and Boston Marathon bomber Dzhokhar Tsarnaev. At the close of 2024, Roof remained on death row at the United States Penitentiary in Terre Haute, Indiana, awaiting the outcome of further appeals.

XVII.

The Healing

God is our refuge and strength, a very present help in trouble,
therefore will not we fear though the earth be removed,
and though the mountains be carried into the midst of the sea.

—PSALM 46:1–2 (KJV)

There is no playbook, of course, for a church's recovery from a terrorist attack in its fellowship hall, and the attendant decimation of its ministerial staff. It is not taught in seminary or workshopped at summer retreats. There is no real way to prepare. That said, it would be hard to imagine a more destabilizing aftermath than the one experienced by Mother Emanuel. Tragedy can inspire unity and reveal superhuman stores of dignity and strength. It also can tear people apart and exacerbate preexisting stresses and strife. The massacre in Emanuel's fellowship hall managed to do both.

Within two weeks of the shootings on June 17, 2015, Mother Emanuel and Charleston had been seared into the world's consciousness as symbols of an otherworldly grace. Across the state, and then the nation, the murders brought together people of different races and persuasions in ways both conspicuous and imperceptible. Inside the church, however, the intimacy of all that had happened made it difficult to move beyond the trauma, and the congregation struggled to navigate its new normal. Starting with Rev. Pinckney's death, when continuity should have been a priority, Emanuel changed pastors three times in just more than a year. The familial vibe of Sunday worship dissipated as the church became a mecca for well-meaning pilgrims, many of them white visitors who came to pay respects, offer prayers, and work out their guilt by association. The new leadership soon faced bitter criticism from family members and survivors who felt ignored and disrespected in their time of utmost spiritual need. Shooting survivors Felicia Sanders and Polly Sheppard moved to other churches, and some family members could not bring themselves to return, a gut punch to a reeling congregation. The church's casual handling of millions of dollars in unsolicited donations generated further ill will, along with negative press and a state criminal investigation.

At the time of the shootings, the presiding AME bishop in South Carolina, Richard Franklin Norris, Sr., had just undergone kidney transplant surgery, deepening the leadership void. As soon as it was confirmed that Rev. Pinckney was among the victims, Norris appointed Rev. Norvel Goff, Sr., the presiding elder of Emanuel's district, as interim pastor. Goff, of course, had been at Emanuel with his wife earlier that evening to oversee the church's Quarterly Conference. They had left to attend a similar conference at another church and were on their way home when he received the first calls about the shootings.

The demands in the first few days were unimaginable. The church was a crime scene. A combined state and federal police investigation was in full swing. There were nine devastated families to comfort and a succession of funerals to coordinate, one of which would draw the president and vice president of the United States. Throngs of mourners and tourists processed down Calhoun Street day and night to add wreaths and bouquets to the mounds rising from the sidewalk. Journalists arrived in downtown Charleston by the scores, setting up broadcast tents across from the church. There were politicians to be handled. Each night brought renewed fears of rioting and unrest.

On Saturday morning, the new interim pastor met with his trustees and stewards in the library of Burke High School to discuss scheduling the funerals, ministering to families and survivors, and reoccupying the church. Once the tears and reminiscing subsided, Goff explained that he favored a rapid return to Mother Emanuel for Sunday worship, the next morning if authorities would allow. Not everyone found it respectful. The floor below the sanctuary had been a killing field only days earlier. Bodies had yet to be buried. But with the nation's eyes fixed on Charleston, Goff felt it vital to send a message about the resilience of the church and the faith. He also thought that a visible demonstration of Mother Emanuel's permanence, building on the grace shown by the families at Roof's bond hearing, might help cool the temperature on Charleston's jittery streets. There hadn't been much time to think, but he knew the healing process would be a long one. When the police released the scene a few hours later he announced that worship would be held in the sanctuary at 9:30 the next morning as usual. He was not deterred when church leaders entered the building on Saturday afternoon and found bullet holes in the paneling, masked only by black tape, and blood smears missed by the clean-up crew.

A thousand worshippers of varied hues jammed the pews the next morning, with the front row reserved for South Carolina's Indian American governor, Nikki Haley; its African American U.S. senator, Tim Scott; and Charleston's Irish American mayor, Joe Riley. Outside, hundreds gathered behind police barricades to listen over loudspeakers, as national networks broadcast the service live. As on any Sunday, folding chairs were set up for overflow seating in the fellowship hall, now bleached and scrubbed with lemon disinfectant. Unlike other Sundays, uniformed police officers lined the aisles and bomb-sniffing dogs patrolled the perimeter. Rev. Pinckney's usual chair on the altar sat empty, draped in black cloth. It was already pushing ninety degrees outside, and the air conditioning gave out mid-service. Packed shoulder to shoulder, worshippers swatted away the drenching heat with cardboard fans and folded programs. As sunlight refracted through the Easter-egg pastels of the stained-glass windows, church bells chimed in unison across the city in a nine-minute tribute, one minute per victim.

Inside, they just had church. Emanuel's choir sang one of its rousing standards, "Total Praise." Lisa Washington Wade, a belting soprano with Mavis Staples soul, swayed her way through "I Won't Let You Fall." Black congregants bowed their heads and joined hands with white strangers as the families were remembered. Former pastor John H. Gillison got down on his knees to lead the congregation in prayer, and to give voice to the obvious question: How could an active and benevolent God allow the slaughter of His own, in His house, while worshipping Him? Maintaining conviction in the face of inexplicable loss had always been the church's great challenge. Some turned *to* God while others turned away. "We ask questions, Lord," the white-haired old preacher began, eyes clenched. "We ask why. We cannot help it. It is our human nature. But through it all, those of us who know Jesus, as we find ourselves engulfed with sadness and darkness and as we find ourselves walking through the valley of the shadow of death, for those of us who know Jesus, we can look through the windows of our faith and we see hope and we see light and we can hear your voice saying I'm with you." That is what Emanuel meant, after all, "God with us."

Although a native of the Lowcountry, sixty-five-year-old Norvel Goff barely knew the congregation he now had to console and somehow uplift. He had never preached to a worldwide television audience, nor ever had to consider the political impact of a Sunday sermon on the national mood. But if Goff would later be accused of other shortcomings, preaching was not one of them. As he opened his King James Bible to Psalm 46—"God is our refuge and strength"—his glassy, uprolled eyes gave him the slightly possessed appearance of a street-corner prophet. With little preparation, he proceeded to deliver a pitch-perfect sermon for a difficult day, heartening, defiant, bent but unbroken.

Goff realized it might be too soon for some congregants to return. "Some folk might need some more time in order to walk in," he said, enveloped in a slate-blue robe with indigo-striped sleeves. "But for those of us who are here this morning I want you to know because the doors of Mother Emanuel is open on this Sunday it sends a message to every demon in hell and on Earth that NO WEAPON—somebody say NO WEAPON [and they did]—NO WEAPON! FORMED AGAINST US! SHALL! PROSPER!" Goff was screeching now, bobbing on his toes like a boxer in his corner. Organ riffs punctuated his Gullah inflections. "Some wanted to divide the race Black and white and brown, but NO WEAPON, FORMED AGAINST US, SHALL prosper." It was Father's Day, with two fewer fathers to celebrate, Clementa Pinckney and Daniel Simmons. Anyone who wondered how the families could be so forgiving, Goff said, "ought to know the nine families' Daddy. If you knew the nine families' Daddy, you would know how the children are behaving. After all, our Daddy said we ought to love our neighbors as we love ourselves."

Goff knew that many were "downright angry," and assured the congregation that accountability would be demanded, for the killings as well as for the malignancy they exposed. But he said it should not be surprising that there had been no retributive violence on Charleston's streets. "A lot of folks expected us to do something strange and to break out in a riot," Goff said. "Well, they just don't know us. They just don't know us because we are a people of faith." He wiped his beading forehead with a long white cloth. "The blood of the Mother Emanuel Nine requires us to work until not only justice in this case but for those who are still living in the margin of life, those who are less fortunate than ourselves, that we stay on the battlefield until there is no more fight to be fought."

AS THE FUNERALS BEGAN the following week, one after the next, the spirit of reconciliation spread from downtown Charleston to an unlikely destination, the

State Capitol in Columbia. For decades there, the South Carolina General Assembly had been engaged in the most anachronistic debate in American politics: whether to continue flying the battle flag of the Confederate States of America over its dome and on its grounds. Neither the deep offense taken by 1.3 million Black South Carolinians nor the economic impact of a sixteen-year NAACP boycott had weakened the resolve of Republican lawmakers to keep the standard flying. Sadly, it would take the assassination of one of their own, a beloved state senator, by a man who branded the flag unmistakably as an insignia of hate, not of heritage.

The Confederate banner had first been raised over the statehouse in 1961 as part of the centennial commemoration of the start of the Civil War. A year later, the legislature voted to leave it there permanently in a gesture of defiance against federal intervention in civil rights. In 2000, despite mass protests and an indignant campaign by Black lawmakers, the legislature compromised by lowering the flag from the Capitol dome only to raise a similar version on a pole nearby, still on the grounds. There it stayed until Democratic lawmakers seized the opportunity presented by Clementa Pinckney's murder (investigators had discovered images on Roof's camera of the flag at the statehouse and of him posing with a handheld Confederate flag and burning and standing on American ones).

The Democrats found an unlikely partner in South Carolina's ambitious and opportunistic forty-three-year-old Republican governor, Nikki Haley, who had started her second term. Under growing pressure from multinational companies with large stakes in the state, like Boeing and Michelin, Haley held a press conference at the Capitol five days after the murders to call for the flag's removal. It was a reversal for Haley, who had largely steered clear of the flag debate on grounds that it had been "resolved to the best of its ability." She knew that the last Republican governor who called for mothballing the flag, David Beasley in 1996, had lost reelection largely because of it. Haley would cast her change of heart as at least partly personal. As an Indian American growing up in rural South Carolina, she had experienced bigotry of her own, as when the judges of the "Wee Miss Bamberg" pageant disqualified her rather than decide whether to group her with contestants for the white crown or the Black one. She had been among the many who had called Clementa Pinckney's cell phone number and left a voicemail as soon as she heard about the shootings. The governor had taken her family to Emanuel's first post-massacre service, and they would return later that summer, when the cameras were gone. She visited with Felicia Sanders at her home and attended each of the open-casket funerals, leaving her so traumatized that she sought counseling.

Surrounded by lawmakers from both parties, including South Carolina's two Republican U.S. senators, Haley began by offering an obligatory nod to those who "view the flag as a symbol of respect, integrity, and duty." But the shootings at Emanuel, she said, "call upon us to look at this in a different way." Dylann Roof's appropriation of the Confederate legacy had reinforced that many found it to be a "deeply offensive symbol of a brutally offensive past."

"We are not going to allow this symbol to divide us any longer," Haley announced. "The fact that people are choosing to use it as a sign of hate is something we cannot stand. The fact that it causes pain to so many is enough to move it from the Capitol grounds. It is, after all, a Capitol that belongs to all of us."

Haley's proposal to move the flag to a state museum needed a two-thirds majority in each legislative chamber, a heavy lift, but timing was on her side. The widely disseminated images of the Emanuel shooter with the flag had an impact that decades of Black remonstration had not. "He killed someone I knew and love," explained Sen. Larry Grooms, one of the white Republicans who switched positions. "When the flag becomes a symbol of hate, it dishonors the memory of the Confederate soldiers who fought and defended our state." Both sides took note when state Sen. Paul Thurmond, the son of the late segregationist governor and U.S. senator Strom Thurmond, announced his support. The state senate acted first, voting 36 to 3 for removal. After an impassioned fifteen-hour debate that ended past 1:00 a.m., the house provided final passage by a margin of 94 to 20. Haley signed the bill the same day using nine pens, one to be given to each of the Emanuel victims' families. The next morning, July 10, 2015, a (mostly) festive crowd of more than eight thousand people gathered at the Capitol under powder-blue skies to watch a gray-uniformed trooper crank down the flag.

Haley would later make her handling of the Emanuel aftermath a focal point of her unsuccessful 2024 presidential primary campaign against Donald Trump, asserting in ads that she had provided "moral clarity during our darkest hours." Not everyone viewed it so uncynically. "It's sad to say, but basically we just shamed everybody," said former Sen. Vincent Sheheen, a Democrat from Camden who sponsored the bill. "If it had not been for Clem sitting there in the South Carolina Senate, I don't think it would have gone down. We passed it, but Clem brought it down. People say what a proud moment it was, and I say that's such bullshit because it took nine people getting killed, including our friend, to do what was right." As if to prove Sheheen's point, senate Republicans subsequently bottled up legislation—named for Pinckney—to create a state hate-crimes law. As of 2024, South Carolina remained one of two states without one, along with Wyoming.

For a moment, however, June 17 seemed to be the night old Dixie died. Legislators in other states soon proposed measures to banish the Confederate flag from specialty license plates. Walmart, Sears, Amazon, and eBay stopped selling Confederate-themed merchandise. NASCAR asked fans to stop displaying the flag at its speedways, where it had long been a staple. A statue of Robert E. Lee came down from its sixty-eight-foot column in New Orleans, while the school named for him in Jacksonville, Florida, became Riverside High. The nationwide protests following the death of George Floyd, a Black man, at the hands of a white Minneapolis police officer in May 2020 gave further impetus to the cause. Mississippi's legislature voted to remove the Confederate cross from the canton of its state flag. A giant bronze bust of Confederate general Nathan Bedford Forrest, the first grand wizard of the Ku Klux Klan, was hauled out of Tennessee's statehouse. In Richmond, once the capital of the breakaway republic, a dozen Confederate memorials were removed, including the iconic sculpture of Lee on horseback. U.S. military bases dropped the names of Confederate officers like Benning and Bragg. By 2024, 484 of the roughly 2,600 Confederate memorials inventoried by the Southern Poverty Law Center had been removed or renamed.

IT TOOK SOME FOLKS longer than others, but Charleston's African Methodists gradually came to recognize that their beloved Mother Emanuel, the safe harbor of two centuries of collective memory, would never, could never, be the same. The latest chapter in the church's storied narrative had changed its trajectory altogether. To begin with, it was no longer just a church. It was now a shrine, one that beckoned with a spiritual power that people had witnessed on television and wanted to feel for themselves. When Sunday worship ended, Emanuel members might find strangers outside with their hands and heads pressed against the white stucco, as if praying at the Wailing Wall. "People come, not necessarily to make themselves feel better, but simply to show that I am not Dylann Roof, that there is love in my heart," said Leon Alston, the head of the steward board. "I see people cry just being around the church." There were Sunday mornings when visitors filled nearly as many seats as the old faithful. They slid into empty pews once occupied by members who could not yet handle being back in the building. Pastor Goff would dutifully call the visitors down front so they could convey condolences and present a check or handcrafted gift. Despite the generosity of spirit, there often seemed a weariness to the ritual, as if the church was indulging houseguests who had stayed one night too many.

Before long, sightseeing buses began parking out front and church historians were fielding near daily requests for tours. Celebrities started dropping by, with singer Pharrell Williams showing up one Sunday, and Facebook founder Mark Zuckerberg another. Emanuel became a mandatory stop for politicians courting Black voters in South Carolina's early presidential primaries. Eight Democratic candidates visited the church during the wide-open 2020 race, including Sens. Cory Booker of New Jersey, Kamala Harris of California, and Elizabeth Warren of Massachusetts.

The ultimate winner of that race, Joe Biden, did not campaign at Emanuel that year. But as both vice president and president, Biden built a relationship with the congregation that was as intimate as any national politician's. When Vice President Biden and his wife, Jill, joined Barack and Michelle Obama at the Pinckney memorial service in June 2015, they still were deep in mourning for Biden's elder son, Beau, who had died of brain cancer less than a month earlier. The Biden family happened to be vacationing nearby on Kiawah Island, and on the following Sunday Biden and other family members returned to Charleston to worship at Emanuel. He felt his own grief intersecting with that of the congregants. "My family and I wanted to show solidarity," Biden said when Rev. Goff asked him to say a few words. "But to be selfish about it, Reverend, the reason we came was to draw some strength from all of you, to draw some strength from the church."

Biden choked up while recounting that moment when he returned to a packed Emanuel on January 8, 2024, this time as president, to deliver the opening argument in his abbreviated reelection rematch against former President Donald Trump. Polls showed the eighty-one-year-old incumbent losing ground with the Black voters who had carried him to victory four years earlier. To reinvigorate that base, Biden sought to link Trump to the kind of hate-fueled violence that had revealed itself in Charleston in June 2015 and again, during Trump's presidency, in the neo-Nazi rally in Charlottesville, Virginia, in August 2017, and the insurrectionist assault on the U.S. Capitol in January 2021.

"The word of God was pierced by bullets in hate and rage," Biden said of the Emanuel shootings, "propelled by not just gunpowder but by a poison, a poison that's for too long haunted this nation. What is that poison? White supremacy." The president then pivoted to compare Trump's refusal to accept his loss in the 2020 election to the revisionism adopted by defeated Confederates after the Civil War. Both lost causes, he said, had waged an assault on truth and history, at considerable peril to the union, and particularly to African Americans. The political lie that Trump had propagated since 2020, Biden asserted, was nothing more than an "old ghost in new garments."

THE WORLDWIDE FOCUS on Emanuel proved double-edged, as the church also perversely became a target for racist threats and rants. One telephone caller claimed to be Dylann Roof and warned that he was "coming back for round two." On the morning of Sen. Booker's appearance, the pastor found a message on his phone that repeatedly referred to the candidate by the N-word. "And you have him talk at your fucking church?" the man said. "Fuck you too."

Entrenched Emanuel members, the ones who proved their pedigrees by sitting in the same pews as their parents and grandparents, reacted in varying ways to the disruption. Many just longed to reclaim their space. "We want our church back, knowing that it will never, ever be the same," explained William Dudley Gregorie, a fifth-generation member and a city councilman. "Our family for one hundred years sat in the center of the fifth row. It doesn't happen anymore. You get there and your pew is filled. It's very difficult. The church has become a destination." With all the visitors and outside attention, which revived with each June's anniversary, Emanuel's people found it difficult to move on. There was no real way to forget. Bishop Green, whose tenure in South Carolina began the year after the killings, observed that "there are members in Emanuel who do not feel Emanuel is their Emanuel anymore, and they are resistant to being the world's church. They want Emanuel to be the church they grew up in, a church steeped in the traditions of African Methodism."

There were others, however, who saw in the arrival of strangers if not a glimpse of God's purpose then at least a glimmer of a silver lining. Whether it possibly compensated in any way for the loss of nine beloved souls was too big a question. But as Emanuel's membership dipped below six hundred, the tragedy was bringing in hundreds of newcomers and making the church a global vessel for Christ's teachings on love and forgiveness. Furthermore, Sunday morning was no longer the most segregated time of the week, at least not at Emanuel. Attendance there was now as diverse as at any church in town. That did not mean that many of the curious stayed long enough to join. And there was plenty of Monday-morning tut-tutting about those who seemed more voyeuristic than prayerful, the ones who underdressed in shorts and polos and brandished iPhone cameras as if attending a high school graduation. Nonetheless, the visitors gave an exhausted church needed vitality and support, while temporarily fattening the collection plate.

"As far as I'm concerned, I love to see the people there, love to see the church full," said Doris Coaxum Sanders, a third-generation member. "I am enjoying them. They're not just local people but people who are coming from all over the States, all over the world, to worship and be with us. Before that we had a dwindling congregation, people had to drive in to church, and we were losing our young people."

Without questioning the cost-benefit, some wondered whether this had been part of the divine plan, a multiracial revival of faith in an age of complacency. Maybe, they suggested, God wanted Emanuel to serve as a living testimony, a reminder of both the destructiveness of hatred and the dominion of belief. "What was the purpose?" asked Charles N. Williams, an army retiree who had attended Emanuel since childhood. "We gave the world a shock that brought them back for a while. I don't know for how long. But it brought them back. May have just been for a minute. But the flag came down. A lot of things were happening, and it was time we needed a shock to let us know that God is still in charge."

THE TORRENT OF GENEROSITY from around the world was beyond anything Emanuel's leaders could have anticipated, or easily managed. It started almost immediately. On the first Sunday, for instance, Patrick Garner, a partner in a Charleston heating and air company, jumped to action after hearing that the cooling system had broken down during the worship service. He summoned a crew that hustled down to the church and fixed the unit, for free, before Pastor Goff arrived at the benediction (a testament to both the technicians' skill and the more than two-hour length of Emanuel's services). The contractor then persuaded a local distributor to donate a new unit and installed it later that week. It would be a sign of things to come. The week after the shootings, church secretary Althea Richardson-Latham unlatched the mailbox, which was fed through a slot in a door to Calhoun Street, and found it so stuffed that the lid sprang open. "The amount of money was scary," she said. "Just cash money, not even in envelopes, hundred-dollar bills, one-dollar bills, change."

Then packages began arriving, sometimes addressed simply to Mother Emanuel Church, Charleston, SC. They bore quilts, shawls, tapestries, teddy bears, crucifixes, candles, inspirational posters, framed poems. There were paintings of the church and sketches of the Nine. Cards of condolence came by the boxload. Thousands contained cash or checks folded into handwritten notes and prayers of comfort. Lee Cohen, a corporate headhunter from Southern California, wrote a personal check for $20,000. Sue McMurray of Durham, North Carolina, sent one for $5, scribbling "In Jesus Name" on the memo line. South Carolina's electric and gas utility contributed $100,000. The state's Baptist convention gave $25,000. Donations came from all manner of other faith groups—an Episcopal church in Deer Isle, Maine; a Unitarian Universalist congregation in Fort Worth, Texas; the Jewish Community Federation of San Francisco. They came from foundations and fraternal groups and the Northeast Philadelphia Dental Implant Periodontal Prosthesis Study Club ($100, offered "with deepest sympathy"). All told, nearly $3.4 million flowed into the church's Moving Forward Fund. Another 6,500 donors gave more than $4 million to a separate city campaign set up by Mayor Riley, the Mother Emanuel Hope Fund.

With money came trouble. Mother Emanuel, naturally, did not have the staff or experience to handle the influx and did not hire professional crisis managers. When envelopes bore the name of an individual—say, a survivor like Felicia Sanders or Jennifer Pinckney—they were supposed to be held apart, unopened, for later delivery. But church volunteers found it wasn't always that simple. Some envelopes and checks might be made out to the church but contain notations like "Donation for families of the Charleston Massacre." At times, according to Richardson-Latham's later testimony, volunteers opened envelopes addressed to individuals, removed checks and cash, and did not properly record the donations. Family members and friends of victims made similar assertions. "They had this whole assembly line," said Rev. Kylon Middleton, who picked up mail for Jennifer Pinckney, his friend's widow. "I saw it with my own eyes, envelopes made out to Jennifer and all the rest and the money taken out and put in piles. Some was cash, some were checks. They were opening things indiscriminately. She received it open and was like, 'Did you open my mail?'" Richardson-Latham alerted the church treasurer, Rosetta Singleton, and various lay leaders to what she considered irregularities and was terminated shortly thereafter. She later sued the church for lost wages and received a small settlement. Goff and Singleton each rejected her allegations and denied she had been fired for whistle-blowing.

The discomfort deepened in early October, however, when Charleston's daily, *The Post and Courier*, published an exposé about Goff's troubled history at two prior churches, in Columbia and Rochester, New York. The paper reported that when Goff was elevated to presiding elder in Charleston in 2014, he left Reid Chapel AME in Columbia with more than half a million dollars in mortgage debt—some assumed to buy a parsonage for him to live in—and liens for nonpayment of payroll taxes. Church leaders contended that the borrowing had not been properly approved. They eventually sued for a full accounting, prompting Goff to countersue for defamation and slander.

Just days after the story dropped, lawyers for Arthur Hurd, Cynthia Hurd's widower, sued Mother Emanuel for records related to the donations, which they had been requesting since July. Hurd's complaint expressed concern that Emanuel would keep the money for itself and charged that the church had "neither been transparent nor forthcoming." A judge ruled that the Moving Forward Fund should be frozen until the church could provide numbers. Emanuel's era of good feelings seemed to be ending, and fast.

To defend himself against the "satanic" report in *The Post and Courier*, an indignant Goff surrounded himself with AME ministers and held a lengthy news conference in Emanuel's sanctuary. He dismissed the allegations of his former parishioners as "fiction" and seemed to analogize the arrival of Sunday's newspaper to that of Dylann Roof four months earlier. "Like pouring salt in an open wound," the pastor said. But among those in attendance was Tyrone Sanders, Tywanza's plain-spoken father, who was in no mood to let Goff go unchallenged. Tyrone and Felicia Sanders had been nursing feelings of abandonment for months because Goff and other Emanuel leaders had not provided the counseling and support that Felicia, in particular, craved from her church. Now, with cameras rolling, Tyrone Sanders demanded accountability. "Within a hundred days, we sort of looked for somebody from the AME circuit to come and pray with us and we hadn't seen one yet," he said. "I'm just wondering why." Caught flat-footed, Goff said attempts to reach out to the Sanders family and others had been stymied because "the coordination has not been there in terms of either coming back to church or extending a welcome to come back." It wasn't quite clear what he meant, but he took the microphone from Sanders and left it at that.

The second-guessing continued when the church finally announced how it would distribute its money. The process had lasted seven months longer than the city's, yet still seemed less deliberative. The city had retained a team of pro bono attorneys and accountants who devised a consensus formula after consultation with the victims' immediate families and the survivors. The nearly $4 million that remained after paying for funerals and burials would be allocated by shares to beneficiaries of the nine victims and to the five survivors—Felicia Sanders and her granddaughter, Ka'mya Manigault, Jennifer and Malana Pinckney, and Polly Sheppard. That meant the Sanderses and Pinckneys would receive multiple shares as both living survivors and heirs of the deceased. Other pots were created to pay education expenses for college-aged children, establish annuities for younger ones, and address special needs. There were few complaints.

Emanuel's leaders, by contrast, came under fire for keeping the lion's share of the donations for the church and then devising a distribution formula that treated the five survivors disparately. Reasoning that the church had itself been victimized, and at some cost, Goff and his lay leaders decided that Mother Emanuel would pocket $1.9 million of the $3.4 million in receipts. Some of it covered direct expenses of the aftermath—off-duty police, lawyers, accountants, staff to handle the press. The rest wound up going to a smorgasbord of projects: repaving the parking lot, installing chimes in the bell tower, fumigating the sanctuary against termites, repairing damaged trusses, initial planning for a memorial to the Nine.

Goff announced in November 2015 that the church, "in its benevolence," would donate the remaining $1.5 million to the families and survivors. But in a choice later regretted by some, the money was split ten ways rather than fourteen, with $150,000 shares allotted to the estates of each deceased and to survivor Polly Sheppard. The payouts would be larger that way, church leaders reasoned. And each family present in the basement that night would get a portion because the Sanderses and Pinckneys would receive shares as heirs of Tywanza and Clementa. But unlike the city's solution, Emanuel's formula did not honor the separate suffering of those survivors as victims themselves, and took no real account of Ka'mya, who eventually required costly inpatient treatment for post-traumatic stress.

Felicia Sanders found it hard to suppress her bitterness over a variety of affronts and moved her membership to Second Presbyterian, a predominantly white church nearby with an entryway plaque that honored the congregation's twenty-two Confederate war dead. "I always love Emanuel AME Church," she explained at a public forum in June 2019. "But since the tragedy, Emanuel has turned their back on me completely." Just days later, coinciding with the fourth anniversary of the Emanuel attack, her lawyer, Andrew J. Savage III, placed unsigned ads in Charleston newspapers demanding to know "Where did the donations go?" and "Why did their church forsake them?" He also lodged a complaint that was routed to the South Carolina Law Enforcement Division, which opened a criminal investigation. After a rather perfunctory three-week probe, the state police agency came up with no specific evidence that donations had been mishandled and closed the case.

It all deeply frustrated church leaders who figured they faced enough challenges without the background noise. How were they supposed to raise money for structural renovations and for a memorial to the Nine while under police scrutiny for financial mismanagement? In their less generous moments, some questioned how Felicia Sanders could so quickly forgive her son's killer yet hold such a grudge against her lifelong church. Then they remembered what she had been through and recognized that they could not, thank God, put themselves in her place.

The Sanders family was not alone in its discontent. Just days after the shootings, Polly Sheppard, still feeling the call to be God's servant, had been back in the church basement, helping to clean the office along with her husband. Yet, like Felicia Sanders, she felt overlooked in the focus on the nine dead and their families. Sometimes it was simple thoughtlessness, like when no one reserved her a seat upstairs for Myra Thompson's jam-packed funeral. The oversight relegated her to the overflow space of the fellowship hall, leaving her to mourn her friend in the very room where she had witnessed her murder. "I expected the whole church to be there to see how we were, but they weren't," Sheppard said. "People called, but I think everybody was in shock." She did not renounce her membership, but worshipped for a while at Mt. Zion AME, where Kylon Middleton was pastor. Ethel Lance's daughter, Nadine Collier, also departed, unable to worship a floor above the room where her mother had been slain. Chris Singleton, Sharonda's son, left for a contemporary non-denominational church in North Charleston.

To combat the aftershocks, the U.S. Department of Justice awarded a $3.6 million grant to the Medical University of South Carolina in Charleston to provide mental-health services to victims, witnesses, and first responders. That led to the creation of the Mother Emanuel Empowerment Center, housed in a building next to the sanctuary, to make counseling available to any who sought it. The clinic's services were underutilized though, and it closed when the grant expired in 2019. The center's counselors found that even trauma as deep as Emanuel's could not overcome a stubborn stigma about mental-health treatment in the Black community, particularly among older people of faith. "People connect counseling with something being wrong," explained Rev. Brenda Nelson, the center's onetime director. "They say, 'We're okay, we just have to pray about it.'"

The tragedy also exacerbated tensions within some victims' families. There were custody disputes involving orphaned children and arguments over which relatives deserved a cut of various pots of donations. There were divides over who spoke for families when it came to forgiveness and whether Dylann Roof should face the death penalty. All of that and more fed into a cringeworthy escalation between Ethel Lance's adult daughters, Sharon Risher and Nadine Collier, who had been feuding for years. Risher had watched in astonishment as her younger sister forgave Roof at the bond hearing on worldwide television. "This girl has to be crazy!" she thought. "Who's going to forgive him so quickly?" Their relationship deteriorated to the point that each sister arranged to have a competing headstone placed on their mother's grave in Emanuel's cemetery, without the other's knowledge. A month after Risher put up her marker, Collier ordered her own black stone lowered into place, obscuring her sister's like a waterfront high-rise.

ON JANUARY 23, 2016, a Saturday, Rev. Betty Deas Clark, the pastor at Mt. Pisgah AME Church in Sumter, South Carolina, found herself in Columbia at a denominational district planning meeting. Toward the end of a rather long oration, Bishop Norris took a moment to pay tribute to Mother Emanuel and its leadership, thanking Elder Goff for stepping into the breach. Then he announced that he was ready to assign a new pastor to the mother church, the church that now had as high a profile as any in America, and he summoned Clark to come forward. Norris had telephoned Clark months before to feel her out. But she had no real forewarning and had assumed—and prayed—that she was out of the bishop's sights. A Lowcountry native, Clark knew well of Emanuel's rocky recovery—everyone did—and understood that the assignment meant cleaning up an unholy mess. "My heart fell into the soles of my feet," she remembered. As Norris presented Clark, he mentioned that he had received more than two hundred inquiries about the opening. Oh well, she thought to herself, "I just got two hundred enemies." She put on her best face and shook all of the hands thrusting toward her, "just in a trance."

Clark would be the first female pastor in Mother Emanuel's 151-year history (and in 198 years going back to the African Church). More than half a century after the AME Church began ordaining women, they remained a rarity in top pulpits. Clark's gender had not been coincidental to her selection. Norris recognized that "there was a need for healing" at Emanuel and thought a woman's touch would help soothe and stabilize the church. A devoted African Methodist from childhood, Clark had come to ministry late after a career as a tailor and had broken barriers with assignments across South Carolina. The bishop did not give her much time to absorb the news; he expected her to be in Emanuel's pulpit the next morning. Clark drove the hour back to Sumter, stayed up past 1:00 a.m. to outline a sermon, and awakened in time to drive nearly two hours to Charleston. Dressed in a black tunic, with a halo of graying hair, she took her text from Jeremiah 29:11 ("For I know the plans I have for you, declares the Lord") and preached about the promise of hope. She did not dwell on the past, nor did she ignore it. "While the dreams, expectations, and bodies of many have been laid to rest, we must not allow nor put our hope to rest," she said.

The church ladies loved it when Clark explained her leadership style by saying that "every cook fries her chicken just a little bit differently." She offered a woman's perspective again the next Sunday when addressing the emotional challenges of the aftermath: "We apply the makeup, but the truth is our eyes are still puffy, our throats are still sore and, yes, there's an emotional numbness," she said. She could feel the brokenness in the place and made a point of hugging all who came to the altar. She also reached out, one by one, to Felicia Sanders and Polly Sheppard and members of the victims' families.

And then, almost as suddenly as she arrived, Betty Clark was gone, ousted by the same Bishop Norris who had appointed her five months earlier. The reason? Clark, in his mind, had committed the most unforgiveable of AME sins: insubordination. Despite the bishop's directive to focus on the congregation, Clark was keeping a high media profile, with a bio that proclaimed her to be "America's Pastor," and a schedule controlled by a gatekeeping assistant. Things came quickly to a head when on June 12, 2016, five days before the anniversary of the Emanuel tragedy, a twenty-nine-year-old gunman shot forty-nine people to death at a gay nightclub in Orlando called Pulse. It was the deadliest mass shooting in the United States to date. As Emanuel's pastor, Clark felt a duty to take stands against gun violence, and when an advocacy group asked her to go to Orlando she quickly agreed even though it meant canceling plans to attend a White House summit on gender equality. While in Florida, she sat in on a counseling session with trauma victims, joined in a media conference call, and appeared on CNN and MSNBC.

But Clark had not cleared the trip with Norris, and when he learned where she was he was displeased. In an interview before his death in 2023, Norris said he let Clark know that he preferred she keep her commitment to the Obama White House and otherwise be in Charleston for the anniversary remembrances. Clark disputed that, saying Norris called her while she was in Orlando but never expressed his dissatisfaction. Regardless, it did not sit well when Clark, driving back from Orlando through heavy rain, arrived too late to make a commemorative Wednesday-night Bible study at Emanuel that she had arranged to teach with Rev. Anthony Thompson. That left Myra Thompson's widower alone with the wrenching task of guiding more than 175 students through the fourth chapter of Mark, just as his wife had a year earlier in the same building.

It all infuriated the bishop. "It was a matter of disobedience," Norris said. "She decided to go to Orlando rather than do what was really the primary responsibility for the pastor of Emanuel." He acknowledged another factor. Because Pulse was a gay club, he felt Clark was associating herself, and her church, not only with the cause of gun control but also with that of LGBTQ rights. Her new congregation might not be ready for that. "That might have had some influence," Norris admitted. "She was taking the church in a new and different direction than the church had previously gone." Clark saw it differently. "I was simply trying to recast the church in a positive light," she said. "When I got there all you could hear them talk about was the money, the money, the money."

The bishop waited for the anniversary to pass, then called Clark the next week.

"As of this moment, you are no longer the pastor of Mother Emanuel," he informed her. "As of this moment, you are the pastor of Bethel AME church in Georgetown." In a swap, he assigned that church's pastor, Rev. Eric S. C. Manning, to Emanuel.

"Bishop, why are you moving me?" Clark asked.

"Out of my godly judgment," the bishop answered, falling back on the authorizing language used in *The Doctrines and Discipline*, the AME bylaws.

Clark couldn't contain herself. "What else did God tell you?"

"Nothing. Get your stuff and move out."

It was, of course, the last thing Mother Emanuel needed. Through no fault of his own, Eric Manning inherited a congregation that seemed more unmoored, if possible, than it had been a year earlier. The pastor's job had become immensely complex, and the forty-eight-year-old army veteran began with considerable liabilities, not least the jarring manner of his ascension. Manning was a Pennsylvania native (his middle initials stood for Sheldon Charles, not South Carolina) who had not been at Emanuel for the tragedy yet suddenly had to speak for and minister to those who had. It was challenging enough to handle the weekly demands of sermons and meetings and funerals and hospital visits for a congregation of that size and age, not to mention the crowded calendar of AME conferences. Now Emanuel's new pastor bore responsibility for healing a deeply wounded flock in a building little changed from the night it became a crime scene. There were unanswerable theological questions to be addressed. Some congregants wanted to know if God had punished the church for some sacrilege. Whether Emanuel's pastor wanted to or not, he also would instantly become a national spokesman for the church's views on gun violence and race relations.

The cluckers in the congregation found Manning's personality aloof, his sermons pedestrian, his managerial style dictatorial. Little escaped their notice. When he recognized his wife on her birthday as "the sugar in my sweet tea," they let him know they found it unnecessarily suggestive. Within sixteen months of his arrival, a delegation of antagonists had taken their complaints to the bishop. Things went from bad to worse in June 2018 when Manning's wife and twenty-one-year-old son were involved in an altercation after church one Sunday with an eighty-four-year-old female congregant. It happened in the fellowship hall following a meeting about the dismissal of an assistant minister that generated words between the two women. As others gathered around, the pastor's son stepped in to defend his mother and took the other woman by the shoulders, according to a police report in which the son acknowledged doing so. The elderly congregant, a lifelong, third-generation member, in turn, reached for the younger Manning's neck, he alleged. An off-duty policeman called for backup to help restore calm, and the woman pressed charges for simple assault (she later withdrew them). One witness told an officer that the woman's eighty-seven-year-old bantam of a husband, who was sixty-six years older, eighty pounds lighter, and three inches shorter than Manning's son, threatened at one point to "get my cousin S&W [meaning his Smith & Wesson]—because you don't touch my wife."

It was quite a scene, and Mother Emanuel's trustees, stewards, and other lay leaders found it beyond disturbing. All of the church's pain, loss, frustration, and disorientation seemed distilled into one inane moment. It was the latest evidence that a congregation made world famous for Christian grace seemed too traumatized to always apply the principle internally. "I have never seen anything like that in my life in my church," said Ruby Martin.

"We've had worse things happen at the church, but we didn't need that," added Leon Alston.

Two Sundays later, Rev. Manning did what he could to repair the damage, seeking out the elderly couple in their seats, placing his hand on their heads in blessing, and apologizing as he embraced them at length. His son then followed his lead as congregants clapped in praise and wiped away tears.

There was a day not long after that Manning became so exasperated by the hostility from some corners of the congregation that he boxed up his office belongings and called Bishop Green to tender his resignation. "Eric, take a breath," the bishop counseled. Manning did, and through perseverance and presence he gradually persuaded some doubters (and outlasted others). He grew more comfortable at the pulpit, and got the parking lot repaved. He shepherded the congregation through Dylann Roof's traumatizing trial, attending each day. He oversaw the church's bicentennial in 2018, featuring a banquet at the grand Francis Marion Hotel, which would have been off limits to Black guests in B. J. Glover's day. Speakers strove to place the events of the prior three years in the context of the 197 that preceded them. "Still we rise," Presiding Elder Goff declared repeatedly as he recounted the sequence of assaults on Black religious freedom in Charleston. Later that year, when an anti-Semite killed eleven people in a Shabbat attack on a Pittsburgh synagogue, Manning flew there to offer comfort and organized an exchange program between the congregations. In 2020, he managed the challenges posed by the Covid-19 pandemic, making worship services virtual and implementing other precautions. In 2024, he hosted President Biden's visit on short notice. He also raised and borrowed enough money to begin needed structural renovations, while co-chairing a separate campaign to build a world-class memorial to the Nine and the survivors.

✦ ✦ ✦

For all of Emanuel's struggles to repair, the tragedy also left an indelible imprint on Charleston, psychologically as well as physically. For those with the deepest connections, there was the Charleston that existed before and the Charleston that came after. They resembled each other, and the cruise-ship tourists detected little difference on their horse-drawn carriage rides through the historic district. But as with New York after 9/11, the Charleston that staggered away from June 17, 2015, could never again be the same place. The attack came at the peak of the city's phenomenal revival, with civic confidence soaring like the price of downtown property. Notwithstanding the flooding threats posed by rising seas and strengthening storms, it was well into what would become a decade-long reign as the best city in America as determined by an annual survey of *Travel + Leisure* readers. In 2016, the year after the massacre, the magazine anointed it the best city *in the world*. But to the extent that the region's shameful legacy and ongoing inequities had been papered over by booms in tourism and real estate, the Emanuel shootings laid them bare for all to see. That the killer had driven down from elsewhere did not matter much. Regardless of ethnicity, Charlestonians were shaken to their core, confronted by a horrific racial attack that echoed their city's horrific racial past. They took it personally, and shared in the heartbreak, whatever their political views. They remembered where they were, what they were doing, who they first called. The town was small enough that many knew victims or survivors. Perhaps Cynthia Hurd had helped them at the library or Felicia Sanders had done their hair. As with any such crime, there was a cry for accountability. But the reckoning demanded was not only for Dylann Roof. It was for Charleston as well.

It began with an outpouring of public remembrance. The city committed itself to memorializing the Nine, and not hiding the slaughter from the 7 million tourists who visited each year. That counted for something in a place accustomed to disunity even in its reconstruction of history, and where the economy relied on romanticism of the past. If there had already been some progress in broadening the public presentation of Charleston's story, the Emanuel tragedy accelerated the momentum. Old times now were not forgotten. Past was transparently prologue. The city hung a green sign across Calhoun Street that rededicated the stretch in front of the church as the Mother Emanuel Way Memorial District, obscuring the segregationist legacy of the boulevard's namesake. A permanent exhibit in Charleston's airport welcomed travelers with a stained-glass replica of the church's façade and a display case bearing Clementa Pinckney's Bible. Trees were planted with markers bearing the victims' names outside the Gaillard Center auditorium. The St. Andrews Regional Library was renamed for Cynthia Hurd. Pinckney's name was given to the Jasper County government building, a middle school in Charleston, and a chapel in Port Royal. A pocket park near Mother Emanuel was dedicated to Susie Jackson, the oldest victim. The baseball complex at Charleston Southern University, where Chris Singleton played outfield, was named for his mother, Sharonda.

There was a flowering of artistic and philanthropic tribute as well. Savannah-based folk artist Panhandle Slim painted a series of iconic portraits of the victims. South Carolina batik painter Leo Twiggs produced nine studies of the church as a "Requiem for Mother Emanuel." Gospel legend Shirley Caesar recorded a ballad entitled "Mother Emanuel" that the church's youth adapted for an interpretive dance. Folk singer Zoe Mulford penned "The President Sang Amazing Grace," a lilting hymn recorded by the legendary Joan Baez: "A young man came to a house of prayer, they did not ask what brought him there, he was not friend, he was not kin, but they opened the door and let him in." Renowned artist Carrie Mae Weems created *Grace Notes*, a performance piece inspired by the shootings that premiered at Charleston's Spoleto Festival. The South Carolina Ballet choreographed a new work entitled *Emanuel: Love is the Answer*. National Book Award–winning poet Nikky Finney wrote "Miss Polly Is Akimbo Underneath the Mother Emanuel Collection Table" about the moment that Dylann Roof confronted Polly Sheppard.

The Emanuel tragedy accelerated fundraising for Joe Riley's valedictory mayoral project—the construction of a $125 million International African American Museum on the site of Gadsden's Wharf, where thousands of captives were marched off slaving ships in the early nineteenth century. It opened in June 2023 with a display dedicated to Emanuel's history, including the 2015 shooting. Cynthia Hurd's family formed a foundation that sponsored an annual book drive for local libraries and literacy programs. The Sanders family staged a five-kilometer road race each spring to raise money for scholarships in Tywanza's memory. Anonymous donors created a separate college scholarship fund in Pinckney's honor to benefit low-income Black students in the Lowcountry. Several family members redirected their life paths in order to wring something constructive from the tragedy. After two seasons in the minor leagues, Chris Singleton found success as an inspirational speaker, preaching on faith and forgiveness at schools, churches, and corporate conferences. Rev. Sharon Risher, Ethel Lance's daughter, left her job as a hospital chaplain to become a crusading voice against gun violence. Daniel Simmons's granddaughter Alana, who vowed at Roof's bond hearing that "hate won't win," built a nonprofit by that name that encourages diversity training in schools.

For a while, at least, Charlestonians made earnest attempts at expanding cross-cultural understanding. The city seemed a softer place in ways, more humble, more aware, particularly as it pertained to race. Ten thousand people had held hands across the Ravenel Bridge. Hoping to harness that spirit, police and citizen leaders initiated the Charleston Illumination Project, which generated strategies for strengthening relationships between law enforcement and minority communities. The police department conducted a racial-bias audit that found disparities in traffic stops, ticketing, and use of force, and redoubled efforts to diversify an agency dominated by white and male officers. The city's colleges opened examinations of their historic ties to slavery. Each June, the city marked the tragedy's anniversary by staging The Charleston Forum, a community assembly on topics related to race. White members of the Episcopalian Grace Church Cathedral began gathering on Tuesday nights with their Black next-door neighbors at Mt. Zion AME for a book study about race. Not far away, Polly and Julian Buxton opened an independent bookstore with the mission of curating an ongoing dialogue about race through talks and readings.

In July 2018, Israeli-born architect Michael Arad, whose breathtaking waterfall design for the 9/11 Memorial in Lower Manhattan had been chosen from among 5,200 entries, unveiled initial drawings for a memorial to the victims and their legacies. He hoped to transform the asphalt lot where Dylann Roof parked into a courtyard featuring a pair of sleekly curving high-backed pews, fabricated from white stone. They would face a fountain etched with the names of the dead. Adjacent would be a rectangular garden surrounded by six benches, one dedicated to each of the five human survivors and the last to the ultimate survivor, Mother Emanuel herself. A foundation was established to raise the $25 million needed to build the complex, with the city and state governments pitching in $4 million apiece.

But Charleston's kumbaya moments, as AME pastor and civil-rights activist Joseph Darby deemed them, did not always extend to the political arena when matters of remembrance gave way to questions of culpability and reparation.

In 2017, the College of Charleston's Avery Research Center for African American History and Culture published a study of racial inequity in the city. Its director, Patricia Williams Lessane, said the inquiry was driven by her desire to rebut Dylann Roof's "false narrative" that African Americans were taking over the world. The report found that the median income for Black families in Charleston County was less than half that of white families, and that the gap far exceeded that in other Southern cities. The share of Black children who lived in poverty, a demoralizing 42 percent, was nearly four times the white rate. Black unemployment was nearly triple that for white people. The comparisons drew on for eighty pages, all revealing similar disparities: jail bookings, school discipline, graduation rates, college readiness, infant mortality, disease prevalence, health coverage.

The data reinforced the argument of civil-rights leaders that the post-massacre forgiveness narrative had let white Charleston off the hook. "It acted as a placebo," said Thomas Dixon, a Black community leader in North Charleston, "instead of allowing the realness of what happened to cut through and empower people to make some change."

At city hall, there was a recognition that centuries of inequity and maltreatment could not be undone with a few pen strokes. But obstacles emerged even to making symbolic amends. In June 2018, near the third anniversary of the Emanuel attack, the city council debated a resolution to apologize for Charleston's "role in regulating, supporting and fostering the institution of slavery in the city and the past wrongs inflicted on African Americans here." The resolution, sponsored by Emanuel member William Dudley Gregorie, unflinchingly recounted Charleston's racial history, committed the city to promoting equity, and called for the creation of an office of racial reconciliation. In the context of the Emanuel tragedy, that might have seemed uncontroversial enough. Yet the measure passed by only a 7 to 5 margin. Each of those who voted against it represented the suburbs west of the Ashley River, a predominantly white area, and most argued that their constituents should not have to apologize for the sins of the city's fathers. The council's eight white members split on the measure, with one dismissing it as "a worthless sentiment."

Then on May 25, 2020, in Minneapolis, Minnesota, a city distant from Charleston in every way, a white police officer killed a handcuffed Black suspect named George Floyd by kneeling on his neck for more than nine minutes. After a bystander's video went public, the city dismissed four officers and prosecutors opened an investigation. Furious protests rocked the normally sedate Midwestern city, and demonstrations soon engulfed much of the country. On May 30, a day of peaceful protest in downtown Charleston devolved into a night of unprecedented civil unrest.

Twenty-two fires were reported and 136 buildings suffered damage in Charleston's rioting. The finely dressed windows of boutiques and hotels were shattered with bricks and bottles. Stores that were just reopening after the coronavirus pandemic shutdown saw their shelves stripped of smart phones, athletic shoes, and jewelry. Historic façades and Confederate statues were spray-painted with "Black Lives Matter" slogans. Restaurateurs evacuated diners into back alleys as staffers locked themselves into walk-in coolers. A photograph in *The Post and Courier* captured a half-eaten dish of cheese tortellini littered with cubes of shattered window glass, hastily abandoned at a King Street wine bar. Gunshots were fired and police cars set aflame. Helmeted officers fired cannisters of tear gas to push the rioters out of downtown, making eighty-one arrests over two days. The city declared a dusk-to-dawn curfew and the governor activated the National Guard. This time, there would be no hand-holding across the Ravenel Bridge.

It was the eruption of violence that had been feared five years earlier after the killings of Walter Scott and the Emanuel Nine. That it had not happened then made it more shocking that it was happening now. Some demonstrators connected the events explicitly, climbing Emanuel's steps as they rambled through town. "Y'all's cousins, aunties, uncles lost their lives at this church, nine beautiful souls," one told the crowd gathered below. He reminded them that the police bought Dylann Roof a hamburger.

Perhaps the Emanuel tragedy in 2015 had been too intimate to unleash a similarly uncontrolled response, the city too bereaved to burn itself down. There had been voices of calm then, local church and political leaders out on the streets, counteracting calls for retribution. Certainly, the family members' expressions of forgiveness set a pacifist tone. Unlike George Floyd's killing, the murders of the Emanuel Nine had been the work of a misguided loner, shaped by amorphous social forces but not attributable to a governmental actor like a police officer. Since 2015, however, reports of sickening abuses against Black victims had only continued to accumulate, often recorded for all to see. In a two-month stretch earlier that year, twenty-five-year-old Ahmaud Arbery had been shot to death by a white assailant as he jogged through a subdivision in south Georgia, and twenty-six-year-old Breonna Taylor had been killed in a botched no-knock police raid in Louisville, Kentucky. It didn't help that the Covid-19 pandemic had upended the world. The American death count had surpassed 100,000 (with minorities victimized disproportionately), schools and businesses had shuttered, and unemployment had soared. It was an edgy time, and fury finally boiled over the rim of Charleston's long-simmering civility.

The Black Lives Matter demonstrations that roiled America that summer were driven by the nation's youth, of all races, while the institutional Black church played a lesser, at times negligible role, certainly compared to the Civil Rights Movement. This twenty-first-century movement bubbled up organically from the streets and social media, catalyzed by videos gone viral, not Sunday-morning calls to protest. Other than Pastor Manning, who broadcast dispatches from the streets via Facebook Live, only one or two Emanuel members joined the demonstrations. The congregation was old and exhausted and socially conservative, particularly when it came to gender and sexuality, while the protesters were young and secular and insistently woke, including about LGBTQ rights. Dorothy Jenkins, the church's social action chair, said there was another obvious factor: fear. "I think people just tried to stay out of harm's way, specifically because of what had happened at the church and to the church," she said. "It was just so fresh in our minds."

On the night of the upheaval, Pastor Manning positioned himself near the corner of Meeting and Calhoun, not far from the church, armed only with his iPhone. "This is a sight that I never thought I would see here in Charleston," he said in the first of several posts, as sirens blared and tear gas yellowed the night sky. "We have just an exuberant amount of chaos taking place. We're trying to come down to just be a voice of reason for so many who have been feeling that their dignity has been robbed." As he tried to calm angry young men, his head shifted left and right in search of danger. A cordon of baton-carrying officers formed over his shoulder.

Like B. J. Glover before him, Manning walked a thin line over the ensuing weeks of marches and demonstrations. He had a building to protect in the heart of the protest zone, and a fretful congregation. But he also felt an obligation to be if not exactly with the young demonstrators then at least among them, bearing witness, showing solidarity, and providing the protection afforded a man wearing a cleric's collar. He condemned the vandalism but did not want it to obscure the violence at the root of the protests. "These things should not be happening in this day and age," he said of the rioting, "but we understand that there are so many who are indeed hurting." As the demonstrations continued day after day, Manning made the church's steps available for rallies and vigils.

Shortly after the protests began, the city council formed a temporary commission, co-chaired by Councilman Gregorie, to guide policy on matters of racial equity. It produced a smorgasbord report with scores of recommendations, several of which made for outsized targets for attack in the hyper-divisive atmosphere of Donald Trump's first term and his 2020 reelection bid. It suggested $100 million in public and private financing for reparations for residents descended from slaves. It embraced the use of critical race theory in city schools to frame the teaching of history. Its call to "reimagine delivery of policing services" was conflated easily enough into "defunding the police." Although merely advisory, the report generated opposition from some of the same corners as the slavery apology, and the council declined by a 7 to 6 vote either to accept it or make the group permanent. Only after five months of negotiation and significant concessions did proponents gain enough support to revive it: the new board could not advocate for reparations, critical race theory, defunding the police, or removing historic monuments, and would require reauthorization every three years. Even then there were four votes against it. The political battle had been distressing enough that the city's inaugural manager of diversity, racial reconciliation, and tolerance resigned before the panel began its work. The commission's difficult birth, reporter Stephen Hobbs wrote in *The Post and Courier*, "showcased a deeply entrenched reality: Despite years of hand-holding and prayers, surveys and reports, community forums and kind words, many in the city are still resistant to acknowledge that racism exists and to discuss potential solutions to racial disparities."

The outrage over the murder of George Floyd, and dismay over the downtown rioting, did present one meaningful opportunity, however. Just as Dylann Roof unwittingly embarrassed the legislature into lowering the Confederate flag, the protests surrounding Floyd's death ratcheted up pressure to bring down Charleston's most durable monument to white supremacy. On June 17, 2020, the fifth anniversary of the Emanuel slayings, Mayor John Tecklenburg, Joe Riley's successor, stood at the base of the John C. Calhoun statue in Marion Square and announced that he would ask the city council to approve its removal. In a city thick with memorials to its past, none carried more potent symbolism. Every Black Charlestonian could describe the disrespect he or she felt, even as children, when walking through the square more than 100 feet beneath Calhoun's scowling gaze. For 124 years, the statue of slavery's great defender had conveyed an image of unassailable white authority, even as the world passing beneath him had changed. Yet there he still stood, twelve feet tall, left foot forward, right hand set imperiously on hip, cape flowing, a racial conquistador set in bronze. For two decades, city leaders had relied on the excuse that the state's Heritage Act, passed in 2000, prevented localities from removing historic monuments. Armed with new legal arguments and the unanimous support of the council, Tecklenburg figured he would take his chances. "That we as Charlestonians must reckon with Mr. Calhoun's towering and deeply troubling legacy is a given," the mayor said. "That we must allow his memorial to continue to divide our city while we do that reckoning, however, is not a given."

During a moment of remembrance, he read the names of the Emanuel Nine. "Their lives were stolen," he said, "but in the days that followed, thanks to amazing grace and the deep faith of the families of the Emanuel Nine, some of which are here today, and the extraordinary act of forgiveness that so moved the world, the miracle of grace came upon our city and set us on this difficult but essential road to racial justice and conciliation."

A week later, just after midnight on June 24, workers begin separating the Calhoun statue from its pedestal with a diamond-tipped band saw. Pastor Manning stood alone in the dark, recording the scene with his iPhone.

Epilogue

On Forgiveness and Grace

*If ye forgive men their trespasses,
your heavenly Father will also forgive you.*

—MATTHEW 6:14 (KJV)

Black Charlestonians have had a lot to forgive.

Nearly two hundred years of forced removal, enslavement, and appropriated labor. The sale of thousands of ancestors, forever separating husbands from wives and children from parents. The brutal subjugation of captives through extrajudicial torture, at times outsourced to government agents. The suppression of religion and literacy. The normalized rape of defenseless women. The hanging of thirty-five men after cursory trials for insurrection. The destruction of the city's only Black church and the exile of its ministers. The four-decade crackdown on Black autonomy that preceded the Civil War. The stolen promise of Reconstruction. The lynchings and unprosecuted murders. The Red Summer race riots. The miscarriages of justice. The decades of Jim Crow humiliation and abuse. The unconstitutional denial of the rights to vote and self-govern. The thirdhand textbooks and off-limits restaurants and back-of-the-bus seating. The segregated theaters and parks and beaches and pools. The dehumanizing treatment by retailers. The inferior schools and inadequate healthcare and unequal pay and dilapidated housing. The jailing of peaceful demonstrators. The overt racism of white politicians and business leaders. The flying of an offensive flag at the State Capitol for fifty-four years. The relocations forced by urban renewal and gentrification. The fatal shooting of an unarmed Black man, in the back, by a white policeman. The ruthless murder of nine faithful churchgoers by a young neo-Nazi during Bible study.

The weight of it all, the duration of it all, takes the breath away. And for many, forgiveness might seem an inadequate response, given available options like anger, bitterness, hatred, revenge, retribution. A more natural one, perhaps a more human one, might even be "Where was God?" But this presupposes that the forgiveness expressed by the family members of the Emanuel Nine *toward* Dylann Roof was *for* Dylann Roof. Such a presupposition misinterprets their intent and misunderstands the distinctive role that the Christian covenants of forgiveness and grace have played in the Black church.

In interviews over the years, each of the six family members who spoke mercifully toward Roof—Chris Singleton, Nadine Collier, Anthony Thompson, Felicia Sanders, Alana Simmons, and Bethane Middleton-Brown—have explained that they did so for their own spiritual release, not his. None have said they meant their words to be read as a grant of exoneration or a pass from accountability or even a prayer for their tormentor's salvation, either in body or soul. They have not forgiven and forgotten. No slate has been wiped.

It also bears repeating that they by no means spoke for all members of their families or congregation or community. "If I have to forgive him to go to heaven," Emanuel trustee Willi Glee told *The New York Times* four months after the shootings, "I'm going to end up in hell with him." Dot Scott, the president of the Charleston NAACP at the time of the shootings, told me that many of her constituents were dumbfounded by the forgiveness for Roof. "I mean, you just killed my mama in the church and I don't even know you and I'm forgiving you?" she said. "No, I'd be begging the Lord to forgive me for not forgiving him. I'm not there yet. I think for the greater part of the minority community it was confusing. Why are they forgiving him when he isn't asking for forgiveness, and if he could do it again would do it again?"

But for those who did forgive, the choice was for them primarily a psychological mechanism, long utilized by African American Christians to purge themselves of self-destructive toxins. It served as an unburdening, not an undoing. "A type of self-medication for African-Americans," the scholars Nadine V. Wedderburn and Robert E. Carey have written. Yes, these Black Christians (not all were African Methodists) shared an understanding that forgiveness is a universal ideal of their faith. But in the African American church it takes on an added dimension, one infused with four centuries of history and culture to carry its own weight and purpose. It is a means not only of moral practice but of emotional self-preservation. Because the choice to forgive is one dignity that cannot be taken away, even by an unrepentant racist murderer, it is also a path to empowerment. It may be mistaken for submission, but in Charleston it reflected a resolve to leave the killer to the courts and to God.

In that way, forgiveness resurrects personal agency for victims who have been robbed of it, breaking chains of psychological enslavement. It imbues the oppressed with leverage over those who have treated them unjustly, trumping assertions of racial superiority with demonstrations of moral superiority. "History has proven over and over again that unmerited suffering is redemptive," Martin Luther King, Jr., declared in eulogizing the four girls killed in the Birmingham church bombing of 1963, more than fifty years before Barack Obama did so for the Emanuel Nine.

This employment of forgiveness is among the manifold ways that African American Christians have repurposed—and repurified—the faith of their enslavers to serve their particular needs. "By some amazing but vastly creative spiritual insight," wrote King's theological mentor, Howard Thurman, "the slave undertook the redemption of a religion that the master had profaned in his midst." The principle applies to Mother Emanuel herself, and to the Black church writ large, as institutions whose power has flowed from their capacity to overcome one trial after the next. It fits hand-in-glove with King's nonviolent approach to civil-rights activism, the holding of racism up to a moral mirror, which changed the country's course in the 1950s and 1960s. To those who argue that forgiveness without remorse is unjust, or worse that it encourages repeat offending, the Black church replies pragmatically: it would be even more unjust, and a magnification of the original offense, to impose a lifetime of anguish on those who suffer on behalf of the victims. In these aspects, the forgiveness of racial hatred and violence qualifies as its own brand of resistance, an insistent protest by spiritual freedom fighters that evil will not prevail over God's people.

"It's victory out of defeat," theologian James H. Cone, an AME minister, told *The New Yorker*'s David Remnick shortly after the Charleston massacre. "It is the weak overcoming the strong. It's 'You can't destroy my spirit. I have a forgiving spirit because that's what God created me to be. You are not going to destroy that.'" Many people, Cone said, misperceived forgiveness as sublimation, a bowing down. Rather, he said, "it's part of that tragic experience of trying to express your humanity in the face of death and not having any power." Similarly, Albert J. Raboteau, the distinguished scholar of African American religion, said in assessing the role of forgiveness in Charleston that "the attitude which [the enslaved] struggled to achieve in imitation of Jesus seems incredible unless one perceives it as a way of holding onto meaning in the midst of the absurdity of unchecked white supremacy." The late AME Bishop John Hurst Adams, who was active in civil-rights causes, noted that the denomination's original slogan was: God Our Father, Christ Our Redeemer, Man Our Brother. "Because of our struggles with slavery and Reconstruction and segregation and prejudice," he told me before his death, "the 'Man Our Brother' has always been a real centerpiece of the teaching and preaching of our church. And in order for us to call whites our brother or sister, it had to include the forgiveness of what they had done to our race."

These understandings are not exclusive to great thinkers and prelates. They filter into the pews on Sunday mornings and Wednesday evenings in a melding of faith and experience, seeping into the soul like eucalyptus balm. Hear out Harold Washington, a Charleston native who joined Emanuel in the 1960s after marrying a lifelong member. "Hatred doesn't do anything for anybody," the octogenarian said. "You're drinking poison while waiting for the other guy to die. But when you've been traumatized for four hundred years it kind of makes you different from someone who has not been traumatized at all. It hurts them more than it hurts you because we've been through it. You're always thinking, 'Yeah, I've seen this before.' It hurts but you don't hold on to it as long because the next day you have to do some other stuff. The world just doesn't change that fast."

Regardless of the common depiction of Christ's pigmentation in sacred art, Black Americans have long had ample reason to identify with the "suffering servant." Some take literally the Bible's prophecies of exodus and resurrection, if not in this life then in the next, mining hope from a belief system that was thrust upon them. They take to heart that the attitude modeled by Christ— forgiveness and love over bitterness and hate—is an essential part of the contract between God and man. That, after all, is typically what they are left with. The imperative to forgive has become so imprinted in the evolutionary genomics of the Black church that it is, for some, an almost unconscious response, even to dehumanization of the worst kind. "Forgiveness is hard-wired into Black Christianity," said Rev. Joseph Darby, the longtime AME and civil-rights leader in Charleston. "People who survived the indignities of antebellum slavery, if they couldn't do anything else, they could forgive. It's learned behavior."

THERE WAS NO PROCESS by which the Emanuel family members concluded that forgiveness was merited or beneficial, no prompting or premeditation.

Years later, they can only describe their actions in mystical terms. Chris Singleton, who started it all, said he was not thinking about how forgiveness might work when he uttered the words to a television reporter. After the fact, he said, he came to understand that he was moved by "something out of this world, because there's no other explanation for it." Ideally, Singleton said, Roof would acknowledge the wrongness of his ways and give his life over to Christ in pursuit of salvation. But that was somewhat secondary. "I honestly believe that forgiveness frees you from being caged in with revenge, vengefulness," he said. "Once you release that—boom—you're good to go. It doesn't mean you forget. You don't forgive and forget. Somebody murdered my mom because she's Black. There's no way around that."

Nadine Collier, the first to speak at Roof's bond hearing, also said the only explanation was that God was with her. "I was angry," she recalled. "I was pissed, I was hurt. I was furious. I'm only human. I felt like I was at my lowest point. And anybody who knows me knows I'm very outspoken. Lord knows, my mouth is very slick. But when the judge asked if anyone wanted to speak, I got up, I said who I was, and something just came over me. I kind of went blank, matter of fact, didn't know what I was going to say." Once she said it, however—"God forgive you and I forgive you"—she could not deny the lasting shift in her outlook. She became calmer, more patient, less judgmental, slower to anger. She had removed Roof's grip on the rest of her life. "Forgiveness is power," she told an audience the following year. "With forgiveness, I find myself rising above all challenges."

Growing up at Emanuel, Collier joined the congregation each Sunday in praying that God would "forgive us our trespasses as we forgive those who trespass against us." But the words tended to flow by without much consideration, and when she spoke in the courtroom she was not contemplating Christ's instruction or example. "People misunderstand why I said forgiveness," she said. "Some liked it, some didn't, but I want people to know I didn't do it for y'all. I did it for me so I can move on with my life." Anthony Thompson, who followed Collier at the bond hearing, made a comparable self-assessment. "He is not a part of my life anymore," Thompson said of his wife's murderer. "Forgiveness has freed me of that, of him, completely. I'm not going to make him a lifetime partner." That one surprising act, he said, had bestowed "a peace that surpasses all understanding."

It merits noting that the final three speakers at Roof's hearing did not explicitly say they had forgiven him, and that two did not use any form of the word (although their sentiments seemed aligned then and subsequently proved to be). Felicia Sanders ended her brief comments to Roof by praying "may God have mercy on you." Alana Simmons told Roof that "everyone's plea for your soul is proof that [the Emanuel Nine] lived in love and their legacies will live in love." Bethane Middleton-Brown couched forgiveness as a goal but suggested that she and her family were works in progress. "We are the family that love built," she said. "We have no room for hate. So we have to forgive and I pray God on your soul."

Sanders has since explained that any forgiveness she felt was not for Roof's benefit. It was simply what allowed her to breathe, to pull herself from bed each morning and continue to care for her family. "Forgiveness is not for the person," she said. "The person doesn't care whether you forgive him or not. Forgiveness is for you. Forgiveness is growth. If you don't have any forgiveness in you, it makes you stagnate. You will never grow. You're giving the individual the power over you, so that means you're still a victim to the person. I want to say that we refuse to be a victim. I want him to know, Prime Evil to know, that just because you took our loved ones, you don't have us."

Simmons and Middleton-Brown said they were only inspired to speak at the hearing after others set the tone. Simmons, who had traveled to Charleston from her home in Virginia, remembered being shocked as she listened to Nadine Collier. "I couldn't believe that with all of the pain that she carried with losing her mother that she had enough strength left to do something that many people can't do for minor things," she said. "For her to do that I thought was a true testament to the people who lost their lives alongside my grandfather." It was all such a blur to Middleton-Brown, who had driven in from North Carolina, that she does not recall hearing Nadine Collier or Anthony Thompson offer forgiveness to her sister's killer. Rather, what made an impression on her was Felicia Sanders's brief account of welcoming Roof to Bible study "with open arms." That simple reminder of the power of love propelled her out of her seat. "I didn't think about what I wanted to say, I didn't know what I was feeling," she said. "I just knew what I didn't want to do: I didn't want to hate."

The other adult survivors eventually adopted the idiom of forgiveness as well. It took some time for Polly Sheppard, who had stared down Roof's gun. But she came around to feeling that if her friend Felicia Sanders could forgive, having lost a son, it would be coldhearted for her not to do so as well. "From that day on I had a release," Sheppard said. "Because forgiveness is, like, you think you're letting somebody else off the hook but you're actually letting yourself off the hook. Because if you keep it, there's no healing with hatred." Jennifer Pinckney, who felt a bullet whiz by her head, could not fully shed her bitterness on behalf of her daughters, who would have no father to walk them down the aisle. But three years after her husband's death she felt she had largely forgiven his killer. "That's what we're taught," she said. "Sometimes I feel like I teeter-totter, but then I know that it's the right thing to do, is to forgive."

THE CONUNDRUMS OF FORGIVENESS have long occupied the great philosophers (Augustine, Kant, Hegel, Nietzsche); theologians (Luther, Butler, Kierkegaard, Tutu); and writers (Shakespeare, Pope, Hugo, Twain), not to mention psychologists and ethicists. Their observations took on fresh relevance during a sixty-year span that included seemingly unforgivable events like the Holocaust, the wartime incarceration of Japanese Americans, South African apartheid, and the September 11 terrorist attacks. The lingering question of reparations for descendants of enslaved Africans, inseparable from matters of generational accountability and forgiveness, has reinforced that the exploration bears real-world implications beyond mere scriptural and philosophical conjecture.

Naturally, interpretations of forgiveness—what it is and how and when it should be practiced—are important to many of the world's religions, including Buddhism, Hinduism, Judaism, and Islam. They can vary significantly. When, for instance, Mother Emanuel's pastor, Eric Manning, traveled to Pittsburgh in 2018 to console survivors of the shootings at the Tree of Life synagogue, he found admiration for his church's commitment to forgiveness but little interest in replicating it. Rather, Pittsburgh's indignant Jewish mourners held fast to the concept of *teshuvah*, or repentance, rooted more in the emphasis on accountability in the Hebrew Scriptures than the love-your-enemies ethos of the New Testament. Under its guidelines, when man sins against God, say by violating the strictures of the Sabbath, he may seek forgiveness from God through confession, remorse, and prayer. But when man sins against man, the offender can only receive such healing grace from the victim, and only after acknowledging fault, asking forgiveness, and, importantly, making restitution. Logically, when the victim has been murdered, this is not possible.

But arguably in no other faith are repentance and forgiveness as central to its theological underpinnings as Christianity. The British theologian Anthony Bash, who has written extensively on the subject, argues that one of the great ethical achievements of the New Testament and the Christian church was to establish forgiveness as a surpassing moral ideal. It is not a commandment, he stresses, but rather an aspiration, in emulation of Christ's teachings and the unmerited grace that God may choose to extend as a gift to his people. "To forgive is to be part of God's redemptive work that includes the moral transformation of human relationships and society," Bash has written. "To forgive, therefore, is to participate in the completion of the work of the cross."

Christianity holds that forgiveness should be unending. When a frustrated Peter asked whether he must continue to forgive a sinner even after a seventh offense, Jesus famously replied that he should do so "until seventy times seven" (Matthew 18:21–22). The gospels of Mark and Luke characterize the sacramental work performed by John the Baptist, the model for the faith's ritual of admission and conversion, as preaching "a baptism of repentance for the forgiveness of sins" (Mark 1:4 and Luke 3:3). In Matthew's recounting of the Last Supper, Jesus offers his cup to his disciples to drink of "the blood of the covenant, which is poured out for many for the forgiveness of sins" (Matthew 26:28), embedding forgiveness in another sacrament, communion. In the Lord's Prayer, as dictated in Matthew 6:14–15, forgiveness is part of a compact bearing profound consequences: God may forgive those who forgive others. And, of course, in perhaps the most defining verse in Scripture, Christ prayed on the cross for his crucifiers, that God would "forgive them, for they know not what they do" (Luke 23:34). The authority to forgive, Bash maintains, is thought to be an essential attribute of the divine, with the corollary that humans, made in God's image, should seek to live out God's example. For believers in God's Word, there could be little doubt as to expectations. "Be kind and compassionate to one another, forgiving each other, just as in Christ God forgave you," it says in Ephesians 4:32.

As they grew into their new faith, embracing the heavenly hope provided by Jesus, Black Christians organically applied its central tenets to their earthly treatment by their enslavers and oppressors. Their practice of forgiveness came to encompass their reality, that while any human of any hue might be victimized on any given day, Black Americans were vulnerable to systemic discrimination every single day.

Around the world, the scene in the Charleston County courtroom inspired the kind of awe reserved for moonshots and miracles. For some, however, it left an aftertaste of acquiescence, with the question hanging of whether Black forgiveness was ultimately radical or regressive. Had Black Christians participated in their own oppression by adopting a white Protestant point of view? How did forgiveness intersect with another moral and political imperative that received heavy contemplation in the Bible, namely justice? Bash wrote that some see forgiveness as "the antonym of justice," particularly when the victim is remorseless. They go so far, he pointed out, as to label forgiveness without repentance as "morally irresponsible" because it may rob victims of self-respect, allow perpetrators to escape accountability, and incentivize recurring misbehavior. The immediacy with which the Emanuel family members forgave ran counter to the view that forgiveness must be a process and perhaps even overtly transactional, requiring recognition, remorse, and reparation on the part of the offender.

Yet if the forgivers are to be believed, their grace toward Dylann Roof was in fact largely transactional. They may not have received the repentance they wanted, but they each acknowledged that their choice was self-serving. Across the generations, their religious training had reinforced that in order to be forgiven they had to forgive, a quid pro quo. Across those same generations, their experience had convinced them viscerally of what researchers have found scientifically, that forgiveness decreases anxiety, depression, anger, and resentment. Whether for individuals or communities, the ability to overcome mistreatment without retaliation is thought to correlate with better overall health.

To some, like the twentieth-century French philosopher Jacques Derrida, this benefit taints the purity of the act. Those closer to the ground typically care less about that. "To forgive is indeed the best form of self-interest," wrote Archbishop Desmond Tutu, who led South Africa's post-apartheid Truth and Reconciliation Commission, "since anger, resentment and revenge are corrosive of that *summum bonum*, that greatest good, communal harmony that enhances the humanity and personhood of all in the community." If Black South Africans had predicated forgiveness on repentance, they would have been "locked into the culprit's whim, locked into victimhood," Tutu held. "That would be palpably unjust."

But what of justice? The state and federal courts would, of course, have the ultimate say about the corporeal fate of the Emanuel killer. But where was the spiritual righteousness in awarding unconditional grace to a miscreant as remorseless as Dylann Roof, whatever the truth of his mental competency? Didn't that matter too? Some twentieth-century philosophers held that certain modern horrors were inexpiable. "Pardoning died in the death camps,"

French philosopher Vladimir Jankélévitch asserted. Not a few of the friends and siblings and fellow congregants of Roof's victims felt it also had died in Emanuel's fellowship hall. If turning the other cheek was intended to restore the power imbalance between victim and victimizer, retribution might be a more direct route, they argued. After all, the Bible also offered backing for taking an eye for an eye.

No one begrudges a traumatized victim the prerogative to respond with Christian empathy. The complications arise when the offender shows no remorse and when his target is not just the forgiving individual but a broader community that may not share the same generous spirit. The Emanuel family members had no reason to think they were representing anyone but themselves at the bond hearing, but much of white America was relieved to think they might be speaking for all of Black America.

There was, in fact, a choice to be made in Charleston after the shootings at Mother Emanuel, a choice between conflagration and peace, between hatred and forgiveness. Once again, the Black community took the high road, the Way of Sorrows, and the streets did not erupt. This left more than a few conflicted, particularly those who already viewed Christianity as a tool of the oppressor class. No one wanted the elegant old city to burn. But neither did they want white Charleston (or white America, for that matter) to be exculpated. In their view, the expressions of forgiveness, the hand-holding across the bridge, the financial support for Mother Emanuel, all served the subversive purpose of making white people feel undeservedly better about themselves. They understood that their white neighbors bore no individual responsibility, and that many had responded with their hearts. But the narrative in Charleston nonetheless risked allowing them to presume absolution for the legacy of white supremacy that produced Dylann Roof and that still prevented Black Carolinians from achieving equity in most every sphere of life.

As throughout Emanuel's history, the 2015 massacre put on full display the competing instincts of African Methodism, the Black Church, and African American resistance. Muhiyidin d'Baha, a Black Lives Matter leader in Charleston who was thirty at the time, told *The New Yorker*'s David Remnick that, for better or worse, the focus on forgiveness had undercut any inclination toward street protest. Like other young activists, he felt it had been written into the DNA of Black Charlestonians, perhaps since Denmark Vesey's execution, that there was a heavy price to pay for making white people too uncomfortable. "When the families give these signals, and the pastors instill in the families a sense of grace and forgiveness, the anger never reverberates," he said. "No leadership arose demanding to have this pain recognized. Again, it's let me accommodate you so you're not scared, we'll just get on the bridge and hold hands, Jesus is good, we're over it. There has been an arrangement here, created over generations, to be able to endure terrorism. At this point, this is the way it is. We endure. We don't ask for more."

This time, however, there had been nine murders. Nine. Why, asked some of the most thoughtful Black voices of the day, was it always on African Americans to forgive in the exhausting choreography of racial violence? Although it captivated the world, the courtroom scene in Charleston "was also in line with society's expectation that the subordinate caste bear its suffering and absolve its transgressors," Isabel Wilkerson wrote in *Caste*. "Black forgiveness of dominant-caste sin has become a spiritual form of having to be twice as good, in trauma, as in other aspects of life, to be seen as half as worthy." In an op-ed for *The New York Times*, Roxane Gay explained why she could not forgive Dylann Roof: "White people embrace narratives about forgiveness so they can pretend the world is a fairer place than it actually is and that racism is merely a vestige of a painful past instead of this indelible part of our present ... We forgive and forgive and forgive and those who trespass against us continue to trespass against us."

Near the fourth anniversary of the shootings, Rev. William H. Lamar IV, pastor of the renowned Metropolitan AME Church in Washington, D.C., hit that point in a radio interview about the events in Charleston. He referenced the Lutheran theologian Dietrich Bonhoeffer and his derision of "cheap grace," which Bonhoeffer defined in part as "the preaching of forgiveness without requiring repentance." Bonhoeffer's critique, Lamar said, was of "a grace that is absent discipline, absent the challenge of living in new ways as communities." So when it came to forgiveness, the AME preacher said, "I am not willing to forgive what has happened in America unless America is willing to repent and willing to atone and America has not done that." Lamar said that modern American Christianity, with its predominant evangelical strains, sought too often "to privatize forgiveness" by limiting it to transactions among individuals while ignoring "the systematic economic, political, and social devastation of communities." In other words, forgiveness requires an earnest attempt to reorder the relationship between victim and offender. Show Black Americans progress toward improving public schools, ridding the streets of guns, and removing bias from policing and they might then open a conversation.

"What the body politic wants," Lamar said, "is a political version of the magical Negro trope in literature and film, that Black people are to help white people come to some sort of self-actualization, some sort of moral discovery, like the Will Smith character in [*The Legend of*] *Bagger Vance* or the character in *Green Book*, this magical Negro, that we are to absolve, that we are to take into our body all of this violence and allow white people on the other end to feel better about themselves ... We refuse to be your magical Negroes."

THAT FRUSTRATION, long fed by cynicism, could be found in the Lowcountry as well, where the suppression of "Black rage" for the reassurance of white folks was as old as plantation culture. "Aren't they wonderful?" Rev. Darby asked mockingly over lunch one day. "We have such good colored people. Don't we have good colored people? We have to do something for them, make them some chicken, go hold hands on the bridge and sing 'Kumbaya.'"

Charleston educator and activist Minerva Brown King, the initial lead plaintiff in the city's school desegregation lawsuit, had her doubts that all the interracial fellowship would translate into progress in education or affordable housing. "I'm sick and tired of the onus of forgiving being on the backs of Black people," she told me. "Why is it always for us to do the work, to do the forgiving? At my age, it's darn well worn me out, and the more we take that responsibility off the perpetrators the more we're going to be victims."

In retrospect, some even felt Barack Obama had been unintentionally complicit. "We've tidied up for the world with a nice little bow, but internally it's a mess," said Rev. Kylon Middleton of Mt. Zion AME. "I love President Obama, but President Obama coopted the whole conversation and made it about forgiveness. It created a whole nostalgia around forgiveness, along with the people holding hands over the Ravenel Bridge. Once it got into the national discourse, and it still is, we can never really take that back."

Allow me to grant the final words on the matter to Melvin L. Graham, Jr., the devoted older brother of Cynthia Graham Hurd, whose life was taken at Mother Emanuel at age fifty-four. A lab technician for a chemical company, Graham retired early after his sister's death because he had trouble focusing at work and worried that he would injure himself or a coworker. I first came across him on a sweltering July afternoon in 2017 in the Emanuel AME Church cemetery, just north of downtown, where I had gone to survey headstones and search for the graves of some of the Nine. Heat radiated off the asphalt lanes like a campfire, and there was no sign of the living until I noticed a man in the distance with a domed head, bent at the waist, sweeping grass clippings with a hand broom from atop Cynthia Hurd's marker. He wore a powder-blue linen shirt tucked neatly into khaki slacks, undampened by sweat. As I got closer, I recognized something about his carriage, call it his dignity, and realized I had seen him before. It had been at Dylann Roof's trial, seven months earlier, when I watched Graham testify to the wrenching loss that his family had suffered.

I introduced myself, and he seemed glad for the company. "I still come here from time to time to talk to her," Graham told me. He pointed at nearby graves. "There's Susie, and Ethel. And there's Tywanza. Brave young man."

I later visited Graham for the first of several conversations about Hurd and her death and what it all meant. Few who I interviewed have been as thoughtful—and humble—about the bewildering place of forgiveness within the context of unimaginable evil.

"For me," Graham told me, "I question. I want to ask the question you're not supposed to ask: Why? And as time goes on, I understand that there were sacrifices, that God used them to open up the hearts and the minds of people. In order to open your heart and mind, I have to put something in front of you that's going to open your eyes. A random killing might not do it. But killing nine people in a church, all innocent, different ages, that shakes you to your core. The one place that's supposed to be safe has been violated. Now what are you going to do?"

Graham attended Roof's bond hearing and was taken aback by the expressions of forgiveness from the other families. He could not summon the same anointing. When the judge asked if the family of Cynthia Hurd wished to speak, he stood formally and responded, "We have nothing to say." Graham sat through each day of Roof's trial, taking in the crime-scene photos and the medical examiner's testimony and the killer's assertion that he had not shed a tear. Over the years, he and his brother, Malcolm, pointedly declined to jump on the forgiveness bandwagon. They were works in progress, they would say, walking their own walk on their own timetable. They might have felt differently had Roof shown any remorse, but that was moot. Instead, they found solace in securing their sister's memory, largely by staging an annual book drive in her name for the public library she served. If they could not yet arrive at Christian forgiveness, they would at least respond with Christian works.

The empathy shown by Charleston's people, including its white people, helped sustain them. "We feel as a family that we need to move on, not get eaten up by hatred," Graham said. "But you have to show us some remorse.

You can't execute my sister and expect me to forgive you for it. So we're going to keep Cynthia's legacy going and not concentrate on him. You can't hate when all these people are doing all these wonderful things for your family and your sister. It eases the pain, melts the pain around your heart."

Graham has, of course, struggled to comprehend what happened at the bond hearing. "That was just God's hand," he said. "I'm still baffled. I don't understand it. That's why I'm saying it must be God talking. This is your whole religious background and training and experience put to the test. Rev. Thompson is a man of faith. The Simmons family, the grandfather, a man of faith. I can see them saying this is what we've been taught over and over again and your hatred is not going to destroy our beliefs and who we are. To some extent, African Americans have always had to be that forgiving type of people, that you forgive so you can move on. Our history is such that if you don't, you can't survive."

He understands the challenge before him, and that time is short, perhaps too short. "My faith teaches me that I've got to let go of a lot of personal feelings, let go of a lot of selfishness and look beyond my pain, and that's hard to do," he said. "Forgiveness is the basic teaching of the church. We practice forgiveness in terms of if you cheated me out of a dollar, I forgive you. But when something so egregious happens it's taken to the extreme, the ultimate test. And you bring it back to Jesus—'forgive them, Father'; 'forgive us our trespasses.' As time goes on, it's going to be easier to let the pain and hurt go and focus on the joy and the positive. At that point, we may be able to forgive. We're on the right path. Maybe we'll get there."

MOTHER EMANUEL HAS BEEN working to get there as well. The church I encountered during ten years of immersion showed itself to be both achingly beautiful and immeasurably broken. It is too trite to say that "The Tragedy" left the congregation shattered or forever altered. Unsurprisingly, it is still seeking its footing even a decade later. In reality, of course, Emanuel was already a diminished version of itself, owing to its aging, shrinking membership and deteriorating physical plant. But the aftermath of the massacre in the fellowship hall reinforced that it could never fully revert, and that realization has been unsettling to many. Membership has remained a challenge, as has Sunday attendance in the wake of the Covid-19 pandemic. Fundraising for ongoing renovations and repairs has progressed dollar by dollar.

Yet it was still possible during my regular visits to lose oneself in the earworm hymns and excitable preaching and forget momentarily what had happened downstairs. It could still just be church. The robed choir and white-gloved ushers still sashayed down the aisles to "This Is the Day" on communion Sundays. Impish children still snuggled up in the pews to church matriarchs like Doris Coaxum Sanders, knowing it might win them a dollar or a piece of hard candy. Lisa Washington Wade still belted out solos that set folks to swaying and waving toward the heavens in praise, for both the gift of her voice and of seeing another morning. If you closed your eyes while the congregation kept beat with a Lowcountry clap, you might still be transported to a hush harbor ring shout.

The mood of the place, however, was necessarily more somber and reflective. The dead were always present. It was difficult to spot Sharon Coakley and Blondelle Gadsden in their usual seats and not think of them as the late Myra Thompson's sisters, or to lean back over the pew to chat with Willi Glee and not recall that he was alive only because he skipped Bible study to grab a bite at Ruby Tuesday. Each evening at 5:00 p.m., the church's electronic carillon—purchased with donations received after the shootings—slowly chimed "Amazing Grace" in remembrance of the Nine. Every sermon, prayer, and hymn was now received through the filter of June 2015. Whether the point was made explicitly or not, and often it was, each Sunday paid tribute to two centuries of resilience. Mother Emanuel had become sacred space, now more than ever, and its walls told a sacred story. It revealed Charleston to have been an epicenter of both enslavement and resistance, and the Black church to have been steadfast in holding both American Christianity and American democracy to account for their betrayals. It stood proudly as a landmark of African Methodism, and thus a singular monument to the theological autonomy and political audacity of African Americans.

In July 2023, Emanuel hosted a special service with dual purposes, to celebrate the return of its beloved pipe organ, which had been out for repair for more than a year, and to break ground ceremonially on the memorial to the Emanuel Nine. The church's past and present melded that steamy Saturday morning, and Bishop Samuel L. Green, Sr., nearing the end of his eight years in South Carolina, marked the occasion with an impassioned sermon. Making a metaphor of the more-than-century-old organ, he led the congregation through the odyssey of all that the church had overcome, observing that with each setback, from the hanging of Denmark Vesey to the earthquake of 1886, "the music has invariably never stopped."

"In June of 2015, when a demented evil bigot came into this church and shot and killed nine of the members, including its pastor, somehow the music of this church survived," Green preached. "In spite of what the bigots wanted and in spite of what the racists were hoping for, in spite of what the white supremacists believed would happen, the music of this congregation never stopped." The faith of the ancestors, Green said, had enabled the South's oldest African Methodist Episcopal congregation "to make melody out of melancholy," time and again. And what better ministry, he wondered? What better testimony to God's existence and grace? "You can say a lot of great things about Mother Emanuel AME Church," the bishop went on, "but the one thing you have to say is that this church is good at driving the devil crazy. This church, this church, will make the devil pull his hair out." The crowd was clapping now, rising to its feet. "The devil has never seen a congregation like this before and every time evil hears that organ the devil thinks to himself, 'Ah, they're at it again.'"

Emanuel's tumultuous history may temper its spirituality at times, but also magnifies it. Rarely have I been so affected as at a worship service in 2019 when the congregation, in powerful unison, sang the anthem "Lift Every Voice and Sing." I had heard the lyrics enough times to mouth a few stanzas. But never had I felt them as when standing next to my septuagenarian seatmate, Lois Gethers, gray braids coiled regally atop her head, as her eyes welled to James Weldon Johnson's defiant words from nearly 120 years earlier. Proof of their relevance could be found in the bullet-scarred linoleum one floor below.

We have come over a way that with tears has been watered,
We have come, treading our path through the blood of the slaughtered.

Several months later, during a service commemorating Veterans Day, I watched with another tremor as nineteen men and women, some in full dress, stood stiffly before the congregation while a trumpeter played "Taps" from the balcony. They averaged more than a decade of military service and included Rev. Manning and his wife, who had met while in the army three decades earlier. Their pride in serving was palpable, as was the knowledge that the country they fought for had not always reciprocated with fairness or dignity. It occurred to me that the late Rev. Daniel L. Simmons, Sr., a Vietnam veteran and recipient of a Purple Heart, should have been among them.

That year's Watch Night service, a New Year's Eve remembrance of slavery and freedom, also assumed added gravitas. As in Black churches around the country, the service recalled the night of December 31, 1862, when congregants gathered to await the dawn of 1863 and Abraham Lincoln's promised Emancipation Proclamation. As midnight approached, four men stationed in the corners of the gallery shouted their ritualized call, one after the next: "Watchman, watchman," boomed Lee Bennett, Jr., a second-generation Emanuel trustee, "pleeee-ase tell me the hour of the night." When Rev. Manning finally declared that the year had passed, there seemed more relief than joy.

Given their ongoing trauma, members of Mother Emanuel have every reason to be wary of white people, not unlike B. J. Glover after his brutal beating. Yet in my experience, they welcomed interlopers and curiosity-seekers with graciousness and goodwill. After my wife, Dina, and I attended our first worship service, three Sundays after the shootings, we were invited down to the fellowship hall, where blood had pooled only eighteen days earlier, to join in a repast of fried chicken and sweet tea (the space remains in daily use, and I conducted dozens of interviews there). We were received as warmly as if at a wedding—I remember being introduced to the church's eldest member, 104-year-old Marguerite Michel—and that has not changed in the ten years since. I have endeavored to tell the congregation's story in a way that reciprocates that respect, recognizing that my own race, background, and privilege make it impossible for me to experience or understand it in the way that African Americans do. To that end, I have compensated in the only way I know how, in the way I have been trained, by putting in the work: by reading and interviewing voluminously, by relentlessly pursuing and adhering to the facts, and by thinking and writing with as much humility, empathy, and care as I can summon.

Faith groups everywhere lost a degree of innocence on the night of June 17, 2015, and with the deadlier attacks that followed at a synagogue in Pittsburgh, Pennsylvania, a Baptist church in Sutherland Springs, Texas, and a pair of mosques in Christchurch, New Zealand. I felt it intensely as I visited Black churches across the Lowcountry. No longer did it make sense to welcome a white stranger into a sanctuary without scrutiny, perhaps a polite question or two or even a request to search his bag. Emanuel trustees Willi Glee and Lee Bennett recounted for me that on one of my early Sunday visits, not long after the shootings, they had watched anxiously from the choir loft as I unzipped my black canvas briefcase, large enough to conceal a weapon, and then exhaled when I removed only a laptop. Who could blame them?

Emanuel has continued to receive threats over the years. Longtime members who were instructed as children to close their eyes in prayer no longer feel safe doing so. The church has formed a security ministry and charged it with thwarting any future attack. Until in-person services were temporarily suspended by the Covid-19 pandemic, a uniformed Charleston police officer stationed himself at the rear of the sanctuary each Sunday and parked his marked car conspicuously in the lot that Dylann Roof had used. A squad of hand-selected congregants, some with police or military backgrounds, have received tactical training and carry concealed handguns in the House of the Lord. Additional surveillance cameras and monitors have been installed, and strangers are required to announce themselves over an intercom before being buzzed into the locked fellowship hall.

The doors of the church are no longer always open.

Acknowledgments

It is no exaggeration to say that *Mother Emanuel*, a decade in the making, could not have been completed without the generosity of four benefactors—the Ford Foundation, the Washington-based think tank New America, the Emerson Collective, and the National Endowment for the Humanities. In addition to financial support that enabled a lengthy leave from daily journalism, each provided an enormous shot of confidence that this book might one day matter. I owe incalculable debts to Darren Walker, Juliet Mureriwa, and Dave Mazzoli at Ford; to Anne-Marie Slaughter, Awista Ayub, and the brilliant fellows at New America; to the late Amy Low and Patrick D'Arcy at Emerson; and to the NEH's taxpayer-supported Public Scholar program (any views, findings, conclusions, or recommendations expressed in this book do not necessarily reflect those of the NEH). They may not remember or be aware of their contributions, but Terry Adamson, Kent Alexander, Michael Gilligan, Peter Lattman, and Earl Lewis facilitated contacts that led to Hail Mary successes in the grant-seeking process.

My deepest gratitude goes to the people of Emanuel African Methodist Episcopal Church, and to the survivors and families of the victims of the 2015 tragedy. Their grace in allowing me to intrude on their grief made my years at the church a revelation and a joy. Scores of congregants suffered my incessant questioning with good humor and learned to ignore the blasphemous glare of my open laptop as I tapped out notes during worship services. Even when not cited directly, their reminiscences infuse this book. I am particularly grateful to Pastor Eric S. C. Manning, who allowed me generous access to the church's archives and activities. Pastor Manning's executive assistant, Sylvia Blake, has been a regular source of help and good cheer. I also appreciated the good will of Emanuel's AME overseers, Bishop Samuel L. Green, Sr., and former Presiding Elder Norvel Goff, Sr., who welcomed me to observe Annual and General Conferences. I was fortunate to have a pair of soulmates in my obsessive pursuit of Emanuel arcana, church trustees Lee Bennett, Jr., and Willi Glee, and regularly taxed the memories of longtime members like Leon Alston,

Cathy Bennett, Timothy Brown, Marlena Davis, Lois Gethers, Melvin Graham, Jr., Kay Taylor Hightower, Ruby Nesbitt Martin, and Doris Coaxum Sanders. I counted every minute spent with Polly Sheppard and Felicia and Tyrone Sanders as a blessing, and appreciated the help of the Sanders's attorney, Andrew J. Savage III. I also thank members of the late Rev. Benjamin J. Glover's family, particularly daughters Oveta Glover and Gail A. Glover, for their guidance in telling his amazing story.

No one has been more central to the making of this book than my incomparable literary agent, Kathy Robbins, a true friend and the sagest of counsels. Thank you for everything, Robbins person. Kathy's assistants—Janet Oshiro, Alexandra Sugarman, and Grace Garrahan—could not have been more professional. My manuscript had a series of godparents at Crown, first Tim Duggan, who procured it, then publisher and editor in chief Gillian Blake, who kept it on track, and, finally, executive editor Kevin Doughten, who brought it to fruition with a convert's enthusiasm. Kevin's smart and nimble work, along with that of associate editor Amy Li, vastly improved the book's structure and focus and made it a more elegant read. I also owe thanks to copy editor Rachelle Mandik, production editors Terry Deal and Craig Adams, editorial assistant Jess Scott, proofreaders Tracy Lynch and Chris Jerome, associate general counsel Dan Novack, designer Aubrey Khan, production manager Heather Williamson, marketer Mason Eng, publicist Tammy Blake, and Penguin Random House publicity director Dyana Messina. I valued sound outside advice from Jen Marshall, Elizabeth Stordeur Pryor, and Jonathan Eig.

My deepest gratitude goes to the immensely gifted Jonathan Green, a Charleston-based artist of international renown, and to Kim Cliett Long and Cameron Hall, for the use of Jonathan's captivating 1995 image *First Sunday*, which art director Christopher Brand transformed into an inspired cover.

I could not have pursued my interest in Mother Emanuel without support from editors at *The New York Times* who allowed me to cover the aftermath of the shootings and then permitted me an extended leave. I am forever grateful to Dean Baquet, Joe Kahn, Matthew Purdy, Marc Lacey, Carolyn Ryan, Rebecca Corbett, Paul Fishleder, Peter Applebome, and the late great Christine Kay. Numerous colleagues from the *Times* have been ongoing sources of encouragement, including James Dao, Jason DeParle, Andrea Elliott, Richard Fausset, David Firestone, Jodi Kantor, and Adam Nagourney, while Alan Blinder, the other half of my Roof-trial double byline, has remained a valued sounding board. Scott Kraft, long a top editor at the *Los Angeles Times*, did me a much-appreciated solid, as did my pal, political writer John Harwood.

Although my background (beyond majoring in history) is in journalism, I have done my best to pursue this project with academic rigor and have relied on generous feedback from professional historians and theologians. Anyone doing such work in Charleston these days has the fortune to be tutored by a pair of public scholars of the first order: Nic Butler, a historian at the Charleston County Public Library, and Harlan Greene, formerly the special collections archivist at the College of Charleston's Addlestone Library. Each has been recurringly gracious in addressing questions and directing me to sources. Among others in the field who went out of their way are Dee E. Andrews of California State University, East Bay; Bobby Donaldson of the University of South Carolina; Douglas R. Egerton of Le Moyne College; Damon L. Fordham of The Citadel; Michael P. Johnson of Johns Hopkins University; Ethan J. Kytle and Blain Roberts of California State University, Fresno; Richard S. Newman of Rochester Institute of Technology; Gregory O'Malley of University of California, Santa Cruz; Robert L. Paquette of Hamilton College; Bernard E. Powers, Jr., and Dale and Ted Rosengarten of College of Charleston; James O'Neil Spady of Soka University of America; and Julie Winch of University of Massachusetts, Boston. My friend Edward Ball, a groundbreaker in the study of Charleston's African American history, has been an enlightening guide. I've also appreciated the help of outstanding Charleston journalists like Tony Bartelme, Andy Brack, Herb Frazier, Jennifer Berry Hawes, Hanna Raskin, and Glenn Smith. My understanding of African Methodist history and governance was enhanced by Rev. Joseph Darby, Rev. Kylon J. Middleton, Dr. John Thomas III, and Rev. Mark Kelly Tyler. Alfred T. Day III, Jean K. Wolf, and Margaret Jerrido aided my understanding of Philadelphia's early church history.

With few exceptions, the research reflected in these pages is mine. I did, however, employ several talented diggers for discrete tasks: Doreen Larimer and Jesse Bustos-Nelson for assistance with property and genealogical searches, respectively, in Charleston, and Jay W. Driskell for a survey of NAACP records at the Library of Congress. Throughout the process, my admiration deepened for the quiet work of archivists and librarians. Of particular assistance were Aaisha Haykal at Charleston's Avery Research Center for African American History and Culture; Steve Tuttle and Wade H. Dorsey at the South Carolina Department of Archives and History; Virginia Ellison at the South

Carolina Historical Society; and the ever-diligent staffs of the Charleston County Public Library's South Carolina Room, the College of Charleston's Addlestone Library, the University of South Carolina's South Caroliniana Library and its Center for Civil Rights History and Research, the Historic Charleston Foundation, the Charleston Library Society, the Preservation Society of Charleston, and the Charleston County Register of Deeds. Sociologist Elizabeth Rauh Bethel kindly directed me to her archived interviews with B. J. Glover, a mother lode.

It tends toward cliché, but Hilary McClellan, an eagle-eyed fact-checker, saved me from myself more times than I can count. Several early readers also did me the great favor of reviewing all or portions of the manuscript and making valuable suggestions. They include Frank Allen, Edward Ball, Anthony Bash, Lee Bennett, Jr., Eddie S. Glaude, Jr., Harlan Greene, Micah Greenstein, Michael L. Lomax, Eric S. C. Manning, Richard S. Newman, Polly Sheppard, John Thomas III, and Dale Rosengarten.

I have been grounded and sustained throughout this process by the love and support of my extended family and a life's collection of wonderful friends, some old, some new, who occasionally succeeded in distracting me from the work. I send love and appreciation to my brother and sister-in-law, Andrew and Merijoy Sack, nephew Devon Martin Sack, aunt and uncle Sharon and Stanley Kantor, uncle Michael Sack, future son-in-law Davey Tevis, and cousins Peri Kantor, Joe Fuhrman, Zoe Markowitz, Celia Sack, Paula Harris, April Sack, Mark Nevin, Samuel Nevin, and Rhonda, Ricky, Lyle, Ali, and Ainsley Passink. My longtime wingman, photographer Alan S. Weiner, was good enough to take my author headshot despite the obvious challenges. College buddies Frank and Amy Allen offered lodging and good fellowship on a research trip to Philadelphia. Another college friend, Denise McCain-Tharnstrom, and her husband, Charles Tharnstrom, extended deeply appreciated invitations to the Los Angeles Library Council's bountiful Literary Feasts. John White and Vincent Fraley of the College of Charleston Libraries accommodated an important weeklong visit to Charleston in 2018.

My incredible wife, Dina, has been an enthusiastic partner through every step of this process, including a temporary relocation to Charleston in 2019, and has supported me and this mission in countless ways with her love and wisdom, not to mention her research prowess. My gratitude for her friendship and sacrifice is endless.

Dina and I fell hard enough for Charleston and its people that we moved there in 2022. Few writers are fortunate enough to take a sunset walk each evening through the very history they have been contemplating on their laptops all day. Depending on whether I turn left or right, I might pass the site of the "Sugar House" on Magazine Street, or of Denmark Vesey's house on Bull Street, or the house on Tradd Street where Daniel Alexander Payne taught school, or the Kress soda fountain on King Street (now an H&M clothing store) where civil rights demonstrators sat in. The city's churches, including Mother Emanuel, are architectural marvels, and to meander the narrow streets on a bright autumn Sunday as their bells peal is, quite simply, to be transported.

My late father, Martin Sack, Jr., died three years before the shootings at Emanuel, but his legacy lives in these pages if the reader finds the writing even a little "breezy" (his highest compliment). Finally, this book is dedicated to three extraordinary women across three generations: my indomitable and nurturing mother, Carol, my devoted and beloved wife, Dina, and my sweet and precious daughter, Laura. Along with my delightful, insightful, and much-adored stepchildren, Alan and Sara Srochi, who keep us all smiling, they have been my greatest cheerleaders through a process that has lasted longer than anticipated. They are the ones I hope this book might make proud. May they forgive my manifold trespasses during its making.

Pastors of Emanuel African Methodist Church

Morris Brown*—1817–1822

Richard H. Cain—1865–1868

William H. Brown—1868–1871

Augustus Thomas Carr—1871–1875

Moses B. Salter—1875–1879

Norman Bascom Sterrett—1879–1882

Lewis Ruffin Nichols—1883–1886

Bruce H. Williams—1887–1890

Lewis Ruffin Nichols—1890–1894

William Wesley Beckett—1895

Norman Bascom Sterrett—1896–1900

A. E. Peets—1900–1901

J. H. Welch—1901–1905

H.W.B. Bennett—1906–1910

Norman Bascom Sterrett—1911–1915

A. E. Peets—1915–1917

Thomas B. Nelson—1917–1923

Priestly Jarvis Chavis—1924–1926

I. W. Wilborn—1927–1929

Jesse E. Beard—1929–1931

E. H. McGill—1931–1935

J. E. Thomas—1936

R. E. Brogdon—1937–1948

Frank R. Veal—1948–1953

Samuel R. Higgins—1953

Benjamin J. Glover—1953–1965

Henry B. Butler, Jr.—1965–1973

Willie J. Jefferson, Jr.—1973–1978

Alonzo W. Holman—1978–1988

John H. Gillison—1988–1996

William Smith, Jr.—1996–2004

Lavern Witherspoon—2004–2006

Stephen Singleton—2006–2010

John H. Gillison—2010 (interim)

Clementa C. Pinckney—2010–2015

Norvel Goff, Sr.—2015–2016 (interim)

Betty Deas Clark—2016

Eric S. C. Manning—2016–

---

* Pastor of Emanuel's predecessor congregation, the African Church, dated from its breakaway from white churches.

A Note on Sources

As this history stretches from the eighteenth century into the twenty-first, its sourcing naturally includes archival documents like letters, memoirs, articles, court transcripts, and property records, as well as extensive interviewing. Between 2015 and 2024, the author interviewed nearly two hundred people, most in person, some multiple times. They included current and former members and leaders of Mother Emanuel, bishops and others in the hierarchy of the African Methodist Episcopal Church, survivors and family members and friends of the victims of the 2015 massacre, historians, theologians, elected officials, and community activists. A list is appended.

The chapters regarding the 2015 massacre and its aftermath, including the trial of Dylann Roof, rely heavily on the author's contemporaneous reporting for *The New York Times*. By order of U.S. District Judge Richard M. Gergel, most exhibits from that trial remain accessible online. The author also reviewed documents and videos unsealed after the trial pertaining to Roof's mental competency, listened to recordings of forty-five jailhouse phone calls placed by Roof to family members from 2015 to 2017 (obtained through an open records request), and exchanged letters with Roof on death row in 2020.

News accounts served as a primary resource, and the endnotes that follow regularly cite the African Methodist Episcopal Church publication, *The Christian Recorder* (*CR*), founded in 1852, as well as leading South Carolina newspapers from various eras: *The Anderson Intelligencer* (*AI*); *The Beaufort Gazette* (*BG*); *Bluffton Today* (*BT*); *Charleston City Paper* (*CCP*); *The Charleston Courier/The Charleston Daily Courier* (*CC*); *Charleston Daily News* (*CDN*); *The Charleston Mercury* (*CM*); *City Gazette and Commercial Daily Advertiser* (*CGCDA*); *City-Gazette and Daily Advertiser* (*CGDA*); *The Evening Post* (*EP*); *The Greenville News* (*GN*); *The* (Greenwood) *Index-Journal* (*IJ*); *The News and Courier* (*NC*); *The Post and Courier* (*PC*); *The South-Carolina Gazette* (*SCG*); *South Carolina Leader* (*SCL*); *Southern Patriot, And Commercial Advertiser* (*SPCA*); *The* (Columbia) *State* (*TS*); *The Sunday News* (*SN*); and *The* (Orangeburg) *Times and Democrat* (*TD*). Also cited frequently are *The New York*

Times (NYT); *The Washington Post* (WP); *The Chicago Defender* or *Chicago Daily Defender* (CD); and the *Congressional Record* (*Cong. Rec.*).

This work benefitted from periodic histories of South Carolina, Charleston, and the AME denomination, as well as the rich literature left by early Methodist and African Methodist leaders like John Wesley, Francis Asbury, Richard Allen, and Daniel Alexander Payne. The ability of historians to draw a fuller picture of antebellum African American life, including its religious aspects, is limited, of course, by restrictions placed on Black literacy. Much of the record of those years necessarily comes from white hands. For instance, our understanding of the 1822 insurrection plot and its aftermath relies heavily on the remarkable, yet deeply flawed, reports of white officials about the trials of Denmark Vesey and others. By contrast, taped interviews with Rev. Benjamin J. Glover and Rev. Clementa C. Pinckney illuminate their times through their own eyes and words.

The author attended worship services and other functions at Emanuel on a regular basis from 2015 to 2024, as well as the AME Church's quadrennial General Conference in Orlando in 2021 and its South Carolina Annual Conference in 2019. Minutes and journals from prior regional and national AME conferences proved invaluable in documenting the denomination's path over the centuries. Mother Emanuel's own archive includes documents dating back only to the 1940s, leaving much of the church's story scattered and incomplete. Gaps were filled through archival research at repositories in South Carolina and elsewhere. They are cited in the endnotes according to the list of abbreviations that follows.

GUIDE TO ABBREVIATIONS

AMEC—African Methodist Episcopal Church

AMISTAD—Amistad Research Center, Tulane University, New Orleans, LA

ARC—Avery Research Center for African American History and Culture, Charleston, SC

CCCC—Charleston County Clerk of Court, Charleston, SC

CCDB—Charleston County Deed Book

CCPL—Charleston County Public Library, Charleston, SC

CCROD—Charleston County Register of Deeds, Charleston, SC

A NOTE ON SOURCES

CLS—Charleston Library Society, Charleston, SC

CTM—Charleston Time Machine, Charleston County Public Library

DUL—Duke University Libraries, Durham, NC

DVA—Douglas R. Egerton and Robert L. Paquette, eds., *The Denmark Vesey Affair: A Documentary History* (Gainesville: University Press of Florida, 2017)

EAMECA—Emanuel African Methodist Episcopal Church Archives, Charleston, SC

FB—U.S. Freedman's Bank Records

GVX—Government video exhibit

GX—Government exhibit

HCF—Historic Charleston Foundation, Charleston, SC

HSP—Historical Society of Pennsylvania, Philadelphia, PA

JNH—*The Journal of Negro History*

JSH—*The Journal of Southern History*

LAJL—Larry A. Jackson Library, Lander University, Greenwood, SC

LCDL—Lowcountry Digital Library, Charleston, SC

LCP—The Library Company of Philadelphia, Philadelphia, PA

LEGL—Richard Allen, *The Life, Experiences, and Gospel Labours of the Rt. Rev. Richard Allen* (Philadelphia: Martin & Boden, 1833)

LOC—Library of Congress, Washington, D.C.

MIRC—Moving Image Research Collections, University of South Carolina Libraries, Columbia

MSRC—Moorland-Spingarn Research Center, Howard University, Washington, D.C.

NARA—National Archives and Records Administration, Washington, D.C.

NP—James Hamilton, *Negro Plot: An Account of the Late Intended Insurrection Among a Portion of the Blacks of the City of Charleston, South Carolina* (Boston: Joseph W. Ingraham, 1822)

OR—Lionel H. Kennedy and Thomas Parker, *An Official Report of the Trials of Sundry Negroes, Charged with an Attempt to Raise an Insurrection in the State of South-Carolina* (Charleston: James R. Schenk, 1822)

ROSE—Stuart A. Rose Manuscript, Archives, and Rare Book Library, Emory University, Atlanta, GA

SCDAH—South Carolina Department of Archives and History, Columbia

SCHM—*The South Carolina Historical Magazine*

SCHS—South Carolina Historical Society, Charleston, SC

SCRBC—Schomburg Center for Research in Black Culture, New York Public Library, New York

SHC—Southern Historical Collection, Louis Round Wilson Special Collections Library, University of North Carolina, Chapel Hill

UMAL—Special Collections and University Archives, University of Massachusetts Amherst Libraries, Amherst

USCSCL—University of South Carolina South Caroliniana Library, Columbia

WMQ—*The William and Mary Quarterly*

Interviews

John Hurst Adams	James E. Clyburn	Patrick Garner
Stephanie Alexander	Sharon Coakley	Madrian Glover Garrick
Elizabeth Alston	Nadine Collier	Lois Gethers
Leon Alston	Esther Collins	James L. Gilliard
Delores Anderson	Philip Crawford	Gloria Gillison
Anthony Bash	Joseph Darby	Jean Gillison
Cathy Bennett	Cress Darwin	Willi Glee
Craig M. Bennett, Jr.	Delores Davis	Gail A. Glover
Lee Bennett, Jr.	Marlena Davis	Gean Glover
Marian C. Bennett	Alfred T. Day III	Oveta Glover
Sue Bennett	Regina Deadwyler	Shawn Glover
Elizabeth Rauh Bethel	Carlotta Dennis	Norvel Goff, Sr.
Walter Boags	Armand Derfner	Carey A. Grady
Lonnie Boston	Dennis C. Dickerson	Malcolm Graham
Wilhelmenia Boston	Thomas Dixon	Melvin L. Graham, Jr.
Timothy J. Bowman	Bobby Donaldson	Alana Simmons Grant
Paula Brady	Monique Douglas	Jonathan Green
Ronnie E. Brailsford, Sr.	Joshua DuBois	Samuel L. Green, Sr.
Felicia Breeland	Josh Earnest	Marguerite Dudley Gregorie
Floyd Breeland	James Edwards	
Thomas Broadwater	Laura J. Evans	William Dudley Gregorie
John Paul Brown	Charles Traynor (Bud) Ferillo, Jr.	Larry Grooms
Millicent E. Brown		Jon Hale
Timothy Brown	Bernard R. Fielding, Sr.	Christine W. Hampton
Ruth Buck	Damon L. Fordham	James Hampton
Carieta Cain-Grizzell	Sonya Fordham	Joseph Hamski
Corletta Nichole Campbell	Robert M. Franklin, Jr.	Denise Harper
	Roslyn Fulton-Warren	Edward B. Hart
Leila Carson	Blondelle Gadsden	Bill Herbkersman
Betty Deas Clark	Jamila Gadsden	Kay Taylor Hightower
Jerome Clemons	Harvey B. Gantt	Gerald Holman

Neil Hunt
Alverta Hunter
Darrell Jackson
Ellen Jackson
Sheri Jackson
Susan Jackson
Vanessa Jackson
Frederick Calhoun James
Valerie Jarrett
Dorothy Jenkins
Joanne Jenkins
Margaret Jerrido
Amber Johnson
Michael P. Johnson
Sylvia Stevenson Johnson
Wilbur E. Johnson
Carla Jones
Cynthia Jones
Cody Keenan
Akil Khalif (Bruce Glover)
Marlon Kimpson
Minerva Brown King
Gregory M. Kinsey
Debra Lamb
Jennifer S. Leath
Edward S. Lee
Joel Lourie
Eric S.C. Manning
Daniel E. Martin, Jr.
Daniel E. Martin, Sr.
Jacob Joseph Martin
Ruby Nesbitt Martin
Johnette Pinckney Martinez
Patrick Marzett
Glenn F. McConnell
Arthur C. McFarland
Vashti Murphy McKenzie
Tony Metze
Kylon J. Middleton
Bethane Middleton-Brown
Alfonzia Miller
Bruce Miller
Robert Mitchell
Effie Moon
Michael Boulware Moore
Brenda Nelson
Richard S. Newman
Phil Noble
Richard Franklin Norris, Sr.
Gregory O'Malley
Jean Ortiz
John Parker
Ravi Perry
George Pettigrew
John Pinckney
Helen Pittman
Bernard E. Powers, Jr.
Bobby Rankin
Arthur Ravenel, Jr.
Althea Richardson-Latham
Joseph P. Riley, Jr.
Nelson B. Rivers III
Lorenzo Roberts
Marilynne Robinson
Todd Rutherford
Doris Coaxum Sanders
Robert Sanders
Felicia Sanders
Tyrone Sanders
Andrew J. Savage III
Dot Scott
Antjuan Seawright
Oren Segal
Cleveland Sellers, Jr.
Mike Shealy
Vincent A. Sheheen
Polly Sheppard
Chris Singleton
Rosetta Singleton
Stephen Singleton
Wayne Singleton
Steve Skardon
Kelly Small
Maxine Smith
Bruce Levern Stevenson
Donald Stevenson
Emma Stevenson
Hilda Stevenson-Stewart
Marvin Stewart
Elnora Cohen Taylor
John Thomas III
Thomas S. Tisdale
Mark Kelly Tyler
Thomasina Tyler
Harold Washington
McKinley Washington, Jr.
Rosalee W. Washington
Theodora Watson
Lovett H. Weems, Jr.
Charles N. Williams
Nathan S. Williams
Preston Warren Williams II
Walter Williams
Lavern Witherspoon
Jean K. Wolf
Andre Woods
Vivian Wright

Notes

CHAPTER 1: THE OPEN DOOR

1 **In the African American church:** Examples include the fire-bombings of Sixteenth Street Baptist Church in Birmingham, Alabama, on September 15, 1963, and Friendship Missionary Baptist Church in Maury County, Tennessee, on January 29, 1995.

2 **Once again, history had been made:** Data for the slave trade come from *Slave Voyages: The Trans-Atlantic Slave Trade Database*, produced by a consortium of university researchers, as well as Gregory E. O'Malley, "Beyond the Middle Passage: Slave Migration from the Caribbean to North America, 1619–1807," WMQ 66, no. 1 (January 2009): 125–172. In 2024, the Slave Voyages database reported that of the 352,649 enslaved persons known to have disembarked in mainland North America, 163,072 did so in Charleston, or 46 percent. That included those shipped directly from Africa and a smaller number sent from the Caribbean and elsewhere in the Americas. The mortality rate during the crossing from Africa to Charleston was roughly 13 percent. These figures, while the best count available, are assumed to be incomplete, both because of missing records and the difficulty of quantifying smuggling after the U.S. ban on slave importation took effect in 1808.

3 **The shooter's target:** The White House, "Remarks by the President in Eulogy for the Honorable Reverend Clementa Pinckney," Charleston, SC, June 26, 2015.

4 **As soon as the Civil War receded:** Bureau of the Census, Department of Commerce, *Religious Bodies, 1916*, Part 1 (Washington, D.C.: Government Printing Office, 1919), 554, 575; General Board 2017 Reports, AMEC; Clifford Grammich, et al., *2020 U.S. Religion Census: Religious Congregations & Adherents Study* (Association of Statisticians of American Religious Bodies, 2023).

Church membership statistics are notoriously imprecise. Although the AME Church claims 2.5 million members worldwide, the 2020 U.S. Religion Census counted only about 1.1 million adherents in the U.S., where the bulk of AME members live.

5 **"the greatest voluntary organization":** W.E.B. Du Bois, *The Negro Church* (Atlanta: The Atlanta University Press, 1903), 123.

5 **"A sacred place":** White House, "Remarks by the President in Eulogy."

6 **The lack of an elevator:** Interviews with Bernard R. Fielding, Sr., Willi Glee, and Maxine Smith.

7 **The images captured by Emanuel's surveillance cameras:** *United States of America v. Dylann Storm Roof* (2:15-CR-472), Trial transcript, December 8, 2016, 232; January 4, 2017, 215; GVX 23H, 23K, 23O.

7 **Five minutes after that:** *U.S.A. v. Roof* (GVX 23I, 23J, 23P, 23U; January 5, 2017, 358–395).

8 **About sixty people attended:** Interviews with Carlotta Dennis and Charles T. (Bud) Ferillo, Jr.; *U.S.A. v. Roof* (GX 63).

8 **In it lay the remains:** "Service Will Honor Founders of Emanuel, Bethel Churches," *EP*, September 20, 1952, 2; Interview with Lee Bennett, Jr.

8 **Per AME practice:** *The Doctrine and Discipline of the African Methodist Episcopal Church, 2021* (Nashville: The A.M.E. Sunday School Union, 2022), 306; Interview with Carlotta Dennis.

9 **The church and its precursor:** "Booker Washington Here. He and His Party Spent Yesterday in Charleston," *NC*, March 20, 1909, 5; Advertisement for W.E.B. Du Bois appearance at Emanuel AME Church, *EP*, February 10, 1921, 6; Michael Soper, "Negro Leader Urges Voter Registration," *NC*, April 13, 1962, 12; Dennis C. Dickerson, *The African Methodist Episcopal Church: A History* (Cambridge, UK: Cambridge University Press, 2020), 560–564.

The five pastors who became bishops were Morris Brown, leader (of the African Church) from 1817 to 1822, elected bishop in 1828; Richard H. Cain, pastor from 1865 to 1868, elected bishop in 1880; Moses B. Salter, pastor from 1875 to 1879, elected bishop in 1892; William W. Beckett, pastor in 1895, elected bishop in 1916; and Samuel R. Higgins, pastor in 1953, elected bishop in 1956. Twenty-five of 148 AME bishops elected as of 2024 were born in South Carolina.

10 **"If Monday night was good enough":** Interview with Joseph Darby.
10 **Across two centuries, the average tenure:** Interviews with William Dudley Gregorie, Stephen Singleton, and Lavern Witherspoon.
11 **On this night, when Elder Goff opened:** Interview with Theodora Watson.
11 **He had long been a prodigy:** Kevin Sack, "Clementa Pinckney Called to Pulpit and Politics in a Life Cut Short," *NYT*, June, 26, 2015, A-1; Interview with John Pinckney.
12 **When in recess, he had to tend:** Interview with Helen Pittman.
12 **He rose well before dawn:** Interviews with Polly Sheppard, Althea Richardson-Latham, and Rosetta Singleton; South Carolina Senate Finance Committee Video Archives, June 17, 2015.
12 **After lunch with fellow senate Democrats:** Interviews with Antjuan Seawright, Mike Shealy, and Vincent Sheheen; *U.S.A. v. Roof* (January 4, 2017, 109–111).
12 **From the road, Pastor Pinckney called:** Interview with Althea Richardson-Latham.
13 **Pinckney followed in a storied AME tradition:** Interview with Clementa C. Pinckney by Mark K. Tyler, August 18, 2013, Council of Bishops of the AMEC (the author is indebted to Tyler, an AME minister as well as a filmmaker, and his co-producer, Philip Katz, for transcripts of this and other interviews conducted for several documentary projects); Interview with Lovett H. Weems, Jr.
13 **Carlotta Dennis could see:** Interviews with Carlotta Dennis, Theodora Watson, and Polly Sheppard.
13 **The meeting broke:** *U.S.A. v. Roof* (GVX 23A, 23V).
14 **As Hurd unfolded the display:** Photograph of the display provided by Herb Frazier, former marketing and public relations manager, Magnolia Plantation & Gardens.
14 **There was a picture of the golden-piped organ:** Interviews with Wayne Singleton, Willi Glee, and Eric S. C. Manning.
14 **On an evening radiating with heat:** Interviews with Brenda Nelson, Willi Glee, Ruby Nesbitt Martin, Ruth Buck, Carlotta Dennis, and Jean Ortiz; *U.S.A. v. Roof* (GVX 23V).
15 **Although few institutions were more patriarchal:** Women were not allowed full ordination by the AME church until 1960, and the denomination elected its first female bishop in 2000. Dickerson, *African Methodist Episcopal Church*, 515; Interview with Sharon Coakley.
15 **Polly Sheppard made the mistake:** Interview with Polly Sheppard; *U.S.A. v. Roof* (December 14, 2016, 1112).
16 **Cynthia Hurd, who juggled librarian jobs:** *U.S.A. v. Roof* (December 7, 2016, 50–52, 66–67, 78).
16 **Finally, near 8:00 p.m.:** *U.S.A. v. Roof* (December 7, 2016, 79–80; January 4, 2017, 111–114; January 10, 2017, 806); Interview with Polly Sheppard.
17 **Myra Thompson was sufficiently devoted:** Anthony B. Thompson, with Denise George, *Called to Forgive: The Charleston Church Shooting, A Victim's Husband and the Path to Healing and Peace* (Bloomington, MN: Bethany House, 2019), 10–13; Interviews with Sharon Coakley and Blondelle Gadsden.

CHAPTER II: THE TRAGEDY

18 **As Myra Thompson and her Bible students:** *U.S.A v. Roof* (GX 120; GVX 23C).
18 **It was 8:16 p.m.:** *U.S.A v. Roof* (GX 239; GVX 23C); Incident/Investigation Report, Dylann Storm Roof, June 18, 2015, Shelby (NC) Police Department.
18 **"Pastor, we have a visitor":** The description of the shootings that begins here is generally sourced from testimony in *U.S.A. v. Roof*, including that of investigators, pathologists, and the adult survivors—Felicia Sanders (December 7, 2016, 49–90); Polly Sheppard (December 14,

2016, 1104–1131); and Jennifer Pinckney (January 4, 2017, 51–132)—as well as interviews with Sanders, Sheppard, and Pinckney.

19 **"There are people . . .":** *U.S.A. v. Roof* (GVX 99); Anthony B. Thompson, *Called to Forgive: The Charleston Church Shooting, A Victim's Husband and the Path to Healing and Peace* (Bloomington, MN: Bethany House, 2019), 13.

19 **He was about to begin:** *U.S.A. v. Roof* (December 13, 2016, 991; December 14, 2016, 1093–1094; GX 108, 298; GVX 5; Competency Evaluation of Dylann Roof, Mark Wagner, November 14, 2016, 5).

20 **Then he methodically assassinated:** *U.S.A. v. Roof* (December 14, 2016, 1102–1103; GX 87).

20 **"See what you made me do":** Interview with Polly Sheppard.

20 **Roof seemed unnerved:** *U.S.A. v. Roof* (GVX 5).

20 **Sanders clutched the child:** Brian Tetsuro Ivie, *Emanuel* (film), Arbella Studios, 2019.

21 **"I have to do this":** *U.S.A. v. Roof* (December 7, 2016, 49–90; December 14, 2016, 1104–1131); Interviews with Felicia Sanders and Polly Sheppard; Jennifer Berry Hawes, "'Forgotten' Survivors Search for Meaning: 2 Women Face Tough Road After Emanuel Tragedy Shatters Their Lives," *PC*, September 7, 2015.

Sheppard and Sanders have differed slightly in their recall of Dylann Roof's words. Sheppard, in an interview, reconstructed the comment as: "I have to do this because you are raping our women and taking over the world." This mirrors Sanders's trial testimony on December 7, 2016: "I have to do this because you raping our womens and y'all taking over the world." Sheppard used somewhat different wording when she testified on December 14 that Roof said: "I have to. I just have to. You're raping our women and taking over the nation." Sheppard told police in her first interview on the night of the massacre that Roof said "Black men were raping white women and killing the white race so he had to do this." (A recording was obtained through an open records request.) In her first media interview, with *The Post and Courier* three months after the shootings, Sanders quoted Roof as saying: "Y'all raping all our white women and taking over the nation."

Roof provided a similar but not identical account in a recorded post-arrest interview with the FBI the day after the shootings: "I had to do it because somebody had to do something. Because, you know, Black people are killing white people every day on the streets, and they rape, they rape white women, a hundred white women a day."

21 **A few years earlier:** Lizette Alvarez and Nikita Stewart, "A Day of Determined Hope as Charleston Mourns 3 More," *NYT*, June 28, 2015, A-16.

21 **"Please answer, oh God":** *U.S.A. v. Roof* (GX 8).

22 **"My life has ended":** Polly Sheppard statement to police, June 17, 2015.

22 **In the pastor's study:** Interview with Jennifer, Eliana, and Malana Pinckney, "The Charleston Church Shootings: Six Years Later," June 20, 2021, *CBSN*.

23 **There had already been an abundance:** *U.S.A. v. Roof* (December 13, 2016, 1044; GVX 5, 23D); Dylann Roof to the author, April 30, 2020.

23 **The killer's luck continued:** *U.S.A. v. Roof* (GVX 23D). Wyoming was the other state without a hate-crimes law as of 2024. Arkansas, Georgia, and Indiana did not have laws at the time of the Emanuel massacre. Georgia enacted one in 2020 after the killing of Ahmaud Arbery, a Black man assailed by whites while jogging near Brunswick. Indiana passed a law in 2019 and Arkansas followed in 2021, although both measures were criticized by civil-rights advocates as too vague to be meaningful.

24 **In the months before:** *U.S.A. v. Roof* (GX 186a, 204a, 204b, 204c; GVX 5); *United States of America v. Joseph Carlton Meek* (2:15-CR-633, Memorandum to File from Deborah Barbier, September 23, 2016).

24 **But there is little evidence:** *U.S.A. v. Roof* (GVX 5).

In an exchange of letters with the author in 2020, Dylann Roof declined to answer questions about his foreknowledge of Emanuel.

24 **The massacre inspired a Black president:** Kevin Sack and Gardiner Harris, "Obama Scorns Racism in Soaring, Singing Eulogy," *NYT*, June 27, 2015, A-1.

25 **Roof's trial in 2016 and 2017:** Emma Dumain, "Emotional Appeals Electrify Convention,"

PC, July 26, 2016; Dan Morse, "Biden, Suffering in His Own Grief, Visits Church Where Nine People Were Killed," *WP*, June 28, 2015; John Lewis, "Together, You Can Redeem the Soul of Our Nation," *NYT*, July 30, 2020, A-23; Kevin Sack, "Politics Often Preached from a Historic Pulpit," *NYT*, January 9, 2024, A-12.

25 **The killer's self-identification:** Richard Fausset and Alan Blinder, "Era Ends as South Carolina Lowers Confederate Flag," *NYT*, July 11, 2015, A-9.

25 **On the night after the shootings:** Rajini Vaidyanathan, "Charleston Victim's Children: 'We Forgive Him,'" *BBC News*, June 19, 2015; Interview with Chris Singleton.

27 **First came Nadine Collier:** Interview with Nadine Collier.

27 **Next up was Anthony Thompson:** Thompson, *Called to Forgive*, 45–49; Brian Tetsuro Ivie, dir., *Emanuel* (film), 2019.

28 **Some of the emotion on the streets:** Melissa Boughton, "Thousands Gather for Bridge to Peace Event: 'We Will Rise Above the Hate,'" *PC*, June 20, 2015.

28 **Pinckney's service was held:** Sack and Harris, "Obama Scorns Racism"; Meg Kinnard, Jeffrey Collins, and Jonathan Drew, "Obama Gives Unvarnished Lecture on Race at Eulogy," *PC*, June 27, 2015.

29 **"a reactionary sense of fear":** Michelle Obama, *Becoming* (New York: Crown, 2018), 397.

29 **The words were all his:** Cody Keenan, *Grace: President Obama and Ten Days in the Battle for America* (New York: Mariner Books, 2022), 201–202; Barack Obama with Bruce Springsteen, "American Music," *Renegades/Born in the USA Podcast*, 2021; Interviews with Cody Keenan, Valerie Jarrett, Joshua DuBois, and Josh Earnest.

29 **Obama had been raised:** Barack Obama, *Dreams from My Father: A Story of Race and Inheritance* (New York: Three Rivers Press, 1995), 272–287; Barack Obama, *The Audacity of Hope: Thoughts on Reclaiming the American Dream* (New York: Vintage, 2006), 240–246; Janny Scott, *A Singular Woman: The Untold Story of Barack Obama's Mother* (New York: Riverhead Books, 2011), 60–61, 271–272; The White House, "Remarks by the President in Eulogy."

31 **He quoted:** Interviews with Marilynne Robinson and Vashti Murphy McKenzie.

CHAPTER III: CHARLESTON'S AFRICAN DIASPORA, FREE AND ENSLAVED

32 **It was no coincidence:** The other state with a Black majority was Louisiana, where African Americans constituted 51.8 percent of the population in 1820, the first census year after it gained statehood in 1812. The comparable figure for South Carolina in 1820 was 52.8 percent.

32 **It was in 1526:** Peter H. Wood, *Black Majority: Negroes in Colonial South Carolina from 1670 Through the Stono Rebellion* (New York: W. W. Norton & Company, 1974), 3–4; Herbert Aptheker, *American Negro Slave Revolts* (New York: International Publishers, 1963), 163.

33 **Not until 1670:** Wood, *Black Majority*, 20–22; Joseph I. Waring, *The First Voyage and Settlement at Charles Town, 1670–1680* (Columbia: University of South Carolina Press, 1970), 22–40; Walter J. Fraser, Jr., *Charleston! Charleston!: The History of a Southern City* (Columbia: University of South Carolina Press, 1989), 1–9; Nic Butler, "Commemorating the African-ness of Charleston's History," *CTM*, February 1, 2019; Nic Butler, "The Evolution of Charleston's Name," *CTM*, August 9, 2019.

Variants that appear in early records include Charles Towne, Charlestowne, and Charlestown. The city would be redesignated Charleston in 1783 as the Revolutionary War against the British was ending.

33 **The settlers began:** Wood, *Black Majority*, 21.

33 **With the introduction of rice cultivation:** Wood, *Black Majority*, 151–152; Slave Voyages database; Gregory E. O'Malley, "Beyond the Middle Passage: Slave Migration from the Caribbean to North America, 1619–1807," *WMQ* 66, no. 1 (January 2009): 166.

34 **South Carolina reported:** Wood, *Black Majority*, 144, 163; Bernard E. Powers, Jr., *Black Charlestonians: A Social History, 1822–1885* (Fayetteville: The University of Arkansas Press, 1994), 267.

34 **Starting with its first slave laws:** L. H. Roper, "The 1701 'Act for the Better Ordering of Slaves': Reconsidering the History of Slavery in Proprietary South Carolina," *WMQ* 64, no. 2 (April 2007): 395–418; M. Eugene Sirmans, "The Legal Status of the Slave in South Carolina,

1670–1740," *JSH* 28, no. 4 (November 1962): 462–473; David J. McCord, *The Statutes at Large of South Carolina* (Columbia: A. S. Johnston, 1840), 7:343–349, 367, 371, 371–384; Thomas Cooper, *The Statutes at Large of South Carolina* (Columbia: A. S. Johnston, 1838), 3:272, 395–399, 456–461; Frank J. Klingberg, ed., *The Carolina Chronicle of Dr. Francis Le Jau, 1706–1717* (Berkeley: University of California Press, 1956), 55.

35 **Over time, new provisions:** McCord, *Statutes*, 368, 382, 394, 396, 408–410, 413, 462; *Digest of the Ordinances of the City Council of Charleston From the Year 1783 to July 1818* (Charleston: Archibald E. Miller, 1818), 180–182, 189–190.

35 **To preclude any scheming:** McCord, *Statutes*, 347, 354, 371; "South-Carolina," *SCG*, August 18, 1739, 1.

35 **Capital punishment was sanctioned:** McCord, *Statutes*, 343, 355, 360, 383, 397–417, 677; Cooper, *Statutes*, 272, 395–399, 456–461, 556–568; *Digest of the Ordinances*, 254–263; Fraser, *Charleston!*, 203.

The derivation of "Sugar House" dates to 1780, when the city's workhouse at the intersection of Magazine and Mazyck (now Logan) Streets burned and was temporarily replaced by a former sugar warehouse on Broad Street. Even once the structure was rebuilt, "the conflation between the 'sugar house' and the 'workhouse'" remained, Joseph Williams wrote in "Charleston Work House and 'Sugar House,'" *Discovering Our Past: College of Charleston Histories*. Fraser wrote that enslaved Charlestonians well understood the threat of being sent for "a little sugar."

36 **The paranoia of white South Carolinians:** Aptheker, *Slave Revolts*, 140–149, 162; Wood, *Black Majority*, 285–307; Lathan A. Windley, *Runaway Slave Advertisements: A Documentary History from the 1730s to 1790*, Vol. 3, *South Carolina* (Westport, CT: Greenwood Publishing Group, 1983).

36 **In the Lowcountry:** Aptheker, *Slave Revolts*, 85–86, 173–176; Walter Edgar, *South Carolina: A History* (Columbia: University of South Carolina Press, 1998), 73–76; Eugene D. Genovese, *Roll, Jordan, Roll: The World the Slaves Made* (New York: Vintage Books, 1972), 587–598; Fraser, *Charleston!*, 144–147; *Commons House Journals*, February 3, 1720–March 10, 1722, 4–5, SCDAH; Wood, *Black Majority*, 314–319.

37 **Yet slaveholding was pervasive:** Richard C. Wade, *Slavery in the Cities: The South 1820–1860* (New York: Oxford University Press, 1964), 20–23.

37 **Enslaved Black tradespeople:** Harlan Greene, Harry S. Hutchins, Jr., and Brian E. Hutchins, *Slave Badges and the Slave-Hire System in Charleston, South Carolina, 1783–1865* (Jefferson, NC: McFarland & Company, 2004).

38 **By the time Charleston incorporated:** Edgar, *South Carolina*, 285–286; Alice Hanson Jones, *Wealth of a Nation to Be: The American Colonies on the Eve of the Revolution* (New York: Columbia University Press, 1980), 171, 377–380; Peter A. Coclanis, *The Shadow of a Dream: Economic Life and Death in the South Carolina Low Country, 1670–1920* (New York: Oxford University Press, 1989), 126–128.

38 **At times, childhood mortality:** Edgar, *South Carolina*, 156.

39 **In the 1680s, the Anglicans built:** Fraser, *Charleston!*, 11, 40.

39 **It is not clear when the first:** McCord, *Statutes*, 352; H. M. Henry, *The Police Control of the Slave in South Carolina*, PhD dissertation, Vanderbilt University, 1914, 176.

40 **Virginia, Maryland, and North Carolina:** Marina Wikramanayake, *A World in Shadow: The Free Black in Antebellum South Carolina* (Columbia: University of South Carolina Press, 1973).

40 **But the largest component:** Wood, *Black Majority*, 100; Ira Berlin, *Slaves Without Masters: The Free Negro in the Antebellum South* (Oxford: Oxford University Press, 1974), 151–152.

40 **South Carolina's colonial assembly:** McCord, *Statutes*, 384–385, 436–443, 459–460, 464–465; John Belton O'Neall, *The Negro Law of South Carolina* (Columbia: John G. Bowman, 1848), 12–16.

41 **Indeed, there were at least three dozen:** Thomas Cooper, *The Statutes at Large of South Carolina* (Columbia: A. S. Johnston, 1839), 5: 150, 209; O'Neall, *Negro Law*, 12–16; Larry Koger, *Black Slaveowners: Free Black Slave Masters in South Carolina, 1790–1860* (Jefferson, NC: McFarland & Company, Inc., 1985), 18–19, 209–210; Judith M. Brimelow and Michael E. Stevens, *State Free Negro Capitation Tax Books, Charleston, South Carolina, ca. 1811–1860* (Columbia: South Carolina Department of Archives and History, 1983), 2–3; Herbert Aptheker, "South Carolina

Poll Tax, 1737–1895," *JNH* 31, no. 2 (April 1946): 132–133; Wikramanayake, *World*, 50–51, 58–65, 151; Nic Butler, "Defining Charleston's Free People of Color," *CTM*, February 7, 2020.

41 **The city had 3,237 free persons of color:** Berlin, *Slaves*, 271.

42 **In 1809, for instance:** "Petition of Sundry People of Color Asking That Free Blacks Paying Taxes on Property Be Exempted from Paying a Capitation Tax," 1809, series S165015, no. 1877, SCDAH; SC Senate Journal, 1809, 15, 71; Nic Butler, "South Carolina's Capitation Tax on Free People of Color, 1756–1864," *CTM*, January 28, 2022.

42 **In 1790, five free Charlestonians:** *Rules and Regulations of the Brown Fellowship Society* (Charleston: J.B. Nixon, 1844), 1–27, ARC; Robert L. Harris, Jr., "Charleston's Free Afro-American Elite: The Brown Fellowship Society and the Humane Brotherhood," *SCHM* 82, no. 4 (October 1981).

CHAPTER IV: CHURCH AND STATE

45 **Among the most concerning aspects:** C. Eric Lincoln and Lawrence H. Mamiya, *The Black Church in the African American Experience* (Durham, NC: Duke University Press, 1990), 203; Janet Duitsman Cornelius, *When I Can Read My Title Clear: Literacy, Slavery, and Religion in the Antebellum South* (Columbia: University of South Carolina Press, 1991), 3–4, 39; Nicholas May, "Holy Rebellion: Religious Assembly Laws in Antebellum South Carolina and Virginia," *The American Journal of Legal History* 49, no. 3 (July 2007): 237; David J. McCord, *The Statutes at Large of South Carolina* (Columbia: A. S. Johnston, 1840), 7:440–441; Lacy K. Ford, *Deliver Us from Evil: The Slavery Question in the Old South* (New York: Oxford University Press, 2009), 92–93.

46 **In the first of two charters:** "The First Charter Granted by King Charles the Second, to the Lords Proprietors of Carolina," in *The Colonial Records of North Carolina*, ed. William L. Saunders (Raleigh: P. M. Hale, 1886), 1:20–34.

46 **The proprietors themselves:** *The Fundamental Constitutions of Carolina*, 1669, 63–64, CLS, LCDL; James Lowell Underwood, "The Dawn of Religious Freedom in South Carolina: The Journey from Limited Tolerance to Constitutional Right," in *The Dawn of Religious Freedom in South Carolina*, eds. James Lowell Underwood and W. Lewis Burke (Columbia: University of South Carolina Press, 2006), 1–8; Bernard E. Powers, Jr., "Seeking the Promised Land: Afro-Carolinians and the Quest for Religious Freedom to 1830," in Underwood and Burke, *Dawn of Religious Freedom*, 126; Walter Edgar, *South Carolina: A History* (Columbia: University of South Carolina Press, 1998), 43.

46 **Until Virginia closed:** Albert J. Raboteau, *Slave Religion: The "Invisible Institution" in the Antebellum South* (New York: Oxford University Press, 1978), 98–99; Powers, "Seeking," 126.

46 **Some feared that schooling:** Frank J. Klingberg, ed., *The Carolina Chronicle of Dr. Francis Le Jau, 1706–1717* (Berkeley: University of California Press, 1956), 55, 60–61, 125.

47 **In 1701, they founded:** Raboteau, *Slave Religion*, 114–115; Peter H. Wood, *Black Majority: Negroes in Colonial South Carolina from 1670 Through the Stono Rebellion* (New York: W. W. Norton & Company, 1974), 132–140; Edmund Gibson, *Two Letters of the Lord Bishop of London* (London: Joseph Downing, 1727), 3–13.

48 **By midcentury, Methodism would claim:** Roger Finke and Rodney Stark, "Turning Pews into People: Estimating 19th Century Church Membership," *Journal for the Scientific Study of Religion* 25, no. 2 (June 1986): 190; Joseph C. Hartzell, "Methodism and the Negro in the United States," *JNH* 8, no. 3 (July 1923): 306–309.

48 **John and Charles Wesley:** The depiction of the Wesleys' journey to America is taken primarily from: Nehemiah Curnock, ed. *The Journal of the Rev. John Wesley, A.M.* (New York: Eaton & Mains, 1909), 1:94, 98, 106–109, 112–113, 166, 185, 197–209, 234, 251–255, 263, 282, 347–353, 371, 376–418, 422, 426, 475–476; 2:218; 4:292; 5:445–446; Thomas Jackson, *The Life of the Rev. Charles Wesley, M.A.* (London: John Mason, 1841), 55, 58, 72–73, 133–134; John Wesley, *Thoughts Upon Slavery* (London: R. Hawes, 1774), 16–17, 21–22, 27; John Wesley, *A Short History of the People called Methodists* (London: J. Paramore, 1781), 5–6.

49 **The brothers' first visit:** Charles Wesley's frustrations in America, which he fled after five months, make it all the more striking that he later achieved such immense success. Back in En-

gland, he became one of the most prolific composers of hymns of all time as well as his brother's collaborator in Methodism's development. Among the more than 6,000 works he penned over fifty years were "Hark! The Herald Angels Sing" and "O For a Thousand Tongues to Sing."

Rev. Alexander Garden opened a school in Charleston in the early 1740s so that Black children might be taught to read the Bible. Funded by the Society for the Propagation of the Gospel, he purchased two young enslaved men to be trained as teachers, on the theory that Black students would learn best from their own. The school closed after two decades. Walter J. Fraser, Jr., *Charleston! Charleston!: The History of a Southern City* (Columbia: University of South Carolina Press, 1989), 70; Carter G. Woodson, *The History of the Negro Church* (Washington, D.C.: The Associated Publishers, 1921), 3.

51 **"I ask you":** *Born in Slavery: Slave Narratives from the Federal Writers' Project, 1936–1938* (Washington, D.C.: Library of Congress, 1941), 14:53–54.

The dialect in this passage and others from the Slave Narrative Project are as transcribed by the interviewers. In "A Note on the Language of the Narratives," the Library of Congress explains that the slave narratives derived from oral interviews that were transcribed with an effort to reproduce spoken language. But interviewers were not always well trained in phonetic transcription and their directions were not always clear. Furthermore, as the LOC points out, all the subjects were Black residents and most interviewers were white people and "by the 1930s, when the interviews took place, white representations of black speech already had an ugly history of entrenched stereotype." The LOC has acknowledged that modern readers may justifiably take offense at the racial idiom.

52 **In *Thoughts Upon Slavery*:** Wesley, *Thoughts*, 46–49, 56–57.

53 **One of Whitefield's earliest Black converts:** John Marrant, *A Narrative of the Lord's Wonderful Dealings with John Marrant, A Black* (London: Gilbert and Plummer, 1785), 10–11.

53 **Whitefield, who became a central figure:** J. Gordon Melton, *A Will to Choose: The Origins of African American Methodism* (Lanham, MD: Rowman & Littlefield Publishers, 2007), 18–23; "A Letter from the Rev. Mr. George Whitefield, to the Inhabitants of Maryland, Virginia, North and South-Carolina," *The Pennsylvania Gazette*, April 17, 1740, 1; William A. Sloat II, "George Whitefield, African-Americans, and Slavery," *Methodist History* 33, no. 1 (October 1994): 3–9.

53 **But unlike Wesley:** *Pennsylvania Gazette*, "A Letter."

54 **"Wherever one stands":** James T. Campbell, *Songs of Zion: The African Methodist Episcopal Church in the United States and South Africa* (Chapel Hill: The University of North Carolina Press, 1998), ix; Vincent Harding, "Religion and Resistance Among Antebellum Negroes, 1800–1860," in *The Making of Black America,* ed. August Meier and Elliott Rudwick (New York: Atheneum, 1969), 180–190.

55 **In their 1998 study:** Sylvia R. Frey and Betty Wood, *Come Shouting to Zion: African American Protestantism in the American South and British Caribbean to 1830* (Chapel Hill: The University of North Carolina Press, 1998), 1.

55 **"Perhaps the religious heritage":** Raboteau, *Slave Religion*, 5–16, 48–55, 58–59.

56 **"Out of black religious life":** Eddie S. Glaude, Jr., *Exodus! Religion, Race, and Nation in Early Nineteenth-Century Black America* (Chicago: The University of Chicago Press, 2000), 6; Eugene D. Genovese, *Roll, Jordan, Roll: The World the Slaves Made* (New York: Vintage Books, 1972), 281.

56 **Genovese also argued:** Genovese, *Roll*, 244–247, 280–284, 659–660; *Born in Slavery*, 14.3:194–196; "Court Week," *Fairfield Herald*, November 7, 1866, 2; "Death of Mr. Bolick," *Fairfield Herald*, November 5, 1873, 3.

Cureton Milling neglects to mention Bolick's record after the Civil War, including his 1866 manslaughter conviction for killing a laborer and his shooting death during an argument seven years later.

56 **"He take 'vantage":** *Born in Slavery*, 14.3:194–196.

57 **As lifelong Anglicans:** Dee E. Andrews, *The Methodists and Revolutionary America, 1760–1800: The Shaping of an Evangelical Culture* (Princeton, NJ: Princeton University Press, 2000), 39–40, 62–72.

57 **Late in December 1784:** Andrews, *Methodists*, 69–72; *LEGL*, 10–11.

Allen, in his autobiography, refers to the Christmas Conference but does not assert that he attended. His biographers and other historians are somewhat divided. Jean K. Wolf, a historical preservationist in Philadelphia, generously shared unpublished research that presents persuasive circumstantial evidence that both Allen and Hosier were at the founding conference. An address by the AME bishops at the denomination's 1896 General Conference asserted that both Allen and Hosier were there (*The Quadrennial Address of the Bishops of the A.M.E. Church to the General Conference Convened in Wilmington, N.C., May 4, 1896*, 89), as have AME historians Dennis C. Dickerson in *The African Methodist Episcopal Church* (Cambridge, UK: Cambridge University Press, 2020), 30; George A. Singleton in *The Romance of African Methodism: A Study of the African Methodist Episcopal Church* (New York: Exposition Press, 1952), 6–7; and James A. Handy in *Scraps of African Methodist Episcopal History* (Philadelphia: A.M.E. Book Concern, 1902), 23. Charles H. Wesley, in *Richard Allen: Apostle of Freedom* (Washington, D.C.: The Associated Publishers, 1935), 31–32, and Richard S. Newman, in *Freedom's Prophet: Bishop Richard Allen, the AME Church, and the Black Founding Fathers* (New York: New York University Press, 2008), 50, speculate that Allen and Hosier probably attended. Carol V. R. George, in *Segregated Sabbaths: Richard Allen and the Emergence of Independent Black Churches, 1760–1840* (New York: Oxford University Press, 1973), 43, concludes that Allen "may have attended the meeting himself, although such a possibility seems remote."

57 **In one of the notable acts:** Donald G. Mathews, *Slavery and Methodism: A Chapter in American Morality 1780–1845* (Princeton: Princeton University Press, 1965), 295–298; Melton, *Will*, 28–30; Andrews, *Methodists*, 150.

58 **Numbers nearly doubled:** Mathews, *Slavery and Methodism*, 12–13; *Minutes of the Annual Conferences of the Methodist Episcopal Church for the Years 1773–1828* (New York: T. Mason and G. Lane, 1840), 1:11, 20, 38–39, 42–43, 92–93; *Minutes of the Annual Conferences of the Methodist Episcopal Church, for the Years 1839–1845* (New York: T. Mason and G. Lane, 1840), 3:63.

Northern states began to outlaw slavery in 1780 with Pennsylvania's passage of An Act for the Gradual Abolition of Slavery, which ended the importation of enslaved people and allowed for the eventual manumission of children.

58 **Construction began the next year:** John O. Willson, *Sketch of the Methodist Church in Charleston, S.C., 1785–1887* (Charleston: Lucas, Richardson, & Co., Steam Book Printers, 1888), 4–10; F. A. Mood, *Methodism in Charleston: A Narrative of the Chief Events Relating to the Rise and Progress of the Methodist Episcopal Church in Charleston, S.C.* (Nashville: E. Stevenson and J. E. Evans, 1856), 23–32, 37–39, 80–83.

58 **The Methodists' unconventional practices:** *Minutes of the Annual Conferences 1773–1828*, 1:60; Mood, *Methodism in Charleston*, 64; Albert M. Shipp, *The History of Methodism in South Carolina* (Nashville: Southern Methodist Publishing House, 1884), 471; James Osgood Andrew, "Letters on Methodist History: Rise and Progress of Methodism in Charleston, South Carolina," *Methodist Magazine and Quarterly Review* 12 (1830): 19; *Articles of Agreement Amongst the Preachers*, January 2, 1795, box 1, South Carolina Conference Papers, Archives, Wofford College, Spartanburg, SC.

Ford, in *Deliver*, 167, reports that Black membership in Lowcountry Methodist churches was "more than 53 percent in 1810 and more than 60 percent in 1815."

59 **Despite their modest numbers:** "Presentments of the Grand Jury of Beaufort District, at April Term, 1795," *CGDA*, May 6, 1795, 3; "Presentment Concerning Court Fees, The Assembling Of Negroes, Observing The Sabbath, And The Reputation Of Constables," February 16, 1790, series S165010, SCDAH; Mood, *Methodism in Charleston*, 42–43; Francis Asbury, *The Journal of the Rev. Francis Asbury, Bishop of the Methodist Episcopal Church from August 7, 1771, to December 7, 1815, in Three Volumes* (New York: N. Bangs and T. Mason, 1821), 2:28.

59 **In 1800:** *The Address of the General Conference of the Methodist Episcopal Church, to all their Brethren and Friends in the United States*, May 20, 1800, LOC; *Journals of the General Conference of the Methodist Episcopal Church, Volume 1, 1796–1836* (New York: Carlton & Phillips, 1855), 40–41; Jacob Read to John Drayton, July 18, 1800, Governor's Messages, November 25, 1800, series 165009, no. 768, SCDAH; Ford, *Deliver*, 86–88.

59 **Later that year, word spread:** Ezekiel Cooper and George A. Phoebus, *Beams of Light on Early Methodism in America* (New York: Phillips & Hunt, 1887), 329–333; Andrew, "Letters," 17–22; Willson, *Sketch*, 10; Mood, *Methodism in Charleston*, 87–91, 175–176.

60 **Harper's friends suggested:** Cooper and Phoebus, *Beams*, 332–333; Mood, *Methodism in Charleston*, 102–105.
60 **Eager to dodge further conflict:** Mood, *Methodism in Charleston*, 106–107; Henry J. Nott and David J. McCord, *Nott and McCord's Reports of Cases Determined in the Constitutional Court of South Carolina* (Charleston: McCarter & Dawson, 1860), 168–171; Ford, *Deliver*, 179–180.
60 **Asbury, deeply invested:** Mood, *Methodism in Charleston*, 47, 73, 108; Asbury, *Journal*, 2:95, 185, 214–215; 3:184.
61 **Less than a year:** Mathews, *Slavery and Methodism*, 11–12, 23–26, 300–302; *Minutes of the Annual Conferences 1773–1828*, 1:93, 183; *Minutes of the Annual Conferences 1839–1845*, 3:31; *Minutes of the Annual Conferences of the Methodist Episcopal Church, South, for the Year 1860* (Nashville: Southern Methodist Publishing House, 1861), 254, 293; James Jenkins, *Experience Labours and Suffering of Rev. James Jenkins* (Printed for the author, 1842), 58.
61 **As the years passed:** Ford, *Deliver*, 141–149; Shipp, *Methodism in South Carolina*, 498.

CHAPTER V: RICHARD ALLEN AND THE INSURGENCY OF AFRICAN METHODISM

63 **It was there, in the cradle of freedom:** The elevation of Richard Allen to founding father status is posited by both Gary B. Nash in "New Light on Richard Allen: The Early Years of Freedom," *WMQ* 46, no. 2 (April 1989): 332, and Richard S. Newman in his superb biography, *Freedom's Prophet: Bishop Richard Allen, the AME Church, and the Black Founding Fathers* (New York: New York University Press, 2008), 1. Other seminal works on Allen include, foremost, his own: *The Life, Experience, and Gospel Labours of the Rt. Rev. Richard Allen* (Philadelphia: Martin & Boden, 1833), as well as Dee E. Andrews, *The Methodists and Revolutionary America, 1760–1800: The Shaping of an Evangelical Culture* (Princeton, NJ: Princeton University Press, 2000); Carol V. R. George, *Segregated Sabbaths: Richard Allen and the Emergence of Independent Black Churches, 1760–1840* (New York: Oxford University Press, 1973); Charles H. Wesley, *Richard Allen: Apostle of Freedom* (Washington, D.C.: The Associated Publishers, 1935); and Gary B. Nash, *Forging Freedom: The Formation of Philadelphia's Black Community, 1720–1840* (Cambridge: Harvard University Press, 1988). See also, James T. Campbell, *Songs of Zion: The African Methodist Episcopal Church in the United States and South Africa* (Chapel Hill: The University of North Carolina Press, 1998), 5.
63 **"Already he has become":** Frederick Douglass, "Richard Allen," undated, The Frederick Douglass Papers, Manuscript Division, LOC, 1.
64 **Little is known of Allen's upbringing:** Daniel A. Payne, *History of the African Methodist Episcopal Church* (Nashville: Publishing House of the A.M.E. Sunday-School Union, 1891), 85–86; Newman, *Freedom's Prophet*, 28–30, 33–35; Nash, *Forging Freedom*, 15–16; Nash, "New Light," 333–335.
64 **In his memoir:** *LEGL*, 6–7; Payne, *History*, iv–v.
    Payne, a Charleston-born minister and educator who became an AME bishop and historian, found the manuscript of Allen's autobiography, written in his son's hand, in "a large old trunk" in the possession of Allen's daughter.
64 **At about seventeen:** Nash, *Forging Freedom*, 95–96; Newman, *Freedom's Prophet*, 40; *LEGL*, 5.
    Allen likely borrows here from both the story of St. Peter's rescue by an angel (Acts 12:7: "He struck Peter on the side and woke him up. 'Quick, get up!' he said, and the chains fell off Peter's wrists.") and Charles Wesley's 1738 hymn "And Can It Be" ("Thine eye diffused a quick'ning ray, I woke, the dungeon flamed with light; My chains fell off, my heart was free; I rose, went forth, and followed Thee.").
65 **Convinced that his sins had been pardoned:** *LEGL*, 6–7; Asbury, *Journal*, 248.
65 **Acclaimed as the "Paul Revere":** Nathan Bangs, *The Life of the Rev. Freeborn Garrettson: Compiled from His Printed and Manuscript Journals and Other Authentic Documents* (New York: Carlton & Lanahan, 1832); Robert Drew Simpson, ed. *American Methodist Pioneer: The Life and Journals of the Rev. Freeborn Garrettson, 1752–1827: Social and Religious Life in the U.S. During the Revolutionary and Federal Periods.* (Rutland, VT: Academy Books, 1984), 48,

159; Freeborn Garrettson, *A Dialogue Between Do-Justice and Professing-Christian* (Wilmington: Peter Brynberg, undated), 35–36; Nash, "New Light," 332–340; Ian B. Straker, "Black and White and Gray All Over: Freeborn Garrettson and African Methodism," *Methodist History* 37, no. 1 (October 1998); Newman, *Freedom's Prophet*, 40–43; Andrews, *Methodists*, 140–141; George, *Segregated Sabbaths*, 27–29; *LEGL,* 7–8; "Manumission Book A, 1780–1793," January 25, 1780, 2, Pennsylvania Abolition Society Papers, HSP.

Straker dates Garrettson's visit to November 19, 1779, Newman to "perhaps in September 1779," and Andrews to "sometime in September 1778 or July 1779."

65 **On September 3:** *LEGL,* 8; Newman, *Freedom's Prophet,* 38–39.
66 **The newly liberated Allen:** Newman, *Freedom's Prophet,* 44–46.
66 **As he contemplated the reversal:** *LEGL,* 7.
66 **Relying on his wit:** *LEGL,* 7–12; Nash, "New Light," 339.

Nash reproduces a letter of testimonial to Allen written by three men that asserts that the itinerant Allen also ventured into Virginia, North and South Carolina, and New York, but Allen does not mention such travels in his autobiography.

67 **The abolitionist minister:** Henry Highland Garnet, "The Pioneers of the African Methodist Episcopal Church, No. 1," *CR,* February 20, 1869.
67 **Allen stood of medium build:** Garnet, "Pioneers."
67 **With Allen gaining favor:** *LEGL,* 11; Newman, *Freedom's Prophet,* 47–49.
68 **Although not yet ordained:** *LEGL,* 12.
68 **Allen and Jones agreed:** "Preamble of the Free African Society," in William Douglass, *Annals of the First African Church in the United States of America, Now Styled the African Episcopal Church of St. Thomas, Philadelphia* (Philadelphia: King & Baird, 1862), LCP, 15–24; Newman, *Freedom's Prophet,* 60–61.
69 **The Free African Society:** "Preamble of the Free African Society," 21–24.
69 **Allen continued to preach:** *LEGL,* 12–13.
69 **"Meeting had begun":** *LEGL,* 12–13.
70 **But in a historical note:** Richard Allen and Jacob Tapsico, *The Doctrines and Discipline of the African Methodist Episcopal Church,* First Edition (Philadelphia: John H. Cunningham, 1817), 3; Milton C. Sernett, *Black Religion and American Evangelicalism: White Protestants, Plantation Missions, and the Flowering of Negro Christianity, 1787–1865* (Metuchen, NJ: The Scarecrow Press and the American Theological Library Association, 1975), 117, 218–220; *LEGL,* 13.

Advocates for the earlier date include Dennis C. Dickerson in *The African Methodist Episcopal Church: A History* (Cambridge, UK: Cambridge University Press, 2020), 31–32; Philadelphia historical preservationist Jean K. Wolf (communications with the author); and two Allen biographers who wrote before Sernett's discovery: Wesley, *Richard Allen,* 52–53, and George, *Segregated Sabbaths,* 55. Siding with Sernett on the 1792 date are Andrews, *Methodists,* 146, 318 (fn. 111); Nash, *Forging Freedom,* 118–119; Albert J. Raboteau, "Richard Allen and the African Church Movement," in *Black Leaders of the Nineteenth Century,* eds. Leon Litwack and August Meier (Urbana: University of Illinois Press, 1988), 1; and Jean Williams, "Richard Allen: from the Free African Society to Bethel AME Church," *The Annals of Eastern Pennsylvania,* 2010, 66–67. Newman, in *Freedom's Prophet,* 64–66, does not choose between the dates.

71 **"the evil of racism":** James H. Cone, *Black Theology and Black Power* (Maryknoll, NY: Orbis Books, 1969), 155.
71 **It frowned on the pleasures:** Douglass, *Annals,* 16, 20, 31–32, 40–43; *LEGL,* 14–15.
71 **"We told him we were dragged":** *LEGL,* 14–15.
71 **Allen and Jones helped:** *LEGL,* 14–15; L. H. Butterfield, ed., *Letters of Benjamin Rush,* Vol. 1, *1761–1792* (Princeton: Princeton University Press, 1951), 602; Absalom Jones, et al., "To the Friends of Liberty and Religion in the City of Philadelphia," *Gazette of the United States,* September 7, 1791, 1.
72 **In 1792, with little dissent:** Douglass, *Annals,* 44–48; Campbell, *Songs,* 10–11; *LEGL,* 15–17.
72 **Allen and Jones stood:** *LEGL,* 17; Douglass, *Annals,* 102–105; "Deed of Mark Wilcox to Richard Allen," Philadelphia Deed Book E.F. 2, 563–566 (microfilm), HSP; Newman, *Freedom's Prophet,* 140–142.

73 **On June 29, 1794:** "Sketch of Churches and Ecclesiastical Organization Among the People of Color," *The Colored American*, October 14, 1837; Asbury, *Journal*, 2:195; *LEGL*, 18; Newman, *Freedom's Prophet*, 71–72; Wesley, *Richard Allen*, 78–79; Andrews, *Methodists*, 319, fn. 122.

In his contemporaneous journal, Asbury, a meticulous diarist, dated the dedication of Bethel to June 29, 1794, as did the unknown scribe in *The Colored American*. Allen, however, remembered it as "July, 1794" and several of his biographers, including Wesley and Newman, have pinpointed it as July 29, 1794.

73 **Allen put forth the rationale:** B. T. Tanner, *An Outline of Our History and Government for African Methodist Churchmen, Ministerial and Lay* (Philadelphia: A.M.E. Book Concern, 1884), 145–149; *Articles of Association of the African Methodist Episcopal Church, of the City of Philadelphia, in the Commonwealth of Pennsylvania* (Philadelphia: John Ormrod, 1799), 6–7, 8–10; *The Colored American*, "Sketch of Churches."

74 **Years later, African Methodism:** The AME motto, first formally adopted at the General Conference of 1856, was updated in 2008 to be somewhat less gendered and more inclusive: "God Our Father, Christ Our Redeemer, the Holy Spirit Our Comforter, Humankind Our Family."

74 **He hypothesized, incorrectly:** Butterfield, *Letters of Benjamin Rush*, 654; Benjamin Rush to Richard Allen, 1793, Rush Family Papers, 38:leaf 32, LCP; *Minutes of the Proceedings of the Committee Appointed on the 14th September 1783* (Philadelphia: R. Aitken & Son, 1784), 187; Newman, *Freedom's Prophet*, 85–88.

75 **Among the tasks they carried out:** Absalom Jones and Richard Allen, *A Narrative of the Proceedings of the Black People During the Late Awful Calamity in Philadelphia in the Year 1793: And a Refutation of Some Censures Thrown Upon Them in Some Late Publications* (Philadelphia: William W. Woodward, 1794), 3–20; Mathew Carey, *A Short Account of the Malignant Fever Lately Prevalent in Philadelphia: With a Statement of the Proceedings That Took Place on the Subject in Different Parts of the United States* (Philadelphia: Printed by the Author, 1793), 76–77.

75 **Jones and Allen could not:** James Gilreath, ed., *Federal Copyright Records, 1790–1800* (Washington, D.C.: Library of Congress, 1987), 16; Newman, *Freedom's Prophet*, 101–104; Jones and Allen, *Narrative*, 3–28.

76 **They appended a letter of commendation:** Jones and Allen, *Narrative*, 21–28.

76 **Jones and Allen nonetheless granted:** Jones and Allen, *Narrative*, 24–27; Newman, *Freedom's Prophet*, 191–192.

76 **Richard Allen's Bethel Church:** Dee E. Andrews, "The African Methodists of Philadelphia, 1794–1802," *Pennsylvania Magazine of History and Biography* 108, no. 4 (October 1984): 482–484; Andrews, *Methodists*, 149–150, 251; Richard Allen and Absalom Jones, "Some Letters of Richard Allen and Absalom Jones to Dorothy Ripley," *JNH* 1, no. 4 (October 1916): 441; Newman, *Freedom's Prophet*, 72–76; Nash, *Forging Freedom*, 192–193; *LEGL*, 18; Pavel P. Svin'in, William Benton Whisenhunt, Christopher Ely, and Marina Swoboda, *A Russian Paints America: The Travels of Pavel P. Svin'in, 1811–1813* (Montreal: McGill-Queen's University Press, 2008), 69–73.

77 **Bethel's "warfare and troubles":** Allen and Tapsico, *Doctrines and Discipline*, 4–5; *LEGL*, 18.

77 **Their remedy called for amending:** *LEGL*, 18–19, 22–25.

78 **Allen specified in a letter:** *LEGL*, 19–21; "Letter of Richard Allen to Francis Asbury," April 8, 1807, and "To the Trustees of the African Methodist Episcopal Church," April 9, 1807," in *The Journal and Letters of Francis Asbury*, ed. J. Manning Potts (London: Epworth Press, 1958), 3:366–367; Sarah Barringer Gordon, "The African Supplement: Religion, Race, and Corporate Law in Early National America," *WMQ* 72, no. 3 (July 2015): 385–422; Newman, *Freedom's Prophet*, 163–166.

78 **The power struggle eventually wound up:** Newman, *Freedom's Prophet*, 159–170.

79 **The Pennsylvania court ruling:** Wesley, *Richard Allen*, 128–134; Carter G. Woodson, *The History of the Negro Church* (Washington, DC: The Associated Publishers, 1921), 15–19; Edward D. Smith, *Climbing Jacob's Ladder: The Rise of Black Churches in Eastern American Cities, 1740–1877* (Washington, D.C.: Smithsonian Institution, 1988), 33; Sernett, *Black Religion*, 110–113.

The African Union Church, which descended from Peter Spencer's Union Church of Africans, justifiably stakes a claim to predating the AME church as an independent Black denomination by three years. AME partisans counter that although Richard Allen's independence movement did not fully succeed until 1816 it had started twenty years earlier, and that Spencer's church never grew beyond its limited regional roots.

79 **In April 1816:** Payne, *History*, 13–14; Allen, *LEGL*, 21; Allen and Tapsico, *Doctrines and Discipline*, 8; "Convention of the African Church," *American and Commercial Daily Advertiser*, May 2, 1816, 2.
80 **At 192 pages, the book:** Allen and Tapsico, *Doctrines and Discipline*.
80 **The African Methodists made sure:** Allen and Tapsico, *Doctrines and Discipline*, 190.
81 **But with the largest voting bloc:** Payne, *History*, 14; Daniel Alexander Payne, *Recollections of Seventy Years* (Nashville: Publishing House of the A.M.E. Sunday School Union, 1888), 100–101; Daniel A. Payne, *The Semi-Centenary and the Retrospection of the African Meth. Episcopal Church in the United States of America* (Baltimore: Sherwood & Co., 1866), 22; David Smith, *Biography of Rev. David Smith of the A.M.E. Church, Being a Complete History, Embracing over Sixty Years' Labor in the Advancement of the Redeemer's Kingdom on Earth* (Xenia, OH: Xenia Gazette, 1881), 33–34; Singleton, *Romance*, 22; Wesley, *Richard Allen*, 151–155; "Convention of the African Church," *American and Commercial Daily Advertiser*, May 2, 1816, 2; Allen and Tapsico, *Doctrines and Discipline*, 10; Handy, *Scraps*, 56–57; "Daniel Coker's Letter," *Southern Evangelical Intelligencer*, July 29, 1820, 141.

Payne and the newspaper differ on the dates of the first conference. Payne, publishing in 1891 after decades of research, wrote that the delegates elected Coker on the conference's first day, April 9, that he resigned on April 10, and that Allen was consecrated as bishop on April 11. That date also appears in Bethel AME Church records and the 1817 edition of *The Doctrines and Discipline*. The real-time report in Baltimore's *American and Commercial Daily Advertiser* dated the convention's start to April 11. It said that Allen and Coker were unanimously chosen to be ordained as elders on April 25, and that Allen was ordained as general superintendent, or bishop, on April 26, by the "imposition of hands of two regularly ordained Elders and three regularly ordained Deacons." The meeting adjourned the next day, according to the article. The author thanks Jean K. Wolf for highlighting the article.

81 **He knew, of course:** *LEGL*, 13, 19; Jones and Allen, *Narrative*, 11; Payne, *History*, 86–88; Handy, *Scraps*, 343–344.
82 **The denomination's early struggles:** Jarena Lee, *The Life and Religious Experience of Jarena Lee, A Colored Lady, Giving an Account of Her Call to Preach the Gospel* (Cincinnati: Printed and published for the author, 1839).
82 **Lee kept after Allen:** Lee, *Life and Religious Experience*.
83 **He had published the first:** Richard Allen, *A Collection of Spiritual Songs and Hymns from Various Authors* (Philadelphia: T. L. Plowman, 1801); Gordon, "African Supplement," 403–404; Newman, *Freedom's Prophet*, 183–207, 268–275; Nash, *Forging Freedom*, 233–245.
83 **And yet, that still understates:** "Letter from Bishop Allen," *Freedom's Journal*, November 2, 1827, 2; Payne, *History*, 83–87.
83 **Allen's denomination grew:** Payne, *History*, 26–27.
84 **No one from Charleston:** Payne, *History*, 26–27; Payne, *Semi-Centenary*, 21.

CHAPTER VI: THE AFRICAN CHURCH

85 **Rev. Anthony Senter:** *Minutes of the Annual Conferences of the Methodist Episcopal Church for the Years 1773–1828* (New York: T. Mason and G. Lane, 1840), 1:307.
85 **While it is not known:** A. M. Chreitzberg, *Early Methodism in the Carolinas* (Nashville: Publishing House of the Methodist Episcopal Church, South, 1897), 156.

The 1820 census shows that Senter's widow, Elizabeth, who he married only seven months before his death, enslaved seven people. Her first husband, a mariner named Roger Shackelford, was recorded as owning the same number in the 1810 census. Shackelford died in 1814 and Elizabeth presumably inherited his property before marrying Senter in May 1817.

86 **When Senter got to Charleston:** *Minutes of the Annual Conferences for 1773–1828*, 1:109–

111, 258; William M. Wightman, *Life of William Capers, D.D., One of the Bishops of the Methodist Episcopal Church, South; Including an Autobiography* (Nashville: Southern Methodist Publishing House, 1859), 138; F. A. Mood, *Methodism in Charleston: A Narrative of the Chief Events Relating to the Rise and Progress of the Methodist Episcopal Church in Charleston, S.C.* (Nashville: E. Stevenson and J. E. Evans, 1856), 187–188; Harlan Greene and Jessica Lancia, "The Holloway Scrapbook: The Legacy of a Charleston Family," *SCHM* 111, no. 1–2 (January–April 2010); 11–12.

86 **Over time:** Mood, *Methodism in Charleston*, 130; Wightman, *Life of William Capers*, 139–140.

There are scattered and unverified indicators of an independent Black religious presence in Charleston as early as 1806, when a Charleston County deed shows that two men, Isaac Austin and Joseph Creighton, bought property on Beaufain Street "in trust for use by the African Society." That is the same name later used to purchase property for the first African Methodist church in the city (CCDB, October 30, 1806, U7:438, CCROD). But records show that Austin and Creighton, although free persons of color, were affiliated with St. Philip's (Episcopal) Church, not one of the Methodist congregations. The common use of "African Society" may have been coincidental. Daniel Coker, in *A Dialogue Between a Virginian and an African Minister* (Baltimore: Benjamin Edes, for Joseph James, 1810), included a Methodist congregation in Charleston on a list of fifteen "African churches" of various denominations in America at the time (39–43). He provided no detail and no Charlestonians were included on an accompanying list of African ministers. Coker may have been referring to the overwhelmingly Black membership of the city's white-run Methodist churches.

87 **They were recognized:** Wightman, *Life of William Capers*, 139–140.

87 **"That the meeting of a numerous":** H.T.F., "To the Editors of the Times," *The Times*, July 17, 1816, 3.

87 **His sensitivities already heightened:** Albert Deems Betts, *History of South Carolina Methodism* (Columbia, SC: The Advocate Press, 1952), 237–238; James Osgood Andrew, "Letters on Methodist History: Rise and Progress of Methodism in Charleston, South Carolina," *Methodist Magazine and Quarterly Review* 12 (1830), 23; Mood, *Methodism in Charleston*, 130.

Unfortunately, the only known accounts of the schism come from white Methodist historians. In his 1830 account, Andrew wrote of Charleston's Black Methodists: "Among the leaders were several men of intelligence, and some of them of considerable property. The preachers, confiding in the intelligence and integrity of these men, committed a very large portion of the management of the coloured society to them. They made numerous collections among themselves, all of which, with the exception of the class and sacramental collections, they disbursed among themselves, either for the relief of their sick and poor, or for the purchase of the freedom of such as were to be sold." Mood wrote in 1856 that "upon a close investigation of the conduct and management of their monetary affairs, much corruption was found to exist." Betts wrote in 1952 that "Negro class-leaders were not using all the money they collected from the colored Methodists (slave and free) for relief of the poor and other Church purposes (our pastors had let them handle the funds, trusting to their integrity and wisdom), but were using some of the funds to buy slaves out of serfdom to set them free."

The surviving manumission records at the South Carolina Department of Archives and History include only a partial index of formerly enslaved people, those whose first names begin with the letters A through D.

88 **But whatever precisely:** Mood, *Methodism in Charleston*, 64, 108–109, 130–131; Wightman, *Life of William Capers*, 140.

Mood, Capers, and other Methodist historians assert that the fledgling denomination's exuberant services attracted large numbers of white Charlestonians and won converts but few who committed to membership. "Under all the obloquy cast upon them, the Methodists were, nevertheless, much esteemed," Capers wrote. "But it seemed to be an esteem like that one might have for inferior animals which render service, rather than a recognition of their proper claims as a flock of Christ's own fold. Their preaching might be attended with great propriety, for almost everybody did so, but who might join them? No, it was vastly more respectable to join some other Church, and still attend the preaching of the Methodists, which was thought to answer all purposes." Wrote Mood: "The crowded audiences who so constantly attended the

Methodist meetings were frequently moved under their earnest appeals, but, unwilling to identify themselves with those who were the instruments of their salvation, they joined other churches."

88 **Brown, who had been born free:** Daniel A. Payne, *History of the African Methodist Episcopal Church* (Nashville: Publishing House of the A.M.E. Sunday-School Union, 1891), 261–262; Daniel Alexander Payne, *Recollections of Seventy Years* (Nashville: Publishing House of the A.M.E. Sunday School Union, 1888), 94.

88 **In Brown's first known transaction:** Bill of Sale, August 16, 1810, Misc. Records, series S213003, 4D:5, SCDAH; Will of Isaac Lesesne, Wills, Charleston County Will Book B, 1786–1793, 1173–1174, SCDAH; Manumissions (Index A–D), 1801–1848, SCDAH; David J. McCord, *The Statutes at Large of South Carolina* (Columbia: A. S. Johnston, 1840), 7:442–443.

Deeds in Charleston establish the name of Morris Brown's wife as Elizabeth, but numerous other records, including his will, obtained from the Philadelphia Register of Wills, show that he was married at the time of his death to a woman named Maria.

After his family, Brown's known purchases of enslaved people began with his payment of $350 on March 30, 1813, for "a certain negro man named Lango about forty five years of age" and $550 for "a mulatto slave named Marcus, a carpenter." Eight months later, he put up $200 to secure the release of an enslaved mulatto painter named London, who had already managed to pay $600 to his owner, Foster Burnet. Burnet had paid $800 for London three years earlier and apparently was content to break even on the investment. That it fell to Brown to pay London's final installment suggests that the purpose was manumission. In November 1815, Brown bought "a Negro wench named Amelia and her future issue" for $400 from Sarah Bampfield, the wife of a merchant and slave auctioneer. Documents show that he freed her eleven months later. In 1816, he paid $600 to Elisabeth Bonsell for "a negroe man named Billy." That same year, he paid $400 to buy "a certain negro fellow named Marcus," about forty-five years old, from the estate of William Soranzo Hasell, a Yale-educated newspaper editor who had died young without an heir. In 1817, he transacted with Hannah Lesesne again, paying $650 for a thirty-year-old "mulatto" carpenter named Maurice. Two years after that, he bought Sam, a tailor by trade, for $1,000 from Susanna Cochran, the elderly widowed mother of Sarah Bampfield.

Bills of Sale, Misc. Records, series S213003, SCDAH: March 30, 1813, 4F:288–289; November 18, 1813, 4G:249–250; November 10, 1815, 4K:79, 123; December 17, 1816, 4M:40; June 24, 1817, 4M:290; March 19, 1819, 4S:11; CCDB, March 8, 1823, L9:259–260; December 14, 1829, Y9:402–403, CCROD.

89 **Other free Black Methodist leaders:** For example, Smart Simpson, one of the Black Methodists so admired by Bishop Capers, bought slaves in 1810 and 1813 and was recorded as owning eight in the 1830 census. They were not his immediate family.

Not surprisingly, Black churchmen at times slave-traded with one another, as when William Eden sold "one Negro man named James" to Amos Cruckshanks for $550 in 1818 after buying James and another slave for $700 in 1814. Morris Brown's own son, Malcolm, who had just turned sixteen when purchased out of slavery by his father, would become one of Charleston's largest and wealthiest free Black slaveholders. A shoemaker like his father, Malcolm M. Brown bought at least fifteen slaves in eleven purchases between 1830 and 1843 and sold at least four to white buyers. His household included seven slaves in 1840 and ten in 1850.

McCord, *Statutes*, 7:459; Bills of Sale, June 7, 1810, Misc. Records, series S213003, 4A: 525, SCDAH; November 18, 1813, 4F:476; March 17, 1830, 5K:176; February 24, 1831, 5K:356; November 22, 1834, 5O:589; December 9, 1834, 5O:589–590; March 12, 1835, 5O:664; May 31, 1837, 5T:182; February 19, 1839, 5T:494; September 18, 1839, 5W:69; January 31, 1840, 5W:14; January 24, 1843, 5W:567; April 23, 1839, 5T:549; March 14, 1843, 6A:4; October 7, 1814, 4I:247; May 23, 1818, 4P:186; U.S. FB, roll 7, Augusta, GA, November 23, 1870–June 29, 1874, no. 6503.

89 **In the recounting of Methodist historians:** Andrew, "Letters," 23; *Minutes of the Annual Conferences for 1773–1828*, 1:283.

89 **The search by churches:** "The Presentments of the Grand Jury, at a Court of General Sessions of the Peace," *CGDA*, September 25, 1799, 3; Mood, *Methodism in Charleston*, 70.

90 **The Methodists designed:** Mood, *Methodism in Charleston*, 80–83, 92–95, 97–98, 101–104.

90 **The final insult:** Mood, *Methodism in Charleston*, 131–132.
90 **For at some point that year:** Mood, *Methodism in Charleston*, 131–132; Andrew, "Letters," 23–24.
91 **The next Sunday:** Mood, *Methodism in Charleston*, 131–132; Andrew, "Letters," 23–24; *Minutes of the Annual Conferences for 1773–1828*, 1:295, 311.
91 **Methodist minister Solomon Bryan:** Charles Cotesworth Pinckney, *An Address Delivered in Charleston, Before the Agricultural Society of South-Carolina, at its Anniversary Meeting on Tuesday, the 18th August, 1829* (Charleston: A. E. Miller, 1829), 20; *The Times*, December 29, 1817, 2.

The article in *The Times* reported that "it appears" that Black Charlestonians had "purchased a lot and erected a building thereon, for the purpose of Divine Worship." This timing does not sync with the purchase of property more than six months later at Hanover and Reid Streets, where the African Church was then built. The author is indebted to historian Robert Paquette for rediscovering this article, which had been cited incorrectly for decades by a series of scholars.

91 **Although Brown would become:** Payne, *Recollections*, 94; Payne, *History*, 262; Daniel A. Payne, "Biography of Morris Brown," in *The Lives of the Bishops of the Methodist Church* (Atlanta: Morris Brown College, undated), ROSE; Daniel Payne, "The Bishopric of the A.M.E. Church—What It Was—What It Is—What It Ought To Be," *CR*, April 22, 1880; McCord, *Statutes*, 7:397; Last Will and Testament of Morris Brown, May 31, 1849, no. 152, Will Book no. 2, 236, Philadelphia Register of Wills.
92 **"He was seldom":** Payne, *History*, 262; Payne, "Biography of Morris Brown"; Henry Highland Garnet, "The Pioneers of the African Methodist Episcopal Church, No. 2," *CR*, March 6, 1869.
92 **Brown had established:** James W. Hagy, *People and Professions of Charleston, South Carolina, 1782–1802* (Baltimore: Clearfield, 1992), 93; James W. Hagy, *Charleston, South Carolina City Directories for the Years 1816, 1819, 1822, 1825 and 1829* (Baltimore: Clearfield, 1996), 3; CCDB, April 19, 1814, I8:275–277; July 4, 1818, A9:267–268; June 13, 1821, I9:90–91; March 8, 1823, L9:259–60, CCROD; Payne, *History*, 263–266.
93 **They considered:** Mood, *Methodism in Charleston*, 131; Andrew, "Letters," 24; "Petition of Free Persons of Color from Charleston Belonging to the Methodist Denomination Asking for a Burial Ground in the Village of Wraggs-Borough," November 24, 1817, series S165015, no. 3997, SCDAH.
93 **On November 24, 1817:** "Petition of Free Persons of Color"; SC House Journal, November 24, 1817–December 18, 1817, 5, 42, SCDAH; SC Senate Journal, November 24, 1817–December 18, 1817, 4, 52, SCDAH; "Committee on Religion Report on the Petition of Certain Free People of Color Asking Permission to Purchase Two Lots of Land in Ragsborough for Use as a Burial Ground," November 28, 1817, series S165005, no. 113, SCDAH; "Committee on Incorporations Report on the Petition of Certain Free People of Color in Charleston Asking Permission to Purchase Two Lots of Land," December 2, 1817, series S165005, no. 119, SCDAH.

The other signatories were: Harry Bull, (Illegible) Hanes, John Ancrum, James Mack, Joseph Brown, Benjamin Berry, James Holmes, Cato Mack, Aleck Harleston, and James Savage.

94 **But it was sufficient:** Payne, *History*, 26.
94 **Some early Methodist histories:** Andrew, "Letters," 23; Mood, *Methodism in Charleston*, 131–132; Daniel A. Payne, *The Semi-Centenary and the Retrospection of the African Meth. Episcopal Church in the United States of America* (Baltimore: Sherwood & Co., 1866), 21.

Payne contradicts himself on this point in his autobiography, *Recollections*, 100 (written twenty-two years after *Semi-Centenary* and three years before *History*), listing Brown—but not Drayton—as among eighteen initial members present at the Philadelphia conference of 1816. The names he provides there, however, are wildly divergent from the identical lists in *Semi-Centenary* and *History*, 13, and would seem to have been confused.

95 **Almost immediately after returning:** CCDB, June 4, 1818, Z8:317–321, and April 9, 1814, I8:275–277, CCROD; Nic Butler, "Hampstead Village: The Historic Heart of Charleston's East Side," *CTM*, October 18, 2019, CCPL; Will of Christopher Williman, *Wills, Charleston County*, Will Book "E," 1807–1818, 744–749, CCPL.

- 95 **Brown and his fellow Black Methodists:** CCDB, June 4, 1818, Z8:317–321, CCROD.
- 95 **On June 7:** *SPCA*, June 8, 1818, 2, and June 10, 1818, 2; *CC*, June 9, 1818, 2.
- 96 **There had been prior rounds of arrests:** "Treatment of Blacks in Charleston, S.C.," *Boston Recorder*, August 29, 1818, 2.
- 96 **"We have rarely":** "Treatment of Negroes in Charleston, S.C.," *Boston Recorder*, July 7, 1818, 3.
- 96 **That earned a scolding:** "Treatment of Blacks," *Boston Recorder*, August 29, 1818, 2.
- 97 **Even after a month:** Payne, *History*, 27–30; Charles Spencer Smith, *A History of the African Methodist Episcopal Church* (Philadelphia: Book Concern of the A.M.E. Church, 1922), 14; *Minutes of the Twelfth Session of the South Carolina Annual Conference of the African Methodist Episcopal Church held at Charleston, S.C., from February 1st to February 10th, 1876* (Charleston: Walker, Evans & Cogswell, 1876), 9, SCHS; Mood, *Methodism in Charleston*, 133; *OR*, 76, 115.

  The location and form of the worship spaces on Anson Street and Cow Alley are not specified in any known document. Two possibilities exist, however, for the site on Anson. One is the property that Morris Brown purchased on the east side of the street in 1821 (and sold in 1823). It is located just south of the corner of Laurens Street at the current address of 66 Anson, the site of the "Chazal House," which was built around 1839. The other is a house that was numbered at the time as 75 Anson Street (Charleston's street numbering has changed), between Calhoun and George Streets. It sits on the west side of the block, bordered now by Menotti Street. That property belonged to a free woman of color named Susannah Hewitt until her death in 1818, when it was bequeathed to her seven children and seven grandchildren. In 1821, one of Hewitt's daughters sued other beneficiaries over her mother's estate, and in February 1822 a judge ordered the Anson Street property sold and the proceeds disbursed. At public auction in May 1822, seven of Susannah Hewitt's descendants, led by daughter Diana Buchanan, submitted a high bid of $3,050 and purchased the house they had been ordered to sell. They did so with the help of a $1,000 mortgage granted by seven leaders of the African Church: Smart Simpson, John B. Mathewes, Peter B. Mathewes, Malcolm Brown, James Eden, James Holmes, and James B. Haig. It is only speculation, but perhaps church officials, hoping to continue using the Hewitt house for their assemblies, helped underwrite the purchase at auction with that understanding. The author is indebted to Doreen Larimer, a Charleston historical property researcher, for assistance in documenting this trail. CCDB, June 13, 1821, I9:90–91; March 8, 1823, L9:259–260; May 7, 1822, H9:415–417; May 7, 1822, N9:86, CCROD; "Last Will and Testament of Susannah Hewitt," November 1, 1815, Charleston County, South Carolina, Record of Wills, 716; "Letter of Testamentary for Susannah Hewitt," April 25, 1818, Q:146; Jonathan H. Poston, *The Buildings of Charleston: A Guide to the City's Architecture* (Columbia: University of South Carolina Press, 1997), 420.
- 98 **White Charleston:** "Communication," *SPCA*, April 14, 1820, 2; "Petition of Inhabitants of Charleston Advocating a Curtailment of Certain Rights Granted to Free Blacks, Persons of Color and Slaves as Well as Citing the Activities of Abolition Societies," October 16, 1820, series S165015, no. 143, SCDAH; "On the Condition of the Blacks in This Country," *The Panoplist, and Missionary Herald*, November 1820, 481–494.

  There is no other known documentation to either support or disprove that Gov. Geddes withdrew initial support for the church-building project.
- 98 **This time he persuaded:** "Petition by Sundry Free Persons of Color, Attached to the African Methodist Episcopal Church in Charleston Called Zion, Asking Permission to Open a Recently Erected House of Worship on Charleston Neck," November 1820, series S165015, no. 1893, SCDAH.
- 99 **To give the African Church:** "Petition by Sundry Free Persons"; General Assembly, SC House Journal, 1820, 13, SCDAH.
- 99 **"Your petitioners are free persons of color":** "Petition by Sundry Free Persons."

  The free persons of color who signed were, in order: Morris Brown, Henry Drayton, Charles Corr, Harry Bull, Amos Cruckshanks (spelled Crukshank here), J. B. Mathewes, Peter B. Mathewes, A. Harleston, Marcus Brown, Malcolm Brown, Sam Cochran, James Savage, James Eden, Robert Milner, J. B. Haig, Quash A. Harleston, Cato Mack, London Turpin, Charles Drayton, Isaac A. Mathewes, Henry Mathewes, John Drayton, Samuel Brown, James Mack, Charles Rogers, and Smart Simpson.

NOTES TO PAGES 99–103

99 **One day before the African Church petition:** Message from Gov. John Geddes, November 27, 1820, series S165009, no. 1271, SCDAH.

100 **In that charged atmosphere:** "Report and Supporting Papers on the Petition of Certain Free Persons of Color, Having Seceded from a Particular Methodist Church, Asking Permission to Worship in a Building Erected by Them in the Suburbs of Charleston," December 2, 1820, series 165005, no. 228, SCDAH; "Legislature of South Carolina," *CC*, December 5, 1820, 2; SC House Journal, November 27, 1820–December 20, 1820, 13, 59, 90, SCDAH; SC Senate Journal, November 27, 1820–December 20, 1820, 10, 47, SCDAH.

100 **Instead, the lawmakers turned their attention:** McCord, *Statutes*, 7:459–460; "South Carolina Law," *Boston Commercial Gazette*, April 30, 1821, 4; *Buffalo Journal*, May 1, 1821, 2; "For the City Gazette," *CGCDA*, September 28, 1821, 2.

101 **Morris Brown attended:** Payne, *History*, 21, 32, 34, 37; "For the City Gazette," *CGCDA*, August 10, 1822, 2; Charleston District Court of General Session, Writs of Prohibition, August 8, 1822, series L10155, no. 5A, SCDAH.

101 **Daniel Payne wrote:** Payne, *Semi-Centenary*, 23; Mood, *Methodism in Charleston*, 133.

CHAPTER VII: HOT BED

102 **On a pleasant May Saturday:** *OR*, 48–53; *NP*, 3–5; Evidence Document (Ev. Doc.) B, Records of the General Assembly, November 28, 1822, Governors' Messages, no. 1328, SCDAH, as compiled in *DVA*, 286. (In this invaluable volume of more than 800 pages, Egerton and Paquette replicate, transcribe, and contextualize hundreds of relevant documents, including a handwritten "transcript" of the trial record and the judges' "Official Report.")

Not surprisingly, William Paul disputed Peter Prioleau's version of their May 25, 1822, meeting when examined by the insurrection court. "I asked him for news & if he had heard anything strange," Paul testified. "When he replied he had heard that there would be a disturbance & interruption shortly between the Blacks & White—I told him I did not understand such talk & stopped the conversation. I did not endeavour to get Col. Prioleau's man to join the rising of the Blacks." Unconvinced, the court convicted Paul, but sentenced him to be exiled out of the country rather than executed.

102 **As whispers of a mass uprising:** *OR*, 26; Archibald H. Grimke, *Right on the Scaffold, or The Martyrs of 1822* (Washington, D.C.: The American Negro Academy, 1901), 18; Thomas Wentworth Higginson, "The Story of Denmark Vesey," *Atlantic Monthly*, June 1861.

103 **That day on the wharf:** *OR*, 48–51.

103 **The authorities quickly rounded up:** *NP*, 5–9; *OR*, 34–35, 52–54, 64–65, 97–98; Ev. Doc. B, *DVA*, 287–290, 627 fn. 1; Gov. Thomas Bennett, Jr., "Message No. 2 to the State Legislature," Records of the General Assembly, November 28, 1822, series S165009, no. 1328, SCDAH; W. Hasell Wilson to Rev. D. Wilson of Charleston, Rev. Robert Wilson Correspondence, Ms. 185, CLS; Higginson, "Story of Denmark Vesey"; Mary Lamboll Beach to Elizabeth L. Gilchrist, July 5, 1822, Mary Lamboll Thomas Beach Letters, 1822–1825, SCHS; Minute Book of Pastor Benjamin M. Palmer, Membership Records, vol. 2, 1814–1836; Circular Congregational Church Records, box 28–692, folder 21, 76, SCDAH; "Large Meeting at Zion Church," *CC*, May 13, 1865, 2.

Like Peter Prioleau, George Wilson was of mixed race, and although enslaved held certain privileges he likely did not care to risk. A literate blacksmith, he was permitted by his owner to hire out his services and share in the earnings. His character and loyalty had earned him an appointment as a class leader in the city's Circular Congregational Church. In fact, Wilson had been tipped to the insurrection by two members of his class, Joe La Roche and Rolla Bennett, the latter of whom was enslaved by the governor himself. It would not be lost on future generations that the chief betrayers of the plot were of mixed race (Prioleau was encouraged to report what he had heard by his friend William Penceel, a free person of color who also was light-skinned). More than four decades later, the prominent Black orator Maj. Martin R. Delany remarked on it during a speech in Charleston after the Civil War. The revelation of the plot by mulattoes, Delany reportedly said, "was the cause of the prejudice existing among the different classes of the colored people" in the city.

103 **The Charleston peninsula:** *NP*, 10; Bennett, "Message No. 2."
By midsummer, the secretary of war, South Carolina's own John C. Calhoun, had acted on Gov. Bennett's request to move a company of reinforcements from Florida to the Lowcountry to ward off possible attack. W. Edwin Hemphill, ed., *The Papers of John C. Calhoun* (Columbia: University of South Carolina Press, 1973), 7:220–221; *SPCA*, July 30, 1822, 2, and August 15, 1822, 2.

104 **The judges concluded:** Ev. Doc. B, *DVA*, 302; *OR*, 22–24, 31–41, 48, 63–65, 91, 95.
The ostensible scheduled date of the insurrection, June 16, is proximate to the June 17 date of Dylann Roof's attack. Some have suggested that Roof's timing was deliberate, but he has not provided evidence of that.

104 **All but 10 of the 130 Black Charlestonians:** *OR*, 44, 91.

105 **"Tell me, are you guilty":** Martha Proctor Richardson to James Screven, August 7, 1822, Arnold and Screven Papers, SHC; *OR*, 102; Ev. Doc. B, *DVA*, 283.

105 **The insurgents:** *OR*, 34–41, 63–68, 75, 82, 96, 121, 166–167; Ev. Doc. B, *DVA*, 291–292, 301, 335; *NP*, 13.

105 **Some modern historians question:** James O'Neil Spady, "Denmark Vesey and the 1822 Charleston Antislavery Uprising: New Themes and New Methods," in *Fugitive Movements: Commemorating the Denmark Vesey Affair and Black Radical Antislavery in the Atlantic World*, ed. James O'Neil Spady (Columbia: University of South Carolina Press, 2022), 38–60; Ev. Doc. B, *DVA*, 286; *OR*, 17, 27, 42, 183, 188; *NP*, 15, 47, 50.

106 **That was just the beginning:** *NP*, 2; *OR*, 183–188; "The Award of Justice," *CGCDA*, July 27, 1822, 2; Michael P. Johnson, "Denmark Vesey's Church," *JSH* 86, no. 4 (November 2020): 805; Paul H. Blackman and Vance McLaughlin, "Mass Legal Executions in America Up to 1865," *Crime, Histoire & Sociétés* 8, no. 2 (2004): 33–61; "Execution," *CC*, July 27, 1822, 2; "Petition of Peter Desverney, A Free Person of Color, and Inhabitants of Charleston, Asking for an Increase in His Annual Bounty, Given to Him by the Act of 1822, for His Services to the State During the Slave Rebellion," October 1857, series S165015, no. 1, SCDAH; Certification of Emancipation of George Wilson, series S213003, vol. 4Z (1823–1825), July 3, 1823, 186, SCDAH; "Message of Governor John L. Wilson Regarding the Appraisal of John C. Prioleau's Slave Peter, and Mrs. Wilson's Slave George," November 11, 1823, series S165009, no. 1343, SCDAH.

107 **The special court:** *OR*, vi-vii, 32–33, 59, 172; *NP*, 11–12, 23, 33; Ev. Doc. B, *DVA*, 350.

108 **The surviving transcript of witness testimony:** Ev. Doc. B, *DVA*, 282, 301–302; *OR*, 72.

108 **"He said, we were deprived":** *OR*, 82; Mary Lamboll Beach to Elizabeth L. Gilchrist, July 5, 1822, Beach Letters, SCHS. (In this letter, Beach wrote that she had heard that Denmark Vesey urged others "to engage in the business on account of their abridgement of religious privileges.")

108 **The trial records and other documents:** Primary sourcing for the analysis of implicated African Church members includes *OR*, *NP*, and Ev. Doc. B, *DVA*, 74–94, 162–270, 279–365; Brandon M. Stone, "Armed with a Gun & Sword: New Perspectives on the Alleged Denmark Vesey Co-Conspirators and the Workhouse Trials," MA thesis, Graduate School of the University of Charleston, South Carolina at the College of Charleston and the Citadel, 2021, 23–26; Johnson, "Denmark Vesey's Church," 807–809.

The names and dispositions (Execution, Transportation beyond the United States, Acquittal, Acquittal but referred for Transportation, or Discharged before trial) of those arrested who can be directly or inferentially identified through trial records or other documents as being currently or formerly associated with the African Church are: Smart Anderson (E), Paris Ball (T), George Bampfield (T), Ned Bennett (E), Jemmy Clement (E), John Vincent (Cruckshanks) (T), John Enslow (T), George Evans (T), Polydore Faber (E), Lot Forrester (E), Monday Gell (T), Jack Glen (E), Butcher Gibbes (A/T), Prince Graham (T/out of SC), Pompey Haig (A), Quash Harleston (A/T), Denbow Martin (T), Jack McNeil (E), Adam Bellamy (Merritt) (T), Dean Mitchell (E), Dublin Morris (T), George Parker (T), Peter Poyas (E), Jack Pritchard (E), Adam Robertson (E), John Robertson (E), Tom Scott (E), Charles Shubrick (D), Scipio Sims (T), Caesar Smith (E), Perault Strohecker (T), Denmark Vesey (E), Sandy Vesey (T), Peter Ward (D), and Bellisle Yates (E).

Most on this list were identified as current members. Monday Gell is recorded as testifying that Lot Forrester "was one of the African Church, but I believe he had been turned out," that Denbow Martin "did belong to the African Church but now to the Lutheran," and that John Vincent "once belonged to the African Church." Quash Harleston's church membership is not referenced in trial documents, but he signed the 1820 petition to the legislature seeking to open the church. In records of George Bampfield's trial that report the testimony of John Enslow, a parenthetical appears: "(I did belong to the African Church, but they turned me out for keeping a girl.)" In the "Senate Transcript," it is ambiguous as to whether the speaker is Enslow or Bampfield, but the *OR* prefaces that quote by attributing it to "the prisoner on being asked if he belonged to the African Church." That still leaves ambiguity, as both Bampfield and Enslow were prisoners. But the use of the word "prisoner" rather than "witness," along with context, suggests the reference was to Bampfield.

Historian Michael P. Johnson, in his 2020 article, "Denmark Vesey's Church," argues that much of the testimony about church connections qualifies as "dubious hearsay," given that only two defendants—Gell and Enslow—testified to their own current membership.

109 **"This business originates":** *OR*, 23, 44, 75–76.
109 **"Religious fanaticism":** *NP*, 31.
110 **Indeed, the trial included evidence:** *OR*, 98.
110 **Morris Brown, Henry Drayton, and other church founders:** "For the City Editor," *CGCDA*, August 10, 1822, 2; "Communication," *Baltimore Patriot & Mercantile Advertiser*, April 12, 1822, 2; Payne, *History*, 31–34; *OR*, 126, 128; Ev. Doc. B, *DVA*, 303, 316.
111 **Numerous histories have declared:** Ev. Doc. B, *DVA*, 664; *OR*, 22–23, 44, 124; Mary Lamboll Beach to Elizabeth L. Gilchrist, July 25, 1822, Beach Letters, SCHS.
111 **Further complicating the question:** Johnson, "Denmark Vesey's Church," 810–821; *Session Book of the Second Presbyterian Church of the City and Suburbs of Charleston*, 9, 27, Second Presbyterian Church Records, box 9, SCHS; *OR*, 17–18, 67–68.
112 **Rolla Bennett testified:** *OR*, 17–18, 61–62, 66–68, 86, 89, 121; *NP*, 36; Ev. Doc. B, *DVA*, 301, 326.
112 **The religious practices of Africa:** Zephaniah Kingsley, *A Treatise on the Patriarchal or Co-operative System of Society as It Exists in Some Governments, and Colonies in America, and in the United States, Under the Name of Slavery with Its Necessity and Advantages* (1829), 13; Douglas Egerton, *He Shall Go Out Free: The Lives of Denmark Vesey* (Lanham, MD: Rowman & Littlefield, 2004), 118–119; *OR*, 21, 103–107, 179; Ev. Doc. B, *DVA*, 282, 285.
113 **Whatever Denmark Vesey's actual agency:** *OR*, 19, 64, 85–86; Ev. Doc. B, *DVA*, 296.
113 **It was only by a stunning bit of fortune:** *OR*, 42–43; Nic Butler, "Denmark Vesey's Winning Lottery Ticket," *CTM*, February 23, 2018, CCPL; "The Commissioners of East Bay-Street Lottery," *CGDA*, August 12, 1799, 2; "East-Bay Lottery," *CGDA*, October 8, 1799, 3; "East-Bay-Street Lottery," *CGDA*, November 9, 1799, 3; Manumission of Telemaque, December 31, 1799, Misc. Records, 3M:427–428, SCDAH.
113 **Vesey's given name:** *OR*, 42–43; Egerton, *He Shall Go*, 15–16, 20, 27, 33.
114 **"It is difficult to imagine":** *OR*, 22, 177.
114 **Having exceeded the average lifespan:** *OR*, 87–88, 95; Ev. Doc. B, *DVA*, 335; Jack Ericson Eblen, "New Estimates of the Vital Rates of the United States Black Population During the Nineteenth Century," *Demography* 11, no. 2 (May 1974): 309.

Little is known of Vesey's wives, but Egerton and Paquette found no evidence of polygamy, to wit: "The Senate transcript reads 'several' for the number of Vesey's wives. The extant record reveals three, Beck and then Dolly and then later the much younger Susan. Although it is unclear as to exactly when Vesey's relationships with Beck or Dolly ended, no contemporary source suggested that these relationships were polygamous, and the rough ages of his children indicate that the marriages did not overlap."

114 **At sentencing, the judges acted:** *OR*, 177–178, 180–182; *NP*, 17.
115 **Like most of the accused:** *OR*, 44–45, 177; John Potter to Langdon Cheves, July 5, 1822, Langdon Cheves Papers, Container 12/44–45, SCHS.
115 **"Your professed design":** *OR*, 45, 177.
115 **Vesey is said to have awaited the hangman:** Mary Lamboll Beach to Elizabeth L. Gilchrist,

July 5, 1822, Beach Letters, SCHS; Untitled article, *The Liberator*, August 25, 1837, 1; *NP*, 19; Ev. Doc. B, *DVA*, 323; Moses Stuart, *Conscience and the Constitution with Remarks on the Recent Speech of the Hon. Daniel Webster in the Senate of the United States on the Subject of Slavery* (Boston: Crocker & Brewster, 1850), 92–94.

116 **Large numbers of Black and white Charlestonians:** *DVA*, 168–169, fn. 12; Memoirs of S. W. Ferguson: Family History and Boyhood, April 26, 1900, Heyward and Ferguson Family Papers, SHC; John B. Adger, *My Life and Times, 1810–1899* (Richmond: The Presbyterian Committee of Publication, 1899), 50–54, 165; Charleston City Council Proceedings on Microfilm, 1821–1980, Charleston Archive, CCPL (In a remarkable bit of both luck and misfortune, the only volume of the council's handwritten minutes from between 1783 and 1865 that survived the Civil War covered this critical period).

116 **"Billy was hung":** "Melancholy Effect of Popular Excitement," *CC*, June 21, 1822, 2.

117 **The next day, Intendant Hamilton responded:** "To the Public," *SPCA*, June 22, 1822, 2; William Johnson, "To The Public," *CC*, June 29, 1822, 2; "Communication," *CC*, June 29, 1822, 2; William Johnson, *To the Public of Charleston* (Charleston: C.C. Sebring, 1822), 3–7, 11–12; William Johnson to Thomas Jefferson, December 10, 1822, Thomas Jefferson Papers, General Correspondence, series 1, reel 53, LOC.

Justice Johnson wrote this to former President Thomas Jefferson in December 1822: "I have lived to see what I really never believed it possible I should see, —Courts held with closed Doors, and Men dying by scores who had never seen the Faces nor heard the Voices of their Accusers." Taking a pointed swipe at Intendant Hamilton, he mused about the capacity of crisis to move public opinion. "You know the best way in the World to make them tractable is to frighten them to Death; and to magnify danger is to magnify the claims of those who arrest it."

117 **Ten days later:** Gov. Thomas Bennett, Jr., to Attorney General Robert Y. Hayne, July 1, 1822, Evidence Document D, Records of the General Assembly, Governors' Messages, no. 1328, SCDAH; Attorney General Robert Y. Hayne to Gov. Thomas Bennett, Jr., July 3, 1822, Evidence Document E, Records of the General Assembly, Governors' Messages, no. 1328, SCDAH; Bennett, "Message No. 2."

117 **Despite such contemporaneous skepticism:** Henry Highland Garnet, *Walker's Appeal, With a Brief Sketch of His Life* (New York: J. H. Tobitt, 1848), 95–96.

To explore the academic debate over Vesey, see: Richard C. Wade, "The Vesey Plot: A Reconsideration," *JSH* 30, no. 2 (May 1964): 143–161; Michael P. Johnson, "Denmark Vesey and His Co-Conspirators," *WMQ* 58, no. 4 (October 2001): 915–976; Douglas R. Egerton, "Forgetting Denmark Vesey; Or, Oliver Stone Meets Richard Wade," *WMQ* 59, no. 1 (January 2002): 143–152; Robert L. Paquette, "Jacobins of the Lowcountry: The Vesey Plot on Trial," *WMQ* 59, no. 1 (January 2002): 185–192; James O'Neil Spady, "Power and Confession: On the Credibility of the Earliest Reports of the Denmark Vesey Slave Conspiracy," *WMQ* 68, no. 2 (April 2011): 287; Robert L. Paquette and Douglas R. Egerton, "Of Facts and Fables: New Light on the Denmark Vesey Affair," *SCHM* 105, no. 1 (January 2004): 8–48; Robert L. Paquette, "From Rebellion to Revisionism: The Continuing Debate About the Denmark Vesey Affair," *The Journal of the Historical Society* 4, no. 3 (Fall 2004): 291–334; Michael P. Johnson, "Telemaque's Pilgrimage? A Tale of Two Charleston Churches, Three Missionaries, and Four Ministers, 1783–1817," *SCHM* 118, no. 1 (January 2017): 4–36; Johnson, "Denmark Vesey's Church," 805–848; Dinitia Smith, "Challenging the History of a Slave Conspiracy," *NYT*, February 23, 2002, B-11.

118 **After suggestions to rename a school:** Ethan J. Kytle and Blain Roberts, *Denmark Vesey's Garden: Slavery and Memory in the Cradle of the Confederacy* (New York: The New Press, 2018), 287–290.

118 **"If black leaders":** Ashley Cooper, "Doing The Charleston," *NC*, August 13, 1976, 11; Shirley J. Holcombe, "Honoring Sedition," *NC*, August 9, 1976, 8.

118 **At the painting's unveiling:** Mary A. Glass, "Slave's Picture Hung in Auditorium," *NC*, August 10, 1976, 13; Bobby Isaac, "Vesey Painting Missing From Auditorium," *NC*, September 19, 1976, 32; Edward C. Fennell, "Reporter Finds Vesey Portrait," *NC*, September 21, 1976, 1; "Vesey Painting Is Returned to City Auditorium," *NC*, October 6, 1976, 5.

The stolen Vesey painting reappeared after three days, deposited against an auditorium door. The city reinstalled the piece, this time high out of reach. It was removed during a 2012 renovation and eventually found its way to Charleston's Old Slave Mart Museum.

118 **History repeated four decades later:** Bo Peterson, "Vesey Evokes Honor, Horror," *PC*, March 8, 2010, B-1; Kytle and Roberts, *Denmark Vesey's Garden*, 331–336.

118 **On May 29:** "City of Charleston Investigates Vandalism of Denmark Vesey Monument," City of Charleston news release, May 30, 2021.

CHAPTER VIII: CRACKDOWN

120 **The auctioneer's advertisements:** "By William A. Caldwell," *CC*, August 14, 1822, 3; *CGCDA*, August 14, 1822, 3; *SPCA*, August 14, 1822, 3.

120 **This vendue master's ads, however:** *CC*, "By William A. Caldwell" (Credit for discovering the Caldwell advertisements through an electronic search goes to Ethan J. Kytle, a historian at California State University, Fresno, and coauthor of the previously cited *Denmark Vesey's Garden*); "Estate Sale," *CC*, December 27, 1822, 3.

121 **Barack Obama said so:** The White House, "Remarks by the President in Eulogy for the Honorable Reverend Clementa Pinckney," Charleston, SC, June 26, 2015.

121 **There is no known record:** Daniel A. Payne, *The Semi-Centenary and the Retrospection of the African Meth. Episcopal Church in the United States of America* (Baltimore: Sherwood & Co., 1866), 23–25; Daniel A. Payne, "Organization Essential to Success of Quarto-Centennial of African Methodism in the South," *Sermons and Addresses 1853–1891* (New York: Arno Press, 1972), 39; F. A. Mood, *Methodism in Charleston: A Narrative of the Chief Events Relating to the Rise and Progress of the Methodist Episcopal Church in Charleston, S.C.* (Nashville: E. Stevenson and J.E. Evans, 1856), 133; Benjamin W. Arnett, ed., *Proceedings of the Quarto-Centennial Conference of the African M.E. Church of South Carolina, May 15, 16 and 17, 1889* (Published by the editor, 1890), 29; *NP*, 31.

122 **The city fathers:** *NP*, 31; "For the City Gazette," *CGCDA*, August 10, 1822, 2; *Henry Drayton v. John B. White*, August 8, 1822, Charleston County Court of General Sessions, Writs of Prohibition, series L10155, no. 5A, SCDAH; David J. McCord, *The Statutes at Large of South Carolina* (Columbia: A. S. Johnston, 1840), 7:459–460.

122 **Even as the specially appointed Court of Magistrates:** Daniel A. Payne, *History of the African Methodist Episcopal Church* (Nashville: Publishing House of the A.M.E. Sunday-School Union, 1891), 261–262; Daniel Alexander Payne, *Recollections of Seventy Years* (Nashville: Publishing House of the A.M.E. Sunday School Union, 1888), 21, 37, 58; "For the City Gazette," *CGCDA*, August 10, 1822, 2.

122 **The justice of the peace:** "For the City Gazette"; "Insurrection," *The National Advocate*, August 20, 1822, 2.

The *National Advocate* article suggests that both Brown and Drayton appealed their convictions, but only records of Drayton's case have been found at SCDAH.

123 **Brown and Drayton made hasty arrangements:** Payne, *Semi-Centenary*, 23–24; Payne, "Biography of Morris Brown," 4; *NP*, 31; Morris Brown to Thos. W. Bacot and Jas. Hamilton, Power of Attorney, August 19, 1822, CCDB, M9:38–39, CCROD.

In the account he published in mid-August 1822, Hamilton did what he could to clear the African Church's leaders: "After the most diligent search and scrutiny, no evidence entitled to belief, has been discovered against them. A hearsay rumour, in relation to Morris Brown, was traced far enough to end in its complete falsification."

123 **The younger of Morris Brown's children:** CCDB, March 8, 1823, L9:259–260, and December 14, 1829, Y9:402–403, CCROD; Payne, *History*, v, 58–59, 261–262; "Obituary," *Public Ledger*, May 12, 1849, 2; Last Will and Testament of Morris Brown, May 16, 1849, Philadelphia Register of Wills, 22:236; Charles Spencer Smith, *A History of the African Methodist Episcopal Church* (Philadelphia: Book Concern of the A.M.E. Church, 1922), 14–15; Arnett, *Proceedings*, 39; Richard S. Newman, *Freedom's Prophet: Bishop Richard Allen, the AME Church, and the Black Founding Fathers* (New York: New York University Press, 2008), 243; "Minute and Trial Book, 1822–1835," October 2, 1822, October 15, 1822, April 4, 1824, Records of Mother Bethel AME Church, microfilm reel 8, HSP.

Brown had arrived in Philadelphia by October 2, 1822, when Mother Bethel records show that trustees agreed to cover his board. Within two weeks, he had been integrated into Bethel's leadership, as records on October 15 show him sitting as one of five judges in a church trial.

124 **A number drifted back:** "Session Book of the Second Presbyterian Church," 39; James Osgood Andrew, "Letters on Methodist History: Rise and Progress of Methodism in Charleston, South Carolina," *Methodist Magazine and Quarterly Review* 12 (1830): 24; Payne, "Organization," 39; Payne, *Semi-Centenary*, 24; Smith, *History*, 14.

124 **They gathered after dark:** Janet Duitsman Cornelius, *Slave Missions and the Black Church in the Antebellum South* (Columbia: University of South Carolina Press, 1999), 8–10, 16–20.

124 **A kettle or wash pot:** Cornelius, *Slave Missions,* 8–10; Arnett, *Proceedings*, 30; "Bishop M.B. Salter," *African Methodist Episcopal Church Review* 9, no. 2 (October 1892): 8.

124 **The trustees of the African Church:** Michael Trinkley, Debi Hacker, and Nicole Southerland, *The Silence of the Dead: Giving Charleston Cemeteries a Voice* (Columbia: Chicora Foundation, 2010), 14–16, 72–75.

125 **The cemetery was managed:** *Peter Mathewes Frost as Trustee and Individually v. The Olivet Presbyterian Church and Martin P. Rowland*, filed November 7, 1921, Metallic Case 330, no. 12, Charleston County Court of Common Pleas, CCCC; CCDB, October 10, 1917, W28:2–3; July 28, 1919, W28:450; August 23, 1940, Z41:312; May 26, 1978, X115:74, CCROD.

126 **In Charleston, militias redoubled their patrols:** "Communication," *CC*, July 17, 1822, 2.

126 **Paternalism's goal:** Lacy K. Ford, *Deliver Us from Evil: The Slavery Question in the Old South* (New York: Oxford University Press, 2009), 7–9; Mary Lamboll Beach to Elizabeth L. Gilchrist, July 5, 1822, Beach Letters, SCHS; Henry William DeSaussure to Joel Roberts Poinsett, July 6, 1822, Joel Roberts Poinsett Papers, vol. 2, folder 7, HSP.

126 **"Far be it from me":** "For the Southern Patriot," *SPCA*, September 12, 1822, 2; Henry William DeSaussure, *A Series of Numbers Addressed to the Public, on the Subject of Slaves and Free People of Color* (Columbia: State Gazette Office, 1822), 5, 7–8, 20–21; Thomas Pinckney (writing as Achates), *Reflections, Occasioned by the late Disturbances in Charleston* (Charleston: A. E. Miller, 1822); Edwin C. Holland (writing as A South-Carolinian), *A Refutation of the Calumnies Circulated Against The Southern & Western States, Respecting the Institution and Existence of Slavery Among Them* (Charleston: A. E. Miller, 1822), 83–86; *Memorial of the Citizens of Charleston to the Senate and House of Representatives of the State of South-Carolina* (Charleston: Duke & Browne, 1822), 1, 7–11.

127 **Gov. Bennett, surely embarrassed:** "Executive Department," *CC*, August 23, 1822, 2; Bennett, "Message No. 2"; City Council of Charleston, "Petition Asking for the Passage of Laws to Further Regulate the Actions, Employment and Distribution of the Population of Slaves and Free Persons of Colour," undated (ca. 1822), series S165015, no. 2059, SCDAH; "Charleston," *CC*, December 5, 1822, 2.

127 **The legislature did not adopt:** "Private Correspondence," *CC*, December 11, 1822, 2; McCord, *Statutes*, 7:461–469.

128 **The enactment that left the deepest impression:** McCord, *Statutes*, 7:461–464; Michael Schoeppner, "Peculiar Quarantines: The Seamen Acts and Regulatory Authority in the Antebellum South," *Law and History Review* 31, no. 3 (August 2013): 559–560, 565, 575, 577, 579, 584.

128 **In Charleston, more than 150:** Philip M. Hamer, "Great Britain, the United States, and the Negro Seamen Acts, 1822–1848," *JSH* 1, no. 1 (February 1935): 3–28; Michael Alan Schoeppner, "Navigating the Dangerous Atlantic: Racial Quarantines, Black Sailors and United States Constitutionalism," PhD dissertation, University of Florida, 2010; Michael A. Schoeppner, *Moral Contagion: Black Atlantic Sailors, Citizenship, and Diplomacy in Antebellum America* (Cambridge, UK: Cambridge University Press, 2019), 35–39; Schoeppner, "Peculiar Quarantines," 559–586; Alan F. January, "The South Carolina Association: An Agency for Race Control in Antebellum Charleston," *SCHM* 78, no. 3 (July 1977): 192–195.

128 **The initial federal test case:** *Elkison v. Deliesseline*, United States Circuit Court, District of South Carolina, August 1823, no. 4, 366; Benjamin F. Hunt, *The Argument of Benj. Faneuil Hunt, in the case of the arrest of the Person claiming to be a British Seaman, under the 3d section of the State Act of Dec. 1822, in relation to Negroes, &c. before the Hon. Judge Johnson, Circuit*

Judge of the United States, for the 6th Circuit (Charleston: A. E. Miller, 1823), LOC, 7, 13; Scott Wallace Stucky, "*Elkison v. Deliesseline*: Race and the Constitution in South Carolina, 1823," *North Carolina Central Law Review* 14, no. 2 (1984): 380–383.

129 **Justice Johnson concluded:** *Elkison v. Deliesseline*; Schoeppner, "Navigating," 70–76; Stucky, "*Elkison*," 362, 383–386; Hamer, "Great Britain," 7–8.

Justice Johnson's opinion in *Elkison* found renewed relevance more than a century later in an even more consequential bit of South Carolina jurisprudence. In December 1952, Thurgood Marshall of the NAACP Legal Defense Fund dusted off the *Elkison* opinion in arguing successfully to the U.S. Supreme Court that segregated state schools were inherently unequal. Marshall cited *Elkison* in his brief and oral presentation to the Warren court while representing Black parents in *Briggs v. Elliott*, the South Carolina challenge that would be consolidated with others into the landmark desegregation case, *Brown v. Board of Education of Topeka*. After explaining that *Elkison* shared with *Briggs* a conflict between federally guaranteed individual rights and South Carolina's perceived public interest, he quoted at length from Johnson's "rope of sand" warning. "Where is this to land us?" Marshall, the future justice asked, quoting Johnson, the former justice. "Is it not asserting the right in each state to throw off the Federal Constitution at its will and pleasure? If it can be done as to any particular article," Marshall echoed Johnson, "it may be done as to all."

Reply Brief for Appellants, *Harry Briggs, Jr., et al., Appellants, v. R.W. Elliott, Chairman, J.D. Carson, et al., Members of Board of Trustees of School District No. 22, Clarendon County, S.C., et al., Appellees*, December 9, 1952, Supreme Court of the United States, 5; *Briggs v. Elliott*, Oral Argument, December 9, 1952, Supreme Court of the United States, 6.

130 **In interviews conducted for the Depression-era Slave Narrative Project:** *Born in Slavery: Slave Narratives from the Federal Writers' Project, 1936–1938* (Washington, D.C.: Library of Congress, 1941), 14.4:192; John Andrew Jackson, *The Experience of a Slave in South Carolina* (London: Passmore & Alabaster, 1862), 22.

130 **Above all, white pastors were eager:** Benjamin M. Palmer, *Religion Profitable: with a Special Reference to the Case of Servants. A Sermon, Preached on September 22, 1822, in the Circular Church, Charleston, S.C.* (Charleston: J. R. Schenck, 1822); Richard Furman, *Exposition of the Views of the Baptists, Relative to the Coloured Population of the United States, in a Communication to the Governor of South-Carolina* (Charleston: A. E. Miller, 1823), 16–17; Frederick Dalcho, *Practical Considerations Founded on the Scriptures, Relative to the Slave Population of South-Carolina* (Charleston: A. E. Miller, 1823), 33.

130 **Furman, the president of the state Baptist convention:** Furman, *Exposition*, 7–9.

130 **Dalcho maintained that the enslaved merited:** Dalcho, *Practical Considerations*, 6, 32–33; Charles C. Jones, *The Religious Instruction of the Negroes in the United States* (Savannah: Thomas Purse, 1842), 105, 235, 255–256.

131 **"In general, our religious instructors":** Whitemarsh B. Seabrook, *An Essay on the Management of Slaves, and Especially, on Their Religious Instruction; Read Before the Agricultural Society of St. John's Colleton* (Charleston: A. E. Miller, 1834), 13–15, 20–26.

131 **The same year:** Ford, *Deliver*, 463–473; Janet Duitsman Cornelius, *When I Can Read My Title Clear: Literacy, Slavery, and Religion in the Antebellum South* (Columbia: University of South Carolina Press, 1991), 39–42, 53–58; Nicholas May, "Holy Rebellion: Religious Assembly Laws in Antebellum South Carolina and Virginia," *The American Journal of Legal History* 49, no. 3 (July 2007); McCord, *Statutes*, 7:468.

132 **By the mid-1840s:** Donald G. Mathews, *Slavery and Methodism: A Chapter in American Morality 1780–1845* (Princeton: Princeton University Press, 1965), 246–282; J. Gordon Melton, *A Will to Choose: The Origins of African American Methodism* (Lanham, MD: Rowman & Littlefield Publishers, 2007), 181; Milton C. Sernett, *Black Religion and American Evangelicalism: White Protestants, Plantation Missions, and the Flowering of Negro Christianity, 1787–1865* (Metuchen, NJ: The Scarecrow Press and the American Theological Library Association, 1975), 47–51; *Journals of the General Conference of the Methodist Episcopal Church, Volume 1, 1796–1836* (New York: Carlton & Phillips, 1855), 447; Lewis M. Purifoy, "The Southern Methodist Church and the Proslavery Argument," *JSH* 32, no. 3 (August 1966): 325.

132 **Not long after:** *Proceedings of the Meeting in Charleston, S.C., May 13–15, 1845, on the Reli-*

gious Instruction of the Negroes, Together with the Report of the Committee and the Address to the Public (Charleston: B. Jenkins, 1845), 3, 21–22, 25, 36, 72; "Negroes at Private Sale," *CM*, May 13, 1845, 3; Luther P. Jackson, "Religious Instruction of Negroes, 1830–1860, With Special Reference to South Carolina," *JNH* 15, no. 1 (January 1930): 88–89; Ford, *Deliver*, 527–532.

133 **The author:** William Capers, *Catechism for the Use of the Methodist Missions. First Part* (John Early, for the Methodist Episcopal Church, South, 1853), 3–25.

133 **The religion shaped:** John B. Adger, *The Religious Instruction of the Colored Population. A Sermon Preached by the Rev. John B. Adger, in the Second Presbyterian Church, Charleston, S.C., May 9th, 1847* (Charleston: T. W. Haynes, 1847), 3, 6; Henry M. Turner, *Celebration of the First Anniversary of Freedom Held in Springfield Baptist Church, January 1, 1866, and Containing an Outline of an Oration Delivered on the Occasion by Chaplain Henry M. Turner* (Augusta: G.U.L., of Georgia, 1866), 13.

133 **Regardless of denomination:** Edward D. Smith, *Climbing Jacob's Ladder: The Rise of Black Churches in Eastern American Cities, 1740–1877* (Washington, D.C.: Smithsonian Institution, 1988), 91–97; Erskine Clarke, *Wrestlin' Jacob: A Portrait of Religion in Antebellum Georgia and the Carolina Low Country* (Tuscaloosa: The University of Alabama Press, 2000), 140–158; Melton, *Will*, 161–163.

133 **Seating for Black congregants:** *Minutes of the Annual Conferences*, 2:17, 308; *Minutes of the Annual Conferences of the Methodist Episcopal Church, South for the Years 1849–1850* (Richmond: John Early, 1850), 246; Mood, *Methodism in Charleston*, 145–151; John O. Willson, *Sketch of the Methodist Church in Charleston, S.C., 1785–1887* (Charleston: Lucas, Richardson, & Co., Steam Book Printers, 1888), 13–14; Albert Deems Betts, *History of South Carolina Methodism* (Columbia, SC: The Advocate Press, 1952), 241; Adger, *Religious Instruction*, 7–8; A. M. Chreitzberg, *Early Methodism in the Carolinas* (Nashville: Publishing House of the Methodist Episcopal Church, South, 1897), 159–160.

134 **It chafed Charleston's white ministers:** George A. Blackburn, ed. *The Life Work of John L. Girardeau, D.D. L.L.D., Late Professor in the Presbyterian Theological Seminary, Columbia, S.C.* (Columbia: The State Company, 1916), 40; "Critical Notices," *Southern Presbyterian Review* 1, no. 2 (September 1847): 146.

134 **On a May Sunday:** Adger, *Religious Instruction*, 1–18; Adger, *My Life*, 164–200.

134 **Adger's proposal struck some:** Adger, *My Life*, 178.

135 **A brick chapel with seating:** Blackburn, *The Life Work*, 31–38, 74, 81–84; Otis Westbrook Pickett, "'We Are Marching to Zion': Zion Church and the Distinctive Work of Presbyterian Slave Missionaries in Charleston, South Carolina, 1849–1874," *The Proceedings of the South Carolina Historical Association* (May 2010): 91–104; "Zion Church," *CM*, April 5, 1859, 1.

135 **In the Episcopal denomination:** "To the Public," *CM*, July 16, 1849, 2; "Excitement in Charleston," *The Commercial*, July 19, 1849, 2; "We Find in the Wilmington Commercial," *CM*, July 21, 1849, 2; "Calvary Church," *CM*, July 23, 1849, 2; "To the Editor of the Mercury," *CM*, July 24, 1849, 2; "Public Meeting," *CC*, July 24, 1849, 2; "Public Meeting," *CC*, November 14, 1849, 2; *Public Proceedings Relating to Calvary Church and the Religious Instruction of Slaves* (Charleston: Miller & Browne, 1850), 9, 28–34; Robert F. Durden, "The Establishment of Calvary Protestant Episcopal Church for Negroes in Charleston," *SCHM* 65, no. 2 (April 1964): 63–84; Jeff Strickland, *All for Liberty: The Charleston Workhouse Slave Rebellion of 1849* (Cambridge, UK: Cambridge University Press, 2022), 145–166.

135 **Hutchinson personally presided:** *Public Proceedings Relating to Calvary Church*, 9, 28–34; Durden, "The Establishment of Calvary": 63–84

136 **Once Black and white:** Michael Lipka, "Many U.S. Congregations Are Still Racially Segregated, but Things Are Changing," Pew Research Center, December 8, 2014.

136 **But for reasons of both math and memory:** *Minutes, Annual Conferences, M.E.C., South, 1860*, 253, 293; *Public Proceedings Relating to Calvary Church*, 39, 42–43; Chreitzberg, *Early Methodism*, 158–160; Ann Taylor Andrus, *The Name Shall Be Bethel: The History of Bethel United Methodist Church 1791–1997* (Columbia: The R. L. Bryan Company, 1997), 21–25.

CHAPTER IX: REVIVAL

137 **Born in Charleston:** Daniel Alexander Payne, *Recollections of Seventy Years* (Nashville: Publishing House of the A.M.E. Sunday School Union, 1888), 11, 14–15, 19–20, 72–74; C.S. Smith, *The Life of Daniel Alexander Payne, D.D., L.L.D* (Nashville: Publishing House A.M.E. Church Sunday School Union, 1894), 18.
137 **Payne's father:** Payne, *Recollections*, 11–12; Smith, *Life of Daniel Alexander Payne*, 9–11.
138 **Payne was "naturally":** Payne, *Recollections*, 6.
138 **Orphaned at age nine:** Payne, *Recollections*, 12–14, 20–22; Smith, *Life of Daniel Alexander Payne*, 13.
138 **Payne began his teaching career:** Payne, *Recollections*, 19–20, 23, 25, 34, 36; Smith, *Life of Daniel Alexander Payne*, 19.
139 **Payne observed that it may:** Payne, *Recollections*, 25–26.
139 **Payne was traumatized by the stranglehold:** Payne, *Recollections*, 28.
140 **He collected letters:** Payne, *Recollections*, 24, 34–44.
140 **The young tutor:** Payne, *Recollections*, 35–36, 41, 43–44.
140 **Bachman's letter of introduction:** Payne, *Recollections*, 44–46, 64–75; Daniel A. Payne, *History of the African Methodist Episcopal Church* (Nashville: Publishing House of the A.M.E. Sunday-School Union, 1891), 139; Douglas C. Stange, "Bishop Daniel Alexander Payne's Protestation of American Slavery," *JNH* 52, no. 1 (January 1967): 61–62.
140 **Soon after his appointment:** Payne, *Recollections*, 74–77; Payne, *History*, 168–170, 194–196.
141 **Payne's disregard for the emotionalism:** Payne, *Recollections*, 93–94; Payne, *History*, 115–116, 269.
141 **"Then, as water rises":** Payne, *History*, 277; Daniel A. Payne, *The Semi-Centenary and the Retrospection of the African Meth. Episcopal Church in the United States of America* (Baltimore: Sherwood & Co., 1866), 184; James T. Campbell, *Songs of Zion: The African Methodist Episcopal Church in the United States and South Africa* (Chapel Hill: The University of North Carolina Press, 1998), 51; Benjamin T. Tanner, *An Apology for African Methodism* (Baltimore: Publisher not identified, 1867), 75.
142 **At the 1844 AME General Conference:** Payne, *History*, 168–169, 400, 421, 423–438; Payne, *Recollections*, 133–134, 150–154.

The other freestanding AME institutions of higher learning are Allen University in Columbia, SC; AME University in Monrovia, Liberia; Edward Waters College in Jacksonville, FL; Morris Brown College in Atlanta, GA; Paul Quinn College in Dallas, TX; and Shorter College in North Little Rock, AR.

142 **Payne was elected:** Payne, *Recollections*, 109–112, 144–148.
142 **The first opportunity:** Payne, *History*, 466–467; Daniel A. Payne, "Organization Essential to Success of Quarto-Centennial of African Methodism in the South," *Sermons and Addresses 1853–1891* (New York: Arno Press, 1972), 40; Charles Spencer Smith, *A History of the African Methodist Episcopal Church* (Philadelphia: Book Concern of the A.M.E. Church, 1922), 51–52; "The Society of Old Brooklynites," *The National Magazine: A Monthly Journal of American History* 19, no. 6–7 (April-May 1894): 415–419; *Brief History of the New York National Freedman's Relief Association* (New York: N.Y.N.F.R.A., 1866), 5–7, 27; H. J. Rhodes, "The Baltimore A.M.E. Annual Conference," *CR*, May 9, 1863.
143 **In no other state:** Walter Edgar, *South Carolina: A History* (Columbia: University of South Carolina Press, 1998), 311.

Edgar reports that 46 percent of white South Carolina families enslaved people in 1860.

143 **After years of resentment:** A standard source on nullification remains William W. Freehling, *Prelude to Civil War: The Nullification Controversy in South Carolina 1816–1836* (New York: Oxford University Press, 1965). See also Edgar, *South Carolina*, 332–337, and John Lofton, *Insurrection in South Carolina: The Turbulent World of Denmark Vesey* (Yellow Springs, OH: The Antioch Press, 1964), 220–231.
144 **On July 29, the steam packet:** "Incendiary Tracts and Papers," *SP*, July 29, 1835, 2; "Incendiary Publications," *CC*, July 30, 1835, 2; "Incendiaries," *CM*, July 30, 1835, 2; "To the Edi-

tors," *CC*, July 31, 1835, 2; "Incendiary Publications," *SP*, July 30, 1835, 2; "Attack on the Post Office," *CC*, July 31, 1835, 2; "Destruction of the Incendiary Pamphlets," *CM*, July 31, 1835, 2; Frank Otto Gatell, ed., "Postmaster Huger and the Incendiary Publications," *SCHM*, 64, no. 4 (October 1963): 193–201; Bertram Wyatt-Brown, "The Abolitionists' Postal Campaign of 1835," *JNH* 50, no. 4 (October 1965): 227–230; Freehling, *Prelude*, 340–348; Lacy K. Ford, *Deliver Us from Evil: The Slavery Question in the Old South* (New York: Oxford University Press, 2009), 481–486, 496–499; Lofton, *Insurrection*, 216–217; Joseph Kelly, *America's Longest Siege: Charleston, Slavery, and the Slow March Toward Civil War* (New York: The Overlook Press, 2013), 204–206; Theodore D. Jervey, *Robert Y. Hayne and His Times* (New York: The MacMillan Company, 1909), 379–381; Harvey S. Teal, "Attacks on the Charleston, S.C. Post Office," *La Posta: A Journal of American Postal History* 17, no. 5 (October–November 1986): 54–55; "Letters from Alfred Huger to Amos Kendall," *Richmond Enquirer*, August 25, 1835, 2.

144 **The city offered:** "Attack on the Post Office"; "Destruction of the Incendiary Pamphlets"; Walter J. Fraser, Jr., *Charleston! Charleston!: The History of a Southern City* (Columbia: University of South Carolina Press, 1989), 213; Ford, *Deliver*, 482–483.

144 **In 1837, the state's most prominent:** "Remarks on Receiving Abolition Petitions," February 6, 1837, in Clyde N. Wilson, ed., *The Papers of John C. Calhoun* (Columbia: University of South Carolina Press, 1980), 13:387–398; Fraser, *Charleston!*, 243–246; Edgar, *South Carolina*, 344–345; *Declaration of the Immediate Causes Which Induce and Justify the Secession of South Carolina from the Federal Union; and the Ordinance of Secession* (Charleston: Evans & Cogswell, 1860), 7–10.

145 **Charleston would not be occupied:** Edgar, *South Carolina*, 360–367; Fraser, *Charleston!*, 247–269.

145 **In the first reconstructionist experiment:** Edgar, *South Carolina*, 366–367; "New Year's Day in Port Royal, South Carolina," *CR*, January 17, 1863; "Interesting From Port Royal," *NYT*, January 9, 1863, 2.

145 **By way of example:** Payne, *History*, 273, 300–301; Tanner, *Outline*, 185–186; Dennis C. Dickerson, *African Methodist Episcopal Church* (Cambridge, UK: Cambridge University Press, 2020), 78; *Proceedings of the Eighth General Conference of the African M.E. Church, Held in the City of Philadelphia, May 1st, 1848, and Continued in Session Twenty-One Days* (Pittsburgh: Benj. F. Peterson, 1848), 30.

146 **Given the tension:** Milton C. Sernett, *Black Religion and American Evangelicalism: White Protestants, Plantation Missions, and the Flowering of Negro Christianity, 1787–1865* (Metuchen, NJ: The Scarecrow Press and the American Theological Library Association, 1975), 157; Payne, *History*, 130, 171, 201, 237–238, 250–252, 306–308, 326–327, 338, 471–472; "An Important Gathering," *NC*, January 28, 1890, 8.

146 **Only in 1856:** Payne, *History*, 328–345; *Eleventh General Conference of the African M.E. Church, Held in Cincinnati, Ohio, May 5, 1856* (Philadelphia: William S. Young, 1856), 22–23.

146 **Hardline abolitionists called for:** *Eleventh General Conference*, 22–23; Dickerson, *African Methodist Episcopal Church*, 4–7, 53.

147 **"We have neither civil nor political":** Payne, *History*, 328, 336–337, 340, 345; *Eleventh General Conference*, 23; *Twelfth General Conference of the African M.E. Church, Held in Pittsburgh, PA., May 7, 1860* (Philadelphia: Wm. S. Young, 1860), 14.

147 **Those preparations took on urgency:** Daniel A. Payne, *Welcome to the Ransomed; or, Duties of the Colored Inhabitants of the District of Columbia* (Baltimore: Bull & Tuttle, 1862), 6–10; H. M. Turner, "A Call to Action," *CR*, October 4, 1862.

148 **In considering Charles Leigh's request:** Payne, *History*, 467; Smith, *History*, 46.

148 **Born free in Baltimore:** Payne, *History*, 286, 294, 467–468; Benjamin W. Arnett, ed., *Proceedings of the Quarto-Centennial Conference of the African M.E. Church of South Carolina, May 15, 16 and 17, 1889* (Published by the editor, 1890), 57, 153; Alexander W. Wayman, *Cyclopaedia of African Methodism* (Baltimore: Methodist Episcopal Book Depository, 1882), 101–102; James Lynch, "Missions," *CR*, April 4, 1863; A. C. McDonald, "Funeral Sermon of the Late Rev. James Lynch," *CR*, January 16, 1873; R. H. Cain, "The First Missionaries to the South, From the A.M.E. Church," *CR*, May 30, 1863; William B. Gravely, "James Lynch and the Black Christian Mission During Reconstruction," in *Black Apostles at Home and Abroad: Afro-Americans and the Christian Mission from the Revolution to Reconstruction*, ed. David W. Wills

and Richard Newman (Boston: G.K. Hall & Co., 1982), 162–166; William C. Harris, "James Lynch: Black Leader in Southern Reconstruction," *The Historian* 34, no. 1 (November 1971): 40–61.

148 **At twelve minutes before noon:** Payne, *History*, 468; Cain, "First Missionaries."
149 **Cain shared in Payne's delight:** Cain, "First Missionaries."
149 **"None are so eminently qualified":** Cain, "First Missionaries."
149 **Lynch and Hall were in fact:** Reginald F. Hildebrand, *The Times Were Strange and Stirring: Methodist Preachers and the Crisis of Emancipation* (Durham, NC: Duke University Press, 1995), xvii; Clarence E. Walker, *A Rock in a Weary Land: The African Methodist Episcopal Church During the Civil War and Reconstruction* (Baton Rouge: Louisiana State University Press, 1982), 63; William E. Montgomery, *Under Their Own Vine and Fig Tree: The African-American Church in the South, 1865–1900* (Baton Rouge: Louisiana State University Press, 1993), 52–53.
150 **The AME missionaries set to the task:** J.D.S. Hall, "South Carolina Correspondent," *CR*, June 27, 1863; James Lynch, "The Beaufort, S.C. Correspondence," *CR*, July 25, 1863; James Lynch, "Letter from the South," *CR*, December 31, 1864; Gravely, "Lynch," 167.
150 **"Ignorant though they be":** James Lynch, "South Carolina Correspondence," *CR*, June 27, 1863; Leon F. Litwack, *Been in the Storm So Long: The Aftermath of Slavery* (New York: Vintage Books, 1979), 455–456.
150 **Wherever they trekked:** Gravely, "Lynch," 167; J.D.S. Hall, "South Carolina Correspondent," *CR*, June 27, 1863; James Lynch, "South Carolina Correspondence," *CR*, August 22, 1863; "Celebration of Freedom's Birthday in the South," *CR*, December 26, 1863; James Lynch, "Letter from South Carolina," *CR*, January 16, 1864; James Lynch, "Letter from James Lynch," *CR*, February 27, 1864; James Lynch, "An Instance of Respect, Regardless of Color," *CR*, September 24, 1864; James Lynch, "Letter from the South," *CR*, December 31, 1864; Edgar, *History*, 364.
151 **By the fall of 1863:** James D. S. Hall, "South Carolina Correspondence," *CR*, November 14, 1863; J.D.S. Hall, "An Important Letter from One of Our Missionaries South," *CR*, March 12, 1864; "Is There to Be Any Unpleasant Conflict Between the M.E. Church and the A.M.E. Church?" *CR*, April 2, 1864; Elisha Weaver, "Editorial Correspondence," April 29, 1865; Elisha Weaver, "A Continuation," *CR*, May 6, 1865; Hildebrand, *Times Were Strange*, 79.
152 **Despite Hall's vigorous defense:** Gravely, "Lynch," 173–178; "Let the Word 'African' Be Stricken from the Pages of Our Discipline," *CR*, November 21, 1863; James Lynch, "The Word 'African' in the Discipline of the A.M.E. Church," *CR*, April 9, 1864; James Lynch, "Let the Word African Be Stricken from the Discipline of the Church," *CR*, March 25, 1865; James Lynch, "Letter from Rev. James Lynch," *CR*, September 9, 1865; A. C. McDonald, "Funeral Sermon of the Late Rev. James Lynch," *CR*, January 16, 1873.
152 **As disputes multiplied:** James Lynch, "Important in Regard to Churches South," *CR*, June 25, 1864; James Lynch, "Letter from the South," *CR*, December 31, 1864; Walker, *Rock*, 84–85.
152 **The Union siege:** Edgar, *South Carolina*, 361, 364–366, 372–375; Fraser, *Charleston!*, 247–269; Francis Butler Simkins and Robert Hilliard Woody, *South Carolina During Reconstruction* (Chapel Hill: The University of North Carolina Press, 1932), 10–11; Maj. Gen. W. T. Sherman to Lieut. Gen. Ulysses S. Grant, December 24, 1864, *Supplemental Report of the Joint Committee on the Conduct of the War* (Washington, D.C.: Government Printing Office, 1866), 1:288–289.
153 **James Lynch had been:** "The Freedmen in Georgia," *New-York Daily Tribune*, February 13, 1865, 5; "Minutes of an Interview Between the Colored Ministers and Church Officers with the Secretary of War and Major-General Sherman," *The Liberator*, February 24, 1865, 1; James Lynch, "Charleston Correspondence," *CR*, March 18, 1865.

Lynch was reported to have spoken at several junctures during the meeting with Sherman and Stanton, including once when the group was asked whether freed people preferred to live communally with white Southerners or "in colonies by yourselves." Lynch was the only one to suggest the races live together. Following Lincoln's assassination, Andrew Johnson rescinded Sherman's order in the fall of 1865 and reverted formerly confiscated land to its prior owners. "Forty acres and a mule" became emblematic of the broken promises of Reconstruction.

153 **In mid-March, Alexander Wayman:** Wayman, *Cyclopaedia*, 6; Elisha Weaver, "Editorial

Correspondence," *CR*, April 1, 1865, April 15, 1865, April 22, 1865, April 29, 1865; "A Continuation," May 6, 1865, *CR*; A. W. Wayman, *My Recollections of African M. E. Ministers, or Forty Years' Experience in the African Methodist Episcopal Church* (Philadelphia: A.M.E. Book Rooms, 1881), 104–111; T. G. Steward, *Fifty Years in the Gospel Ministry* (Philadelphia: A.M.E. Book Concern, 1921), 42–50; Smith, *History*, 59; Hugh T. Harrington, "John C. Calhoun's Casket," *Carologue* (Fall 2009), SCHS.

Calhoun's tomb was empty when Wayman and Weaver visited as his coffin had been temporarily removed in 1863 to protect it from possible desecration by Union soldiers. It was returned in 1871.

154 **At a meeting at Zion:** Elisha Weaver, "Editorial Correspondence," *CR*, April 29, 1865; Elisha Weaver, "A Continuation," *CR*, May 6, 1865; James Lynch, "Organization of the African Methodist Church in Charleston," *CR*, May 6, 1865; "For the Christian Recorder," *CR*, May 6, 1865.

154 **They thronged to mass meetings:** "Department of the South," *NYT*, April 4, 1865, 9; "Large Meeting at Zion Church," *CC*, April 29, 1865, 2; "Large Meeting at Zion Church," *CC*, May 13, 1865, 2; Richard H. Cain, "Charleston Correspondence," *CR*, August 26, 1865; Richard H. Cain, "Our Charleston Letter," *CR*, September 30, 1865.

154 **Most everyone in town:** "Freedmen's Jubilee," *CC*, March 22, 1865, 2; "Fort Sumter," *NYT*, April 18, 1865, 8; "Charleston," *The New York Herald*, April 18, 1865, 4; Frank A. Rollin, *Life and Public Services of Martin R. Delany* (Boston: Lee and Shepard, 1883), 193–194.

155 **The grand culmination of the AME reoccupation:** Payne, *History*, 469–470; Payne, *Recollections*, 161–165.

155 **Payne and his young companions:** Payne, *Recollections*, 162; Steward, *Fifty Years*, 28–31; Arnett, *Proceedings*, 49; Richard H. Cain, "South Carolina Correspondence," *CR*, May 27, 1865.

156 **Bishop Payne saw:** Payne, *Recollections*, 162–163; Arnett, *Proceedings*, 74–75; Cain, "South Carolina Correspondence," *CR*, May 27, 1865; Payne, *History*, 469–470; Smith, *History*, 60.

156 **At 10:00 a.m. the next morning:** Payne, *History*, 469–470; Arnett, *Proceedings*, 40, 49–52; Tanner, *Apology*, 366–368; "South Carolina Conference of the African Methodist Episcopal Church," *CC*, May 16, 1865, 2; "Methodist Conference," *CC*, May 17, 1865, 3; "Meeting of the South Carolina Conference," *CR*, June 3, 1865; Gravely, "Lynch," 171.

156 **"Thus equipped":** Payne, "Organization," 40–41.

156 **The conference pioneers:** "Meeting of the South Carolina Conference," *CR*, June 3, 1865; Steward, *Fifty Years*, 31 (contradicting Steward, the *CC* of May 19, 1865, 2, titled Delany's address "The Origin of the Races," not "The Unity of the Races").

157 **The conference proceedings:** Richard H. Cain, "Charleston Correspondence," *CR*, June 3, 1865.

157 **Cain wrote:** Cain, "Charleston Correspondence," June 3, 1865.

157 **On the conference's fourth day:** "Meeting of the South Carolina Conference," *CR*, June 3, 1865; "Methodist Conference," *CC*, May 19, 1865, 2.

157 **He did not want to appear:** T. Willard Lewis, "Methodist Episcopal Church," *CC*, June 1, 1865, 2; Cain, "Charleston Correspondence," *CR*, June 3, 1865.

158 **By the end of May:** "The African M.E. Church," *CC*, May 31, 1865, 2; R. H. Cain, "Charleston Correspondence," *CR*, August 5, 1865.

158 **The denomination's growth:** Smith, *History*, 504, 508, 514, 517–519, 524.

158 **Thanks to the voracious appetite:** *Minutes of the Thirteenth General Conference of the African M.E. Church, Held in Philadelphia, PA., May 2, 1864* (Philadelphia: William S. Young, 1864), 30; Benjamin W. Arnett, ed., *The Budget for 1881* (Xenia, OH: Torchlight Printing Company, 1881), 41; Benjamin W. Arnett, ed., *The Budget for 1884* (Dayton: Christian Publishing House, 1884), 70; Benjamin W. Arnett, ed., *Journal of the 17th Session and the 16th Quadrennial Session of the General Conference of the African Methodist Episcopal Church in the United States, Held at St. Louis, Missouri, May 3–25, 1880* (Xenia, Ohio: Torchlight Printing Company, 1882), 122–123; *The Sixteenth Session, and the Fifteenth Quadrennial Session of the General Conference of the African Methodist Episcopal Church. Place of Session, Atlanta, Georgia, from May 1st to 18th, 1876*, 68, 87–88; *Minutes of the Annual Conferences of the Methodist Episcopal*

Church, South, for the Year 1861 (Nashville: Southern Methodist Publishing House, 1870), 336–337; *Minutes of the South Carolina Conference of the Methodist Episcopal Church, South, for 1864, 1865, and 1866* (Charleston: Weekly Record Publishing House, 1867), 22, 26; Smith, *History*, 496, 519, 524.

159 **Cain's timetable:** R. H. Cain, "Charleston Correspondence," *CR*, August 5, 1865.

CHAPTER X: RESURRECTION

160 **As the Civil War drew to its close:** Wesley Loy, "10 Rumford Place: Doing Confederate Business in Liverpool," *SCHM* 98, no. 4 (October 1997): 349–374; "Mr. George Trenholm," *NYT*, February 13, 1868, 1; Ethel Trenholm Seabrook Nepveux, *George A. Trenholm: Financial Genius of the Confederacy, His Associates and His Ships That Ran the Blockade* (Anderson, SC: The Electric City Printing Company, 1999), 14, 17, 98, 107; Ethel Trenholm Seabrook Nepveux, *George Alfred Trenholm and the Company That Went to War, 1861–1865* (Charleston: Comprint, 1973); E. Lee Spence, *Treasures of the Confederate Coast: The Real Rhett Butler & Other Revelations* (Miami: Narwhal Press, 1995).

160 **When the Confederate government evacuated:** Nepveux, *George A. Trenholm*, 157–167; CCDB, September 6, 1865, B15:101–102, and September 6, 1865, A14.5:109–111, CCROD; Letter from George A. Trenholm, September 10, 1865, George Alfred Trenholm Papers, USCSCL.

161 **Five original church trustees:** CCDB, September 6, 1865, B15:101–102, September 6, 1865, A14.5:109–111, June 24, 1863, T14.2:31–32, CCROD.

The author is indebted to Charleston archivists and researchers Nic Butler, Harlan Greene, and Doreen Larimer for their analysis of the deed and mortgage.

161 **The lot ran 50 feet:** CCDB, September 6, 1865, B15:101–102; Nic Butler, "Squeezing Charleston Neck, from 1783 to the Present," *CTM*, August 31, 2018, CCPL; R. H. Cain, "Charleston Correspondence," *CR*, October 14, 1865; "The Colored Churches," *SN*, October 2, 1881, Willis Pamphlets, 1878–84, CLS.

162 **It seemed fitting:** Cain, "Charleston Correspondence," *CR*, October 14, 1865; "African Methodist Church," *CDN*, May 28, 1866, 5 (This article ballparks capacity at "about two thousand").

162 **Rev. Cain presided over an afternoon:** Cain, "Charleston Correspondence," October 14, 1865; "New Emanuel Church," *CR*, September 17, 1891; Arnett, *Proceedings*, 30; Al Dunmore, "Annie and Her Church," *Courier*, February 23, 1952.

163 **The pastor estimated the cost:** Cain, "Charleston Correspondence," October 14, 1865; E. J. Adams, "Religious Progress at Charleston," *CR*, April 28, 1866; "The Colored Churches," *SN*, October 2, 1881, CLS; FB, Registers of Signatures of Depositors, 1865–1874, roll 21, no. 3364.

163 **Until the Calhoun Street site could be occupied:** Cain, "Charleston Correspondence," *CR*, October 14, 1865; Arnett, *Proceedings*, 105; "The Methodist Episcopal Church, South, and the Colored People," *CC*, October 14, 1865, 2.

163 **"These persons prefer":** "The Methodist Episcopal Church, South, and the Colored People."

163 **Although still under construction:** "African M.E. Church," *SCL*, February 24, 1866, 2; "Grand Fair for the Benefit of the African M.E. Church," *SC*, March 31, 1866, 3; Charlotte S. Riley, *A Mysterious Life and Calling: From Slavery to Ministry in South Carolina*, Crystal J. Lucky, ed. (Madison: The University of Wisconsin Press, 2016), 46–47; "An Appeal to the Charitable," *CDN*, February 22, 1867, 3; A. W. Wayman, "Communications: A Tour South," *CR*, March 9, 1867; "Old Folk's Home," *CR*, May 4, 1867; "Camp Meeting," *SCL*, May 12, 1866, 2; "Camp Meeting," *CDN*, May 14, 1866, 5; Richard H. Cain, "South Carolina Correspondence," *CR*, May 19, 1866; "Colored Maroon," *CDN*, June 7, 1866, 5.

164 **Missionaries' dispatches from Charleston:** E. J. Adams, "Religious Progress at Charleston," *CR*, April 28, 1866; "Personal Items," *CR*, July 28, 1866; Wayman, "Communications," *CR*, March 9, 1867; "Procession of Colored Children," *CDN*, October 19, 1867, 3; "Emancipation Anniversary," *CM*, January 4, 1868, 4; "Notice," *CDN*, August 6, 1870, 3; "Major Delany on The African Race," *The South Carolina Republican*, January 23, 1869, 3; "The Batson Concert," *NC*, January 23, 1889, 2; "The Dying Year," *NC*, January 1, 1885, 12; "Remarkable Religious Manifestations," *NC*, May 27, 1879, 4.

165 **The *South Carolina Leader*:** "African M.E. Church," *SCL*, February 24, 1866, 2; *SCL*, March 31, 1866, 2.

165 **Bishop Payne returned:** "AME Conference," *SCL*, May 12, 1866, 2; "Savannah Items," *CDN*, May 19, 1866, 5; "Religious Notice," *CDN*, May 26, 1866, 1; "African Methodist Church," *CDN*, May 28, 1866, 5; Riley, *Mysterious Life*, 110–111; Smith, *History*, 506–508; Richard Harvey Cain, "Communications: Charleston Correspondence," *CR*, June 29, 1867.

Although it is not clear when, the church had been named before the dedication service on May 27, 1866, as it was presented as "Immanuel Church" in the minutes of the second session of the South Carolina Annual Conference, held the week prior in Savannah and attended by Bishop Payne and Reverend Cain. The name "Emanuel Church" seems to first appear in a Charleston newspaper in a front-page funeral notice in *CDN* on October 8, 1867.

165 **In these churches:** Daniel A. Payne, "The African M.E. Church in Its Relations to the Freedmen," *Bishop Payne's Address Before the College Aid Society* (Xenia, OH: Torchlight Co., 1868), 4, LCP; Adams, "Religious Progress," *CR*, April 28, 1866; R. H. Cain, "Correspondence from South Carolina," *CR*, June 23, 1866; Wayman, "Communications," *CR*, March 9, 1867; P. W. Johnson, "From the Edisto District," *CR*, December 13, 1883; *Minutes of the Eleventh Session of the South Carolina Annual Conference of the African Methodist Episcopal Church Held at Abbeville, C.H., S.C., From February 6 to February 16, 1875* (Charleston: Walker, Evans & Cogswell, 1875), Tables A and B, SCHS; *Minutes of the Nineteenth Session of the South Carolina Annual Conference of the African Methodist Episcopal Church Held at Charleston, S.C., from February 14th to February 20th, 1883* (Charleston: Walker, Evans & Cogswell, 1883), 44, SCHS.

166 **He had been born free:** Bernard E. Powers, Jr., "'I Go to Set the Captives Free': The Activism of Richard Harvey Cain, Nationalist Churchman and Reconstruction-Era Leader," in *The Southern Elite and Social Change*, ed. Randy Finley and Thomas A. DeBlack (Fayetteville: The University of Arkansas Press, 2002), 34–43; William J. Simmons, *Men of Mark: Eminent, Progressive and Rising* (Cleveland: Geo. M. Rewell & Co., 1887), 866–871; Martin A. Parlett, "Like a Lion Bound, Hear Him Roar: Richard Harvey Cain and a Rhetoric of Reconstruction," in *Before Obama: A Reappraisal of Black Reconstruction Era Politicians*, Vol. 2, *Black Reconstruction Era Politicians: The Fifteenth Amendment in Flesh and Blood*, ed. Matthew Lynch (Santa Barbara: Praeger, 2012), 2:285–312; "Programme of the Funeral Services of Bishop Richard H. Cain, January 21, '87," *CR*, February 3, 1887; Rayford W. Logan and Michael R. Winston, eds., *Dictionary of American Negro Biography* (New York: W. W. Norton & Company, 1982), 84.

166 **In the late 1850s:** Payne, *Recollections*, 332; Cain, "First Missionaries"; "Brooklyn Correspondence," *CR*, June 20, 1863; *Cong. Rec.*, House, 43rd Congress, 1st Session, January 10, 1874 (Washington, D.C.: Government Printing Office, 1875), 566.

167 **In both the Midwest and in New York:** Powers, "'I Go to Set'"; Parlett, "Like a Lion"; "Brooklyn Correspondence," *CR*, January 23, 1864; Cain, "First Missionaries"; Cain, "Brooklyn Correspondence," *CR*, June 20, 1863.

167 **Cain felt he could employ:** R. H. Cain, "Highly Important from South Carolina," *CR*, February 24, 1866; "South Carolina Correspondence," *CR*, September 29, 1866.

168 **Dozens of preachers:** Smith, *History*, 508, 512; Benjamin T. Tanner, *An Apology for African Methodism* (Baltimore: Publisher not identified, 1867), 377–379; Bernard E. Powers, Jr., *Black Charlestonians: A Social History, 1822–1885* (Fayetteville: The University of Arkansas Press, 1994), 204–205; Reginald F. Hildebrand, *The Times Were Strange and Stirring: Methodist Preachers and the Crisis of Emancipation* (Durham, NC: Duke University Press, 1995), 62; Harry V. Richardson, *Dark Salvation: The Story of Methodism as It Developed Among Blacks in America* (Garden City, NY: Anchor Press-Doubleday, 1976), 199; C. H. Phillips, *The History of the Colored Methodist Episcopal Church in America: Comprising its Organization, Subsequent Development and Present Status* (Jackson, TN: Publishing House C.M.E. Church, 1925), 204–208; "Death of Bishop Vanderhorst," *CDN*, July 19, 1872, 1.

168 **Rarely one to shun hyperbole:** Richard Harvey Cain, "Our Charleston Correspondence," *CR*, October 21, 1865; Cain, "Highly Important"; Cain, "South Carolina Correspondence," *CR*, May 19, 1866.

169 **But as the pioneering historian:** Carter G. Woodson, *The History of the Negro Church*

(Washington, D.C.: The Associated Publishers, 1921), 66; "The African Methodist Episcopal Church and the Methodist Episcopal Church and the Coming General Conferences," *CR*, April 2, 1864.

169 **"Our success has been abundant":** *The Fifteenth Quadrennial Session of the General Conference of the African Methodist Episcopal Church, Place of Session, Nashville, Tennessee, May 6, 1872*, 39.

169 **Other denominations competed vigorously:** Wilbert L. Jenkins, *Seizing the New Day: African-Americans in Post–Civil War Charleston* (Bloomington: Indiana University Press, 1998), 125–126; William E. Montgomery, *Under Their Own Vine and Fig Tree: The African-American Church in the South, 1865–1900* (Baton Rouge: Louisiana State University Press, 1993), 259–260; Powers, *Black Charlestonians*, 214–216; "Impressions of Charleston," *CR*, September 8, 1866; "It Depends on the Dye," *NC*, June 22, 1888, 6; Interview with Minerva King and Walter Boags.

170 **That was decidedly not the milieu:** "Impressions of Charleston"; R. H. Cain, "South Carolina Correspondence," *CR*, April 21, 1866; Arnett, *Proceedings*, 105–107.

170 **"The reason that the Church is":** Arnett, *Proceedings*, 105–107.

171 **"Conversion from the Negroes' point of view":** A. A. Taylor, "Religious Influences," *JNH* 9, no. 3 (July 1924): 346–347.

171 **Ever covetous of white respectability:** Payne, *Recollections*, 253–256.

172 **Rev. James H. A. Johnson:** Arnett, *Proceedings*, 48, 53–54.

172 **"If a pine tree that is to stand":** "From Charleston. A Sermon by Rev. Henry Ward Beecher," *NYT*, April 23, 1865, 2.

173 **Alcohol was an evergreen concern:** *Minutes of the General and Annual Conferences, of the African Methodist Episcopal Church, Comprising Four Districts, For A.D. 1839–40* (Brooklyn: George Hogarth, 1840), 21–22; *Minutes of the Twelfth Session of the South Carolina Conference of the African Methodist Episcopal Church held at Charleston, S.C., from February 1st to February 10th, 1876* (Charleston: Walker, Evans & Cogswell, 1876), 19, 23; *Fifteenth Quadrennial Session*, 30, 44, 85; *Minutes of the Thirteenth General Conference of the African M.E. Church, Held in Philadelphia, PA, May 2, 1864* (Philadelphia: William S. Young, 1864), 11, 12, 19.

173 **"We wore calicoes":** Lisa Foster with Mary Lou Murray Coombs, *Janie Mitchell, Reliable Cook: An Ex-Slave's Recipe for Living, 1862–1931* (Charleston: Evening Post Books, 2011), 91.

173 **To men like Bishop Payne:** Smith, *History*, 520; Tanner, *Apology*, 372; James T. Campbell, *Songs of Zion: The African Methodist Episcopal Church in the United States and South Africa* (Chapel Hill: The University of North Carolina Press, 1998), 60–61; "The Rights of Colored Men and Women," *CR*, January 7, 1865; Richard H. Cain, "Charleston Correspondence," *CR*, June 29, 1867.

174 **When Black congregants experienced:** Richard H. Cain, "Our Charleston Letter," *CR*, September 30, 1865; Cain, "Charleston Correspondence," June 29, 1867; Foster, *Janie Mitchell*, 95.

174 **There was a cadre:** Details on occupations were obtained from Charleston city directories for various years and U.S. Freedman's Bank records.

174 **Moses Vanderhorst:** Arnett, *Proceedings*, 75; Bill of Sale, April 18, 1849, Misc. Records, series S213050, 6B:579, and Bill of Sale, June 1, 1849, Misc. Records, series S213050, 6B:580, SCDAH; FB for George Garrett, September 12, 1871; Census of 1850 for Free Inhabitants of the Parishes of St. Philip and St. Michael, 144, and Schedule of Slave Inhabitants, 112–113; Confederate Papers Relating to Citizens or Business Firms, Publication M346, no. 299, roll 153, 3, NARA.

The author found no manumission or capitation tax records to suggest that Moses Vanderhorst had been freed before 1865. Robert Cattle's surname is spelled "Cattel" in some records.

175 **Henry C. Hammond:** "African M.E. Church—Calhoun Street Charge," *CDN*, March 15, 1873, 4; "Election of Officers," *CDN*, May 5, 1870, 3; "Mechanics' Association," *SCL*, December 23, 1865, 3; "Grand Fair," *SCL*, March 31, 1866, 3; FB, roll 21, Charleston, SC, December 19, 1865–December 2, 1869, no. 2319, and roll 22, Charleston, SC, December 4, 1869–February 25, 1871, no. 4158; "An Appeal to the Charitable," *CDN*, February 22, 1867, 3; "Result of the Municipal Election," *NC*, October 8, 1875, 4; "Installation of the New Council," *NC*, November 16, 1875, 4; "Mass Meeting!" *SCL*, October 21, 1865, 3; "Mass Meeting of the

Colored Citizens of Charleston," *CDN*, March 22, 1867, 1; "The Convention of the Union Republican Party of South Carolina," *CC*, July 26, 1867, 1; "Celebration of the 91st Anniversary of American Independence," *CDN*, July 3, 1867, 2; "Grand Celebration in Honor of the Emancipation Proclamation of President Lincoln," *SCL*, December 16, 1865, 3; "The Day We Celebrate," *SCL*, January 6, 1866, 2.

175   **For on March 22:** "A Fowl Thief Shot," *NC*, March 23, 1875, 4; "The Fowl-Thief Shooting Affair," *NC*, March 24, 1875, 4.

176   **One such neighborhood:** *Born in Slavery: Slave Narratives from the Federal Writers' Project, 1936–1938* (Washington, D.C.: Library of Congress, 1941), 14.2:223–236; "WPA Writers' Program Records Appraisal Sheet," LOC, WPA Records, box A906.

Susan Hamlin actually had two conversations with Jessie Butler as Butler later happened upon her strolling down King Street, stopped to chat, and wrote up Hamlin's comments, apparently from memory, as if verbatim. Further evidence of Butler's mindset is provided by her depiction in another slave narrative of her subject's home as "clean and neat," with "none of the musty, stale odor about the place common to negro dwellings." *Born in Slavery*, 14.3:197.

177   **Hamlin described herself to her visitors:** *Born in Slavery*, 14.2:223–236.

177   **Hamlin was born not in Charleston:** *Born in Slavery*, 14.2:223–236; Townsend Mikell, *The Mikell Genealogy of South Carolina* (Charleston: Walker, Evans and Cogswell Company, 1910), 20–22.

178   **After Ephraim Mikell's death:** *Born in Slavery*, 14.2:223–236; "Will of Ephraim Mikell," *Wills, Charleston County, South Carolina, 1740–1747*, 5:717–721; *Catalogue of the Officers and Students of the College of New Jersey for 1837 and 1838* (Princeton: John Bogart, 1838); "Mr. Edward N. Fuller," *NC*, May 23, 1896, 8; CCDB, T13:95, CCROD.

CHAPTER XI: MOTHER CHURCH, AND THE DADDY OF RECONSTRUCTION

180   **A year before the Civil War ended:** Richard Harvey Cain, "Our Duty in the Crisis," *CR*, May 7, 1864; *Cong. Rec.*, House of Representatives, 43rd Congress, 2nd Session, February 3, 1875, 956.

180   **Cain was not alone:** R. H. Cain, "South Carolina Correspondence," *CR*, April 21, 1866; Reginald F. Hildebrand, *The Times Were Strange and Stirring: Methodist Preachers and the Crisis of Emancipation* (Durham, NC: Duke University Press, 1995), 51; Eric Foner, *Freedom's Lawmakers: A Directory of Black Officeholders during Reconstruction, Revised Edition* (Baton Rouge: Louisiana State University Press, 1993), xiii–xv.

Mississippi and Louisiana also had Black majorities in 1870.

181   **He also became an exemplar:** "National Freedman's Savings and Trust Company," *CC*, January 12, 1867, 3; "The Enterprise Railroad Company," *CDN*, March 25, 1870, 3; "The Details of the Legislative Proceedings of Wednesday," *CDN*, December 15, 1871, 1; "A Storm Abrewing," *CDN*, February 17, 1870, 1; "Famous Indignation Meeting," *CDN*, February 18, 1870, 1; Bernard E. Powers, Jr., *Black Charlestonians: A Social History, 1822–1885* (Fayetteville: The University of Arkansas Press, 1994), 168–170; "Our Paper," *Missionary Record*, April 1, 1876, 3.

In 1870, Cain introduced the South Carolina senate bill to incorporate the Enterprise Railway Company, which he owned in part and served as president.

181   **As pastor, Cain regularly made:** "Mass Meeting of Freedmen," *CC*, February 15, 1867, 2; "Mass Meeting of the Freedmen," *CM*, February 15, 1867, 1; "The African Meeting," *CDN*, February 15, 1867, 1.

181   **When a Black teenager:** R. H. Cain (November 14, 1867) and D. W. Logan (November 21, 1867) to R. K. Scott, FB, Assistant Commissioner, Letters Received, November 1866–December 1867, A-E, roll 12, images 524–530, NARA; "Jefferson Williams: Death of a Well Known and Respectable Negro," *EP*, May 2, 1898, 4.

Williams's funeral was held at Emanuel and he is buried in its graveyard.

182   **When Emanuel developed plans:** FB, Assistant Commissioner, Letters Received, 1865–1872, roll 5, January 14, 1867, 54; January 18, 1867, 56; May 20, 1867, 70; June 19, 1867, 74; Endorse-

ment Sent, vol. 1–5, 1865–1870, roll 3, January 17, 1867, 28; January 24, 1867, 48; February 5, 1867, 58; February 11, 1867, 88; February 23, 1867, 96; June 21, 1867, 417, NARA.

182 **In short order:** "South Carolina: The Educational Interests of the State," *NYT*, July 3, 1874, 1; "Appointments of the South Carolina Conference," *CR*, February 13, 1869; "Count of the Canvassers," *NC*, November 25, 1882, 1; "The State Legislature: Biographical Sketches of the Members," *NC*, December 1, 1884, 3; Thomas Holt, *Black over White, Negro Political Leadership in South Carolina during Reconstruction* (Urbana: University of Illinois Press, 1977), 39, 228–241; Foner, *Freedom's Lawmakers*, xiv, xxi.

Emanuel's later history of direct political involvement by its ministers, in addition to Sen. Pinckney, included an unsuccessful race by Rev. Frank Veal for the state house of representatives in 1952, while he was pastor. "S.C. House to Have Many New Faces; Few Senate Changes," *NC*, July 9, 1952, 6-A.

183 **Once the Civil War ended:** Eric Foner, *Reconstruction: America's Unfinished Revolution, 1863–1877* (New York: Harper & Row, 1988), 176–184, 187–188, 193.

Certain categories of Southerners, including former Confederate officials and wealthy property owners, were exempted from the general amnesty and had to apply for individual presidential pardons.

183 **As it happened:** Herbert Aptheker, "South Carolina Negro Conventions, 1865," *JNH* 31, no. 1 (January 1946): 91–92.

184 **The provisional governor:** "Message of Gov. Perry," *NYT*, September 20, 1865, 1; *Journal of the Convention of the People of South Carolina, Held in Columbia, S.C., December 1865* (Columbia: J. A. Selby, 1865), 166.

Black citizenship was not guaranteed until the Dred Scott decision was effectively repealed by ratification of the Fourteenth Amendment on July 9, 1868, when South Carolina and Louisiana provided the final needed approvals.

184 **Three days after the constitutional convention adjourned:** "Our Charleston Letter," *CR*, September 30, 1865.

185 **In late November:** *Proceedings of the Colored People's Convention of the State of South Carolina, Held in Zion Church, Charleston, November, 1865* (Charleston: South Carolina Leader Office, 1865), 5–8; Aptheker, "Negro Conventions," 91–97.

It is not clear whether Joseph Russel became a trustee before the November 1865 convention or shortly thereafter. He was not among the five who signed the deed for the Calhoun Street property in September 1865 but is listed as a trustee in an advertisement for the church fair, *SCL*, March 31, 1866, 3. Some documents spell his surname "Russell."

185 **Frustrated that freedom had not translated:** *Proceedings of the Colored People's Convention*, 22–31; Powers, *Black Charlestonians*, 82–84; "The Mass Meeting," *SCL*, October 28, 1865, 2; Michael E. Ruane, "In 1865, Thousands of Black South Carolinians Signed a 54-Foot-Long Freedom Petition," *WP*, September 23, 2021; Holt, *Black over White*, 14–23.

The petition went on display at the Smithsonian's National Museum of African American History and Culture in 2021.

185 **"We ask for no special privileges":** *Proceedings of the Colored People's Convention*, 13–14, 24–25.

185 **On the meeting's third night:** *Proceedings of the Colored People's Convention*, 13–14; "State Convention: Colored People In Council," *SCL*, November 25, 1865, 2.

186 **To no one's surprise:** *Acts of the General Assembly of the State of South Carolina, Passed at the Sessions of 1864–65* (Columbia: Julian A. Selby, 1866), 271–304; Walter Edgar, *South Carolina: A History* (Columbia: University of South Carolina Press, 1998), 383–384; Francis Butler Simkins and Robert Hilliard Woody, *South Carolina During Reconstruction* (Chapel Hill: The University of North Carolina Press, 1932), 48–50; Foner, *Reconstruction*, 199–200; Powers, *Black Charlestonians*, 80–82.

186 **The new laws:** *Acts of the General Assembly*, 271–304.

187 **In electing constitutional convention delegates:** Edgar, *South Carolina*, 386–387; Joel Williamson, *After Slavery: The Negro in South Carolina During Reconstruction, 1861–1877* (New York: W. W. Norton & Company, 1965), 343, 369, 377; Monroe N. Work, et al., "Some Negro Members of Reconstruction Conventions and Legislatures and of Congress," *JNH* 5, no. 1

(January 1920): 79–81; Nic Butler, "The South Carolina Constitutional Convention of 1868," *CTM*, March 2, 2018; Holt, *Black over White*, Table 5; A. A. Taylor, "The Convention of 1868," *JNH* 9, no. 4 (October 1924): 381–408.

Contemporaneous news reports and calculations by historians have produced a range for the number of Black delegates at the 1868 constitutional convention, from as low as 69 to as high as 76 of the 124 total. They always comprise a majority.

187 **Cain's reach was already expanding:** "Our New Exchanges," *CR*, June 30, 1866; "Our Paper," *Missionary Record*; "Famous Indignation Meeting," *CDN*, February 18, 1870, 1; "Public Meeting," *CC*, March 22, 1867, 1; "Mass Meeting of Freedmen," *CC*, March 27, 1867, 2; "The State Union Convention, So-Called," *CDN*, May 9, 1867, 3.

Cain converted his newspaper, by then renamed the *Missionary Record*, into a mouthpiece for the South Carolina Conference of the AME Church in 1876.

187 **Cain played a central role:** *Proceedings of the Constitutional Convention of South Carolina, Held at Charleston, S.C., Beginning January 14th and ending March 17th, 1868* (Charleston: Denny & Perry, 1868), 107–110, 196–197, 379–381, 409–424; "The Convention," *CDN*, February 19, 1868, 1; "The Convention," *CDN*, February 22, 1868, 1; "The Freedmen's Bureau," *NYT*, October 9, 1868, 1.

188 **The arch-conservative *Charleston Mercury*:** "The Great Ringed-Streaked and Striped," *CM*, January 24, 1868, 1; "Sketches of the Delegates to the Great Ringed-Streaked-and-Striped," *CM*, January 28, 1868, 1.

189 **At another juncture:** "The Great Ringed-Streaked and Striped"; "The Convention," *CDN*, January 28, 1868, 1; "Cain's Pony," *CM*, May 27, 1868, 1; "Alderman Cain in Danger of Losing His Pony," *CM*, June 1, 1868, 1; "A Reverend Senatorial Alderman's Pony Seized for Debt," *CM*, June 10, 1868, 1; "Fire Brands," *CM*, June 23, 1868, 2; "Cain's Pony Once More," *CM*, June 24, 1868, 1; "The Rev. Cain Reduced to the Ranks," *CDN*, June 10, 1868, 3; Cal M. Logue, "Racist Reporting During Reconstruction," *Journal of Black Studies* 9, no. 3 (March 1979): 335–349.

189 **"The colored men":** "South Carolina," *NYT*, January 21, 1868, 2.

189 **The new state constitution:** *Proceedings of the Constitutional Convention*, 789–793; Butler, "South Carolina Constitutional Convention of 1868"; Edgar, *South Carolina*, 387; Williamson, *After Slavery*, 343.

190 **Within two weeks:** "The District Nominating Convention," *CDN*, March 28, 1868, 3; "Election of 1868," *The Free Press*, April 5, 1868, 2; "Politics in the State," *CDN*, April 10, 1868, 1; "The Election," *CC*, April 25, 1868, 2; Holt, *Black over White*, 97.

190 **A month after his election:** "Removal of Aldermen," *CDN*, May 27, 1868, 2; "Municipal Changes," *CDN*, May 27, 1868, 3; "Our City Government," *CDN*, May 27, 1868, 3; Bernard E. Powers, Jr. "Community Evolution and Race Relations in Reconstruction Charleston, South Carolina," *SCHM* 101, no. 3 (July 2000): 217–218; "The Whirlwind Cometh—Beware!" *CDN*, June 23, 1868, 1; "Fire Brands," *CM*, June 23, 1868, 2; "The Incendiary Torch," *CDN*, June 23, 1868, 2; "Two More New Aldermen," *CDN*, July 13, 1868, 3.

190 **Cain left Emanuel's pulpit:** "Appointments of the South Carolina Conference," *CR*, February 13, 1869; "Jottings About the State," *CDN*, March 1, 1872, 1; "South Carolina Conference Appointments," *CR*, February 24, 1876; "Fourth of July Sermon," *CC*, July 6, 1869, 1; "The Fourth," *CC*, July 6, 1869, 1.

191 **Among his first proposals:** "The State Legislature," *CC*, July 9, 1868, 1; "From the State Capital," *CDN*, July 11, 1868, 1; "Our Columbia Letter," *CC*, September 5, 1868, 4.

191 **"He said that prejudices":** "The Debate on the Discrimination Bill," *CDN*, September 5, 1868, 1; Powers, *Black Charlestonians*, 231–232.

192 **He was acutely aware:** *Proceedings of the Colored People's Convention*, 24; "A Colored Man to the Colored People," *CDN*, November 16, 1868, 2; "R.H. Cain," *CM*, November 10, 1868, 1.

192 **The *Courier* called Cain's speech:** "The Debate on the Discrimination Bill," *CDN*, September 5, 1868, 1; "Our Columbia Letter," *CC*, September 5, 1868, 4; "R.H. Cain," *CM*, November 10, 1868, 1; "A Colored Man to the Colored People," *CDN*, November 16, 1868, 1; "Sound and Sensible Advice," *CDN*, November 9, 1868, 2; "What Is the Real Duty of the Colored Man in the South Under the Present Circumstances?" *CC*, November 17, 1868, 1.

192 **The state house of representatives again sent:** "The Last Day of Legislation," *CDN*,

March 2, 1870, 1; *Acts and Joint Resolutions of the General Assembly of the State of South Carolina, Passed at the Regular Session of 1869–'70* (Columbia: John W. Denny, 1870), 386–388; *Journals of the General Assembly of the State of South Carolina Being the Regular Session of 1869–'70* (Columbia: John W. Denny, 1870), 447–448, 529.

193 **"When he secures the floor":** "The New Regime," *CDN*, March 8, 1870, 1.

193 **Both on the floor of the state senate:** "Out of Their Mouths," *CDN*, December 11, 1869, 2; "Cain for Reform," *CDN*, May 2, 1870, 1; "Cheating the People out of their Schools," *CDN*, May 16, 1870, 2; "Taken the Back Track," *CDN*, May 30, 1870, 2; "Coming Up," *CDN*, June 20, 1870, 2; "Hard on the Carpet-Baggers," *AI*, July 7, 1870, 3; "To the Editor of the Charleston Daily Courier," *CC*, August 8, 1871, 2.

Interestingly, given Cain's demands for Black representation, when he had control of the selection of a West Point cadet from his congressional district, he chose a white candidate. "Minor Topics," *NYT*, May 19, 1873, 4; "Our Swivel," *CR*, May 29, 1873.

193 **"Colored men must place":** "Senator Cain and the Radical Politicians," *CDN*, May 26, 1869, 2; "Cuffee's Chance to go to Congress—A Bugle Blast from Parson Cain," *CDN*, September 27, 1869, 2.

194 **Cain alienated party regulars:** "The Radical Nominations," *CDN*, September 16, 1870, 2; "The Bowen–DeLarge War," *CDN*, September 19, 1870, 3; "War to the Knife," *CDN*, September 29, 1870, 3; "The State Senatorship," *CDN*, October 19, 1870, 1; "Official Vote of the City," *CDN*, October 29, 1870, 1; *Reports and Resolutions of the General Assembly of the State of South Carolina at the Regular Session, 1872–'73* (Columbia: Republican Printing Company, 1873), 62; "The Rival Tickets," *CDN*, August 20, 1872, 1; "The State House Convention," *CC*, August 24, 1872, 1; "The Warring Factions," *CDN*, August 26, 1872, 1; "State Notices," *CDN*, November 20, 1872, 3.

194 **Four Republican officials:** "Murder of B.F. Randolph, Negro Senator from Orangeburg," *CDN*, October 19, 1868, 3; "The Violation of the Public Peace," *CC*, October 19, 1868, 2; "Funeral of B.F. Randolph," *CC*, October 21, 1868, 2; "The Mass Meeting Yesterday," *CM*, October 22, 1868, 1; "The Republican Meeting Yesterday," *CC*, October 22, 1868, 1; "Proclamations by His Excellency Robert K. Scott Governor of South Carolina," *CM*, October 22, 1868, 1; Holt, *Black over White*, 141–142.

The other Republicans killed were state representatives S.G.W. Dill and James Martin, both white, and Lee Nance, a Black delegate to the constitutional convention.

195 **It would later be learned:** Testimony of William K. Tolbert, *Testimony Taken by the Joint Select Committee to Inquire into the Condition of Affairs in the Late Insurrectionary States: South Carolina* (Washington, D.C.: Government Printing Office, 1872), 2:1256–1260.

195 **Naturally, Randolph's murder:** "The Randolph Murder," *CC*, October 20, 1868, 2; "The Republican Meeting Yesterday," *CC,* October 22, 1868; "The Mass Meeting Yesterday," *CM* October 22, 1868; "Proclamations by His Excellency Robert K. Scott," *CM*, October 22, 1868, 1; Richard H. Cain to Robert K. Scott, October 24, 1868, Scott Papers, series S516002, box 3, folder 12, SCDAH; Powers, *Black Charlestonians*, 230; "The Negro Military Organizations in Charleston," *CDN,* August 12, 1868, 2; "The Charleston Negroes on the 'Hamburg Massacre,'" *AI*, July 27, 1876, 2.

195 **Cain's family felt shadowed:** *Born in Slavery: Slave Narratives from the Federal Writers' Project, 1936–1938,* vol. 16, Texas, part 2 (Washington, D.C.: Library of Congress, 1941), 10–14.

In interviews with the author, several of Anna Jane Edwards's descendants recalled being warned by older family members not to pry too deeply into her background. Some heard whispers that Anna was not Cain's adopted daughter, but rather his biological one, fathered with a white woman from a prominent family. Interviews and emails with Corletta Nichole Campbell, Esther Collins, and Carieta Cain-Grizzell.

196 **Edwards, a formerly enslaved woman:** *Born in Slavery* 16, 2:10–14.

196 **"Attempts were made":** *Born in Slavery* 16, 2:10–14.

196 **Cain served two terms:** *The Fifteenth Quadrennial Session of the General Conference of the African Methodist Episcopal Church, Place of Session, Nashville, Tennessee, May 6, 1872,* 74–75.

Equity in public accommodations remained an abiding concern of Cain's after his political career. *CR* reported on January 19, 1882, and April 6, 1882, that then Bishop Cain and his wife sued a Texas railroad company for $25,000 in damages after being denied admission to first-class seats they had purchased. Upon the instruction of the judge that damages could only be awarded in the amount of the Cains' actual inconvenience, the federal jury returned a verdict of $4.80 in their favor.

197 **Cain used:** House of Representatives, *Cong. Rec.*, 43rd Congress, 1st Session, January 10, 1874, 565–566, and 2nd Session, February 3, 1875, 957, and February 4, 1875, 981.

197 **In his final address:** *Cong. Rec.*, 43rd Congress, 2nd Session, February 10, 1875, 1153; "Barack Obama's Remarks to the Democratic National Convention," *NYT*, July 27, 2004; Marie Le Baron, "Colored Congressmen," *National Republican*, April 16, 1874, 6.

198 **Cain's at-large seat:** "State Political Items," *Yorkville Enquirer*, October 1, 1874, 2.

198 **That troublesome sideline began one day:** Philip Dray, *Capitol Men: The Epic Story of Reconstruction Through the Lives of the First Black Congressmen* (New York: Houghton Mifflin, 2008), 368–370; Christine W. Hampton and Rosalee W. Washington, *The History of Lincolnville, South Carolina* (Charleston: BookSurge, 2007), 1–3; CCDB, Grantee Index, 1800–1881, CCROD.

The story of Cain's train trip and discovery of land for sale is related in several books, and is repeated by longtime Lincolnville residents. It does not appear to be documented in any primary source.

198 **It would eventually come to light:** "The Courts," *CDN*, January 14, 1873, 4; "Parson Cain's Peculiarities," *CDN*, January 14, 1873, 4; "Parson Cain's Defence," *CDN*, January 17, 1873, 1; "Daddy Cain's Legacy," *NC*, September 25, 1885, 8; "'Daddy' Cain's Legacy," *NC*, February 23, 1887, 12; "Daddy Cain's Dupes," *NC*, February 23, 1887, 6; "The Lincolnville Litigation," *NC*, February 25, 1887, 8; "A Congressman in Trouble," *Edgefield Advertiser*, May 1, 1873, 4; "South Carolina. The Men Who Hold Office in the State," *NYT*, June 15, 1874, 1.

The *NYT* article, which was based on an interview with Buttz, asserts that after Cain arrived in Charleston he was "charged with several petty offenses" and thus "fell into disfavor among the religious portion of the negro community, and was compelled to leave the church." If so, there is no record of either the offenses or the ouster. After Cain left Emanuel, AME bishops continued to assign him to significant posts throughout his tenure in South Carolina.

198 **No event in South Carolina:** Dray, *Capitol Men*, 234–244; Edgar, *South Carolina*, 402–404; Foner, *Reconstruction*, 570–572; "Bloody Work in Hamburg," *NC*, July 10, 1876, 1.

199 **Nine days after:** "The Meeting Last Night," *NC*, July 18, 1876, 4; "The Meaning of Hamburg," *NYT*, July 24, 1876, 6; "The Charleston Negroes on the 'Hamburg Massacre,'" *AI*, July 27, 1876, 2.

200 **He had won the Republican nomination:** Stanley B. Parsons, William W. Beach, and Michael J. Dubin, *United States Congressional Districts and Data, 1843–1883* (New York: Greenwood Press, 1986); *Reports and Resolutions of the General Assembly of the State of South Carolina at the Regular Session, 1876–'77* (Columbia: Republican Printing Company, 1877), 217.

200 **Despite his victory margin:** Martin A. Parlett, "Like a Lion Bound, Hear Him Roar: Richard Harvey Cain and a Rhetoric of Reconstruction," in *Before Obama: A Reappraisal of Black Reconstruction Era Politicians*, Vol. 2, *Black Reconstruction Era Politicians: The Fifteenth Amendment in Flesh and Blood*, ed. Matthew Lynch (Santa Barbara: Praeger, 2012), 308; Papers in the Case of *O'Connor v. Cain,* Second District, SC, 45th Congress, House of Representatives, 2nd Session, Mis. Doc. No. 45, March 22, 1878; "The Contest for Congress," *NC*, October 1, 1877, 1; "A Well Timed Protest," *The News and Herald*, October 4, 1877, 2; "Washington: Business in the House," *NYT*, October 17, 1877, 1; "Timid Democrats," *AI*, April 18, 1878, 2; "General Washington Despatches," *The New York Herald*, March 10, 1877, 5; "Interviewing Hayes," *AI*, March 15, 1877, 2; "The Last of the Usurpation," *AI*, April 19, 1877, 1; Edgar, *South Carolina*, 405–407.

200 **Over the next dozen years:** Edgar, *South Carolina*, 413–416, 443–448; George G. Tindall, "The Campaign for the Disenfranchisement of Negroes in South Carolina," *JSH* 15, no. 2 (May 1949): 216–217.

201 **In 1890, the state elected:** Edgar, *South Carolina*, 443–448; *Inaugural Address of B. R. Tillman, Governor of South Carolina, Delivered at Columbia, S.C., December 4, 1890* (Columbia:

James H. Woodrow, 1890); *Constitution of the State of South Carolina, Ratified in Convention, December 4, 1895* (Abbeville, SC: Hugh Wilson, 1900), 9–12, 18, 45; *Civil Rights Cases*, 109 U.S. 3 (1883).

201 **Cain's faith in radical Republicanism:** "Coming Up," *CDN*, June 20, 1870, 3; Robert J. Holland, "Missionary Meeting," *CR*, January 24, 1878; *Minutes of the Eleventh Session of the South Carolina Annual Conference*, 27–29.

Cain's disenchantment was broadly shared within the AME leadership. In 1875, the bishops issued an "Address to the American People" that declared Reconstruction to have been "a miserable disappointment." It added: "We feel that we are at the very mouth of another lion's den, at the very door of another fiery furnace; nor do those whom we have served with the utmost fidelity seem to hesitate to push us in . . . Alas! all is changed, and, instead of assuring us an equal chance in the race of life, we are called upon to answer for all the country's woes."

202 **Melding his primary:** Parlett, "Like a Lion," 308–311; House of Representatives, *Cong. Rec.*, 43rd Congress, 1st Session, January 24, 1874, 902; 45th Congress, 2nd Session, March 11, 1878, 1646, and 3rd Session, January 23, 1879, 683–688; Richard H. Cain to William Coppinger, January 25, 1877, American Colonization Society Papers, vol. 196, LOC; George B. Tindall, "The Liberian Exodus of 1878," *SCHM* 53, no. 3 (July 1952): 134; "The African Exodus," *NC*, April 16, 1878, 1; "Coming Home," *Orangeburg Times*, January 23, 1880, 2; Lahnice McFall Hollister, ed., *Resisting Jim Crow: The Autobiography of Dr. John A. McFall* (Simpsonville, SC: Kittawah Press, 2021), 11.

Mass emigration to Africa may not have been Cain's only radical solution to the end of Reconstruction. John McFall, a prominent Black druggist who was born in Charleston in 1878, wrote in a memoir that Cain also advocated making South Carolina a Black state. Cain "insisted that so long as the whites were able to dominate the Negroes, so long would injustice and strife continue. He wanted to have South Carolina a solidly black state to which the Negroes from elsewhere in the United States could settle and there work out their destiny."

202 **Under the circumstances:** "The Radical Convention," *NC*, October 26, 1878, 1.

202 **Cain's political obligations:** Daniel Alexander Payne, *Recollections of Seventy Years* (Nashville: Publishing House of the A.M.E. Sunday School Union, 1888), 332; Daniel A. Payne, *History of the African Methodist Episcopal Church* (Nashville: Publishing House of the A.M.E. Sunday-School Union, 1891), 470–71; *Journal of the 17th Session and the 16th Quadrennial Session of the General Conference of the African Methodist Episcopal Church in the United States, Held at St. Louis, Missouri, May 3–25, 1880* (Xenia, OH: Torchlight Printing Company, 1882), 169–191.

203 **Payne likely was thinking:** *Journal of the 17th Session*, 205–208; James T. Campbell, *Songs of Zion: The African Methodist Episcopal Church in the United States and South Africa* (Chapel Hill: The University of North Carolina Press, 1998), 58–59; "Episcopal Notes and Meetings," *CR*, July 15, 1880; "Brief History of Paul Quinn College," *CR*, July 13, 1899; Wesley J. Gaines, *African Methodism in the South; or Twenty-Five Years of Freedom* (Atlanta: Franklin Publishing House, 1890), 188.

Paul Quinn College, named like many AME colleges after an early bishop of the church, relocated from Waco to Dallas in 1990.

203 **In South Carolina, however:** T. G. Steward, *Fifty Years in the Gospel Ministry* (Philadelphia: A.M.E. Book Concern, 1921), 72–73; "All Around Town," *NC*, January 23, 1887, 8; "All Around Town," *NC*, January 24, 1887, 8; "A Glance at Some of the Conference Leaders," *NC*, February 4, 1887, 8.

CHAPTER XII: THE LONG AND STORMY NIGHT

204 **Before the departure:** Richard R. Wright, Jr., ed., *Centennial Encyclopaedia of the African Methodist Episcopal Church* (Philadelphia: Book Concern of the A.M.E. Church, 1916), 299; "The Colored Churches," *SN*, October 2, 1881, CLS; A. Thos. Carr, "Emanuel Chapel," *CR*, April 15, 1875; "To the Rev. L.R. Nichols," *CR*, November 29, 1883; B. T. Tanner, "Letter from the Editor of the Review," *CR*, February 4, 1884; N. B. Sterrett, "History of Mt. Zion A.M.E. Church," Mount Zion A.M.E. Church Records, box 1, Finding Aid folder, ARC; *Minutes of the*

Nineteenth Session of the South Carolina Annual Conference of the African Methodist Episcopal Church Held at Charleston, S.C., from February 14th to February 20th, 1883 (Charleston: Walker, Evans & Cogswell, 1883), SCHS; *Minutes of the Twentieth Session of the South Carolina Annual Conference of the African Methodist Episcopal Church held at Georgetown, S.C., from February 13th to February 19th, 1884* (Charleston: Walker, Evans & Cogswell, 1884), SCHS; Bureau of the Census, Department of Commerce, *Religious Bodies, 1916*, Part 1 (Washington, D.C.: Government Printing Office, 1919), 374.

There is, as might be expected, some imprecision in the reporting of Emanuel's membership at the time, although little question that it was massive relative to its catchment area. The pastor in 1875, Augustus T. Carr, reported 2,764 members and 372 probationers. An article in NC in 1881 said there were 2,932 members and 946 probationers, the same figure used by Wright in his encyclopedia. Rev. N. B. Sterrett, who led Emanuel until 1882 and then founded Mt. Zion AME, claimed 4,200 members and 800 probationers at the time of that departure. His successor, Pastor Lewis Ruffin Nichols, said there were 3,569 members and probationers in 1883 and 4,400 in 1884. He asserted that there would be more than 7,000 "if we were to hunt up and recognize all who claim to be members of Emanuel." Available minutes of the South Carolina Conference record Emanuel as having 2,870 members and 863 probationers in 1883 and 3,030 members and 555 probationers in 1884.

204 **The numerical strength:** *Religious Bodies, 1916*, 21, 25–26, 30, 130, 306, 336–353, 374–375; U.S. Bureau of the Census, *Negroes in the United States, 1920–32* (Washington, D.C.: Government Printing Office, 1935), 532.

Given the vagaries of census-counting, the religious census figures are best taken as indicators of relative denominational strength rather than absolute measures. Atlanta was tied with Charleston behind Chicago in the count of AME members in 1916.

205 **Before the gentrification:** Membership records for Verdelle C. Green and Marguerite Michel, box 2, EAMECA; Class Address Lists, box 2, folder 6, EAMECA; Trustees Reports, box 3, folder 6, EAMECA; *Religious Bodies, 1916*, 40.

205 **Emanuel's pastors reported:** "News from the Churches," *CR*, September 25, 1873; "Emanuel Chapel," *CR*; "Large Religious Gathering," *NC*, May 12, 1875, 4; "The Dying Year," *NC*, January 1, 1885, 12; James M. Townsend, "Glimpses and Gleanings," *CR*, February 2, 1882.

206 **Satellite branches soon opened:** "The Mission Church Nuisance," *NC*, July 6, 1883, 4; "In Honor of 'Daddy' Cain," *NC*, July 15, 1888, 8; "Colored Churches," *SN*; "A Black Bishop," *NC*, September 26, 1881, 1; CCDB: December 10, 1872, J16:22; May 20, 1873, M14:339–340; November 2, 1875, B17:230; September 17, 1883, B20:15; March 5, 1885, H20:261, CCROD.

206 **Once Rev. Sterrett determined in 1882:** N. B. Sterrett, "Charleston Letter," *CR*, June 8, 1882; Wright, *Encyclopaedia*, 214; A. B. Caldwell, ed. *History of the American Negro, South Carolina Edition* (Atlanta: A. B. Caldwell, 1919), 570–572.

Sterrett pastored Emanuel a record three times: 1879–1882, 1896–1900, and 1911–1915 (three men have done so twice).

206 **It had fallen:** Sterrett, "History of Mt. Zion."

207 **When Sterrett arrived:** Sterrett, "History of Mt. Zion"; "A Church Consolidation," *NC*, January 31, 1882, 1; "Sale of Glebe Street Church," *NC*, August 18, 1882, 4; "Central Presbyterian Church," *NC*, September 24, 1882, 4; CCDB, April 9, 1881, Z18:88, and March 30, 1883, E18:562; Westminster Presbyterian Church (Charleston, S.C.) Session Minutes and Registers, 1852–1885, microfilm 45–385, 337, SCHS.

207 **McPherson informed Sterrett:** Sterrett, "History of Mt. Zion."

207 **McPherson recommended that Sterrett enlist:** Sterrett, "History of Mt. Zion."

208 **As it was, Sterrett was a bit:** A. W. Wayman, "Notes by the Way," *CR*, October 20, 1881; "Close of the Northeast South Carolina Conference," *CR*, December 30, 1897; Attorney notes, *St. Philip's Church v. Zion Presbyterian Church*, Rutledge & Young Records, box 5, folder 308.01 (S) 01, SCHS; Loraine Elizabeth Moultrie, "This Is my Life at Emanuel A.M.E. Church," box 13, folder 9, EAMECA; Interviews with Robert Mitchell and Kylon J. Middleton.

208 **"It was a tonal split":** Interview with Kylon J. Middleton.

As evidenced by Middleton's pastorship, and Mt. Zion's diversified membership, it is no longer known as a "light-skinned church."

208 **In the summer of 1883:** "Riotous Doings Rebuked," *NC*, July 4, 1883, 1; "Mission Church Nuisance," *NC*; "A Word in Season," *NC*, September 10, 1886, 8.
209 **It produced a schism:** "The Morris Brown Muss," *NC*, May 6, 1884, 1; "A Religious Rebellion," *NC*, May 7, 1884, 1.
209 **In April 1884:** "The Morris Brown Muss"; "A Religious Rebellion"; "Church Troubles in the South," *NYT*, May 7, 1884, 8; "The African Methodist Riot," *NC*, May 8, 1884, 4; "The African M.E. Church Conference and the Morris Street Rebellion," *NC*, June 2, 1884, 1; "The Colored Church Row," *NC*, June 15, 1884, 4; "The Morris Brown Muddle," *NC*, June 16, 1884, 1; "'Pot and Kettle' Illustrated," *NC*, June 17, 1884, 4; "Morris Brown's Ministers," *NC*, June 18, 1884, 4; "Morris Brown," *NC*, June 19, 1884, 4; George Brown Tindall, *South Carolina Negroes, 1877–1900* (Columbia: University of South Carolina Press, 1952), 193–194; Bernard E. Powers, Jr., *Black Charlestonians: A Social History, 1822–1885* (Fayetteville: The University of Arkansas Press, 1994), 206–209.
210 **In late June:** "The General Conference," *CR*, May 22, 1884; "The Morris Brown Mob," *NC*, July 1, 1884, 1; "All's Well That Ends Well," *NC*, July 2, 1884, 1; "A Talk with Bishop Turner," *NC*, July 3, 1884, 4; "An Independent Colored Church," *NC*, July 6, 1884, 4; "The African Church Rebellion," *NC*, July 8, 1884, 4; "Bishop H. M. Turner in Charleston, S.C.," *CR*, July 17, 1884; "All's Well That Ends Well," *CR*, July 17, 1884.

After successfully presenting his compromise to the Morris Brown congregation, Bishop Turner told a reporter: "You see, nothing puts us on our good behavior like having our misbehavior published."
210 **When Bishop Wayman graced Emanuel:** "Black Bishop," *NC*.
211 **The first test:** Carl McKinley, *The August Cyclone: A Descriptive Narrative of the Memorable Storm of 1885* (Charleston: The News and Courier Book Presses, 1886), 3–20; Walter J. Fraser, Jr., *Charleston! Charleston!: The History of a Southern City* (Columbia: University of South Carolina Press, 1989), 314–318; Walter Edgar, *South Carolina: A History* (Columbia: University of South Carolina Press, 1998), 426; "Music in the Air," *NC*, August 29, 1885, 1.
211 **The church would not:** Otto W. Nuttli, G. A. Bollinger, and Robert B. Herrmann, *The 1886 Charleston, South Carolina, Earthquake—A 1986 Perspective* (Washington, D.C.: United States Government Printing Office, 1986), iii, 15–17, 20, 42; Robert P. Stockton, *The Great Shock: The Effects of the 1886 Earthquake on the Built Environment of Charleston, South Carolina* (Easley, SC: Southern Historical Press, Inc., 1986), 47; Ivan Wong et al., "Potential Losses in a Repeat of the 1886 Charleston, South Carolina, Earthquake," *Earthquake Spectra* 21, no. 4 (2005): 1157–1184; Richard N. Côté, *City of Heroes: The Great Charleston Earthquake of 1886* (Mt. Pleasant, SC: Corinthian Books, 2006), xii–xiii; *Charleston As It Is After the Earthquake Shock* (Charleston, 1886), 42, SCHS; "Scenes on the Streets," *NC*, September 4, 1886, 2; Email from Thomas L. Pratt, Research Geophysicist, U.S. Geological Survey.
211 **Rev. Sterrett had been seeking:** N. B. Sterrett, "The Earthquake: An Eyewitness Tells of the Sights and Sounds in Summerville, S.C.," *CR*, September 30, 1886.
212 **Although Emanuel's lore:** "Faint Dawn of Hope," *NC*, September 4, 1886, 2; "The Dead and Wounded," *NC*, September 5, 1886, 2; City of Charleston, South Carolina, *Record of Earthquake Damages* (Atlanta: Winham and Lester, 1886), 70–71, CCPL.

The only known photograph of the original Emanuel, taken nearly four years after the earthquake, during a celebration of the twenty-fifth anniversary of the South Carolina Conference, shows it standing.
212 **The pastors of Charleston's AME churches:** W. H. Heard, "The Charleston Disaster," *CR*, September 16, 1886; "Appeal for Help," *CR*, September 23, 1886; "The Colored Clergy," *NC*, September 7, 1886, 1; "No Sectional Line—No Color Line," *NC*, September 8, 1886, 4; "Round About Town," *NC*, September 8, 1886, 2.
212 **By mid-October:** L. Ruffin Nichols, "An Appeal," *CR*, October 21, 1886; "All About Town," *NC*, October 26, 1886, 8; "The President's Sympathy," *NC*, October 27, 1886, 8; "The Confederate Home," *NC*, October 5, 1886, 1.
213 **But Nichols soon decided:** W. H. Heard, "Charleston Letter," *CR*, November 18, 1886; "The Afro-American Methodists," *NC*, May 17, 1890, 8; Arnett, *Proceedings*, 14, 34, 318–319; "An Appeal," *CR*, September 21, 1893; "The Tenth Episcopal District and Charities," *CR*,

September 28, 1893; "Emanuel A.M.E. Church," *NC*, September 10, 1887, 8; "Emanuel's Grand Rally," *NC*, June 25, 1888, 8; "The New Emanuel," *NC*, November 13, 1889, 8; "The New Emanuel Church," *NC*, February 27, 1890, 8; "The Equitable Building and Loan Association, of Augusta, GA.," *NC*, October 16, 1891, 4.

213 **The old building:** "Charleston, Columbia, Abbeville, and Spartanburg," *CR*, March 19, 1891; "Gathered from All Points of the Compass," *CR*, April 2, 1891; "Gathered from All Points of the Compass," *CR*, July 9, 1891; W. W. Heard, "As I Saw It," *CR*, July 16, 1891; "A Good Day's Work," *NC*, August 18, 1891, 2; "New Emanuel Church," *CR*, September 10, 1891; A. B. Caldwell, ed., *History of the American Negro, South Carolina Edition* (Atlanta: A. B. Caldwell, 1919), 538–541.

214 **A share of the $50,000 cost:** "John H. Devereux Has Passed Away," *NC*, March 17, 1920, 4; "S.C. Birthday," *NC*, July 26, 1947, 4; Robert P. Stockton, "Devereux Dominated His Architectural Era," *NC*, October 26, 1981, 1-B; John E. Wells and Robert E. Dalton, *The South Carolina Architects, 1885–1935: A Biographical Dictionary* (Richmond: New South Architectural Press, 1992), 40–41; Beatrice St. Julien Ravenel, *Architects of Charleston* (Charleston: Carolina Art Association, 1964), 265–266; Côté, *City of Heroes*, 75–77; "The Condition of the City," *NC*, September 9, 1886, 1.

214 **The Gothic Revival façade:** Benjamin W. Arnett, ed. *Proceedings of the Quarto-Centennial Conference of the African M.E. Church of South Carolina, May 15, 16 and 17, 1889* (Published by the editor, 1890), 409; "Story of Emanuel Church," *NC*, July 29, 1907, 6; "Conference of A.M.E. Church," *NC*, December 6, 1907, 6; "Organ Recital at Emanuel Church," *NC*, March 6, 1908, 10; "Organ Recital at Emanuel Church," *NC*, March 7, 1908, 8; "Murals Painted for Emanuel Church by Green," *NC*, November 25, 1945, 24; Contract for stucco work, December 9, 1948, box 9, EAMECA; National Register of Historic Places Registration Form for Emanuel African Methodist Episcopal Church, April 24, 2018.

214 **By late 1891:** "Filling the Contribution Box," *NC*, November 23, 1891, 2; "Perhaps the Best in the South," *NC*, December 1, 1891, 8; Zenette Thomas, "Rambles in the South," *CR*, February 16, 1893; Wm. D. Johnson, "Charleston and Other Points," *CR*, June 1, 1893; "Here, There and Everywhere," *NC*, August 24, 1893, 4; "The New Emanuel," *NC*, July 26, 1894, 8; Wm. D. Johnson, "On the Rounds," *CR*, December 20, 1894; "Here and There," *CR*, January 13, 1898; "Topics of the Town," *EP*, September 16, 1899, 5; Arnett, *Proceedings*, 106; Interview with Sonya Fordham.

215 **As the new century:** "When Emanuel A.M.E. Church, Charleston, S.C., Is Completed," *CR*, April 12, 1900; "Another League Formed," *NC*, September 20, 1909, 6; "All Around Town," *NC*, January 20, 1902, 8; Hollister, *Resisting Jim Crow*, 128–130; Interview with Sonya Fordham.

Although Emanuel hosted many notable lecturers, there is no record of any appearance by the best known orator of the day, Frederick Douglass. The seventy-year-old Douglass did, however, deliver his lecture on "Self-Made Men" at Mt. Zion AME Church during his first visit to Charleston on March 5, 1888, six years after the church was founded as an offshoot of Emanuel. "Frederick Douglass," *NC*, March 6, 1888, 2.

In telling the story of Paul Laurence Dunbar's appearance, John A. McFall wrote that the night stood out in his memory. That was because a box of matches somehow ignited in his coat pocket when he sat down, prompting him "to hastily beat it downstairs to the pastor's study where I could extinguish it without the audience knowing about it."

215 **One stiflingly hot afternoon in July:** "A Panic at a Funeral," *NC*, July 7, 1902, 8; "Went to See the Wreck," *NC*, July 8, 1902, 9.

215 **After enacting more conventional laws:** *Code of Laws of South Carolina, 1952* (Charlottesville: The Michie Company, 1952), 1:287, 293–294; 2:821–822; 4:554; 5:265; Wm. D. Chappelle, "Presiding Elders of South Carolina in Council," *CR*, September 20, 1894.

216 **In November 1900:** "Burton Out on Bail," *NC*, November 24, 1900, 8; "Want Burton Dismissed," *EP*, November 27, 1900, 2; "Object to Special Seats," *NC*, February 2, 1904, 8; *Acts and Joint Resolutions of the General Assembly of the State of South Carolina Passed at the Regular Session of 1904* (Columbia: The State Company, 1904), 438–439.

216 **One of the first such cases:** "Stephney Riley Slain," *NC*, October 3, 1885, 1; "The Riley In-

quest," *NC*, October 6, 1885, 1; "The Riley Homicide," *NC*, November 12, 1885, 1; "The Riley Homicide," *NC*, November 13, 1885, 1; "The Riley Homicide," *NC*, November 14, 1885, 8; "Dr. Bellinger," *NC*, November 14, 1885, 4; "The Court of Sessions," *NC*, July 2, 1886, 1; "The Bellinger Trial," *The Manning Times*, November 18, 1885, 4; "Dr. Bellinger's Trial Begun," *The Morning Times*, November 11, 1885, 1; Susan Millar Williams and Stephen G. Hoffius, *Upheaval in Charleston: Earthquake and Murder on the Eve of Jim Crow* (Athens: The University of Georgia Press, 2011), 81–84.

217 **The doctor testified:** "The Riley Inquest"; "The Riley Homicide," November 12, 1885; "The Riley Homicide," November 13, 1885; "The Riley Homicide," November 14, 1885; "Dr. Bellinger"; "The Court of Sessions."

There is some dispute as to whether the jury that deadlocked 11–1 for acquittal in Bellinger's trial consisted only of white citizens. At least two contemporaneous newspaper accounts say that it did. But Williams and Hoffius assert in *Upheaval in Charleston* that the lone holdout for a manslaughter conviction—John E. Foster, according to newspaper accounts—also was the jury's sole Black member. The 1886 Charleston City Directory includes a John E. Foster, a school janitor, who was designated as "colored." But the 1892 edition lists someone with the same name as being a white traveling salesman. The 1880 census, meanwhile, shows John E. Foster of Charleston as being a sailor and "mulatto."

217 **A month after the Riley shooting:** "Colored Folks in Council," *NC*, November 3, 1885, 1.
217 **The session produced:** "Stirring Up Strife," *NC*, November 23, 1885, 1; "An Address to the Races," *NC*, November 25, 1885, 1.
218 **Lynching reached its peak:** *Thirty Years of Lynching in the United States, 1889–1918* (New York: National Association for the Advancement of Colored People, 1919), 89; *Lynching in America: Confronting the Legacy of Racial Terror* (Montgomery, AL: Equal Justice Initiative, 2017), 4, 40; George Brown Tindall, *South Carolina Negroes, 1877–1900* (Columbia: University of South Carolina Press, 1952), 250–254; Pauli Murray, ed. *States' Laws on Race and Color* (Woman's Division of Christian Service, Methodist Church, 1951), 406–407.
218 **The victims in the peak year:** J. L. Dart, *The Famous Trial of the Eight Men Indicted for the Lynching of Frazier B. Baker and His Baby, Late U.S. Postmaster of Lake City in the U.S. Circuit Court, at Charleston, SC April 10–22, 1899*, John L. Dart Family Papers, 1844–1947, box 1, folder 7, ARC; Damon L. Fordham, *True Stories of Black South Carolina* (Charleston: The History Press, 2008), 66–74. (The author is indebted to Fordham for assistance in locating documents.)
219 **Ten weeks later:** *Charleston Messenger*, May 7, 1898, 2, SC Room, CCPL; Dart, *Famous Trial*; Trichita M. Chestnut, "Lynching: Ida B. Wells-Barnett and the Outrage over the Frazier Baker Murder," *Prologue* 40, no. 3 (Fall 2008), 21–28, NARA.
219 **After state authorities declined:** "A Mistrial in the Lake City Case," *NC*, April 24, 1899, 4; Caitlin Byrd, "'The Darkest Blot Upon South Carolina's History,'" *PC*, January 13, 2019, 3.
219 **The ever-looming risk:** Stewart E. Tolnay and E. M. Beck, "Racial Violence and Black Migration in the American South, 1910–1930," *American Sociological Review* 57, no. 1 (February 1992): 103–116; Idus A. Newby, *Black Carolinians: A History of Blacks in South Carolina from 1895 to 1968* (Columbia: University of South Carolina Press, 1973), 193–195; *Negroes in the United States, 1920–32*, 32–43.
220 **The flight of so many Black South Carolinians:** *Religious Bodies, 1916* and *1926*; *Minutes of the Eighty-Fourth Session of the South Carolina Annual Conference of the Seventh Episcopal District Held in Emanuel A.M.E. Church, Charleston, South Carolina, November 12–16, 1947* (Columbia: The Allen University Press, 1947), 52, Julia Alston Gourdine Papers, series 2, box 11, folder 14, ARC.
220 **On March 19, 1909:** "Lecture by Dr. Washington," *EP*, March 12, 1909, 5; "Booker T. Washington to Speak in Charleston," *NC*, March 13, 1909, 10; "Booker Washington Here," *NC*, March 19, 1909, 10; "Dr. W.E.B. DuBois Here February 16," *EP*, February 10, 1921, 10.
221 **Washington's appearance:** "Tours South Carolina," *The Washington Bee*, April 3, 1909, 1; "Washington in South Carolina," *The New York Age*, March 18, 1909, 1; "The March of Triumph," *The Freeman*, April 3, 1909, 1; "Booker Washington Here," *NC*, March 20, 1909, 5; "Washington Urges Negroes to Labor," *EP*, March 20, 1909, 6; David H. Jackson, Jr., "Booker T. Washington in South Carolina, March 1909," *SCHM* 113, no. 3 (July 2012): 192–220.

221 **Washington's South Carolina tour:** Jackson, Jr., "Booker T. Washington."
222 **The speech at Emanuel:** "Booker Washington Here," *NC*, March 20, 1909, 5.
222 **If blame was to be placed:** "Booker Washington Here," *NC*, March 20, 1909, 5.
223 **"In all that concerns":** "Booker Washington Here," *NC*, March 20, 1909, 5.
223 **He spoke regularly:** Dennis C. Dickerson, *The African Methodist Episcopal Church: A History* (Cambridge, UK: Cambridge University Press, 2020), 180–188; Booker T. Washington, "Taking Advantage of Our Disadvantages," *A.M.E. Church Review* 10 (April 1894), reprinted in *The Booker T. Washington Papers*, ed. Louis R. Harlan (Charlottesville: University of Virginia Press, Rotunda, 2021), 3:478–483; "Mass Meeting for the Negroes Here," *EP*, July 6, 1910, 9; "Negroes Held Mass Meeting," *NC*, July 11, 1910, 7.
224 **When Du Bois showed:** Nic Butler, "The Charleston Riot of 1919," *CTM*, May 10, 2019, CCPL; Fraser, *Charleston!*, 363; Cameron McWhirter, *Red Summer: The Summer of 1919 and the Awakening of Black America* (New York: Henry Holt and Company, 2011), 13.
224 **In 1910, when Black and white numbers were comparable:** Theodore Hemmingway, "Prelude to Change: Black Carolinians in the War Years, 1914–1920," *JNH* 65, no. 3 (Summer 1980): 212–227; Bureau of the Census, *Mortality Rates, 1910–1920* (Washington, D.C.: Government Printing Office, 1924), 20–21; Robert A. Margo, *Race and Schooling in the South, 1880–1950: An Economic History* (Chicago: The University of Chicago Press, 1990), 54.

Despite their second-class citizenship at home and in the military, Black South Carolinians, incentivized by both patriotism and pay, comprised more than half of those who registered for the World War I draft in the state, according to Hemmingway.

225 **Although Washington and Du Bois:** David Levering Lewis, *W.E.B. Du Bois: A Biography* (New York: Henry Holt and Company, 2009), 165–174, 201, 204–205; W.E.B. Du Bois, "The Evolution of Negro Leadership," *The Dial* 31, no. 362 (July 16, 1901): 53–55; W.E.B. Du Bois, *The Souls of Black Folk: Essays and Sketches* (Chicago: A. C. McClurg & Co., 1903), 41–59, 105; W.E.B. Du Bois, "The Talented Tenth," in *The Negro Problem: A Series of Articles by Representative Negroes of To-day*, ed. Booker T. Washington (New York: James Pott & Company, 1903), 33–75.
225 **By assailing Washington in print:** Du Bois, *Souls*, 50, 52.
225 **He first spoke:** "For Colored Y.W.C.A.," *NC*, February 22, 1917, 10; "A Grand Lecture," *SN*, February 25, 1917, 3; "Negro Editor to Lecture," *NC*, March 2, 1917, 6; "A Great Lecture," *The Charleston Messenger*, 1817, W.E.B. Du Bois Papers, UMAL; Application for Charter of Charleston Branch, NAACP Papers, LOC; Dr. W.E.B. Du Bois and Sight Seeing Party, Charleston, SC, March 1917, Avery Photograph Collection, folder 60–9, ARC; Peter F. Lau, *Democracy Rising: South Carolina and the Fight for Black Equality Since 1865* (Lexington: The University Press of Kentucky, 2006), 34; Edward Ball, *The Sweet Hell Inside: The Rise of an Elite Black Family in the Segregated South* (New York: Perennial, 2001), 109–111, 191–196; "Aged Negro Dies," *NC*, April 25, 1931, 7.

The funeral service for Edwin G. (Captain) Harleston (1854–1931), the father of Edwin Augustus (Teddy) Harleston, was held at Emanuel, and a stained-glass window is dedicated to his memory. Captain Harleston founded Charleston's landmark Harleston Funeral Home in 1913 and housed it in a newly constructed building across Calhoun Street from the church.

The organizational meeting of the Charleston branch was held on February 27, 1917. Its application to the NAACP for a charter was approved a month later on March 27.

Du Bois later wrote a Charleston-based novel, *The Ordeal of Mansart* (1957), the first of a trilogy, that referenced Emanuel several times.

226 **At the point Du Bois returned:** "Awake," *The Crisis* 13, no. 6 (April 1917): 270; Advertisement for Du Bois lecture, *EP*, February 10, 1921, 6; "Dr. W.E.B. Du Bois Here February 16," *EP*, February 10, 1921, 10; "Colored Teachers in Charleston Schools," *The Crisis* 22 no. 2 (June 1921): 58–60; W.E.B. Du Bois, "Diary of a Journey," ca. 1921, 6, W.E.B. Du Bois Papers, UMAL.
226 **Du Bois's interests:** "The Second Pan-African Congress," *The Crisis* 21, no. 6 (April 1921): 248; W.E.B. Du Bois, "The Second Pan-African Congress," *The Crisis* 22, no. 2 (June 1921): 57;

"N.A.A.C.P. Campaign Gets Under Way Through-Out the Entire Country," *New Journal & Guide*, March 5, 1921, 1.

226 **There is no known record:** Edward C. Mickey to NAACP, April 3, 1921, Edwin A. and Elise F. Harleston Papers, ROSE; "Noted Negro Speaker Gives Lecture Here," *The Topeka Daily Capital*, March 16, 1921, 1.

227 **"We who resent":** W.E.B. Du Bois, "To the World," *The Crisis* 23, no. 1 (November 1921): 5.

Marcus Garvey made his own appearance in Charleston at Morris Street Baptist Church on September 24, 1924 ("Meeting Notices," *EP*, September 22, 1924, 11).

CHAPTER XIII: B. J. GLOVER AND THE GOSPEL OF RESISTANCE

228 **Rev. Benjamin James Glover:** Elizabeth Rauh Bethel, *Promiseland: A Century of Life in a Negro Community* (Columbia: University of South Carolina Press, 1997), 17–33; Interview with Gean Glover; World War II Draft Card for Benjamin James Glover, October 16, 1940, NARA.

229 **In her packed pews:** Video outtakes of civil-rights rally at church (News Story 63-747), WIS-TV News Collection, MIRC; Interview with James G. Blake by Tom Dent, May 15, 1991, box 147, item 14, Dent Collection, AMISTAD; Michael Soper, "Negro Leader Urges Voter Registration," *NC*, April 13, 1962, 1-B; "Three Memorial Services Set for Dr. King," *EP*, April 6, 1968, 7-A; "Memorial Services for King Scheduled," *NC*, April 6, 1968, 6-A.

The popularization of "We Shall Overcome" as a civil-rights anthem originated in a labor strike in 1945 at Charleston's Cigar Factory, where protesters, many of them Black women, sang the gospel hymn, "I'll Overcome Someday."

230 **"B. J. Glover was the ultimate":** Interview with James E. Clyburn.

230 **Another United Methodist:** Peter F. Lau, *Democracy Rising: South Carolina and the Fight for Black Equality Since 1865* (Lexington: The University Press of Kentucky, 2006), 120; Patricia Sullivan, *Lift Every Voice: The NAACP and the Making of the Civil Rights Movement* (New York: The New Press, 2009), 245; Email from Oveta Glover; "Funeral services Monday for the Rev. Dr. James G. Blake," *TD*, December 19, 1999, 4A.

231 **Crawford presented:** Roy Nash, "The Lynching of Anthony Crawford: South Carolina Declares an End to Mob Rule," NAACP/LOC; "Anthony Crawford," *The Crisis* 13, no. 2 (December 1916): 67; "Farming that Pays," *The Abbeville Medium*, December 15, 1904, 6, USCSCL.

231 **The day Crawford was killed:** Nash, "Lynching of Anthony Crawford"; "Anthony Crawford"; *Thirty Years of Lynching in the United States, 1889–1918* (New York: National Association for the Advancement of Colored People, 1919), 24–25; Sullivan, *Lift Every Voice*, 75; George A. Devlin, *South Carolina and Black Migration, 1865–1940: In Search of the Promised Land* (New York: Garland Publishing, 1989), 357–359, 383–386; W. C. Crawford to R. I. Manning, November 25, 1916, Manning Papers, SCDAH.

232 **One family that refused to flee:** Interview with Oveta Glover; Funeral program for Rev. Charles George Glover; Bethel, *Promiseland*, 186.

Among the suggestions that the Glovers likely knew the Crawfords is that Anthony Crawford's eldest son was the pastor of the AME church in neighboring Due West at the time of his father's death.

232 **Violence found the Glover homestead:** Interviews with B. J. Glover by Elizabeth Rauh Bethel, March 16, 1979, and June 11, 1979, from Bethel's research records, LAJL; Interview with Benjamin J. Glover by Marvin Lare, October 11, 2005, "Champions of Civil and Human Rights in South Carolina," vol. 1, part 1, USCSCL.

232 **The indignities she confronted:** Bethel and Lare interviews with Glover.

233 **Despite the size:** Bethel and Lare interviews with Glover; "The Omega Celebration of Life for Rev. Dr. Benjamin 'BJ' James Glover," July 1, 2010; Benjamin J. Glover to Bishop Samuel R. Higgins, June 12, 1961, USCSCL; Interview with B. J. Glover by WXRY radio, undated but likely 1975, recording courtesy of Herb Frazier and the Glover family.

233 **A rougher education:** Bethel and Lare interviews with Glover; "Assignments for A.M.E.," *IJ*,

November 27, 1940, 5; "Negro Pays $300 Fine," *IJ*, September 30, 1941, 5; "A.M.E. Minister Brutally Beaten, Courier Is Told," *The Pittsburgh Courier*, November 1, 1941, 1; "Ohio Pastor Is Beaten by Georgia Cops," *CD*, November 15, 1941, 1; Leona Purifoy White, "Middletown," *CD*, January 24, 1942, 11.

233 **"You must take your hat off":** Bethel and Lare interviews with Glover; Glover's Draft Card.
234 **The *Courier* characterized Glover's beating:** Bethel and Lare interviews with Glover; "Day Book of B.J. Glover," box 7, folder 1, EAMECA; "Due West News," *The Palmetto Leader*, October 4, 11, 18, and 25, 1941, and November 1, 8, and 15, 1941.
234 **While Glover's alleged offense:** Bethel and Lare interviews with Glover; Speech by B. J. Glover at James Island Voter Registration Meeting of Palmetto Voters Association, 1959, recording courtesy of Herb Frazier and the Glover family; E. Philip Ellis, "AME Pastor Assignments Are Listed," *TS*, November 27, 1940, 3; "Day Book"; Interviews with Thomas Broadwater, Madrian Glover Garrick, Gail A. Glover, Oveta Glover, Shawn Glover, Akil Khalif, and Vivian Wright.

The depiction of the Klan incident in subsequent paragraphs relies on the interviews with Glover by Lare and Bethel, and the author's interviews with Glover's children and friends. In the recollections of Vivian Wright, Glover's niece, and Thomas Broadwater, a friend, Glover said the abduction happened immediately after he left the Abbeville courthouse, suggesting that his assailants had been notified as a result of the voter registration clerk's telephone call. That conflicts with Glover's own telling in the Lare interview, in which he distanced the attack from the courthouse visit ("shortly thereafter, in 1937") and Bethel's interviews, in which he dated the beating to 1939 and said he was snatched in Greenwood after he "had gotten off the bus and was walking down the street."

236 **For a time, Glover said:** Bethel and Lare interviews with Glover.
236 **By the time Glover was assigned:** "Bishop Reid Announces State AME Appointments," *EP*, November 9, 1953, 2; "Assignments Listed For Lowcountry AME Churches," *NC*, November 14, 1950, 13; Glover to Higgins; Interview with Doris Coaxum Sanders.
237 **Those who grew up in the church:** Interviews with Shawn Glover and Ruby Nesbitt Martin.
237 **"We were a massive body":** Interview with Sharon Coakley.
237 **A Black South Carolinian in the 1930s:** Gov. Olin B. Johnston to J. Arthur Brown, June 21, 1937, Brown Papers, box 1, folder 1, ARC; Interviews with Ruby Nesbitt Martin and Harold Washington.
238 **Indeed, one study found:** Karl E. Taeuber and Alma F. Taeuber, *Negroes in Cities: Residential Segregation and Neighborhood Change* (Chicago: Aldine Publishing, 1965), 45–47; "Defense Map Shows Emergency Refuge Centers and Casualty Stations," *NC*, February 21, 1942, 7; Interview with Sharon Coakley.
238 **Born in Charleston in 1914:** Service of Triumph and Home-Going Celebration for the Late Rev. Hilda B. Scott, January 3, 2003; Emanuel A.M.E. Church Gives Tribute to Rev. Hilda B. Scott, December 10, 1994, box 4, folder 3, EAMECA; Eric Frazier, " 'Mama Hilda': Her Interest Made the Difference for Youngsters," *PC*, December 18, 1994, 9-G.
238 **"She knew everybody":** Interview with Dorothy Jenkins.
239 **It was during Glover's pastorship:** *Combined Minutes of the General Conference, African Methodist Episcopal Church, 1948 (Kansas City, Kansas)—1952 (Chicago, Illinois)—1956 (Miami, Florida)* (Nashville: A.M.E. Sunday School Union, 1956), 309, 379, 391; Interviews with Marlena Davis and Charles N. Williams.
239 **"She just taught":** Interview with Ruby Nesbitt Martin.
240 **"Dad would slap":** Interviews with Oveta Glover, Shawn Glover, and Gean Glover.
240 **When guest-preaching:** Sermon by B. J. Glover at Bethel AME Church, Columbia, SC, June 12, 1966, recording courtesy of Herb Frazier and the Glover family; Letter from B. J. Glover, July 26, 1960, box 5 folder 3, EAMECA.
240 **Glover's pulpit style:** "The Four People Who Go to Church," undated sermon, B. J. Glover Papers, USCSCL.
241 **"I still have an appreciation":** Interviews with Sonya Fordham and Melvin L. Graham, Jr.
241 **But until then, the global AME church:** *The Episcopal Address to the Thirty-Fifth Quadrennial Session of the General Conference of the African Methodist Episcopal Church Convening in Miami, Florida, May 2–16, 1956* (Prepared by Bishop Alexander Joseph Allen, n.p.).

241 **Only in Mississippi:** Idus A. Newby, *Black Carolinians: A History of Blacks in South Carolina from 1895 to 1968* (Columbia: University of South Carolina Press, 1973), 23, 152; J. Edward Arbor, "Upon This Rock," *The Crisis* 42, no. 4 (April 1935): 110–111.

242 **Every four years:** *The Quadrennial Address of the Bishops of the A.M.E. Church to the General Conference Convened in Wilmington, N.C., May 4, 1896*, (Xenia, OH: Chew, Pr.), 11, 65–66, LOC; *Quadrennial Address of Bishops to the Twenty-First Session of the General Conference of the A.M.E. Church, Held in Columbus, Ohio, May 1900* (Benjamin F. Lee), 64–66; NAACP, *Thirty Years of Lynching*, 29.

242 **The AME bishops gradually grew:** *The Episcopal Address to the Thirty-First Quadrennial Session of the General Conference of the African Methodist Episcopal Church at Detroit, Michigan, May 1940*, 35, ROSE.

242 **In 1952, the bishops' tone:** *The Episcopal Address to the Thirty-Fourth Quadrennial Session of the General Conference of the African Methodist Episcopal Church at Chicago, Illinois, May 1952*, 27–28, ROSE; *The Episcopal Address to the Thirty-Seventh Quadrennial Session of the General Conference of the African Methodist Episcopal Church Meeting in Cincinnati Gardens, Cincinnati, Ohio, May 6–18, Nineteen Hundred Sixty-Four*, 52–55, ROSE.

243 **The NAACP considered:** Dear Sir Letter from Richard H. Mickey, May 16, 1917, Harleston Papers, ROSE; "Meeting Notice," *EP*, June 21, 1919, 13; "N.A.A.C.P. Speaker," *EP*, September 11, 1920, 11; "The Local Branch of the National Association for the Advancement of Colored People," *SN*, October 30, 1921, 30; Herb Frazier, "Charleston NAACP Elects New Officers During Much Delayed Election," *CCP*, March 31, 2023, 6; Application for Charter of Charleston Branch, NAACP/LOC; "Desegregation and Racial Tensions," Address of Roy Wilkins, February 24, 1956, Charleston S.C., NAACP/LOC; "17th Annual Meeting of the South Carolina Conference of Branches of National Association for Advancement of Colored People," October 16, 1958, NAACP/LOC.

Among the twenty-nine signatories to Charleston's NAACP charter application were physicians, a druggist, a lawyer, businessmen, dressmakers, and undertakers. Some were, like Harleston, members of Plymouth Congregational Church, according to newspaper articles. Others attended Centenary Methodist, St. Mark's Episcopal, Zion Presbyterian, and Morris Brown AME, but none could be identified as Emanuel members.

The tradition of NAACP leadership from Emanuel continued in 2023 when Dorothy Jenkins, a third-generation Emanuel member and longtime chair of its social action committee, was elected president of the Charleston branch.

244 **Within a few years:** Edwin A. Harleston to John R. Shillady, November 2, 1918, Harleston Papers, ROSE; James M. Hinton, Backward Glance of Past (19) Years, October 17, 1958, NAACP/LOC; Memorandum from Gloster B. Current, May 9, 1958, NAACP/LOC; Ruby Hurley to Gloster B. Current, May 23, 1958, NAACP/LOC; 17th Annual Conference Report, October 16–19, 1958, NAACP/LOC; Lucille Black, "Memorandum to the South Carolina Branches," October 19, 1953, NAACP/LOC; Monthly report from H. D. Anderson, Jr., Field Secretary, SC Conference of Branches, March 23, 1959, NAACP/LOC; I. DeQuincey Newman, Annual Report, December 1960, NAACP/LOC; Robert W. Bagnall to J. E. Beard, May 15, 1929, Harleston Papers, ROSE; Mary White Ovington, "Along the N.A.A.C.P. Battlefront," *The Crisis* 43, no. 4 (April 1936): 116; Robert W. Bagnall, "Lights and Shadows in the South," *The Crisis* 39, no. 4 (April 1932): 125; W. H. Miller to E. Frederic Morrow, March 15, 1939, NAACP/LOC; Sullivan, *Lift Every Voice*, 78–79; Richard Gergel, *Unexampled Courage: The Blinding of Sgt. Isaac Woodard and the Awakening of President Harry S. Truman and Judge J. Waties Waring* (New York: Sarah Crichton Books, 2019), 31–34.

244 **Boosted by a series of successful court fights:** "Membership Status—Southeast Region," November 16, 1953, NAACP/LOC; Memorandum from Current, May 9, 1958, NAACP/LOC; 17th Annual Conference Report; Walter F. Murphy, "The South Counterattacks: The Anti-NAACP Laws," *The Western Political Quarterly* 12, no. 2 (June 1959): 380; R. Scott Baker, *Paradoxes of Desegregation: African American Struggles for Educational Equity in Charleston, South Carolina, 1926–1972* (Columbia: University of South Carolina Press, 2006), 111–115; *The Bulletin* (Kentucky State College) 12, no. 2 (1961–63): 122; Interview with Oveta Glover.

Septima Poinsette Clark, an educator and organizer who was considered "The Mother of the Movement" by Martin Luther King, Jr., lived at the time in the house she owned at 17 Henrietta Street, directly behind Mother Emanuel. The church bought the property from Clark in 1972 for $3,000 and leveled it to expand its parking lot. Clark's prior ownership of the site is marked by a disc embedded in the sidewalk. Clark occasionally attended services and events at Emanuel but joined Old Bethel United Methodist as an adult. CCDB, August 7, 1972, V99:464, CCROD; Katherine Mellon Charron, *Freedom's Teacher: The Life of Septima Clark* (Chapel Hill: The University of North Carolina Press, 2009), 36.

245 **Waring made:** Richard Kluger, *Simple Justice: The History of Brown v. Board of Education and Black America's Struggle for Equality* (New York: Vintage Books, 1975), 298–305; Tinsley E. Yarbrough, *A Passion for Justice: J. Waties Waring and Civil Rights* (New York: Oxford University Press, 1987), 35; Brian Hicks, *In Darkest South Carolina: J. Waties Waring and the Secret Plan That Sparked a Civil Rights Movement* (Charleston: Evening Post Books, 2018); Samuel Grafton, "Lonesomest Man in Town," *Collier's*, April 29, 1950, 20–21, 49–50; Gergel, *Unexampled Courage*, 111, 203–204.

245 **Few cases would be more important:** Kluger, *Simple Justice*, 3–25, 302–305; Gergel, *Unexampled Courage*, 216–239; Baker, *Paradoxes*, 96–98.

246 **The Briggs litigation:** Kluger, *Simple Justice*, 3–25, 302–305; Sue Anne Pressley, "After 45 Years, S.C. Pioneer of Civil Rights Is Cleared," *WP*, October 11, 2000.

246 **When Judge Waring retired:** "Negro-Right Judge Comes Here to Live," *NYT*, February 24, 1952, 33; "NAACP Has Dinner for Judge Waring," *NC*, November 7, 1954, 8-A; Brian Hicks, "Judge No Longer Lost to History," *PC*, December 28, 2022; J. Waties Waring to Benjamin J. Glover, May 27, 1961, Papers of Ruby Pendergrass Cornwell, box 3, folder 5, ARC; Benjamin J. Glover to J. Waties Waring, June 25, 1951, and Waring to Glover, June 27, 1951, Waring Papers, box 110–11, folder 280, MSRC.

247 **Glover may have been stunned:** J. Waties Waring to Benjamin J. Glover, May 27, 1961, Papers of Ruby Pendergrass Cornwell, box 3, folder 5, ARC; Jack Bass and Marilyn W. Thompson, *Strom: The Complicated Personal and Political Life of Strom Thurmond* (New York: Public Affairs, 2005), 117.

CHAPTER XIV: THE MOVEMENT CHURCH

250 **"If Negroes would":** B. J. Glover, "Let's Free America," *The Allen University Bulletin* 12, no. 4 (January 1949): 6, USCSCL.

250 **It would be another decade:** Interview with Minerva Brown King; William H. Chafe, *Civilities and Civil Rights: Greensboro, North Carolina, and the Black Struggle for Freedom* (New York: Oxford University Press, 1980), 99; R. Scott Baker, *Paradoxes of Desegregation: African American Struggles for Educational Equity in Charleston, South Carolina, 1926–1972* (Columbia: University of South Carolina Press, 2006), 139–146; Jon Hale, "'The Fight Was Instilled in Us': High School Activism and the Civil Rights Movement in Charleston," *SCHM* 114, no. 1 (January 2013): 23; Millicent Ellison Brown, "Civil Rights Activism in Charleston, South Carolina, 1940–1970," PhD dissertation, Florida State University, 1997, 166–167; "Negro Lunch Counter Move Spreads to S.C.," *EP*, February 12, 1960, 4-D; "Negroes Foiled in Sitdown Try at Orangeburg," *NC*, February 26, 1960, 1; "50 Negroes Demonstrate at Columbia," *EP*, March 2, 1960, 8-A; "Negro Demonstrators Arrested at Sumter," *EP*, March 4, 1960, 8-C; "7 Greenville Negroes Arrested in Library," *NC*, March 17, 1960, 5-D; "24 Arrested Here in Demonstration," *NC*, April 2, 1960, 1-B.

251 **Gantt, who was both an outstanding student:** Interview with Harvey Gantt; "Negro Trespass Convictions Reversed by Supreme Court," *EP*, June 24, 1964, 9; "NAACP Informs Units Not to Buy at Stores," *NC*, March 17, 1960, 5-D.

251 **Five days after the initial Charleston sit-in:** W. Glenn Robertson, "Negroes Here Asked to Boycott 3 Stores," *NC*, April 7, 1960, 7-A.

252 **Regular picketing:** "Negro Urges Boycott of Three Chains," *EP*, April 7, 1960, 13; "Negroes Picket Two Local Stores," *EP*, April 29, 1960, 1-B; "Eleven Negroes Stage 'Sitdown' in Local Store," *EP*, July 25, 1960, 2; "Lunch Counter Sit-In Staged at Store Here," *NC*, July 27, 1960, 9; "Negro Youths Picket Local Variety Stores," *NC*, July 28, 1960, 5-A; "14 Negroes Stage Sit-

In; 9 Post Bond," *NC,* February 12, 1961, 12; "Nine Negroes Sentenced in Sit-In Case," *NC,* March 2, 1961, 11; Mary Goodfellow, "S.C. Prosperity Rests on Negro's Participation," *The Charlotte Observer,* June 2, 1965, 2; Order of Service, Emanuel African Methodist Episcopal Church, January 3, 1960, and December 11, 1960, EAMECA.

252 **In the wake of the *Brown v. Board* ruling:** Baker, *Paradoxes,* 94; Mary C. Simms Oliphant, *The History of South Carolina* (River Forest, IL: Laidlaw Brothers, 1964), 277–281.

253 **"We used to run":** Interview with Oveta Glover.

Oveta Glover followed in her father's footsteps by serving as president of the Columbia, SC, branch of the NAACP, beginning in 2019.

253 **That made it all the more amazing:** Interview with Oveta Glover; "3 Negro Children Seek Admission to White Schools," *EP,* October 10, 1960, 1; "Negroes Denied School Transfer," *NC,* October 11, 1960, 1-B.

254 **The Glovers were not alone:** "3 Negro Children Seek Admission"; "Negroes Denied School Transfer"; "Negro Parents at Charleston Protest Overcrowded Schools," *IJ,* October 11, 1960, 5; "Negroes Discard Boycott Tactics," *NC,* October 13, 1960, 1; "5 Student Transfers Rejected," *NC,* October 21, 1960, 17; "Petition Is Answered by Board," *NC,* December 8, 1960, 9; I. DeQuincey Newman, "Annual Report, South Carolina Conference of Branches," December 1960, NAACP/LOC.

254 **It would take another three years:** "School Mixing Suit to Be Aired Monday," *The Sumter Daily Item,* August 1, 1963, 8-A; "White and Negro Pupils' Ability Is Argued in Suit," *GN,* August 6, 1963, 1; "Charleston Schools Ordered to Admit 13 Negro Children," *GN,* August 23, 1963, 1; Robert McHugh, "Charleston Schools Ordered to Admit 13," *TS,* August 23, 1963, 1-A; "Text of Judge's Opinion and Finding," *NC,* August 24, 1963, 7; "Negroes to Attend 4 Schools," *The Columbia Record,* August 23, 1963, 2-A; Opinion and Order, *Brown v. School District No. 20,* 2, NARA.

255 **Because the ruling came down:** "Charleston Schools Ordered to Admit 13"; McHugh, "Charleston Schools Ordered"; "Text of Judge's Opinion and Finding"; Baker, *Paradoxes,* 166, 170.

255 **On September 3:** "Five Negro Students Enter Charleston White Schools," *The Columbia Record,* August 30, 1963, 1; Barbara Stambaugh, "Bomb Scare Mars Mixing of Schools," *The News and Record,* September 3, 1963, 1; "Bomb Call Empties School," *The Columbia Record,* September 3, 1963, 1; Transcript of hearing in *Millicent F. Brown v. School District Number 20,* vol. 1, August 5, 1963, 26, 28–29, NARA; Interview with Oveta Glover.

255 **The most consequential demonstration:** "State House March Lands 189 in Jail," *TS,* March 3, 1961, 31; "190 Are Arrested in Demonstration at State Capitol," *EP,* March 3, 1961, 1; "Segregation 'Protesters' Out on Bond," *TS,* March 4, 1961, 3; "36 Negro Students Convicted," *TS,* March 17, 1961, 5-A.

256 **Almost all of the accused:** *State v. Edwards,* 239 S.C. 339 (1961); *Edwards v. South Carolina,* 372 U.S. 229 (1963).

256 **Glover's arrest in Columbia:** "King Street, U.S.A.," *The Afro-American,* April 21, 1962, 3; "Charleston Youths Continue Picketing," *Mississippi Free Press,* May 5, 1962, 3, NAACP Papers, Part 25: Branch Department Files, series C, LOC; "Negroes Get Jobs During S.C. NAACP Buying Drive," *CD,* May 9, 1962, 8; Interview with Benjamin J. Glover by Marvin Lare, October 11, 2005, "Champions of Civil and Human Rights in South Carolina," vol. 1, part 1, USCSCL.

257 **It grated on him:** Lare interview with Glover.

257 **"Where am I violating":** Lare interview with Glover; Interviews with Gail A. Glover and Vivian Wright.

Glover did not date the launderette incident in his interviews, and it is documented only in his telling. Given the police officer's ostensible reaction, it is possible it took place in summer 1964, shortly after the enactment of the federal Civil Rights Act, which ended segregation in public accommodations. Glover and other Black leaders in Charleston set out immediately to test the new law by seeking admission to hotels and restaurants where they previously had been banned.

257 **In April 1962:** Michael Soper, "Negro Leader Urges Voter Registration," *NC,* April 13, 1962,

12; "King Vote Team Hits Charleston," *The Afro-American*, April 21, 1962, 7; Clayborne Carson et al., eds., *The Papers of Martin Luther King, Jr.*, Vol. 7, *To Save the Soul of America, January 1961–August 1962* (Berkeley: University of California Press, 2014), 35–37, 69; David J. Garrow, *Bearing the Cross: Martin Luther King, Jr., and the Southern Christian Leadership Conference* (New York: Vintage Books, 1986), 194–198.

257 **As the most spacious Black church:** Interview with Sharon Coakley.

258 **King's appearance at Emanuel:** "Negro Leader Urges," *NC*; Photograph of Martin Luther King, Jr., at Emanuel AME Church, April 12, 1962, ARC; Interview with Charles (Bud) Ferillo.

258 **Other than to visit:** Glenn Robertson, "King Says 'Build' Rather Than 'Burn,'" *EP*, July 31, 1967, 1-A; Interview with James G. Blake by Tom Dent, May 15, 1991, box 147, item 14, Dent Collection, AMISTAD; Interview with Andrew Young.

259 **Two months after King's 1962 visit:** Philip B. Hill, "Big Audience Hears NAACP's Wilkins," *NC*, June 18, 1962, 11; "Negroes Hear Roy Wilkins, Then Stage Orderly March," *NC*, July 8, 1963, 9; Nic Butler, "Segregation and Integration at CCPL, 1931–1965," The Charleston Archive, February 10, 2012, CCPL.

259 **The move from the courtroom:** Interview with Harvey Jones, "Veterans of the Civil Rights Movement," Civil Rights Movement Archives, DUL; Leverne Prosser, "NAACP Lists Integration Strategy in 8 S.C. Cities," *NC*, May 22, 1963, 14; John P. O'Keefe, "Prayer March Held Downtown," *NC*, June 10, 1963, 11; Gus J. Chigges, "Charleston Negroes Hold Quiet March," *TS*, June 10, 1963, 1; "Sit-Ins Continue Downtown," *NC*, June 12, 1963, 13; "Charleston, S.C. Braces for More Race Protests," *CD*, June 13, 1963, 11; John P. O'Keefe, "46 Demonstrators Are Arrested Here," *NC*, June 14, 1963, 1; "8 Negroes 'Wade In' at Folly," *EP*, July 6, 1963, 12; "Playground in City Entered by Negroes," *NC*, July 16, 1963, 15.

260 **Marches to and from those sites:** Interview with Ellen Jackson.

260 **"Emanuel was very well placed":** Interviews with Millicent Brown, Minerva Brown King, Ellen Jackson, and Charles (Bud) Ferillo.

261 **"There was so much singing":** Interview with Millicent Brown.

262 **During the summer:** Letter to B. J. Glover from anonymous Emanuel member, July 2, 1962, provided by Marlena Davis.

262 **"He blasted them":** Interview with Daniel Martin, Sr.

262 **On occasion, they withheld:** Interviews with Ruby Nesbitt Martin and Doris Coaxum Sanders.

262 **Ruby Martin said she did not:** Interviews with Ruby Nesbitt Martin, Sonya Fordham, Melvin L. Graham, Jr., and Elnora Taylor.

263 **As a veteran jail-goer:** "Numbers Dwindle in Demonstrations," *NC*, July 21, 1963, 1; Interview with Oveta Glover; Lare interview with Glover.

263 **One night in June:** "300 Negroes Rally at Police Station," *NC*, June 26, 1963, 9; "40 Arrested Protesting Segregation," *EP*, July 3, 1963, 13; Ed Harrill, "Order Restrains Demonstrations," *EP*, July 6, 1963, 1; "5 Local Policemen Hurt in Near Riot," *NC*, July 17, 1963, 1; "Violence Erupts for First Time in Charleston; 6 Hurt," *The Bee*, July 17, 1963, 1; Robert McHugh, "Protests Continue in S.C. Port City," *TS*, July 18, 1963, 1.

264 **The incident put pressure:** "Negroes Vow to Continue Demonstrating," *TD*, July 18, 1963; "Troopers in Charleston After Negroes Fight Police," *The Courier-Journal*, July 18, 1963, 4; Claude Sitton, "State Police Sent into Charleston," *NYT*, July 18, 1963, 10; "68 Negroes Are Charged with Rioting," *NC*, July 18, 1963, 1; Robert McHugh, "Protests Continue in S.C. Port City," *TS*, July 18, 1963, 1.

264 **The arrests outside the newspaper building:** "'Mournful March' Opens Seventh Week of Protests," *The Columbia Record*, July 22, 1963, 2; "South Carolina One Hundred Years After the Emancipation Proclamation: Annual Report of I. DeQuincey Newman, Field Secretary for South Carolina National Association for the Advancement of Colored People," 1963, Newman Papers, USCSCL; Baker, *Paradoxes*, 151–153; Stephen O'Neill, *From the Shadow of Slavery: The Civil Rights Years in Charleston*, PhD dissertation, University of Virginia, 1994, 227–228; Interview with Minerva Brown King.

264 **Rev. Glover found:** "14 Negroes Convicted of Trespassing," *EP*, June 24, 1963, 11; "11 Convicted in Sit-Ins Court Cases," *EP*, June 25, 1963, 2; "300 Negroes Rally at Police Station," *NC*, June 26, 1963, 9; "8 Negroes 'Wade In' at Folly," *EP*, July 6, 1963, 12; "Demonstrators Con-

tinuing Integration Marches Here," *EP*, July 20, 1963, 1; "AME Bishop Arrested in Civil Rights Protests," *CD*, July 25, 1963, A-3.

265 **Eventually, the economic pressure:** "NAACP Lists Integration Strategy," *NC*; "Charleston, S.C. Braces," *CD*; "Mayor and Negro Leaders Meet in Closed Session," *NC*, July 11, 1963, 11; "Mayor, Negro Leaders Arrive at No Agreement at Meeting," *EP*, July 11, 1963, 13.

265 **In July, Charleston's movement leaders:** "Movement's Aims Are Outlined," *EP*, July 12, 1963, 13; "Merchants Back Charleston Pact," *NYT*, July 24, 1963, 17.

265 **Some organizers were ready:** "Merchants Back Charleston Pact"; Interview with Blake by Dent; "87 City Merchants Agree to Desegregation Program," *NC*, August 2, 1963, 9.

266 **With that victory:** "Charleston Marchers to Return Tonight," *EP*, August 28, 1963, 20.

266 **"That summer certainly produced":** Interview with Arthur C. McFarland.

266 **Even though the color barrier:** "Negroes Here Test Civil Rights Law," *NC*, July 4, 1964, 9; B. J. Glover to William McCord, January 5, 1965, box 5, folder 5, EAMECA.

267 **With Jim Crow limping:** "Negroes Acting to Halt Dropouts," *NC*, September 23, 1963, 9; "Negro Voter Registration Drive Scheduled," *EP*, March 31, 1964, 19; "Rev. B. J. Glover Named President of Allen University," *EP*, June 19, 1965, 1; Tom English, Jr., "Votes, Schools, Weapons Cited," *Florence Morning News*, October 1, 1966, 1.

267 **He was succeeded by another NAACP firebrand:** "The Heritage of Slavery," CBS News Special Report, 1968; "Concept of 'Black Power' Explained by Julian Bond," *NC*, August 1, 1966, 13-A.

268 **"exploded, once and for all":** O'Neill, *Shadow*, 248–287.

268 **The-more-than-one-hundred-day strike:** William L. Walker, Jr., "Medical College Strike Ends After 100 Days," *NC*, June 28, 1969, 1; O'Neill, *Shadow*, 254–255, 258–259; Claudia Smith Brinson, *Stories of Struggle: The Clash over Civil Rights in South Carolina* (Columbia: University of South Carolina Press, 2020), 212–213, 229.

268 **The dispute began in December 1967:** Interview with Mary Moultrie, William Saunders, and Rosetta Simmons by Kerry Taylor, March 5, 2009, Charleston Oral History Program, LCDL, 4; Interview with Zedekiah L. Grady by Mark K. Tyler, August 19, 2013; O'Neill, *Shadow*, 262; Brinson, *Stories of Struggle*, 212–217.

268 **Although not recognized:** Steve Hoffius, "Charleston Hospital Workers' Strike, 1969," in *Working Lives: The Southern Exposure History of Labor in the South* (New York: Pantheon Books, 1974), 245; Brinson, *Stories of Struggle*, 211–276; O'Neill, *Shadow*, 267–268; James T. Wooten, "Charleston Is Armed Camp as 142 More Are Held," *NYT*, April 29, 1969, 42; Betty Walker, "Curfew Fails to Halt Violence," *NC*, May 2, 1969, 1-A; Interview with Theodora Watson.

269 **Seeking revival in the aftermath:** Sam McCuen, "Abernathy Leads March," *TS*, April 23, 1969, 17-A; William Walker, Jr., "Mr. Abernathy Leads 800 on Medical Center March," *NC*, April 23, 1969, 1-B; James T. Wooten, "100 Negroes Seized in Charleston Protest March," *NYT*, April 27, 1969, 60; Don McKee, "Thousands Join March," *GN*, May 12, 1969, 1; Sam E. McCuen, "Abernathy Leads Peaceful March," *TS*, May 12, 1969, 1-A; Brinson, *Stories of Struggle*, 225; Interviews with Lee Bennett, Jr., and Andrew Young.

Among the hospital officials that Young and other SCLC leaders negotiated with was Dr. James W. Colbert, Jr., the medical university's vice president for academic affairs and the father of television host and comedian Stephen Colbert, who grew up in Charleston as the youngest of Dr. Colbert's eleven children.

269 **Few gatherings were as electric:** Stewart R. King, "Coretta King Pledges Support of Hospital Strike," *NC*, April 30, 1969, 1-A; Don McKee, "Coretta King Tells Workers 'We Can Win a Victory,'" *IJ*, April 30, 1969, 19; Sam E. McCuen, "Mrs. King Defends Charleston Strikers," *TS*, April 30, 1969, 1-A; "Mrs. King Joins Hospital Strikers," *GN*, April 30,1969, 1; Ron Brinson and Clyde Johnson, "Mrs. King Leads Strike Supporters," *EP*, April 30, 1969, 1; Bruce Golphin, "Mrs. King to Lead Charleston March," *WP*, April 30, 1969, A-3.

The phrase "I Am Somebody" originated as a civil-rights slogan with Reverend William Holmes Borders, the activist pastor of Wheat Street Baptist Church in Atlanta, who published a poem by that title in the 1940s. The phrase later became central to Reverend Jesse L. Jackson's civil-rights messaging. "Courier Presents Readers Famous Poem," *The Pittsburgh Courier*, February 20, 1943, 14.

270   **King told:** Stewart R. King, "Coretta King Pledges Support of Hospital Strike," *NC*, April 30, 1969, 1-A; Don McKee, "Coretta King Tells Workers 'We Can Win a Victory,'" *IJ*, April 30, 1969, 19; Sam E. McCuen, "Mrs. King Defends Charleston Strikers," *TS*, April 30, 1969, 1-A; "Mrs. King Joins Hospital Strikers," *GN*, April 30,1969, 1; Ron Brinson and Clyde Johnson, "Mrs. King Leads Strike Supporters," *EP*, April 30, 1969, 1; Bruce Golphin, "Mrs. King to Lead Charleston March," *WP*, April 30, 1969, A-3; Madeline Anderson, Dir., *I Am Somebody*, Icarus Films, 1970; Brinson, *Stories of Struggle*, 248–249; O'Neill, *Shadow*, 273.

270   **"The greatest power":** McCuen, "Mrs. King Defends Charleston Strikers"; Anderson, *I Am Somebody*.

270   **The strike resolved only:** Brinson, *Stories of Struggle*, 258–276.

271   **Their share of the voting pool:** *Report of the South Carolina Election Commission for the Period Ending June 30, 1974* (State Budget and Control Board), 391; *Report of the Secretary of State O. Frank Thornton to the General Assembly of South Carolina for the Fiscal Year Beginning July 1, 1965 and Ending June 30, 1966*, 333.

271   **The impact was felt immediately:** O'Neill, *Shadow*, 310–314; Brian Hicks, *The Mayor: Joe Riley and the Rise of Charleston* (Charleston: Evening Post Books, 2015), 87–89, 100–102, 109, 114, 128; Margaret M. Wilcox, "Negro Attorney Is Named Associate Judge for City," *NC*, February 26, 1969, 1; Steve Estes, *Charleston in Black and White: Race and Power in the South after the Civil Rights Movement* (Chapel Hill: The University of North Carolina Press, 2015), 48–56.

271   **Riley campaigned on pledges:** Hicks, *Mayor*, 115, 309; Walter J. Fraser, Jr., *Charleston! Charleston!: The History of a Southern City* (Columbia: University of South Carolina Press, 1989), 428; Henry O. Counts, "Riley Promises Unification for City," *NC*, December 16, 1975, 1-A; Barbara S. Williams, "Inaugural Departs from Old Customs," *NC*, December 16, 1975, 1-B.

CHAPTER XV: CLEMENTA PINCKNEY AND THE PARADOX OF BLACK POWER

273   **The morning worship had ended:** Interviews with Gregory Kinsey, John Paul Brown, and Brenda Nelson; Kevin Sack, "Clementa Pinckney Called to Pulpit and Politics in a Life Cut Short," *NYT*, June, 26, 2015, A-1.

273   **It was the mid-1980s:** Interviews with John Pinckney and Gracie Stevenson Broome.

273   **Pinckney came from a line:** "Boycott Continues," *IJ*, February 9, 1971, 9; Interviews with Johnette Pinckney Martinez and John Pinckney.

274   **Within months of his calling:** Interviews with Gregory Kinsey and John Paul Brown; "State Sen. Pinckney appointed Presiding Elder in AME Church," *TD*, December 29, 2006, 8-C.

274   **Child-prodigy preachers:** Interviews with Helen Pittman, Gracie Stevenson Broome, Johnette Pinckney Martinez, and John Pinckney; Tim Lockley, "The Forming and Fracturing of Families on a South Carolina Rice Plantation, 1812–1865," *The History of the Family*, 2017; Sermon by Clementa Pinckney at Campbell Chapel AME Church, Bluffton, SC, January 26, 2010; Stephanie Harvin, "Clementa Pinckney: Legislator Sees Public Life As Extension of His Ministry," *PC*, January 13, 2001, D-1.

275   **Even as a preteen:** Interviews with Sylvia Stevenson Johnson and Carey A. Grady.

275   **Pinckney preferred 4-H debate competitions:** Interviews with Thomasina C. Tyler and Roslyn Fulton-Warren.

275   **He presided over the student government:** Interview with Helen Pittman.

276   **He had been a page:** Vicky Agnew, "White Joins Political Exodus," *BG*, March 31, 1996, 1; "State Sen. Pinckney appointed Presiding Elder in AME Church," *TD*, December 29, 2006, 8-C; Harvin, "Clementa Pinckney"; Meg Kinnard, "Widow, Daughters of Slain Emanuel AME Pastor, Senator Receive Posthumous Degree," Associated Press, May 8, 2016; Interview with Lovett H. Weems, Jr.

In 2016, Wesley Theological Seminary granted Pinckney's doctoral degree posthumously in a commencement ceremony at Washington National Cathedral attended by his wife and two daughters.

277   **The stucco façade:** Elsa McDowell, "Low Country Takes Time to Give Thanks," *PC*, Sep-

277 **After three decades:** Regina M. Bures and Colleen Cain, "Dimensions of Gentrification in a Tourist City," University of Florida, paper presented to the Population Association of America, 2008; "City of Charleston Gentrification Task Force Report to City Council," July 10, 2001; Yuqing Pan, "The U.S. Cities That Are Gentrifying the Fastest—You'll Never Guess No. 1," Realtor.com, January 23, 2017.

277 **The City of Charleston lost:** Adam Parker, "Last Black Homeowners Leave Charleston's Ansonborough Neighborhood," *PC*, August 7, 2022, A-1.

278 **Younger ones:** *The Doctrine and Discipline of the African Methodist Episcopal Church, 2021* (Nashville: The AME Sunday School Union, 2022), 376–377; Christina Lee Knauss, "AME Rejects Same-Sex Unions," *TS*, July 8, 2004, B1; Interview with Neil Brady and Paula Hunt.

278 **"On a couple of occasions":** Interviews with Lavern Witherspoon and Eric S. C. Manning; 2008 Members Directory, Pinckney File, EAMECA; Emanuel AME Church Quarterly Conference Minutes, April 24, 2014, EAMECA; Adam Parker, "Disappearing Churches: Downtown Charleston Congregations Cope with Big Changes," *PC*, March 26, 2017, G-1; Warren L. Wise, "Downtown Charleston Church Could Soon See the Wrecking Ball," *PC*, September 24, 2018, A-7; Rickey Ciapha Dennis, Jr., "An Exodus of Churches in Heart of Holy City," *PC*, November 5, 2018, A-1; Warren L. Wise, "Charleston Church Site Slated to Be Redeveloped into $40M, 250-Unit Apartment Building," *PC*, April 29, 2021; Rickey Ciapha Dennis, Jr., "Downtown Charleston Church Building to Be Repurposed as Cycling Studio," *PC*, August 14, 2022, A-1; Warren L. Wise, "Charleston Church Slated to Be Converted into Condominium Units," *PC*, August 30, 2022, B-1.

279 **An engineering firm:** "A Structural Investigation of Emanuel AME Church, Charleston, South Carolina," Bennett Preservation Engineering PC, June 15, 2015; Minutes of the Official Board, Emanuel AME Church, October 6, 2010, EAMECA; Mother Emanuel African Methodist Episcopal Church, Board of Trustees Meeting Minutes, December 13, 2011, EAMECA; Minutes of the Board of Stewards, Emanuel AME Church, June 2, 2014, EAMECA; Emanuel AME Church Revenue & Expense Budget Performance, 01/01/2011 through 12/31/2011, EAMECA.

279 **The building had been included:** "Emanuel Church A Shrine," *NC*, July 10, 1982, 5-A; Interview with Samuel L. Green, Sr..

279 **He also was charged:** Mortgage Club of Emanuel AME Church tickets, Gourdine Papers, series 2, box 6, folder 9, ARC; Interview with Willi Glee.

280 **"I believe in heaven":** Harvin, "Clementa Pinckney."

280 **Two years before:** Interview with Sylvia Stevenson Johnson; Telegram from Isaac W. Williams to Roy Wilkins, March 11, 1971, NAACP/LOC.

281 **"We don't see ourselves":** Remarks by Clementa Pinckney to Northeastern University students, October 2013.

281 **"To just have the vote":** Interview with Clementa Pinckney by Henry Louis Gates, Jr., October 26, 2012; Sarita Chourey, "Okatie Crossings Bill Clears Committee," *Savannah Morning News*, February 2, 2010; Josh McCann, "Davis: Bill Is 'Pretty Much Dead,'" *BG*, March 19, 2010, 1A; Bruce Smith, "Savannah Port Would Benefit Border Rivals," *Statesville Record and Landmark*, March 13, 2007, 10; "Minister Lawmakers Leading Lottery Opposition," *IJ*, March 8, 2000, 3A; Gwyneth J. Saunders, "Haley Not Ready to Gamble on Hardeeville Resort-Casino," *Savannah Morning News*, March 2, 2012; Sarita Chourey, "Push Begins to Raise Hourly Wage in S.C.," *BT*, December 17, 2014; Interview with Helen Pittman.

282 **"We are in an American system":** Gates interview with Pinckney.

283 **The men met briefly:** Email from Jennifer Pinckney; Gates interview with Pinckney.

283 **"He would say, 'Mmm-hmm' ":** Interviews with Joseph Darby and James L. Gilliard; Sack, "Clementa Pinckney Called."

283 **Pinckney made a point:** Interview with Bill Herbkersman; Sack, "Clementa Pinckney Called."

284 **In the house in 2000:** Rachel Graves, "House: Bring It Down," *PC*, May 11, 2000, 1-A; Brian Whitmore, "Pinckney Defends No-Vote on Flag," *BG*, June 9, 2000, 1B.

Pinckney voted no on a preliminary vote on the flag compromise but missed the final vote to attend a funeral. It is not clear from news accounts whether he attended as an officiant or mourner. The flag first was raised over the statehouse in 1961 to commemorate the centennial of the start of the Civil War. The following year, a state law was passed requiring that it continue to fly.

284 **"There were many who said":** SC Senate, Video Archive, April 14, 2015, 12 p.m.

285 **"We thought we had the votes":** Interview with Marlon Kimpson.

285 **"He said, 'Darrell, I don't ask for much'":** Interview with Darrell Jackson.

285 **After the 2010 census:** Interviews with Larry Grooms, Darrell Jackson, and Glenn F. McConnell.

286 **Pinckney's reputation as the "conscience of the senate":** Interviews with Kay Taylor Hightower, Shaquanda Stevenson, Helen Pittman, and Althea Richardson-Latham; Casey Conley, "Questions Still Surround State Sen. Clementa Pinckney's Residency," *The Island Packet*, November 14, 2012; Kelly Champlin, "Pinckney Answers Address Questions," *BT*, November 14, 2012; Sarita Chourey, "State Election Commission Sides with Pinckney in Residency Challenge," *BT*, November 27, 2012; Clementa Pinckney, Statement of Economic Interests, 2008 and 2015, SC State Ethics Commission; *Clementa Pinckney v. The Senate*, Petition for Approval of Compromise Settlement Agreement, SC Workers' Compensation Commission, January 20, 2011.

Available documents do not detail the nature of the accident in the workers' compensation claim. The settlement agreement stated that "an actual bona fide disagreement exists" between Pinckney and the state about the extent of his disability and the amount owed for it. Neither of Pinckney's lawyers, Gerald Malloy and Ann Mickle, responded to requests to discuss the case.

286 **"He came to me and he said":** Interview with Mike Shealy.

287 **Shealy did some research:** Interview with Mike Shealy; Emails from Mike Shealy; An Act to Make Appropriations and Provide Revenues to Meet the Ordinary Expenses of State Government for the Fiscal Year Beginning July 1, 2013, General Assembly of SC; Willi Glee to P. George Benson, March 6, 2014, EAMECA; College of Charleston Expenditure Authorization/Travel Payment Voucher to Emanuel AME Church, March 11, 2014.

287 **But Congress in 1954 had prohibited:** Interview with William Dudley Gregorie; Sermon by Clementa Pinckney at Campbell Chapel AME Church, Bluffton, SC, January 26, 2010.

288 **More pointedly, like other denominations, the AME Church:** Susan Schmidt and Michael Abramowitz, "AME Bishop, Leaving Questions in L.A., Seeks Deals Here," *WP*, February 9, 1990; Stephen Clark, "New Pastor Buoys Spirits at Ward AME Church," *Los Angeles Times*, June 18, 2006; Joe Lambe, "Minister Sues Elder and Church," *The Kansas City Star*, November 30, 1999, B3; Ruth E. Igoe, "$6 Million Award in Harassment Case," *The Kansas City Star*, December 4, 1999, B1; Dan Margolies, "$4 Million Award Tossed Out," *The Kansas City Star*, March 31, 2001, B8; Angel Jennings, "Former Pastor Is Troubled by Church Upheaval," *Los Angeles Times*, October 20, 2013; Bob Smietana, "N.Y. Clergy to Repay $800K in Kickbacks from Sale of Black Churches," *WP*, September 8, 2022; Assurances of Discontinuance no. 21-066, In the Matter of Gregory G. M. Ingram, and no. 21-067, In the Matter of Melvin Wilson, Attorney General of the State of New York, October 8, 2021.

288 **The church began to confront:** Adam Parker, "Class-Action Suit Filed Against AME Church over $90M in Lost Pension Funds," *PC*, April 6, 2022; Jennifer Berry Hawes and Thad Moore, "AME Church Pension Scandal, Shrouded in Mystery, Rooted in Risky Investments," *PC*, May 6, 2022; Jennifer Berry Hawes and Thad Moore, "AME Church Sues Former Pension Fund Director, Alleging He Stole Millions," *PC*, May 26, 2022; "AME Church Files Lawsuit Against Dr. Jerome Harris and Others for Conspiracy to Defraud and Embezzle Clergy Retirement Funds," *CR*, May 25, 2022; "AME Church Alleges Ex-Retirement Services Executive Embezzled Millions," *WP*, May 27, 2022; John Thomas III, "It's the Ethics for Me," *CR*, October 4, 2022.

288 **The base salary:** *The Connectional Budget of the African Methodist Episcopal Church, 2021–2024* (Nashville: AMEC Publishing House, 2022), 17.

290 **The perceived value of becoming a bishop:** Interviews with Preston Warren Williams II and Carey A. Grady.

Mandatory retirement for AME pastors and general officers is seventy-five, but bishops must retire "at that General Conference when the Bishop's 73rd birthday is on or before July 15th of the General Conference year." General Conferences are quadrennial, although the Covid-19 pandemic delayed the 2020 event in Orlando until 2021. *Doctrine and Discipline, 2021*, 171, 182.

290 **Every AME district:** Emanuel AME Church Income Budget for the Period January 1 Thru December 31, 2010, and Emanuel AME Church Budget of Expenditures for the Period January 1 Thru December 31, 2010, Pinckney Files, EAMECA.
290 **"You find the money":** Interview with Joseph Darby.
291 **In 2024, the AME churches of South Carolina:** *Connectional Budget*, 32–33; Emanuel AME Church Revenue and Expense Budget Performance: 01/01/2011 through 12/31/2011, Pinckney Files, EAMECA.

Pinckney was earning about $70,000 a year from Emanuel at the time of his death, according to a "Decision and Order of the South Carolina Workers' Compensation Commission" (File No. 1512493), dated January 15, 2016.

291 **The since-retired bishop:** Interviews with Preston Warren Williams II and Kylon J. Middleton; *Doctrine and Discipline, 2021*, 694.
292 **"He was hurt":** Email from Jennifer Pinckney.
292 **Pinckney initially resisted:** Email from Jennifer Pinckney; Interview with Kay Taylor Hightower.
292 **"definitely a product of the system":** Interview with Kylon J. Middleton.
292 **Another Pinckney friend:** Interview with Kay Taylor Hightower.
293 **"It's turning":** Interviews with Lavern Witherspoon and Preston Warren Williams II.
293 **In a New Year's Day sermon:** Videotapes of service, January 1, 2012, unmarked box, EAMECA.

CHAPTER XVI: JUDGMENT DAY

295 **Dylann Roof's federal:** *U.S.A. v. Roof* (Evaluation of Competency to Stand Trial, James C. Ballenger, November 15, 2016, 22; Second Competency Evaluation, James C. Ballenger, January 1, 2017, 6, 9; GX 3).
296 **But in his bizarre and disquieting trial:** *U.S.A. v. Roof* (GVX 5; Sealed Ex Parte Hearing, November 7, 2016, 14–15, 38–39; Competency Hearing, November 21, 2016, 29–31; November 22, 2016, 82, 273–274; Ballenger, 53–54).
296 **With considerable cunning:** *U.S.A. v. Roof* (Telephone Conference, October 25, 2016, 4–5; Sealed Ex Parte Hearing, November 7, 2016, 27–29, 53; Psychological Evaluation of Dylann Roof, Rachel Loftin, 41–42).
296 **Rather than hearing:** *U.S.A. v. Roof* (GX 107A-D; GX 500, 18–19; January 4, 2017, 49–50; January 10, 2017, 833); Kevin Sack and Alan Blinder, "'I Had to Do It,' Defendant in Church Rampage Says in Video," *NYT*, December 10, 2016, A-1; Alan Blinder and Kevin Sack, "Insisting He Is Not Mentally Ill, Church Killer Rejects a Lifeline," *NYT*, January 5, 2017, A-1; Alan Blinder and Kevin Sack, "Charleston Church Killer Is Sentenced to Death," *NYT*, January 11, 2017, A-1.
297 **To preserve his chosen narrative:** *U.S.A. v. Roof* (Telephone Conference, October 25, 2016, 4–5); Kevin Sack and Alan Blinder, "With His Life Now at Stake, Killer Rejects Best Defense," *NYT*, January 2, 2017, A-8.
297 **Roof's shrewdness:** *U.S.A. v. Roof* (Docket Entry 545; Sealed Ex Parte Hearing, November 2, 2016, 11; November 7, 2016, 40, 42, 47–49; Competency Hearing, November 22, 2016, 273–275).
297 **Gergel, an Obama appointee:** *U.S.A. v. Roof* (Competency Hearing, November 22, 2016, 282; January 2, 2017, 197–223).

Judge Gergel began working on *Unexampled Courage* after organizing a conference about Judge Waring in 2011. The book was published two years after Dylann Roof's trial.

298 **The competency assessments:** *U.S.A. v. Roof* (Sealed Ex Parte Hearing, November 7, 2016, 52–53; Psychiatric Evaluation of Dylann Storm Roof, Donna Schwartz Maddox, 6–11, 15–16; Neuropsychological and Facial Anthropometric Evaluation of Dylann Roof, Paul J. Moberg, 4–5; Competency Evaluation of Dylann Roof, Mark Wagner, November 14, 2016, 5; Loftin,

2–4, 7, 11, 13–14, 22–23, 44–45); Kevin Sack, "Evidence Not Seen by Jury Raises Questions About Gunman's Death Sentence," *NYT*, June 1, 2017, A-17.

298 **He developed a daily marijuana habit:** *U.S.A. v. Roof* (Final Report for Defense Counsel, John Elder Robison, December 28, 2016, 8; Ballenger, 38; Loftin, 3–4, 22–23, 35–37, 41–47; Maddox, 10–11).

298 **Those who examined Roof:** *U.S.A. v. Roof* (Sealed Ex Parte Hearing, November 2, 2016, 7; Ballenger, 18, 29, 34, 42; Ballenger Second Evaluation, 10; Maddox, 7; Loftin, 30; Wagner, 5–6; Robison, 7).

298 **As evidence, Bruck presented:** The U.S. District Court in Charleston allowed journalists, including the author, to view videos of jailhouse visits from November 19, 2016, December 18, 2016, and December 27, 2016, following their unsealing in 2017 by Judge Gergel.

299 **Roof's unnerving disengagement:** Audio recordings of Dylann Roof telephone calls, produced in 2023 by the Charleston County Sheriff's Office in response to a Freedom of Information Act request.

Dylann Roof's grandfather, Carl Joseph Roof, a former president of the Richland County Bar Association, died in 2021. Dylann's father, Franklin Bennett Roof, died in 2023.

299 **In a pair of letters:** Letters from Dylann Roof to the author, one undated but received on March 17, 2020, and one dated April 30, 2020.

300 **After scores of hours:** *U.S.A. v. Roof* (Loftin, 35, 49–51, 55).

300 **Although Roof's father:** *U.S.A. v. Roof* (GVX 5; Loftin, 13; Ballenger, 49, 53; Robison, 7).

300 **Rather, Roof consistently attributed:** *U.S.A. v. Roof* (GX 3, 500; GVX 5; Maddox, 5; Ballenger, 15; Loftin, 48–49; Wagner, 2–3; December 15, 2016, 1204, 1207–1208).

301 **Roof explained in his FBI interview:** *U.S.A. v. Roof* (Ballenger, 25; Wagner, 3–4; GVX 5).

301 **Roof's living situation:** *U.S.A. v. Roof* (Robison, 7–8; F.B.I. Interview with Jacob Hunter Meek, June 29, 2015, 3–4; Affidavit for Search Warrant, June 18, 2015; Affidavit in Support of an Application for a Search Warrant, June 27, 2015; *United States of America v. Joseph Carlton Meek* (3:15-CR-633) (Memorandum to File, Deborah Barbier, September 23, 2016, 4–5); SC Law Enforcement Division Memorandum to File, Case File 31-15-0060, June 19, 2015; Stephanie McCrummen, "An American Void," *WP*, September 12, 2015.

302 **Investigators would later learn:** *U.S.A. v. Roof* (GX 4, 109e, 361–410; GVX 297–299; December 13, 2016, 994–1002).

302 **Roof bought his weapon:** *U.S.A. v. Roof* (GVX 5; GX 108, 239–242); SC Law Enforcement Division Investigative Report, Case File 31-15-0060, June 18, 2015; Michael S. Schmidt, "Background Check Missed Charleston Suspect," *NYT*, July 11, 2015, A-1.

302 **The dreadful screw-up:** Statement by FBI Director James Comey Regarding Dylann Roof Gun Purchase, July 10, 2015; F.B.I. Inspection Division, *Inspector's Report: A Review of the CJIS Division's National Instant Criminal Background Check System (NICS) in Clarksburg, West Virginia*; U.S. Department of Justice, *National Instant Criminal Background Check System Operations, 2017*, 19–20; Andrew Knapp, "After Dylann Roof 'Mistake,' FBI to Make Change to Gun Background Checks," *PC*, July 10, 2018; Joshua Eaton, "Charleston Mass Murderer Got His Gun Because of Background Check Gaps, Internal Report Shows," *Roll Call*, October 10, 2019; Thomas Novelly, "SC Rep. Jim Clyburn's 'Charleston Loophole' Bill Passes House. Heads to Uncertain Senate," *PC*, March 11, 2021; Jeffrey Collins, "South Carolina Bill to Lengthen Gun Background Checks Stalls," *The Augusta Chronicle*, March 20, 2018; Nick Reynolds, "South Carolinians Can Now Carry Handguns Without Permits. The New Law, Explained," *PC*, March 7, 2024.

303 **"Once again, innocent people":** The White House, Statement by the President on the Shooting in Charleston, South Carolina, June 18, 2015; Cassie Cope, "Pinckney's Widow Joins Obama As He Unveils Action on Guns," *TS*, January 5, 2016; Jennifer Berry Hawes, "Church Shooting Victims' Families Upset Gov. Nikki Haley Not Supporting Gun Law Reforms," *PC*, June 2, 2016; Emma Dumain, "Emanuel AME Shooting Survivors Urge Action on New Gun Laws in Emotional Appeal to DNC," *PC*, July 27, 2016; Joseph Cranney, "Emanuel AME Pastor Advocates for Dylann Roof Gun Loophole Bill at Statehouse," *PC*, February 27, 2018; Jennifer Berry Hawes, "Three Years After Church Shooting, Loved Ones of the Nine Who Died Forge New Paths," *PC*, June 17, 2018; Gregory Yee, "At Charleston's Emanuel 9 Rally for

Unity: Calls for Stricter Gun Laws, Grassroots Action," *PC*, June 23, 2018; Caitlin Byrd, "SC Rep. Jim Clyburn Says Bill Closing 'Charleston Loophole' Will Pass the House," *PC*, February 21, 2019; Christine Hauser and Isabella Grullón Paz, "Families of Charleston Massacre Victims Reach $88 Million Settlement," *NYT*, October 28, 2021; Department of Justice, "Justice Department Announces Multi-Million Dollar Settlement in Principle with Mother Emanuel Charleston Church Mass Shooting," October 28, 2021.

303 **It was an acquaintance of Roof:** *U.S.A. v. Roof* (GVX 5; December 13, 2016, 978–979); Charleston Police Department Supplemental Incident Report, June 24, 2015; Charleston County Sheriff's Office Incident Supplement, June 18, 2015; Search Warrant Affidavits; Abby Phillip, "Dylann Roof's Sister Tried to Crowdfund Her Wedding and Honeymoon," *WP*, July 2, 2015.

303 **The news from Charleston:** Gabe Whisnant, "Tip from Kings Mountain Florists Led to Charleston Shooting Suspect's Arrest," *The Star*, June 18, 2015; *In The Matter of the Search Of 10428 Garners Ferry Road, Eastover, South Carolina 29044,* Affidavit in Support of an Application for a Search Warrant, June 27, 2015.

304 **At 10:52 a.m.:** *U.S.A. v. Roof* (GVX 5; December 9, 2016, 466–467, 473–474); Shelby Police Department Incident/Investigation Report #2015-002966, June 18, 2015; Shelby Police Department Dashcam Video of Dylann Roof Arrest, *NYT*, June 23, 2015; Nikki R. Haley, *With All Due Respect: Defending America with Grit and Grace* (New York: St. Martin's Press, 2019), 14–15.

Three counts of attempted murder, pertaining to the survivors, were added later.

304 **A month later, Loretta Lynch:** *U.S.A. v. Roof* (Indictment); Department of Justice, Attorney General Lynch Statement Following the Federal Grand Jury Indictment Against Dylann Storm Roof, July 22, 2015; Department of Justice, Attorney General Loretta E. Lynch Statement on the Case of Dylann Roof, May 24, 2016; Nick Gass, "Dylann Roof charged with Federal Hate Crime," *Politico*, July 22, 2015; Alan Blinder, "Man Charged in Charleston Massacre Will Face Two Death Penalty Trials," *NYT*, May 25, 2016, A-11; Alan Blinder, "Capital Trial Defies Will of Survivors of Massacre," *NYT*, November 27, 2016, A-20.

The phrase "related to hate crimes" is deliberate here, as the twelve counts charging Roof with a "hate crime act resulting in death" or "involving an attempt to kill" did not themselves carry the death penalty. Rather, the Department of Justice pursued the death penalty for nine counts of "obstruction of religion resulting in death" and nine counts of "use of a firearm to commit murder during and in relation to a crime of violence." The commission of a "hate crime act resulting in death" constituted one of those crimes of violence.

305 **The survivors and family members:** Blinder, "Capital Trial"; Meg Kinnard, "Charleston Church Slaying Families Accept Pursuit of Death Penalty," *TS*, May 25, 2016; Alexandra King, "Charleston Victim's Brother: Dylann Roof Should Get Death Penalty," CNN.com, December 16, 2016; Alan Blinder and Kevin Sack, "White Supremacist Guilty in Charleston Church Massacre," *NYT*, December 16, 2016, A-15; Monique L. Lyle and Robert W. Oldendick, "One Year Later: Race Relations and the Emanuel Nine Shooting," University of South Carolina Institute for Public Service and Policy Research, June 2016, 5; Interview with Polly Sheppard.

305 **There was never any question:** *U.S.A. v. Roof* (GX 22, 424; GVX 5; December 13, 2016, 1010–1047; Sealed Ex Parte Hearing, November 7, 2016, 44); Alan Blinder, "Mistrial Declared for South Carolina Officer Who Killed Unarmed Black Man," *NYT*, December 6, 2016, A-13; Alan Blinder and Kevin Sack, "Churchgoer Was Spared by Gunman to Tell Story," *NYT*, December 15, 2016, A-14; Alan Blinder, "White Officer Who Shot Black Man in the Back Is Sentenced to 20 Years," *NYT*, December 8, 2017, A-15.

After the mistrial in state court in December 2016, North Charleston police officer Michael Slager reached an agreement to plead guilty to federal civil-rights violations and received a sentence of twenty years.

306 **The lead FBI agent:** *U.S.A. v. Roof* (December 13, 2016, 985–986; Motion for Mistrial, Or For Curative and Prospective Relief, December 8, 2016, 4); Kevin Sack, "A Quiet Agony for Congregants in Courtroom 6," *NYT*, December 16, 2016, A-15; Interview with Sharon Risher.

306 **The adult survivors:** *U.S.A. v. Roof* (GX 424; December 7, 2016, 49–90; December 14, 2016, 1104–1131); Alan Blinder and Kevin Sack, "Dylann Roof Found Guilty in Charleston Church Massacre," *NYT*, December 15, 2016.

307 **After a holiday break:** *U.S.A. v. Roof* (January 4, 2017, 49); Alan Blinder and Kevin Sack, "Dylann Roof, Addressing Court, Offers No Apology or Explanation for Massacre," *NYT*, January 4, 2017.

307 **Jurors then sat:** *U.S.A. v. Roof* (GX 643, 746, 768; January 4, 2017, 177; January 6, 2017, 541, 580, 633–634); Kevin Sack and Alan Blinder, "At Charleston Gunman's Trial, a Question of How Many Tears Are Too Many," *NYT*, January 9, 2017, A-9.

308 **The decision had been obvious enough:** *U.S.A. v. Roof* (January 11, 2017, 16–18, 26, 31–33, 57–62, 82–83); Jennifer Berry Hawes, "Summoned to History: Jury Foreman, Alternate in Dylann Roof Trial Speak Publicly for the First Time," *PC*, January 14, 2018; Jennifer Berry Hawes, *Grace Will Lead Us Home: The Charleston Church Massacre and the Hard, Inspiring Journey to Forgiveness* (New York: St. Martin's Press, 2019), 279; Alan Blinder and Kevin Sack, "Dylann Roof Is Sentenced to Death in Charleston Church Massacre," *NYT*, January 10, 2017; Kevin Sack and Alan Blinder, "Anguish, Mercy and Defiance at Roof's Sentencing," *NYT*, January 12, 2017, A-12.

308 **Felicia Sanders clutched:** *U.S.A. v. Roof* (January 11, 2017, 6–8, 9–10, 88-93); Hawes, *Grace*, 139–141.

309 **Judge Gergel did not:** *U.S.A. v. Roof* (January 11, 2017, 93–94); "Jurors in Dylann Roof Case Say They 'Will Forever Be Changed' by Their Emanuel Experience," *PC*, February 25, 2017; Hawes, "Summoned to History."

Repulsively, in the decade following the Emanuel attack, Dylann Roof became something of an antihero to others who endorsed his views and methods. When white nationalists marched by torchlight through Charlottesville, Virginia, in August 2017, some chanted, "Dylann Roof was a hero!" A man who killed two black shoppers in a Louisville, Kentucky, supermarket in 2018 shouted Roof's name after being arrested. A woman convicted in 2019 for plotting to bomb a tavern in Toledo, Ohio, had written to Roof behind bars and created a Tumblr profile called "CharlestonChurchMiracle." The man who killed forty-nine people that same year at two mosques in Christchurch, New Zealand, claimed to have read Roof's writings. In a manifesto much like Roof's, the self-avowed racist who killed ten black shoppers in a Buffalo, New York, supermarket in 2022 credited Roof for inspiring his own graduation from internet hate. The Anti-Defamation League found in 2019 that Roof's iconic bowl haircut had become a white supremacist emblem, incorporated into camouflage jacket patches and internet screen names like "Bowl Gang," "Bowlwaffen Division," and "The Final Bowlution."

In 2017, a Black man killed one parishioner and wounded six others at a white church in Tennessee in an attack that authorities concluded was retaliatory for the Emanuel shootings.

Joe Heim, "Recounting a Day of Rage, Hate, Violence and Death," *WP*, August 14, 2017; Billy Kobin, "Prosecutors: Gregory Bush Shouted 'Dylann Roof' After Killing Two Black Shoppers at Kroger," *Courier Journal*, June 8, 2021; Cleve R. Wootson Jr. and Mark Berman, "A Woman Wanted to Commit a Mass Murder—So She Contacted Dylann Roof, Authorities Say," *WP*, December 11, 2018; Cory Shaffer, "Toledo Woman Who Communicated with South Carolina Church Shooter Dylann Roof Planned Domestic Attack, Officials Say," Cleveland.com, December 10, 2018; "New Zealand Mosque Shooter Mentioned Dylann Roof in Manifesto," *PC*, September 14, 2020; Manifesto of Payton Gendron, May 2022, provided by Anti-Defamation League; Anti-Defamation League, "Hardcore White Supremacists Elevate Dylann Roof to Cult Hero Status," February 6, 2019; Affidavit by Louie Espinosa, Jr., in Support of Complaint, Arrest and Search Warrant for Elizabeth Lecron, December 10, 2018, Case No. 3:18MJ5409, U.S. District Court for the Northern District of Ohio; Devlin Barrett, "Tennessee Church-Shooting Suspect Had Note Referencing Dylann Roof Attack," *WP*, September 29, 2017; Adam Tamburin, "Emanuel Samson Wanted to Kill 'A Minimum of 10 White Churchgoers,' Prosecutor Says at Trial," *The Tennessean*, May 20, 2019.

309 **In late March 2017:** Kevin Sack, "South Carolina Lets Church Gunman Plead Guilty to Avoid a Second Trial," *NYT*, April 1, 2017, A-10; Meg Kinnard and Denise Lavoie, "Charleston Church Shooter Dylann Roof's Conviction, Death Sentence Upheld," *PC*, August 25, 2021; Associated Press, "US Supreme Court Rejects Dylann Roof's Appeal of Sentence for Emanuel AME Shooting," *PC*, October 11, 2022.

CHAPTER XVII: THE HEALING

311 **The church's casual handling:** Gregory Yee, "SLED Finishes Its Emanuel AME Finance Investigation. No Wrongdoing Found," *PC*, November 19, 2019.

311 **At the time of the shootings:** Interview with Norvel Goff, Sr.

311 **On Saturday morning:** Interviews with Norvel Goff, Sr., Althea Richardson-Latham, Carla Jones, Maxine Smith, Carlotta Dennis, and Willi Glee; Jennifer Berry Hawes, "Answering a Prayer," *PC*, June 21, 2015; *Althea Richardson-Latham v. Emanuel African M.E. Church of Charleston, et al.* (Case No. 2016-CP-10-5507) (Deposition of Althea Richardson-Latham, February 28, 2018, 31).

312 **A thousand worshippers:** John Eligon and Richard Fausset, "Defiant Show of Unity in Church That Lost 9 to Racial Violence," *NYT*, June 22, 2015, A-1; Adam Parker, "Bent But Not Broken," *PC*, June 22, 2015, A1; Interview with Carlotta Dennis.

312 **Emanuel's choir sang:** Email from Lisa Washington Wade; "AME Emanuel Church Full Sermon," June 21, 2015; "Charleston's Emanuel AME Church: Scenes from Service," *The Wall Street Journal*, June 21, 2015.

312 **Although a native:** "Charleston's Emanuel AME Church: Scenes from Service."

314 **The Confederate banner had first been raised:** *U.S.A. v. Roof* (GX 4, 445, 447, 448).

314 **The Democrats found an unlikely partner:** Frances Robles, Richard Fausset, and Michael Barbaro, "Governor Joins the Call to Take Down Rebel Flag" (with transcript of Haley remarks), *NYT*, June 23, 2015, A-1; Richard Fausset, "Governor Points to Personal Reasons, Not Politics, for Shift on Confederate Flag," *NYT*, June 24, 2015, A-15; Meg Kinnard, "20 Years On, Ex-SC Gov Beasley's Prayer on Flag Answered," *PC*, July 10, 2015; Jennifer Berry Hawes and Doug Pardue, "Thousands Told Haley: Get Rid of Flag," *PC*, July 5, 2016; Michelin press statement, June 22, 2015; Jennifer Berry Hawes, "Nikki Haley Struggled with PTSD After Emanuel Shooting, Saw Horrors as UN Ambassador," *PC*, November 12, 2019; Nikki R. Haley, *With All Due Respect: Defending America with Grit and Grace* (New York: St. Martin's Press, 2019), 14–51.

315 **Surrounded by lawmakers:** Robles et al., "Governor Joins the Call"; Haley, *With All Due Respect*, 37.

315 **Haley's proposal:** Mark Berman, "South Carolina Governor Signs Bill Removing Confederate Flag from Statehouse Grounds," *WP*, July 9, 2015; Richard Fausset and Alan Blinder, "South Carolina Settles Its Decades-Old Dispute Over a Confederate Flag," *NYT*, July 10, 2015, A-16; Richard Fausset and Alan Blinder, "Era Ends as South Carolina Lowers Confederate Flag," *NYT*, July 11, 2015, A-9; Interview with Larry Grooms.

315 **Haley would later make her handling:** Nikki Haley presidential campaign announcement, February 14, 2023; Interview with Vincent A. Sheheen, June 18, 2020.

Hate-crimes bills that passed the South Carolina house of representatives failed to move out of the state senate in 2022, 2023, and 2024. Both chambers were controlled by Republicans. Jeffrey Collins, "South Carolina House OKs Hate Crimes Bill, Sends It to Senate," AP News, March 8, 2023; Jeffrey Collins, "South Carolina's Push to Be Next-to-Last State with Hate Crimes Law Stalls Again," *WP*, February 28, 2024.

316 **Legislators in other states:** Neil Vigdor, "North Carolina Discontinues License Plates with Confederate Flags," *NYT*, February 1, 2021; MJ Lee, "Walmart, Amazon, Sears, eBay to Stop Selling Confederate Flag Merchandise," CNN.com, June 24, 2015; Michael Levenson, "NASCAR Says It Will Ban the Confederate Battle Flag," *NYT*, June 11, 2020, B-9; Jeff Adelson and Jessica Williams, "New Orleans Completes Removal of Confederate Monuments with Take Down of Robert E. Lee Statue," *The Advocate*, May 19, 2017; Emily Bloch, "Duval School Board Votes to Rename 6 Confederate-Tied Schools, Including Lee," *Florida Times-Union*, June 1, 2021; Rick Rojas, "Mississippi Lawmakers Vote to Retire State Flag Rooted in the Confederacy," *NYT*, June 29, 2020, A-19; Joel Ebert, "Nathan Bedford Forrest Bust at the Tennessee Capitol: What You Need to Know," *The Tennessean*, August 18, 2017; Natalie Allison, "The Bust of Nathan Bedford Forrest Is Out of the Tennessee Capitol. Here's How It Happened," *The Tennessean*, July 23, 2021; Gregory S. Schneider and Laura Vozzella, "Robert E. Lee Statue Is Removed in Richmond, Ex-Capital of Confederacy, After Months of Protests and

Legal Resistance," *WP*, September 8, 2021; Helene Cooper, "Base Names Proposed to Honor New Heroes, Not the Confederacy," *NYT*, May 25, 2022, A-21; "Whose Heritage? Public Symbols of the Confederacy," Southern Poverty Law Center, February 1, 2019 (updated online April 12, 2023).

316   **When Sunday worship ended:** Interviews with Leon Alston and Daniel E. Martin, Jr.

317   **Celebrities started dropping by:** Kelly Rae Smith, "Pharrell Williams Performed 'Freedom' with Mother Emanuel Choir Sunday," *CCP*, November 1, 2015; Thad Moore, "Facebook CEO Mark Zuckerberg Visits Charleston, Attends Emanuel AME Service Sunday," *PC*, March 12, 2017.

317   **When Vice President Biden:** "Joe Biden Shares Story of Faith with Pastor Who Lost His Wife In Charleston Shooting," CNN, February 26, 2020; Joe Biden, *Promise Me, Dad: A Year of Hope, Hardship and Purpose* (New York: Flatiron Books, 2017), 216–221; Dan Morse, "Biden, Suffering in His Own Grief, Visits Church Where Nine People Were Killed," *WP*, June 28, 2015.

Although Joe Biden did not campaign at Emanuel in 2020, a pivotal moment in his come-from-behind victory in the South Carolina Democratic primary turned directly on the Emanuel tragedy. It occurred during a televised forum in Charleston four days before the balloting, when Biden was in freefall after poor finishes in the Iowa caucuses and New Hampshire primary. Then Vice President Biden fielded a question from Anthony Thompson, Myra Thompson's widower, about how faith would influence his decision-making. Biden, a practicing Catholic, didn't quite answer the question. But it prompted him to recount how deeply he had been moved by the melding of his own grief for his son with the losses experienced by the congregation and its families. "Because what you all did was astounding," he told Thompson, choking back emotion. "I don't know if you all know this. All those who died, were killed by this white supremacist, they forgave him. They forgave him. The ultimate act of Christian charity . . . You brought down that Confederate flag. You're the ones who changed the attitude in this state that was profound."

317   **Biden choked up:** The White House, "Remarks by President Biden at a Political Event, Charleston, SC," January 7, 2024.

318   **One telephone caller:** Dustin Waters, "Emanuel AME Church Receives Threatening Call," *CCP*, December 15, 2015; Brian Hicks, "Rumors About the Death of Racism Have Been Greatly Exaggerated," *PC*, July 26, 2015; Interview with Eric S. C. Manning.

318   **"We want our church back":** Interviews with William Dudley Gregorie and Samuel L. Green, Sr.

319   **"As far as I'm concerned":** Interview with Doris Coaxum Sanders.

319   **"What was the purpose?":** Interview with Charles N. Williams.

319   **On the first Sunday:** Interviews with Althea Richardson-Latham, Willi Glee, Kelly Small, and Pat Garner.

320   **Lee Cohen, a corporate headhunter:** Records of Emanuel AME Church Moving Forward Fund; Andrew Knapp and Jennifer Berry Hawes, "$2.5 Million Goes to Emanuel Survivors," *PC*, September 25, 2015; Adam Parker, "Emanuel Survivors to Get Share of $1.5 Million," *PC*, November 24, 2015; Jennifer Berry Hawes, "Emanuel Distributes Donations to Families," *PC*, May 5, 2016; Interview with Laura Evans, August 6, 2019.

320   **When envelopes bore the name:** *Richardson-Latham v. Emanuel* (Complaint; Depositions of Richardson-Latham, 36–41, 58–59, and Rosetta Singleton, February 28, 2018, 23–25); *Arthur S. Hurd v. Emanuel African Methodist Episcopal Church* (Case No. 2015-CP-10-5397) (Complaint; Consent Order, October 26, 2015; Consent Order, March 26, 2016; Affidavits of Rosetta Singleton, October 13, 2015, Norvel Goff, Sr., October 13, 2015, and Althea Latham, October 13, 2015); Interviews with Nadine Collier, Bruce Miller, Laura Evans, Kylon J. Middleton, and Norvel Goff, Sr.

321   **The discomfort deepened:** Jennifer Berry Hawes, "Emanuel AME Leader Faces Questions. Many Demand Answers over Donations, Past Financial Management," *PC*, October 2, 2015; Jennifer Berry Hawes, "Emanuel AME Shooting Victim's Husband Files Suit Seeking Transparency," *PC*, October 5, 2015; Jennifer Berry Hawes, "Parishioners at Goff's Former Church File Lawsuit," *PC*, November 7, 2015; *Norvel Goff v. William M. Toney*, Richland County Court of Common Pleas (2015-CP-40-7220) (Complaint; Stipulation of Dismissal); Email from Wilbur E. Johnson.

The litigation between Norvel Goff and the congregants of Reid Chapel was settled by the parties in 2019 without any admission of liability.

321 **Just days after the story dropped:** *Hurd v. Emanuel* (Complaint; Consent Order).

321 **To defend himself:** Adam Parker, "Goff Slams Critics of How Gifts Managed," *PC*, October 6, 2015; Dustin Waters, "Church Leader Defends Financial History and Handling of Donations to Emanuel AME," *CCP*, October 8, 2015; Jennifer Berry Hawes, "Families Critical of Goff," *PC*, July 8, 2016; Jennifer Berry Hawes, *Grace Will Lead Us Home: The Charleston Church Massacre and the Hard, Inspiring Journey to Forgiveness* (New York: St. Martin's Press, 2019), 141–155.

322 **The city had retained:** Andrew Knapp, "After Emanuel AME Church Shooting, Leaders Vow to Avoid Conflict over Millions in Donations," *PC*, August 26, 2015; Andrew Knapp and Jennifer Berry Hawes, "$2.5 Million Goes to Emanuel Survivors," *PC*, September 25, 2015; Interview with Laura Evans.

322 **Emanuel's leaders:** Adam Parker, "Emanuel Survivors to Get Share of $1.5 Million," *PC*, November 24, 2015; Jennifer Berry Hawes, "Emanuel Distributes Donations to Families," *PC*, May 5, 2016; Robert Behre, "Emanuel AME Being Tented for Termites As It Grapples with Major Repairs," *PC*, September 20, 2017; Interviews with Wilbur E. Johnson and Andrew J. Savage III.

322 **Goff announced in November 2015:** Parker, "Emanuel Survivors to Get Share"; Carolyn Murray, "Youngest Survivor of Emanuel AME Church Shooting Speaks Out Publicly for the First Time," WCBD-TV, August 19, 2021; *K.M. v. Meta Platforms* (Case No. 2:23-CV-1370, US. District Court for the District of South Carolina) (Complaint).

322 **Felicia Sanders found:** Hawes, *Grace*, 141–150, 205–207; Jennifer Berry Hawes, "'Forgotten' Survivors Search for Meaning: 2 Women Face Tough Road After Emanuel Tragedy Shatters Their Lives," *PC*, September 7, 2015; "June 17, 2015," ad, *CCP*, June 12, 2019; Jennifer Berry Hawes, "SLED Opens Investigation in Emanuel AME Church over Finances, Including Donations," *PC*, October 31, 2019; Yee, "SLED Finishes"; Jennifer Berry Hawes and Glenn Smith, "SLED Inquiry into Emanuel AME Church Donations Fails to Dispel Controversy," *PC*, January 7, 2020; Case Status Report, Case Number 31-19-0122, SC Law Enforcement Division, October 21, 2019; Interviews with Felicia and Tyrone Sanders and Andrew J. Savage III.

323 **Just days after the shootings:** Interviews with Polly Sheppard, Nadine Collier, and Chris Singleton.

323 **To combat the aftershocks:** "Responding to the Aftermath of the Mother Emanuel AME Massacre," Department of Justice, Office for Victims of Crime, June 2, 2016; Deanna Pan, "Ahead of Trial, Emanuel AME Church Opens 'Empowerment Center,'" *PC*, November 4, 2016; Interviews with Brenda Nelson and Eric S. C. Manning.

324 **"This girl has to be":** Sharon Risher, "My Mom Was Killed in the Charleston Shooting. Executing Dylann Roof Won't Bring Her Back," *Vox*, June 15, 2016; Hawes, *Grace*, 176–177.

324 **On January 23, 2016:** Interviews with Betty Deas Clark and Richard Franklin Norris, Sr.

325 **Norris recognized:** Interviews with Betty Deas Clark and Richard Franklin Norris, Sr.; Melissa Boughton, "New Emanuel AME Pastor in Sermon About Hope: 'Our Best Days Are In Front of Us,'" *PC*, January 24, 2016; Jennifer Berry Hawes, "New Pastor of Mother Emanuel Seeks Healing Amid the Clamor," *PC*, March 26, 2016.

325 **And then, almost as suddenly:** Interviews with Betty Deas Clark and Richard Franklin Norriss, Sr.; Emma Dumain, "From Orlando, Emanuel AME Pastor Calls for Stricter Gun Laws And Unity After Mass Shooting," *PC*, June 12, 2016; Jennifer Berry Hawes, "Emanuel AME Pastor Moved After Five Months on the Job," *PC*, June 21, 2016.

326 **But Clark had not cleared the trip:** Interviews with Betty Deas Clark and Richard Franklin Norris, Sr.; Melissa Boughton, "'Now Is the Time to Focus on God,' Says Emanuel Victim's Husband," *PC*, June 17, 2016; "Transition of Retired Bishop Richard Franklin Norris, Sr.," *CR*, June 15, 2023.

327 **Within sixteen months:** Incident/Investigation Report, Case 18-09326, Charleston Police Department, June 24, 2018; Interviews with Elnora Cohen Taylor, Theodora A. Watson, and Doris Coaxum Sanders.

328 **It was quite a scene:** Interviews with Ruby Nesbitt Martin and Leon Alston.

328 **There was a day not long after:** Interview with Eric S. C. Manning; Kevin Sack, "Anguished by 'Spiral of Hate,' Rabbi and Pastor Grieve as One," *NYT,* November 24, 2018, A-1; Jennifer Berry Hawes, "Emanuel AME Church, Shooting Survivors Form Bonds with Other Traumatized Houses of Worship," *PC,* June 15, 2019.

329 **Notwithstanding the flooding:** Rachel Chang, "This South Carolina Destination Was Just Named the No. 1 City in the U.S. by T+L Readers—Here's Why," *Travel + Leisure,* July 13, 2022; Melanie Lieberman, "The World's Best Cities in 2016," *Travel + Leisure,* July 6, 2016; Susan Crawford, *Charleston: Race, Water and the Coming Storm* (New York: Pegasus Books, 2023).

329 **The city committed itself to memorializing:** Emily Williams, "Despite Pandemic, Charleston Tourism Had Bigger Impact in 2021 Than Before COVID," *PC,* March 30, 2022; Melissa Boughton, "Dedication, Blessing Planned for Mother Emanuel Way Memorial District," *PC,* September 22, 2015; "Editorial: Sen. Pinckney Building Adds to Legacy," *Jasper County Sun Times,* February 22, 2017; Karl Puckett, "Tiny Chapel Built by Freed Slaves Now Honors Clementa Pinckney and Port Royal History," *TS,* June 16, 2022.

330 **There was a flowering:** Paul Bowers, "Savannah Folk Artist Paints Portraits of the Emanuel Nine," *CCP,* June 25, 2015; Tom Mack, "State Museum and Leo Twiggs Offer Tribute to Mother Emanuel," *Free Times,* February 7, 2018; Robert K. Oermann, "Nashville Song 'Mother Emanuel' Will Be Sung at Memorial for Charleston Church Shooting," *Music Row,* June 15, 2016; Vincent Harris, "Joan Baez Breaks from Her Farewell Tour to Perform at the Emanuel 9 Rally for Unity," *CCP,* June 20, 2018; "South Carolina's Ballet to Present 'Emanuel: Love Is the Answer,'" WCIV-TV, June 19, 2018; Adam Parker, "4 Years After the Charleston Church Shooting, Artists Help Public Digest the Horror," *PC,* June 16, 2019.

330 **Cynthia Hurd's family:** Jesse Naranjo, "Children's Book Drive in Honor of Librarian Killed in Church Shooting to Take Place in July," *PC,* June 27, 2018; "$3.2M Pinckney Scholarship for Students," *Jasper County Sun Times,* March 30, 2016.

331 **Hoping to harness that spirit:** Charleston Illumination Project, "Community Engagement, Strategic Planning and Engagement Report," September 2016; Adam Parker, "MUSC Resolution Atones for Past Discrimination," *PC,* August 14, 2015; Adam Parker, "College of Charleston Coming to Terms with Its Role in Slavery. A Documentary Is One Step," *PC,* August 24, 2019; Glenn Smith, "Illumination Project Unveils Actions to Improve Police, Community Relations," *PC,* November 21, 2016; Angie Jackson, "Pastor of Mount Zion AME Church Takes Helm of Charleston's Illumination Project," *PC,* June 28, 2018; Gregory Yee and Mikaela Porter, "Preliminary Charleston Police Audit Finds Racial Disparities, Paves Path Forward," *PC,* September 30, 2019.

331 **In July 2018, Israeli-born architect:** Kevin Sack, "For Memorial of Racist Church Massacre, A Plan for Benches Extended in Welcome," *NYT,* July 16, 2018, A-13; Ted Loos, "Architect and 9/11 Memorial Both Evolved over the Years," *NYT,* September 4, 2011; Ricky Ciapha Dennis, Jr., "Inflation Delays Groundbreaking, Adds Costs to Charleston's Emanuel Nine Memorial," *PC,* September 24, 2022.

332 **In 2017, the College of Charleston's Avery Research Center:** Stacey Patton, "The State of Racial Disparities in Charleston County, South Carolina, 2000–2015," ARC, 2017; Deanna Pan, "Poverty, Unemployment Disproportionately Affect Charleston County's Black Residents, Report Says," *PC,* November 13, 2017.

332 **"It acted as a placebo":** Interview with Thomas Dixon.

332 **In June 2018, near the third anniversary:** City Council of Charleston, Resolution 2018-011, June 19, 2018; Melissa Gomez, "Charleston Apologizes for City's Role in Slave Trade," *NYT,* June 19, 2018; Hannah Alani, "It's Official: Charleston Apologizes for Its Role in Slavery," *PC,* June 19, 2018; Abigail Darlington, "Why Charleston's Slavery Apology Barely Passed City Council," *PC,* June 24, 2018; Mikaela Porter, "One Year After Charleston Apologized for Slavery, A Broader Conversation Has Begun," *PC,* June 27, 2019.

333 **Twenty-two fires:** Jessica Holdman, Adam Benson, and Sara Coello, "Charleston Protests Turn Violent Overnight After Day of Peaceful Demonstrations," *PC,* May 30, 2020; Thomas Novelly, "2 Men in Trump Hats Cornered, Punched During Protest in Charleston," *PC,* May 30, 2020; Thomas Novelly, "City of Charleston Extends Curfew From 6 P.M. To 6 A.M.

Following Downtown Violence," *PC*, May 31, 2020; Hanna Raskin, "Downtown Charleston Restaurant and Bar Owners Recount Night of Horror as Violence Unfolded," *PC*, May 31, 2020; Adam Benson, "McMaster OKs SC National Guard Support for Charleston, Columbia," *PC*, May 31, 2020; Glenn Smith, "Daylight Reveals Path of Destruction in Charleston from Looting, Vandalism After Protests," *PC*, May 31, 2020; Hanna Raskin, "Restaurants and Bars Form 44 percent of Businesses Damaged in Downtown Charleston Looting," *PC*, June 5, 2020; Hanna Raskin, "911 Calls: Charleston Restaurant Workers Hid in Coolers, Courtyards in Horror Amid Riots," *PC*, June 10, 2020; Gregory Yee and Mikaela Porter, "13 Hours: How the George Floyd Protest and Rioting Changed Charleston," *PC*, August 29, 2020; Gregory Yee, "Charleston Police Say They've Changed Since May 2020 Rioting; Report Details How," *PC*, February 23, 2021; "Strengthening Charleston: Assessment of the Charleston Police Department Response to the May 30–31, 2020, Protests/Riots, Final Report," February 2021, 25–27, 30–39.

333 **"Y'all's cousins":** "Charleston Protests Turn Violent," *PC*; Jennifer Berry Hawes, "After Emanuel and Walter Scott Shootings, Charleston Stayed Nonviolent. What Changed?" *PC*, June 1, 2020.

334 **Other than Pastor Manning:** Interviews with Eric S. C. Manning and Dorothy Jenkins.

335 **Shortly after the protests began:** Special Commission on Equity, Inclusion and Racial Reconciliation, City of Charleston, "Report and Recommendations, August 2021"; Adam Parker, "Charleston's Racial Conciliation Commission Makes Its Recommendations," *PC*, August 4, 2021; Steve Bailey, "Reparations, Defund Police, Critical Race Theory? Read All About It, Charleston," *PC*, August 14, 2021; Edward M. Gilbreth, "Raucous Public Meetings No Way to Resolve Hot-Button Issues," *PC*, August 26, 2021; Adam Parker, "Charleston City Council Votes No on Forming New Racial Conciliation Commission," *PC*, September 20, 2021; Emma Whalen, "Charleston Council Votes to Revive Racial Reconciliation Commission," *PC*, December 21, 2021; Emma Whalen and Adam Parker, "Political Group Targeting Charleston City Council Vote on Racial Reconciliation Commission," *PC*, January 10, 2022; Emma Whalen, "Charleston Race Conciliation Commission Buckling Under Weight of Compromise," *PC*, January 30, 2022; Emma Whalen, "Charleston Approves Amended Racial Conciliation Commission," *PC*, February 9, 2022; Dustin Waters, "Charleston's New Manager of Tolerance and Racial Reconciliation Looks Ahead," *CCP*, July 10, 2019; Stephen Hobbs, "New Charleston Commission Focused on Racial Equality Begins Work Amid Hope, Suspicion," *PC*, July 17, 2022; City Council of Charleston Ordinances 2020-81 and 2022–18; Interview with Amber Johnson.

335 **Just as Dylann Roof unwittingly embarrassed:** Fleming Smith, "'Take It Down': Calhoun Statue Will Be Moved from Marion Square, Charleston Mayor Says," *PC*, June 17, 2020; Stephen Hobbs, Gregory Yee, Jerrel Floyd, Mikaela Porter, Fleming Smith, and Rickey Ciapha Dennis, "John C. Calhoun Statue Taken Down from Its Perch Above Charleston's Marion Square," *PC*, June 23, 2020.

EPILOGUE: ON FORGIVENESS AND GRACE

338 **"If I have to forgive":** Richard Fausset, "Open Doors and Lingering Pain at Church Where 9 Were Killed," *NYT*, October 19, 2015, A-1; Interviews with Dot Scott, Melvin L. Graham, Jr., and Malcolm Graham.

338 **It served as an unburdening:** Nadine V. Wedderburn and Robert E. Carey, "Forgiveness in the Face of Hate," in *Multiculturalism and the Convergence of Faith and Practical Wisdom in Modern Society*, ed. Ana Maria Pascal (Hershey, PA: IGB Global, 2017), 319; Albert J. Raboteau, "Forgiveness and the African American Church Experience," presentation to the Faith Angle Forum, November 2015, 30–31.

339 **"History has proven":** Martin Luther King, Jr., "Eulogy for the Martyred Children," September 18, 1963, in *A Call to Conscience: The Landmark Speeches of Martin Luther King, Jr.*, eds. Clayborne Carson and Kris Shepard (New York: IPM/Warner Books, 2001), 89–100.

339 **This employment of forgiveness:** Howard Thurman, *Deep River and the Negro Spiritual Speaks of Life and Death* (Richmond, IN: Friends United Press, 1975), 36.

NOTES TO PAGES 339–354

339 **"It's victory out of defeat":** David Remnick, "Blood at the Root: In the Aftermath of the Emanuel Nine," *The New Yorker*, September 21, 2015; Raboteau, "Forgiveness," 6; Interview with John Hurst Adams.

James H. Cone and John Hurst Adams died in 2018; Albert J. Raboteau died in 2021.

340 **Hear out Harold Washington:** Interview with Harold Washington.

340 **"Forgiveness is hard-wired":** Joseph Darby, The Faith and Politics Institute, Circular Congregational Church, Charleston, SC, March 19, 2016.

341 **"something out of this world":** Interview with Chris Singleton.

341 **Nadine Collier, the first to speak:** Interview with Nadine Collier; Nadine Collier, The Faith and Politics Institute, Circular Congregational Church, Charleston, SC, March 19, 2016.

341 **Growing up at Emanuel:** Interviews with Nadine Collier and Anthony Thompson; Anthony Thompson, Emanuel AME Church Bible Study, June 12, 2019.

342 **Sanders has since explained:** Michael Schwirtz and Chris Dixon, "Some Forgive, No One Forgets: Charleston, One Year Later," *NYT*, June 17, 2016, A-15; Felicia Sanders, College of Charleston forum, June 6, 2019.

342 **Simmons and Middleton-Brown:** Interviews with Alana Simmons Grant and Bethane Middleton-Brown.

Middleton-Brown died in 2021.

342 **It took some time:** "Charleston Shooting Survivors Open Up About the Power of Forgiveness," *Today*, September 20, 2018.

343 **When, for instance:** Kevin Sack, "Anguished by 'Spiral of Hate,' Rabbi and Pastor Grieve as One," *NYT*, November 24, 2018, A-1.

343 **The British theologian:** Anthony Bash, *Forgiveness and Christian Ethics* (Cambridge, UK: Cambridge University Press, 2007), 26, 79–81, 104, 174, 177–178.

345 **Bash wrote:** Bash, *Forgiveness,* 23, 63, 68.

345 **Across those same generations:** Bash, *Forgiveness*, 37–39.

345 **"To forgive is indeed":** Jacques Derrida, *On Cosmopolitanism and Forgiveness* (London: Routledge, 2001), 32–34, 58–59; Desmond Mpilo Tutu, *No Future Without Forgiveness* (New York: Doubleday, 1999), 31, 35, 272.

345 **"Pardoning died":** Derrida, *On Cosmopolitanism*, 37; Vladimir Jankélévitch, "Should We Pardon Them?" *Critical Inquiry* 22, no. 3 (Spring 1996): 567.

346 **"When the families":** Remnick, "Blood at the Root."

Muhiyidin d'Baha, also known as Muhiyidin Elamin Moye, was shot to death in New Orleans in 2018 in a homicide apparently unrelated to his activism.

347 **Although it captivated:** Isabel Wilkerson, *Caste: The Origins of Our Discontents* (New York: Random House, 2020), 287; Roxane Gay, "Why I Can't Forgive the Killer in Charleston," *NYT*, June 23, 2015, A-23; Stacey Patton, "Black America Should Stop Forgiving White Racists," *WP*, June 22, 2015.

347 **Near the fourth anniversary:** "Forgiveness After a Massacre In Charleston," WAMU-FM, June 4, 2019; Dietrich Bonhoeffer, *The Cost of Discipleship* (New York: Touchstone, 1959), 43–44; Wedderburn and Carey, "Forgiveness in the Face of Hate," 319.

348 **"Aren't they wonderful?":** Interview with Joseph Darby.

348 **"I'm sick and tired":** Interview with Minerva Brown King.

348 **"We've tidied up":** Kylon J. Middleton, College of Charleston forum, June 6, 2019.

349 **"I still come here":** Interview with Melvin L. Graham, Jr.

349 **Graham attended Roof's bond hearing:** Interview with Melvin L. Graham, Jr.; Gene Demby, "The Charleston Story: A Knotted Mix of Race, Grace and Injustice," NPR, December 16, 2016.

354 **Longtime members who were instructed:** Interview with Doris Coaxum Sanders.

Bibliography

Aba-Mecha, Barbara W. "South Carolina Conference of NAACP: Origin and Major Accomplishments, 1939–1954." *The Proceedings of the South Carolina Historical Association* (1981).
Abbott, Martin. *The Freedmen's Bureau in South Carolina, 1865–1872.* Chapel Hill: The University of North Carolina Press, 1967.
Abernathy, Ralph David. *And the Walls Came Tumbling Down.* New York: Harper & Row, 1989.
Acts of the General Assembly of the State of South Carolina Passed at the Sessions of 1864–65. Columbia: Julian A. Selby, 1866.
Acts and Joint Resolutions of the General Assembly of the State of South Carolina, Passed at the Regular Session of 1869–70. Columbia: John W. Denny, 1870.
Acts and Joint Resolutions of the General Assembly of the State of South Carolina Passed at the Regular Session of 1904. Columbia: The State Company, 1904.
The Address of the General Conference of the Methodist Episcopal Church, to All Their Brethren and Friends in the United States, May 20, 1800.
Adger, John B. *My Life and Times, 1810–1899.* Richmond: The Presbyterian Committee of Publication, 1899.
———. *The Religious Instruction of the Colored Population. A Sermon Preached by the Rev. John B. Adger, in the Second Presbyterian Church, Charleston, S.C., May 9, 1847.* Charleston: T. W. Haynes, 1847.
Allen, Richard. *A Collection of Spiritual Songs and Hymns from Various Authors.* Philadelphia: T. L. Plowman, 1801.
———. *The Life, Experience, and Gospel Labours of the Rt. Rev. Richard Allen.* Philadelphia: Martin & Boden, 1833.
Allen, Richard, and Absalom Jones. "Some Letters of Richard Allen and Absalom Jones to Dorothy Ripley." *The Journal of Negro History* 1, no. 4 (October 1916).
Allen, Richard, and Jacob Tapsico. *The Doctrines and Discipline of the African Methodist Episcopal Church.* Philadelphia: John H. Cunningham, 1817.
Andrew, James Osgood. "Letters on Methodist History: Rise and Progress of Methodism in Charleston, South Carolina." *Methodist Magazine and Quarterly Review* 12 (1830).
Andrews, Dee E. "The African Methodists of Philadelphia, 1794–1802." *Pennsylvania Magazine of History and Biography* 108, no. 2 (October 1984).
———. *The Methodists and Revolutionary America, 1760–1800: The Shaping of an Evangelical Culture.* Princeton: Princeton University Press, 2000.
Andrus, Ann Taylor. *The Name Shall Be Bethel: The History of Bethel United Methodist Church 1797–1997.* Columbia: The R. L. Bryan Company, 1997.
Annual Report of the New York National Freedman's Relief Association, of New York, with a Sketch of Its Early History. New York: Holman, 1866.
Aptheker, Herbert. *American Negro Slave Revolts.* New York: International Publishers, 1943.
———. "Eighteenth Century Petition of South Carolina Negroes." *The Journal of Negro History* 31, no. 1 (January 1946).
———. "South Carolina Negro Conventions, 1865." *The Journal of Negro History* 31, no. 1 (January 1946).
———. "South Carolina Poll Tax, 1737–1895," *The Journal of Negro History* 31, no. 2 (April 1946).
Arnett, Benjamin W., ed. *The Budget for 1881.* Xenia, OH: Torchlight Printing Company, 1881.
———. *The Budget of 1884.* Dayton: Christian Publishing House, 1884.

———. *The Budget of 1904*. Philadelphia: E. W. Lampton and J. H. Collett, 1904.
———. *The Centennial Budget*. 1887.
———. *Journal of the 17th Session and the 16th Quadrennial Session of the General Conference of the African Methodist Episcopal Church in the United States, Held at St. Louis, Missouri, May 3–25, 1880*. Xenia, OH: Torchlight Printing Company, 1882.
———. *Proceedings of the Quarto-Centennial Conference of the African M.E. Church of South Carolina, at Charleston, S.C., May 15, 16 and 17, 1889*. Published by the editor, 1890.
Articles of Association of the African Methodist Episcopal Church, of the City of Philadelphia, in the Commonwealth of Pennsylvania. Philadelphia: John Ormrod, 1799.
Asbury, Francis. *The Journal of the Rev. Francis Asbury, Bishop of the Methodist Episcopal Church from August 7, 1771, to December 7, 1815, in Three Volumes*. New York: N. Bangs and T. Mason, 1821.
Ashmore, Nancy V. "The Development of the AME Church in South Carolina, 1865–1965." MA thesis, University of South Carolina, 1969.
Ashton, Susanna. *I Belong to South Carolina: South Carolina Slave Narratives*. Columbia: University of South Carolina Press, 2010.
Baker, R. Scott. *Paradoxes of Desegregation: African American Struggles for Educational Equity in Charleston, South Carolina, 1926–1972*. Columbia: University of South Carolina Press, 2006.
Ball, Edward. *Slaves in the Family*. New York: Farrar, Straus & Giroux, 1998.
———. *The Sweet Hell Inside: The Rise of an Elite Black Family in the Segregated South*. New York: Perennial, 2001.
Bangs, Nathan. *The Life of the Rev. Freeborn Garrettson: Compiled from His Printed and Manuscript Journals and Other Authentic Documents*. New York: Carlton & Lanahan, 1832.
Bash, Anthony. *Forgiveness and Christian Ethics*. Cambridge, UK: Cambridge University Press, 2007.
Bass, Jack, and Jack Nelson. *The Orangeburg Massacre*. Macon, GA: Mercer University Press, 1984.
Bass, Jack, and Marilyn W. Thompson. *Strom: The Complicated Personal and Political Life of Strom Thurmond*. New York: PublicAffairs, 2005.
Berlin, Ira. *Slaves Without Masters: The Free Negro in the Antebellum South*. Oxford: Oxford University Press, 1974.
Bess, Thomas L., Sr., and Garland D. Davis. *Morris Brown: The Invisible Man of the African Methodist Episcopal Church*. Midwest City, OK: Jewell Jordan Publishing, 2019.
Bethel, Elizabeth Rauh. *Promiseland: A Century of Life in a Negro Community*. Columbia: University of South Carolina Press, 1997.
Betts, Albert Deems. *History of South Carolina Methodism*. Columbia, SC: The Advocate Press, 1952.
Biden, Joe. *Promise Me, Dad: A Year of Hope, Hardship and Purpose*. New York: Flatiron Books, 2017.
Blackburn, George A., ed. *The Life Work of John L. Girardeau, D.D. L.L.D., Late Professor in the Presbyterian Theological Seminary, Columbia, S.C.* Columbia: The State Company, 1916.
Bleser, Carol K. Rothrock. *The Promised Land: The History of the South Carolina Land Commission, 1869–90*. Columbia: University of South Carolina Press, 1969.
Bonhoeffer, Dietrich. *The Cost of Discipleship*. New York: Touchstone, 1959.
Born in Slavery: Slave Narratives from the Federal Writers' Project, 1936–1938. Washington, D.C.: Library of Congress, 1941.
Brauer, Simon G. "How Many Congregations Are There? Updating a Survey-Based Estimate." *Journal for the Scientific Study of Religion* 56, no. 2 (June 2017).
Brief History of the New York National Freedman's Relief Association. New York: N.Y.N.F.R.A., 1866.
Brimelow, Judith, and Michael E. Stevens. *State Free Negro Capitation Tax Books, Charleston, South Carolina, ca. 1811–1860*. Columbia: South Carolina Department of Archives and History, 1983.
Brinson, Claudia Smith. *Stories of Struggle: The Clash over Civil Rights in South Carolina*. Columbia: University of South Carolina Press, 2000.
Brown, Cynthia Stokes, ed. *Ready from Within: Septima Clark and the Civil Rights Movement, A First Person Narrative*. Trenton, NJ: Africa World Press, 1990.
Brown, Millicent E. *Civil Rights Activism in Charleston, South Carolina, 1940–1970*. PhD dissertation, Florida State University, 1997.
Buckley, James M. *A History of Methodism in the United States*, Vol. 1. New York: The Christian Literature Co., 1897.
Bureau of the Census. *Religious Bodies, 1916*. Washington, D.C.: Government Printing Office, 1919.

Butler, Nic. "Charles Town's Growing Pains." *Charleston Time Machine*, March 9, 2018.
———. "The Charleston Riot of 1919," *Charleston Time Machine*, May 10, 2019.
———. "Commemorating the African-ness of Charleston's History." *Charleston Time Machine*, February 1, 2019.
———. "Defining Charleston's Free People of Color." *Charleston Time Machine*, February 7, 2020.
———. "Denmark Vesey's Winning Lottery Ticket." *Charleston Time Machine*, February 23, 2018.
———. "The Evolution of Charleston's Name." *Charleston Time Machine*, August 9, 2019.
———. "South Carolina's Capitation Tax on Free People of Color, 1756–1864." *Charleston Time Machine*, January 28, 2022.
———. "The South Carolina Constitutional Convention of 1868." *Charleston Time Machine*, March 2, 2018.
———. "Squeezing Charleston Neck, from 1783 to the Present." *Charleston Time Machine*, August 31, 2018.
Butterfield, L.H., ed. *Letters of Benjamin Rush*, Vol. 1, *1761–1792*. Princeton: Princeton University Press, 1951.
Caldwell, A. B., ed. *History of the American Negro, South Carolina Edition*. Atlanta: A. B. Caldwell Publishing Co., 1919.
Campbell, James T. *Songs of Zion: The African Methodist Episcopal Church in the United States and South Africa*. Chapel Hill: The University of North Carolina Press, 1998.
Cannon, Noah C. W. *A History of the African Methodist Episcopal Church, The Only One in the United States of America, Styled Bethel Church*. Rochester: Strong & Dawson, Printers, 1842.
Capers, William. *Catechism for the Use of the Methodist Missions. First Part*. John Early, for the Methodist Episcopal Church, South, 1853.
Carey, Mathew. *A Short Account of the Malignant Fever Lately Prevalent in Philadelphia: With a Statement of the Proceedings That Took Place on the Subject in Different Parts of the United States*. Philadelphia: Printed by the Author, 1793.
Carson, Clayborne, et al., eds. *The Papers of Martin Luther King, Jr.*, Vol. 6, *Advocate of the Social Gospel, September 1948–March 1963*. Berkeley: University of California Press, 2007.
———. *The Papers of Martin Luther King, Jr.*, Vol. 7, *To Save the Soul of America, January 1961–August 1962*. Berkeley: University of California Press, 2014.
Carson, Clayborne, and Kris Shepard, eds., *A Call to Conscience: The Landmark Speeches of Martin Luther King, Jr*. New York: IPM/Warner Books, 2001.
Chafe, William H. *Civilities and Civil Rights: Greensboro, North Carolina, and the Black Struggle for Freedom*. New York: Oxford University Press, 1980.
Charron, Katherine Mellen. *Freedom's Teacher: The Life of Septima Clark*. Chapel Hill: The University of North Carolina Press, 2009.
Chestnut, Trichita M. "Lynching: Ida B. Wells-Barnett and the Outrage over the Frazier Baker Murder." *Prologue* 40, no. 3 (Fall 2008).
Chreitzberg, A. M. *Early Methodism in the Carolinas*. Nashville: Publishing House of the Methodist Episcopal Church, South, 1897.
Clark, Septima Poinsette. *Echo in My Soul*. New York: E. P. Dutton & Co., 1962.
Clarke, Erskine. *Our Southern Zion: A History of Calvinism in the South Carolina Low Country, 1690–1990*. Tuscaloosa: The University of Alabama Press, 1996.
———. *Wrestlin' Jacob: A Portrait of Religion in Antebellum Georgia and the Carolina Low Country*. Tuscaloosa: The University of Alabama Press, 2000.
Coclanis, Peter A. *The Shadow of a Dream: Economic Life and Death in the South Carolina Low Country 1670–1920*. New York: Oxford University Press, 1989.
Coclanis, Peter A., and Lacy K. Ford. "The South Carolina Economy Reconstructed and Reconsidered: Structure, Output, and Performance, 1670–1985." In *Developing Dixie: Modernization in a Traditional Society*, edited by Winfred B. Moore, Jr., Joseph F. Tripp, and Lyon G. Tyler, Jr. Westport, CT: Greenwood Press, 1988.
Code of Laws of South Carolina, 1952. Charlottesville: The Michie Company, 1952.
Coker, Daniel. *A Dialogue Between a Virginian and an African Minister*. Baltimore: Benjamin Edes, for Joseph James, 1810.
Combined Minutes of the General Conference, African Methodist Episcopal Church, 1948 (Kansas City,

Kansas)—1952 (Chicago, Illinois)—1956 (Miami, Florida). Nashville: A.M.E. Sunday School Union, 1956.

Cone, James H. *Black Theology and Black Power.* New York: Harper & Row, 1969.

The Conservation of Mother Emanuel AME's Cemetery: A Report Completed by the Graduate Program in Historic Preservation at Clemson University and the College of Charleston, 2017.

Cooper, Ezekiel, and George A. Phoebus. *Beams of Light on Early Methodism in America.* New York: Phillips & Hunt, 1887.

Cooper, Thomas. *The Statutes at Large of South Carolina,* Vols. 2, 3, and 5. Columbia: A. S. Johnston, 1837–1839.

Cornelius, Janet Duitsman. *Slave Missions and the Black Church in the Antebellum South.* Columbia: University of South Carolina Press, 1999.

———. *When I Can Read My Title Clear: Literacy, Slavery, and Religion in the Antebellum South.* Columbia: University of South Carolina Press, 1991.

Côté, Richard N. *City of Heroes: The Great Charleston Earthquake of 1886.* Mt. Pleasant, SC: Corinthian Books, 2006.

Crawford, Susan. *Charleston: Race, Water, and the Coming Storm.* New York: Pegasus Books, 2023.

Curnock, Nehemiah, ed. *The Journal of the Rev. John Wesley, M.A., Vols. 1–8.* New York: Eaton & Mains, 1909.

Dalcho, Frederick. *Practical Considerations Founded on the Scriptures, Relative to the Slave Population of South-Carolina.* Charleston: A. E. Miller, 1823.

Dart, J. L. *The Famous Trial of the Eight Men Indicted for the Lynching of Frazier B. Baker and His Baby, Late Postmaster of Lake City in the U.S. Circuit Court, at Charleston, SC, April 10–22, 1899.*

Day, Alfred T. III. "Creaking Timbers and Conflicting Traditions: Richard Allen and the St. George's Walkout." *Journal of the Historical Society of the Eastern Pennsylvania Conference,* 2007.

Debnam, Jewell Charmaine. "Black Women and the Charleston Hospital Workers' Strike of 1969." PhD dissertation, Michigan State University, 2016.

Declaration of the Immediate Causes Which Induce and Justify the Secession of South Carolina from the Federal Union; and the Ordinance of Secession. Charleston: Evans & Cogswell, 1860.

Derrida, Jacques. *On Cosmopolitanism and Forgiveness.* London: Routledge, 2001.

DeSaussure, Henry William. *A Series of Numbers Addressed to the Public, on the Subject of Slaves and Free People of Color.* Columbia: State Gazette Office, 1822.

Devlin, George A. *South Carolina and Black Migration, 1865–1940: In Search of the Promised Land.* New York: Garland Publishing, 1989.

Dickerson, Dennis C. *African Methodism and Its Wesleyan Heritage: Reflections on AME Church History.* Nashville: AMEC Sunday School Union, 2009.

———. *The African Methodist Episcopal Church: A History.* Cambridge, UK: Cambridge University Press, 2020.

———. *A Liberated Past: Explorations in A.M.E. Church History.* Nashville: AMEC Sunday School Union, 2003.

———. "Liberation, Wesleyan Theology and Early African Methodism, 1766–1840." *Wesley and Methodist Studies* 3 (2011).

———. *Religion, Race, and Region: Research Notes on A.M.E. Church History.* Nashville: AMEC Sunday School Union, 1995.

Digest of the Ordinances of the City Council of Charleston From the Year 1783 to July 1818. Charleston: Archibald E. Miller, 1818.

The Doctrine and Discipline of the African Methodist Episcopal Church, 2000. Nashville: AMEC Publishing House, Sunday School Union, 2001.

The Doctrine and Discipline of the African Methodist Episcopal Church, 2021. Nashville: The AME Sunday School Union, 2022.

Douglass, William. *Annals of the First African Church in the United States of America, Now Styled The African Episcopal Church of St. Thomas, Philadelphia.* Philadelphia: King & Baird, 1862.

Drago, Edmund L. *Initiative, Paternalism & Race Relations: Charleston's Avery Normal Institute.* Athens: The University of Georgia Press, 1990.

Dray, Philip. *Capitol Men: The Epic Story of Reconstruction Through the Lives of the First Black Congressmen.* New York: Houghton Mifflin, 2008.

BIBLIOGRAPHY

Du Bois, W.E.B. "The Evolution of Negro Leadership." *The Dial* 31, no. 362 (July 1901).
———. *The Ordeal of Mansart*. New York: Mainstream Publishers, 1957.
———. *The Souls of Black Folks: Essays and Sketches*. Chicago: A. C. McClurg & Co., 1903.
Du Bois, W.E.B., ed. *The Negro Church*. Atlanta: The Atlanta University Press, 1903.
Durden, Robert F. "The Establishment of Calvary Protestant Episcopal Church for Negroes in Charleston." *The South Carolina Historical Magazine* 65, no. 2 (April 1964).
Eblen, Jack Ericson. "New Estimates of the Vital Rates of the United States Black Population During the Nineteenth Century." *Demography* 11, no. 2 (May 1974).
Edgar, Walter. *South Carolina: A History*. Columbia: University of South Carolina Press, 1998.
Egerton, Douglas R. "Forgetting Denmark Vesey; Or, Oliver Stone Meets Richard Wade." *The William and Mary Quarterly* 59, no. 1 (January 2002).
———. *He Shall Go Out Free: The Lives of Denmark Vesey*. Lanham, MD: Rowman & Littlefield, 2004.
———. "'Why They Did Not Preach Up This Thing': Denmark Vesey and Revolutionary Theology." *The South Carolina Historical Magazine* 100, no. 4 (October 1999).
Egerton, Douglas R., and Robert L. Paquette, eds. *The Denmark Vesey Affair: A Documentary History*. Gainesville: University Press of Florida, 2017.
Eleventh General Conference of the African M.E. Church, Held in Cincinnati, Ohio, May 5, 1856. Philadelphia: William S. Young, 1856.
Ellis, Clifton, and Rebecca Ginsburg. *Slavery in the City: Architecture and Landscapes of Urban Slavery in North America*. Charlottesville: University of Virginia Press, 2017.
The Episcopal Address to the Thirtieth General Conference of the African Methodist Episcopal Church, New York City, May 6, 1936.
The Episcopal Address to the Thirty-Eighth Quadrennial Session of the General Conference of the African Methodist Episcopal Church, Philadelphia, Pennsylvania, May 1–14, 1968.
The Episcopal Address to the Thirty-Fifth Quadrennial Session of the General Conference of the African Methodist Episcopal Church Convening in Miami, Florida, May 2–16, 1956.
The Episcopal Address to the Thirty-First Quadrennial Session of the General Conference of the African Methodist Episcopal Church at Detroit, Michigan, May 1940.
The Episcopal Address to the Thirty-Fourth Quadrennial Session of the General Conference of the African Methodist Episcopal Church at Chicago, Illinois, May 1952.
The Episcopal Address to the Thirty-Second Quadrennial Session of the General Conference of the African Methodist Episcopal Church at Philadelphia, Pennsylvania, May 1944.
The Episcopal Address to the Thirty-Seventh Quadrennial Session of the General Conference of the African Methodist Episcopal Church Meeting in Cincinnati Gardens, Cincinnati, Ohio, May 6–18, 1964.
Episcopal Address to the Thirty-Third Session of the General Conference of the African Methodist Episcopal Church, Kansas City, Kansas, May 5, 1948.
The Episcopal Address to the Twenty-Fourth General Conference of the African Methodist Episcopal Church, Kansas City, Missouri. Nashville: Publishing House of the A.M.E. Sunday School Union, 1912.
Episcopal Address to the Twenty-Sixth General Conference of the A.M.E. Church, May 1920, St. Paul A.M.E. Church, St. Louis, Missouri. Nashville: Publishing House of the A.M.E. Sunday School Union, 1920.
Estes, Steve. *Charleston in Black and White: Race and Power in the South after the Civil Rights Movement*. Chapel Hill: The University of North Carolina Press, 2015.
The Fifteenth Quadrennial Session of the General Conference of the African Methodist Episcopal Church, Place of Session, Nashville, Tennessee, May 6, 1872. Philadelphia: Publishing Department of the AME Church, 1876.
Finke, Roger, and Rodney Stark. "Turning Pews into People: Estimating 19th Century Church Membership." *Journal for the Scientific Study of Religion* 25, no. 2 (1986).
"The First Charter Granted by King Charles the Second, to the Lords Proprietors of Carolina." In *The Colonial Records of North Carolina*, Vol. 1, edited by William L. Saunders. Raleigh: P.M. Hale, 1886.
Foner, Eric. *Freedom's Lawmakers: A Directory of Black Officeholders During Reconstruction*. Revised Edition. Baton Rouge: Louisiana State University Press, 1993.
———. *Reconstruction: America's Unfinished Revolution, 1863–1877*. New York: Harper & Row, 1988.

Ford, Lacy K. *Deliver Us from Evil: The Slavery Question in the Old South*. New York: Oxford University Press, 2009.
Fordham, Damon L. *True Stories of Black South Carolina*. Charleston: The History Press, 2008.
———. *Voices of Black South Carolina: Legend & Legacy*. Charleston: The History Press, 2009.
Foster, Lisa, with Mary Lou Murray Coombs. *Janie Mitchell, Reliable Cook: An Ex-Slave's Recipe for Living, 1862–1931*. Charleston: Evening Post Books, 2011.
Fraser, Walter J., Jr. *Charleston! Charleston!: The History of a Southern City*. Columbia: University of South Carolina Press, 1989.
Frazier, E. Franklin. *The Negro Church in America*. New York: Schocken Books, 1963.
Frazier, Herb, Bernard Edward Powers, Jr., and Marjory Wentworth. *We Are Charleston: Tragedy and Triumph at Mother Emanuel*. Nashville: W Publishing Group, 2016.
Freehling, William W. *Prelude to Civil War: The Nullification Controversy in South Carolina 1816–1836*. New York: Oxford University Press, 1965.
Frey, Sylvia R., and Betty Wood. *Come Shouting to Zion: African American Protestantism in the American South and British Caribbean to 1830*. Chapel Hill: The University of North Carolina Press, 1998.
Furman, Richard. *Exposition of the Views of the Baptists, Relative to the Coloured Population of the United States, in a Communication to the Governor of South-Carolina*. Charleston: A. E. Miller, 1823.
Gaines, Wesley J. *African Methodism in the South; or Twenty-Five Years of Freedom*. Atlanta: Franklin Publishing House, 1890.
Garnet, Henry Highland. *Walker's Appeal, With a Brief Sketch of His Life*. New York: J. H. Tobitt, 1848.
Garrettson, Freeborn. *A Dialogue Between Do-Justice and Professing-Christian*. Wilmington: Peter Brynberg, undated.
Garrow, David J. *Bearing the Cross: Martin Luther King, Jr., and the Southern Christian Leadership Conference*. New York: Vintage Books, 1986.
Gatell, Frank Otto, ed. "Postmaster Huger and the Incendiary Publications." *The South Carolina Historical Magazine* 64, no. 4 (October 1963).
Gates, Henry Louis, Jr. *The Black Church: This Is Our Story, This Is Our Song*. New York: Penguin Press, 2021.
———. *Stony the Road: Reconstruction, White Supremacy and the Rise of Jim Crow*. New York: Penguin Press, 2019.
Genovese, Eugene D. *Roll, Jordan, Roll: The World the Slaves Made*. New York: Vintage, 1972.
George, Carol V. R. *Segregated Sabbaths: Richard Allen and the Emergence of Independent Black Churches, 1760–1840*. New York: Oxford University Press, 1973.
Gergel, Richard. *Unexampled Courage: The Blinding of Sgt. Isaac Woodard and the Awakening of President Harry S. Truman and Judge J. Waties Waring*. New York: Sarah Crichton Books, 2019.
Gibson, Campbell. *Population of the 100 Largest Cities and Other Urban Places in the United States, 1790 to 1990*. Washington, D.C.: U.S. Census Bureau, 1998.
Gibson, Campbell, and Kay Jung, *Historical Census Statistics on Population Totals by Race, 1790 to 1990, and by Hispanic Origin, 1970 to 1990, for the United States, Regions, Divisions and States*. Washington, D.C.: U.S. Census Bureau, 2002.
Gibson, Edmund. *Two Letters of the Lord Bishop of London*. London: Joseph Downing, 1727.
Gilreath, James, ed. *Federal Copyright Records, 1790–1800*. Washington, D.C.: Library of Congress, 1987.
Glaude, Eddie S., Jr. *Exodus! Religion, Race, and Nation in Early Nineteenth-Century Black America*. Chicago: The University of Chicago Press, 2000.
Gordon, Sarah Barringer. "The African Supplement: Religion, Race, and Corporate Law in Early National America." *The William and Mary Quarterly* 72, no. 3 (July 2015).
Grammich, Clifford, et al. *2020 U.S. Religion Census: Religious Congregations & Adherents Study*. Association of Statisticians of American Religious Bodies, 2023.
Gravely, William B. "James Lynch and the Black Christian Mission During Reconstruction." In *Black Apostles at Home and Abroad: Afro-Americans and the Christian Mission from the Revolution to Reconstruction*. Edited by David W. Wills and Richard Newman. Boston: G. K. Hall & Co., 1982.

Greene, Harlan, Harry S. Hutchins, Jr., and Brian E. Hutchins. *Slave Badges and the Slave-Hire System in Charleston, South Carolina, 1783–1865.* Jefferson, NC: McFarland & Company, 2004.

Greene, Harlan, and Jessica Lancia. "The Holloway Scrapbook: The Legacy of a Charleston Family." *The South Carolina Historical Magazine* 111, no. 1–2 (January–April 2010).

Grimke, Archibald H. *Right on the Scaffold, or The Martyrs of 1822.* Washington, D.C.: The American Negro Academy, 1901.

Hagy, James W. *Charleston, South Carolina City Directories for the Years 1816, 1819, 1822, 1825 and 1829.* Baltimore: Clearfield, 1996.

———. *Directories for the City of Charleston, South Carolina, for the Years 1830–31, 1835–36, 1836, 1837–38 and 1840–41.* Baltimore: Clearfield, 1997.

———. *People and Professions of Charleston, South Carolina, 1782–1802.* Baltimore: Clearfield, 1992.

Hale, Jon. "'The Fight Was Instilled in Us': High School Student Activism and the Civil Rights Movement In Charleston." *The South Carolina Historical Magazine* 114, no. 1 (January 2013).

Haley, Nikki R. *With All Due Respect: Defending America with Grit and Grace.* New York: St. Martin's Press, 2019.

Hamer, Philip M. "Great Britain, the United States, and the Negro Seamen Acts, 1822–1848." *The Journal of Southern History* 1, no. 1 (February 1935).

Hamilton, James. *Negro Plot: An Account of the Late Intended Insurrection Among a Portion of the Blacks of the City of Charleston, South Carolina.* Boston: Joseph W. Ingraham, 1822.

Hampton, Christine W., and Rosalee W. Washington. *The History of Lincolnville, South Carolina.* Charleston: BookSurge, 2007.

Handy, James A. *Scraps of African Methodist Episcopal History.* Philadelphia: A.M.E. Book Concern, 1902.

Harding, Vincent. "Religion and Resistance Among Antebellum Negroes, 1800–1860." In *The Making of Black America*, edited by August Meier and Elliott Rudwick. New York: Atheneum, 1969.

———. *There Is a River: The Black Struggle for Freedom in America.* New York: Harcourt Brace Jovanovich, 1981.

Harlan, Louis R., ed. *The Booker T. Washington Papers*, Vol. 3. Charlottesville: University of Virginia Press, Rotunda, 2021.

Harris, Robert L., Jr. "Charleston's Free Afro-American Elite: The Brown Fellowship Society and the Humane Brotherhood." *The South Carolina Historical Magazine* 82, no. 4 (October 1981).

Harris, William C. "James Lynch: Black Leader in Southern Reconstruction." *The Historian* 34, no. 1 (November 1971).

Hartzell, Joseph C. "Methodism and the Negro in the United States." *The Journal of Negro History* 8, no. 3 (July 1923).

Hawes, Jennifer Berry. *Grace Will Lead Us Home: The Charleston Church Massacre and the Hard, Inspiring Journey to Forgiveness.* New York: St. Martin's Press, 2019.

Hemmingway, Theodore. "Prelude to Change: Black Carolinians in the War Years, 1914–1920." *The Journal of Negro History* 65, no. 3 (Summer 1980).

Hemphill, W. Edwin, ed. *The Papers of John C. Calhoun*, Vol. 7, *1822–1823*. Columbia: University of South Carolina Press, 1973.

Henry, H. M. *The Police Control of the Slave in South Carolina.* PhD dissertation, Vanderbilt University, 1914.

Hicks, Brian. *In Darkest South Carolina: J. Waties Waring and the Secret Plan That Sparked a Civil Rights Movement.* Charleston: Evening Post Books, 2018.

———. *The Mayor: Joe Riley and the Rise of Charleston.* Charleston: Evening Post Books, 2015.

Higginson, Thomas Wentworth. "The Story of Denmark Vesey." *Atlantic Monthly,* June 1861.

Hildebrand, Reginald F. "Richard Harvey Cain, African Methodism & the Gospel of Freedom in South Carolina." *The A.M.E. Church Review* 117, no. 381 (January–March 2001).

———. *The Times Were Strange and Stirring: Methodist Preachers and the Crisis of Emancipation.* Durham, NC: Duke University Press, 1995.

Hinks, Peter P. *To Awaken My Afflicted Brethren: David Walker and the Problem of Antebellum Slave Resistance.* University Park: The Pennsylvania State University Press, 1997.

Historical Statistics of the United States, Colonial Times to 1970. Washington, D.C.: Bureau of the Census, 1975.

Hoffius, Steve. "Charleston Hospital Workers' Strike, 1969." In *Working Lives: The Southern Exposure History of Labor in the South*, edited by Marc S. Miller. New York: Pantheon Books, 1974.

Holland, Edwin C. (writing as A South-Carolinian). *A Refutation of the Calumnies Circulated Against the Southern & Western States, Respecting the Institution and Existence of Slavery Among Them.* Charleston: A. E. Miller, 1822.

Hollister, Lahnice McFall, ed. *Resisting Jim Crow: The Autobiography of Dr. John A. McFall*. Simpsonville, SC: Kittawah Press, 2021.

Holt, Thomas. *Black over White: Negro Political Leadership in South Carolina During Reconstruction.* Urbana: University of Illinois Press, 1977.

Hunt, Benjamin F. *The Argument of Benj. Faneuil Hunt, in the case of the arrest of the Person claiming to be a British Seaman, under the 3d section of the State Act of December 1822, in relation to Negroes, &c. before the Hon. Judge Johnson, Circuit Judge of the United States, for the 6th Circuit.* Charleston: A. E. Miller, 1823.

Jackson, David H., Jr. *Booker T. Washington and the Struggle against White Supremacy: The Southern Educational Tours, 1908–1912.* New York: Palgrave Macmillan, 2008.

———. "Booker T. Washington in South Carolina, March 1909." *The South Carolina Historical Magazine* 113, no. 3 (July 2012).

Jackson, John Andrew. *The Experience of a Slave in South Carolina.* London: Passmore & Alabaster, 1862.

Jackson, Luther P. "Religious Instruction of Negroes, 1830–1860, with Special Reference to South Carolina." *The Journal of Negro History* 15, no. 1 (January 1930).

Jackson, Thomas. *The Life of the Rev. Charles Wesley.* London: John Mason, 1841.

Jankélévitch, Vladimir, and Ann Hobart. "Should We Pardon Them?" *Critical Inquiry* 22, no. 3 (Spring 1996).

January, Alan F. "The South Carolina Association: An Agency for Race Control in Antebellum Charleston." *The South Carolina Historical Magazine* 78, no. 3 (July 1977).

Jarrett, Valerie. *Finding My Voice: My Journey to the West Wing and the Path Forward.* New York: Viking, 2019.

Jenkins, James. *Experience Labours and Suffering of Rev. James Jenkins.* Printed for the author, 1842.

Jenkins, Wilbert L. *Seizing the New Day: African-Americans in Post-Civil War Charleston.* Bloomington: Indiana University Press, 1998.

Jervey, Theodore D. *Robert Y. Hayne and His Times.* New York: The MacMillan Company, 1909.

Johnson, Andre E., and Earle J. Fisher. "'But I Forgive You?': Mother Emanuel, Black Pain and the Rhetoric of Forgiveness." *The Journal of Communication and Religion* 42, no. 1 (Spring 2019).

Johnson, Michael P. "Denmark Vesey and His Co-Conspirators." *The William and Mary Quarterly* 58, no. 4 (October 2001).

———. "Denmark Vesey's Church." *The Journal of Southern History* 86, no. 4 (November 2020).

———. "Reading Evidence." *The William and Mary Quarterly* 59, no. 1 (January 2002).

———. "Telemaque's Pilgrimage? A Tale of Two Charleston Churches, Three Missionaries, and Four Ministers, 1783–1817." *The South Carolina Historical Magazine* 118, no. 1 (January 2017).

Johnson, Michael P., and James L. Roark. *Black Masters: A Free Family of Color in the Old South.* New York: W. W. Norton & Co., 1984.

———. "'A Middle Ground': Free Mulattoes and the Friendly Moralist Society of Antebellum Charleston." *Southern Studies* (Fall 1982).

Johnson, Michael P., and James L. Roark, eds. *No Chariot Let Down: Charleston's Free People of Color on the Eve of the Civil War.* Chapel Hill: The University of North Carolina Press, 1984.

Johnson, William. *To the Public of Charleston.* Charleston: C. C. Sebring, 1822.

Jones, Absalom, and Richard Allen. *A Narrative of the Proceedings of the Black People During the Late Awful Calamity in Philadelphia in the Year 1793: And a Refutation of Some Censures Thrown Upon Them in Some Late Publications.* Philadelphia: William W. Woodward, 1794.

Jones, Alice Hanson. *Wealth of a Nation to Be: The American Colonies on the Eve of the Revolution.* New York: Columbia University Press, 1980.

Jones, Charles C. *The Religious Instruction of the Negroes in the United States.* Savannah: Thomas Purse, 1842.

Jones, Norrece T., Jr. *Born a Child of Freedom, Yet a Slave: Mechanisms of Control and Strategies of*

Resistance in Antebellum South Carolina. Hanover, NH: Wesleyan University Press/University Press of New England, 1990.
Journal of the Convention of the People of South Carolina, Held in Columbia, S.C., December 1865. Columbia: J. A. Selby, 1865.
Journal of the 17th Session and the 16th Quadrennial Session of the General Conference of the African Methodist Episcopal Church in the United States, Held at St. Louis, Missouri, May 3–25, 1880. Xenia, Ohio: Torchlight Printing Company, 1882.
Journals of the General Assembly of the State of South Carolina Being the Regular Session of 1869–'70. Columbia: John W. Denny, 1870.
Journals of the General Conference of the Methodist Episcopal Church, Vol. 1, 1796–1836. New York: Carlton & Phillips, 1855.
Keenan, Cody. *Grace: President Obama and Ten Days in the Battle for America.* New York: Mariner Books, 2022.
Kelly, Joseph. *America's Longest Siege: Charleston, Slavery, and the Slow March Toward Civil War.* New York: Overlook Press, 2013.
Kennedy, Lionel H., and Thomas Parker. *An Official Report of the Trials of Sundry Negroes, Charged with an Attempt to Raise an Insurrection in the State of South-Carolina.* Charleston: James R. Schenk, 1822.
Kingsley, Zephaniah. *A Treatise on the Patriarchal or Co-operative System of Society as It Exists in Some Governments, and Colonies in America, and in the United States, Under the Name of Slavery with its Necessity and Advantages.* No publisher, 1829.
Klebaner, Benjamin Joseph. "American Manumission Laws and the Responsibility for Supporting Slaves." *The Virginia Magazine of History and Biography* 63, no. 4 (October 1955).
Klingberg, Frank J., ed., *The Carolina Chronicle of Dr. Francis Le Jau, 1706–1717.* Berkeley: University of California Press, 1956.
Kluger, Richard. *Simple Justice: The History of Brown v. Board of Education and Black America's Struggle for Equality.* New York: Vintage Books, 1975.
Koger, Larry. *Black Slaveowners: Free Black Slave Masters in South Carolina, 1790–1860.* Jefferson, NC: McFarland & Co., 1985.
Kytle, Ethan J., and Blain Roberts. *Denmark Vesey's Garden: Slavery and Memory in the Cradle of the Confederacy.* New York: The New Press, 2018.
Lamson, Peggy. *The Glorious Failure: Black Congressman Robert Brown Elliott and the Reconstruction in South Carolina.* New York: W. W. Norton & Company, 1973.
Lau, Peter F. *Democracy Rising: South Carolina and the Fight for Black Equality Since 1865.* Lexington: The University Press of Kentucky, 2006.
Lee, Jarena. *The Life and Religious Experience of Jarena Lee, A Colored Lady, Giving an Account of Her Call to Preach the Gospel.* Cincinnati: Printed and published for the author, 1839.
Lewis, David Levering. *W.E.B. Du Bois: A Biography.* New York: Henry Holt and Company, 2009.
Lincoln, C. Eric, and Lawrence H. Mamiya. *The Black Church in the African American Experience.* Durham, NC: Duke University Press, 1990.
Lineberry, Cate. *Be Free or Die: The Amazing Story of Robert Smalls' Escape from Slavery to Union Hero.* New York: Picador, 2017.
Litwack, Leon F. *Been in the Storm So Long: The Aftermath of Slavery.* New York: Vintage Books, 1979.
Litwack, Leon, and August Meier, eds. *Black Leaders of the Nineteenth Century.* Urbana: University of Illinois Press, 1988.
Lofton, John M., Jr. "Denmark Vesey's Call to Arms." *The Journal of Negro History* 33, no. 4 (October 1948).
Lofton, John. *Insurrection in South Carolina: The Turbulent World of Denmark Vesey.* Yellow Springs, OH: The Antioch Press, 1964.
Logue, Cal M. "Racist Reporting During Reconstruction." *Journal of Black Studies* 9, no. 3 (March 1979).
Loy, Wesley. "10 Rumford Place: Doing Confederate Business in Liverpool." *The South Carolina Historical Magazine* 98, no. 4 (October 1997).
Lynching in America: Confronting the Legacy of Racial Terror. Montgomery, AL: Equal Justice Initiative, 2017.
Margo, Robert A. *Race and Schooling in the South, 1880–1950: An Economic History.* Chicago: The University of Chicago Press, 1990.

Marrant, John. *A Narrative of the Lord's Wonderful Dealings with John Marrant, A Black*. London: Gilbert and Plummer, 1785.
Martis, Kenneth. *Historical Atlas of Political Parties in the United States Congress, 1789–1989*. New York: Macmillan, 1989.
Mathews, Donald G. *Slavery and Methodism: A Chapter in American Morality 1780–1845*. Westport, CT: Greenwood Press, 1965.
May, Nicholas. "Holy Rebellion: Religious Assembly Laws in Antebellum South Carolina and Virginia." *The American Journal of Legal History* 49, no. 3 (July 2007).
McCord, David J. *The Statutes at Large of South Carolina*, Vol. 7. Columbia: A. S. Johnston, 1840.
McKinley, Carl. *The August Cyclone: A Descriptive Narrative of the Memorable Storm of 1885*. Charleston: The News and Courier Book Presses, 1886.
McWhirter, Cameron. *Red Summer: The Summer of 1919 and the Awakening of Black America*. New York: Henry Holt and Company, 2011.
Melton, J. Gordon. *A Will to Choose: The Origins of African American Methodism*. Lanham, MD: Rowman & Littlefield Publishers, 2007.
Memorial of the Citizens of Charleston to the Senate and House of Representatives of the State of South-Carolina. Charleston: Duke & Browne, 1822.
Minutes of the Annual Conferences of the Methodist Episcopal Church for the Years 1773–1828. Vol. 1. New York: T. Mason and G. Lane, 1840.
Minutes of the Annual Conferences of the Methodist Episcopal Church, for the Years 1829–1839. Vol. 2. New York: T. Mason and G. Lane, 1840.
Minutes of the Annual Conferences of the Methodist Episcopal Church, for the Years 1839–1845. Vol. 3. New York: T. Mason and G. Lane, 1840.
Minutes of the Annual Conferences of the Methodist Episcopal Church, South for the Years 1849–1850. Richmond: John Early, 1850.
Minutes of the Annual Conferences of the Methodist Episcopal Church, South, for the Year 1860. Nashville: Southern Methodist Publishing House, 1861.
Minutes of the Annual Conferences of the Methodist Episcopal Church, South, for the Year 1861. Nashville: Southern Methodist Publishing House, 1870.
Minutes of the General and Annual Conferences, of the African Methodist E. Church, Comprising Four Districts; From 1836 to 1839, Inclusive. Brooklyn: George Hogarth, 1839.
Minutes of the General and Annual Conferences, of the African Methodist Episcopal Church, Comprising Four Districts, for A.D. 1839–40. Brooklyn: George Hogarth, 1840.
Minutes of the Proceedings of the Committee Appointed on the 14th September 1783. Philadelphia: R. Aitken & Son, 1784.
Minutes of the South Carolina Annual Conference of the African M.E. Church, 1865, 1866, 1867. Charleston: Charleston Messenger Print, 1914.
Minutes of the Eleventh Session of the South Carolina Annual Conference of the African Methodist Episcopal Church Held at Abbeville, C.H., S.C., From February 6 to February 16, 1875. Charleston: Walker, Evans & Cogswell, 1875.
Minutes of the Twelfth Session of the South Carolina Annual Conference of the African Methodist Episcopal Church Held at Charleston, S.C., from February 1st to February 10th, 1876. Charleston: Walker, Evans & Cogswell, 1876.
Minutes of the Thirteenth General Conference of the African M.E. Church, Held in Philadelphia, PA., May 2, 1864. Philadelphia: William S. Young, 1864.
Minutes of the Nineteenth Session of the South Carolina Annual Conference of the African Methodist Episcopal Church Held at Charleston, S.C., from February 14th to February 20th, 1883. Charleston: Walker, Evans & Cogswell, 1883.
Minutes of the Twentieth Session of the South Carolina Annual Conference of the African Methodist Episcopal Church held at Georgetown, S.C., from February 13th to February 19th, 1884. Charleston: Walker, Evans & Cogswell, 1884.
Minutes of the Eighty-Fourth Session of the South Carolina Annual Conference of the Seventh Episcopal District Held in Emanuel A.M.E. Church, Charleston, South Carolina, November 12–16, 1947. Columbia: The Allen University Press, 1947.

Montgomery, William E. *Under Their Own Vine and Fig Tree: The African-American Church in the South, 1865–1900.* Baton Rouge: Louisiana State University Press, 1993.

Mood, F. A. *Methodism in Charleston: A Narrative of the Chief Events Relating to the Rise and Progress of the Methodist Episcopal Church in Charleston, S.C.* Nashville: E. Stevenson and J. E. Evans, 1856.

Murphy, Walter F. "The South Counterattacks: The Anti-NAACP Laws." *The Western Political Quarterly* 12, no. 2 (June 1959).

Murray, Pauli, ed. *States' Laws on Race and Color.* Woman's Division of Christian Service, Methodist Church, 1951.

Nash, Gary B. *Forging Freedom: The Formation of Philadelphia's Black Community, 1720–1840.* Cambridge: Harvard University Press, 1988.

———. "New Light on Richard Allen: The Early Years of Freedom." *The William and Mary Quarterly* 46, no. 2 (April 1989).

Nepveux, Ethel Trenholm Seabrook. *George Alfred Trenholm and the Company that Went to War, 1861–1865.* Charleston: Comprint, 1973.

———. *George A. Trenholm: Financial Genius of the Confederacy, His Associates and His Ships that Ran the Blockade.* Anderson, SC: The Electric City Printing Company, 1999.

Newby, Idus A. *Black Carolinians: A History of Blacks in South Carolina from 1895 to 1968.* Columbia: University of South Carolina Press, 1973.

Newman, Richard. *Freedom's Prophet: Bishop Richard Allen, the AME Church, and the Black Founding Fathers.* New York: New York University Press, 2008.

Nuttli, Otto W., G. A. Bollinger, and Robert B. Herrmann. *The 1886 Charleston, South Carolina, Earthquake—A 1986 Perspective.* Washington, D.C.: United States Government Printing Office, 1986.

Obama, Barack. *The Audacity of Hope: Thoughts on Reclaiming the American Dream.* New York: Three Rivers Press, 2006.

———. *Dreams from My Father: A Story of Race and Inheritance.* New York: Times Books, 1995.

Obama, Michelle. *Becoming.* New York: Crown, 2018.

Oliphant, Mary C. Simms. *The History of South Carolina.* River Forest, IL: Laidlaw Brothers, 1964.

O'Malley, Gregory E. "Beyond the Middle Passage: Slave Migration from the Caribbean to North America, 1619–1807." *The William and Mary Quarterly* 66, no. 1 (January 2009).

O'Neall, John Belton. *The Negro Law of South Carolina.* Columbia: John G. Bowman, 1848.

O'Neill, Stephen. *From the Shadow of Slavery: The Civil Rights Years in Charleston.* PhD dissertation, University of Virginia, 1994.

Palmer, Benjamin M. *Religion Profitable: with a Special Reference to the Case of Servants. A Sermon, Preached on September 22, 1822, in the Circular Church, Charleston, S.C.* Charleston: J. R. Schenck, 1822.

Paquette, Robert L. "From Rebellion to Revisionism: The Continuing Debate about the Denmark Vesey Affair." *The Journal of the Historical Society* 4, no. 3 (Fall 2004).

———. "Jacobins of the Lowcountry: The Vesey Plot on Trial." *The William and Mary Quarterly* 59, no. 1 (January 2002).

Paquette, Robert L., and Douglas R. Egerton. "Of Facts and Fables: New Light on the Denmark Vesey Affair." *The South Carolina Historical Magazine* 105, no. 1 (January 2004).

Parlett, Martin A. "Like a Lion Bound, Hear Him Roar: Richard Harvey Cain and a Rhetoric of Reconstruction." In *Before Obama: A Reappraisal of Black Reconstruction Era Politicians*, Vol. 2, *Black Reconstruction Era Politicians: The Fifteenth Amendment in Flesh and Blood*, ed. Matthew Lynch. Santa Barbara: Praeger, 2012.

Parsons, Stanley B., William W. Beach, and Michael J. Dubin. *United States Congressional Districts and Data, 1843–1883.* New York: Greenwood Press, 1986.

Payne, Daniel A. "The African M. E. Church in Its Relations to the Freedmen." In *Bishop Payne's Address Before the College Aid Society.* Xenia, OH: Torchlight Co., 1868.

———. "Biography of Morris Brown." In *The Lives of the Bishops of the Methodist Church.* Atlanta: Morris Brown College, undated.

———. *History of the African Methodist Episcopal Church.* Nashville: Publishing House of the A.M.E. Sunday-School Union, 1891.

———. *Recollections of Seventy Years*. Nashville: Publishing House of the A.M.E. Sunday School Union, 1888.
———. *The Semi-Centenary and the Retrospection of the African Meth. Episcopal Church in the United States of America*. Baltimore: Sherwood & Co., 1866.
———. *Sermons and Addresses, 1853–1891,* Charles Killian, ed. New York: Arno Press, 1972.
———. *Welcome to the Ransomed; or, Duties of the Colored Inhabitants of the District of Columbia.* Baltimore: Bull & Tuttle, 1862.
Phillips, C. H. *The History of the Colored Methodist Episcopal Church in America: Comprising its Organization, Subsequent Development and Present Status.* Jackson, TN: Publishing House C.M.E. Church, 1925.
Pickett, Otis Westbrook. "'We Are Marching to Zion': Zion Church and the Distinctive Work of Presbyterian Slave Missionaries in Charleston, South Carolina, 1849–1874." In *The Proceedings of the South Carolina Historical Association*, edited by Robert Figueira and Stephen Lowe, 2010.
Pinckney, Charles Cotesworth. *An Address Delivered in Charleston, Before the Agricultural Society of South-Carolina, at Its Anniversary Meeting on Tuesday, the 18th August, 1829.* Charleston: A. E. Miller, 1829.
Pinckney, Elise, ed. *Register of St. Philip's Church, Charleston, South Carolina, 1810 Through 1822.* Charleston: National Society of the Colonial Dames of America in the State of South Carolina, 1973.
Pinckney, Thomas (writing as Achates). *Reflections, Occasioned by the Late Disturbances in Charleston.* Charleston: A. E. Miller, 1822.
Poston, Jonathan H. *The Buildings of Charleston: A Guide to the City's Architecture.* Columbia: University of South Carolina Press, 1997.
Potts, J. Manning, ed. *The Journal and Letters of Francis Asbury.* Vol. 3, *The Letters.* London: Epworth Press, 1958.
Powers, Bernard E., Jr. *Black Charlestonians: A Social History, 1822–1885.* Fayetteville: The University of Arkansas Press, 1994.
———. "Community Evolution and Race Relations in Reconstruction Charleston, South Carolina." *The South Carolina Historical Magazine* 101, no. 3 (July 2000).
———. "'I Go to Set the Captives Free': The Activism of Richard Harvey Cain, Nationalist Churchman and Reconstruction-Era Leader." In *The Southern Elite and Social Change*, edited by Randy Finley and Thomas A. DeBlack. Fayetteville: The University of Arkansas Press, 2002.
Preservation Society of Charleston. *The Churches of Charleston and the Low Country.* Columbia: University of South Carolina Press, 1994.
Proceedings of the Colored People's Convention of the State of South Carolina, Held in Zion Church, Charleston, November, 1865. Charleston: South Carolina Leader Office, 1865.
Proceedings of the Constitutional Convention of South Carolina, Held at Charleston, S.C., Beginning January 14th and ending March 17th, 1868. Charleston: Denny & Perry, 1868.
Proceedings of the Eighth General Conference of the African M.E. Church, Held in the City of Philadelphia, May 1st, 1848, and Continued in Session Twenty-One Days. Pittsburgh: Benj. F. Peterson, 1848.
Proceedings of the Meeting in Charleston, S.C., May 13–15, 1845, on the Religious Instruction of the Negroes, together with the Report of the Committee and the Address to the Public. Charleston: B. Jenkins, 1845.
Public Proceedings Relating to Calvary Church and the Religious Instruction of Slaves. Charleston: Miller & Browne, 1850.
Purifoy, Lewis M. "The Southern Methodist Church and the Proslavery Argument." *The Journal of Southern History* 32, no. 3 (August 1966).
The Quadrennial Address of the Bishops of the A.M.E. Church to the General Conference Convened in Wilmington, N.C., May 4, 1896. Xenia OH: Chew, Pr.
The Quadrennial Address of the Bishops of the A.M.E. Church to the Twenty-Third General Conference, Convened at Norfolk, Virginia, May 4, 1908.
The Quadrennial Address of Bishops to the Twenty-First Session of the General Conference of the A.M.E. Church, Held in Columbus, Ohio, May 1900. Benjamin F. Lee.

Raboteau, Albert J. "Forgiveness and the African American Church Experience." Transcript of a presentation to the Faith Angle Forum, November 2015.

———. *Slave Religion: The "Invisible Institution" in the Antebellum South*. New York: Oxford University Press, 1978.

Ravenel, Beatrice St. Julien. *Architects of Charleston*. Charleston: Carolina Art Association, 1964.

Remnick, David. "Blood at the Root: In the Aftermath of the Emanuel Nine." *The New Yorker*, September 21, 2015.

Richardson, Harry V. *Dark Salvation: The Story of Methodism as It Developed Among Blacks in America*. Garden City, NY: Anchor Press-Doubleday, 1976.

Riley, Charlotte S. *A Mysterious Life and Calling: From Slavery to Ministry in South Carolina*. Crystal J. Lucky, ed. Madison: The University of Wisconsin Press, 2016.

Risher, Sharon. *For Such a Time as This: Hope and Forgiveness After the Charleston Massacre*. St. Louis: Chalice Press, 2019.

Robertson, David. *Denmark Vesey: The Buried Story of America's Largest Slave Rebellion and the Man Who Led It*. New York: Vintage Books, 1999.

———. "Inconsistent Contextualism: The Hermeneutics of Michael Johnson." *The William and Mary Quarterly* 59, no. 1 (January 2002).

Robinson, Marilynne. *Gilead*. New York: Farrar, Straus and Giroux, 2004.

Rollin, Frank A. *Life and Public Services of Martin R. Delany*. Boston: Lee and Shepard, 1883.

Roper, L. H. "The 1701 'Act for the Better Ordering of Slaves': Reconsidering the History of Slavery in Proprietary South Carolina." *The William and Mary Quarterly* 64, no. 2 (April 2007).

Rose, Willie Lee. *Rehearsal for Reconstruction: The Port Royal Experiment*. New York: Oxford University Press, 1964.

Rubio, Philip F. "'Though He Had a White Face, He Was a Negro in Heart': Examining the White Men Convicted of Supporting the Denmark Vesey Slave Insurrection Conspiracy." *The South Carolina Historical Magazine* 113, no. 1 (January 2012).

Rucker, Walter C. "I Will Gather All Nations: Resistance, Culture and Pan-African Collaboration in Denmark Vesey's South Carolina." *The Journal of Negro History* 86, no. 2 (Spring 2001).

Rules and Regulations of the Brown Fellowship Society. Charleston: J. B. Nixon, 1844.

Rules of the South-Carolina Association Adopted in the City of Charleston on the Fourth Thursday in July Being the 25th Day, A.D. 1823. Charleston: Archibald E. Miller, 1823.

Schoeppner, Michael A. *Moral Contagion: Black Atlantic Sailors, Citizenship, and Diplomacy in Antebellum America*. Cambridge, UK: Cambridge University Press, 2019.

———. "Navigating the Dangerous Atlantic: Racial Quarantines, Black Sailors and United States Constitutionalism." PhD dissertation, University of Florida, 2010.

———. "Peculiar Quarantines: The Seamen Acts and Regulatory Authority in the Antebellum South." *Law and History Review* 31, no. 3 (August 2013).

Scott, Janny. *A Singular Woman: The Untold Story of Barack Obama's Mother*. New York: Riverhead Books, 2011.

Seabrook, Whitemarsh B. *An Essay on the Management of Slaves, and Especially, on Their Religious Instruction; Read Before the Agricultural Society of St. John's Colleton*. Charleston: A. E. Miller, 1834.

Sernett, Milton C. *Black Religion and American Evangelicalism: White Protestants, Plantation Missions, and the Flowering of Negro Christianity, 1787–1865*. Metuchen, NJ: The Scarecrow Press and the American Theological Library Association, 1975.

Shipp, Albert M. *The History of Methodism in South Carolina*. Nashville: Southern Methodist Publishing House, 1884.

Simkins, Francis Butler, and Robert Hilliard Woody. *South Carolina During Reconstruction*. Chapel Hill: The University of North Carolina Press, 1932.

Simmons, William J. *Men of Mark: Eminent, Progressive and Rising*. Cleveland: Geo. M. Rewell & Co., 1887.

Simpson, Robert Drew, ed. *American Methodist Pioneer: The Life and Journals of the Rev. Freeborn Garrettson, 1752–1827: Social and Religious Life in the U.S. During the Revolutionary and Federal Periods*. Rutland, VT: Academy Books, 1984.

Singleton, George A. *The Romance of African Methodism: A Study of the African Methodist Episcopal Church*. New York: Exposition Press, 1952.

Sirmans, M. Eugene. "The Legal Status of the Slave in South Carolina, 1670–1740." *The Journal of Southern History* 28, no. 4 (November 1962).

The Sixteenth Session, and the Fifteenth Quadrennial Session of the General Conference of the African Methodist Episcopal Church. Place of Session, Atlanta, Georgia, from May 1st to 18th, 1876.

Sloat, William A. II. "George Whitefield, African-Americans, and Slavery." *Methodist History* 33, no. 1 (October 1994).

Smith, Charles Spencer. *A History of the African Methodist Episcopal Church.* Philadelphia: Book Concern of the A.M.E. Church, 1922.

———. *The Life of Daniel Alexander Payne, D.D., L.L.D.* Nashville: Publishing House A.M.E. Church Sunday School Union, 1894.

Smith, Charles Spencer, ed. *Sermons Delivered by Bishop Daniel A. Payne, D.D., LL.D., Before the General Conference of the A.M.E. Church, Indianapolis, Ind. May, 1888.* Nashville: Publishing House A.M.E. Sunday School Union, 1888.

Smith, David. *Biography of Rev. David Smith of the A.M.E. Church, Being a Complete History, Embracing over Sixty Years' Labor in the Advancement of the Redeemer's Kingdom on Earth.* Xenia, OH: Xenia Gazette, 1881.

Smith, Edward D. *Climbing Jacob's Ladder: The Rise of Black Churches in Eastern American Cities, 1740–1877.* Washington, D.C.: Smithsonian Institution, 1988.

Spady, James O'Neil. "Belonging and Alienation: Gullah Jack and Some Maroon Dimensions of the 'Denmark Vesey Conspiracy.'" In *Maroons and the Marooned: Runaways and Castaways in the Americas*, edited by Richard Bodek and Joseph Kelly. Jackson: University Press of Mississippi, 2020.

———. "Power and Confession: On the Credibility of the Earliest Reports of the Denmark Vesey Slave Conspiracy." *The William and Mary Quarterly* 68, no. 2 (April 2011).

Spady, James O'Neil, ed. *Fugitive Movements: Commemorating the Denmark Vesey Affair and Black Radical Antislavery in the Atlantic World.* Columbia: University of South Carolina Press, 2022.

Spence, E. Lee. *Treasures of the Confederate Coast: The "Real Rhett Butler" & Other Revelations.* Miami: Narwhal Press, 1995.

Stange, Douglas C. "Document: Bishop Daniel Alexander Payne's Protestation of American Slavery." *The Journal of Negro History* 52, no. 1 (January 1967).

Steward, T. G. *Fifty Years in the Gospel Ministry.* Philadelphia: A.M.E. Book Concern, 1921.

Stockton, Robert P. *The Great Shock: The Effects of the 1886 Earthquake on the Built Environment of Charleston, South Carolina.* Easley, SC: Southern Historical Press, 1986.

Stone, Brandon M. "Armed with a Gun & Sword: New Perspectives on the Alleged Denmark Vesey Co-Conspirators and the Workhouse Trials." MA thesis, Graduate School of the University of Charleston, South Carolina at the College of Charleston and the Citadel, 2021.

Straker, Ian B. "Black and White and Gray All Over: Freeborn Garrettson and African Methodism." *Methodist History* 37, no. 1 (October 1998).

Strickland, Jeff. *All for Liberty: The Charleston Workhouse Slave Rebellion of 1849.* Cambridge, UK: Cambridge University Press, 2022.

Strobert, Nelson T. *Daniel Alexander Payne: The Venerable Preceptor of the African Methodist Episcopal Church.* Lanham, MD: University Press of America, 2012.

Stuart, Moses. *Conscience and the Constitution: With Remarks on the Recent Speech of the Hon. Daniel Webster in the Senate of the United States on the Subject of Slavery.* Boston: Crocker & Brewster, 1850.

Stucky, Scott Wallace. "*Elkison v. Deliesseline*: Race and the Constitution in South Carolina, 1823." *North Carolina Central Law Review* 14, no. 2 (1984).

Sullivan, Patricia. *Lift Every Voice: The NAACP and the Making of the Civil Rights Movement.* New York: The New Press, 2009.

Svin'in, Pavel P., William Benton Whisenhunt, Christopher Ely, and Marina Swoboda. *A Russian Paints America: The Travels of Pavel P. Svin'in, 1811–1813.* Montreal: McGill-Queen's University Press, 2008.

Taeuber, Karl E., and Alma F. *Negroes in Cities: Residential Segregation and Neighborhood Change.* Chicago: Aldine Publishing, 1965.

Tanner, Benjamin T. *An Apology for African Methodism.* Baltimore: Publisher not identified, 1867.

———. *An Outline of Our History and Government for African Methodist Churchmen, Ministerial and Lay.* Philadelphia: A.M.E. Book Concern, 1884.
Taylor, A.A. "The Convention of 1868." *The Journal of Negro History* 9, no. 4 (October 1924).
———. "Religious Influences." *The Journal of Negro History* 9, no. 3 (July 1924).
Teal, Harvey S. "Attacks on the Charleston, S.C. Post Office," *La Posta: A Journal of American Postal History* 17, no. 5 (October–November 1986).
Testimony Taken by the Joint Select Committee to Inquire into the Condition of Affairs in the Late Insurrectionary States, Vol. 2, *South Carolina.* Washington, D.C.: Government Printing Office, 1872.
Thirty Years of Lynching in the United States, 1889–1918. New York: National Association for the Advancement of Colored People, 1919.
Thompson, Anthony B., with Denise George. *Called to Forgive: The Charleston Church Shooting, A Victim's Husband, and the Path to Healing and Peace.* Bloomington, MN: Bethany House, 2019.
Thurman, Howard. *Deep River and the Negro Spiritual Speaks of Life and Death.* Richmond, IN: Friends United Press, 1975.
Tindall, George B. "The Campaign for the Disenfranchisement of Negroes in South Carolina." *The Journal of Southern History* 15, no. 2 (May 1949).
———. "The Liberian Exodus of 1878." *The South Carolina Historical Magazine* 53, no. 3 (July 1952).
———. *South Carolina Negroes, 1877–1900.* Columbia: University of South Carolina Press, 1952.
Tolnay, Stewart E., and E. M. Beck. "Racial Violence and Black Migration in the American South, 1910–1930." *American Sociological Review* 57, no. 1 (February 1992).
Trinkley, Michael, Debi Hacker, and Nicole Southerland. *The Silence of the Dead: Giving Charleston Cemeteries a Voice.* Columbia: Chicora Foundation, 2010.
Turner, Henry M. *Celebration of the First Anniversary of Freedom Held in Springfield Baptist Church, January 1, 1866, and Containing an Outline of an Oration Delivered on the Occasion by Chaplain Henry M. Turner.* Augusta: G.U.L., of Georgia, 1866.
Tutu, Desmond Mpilo. *No Future Without Forgiveness.* New York: Doubleday, 1999.
Twelfth General Conference of the African M.E. Church, Held in Pittsburgh, PA., May 7, 1860. Philadelphia: Wm. S. Young, 1860.
Underwood, James Lowell, and W. Lewis Burke, eds. *The Dawn of Religious Freedom in South Carolina.* Columbia: University of South Carolina Press, 2006.
U.S. Bureau of the Census. *Negroes in the United States, 1920–32.* Washington, D.C.: Government Printing Office, 1935.
Wade, Richard C. *Slavery in the Cities: The South 1820–1860.* New York: Oxford University Press, 1964.
———. "The Vesey Plot: A Reconsideration." *The Journal of Southern History* 30, no. 2 (May 1964).
Walker, Clarence E. *A Rock in a Weary Land: The African Methodist Episcopal Church During the Civil War and Reconstruction.* Baton Rouge: Louisiana State University Press, 1982.
Walker, David. *Walker's Appeal, in Four Articles; Together with a Preamble, to the Coloured Citizens of the World, but in Particular, and Very Expressly, to Those of the United States of America.* Boston: David Walker, 1830.
Waring, Joseph I. *The First Voyages and Settlement at Charles Town, 1670–1680.* Columbia: University of South Carolina Press, 1970.
Washington, Booker T., et al. *The Negro Problem: A Series of Articles by Representative Negroes of Today.* New York: James Pott & Company, 1903.
———. *Up from Slavery: An Autobiography.* Garden City, NY: Doubleday & Company, 1901.
Wayman, Alexander W. *Cyclopaedia of African Methodism.* Baltimore: Methodist Episcopal Book Depository, 1882.
———. *My Recollections of African M. E. Ministers, or Forty Years' Experience in the African Methodist Episcopal Church.* Philadelphia: A.M.E. Book Rooms, 1881.
Wedderburn, Nadine V., and Robert E. Carey. "Forgiveness in the Face of Hate." In *Multiculturalism and the Convergence of Faith and Practical Wisdom in Modern Society*, edited by Ana Maria Pascal. Hershey, PA: IGB Global, 2017.
Wells, John E., and Robert E. Dalton. *The South Carolina Architects, 1885–1935: A Biographical Dictionary.* Richmond: New South Architectural Press, 1992.
Wesley, Charles. *Richard Allen: Apostle of Freedom.* Washington, D.C.: The Associated Publishers, 1935.

Wesley, John. *The Character of a Methodist*. Bristol: Felix Farley, 1742.
———. *A Short History of Methodism*. London: Foundery, 1765.
———. *A Short History of the People called Methodists*. London: J. Paramore, 1781.
———. *Thoughts Upon Slavery*. London: R. Hawes, 1774.
Wightman, William M. *Life of William Capers, D.D., One of the Bishops of the Methodist Episcopal Church, South; Including an Autobiography*. Nashville: Southern Methodist Publishing House, 1859.
Wikramanayake, Marina. *A World in Shadow: The Free Black in Antebellum South Carolina*. Columbia: University of South Carolina Press, 1973.
Wilkerson, Isabel. *Caste: The Origins of Our Discontents*. New York: Random House, 2020.
Williams, Jean. "Richard Allen: from the Free African Society to Bethel AME Church." *The Annals of Eastern Pennsylvania*. Philadelphia: Historical Society of the Eastern Pennsylvania Conference, 2010.
Williams, Susan Millar, and Stephen G. Hoffius. *Upheaval in Charleston: Earthquake and Murder on the Eve of Jim Crow*. Athens: The University of Georgia Press, 2011.
Williamson, Joel. *After Slavery: The Negro in South Carolina During Reconstruction, 1861–1877*. New York: W. W. Norton & Company, 1965.
Willson, John O. *Sketch of the Methodist Church in Charleston, S.C., 1785–1887*. Charleston: Lucas, Richardson, & Co., Steam Book Printers, 1888.
Wilson, Clyde N., ed. *The Papers of John C. Calhoun*. Vol. 13, *1835–1837*. Columbia: University of South Carolina Press, 1980.
Winch, Julie. *Philadelphia's Black Elite: Activism, Accommodation, and the Struggle for Autonomy, 1787–1848*. Philadelphia: Temple University Press, 1988.
Windley, Lathan A. *Runaway Slave Advertisements: A Documentary History from the 1730s to 1790*. Vol. 3, *South Carolina*. Westport, CT: Greenwood Publishing Group, 1983.
Wong, Ivan, et al. "Potential Losses in a Repeat of the 1886 Charleston, South Carolina, Earthquake." *Earthquake Spectra* 21, no. 4.
Wood, Peter H. *Black Majority: Negroes in Colonial South Carolina From 1670 through the Stono Rebellion*. New York: W. W. Norton & Company, 1974.
Woodson, Carter G. *The History of the Negro Church*. Washington, D.C.: The Associated Publishers, 1921.
Work, Monroe N., et al. "Some Negro Members of Reconstruction Conventions and Legislatures and of Congress." *The Journal of Negro History* 5, no. 1 (January 1920).
Wright, Richard R., Jr., ed. *Centennial Encyclopaedia of the African Methodist Episcopal Church*. Philadelphia: Book Concern of the A.M.E. Church, 1916.
Wyatt-Brown, Bertram. "The Abolitionists' Postal Campaign of 1835." *The Journal of Negro History* 50, no. 4 (October 1965).
Yarbrough, Tinsley E. *A Passion for Justice: J. Waties Waring and Civil Rights*. New York: Oxford University Press, 1987.

Index

Abernathy, Ralph David, 269
abolitionists/abolition
   American Anti-Slavery Society, 140, 144
   Methodism and, 57–58, 59, 132, 144–47
   New York National Freedman's Relief Association, 142–43
   in Northern states, 66, 376n58
   Quakerism and, 58
   slaveholders' defense against, 126
Adams, Abraham, 161
Adams, E. J., 164
Adams, John, 161
Adams, John Hurst, 340
Adger, John Bailey, 116, 134
African Americans. *See also entries beginning with* "Black"; free people of color; segregation; slaves/slavery; slave trade; violence against African Americans
   back-to-Africa movement, 202, 405n202
   Black churches as central force in lives of, 3, 5, 149–50, 165, 204, 215, 408n215
   Charleston population of, 34, 39, 41, 277–78
   citizenship of, 149, 196, 401n184
   definition and rights of, in South Carolina, 186
   economic condition of, 249–50, 332
   as emancipated but not free, 173–74
   Emanuel as symbol of new life for, 164–65
   first publication by, with copyright, 75
   forgiveness and grace as survival mechanism for, 31, 338–40
   income of, 241
   life in Charleston of, 224–25
   members of Bethel Methodist Church, 60, 86, 90–91, 93
   mental health treatment and, 324
   Methodism as best denomination for, 72
   as Methodist ministers, 58
   migration to North of, 34, 219–20, 232
   in military, 150–51, 224, 249, 410n224
   as percent of Methodists, 59
   in Philadelphia, 68, 74–76
   in politics during Reconstruction, 181, 182, 189, 194–98, 200, 403n194
   post–Civil War competition among denominations for, 169–70
   public accommodations and, 196–97, 201, 403n196
   skin tone classism and, 42, 81, 170, 208, 385n103, 406n208
   South Carolina population of, 34, 100, 180–81, 372n32
   in state and local government, 244–45, 271–72, 277, 280, 318, 335
   voting by, 184, 187, 190, 200–201, 235, 257, 271
   white people and advancement of, 222–23
African American women
   African Supplement vote and, 81
   as AME itinerant lay preachers, 82
   AME ordination of, 81, 239
   AME patriarchy and, 15, 81, 145, 239
   as backbones of congregations, 15, 81–82
   employment of, in South Carolina, 250
   importance of, at Emanuel, 15, 164, 174, 175, 176, 206, 238–40, 325–27
   level of discrimination against, 270
   as "old mothers" of Charleston's Black Methodists, 157
African Church
   construction of, 97–101, 384n99
   demise of, 120–22, 124–25
   persecution of leaders of, 101
   political divisions within, 110
   Vesey plot and, 108–9, 110–11, 386n108, 387n108
   white Charlestonians' fear of, 109–10
African Civilization Society, 167
African Episcopal Church of St. Thomas, 72
African Methodist Episcopal Church (AME). *See also specific individuals*
   American Black nationalism and, 83
   bishops, 81, 289–90, 370n9, 380n31, 405n202
   Black Charlestonians and, 154, 158
   civil rights movement and, 241, 242–43

African Methodist Episcopal Church (AME) (*cont'd*):
  conferences, 84, 94–95, 101, 142, 146, 147, 156–57, 158, 159, 165, 173, 197, 239, 383n94
  death penalty position of, 305
  educational institutions, 142, 393n142
  education of pastors, 140–41, 142
  establishment of, 4, 79
  finances of, 290–91
  first female itinerant lay preacher, 82
  governance of, 287–88
  growth of, 5, 83–84, 158–59
  guidebook of, 79–80
  importance of Emanuel, 215
  as "instrument to lift African Americans up," 173–74
  membership of, 5, 220, 369n4
  missionaries in South, 142–43, 148–49, 150–52, 153, 155, 167–68, 169, 172, 295n153
  motto of, 74, 379n74
  as patriarchal, 15, 81, 145, 239
  as predominant denomination, 204–5, 406n204
  race and membership, 80
  Reconstruction statement of, 405n202
  redemption of racial manhood from slavery and, 141
  retirement of officials of, 420n290
  rule book, 8
  same-sex marriage prohibition, 145
  schism between Northern and Southern branches of, 209–10
  sexual or financial impropriety by officials of, 288–90
  slavery and, 146–47
  tenets of, 9, 74, 80–81, 173, 174
  Booker T. Washington and, 223
  women as backbone of, 15, 81–82
  worship style in, 141
African Methodist Episcopal Zion Church, 79
African Society, 95
African Union Church, 79, 380n79
Allen, Flora, 76–77
Allen, John, 76
Allen, Richard
  accomplishments of, 75, 83
  African Episcopal Church of St. Thomas and, 72
  on African Supplement, 78
  AME guidebook and, 79–80
  Francis Asbury and, 67–68
  basic facts about, 63, 64, 67
  as bishop, 81, 82–83, 380n81
  Black Methodism establishment and, 69–73, 379n73
  on Black Methodists' autonomy, 78
  Christmas Conference and, 57, 375n57
  conversion of, 64–65, 377n64
  death of, 83
  direct action model of, 63
  Free African Society and, 68–69
  freedom of, 65, 66
  on importance of women, 81–82
  Jarena Lee and, 82
  memoir by, 64, 377n64
  ordination of Morris Brown and Henry Drayton by, 94
  rationale for Black church, 73
  as self-appointed itinerant preacher, 66–67, 68
  yellow fever in Philadelphia and, 74–76
Allen, Sarah Bass, 77, 82
Alston, Leon, 328
"Amazing Grace" (Newton), 29, 31, 351
A.M.E. Church Review, 223
Amelia (enslaved person), 382n88
American and Commercial Daily Advertiser, 380n81
American Anti-Slavery Society, 140, 144
American Bible Society Gullah Bible, 55
American Missionary Association, 156
American Negro Slave Revolts (Aptheker), 36
American Revolution, 65–66
Anderson, Robert, 144–45, 154–55
Anderson, Smart, 112
Andrew, James Osgood, 89, 94, 132, 381n87
Aptheker, Herbert, 36
Arad, Michael, 331
Arbery, Ahmaud, 333, 371n23
Arkansas, 371n23
Arthur Ravenel, Jr., Bridge "unity chain" memorial, 28, 331
Asbury, Francis
  abolition of slavery and, 59
  Richard Allen and, 67–68
  on Charleston as immoral city, 60
  as first Methodist bishop, 57
  Methodist church in Charleston and, 58
  opening of Bethel AME Church and, 73, 379n73
  Stokely Sturgis and, 65
  John Wesley and, 57
Ash, Abraham, 93
Austin, Isaac, 381n86
Axson, Jacob, Jr., 107–8

Bachman, John, 140
Bacot, Thomas W., 94
Bagnall, Robert W., 243, 244

INDEX

Baker, Frazier B., 218–19, 246
Baker, Julia, 218
Baker, Lavinia, 219
Bampfield, Sarah, 382n88
Baptists and slavery, 132
Bash, Anthony, 343–44
Bates, Daisy, 183
Baxter, Amos, 86
Bay, Elihu Hall, 121–22
Beach, Mary Lamboll, 126
Beard, Danny, 301
Beard, Jesse E., 243
Beasley, David, 314
Beck (Denmark Vesey wife), 387n114
Beckett, William Wesley, 182, 370n9
Beecher, Henry Ward, 155, 172–73
Bell, Anne, 51–52
Bellinger, Amos N., 216–17, 409n217
Bennett, Batteau, 117
Bennett, H.W.B, 221
Bennett, Lee, Jr., 269, 353
Bennett, Ned, 109
Bennett, Rolla, 112, 385n103
Bennett, Thomas, Jr., 90, 103, 107, 117, 127
Berlin, Ira, 41
Bethel African Methodist Episcopal Church (Mother Bethel)
  African Supplement, 77–78, 81
  William Capers and, 86–87
  land purchased for, 95
  membership growth of, 76–77
  opening of, 73, 379n73
  treated as adjunct of white St. George's, 77–79
  worship style in, 77
Bethel Circuit, 97
Bethel Methodist Episcopal Church (MEC)
  African American membership, 58, 60, 86
  Black membership of, 58
  construction of, 90, 136
  establishment of, 58
  resignation of African Americans from, 90–91, 93
Betts, Albert Deems, 381n87
Biden, Jill, 29, 317
Biden, Joseph R., Jr., 25, 29, 317–18, 426n317
"Big Bertha" pipe organ, 14
Billy (enslaved person), 382n88
Black Christianity, 56, 169–70, 344–45. *See also* Black churches; Black Methodists/Methodism
Black churches. *See also* Black Methodists/Methodism; civil rights movement and Emanuel; *specific congregations*; *specific sanctuaries*
  Richard Allen on rationale for, 73
  as branches of white churches, 134–36
  as centers of resistance, 56, 217–18, 219, 226
  as central force in African American life, 3, 5, 149–50, 165, 204, 215, 408n215
  as Christianity with African rituals, 55–56
  civil rights movement and, 229–30, 241, 242–44, 261–62, 265, 268, 413n243
  closure of Charleston, 278–79
  desecrations of, 3
  early, 79, 380n79
  1885 hurricane and, 211
  forgiveness and grace as emotional self-preservation, 31, 338–39
  harassment of, in Charleston, 208–9
  Barack Obama and, 29–30
  open-doors of, 1–2, 354
  politics and, 181–83
  resistance to white supremacy and, 3
  Watch Night service in, 352–53
  worship style in, 77, 87, 141, 171–72, 208–9, 213, 381n88
Black Codes, 184, 186, 189
Black Lives Matter, 334–35
Black Majority (Wood), 36
Black Methodists/Methodism
  "burying ground" dispute and, 89–91, 125
  dispute with white Methodism, 77–79
  establishment of, 69–73, 379n73
  establishment of church in Charleston by, 93–94, 383n91
  "old mothers" of, 157
  as outnumbering white Methodists in pre–Civil War Charleston, 133
  resignation from Bethel MEC of, 90–91
  Anthony Senter and, 85–86, 87, 89
Black Over White (Holt), 182
Blackwood, Jesse, 108
Blackwood, Thomas, 105
Blake, James G., 230, 251, 265–66
Blue Meeting House, 58, 59, 60, 86, 89
Boies, Artemas, 98
Bolick, Levi M., 56–57, 375n56
Bonhoeffer, Dietrich, 347
Bonneau, Thomas, 138
Bonsell, Elisabeth, 382n88
Boston Recorder, 96
Boulware, Harold R., Sr., 230
Bowers, William, 283–84
Bradley, Tom, 183
Brawley, Lucinda, 251
Breeland, Floyd, 271
Briggs v. Elliott (1951), 245–46
Broadwater, Thomas, 412n234
Brogdon, R. E., 243

Broughton, Shadrach, 174
Brown, Bella, 88, 89
Brown, Charlotte, 88
Brown, Elizabeth, 88, 123, 382n88
Brown, J. Arthur, 230, 251, 254, 265, 266
Brown, John Mifflin, 169
Brown, John Paul, 274
Brown, Malcolm
  Brown Fellowship Society and, 42
  establishment of Black Methodist church in Charleston and, 93
  land for Mother Bethel, 95
  as leader of African Church, 384n97
  petition to allow independent Black church, 384n99
  purchase of freedom, 88, 89
  as slaveholder, 382n89
Brown, Marcus, 93, 101, 384n99
Brown, Maria, 123, 382n88
Brown, Mary, 88
Brown, Millicent, 255, 260, 261
Brown, Minerva, 251, 254, 255
Brown, Morris
  accomplishments of, 123
  at AME conferences, 84, 94, 142, 383n94
  basic facts about, 88, 91–93, 97, 370n9
  "capitation tax" and, 42
  death of, 123
  establishment of Black Methodist church in Charleston and, 93–94, 95, 97–101, 383n91, 384n99
  expulsion from South Carolina of, 121–22, 389nn122–23
  jailing of, 96
  ordination of, 94
  purchase of slaves' freedom by, 88–89, 382n88
  resignation of African Americans from Bethel MEC and, 93
  sermons by, 93
  Vesey insurrection and, 110
Brown, Samuel, 88, 384n99
Brown, Sarah, 88
Brown, William H., 191
Brown Fellowship Society, 42, 86
Bruck, David I., 296, 298, 301, 307
Bryan, Solomon, 91
Buchan, John, 98
Buchanan, Diana, 384n97
Buck, Ruth, 15
Bull, Harry, 86, 384n99
Burnet, Foster, 382n88
Butler, H. B., 243
Butler, Jessie A, 177, 178, 400n176
Butler, Matthew C., 199
Buttz, Charles W., 198, 404n198

Cain, Laura, 163
Cain, Richard Harvey
  AME conferences, 156–57
  AME missionaries to South Carolina and, 149, 167–68
  back-to-Africa movement and, 202, 405n202
  basic facts about, 5, 148, 166, 167, 180, 185–86, 187, 189, 193, 197, 400n181
  as bishop, 203, 370n9
  on challenges of ministering to former slaves, 170
  during Civil War, 149, 167
  Colored People's Convention and, 185–86
  death of, 203
  on destruction in Charleston during Civil War, 155–56
  on emancipation versus freedom, 173
  land purchases by, 198, 404n198
  massacre of Black militiamen and, 198–99
  Northern Methodists and, 157–58, 168
  Daniel Alexander Payne and, 166–67, 202–3
  on Benjamin Franklin Perry and Black Codes, 184
  political career of, 187–89, 190, 191–94, 195–98, 200, 201–2, 403n193, 405n202
Cain, Richard Harvey and Emanuel
  "Cain's church" moniker, 190–91
  Church as "political machine" and, 181–82
  construction of, 159, 162, 163, 164
  preaching style of, 174
  sister congregations and, 165–66
Caldwell, William A., 120
Calhoun, John C., 144, 396n153
Campbell, James T., 54
Canby, Edward, 190
Capers, William, 86–87, 133, 140, 381n88
Carey, Mathew, 75
Carey, Robert E., 338
Carolina (frigate), 33
Carr, Augustus T., 167, 205, 406n204
Cart, Susannah, 95
Caste (Wilkerson), 347
Cattle, Robert, 161, 174–75
Champion, James, 79–80
Chappelle, William David, 216
Charleston
  African Americans in city government, 271–72, 277, 318, 335
  African Americans in post–Civil War politics, 175
  Black Lives Matter protests, 334–35
  Black population of, 34, 39, 41, 277–78
  caste-consciousness in, 3–4
  Christian denominations and skin tone in, 170

INDEX

civil rights protests in, 250–51, 254, 266, 268–71
Civil War destruction in, 152–53, 155–56
Civil War liberation of, 154–55
closure of Black churches in, 278–79
earthquake (1886), 211–13
effect of Emanuel killings in, 28, 329–32
George Floyd, Ahmaud Arbery, and Breonna Taylor murders and, 332–35
gentrification of, 277
harassment of Black churches in, 208–9
hurricane (1885), 211
life of African Americans in, 224–25, 332
map, xi
NAACP in, 226, 243, 244–45, 410n225, 413n243
predominance of AME in, 204–5, 406n204
race riots and murder of African Americans in, 224
removal of Calhoun statue, 335–36
segregation in, 238
Denmark Vesey portrait and statue, 117–18, 388n118

Charleston, pre–Civil War. *See also* Bethel Methodist Episcopal Church (MEC)
accommodation between white and Black Methodists in, 85–86, 87, 89
actions against autonomous Black congregation, 91, 94, 95–97
Black assembly laws, 95
Black Methodists in, 4, 133, 136
Black population in, 34
"burying ground" dispute, 89–91, 125
campaign of repression of African Americans, 126, 127, 128
"capitation tax" in, 42
caste system in, 32, 38
climate of, 38
first names of, 33, 372n33
illicit religious gatherings of African Americans in, 124
as immoral city, 60
importance of, 38
law prohibiting teaching African Americans to read, 101, 131, 139
low-profile of free people of color in, 42
Methodists in, 58–59, 60–61, 86
paranoia about Black population in, 35–36
percent of slaveholders in, 37
population of free people of color in, 39, 41
regulation of free people of color, 40–41
religious diversity and liberty in, 39
slaves disembarking in, 32, 33, 369n2
states' rights and, 116–17

"Sugar House," 35, 69, 373n35
wealth of, 38
John Wesley's preaching in, 49–50
The Charleston Courier, 116, 192
The Charleston Daily News, 187, 189, 192, 193
Charleston Evening Post, 263
"The Charleston Movement," 228, 260
Chew, Benjamin, 64
The Chicago Defender, 234
Christianity, 52, 125, 129–31. *See also* African American churches; Christianity and slavery; evangelical Christianity; forgiveness and grace
in charter for South Carolina, 45–46
conversion of, into liberation theology, 54, 55–56
egalitarianism in, 44
free will and, 48
grace and, 30, 31, 343–45, 347
literacy and, 45
open doors of churches, 1–2, 354
religion shaped by whites for African Americans, 132–33
segregated services, 134, 136, 157, 169
slavery and, 44, 45–46, 52, 125, 129–31, 132
The Christian Recorder, 148, 149, 150, 152, 153, 154, 156, 162, 164, 167, 169, 170, 184, 212, 289
City Gazette and Commercial Daily Advertiser, 120
Civil Rights Act (1964), 266–67
civil rights movement
Black churches and, 229–30, 241, 242–44, 261–62, 265, 268, 413n243
Richard Harvey Cain and, 167, 191–93
Colored People's Convention, 185–86
groups active in, 230, 257, 258–59
Highlander Folk School, 258
March on Washington, 266
pace of court cases, 249
participation and job loss, 263
Penn Center, 258
protests in Charleston, 250–51, 254, 266, 268–71
skin tone and, 260
student sit-ins, 250–51
J. Waties Waring and, 245–46
civil rights movement and Emanuel
"The Charleston Movement" and, 260
Benjamin J. Glover and, 229, 230, 239–41, 243–44, 246–48, 252, 254, 256, 260, 262, 263, 264–65
hospital strike, 268, 269–70
Martin Luther King, Jr., at, 257–58
NAACP and, 243–44

civil rights movement and Emanuel (*cont'd*):
  protests during 1963, 263–66
  Roger Wilkins at, 259
Civil War
  African American soldiers, 150–51
  AME missionaries to South Carolina during, 142–43, 148–49, 150–52, 153, 155, 295n153
  Richard Harvey Cain during, 167
  destruction in Charleston during, 152–53, 155–56
Clark, Betty Deas, 324–27
Clark, Septima Poinsette, 230, 245, 413n244
Cleveland, Grover, 212
Clinton, Hillary Rodham, 29
Clyburn, James E., 29, 183, 230, 256, 303
Coakley, Sharon, 237, 238, 258
Cochran, Sam, 384n99
Cochran, Susanna, 382n88
Coke, Thomas, 57, 59
Coker, Daniel, 79–80, 81, 380n81, 381n86
Coleman-Singleton, Sharonda, 7, 18, 308
Collier, Nadine, 27, 323, 324, 341
Colored Methodist Episcopal Church, 167
Colored People's Conventions, 167, 185–86, 401n185
Cone, James H., 71, 339
Cooper, Lord Anthony Ashley, 33
Corr, Charles, 42, 93, 384n99
Crawford, Anthony, 231–32
Creighton, Joseph, 381n86
The Crisis, 225
Cross, George W., 107
Cross, Yorrick, 108
the Cross, 124
Cruckshanks, Amos, 93, 95, 101, 384n99

Dalcho, Frederick, 130–31
Darby, Joseph, 10, 283, 290–91, 331, 340, 348
Dawson, Ralph, 254
d'Baha, Muhiyidin, 346–47
De Laine, Joseph A., 230, 246
Delany, Martin R., 155, 157, 385n103
Deliver Us from Evil (Ford), 126
Demings, Val, 183
Dennis, Carlotta, 8, 9, 15
Dennison, William, 167
Derrida, Jacques, 345
DeSaussure, Henry William, 126
Devereux, John Henry, 213, 214
Devine, St. Julian, 271
A Dialogue Between a Virginian and an African Minister (Coker), 381n86
Dill, S.G.W., 403n194

Dills, Debbie, 303–4
Dixon, Thomas, 332
The Doctrines and Discipline of The African Methodist Episcopal Church, 8, 70, 79–80, 146, 380n81
Dolly, 387n114
Dougherty, George, 59–60
Douglass, Frederick, 64, 183, 408n215
Drayton, Charles, 384n99
Drayton, Henry
  at AME conferences, 84, 94, 383n94
  establishment of Black Methodist church in Charleston and, 93
  expulsion from South Carolina of, 121–22, 389nn122–23
  jailing of, 96
  land for Mother Bethel, 95
  ordination of, 94
  petition to allow independent Black church, 384n99
  Vesey plot and, 110–11
Drayton family (white), 13–14
Du Bois, W.E.B., 5, 9, 56, 220, 225–27, 410n225
Dunbar, Paul Laurence, 215

Eastside Missionary Baptist Church, 279
Eden, James, 124, 384n97, 384n99
Eden, Maria, 175, 176
Eden, William, 93, 175, 382n89
Edwards, Anna Jane, 195–96, 403n195
Edwards v. South Carolina (1963), 256
Elkison, Henry, 128–29, 391n129
Elliott, Robert Brown, 187, 194
Emanuel African Methodist Episcopal Church. *See also* civil rights movement and Emanuel; *entries beginning with* Roof, Dylann; *specific pastors*
  bicentennial, 328
  Black Lives Matter and, 334
  as Richard Harvey Cain's church, 190–91
  as central to Black life in Charleston, 4–5, 9, 215, 220–21, 223–24, 226, 237–38, 281
  condition of, at Clementa Pinckney's arrival, 6–7, 279–80
  congregants' displeasure with leadership of, after killings, 321–23
  conservatism of, 9–10, 236
  construction of, 159, 161–64
  construction of new, 213–14
  development of Black leadership community and, 165
  early events/projects of, 164
  1886 earthquake and, 211–13
  first service at, 163, 165

first sitting president to speak at, 25
hurricane damage, 277
interior described, 8
location of, xi, 2
Magnolia Plantation history fair and, 13–14
membership of, 6, 165–66, 174, 204, 205, 237–38, 278, 279, 318, 406n204
money to AME accounts from, 291
name of, 165, 298n165
on National Register of Historic Places, 279
open doors policy of, 1–2, 354
as "pastor-killer," 9, 10, 13
pastors at, 167, 175–76, 198, 205, 206–7, 210, 292, 293, 325–27, 370n9, 406n206
Clementa Pinckney as state senator and, 286–87
pipe organ, 14
as "political machine," 181–82, 187, 401n182
as primary venue for Black advocacy, 216
purchase of land for, 161
purchase of Zion Presbyterian by, 207–8
Quarterly Conference of, 8–9, 11, 12–13
as "sacred place," 5
sister congregations of, 165–66, 206
as symbol of new life for African Americans, 164–65
time capsule, 162
women as backbone of, 15, 174, 175, 176, 206
worship style in, 171–72, 213
Emanuel African Methodist Episcopal Church, after murders, 42
Joe Biden and, 317–18, 426n317
conditions at, 310–13
donations of services and money, 319–22, 323
funerals for victims, 313–14
membership, 322–23
Clementa Pinckney memorial service, 28–30, 317
racist threats and rants received, 318
as shrine, 316–17
as symbol of otherworldly grace, 310
visitors at services, 318–19
Enslow, John, 287n108
evangelical Christianity, 44, 55, 347
Everett, Francis, 176
Everett, John S., 175–76

Federal Writers Project, 52, 56–57, 176–77, 196, 400n176
Fenwick, Catherine, 176
Ferillo, Charles (Bud), 260
Fielding, Herbert U., 266, 271
Fields, Richard E., 271
First African Baptist Church of Savannah, 79

Flake, Floyd H., 183
Floyd, George, 332–33
Ford, Lacy K., 126
Fordham, Sonya, 241, 263
forgiveness and grace
  absolution for white mistreatment offered by Absalom Jones and Richard Allen, 75
  adequacy of response for crimes committed, 337–38
  "cheap grace," 347
  Christianity and, 30, 31, 343–45, 347
  exoneration and, 338
  Judaism and, 343
  justice and, 345–46
  person benefiting from, 342–43
  protests and, 346–47
  remorse of offender and, 346, 350
  of Dylann Roof, 26–28, 341–43, 349
  as survival mechanism for African Americans, 31, 338–40
  white embrace of Black, 347, 348
Foster, John E., 409n217
Fourteenth Amendment, 187
Free African Society, 68–69, 71, 72
free people of color
  benevolent societies, 42–43
  first in South Carolina, 39
  laws about worship by, 45
  literacy of, 131, 138–39
  low-profile of, 42
  mixed-race individuals as percent of, 40
  population of, in pre–Civil War Charleston, 39, 41
  regulation of, 40–41
  skin tone classism of, 42, 81, 385n103
  as slaveholders, 41, 89, 175, 382n89
  St. Mark's Episcopal church and, 170
  stereotypes of slaves and, 41
  treatment of, after Vesey plot, 127–29
  ways of obtaining freedom, 40
  in white churches, 39, 42
Frey, Sylvia R., 55
Friendly Moralist Society, 42
Frost, Peter Mathewes, 125
Fuller, Edward N., 178
Fundamental Constitutions (Locke), 46
Furman, Richard, 130

Gadsden, Charlotte, 174
Gadsden, Christopher, 140
Gaillard, J. Palmer, Jr., 263, 265, 270
Gaines, Wesley J., 203
Gantt, Harvey, 230, 251
Garden, Alexander, Jr., 49, 126–27, 374n49

Garner, Patrick, 319
Garnet, Henry Highland, 67, 92
Garrett, George, 174–75
Garrettson, Freeborn, 65
Garrison, William Lloyd, 140, 155
Garvey, Marcus, 227
Gay, Roxane, 347
Geddes, John, 98, 99–100
Gell, Monday, 104–5, 109, 114, 131, 387n108
Genovese, Eugene D., 56
Georgia, 47–48, 371n23
Gergel, Belinda, 297
Gergel, Richard M., 297–98, 308–9
Gethers, Lois, 15, 352
Gibbons v. Ogden (1824), 129
Gibson, Edmund, 47
Gibson, Emanuel, 124
Gilliard, James L., 283
Gillison, John H., 10, 312
Glaude, Eddie S., Jr., 56
Glee, Willi, 14–15, 338, 353
Glover, Benjamin J. *See also* Glover *under* civil rights movement and Emanuel
    basic facts about, 5, 228–29, 231, 232–33, 240, 266
    beatings of, 233–36, 412n234
    Civil Rights Act (1964) and, 266–67
    civil rights march on State Capitol Building, 255–56
    economic power of African Americans and, 256–57, 350
    ministerial posts held by, before Emanuel, 233, 234, 236
    on results of 1963 protests, 265–66
Glover, Charles G., 232, 233, 235–36
Glover, Gean, 240
Glover, Lydia, 245
Glover, Oveta, 228, 240, 252, 253–54, 255
Glover, Queen Ester, 232
Goff, Norvel, Sr.
    basic facts about, 321, 426n321
    congregants' displeasure with, after killings, 321–22
    donations to Emanuel and, 321
    at Emanuel's bicentennial, 328
    as interim pastor, 311–13, 317
    mention of, 7
    Quarterly Conference and, 8, 13
Grady, Zedekiah L., 290
Graham, Lindsey, 29
Graham, Malcolm, 305, 349
Graham, Melvin L., Jr., 241, 263, 308, 348–50
Grant, James S., 161, 174, 175
Graves, Wesley W., 266
Great Awakening, 45, 53

Greater Macedonia AME Church, 278
Great Migration, 219–20
Green, John H., 214, 318
Green, Samuel L., Sr., 279, 289–90, 328, 351–52
Green, Verdelle, 205
Greenberg, Reuben Morris, 272
Gregorie, William Dudley, 10, 287, 318, 332, 335
Grimke, Francis J., 138
Grooms, Larry, 315
Gullah, 55

Haig, James B., 384n97, 384n99
Haley, Nikki, 29, 282, 312, 314–15
Hall, Clinton, 289–90
Hall, James D. S., 148–49, 150–51, 155, 167
Hamilton, James, Jr.
    on demise of African Church, 121
    expulsion from South Carolina of Morris Brown and Henry Drayton and, 123, 389n123
    Vesey plot and, 103, 104, 106, 107, 109–10, 127
Hamilton, Lonnie, III, 271
Hamilton, Quash, 108–9
Hamlin, Susan, 176–79, 400n176
Hammet, Bacchus, 116
Hammond, Henry C., 175
Hampton, Wade, 199
Hamski, Joseph, 306
Harding, Vincent, 54
Harleston, Alexander, 86, 384n99
Harleston, Edwin Augustus, 226
Harleston, Edwin G., 410n225
Harleston, Quash A., 384n99
Harper, Frances Ellen Watkins, 164
Harper, John, 59, 60
Hasell, William Soranzo, 382n88
hate crimes, 23, 316, 326, 371n23. *See also entries beginning with* Roof, Dylann
Hayes, Rutherford B., 199–200
Hayne, Joseph E., 209, 210
Hayne, Robert Y., 117
Herbkersman, Bill, 283
Hewitt, Susannah, 384n97
Higgins, Samuel R., 370n9
Highlander Folk School, 258
Hightower, Kay Taylor, 292–93
Hildebrand, Reginald F., 150
Hill, Nathaniel, 175
Hinton, James M., Sr., 230
Hobbs, Stephen, 335
Holland, Edwin C., 127
Holloway, Richard, 42, 86

INDEX

Holman, Alonzo W., 243
Holmes, James, 384n97
Holt, Thomas, 182
Horry, Elias, 105
Horry, John, 105
Horton, Myles, 258
Hosier, Harry, 57, 375n57
Humane Brotherhood, 42
Hurd, Arthur S., 305, 321
Hurd, Cynthia Graham, 13, 16, 241, 307
Hurley, Ruby, 243–44
Hutchinson, T. Leger, 135

Indiana, 371n23

Jackson, Darrell, 285
Jackson, David H., Jr., 222
Jackson, Ellen, 260, 261
Jackson, John Andrew, 130
Jackson, Susie, 7, 20, 307
James (enslaved person), 382n89
James, Frederick Calhoun, 274
Jankélévitch, Vladimir, 345–46
Januchowski, Craig, 304
Jefferson, P. W., 210
Jefferson, Thomas, 71
Jenkins, Dorothy, 238–39, 334, 413n243
Jenkins, Esau, 230, 258, 265
Johnson, Andrew, 161, 183, 395n153
Johnson, James H. A., 155, 172
Johnson, Lewis E., 194
Johnson, Michael P., 106, 287n108
Johnson, William, Jr., 116, 117, 128–29, 388n117, 391n129
Jones, Absalom, 68, 69–72, 75–76, 81, 83
Jones, Charles Colcock, 131
Jones, Harvey, 259–60
Jones, Jehu, 42
Jordan, Vernon E., Jr., 183

Kelly, William F., 251
Kennedy, Lionel H., 106, 107, 109, 112, 113, 115, 139
Kimpson, Marlon, 285
King, A. D., 270
King, Coretta Scott, 269–70
King, Martin Luther, Jr., 9, 56, 229–30, 257–58, 266, 339
King, Martin Luther, Sr., 270
King, Minerva Brown, 264, 348
Ku Klux Klan, 195, 200, 232, 253

Ladson, Augustus, 177
Lamar, William H., IV, 347–48

Lance, Ethel, 16, 307
Lango (enslaved person), 382n88
La Roche, Joe, 385n103
Le Baron, Marie, 197
Lee, Jarena, 82
Legare, Charles, 161
Leigh, Charles C., 142–43
Le Jau, Francis, 34–35, 46–47
Leland, A. W., 98
Lesesne, Hannah, 88–89, 382n88
Lessane, Patricia Williams, 332
Lewis, David Levering, 225
Lewis, John, 25
Lewis, T. Willard, 151–52, 154, 157–58, 167–68
liberation theology, 5, 54, 55–56, 261
Lincoln, Abraham, 142, 145, 147, 155
literacy
    of African Americans outlawed, 101, 131, 139
    Africans' capacity to learn and, 46
    of enslaved people, 35, 38, 131
    of free people of color, 131, 138–39
    insurrections and, 45
    religion and, 45
    SPG and, 374n49
Locke, John, 46
Loftin, Rachel, 300
Louisiana, 372n32
Lynch, James, 148–49, 150–52, 153, 155, 156, 167, 395n153
Lynch, Loretta, 304, 305
lynchings, 218, 231–32, 246

Mack, Cato, 384n99
Mack, James, 384n99
Maddox, Donna, 301
Magnolia Plantation & Gardens, 13–14
Magwood, Simon, 94
Malcolm X, 56
Malloy, Gerald, 286, 420n286
Manigault, Ka'mya, 16, 322
Manley, Henry, 69–70
Manning, Eric S. C., 119, 303, 306, 308–9, 326–28, 334–35, 337, 352
Marcus (enslaved person), 382n88
Marrant, John, 53
Marshall, Thurgood, 245–46, 391n129
Martin, Daniel, Sr., 262, 271
Martin, Denbow, 387n108
Martin, J. Robert, 254–55
Martin, James, 403n194
Martin, Ruby, 15, 237–38, 239, 262–63
Martinez, Johnette Pinckney, 274
Mathewes, Henry, 93, 95, 384n97
Mathewes, Isaac A., 93, 384n99
Mathewes, John B., 93, 384n97, 384n99

Mathewes, Peter B., 93, 125, 384n97, 384n99
Maurice (enslaved person), 382n88
McAllister, Julius Harrison, Sr., 31
McConnell, Glenn F., 286
McCray, John Henry, 230
McFall, John, 405n202
McFarland, Arthur C., 266
McKenzie, Vashti Murphy, 31, 81
McPherson, David, 207
Meek, Joey, 301–2
Memminger, Christopher G., 160
Mercury, 135, 189, 192
Methodist Episcopal Church (MEC). *See* Methodists/Methodism
Methodist Episcopal Church, North, 151–52, 154, 157–58, 168
Methodist Episcopal Church, South, 132, 158, 159, 163
Methodists/Methodism. *See also* Black Methodists/Methodism
   Richard Allen as self-appointed itinerant preacher, 66–67, 68
   authority of bishops in, 73–74
   backsliding on slavery by, 61–62
   as best denomination for Black Americans, 72
   Black lay leaders under white ministers, 86–88, 382n87
   in Charleston
      Black, as outnumbering white, in pre–Civil War Charleston, 136
   Christmas Conference, 57–58, 375n57
   circuit riders, 51
   dispute between white and Black, 77–79
   established in America, 57
   growth in America of, 57, 58
   itinerant evangelism of, 48–49
   Northern Branch of, 151–52, 154, 157–58, 168
   ordination of Black ministers, 58
   "Paul Revere of American," 65
   percent of Black adherents, 59
   relationship to Anglicanism of, 57
   Anthony Senter and, 85–86, 87–88
   slavery and, 48, 49, 51–52, 53–54, 57–58, 59, 130, 132
   South branch of, 132, 158, 159, 163
   in South Carolina, 59–60, 87
   theological and liturgical components of, 50–51, 58
   Wesleys and, 47–49, 50–51
   George Whitefield and, 52–53
Methodists/Methodism in Charleston
   early churches, 58
   membership of, 60–61, 86, 133
   pre–Civil War accommodation between white and Black, 85–86, 87, 89
   schism between white and Black, 90–91, 94, 381n87, 383n91
Meynardie, E. J., 163
Michel, Marguerite, 205, 283, 353
Mickey, Edward C., 226
Mickle, Ann, 420n286
Middleton, DePayne, 7, 308, 320–21
Middleton, Kylon J., 182–83, 208, 292, 323, 348
Middleton-Brown, Bethane, 27, 308, 342
Mikell, Ephraim, 177–78
Mikell, Mary, 178
Miller, W. H., 244
Milling, Cureton, 56–57, 375n56
Milner, Robert, 384n99
Missionary Record, 190, 192, 193
Mitchell, Janie, 173, 174
Mood, Francis Asbury
   on building on Black burial ground, 90
   on civil disobedience of African Americans in white Methodist churches, 133–34
   on construction of Mother Bethel, 97
   on early years of African Church, 101
   on resignation of Black Methodists, 91
   on schism between white and Black Methodists, 94, 381n87
   on worship style in Black churches, 381n88
Morris Brown AME Church, 166, 209–10, 217, 229, 236, 290
Morrison, William M., 270
Morris Street Baptist Church, 229
Moss, Henry, Jr., 275–76
Mother Bethel. *See* Bethel African Methodist Episcopal Church (Mother Bethel)
Mother Emanuel Empowerment Center, 323–24
Motley, Constance Baker, 254–55
Moultrie, Mary, 230, 268–69
Mt. Lebanon AME Church, 233, 234
Mt. Zion AME Church, 208, 323, 406n204, 406n208

Nance, Lee, 403n194
Nash, Roy, 231
National Advocate, 389n122
National Association for the Advancement of Colored People (NAACP)
   Black churches and, 230, 243, 413n243
   in Charleston, 226, 243, 244–45, 410n225, 413n243
   "The Charleston Movement," 228, 260
   Emanuel and, 243–44
   establishment of, 221, 225
   membership, 244, 245

South Carolina victories, 245–46
strength of, in South Carolina, 258–59
student sit-ins and, 251
Native Americans as slaves, 34
Negro Seamen Act (South Carolina, 1922), 128–29
Nelson, Brenda, 14, 324
Nesbit, Elisabeth, 174
Nettles, William N., 305
Newby, Idus A., 241–42
Newman, Isaiah DeQuincey, 230
Newman, J. Quincey, 255–56
Newman, Richard S., 66
The News and Courier, 118, 164, 176, 208–9, 215, 217, 219, 238, 263, 264
Newton, John, 29, 31, 351
The New Yorker, 346–47
New York National Freedman's Relief Association, 142–43
The New York Times, 91, 189, 338, 347
Niagara Movement, 225
Nicholas, Henry, 269
Nichols, Anna Elizabeth, crypt of, 8
Nichols, Decatur Ward, 265, 272
Nichols, Lewis Ruffin, 8, 198, 212–14, 217, 218, 406n204
Norris, Richard Franklin, Sr., 311, 324–27
Northern Methodists. *See* Methodist Episcopal Church, North

Obama, Barack
  approach to racial matters by, 29, 30–31
  on availability of guns, 303
  Black church and, 29–30
  on Emanuel as "sacred place," 5
  on importance of African American churches, 3
  Clementa Pinckney and, 282–83
  at Pinckney memorial service, 28–31, 48, 317
Obama, Michelle, 29, 317
O'Connor, Michael P., 200, 202
Oglethorpe, James, 47, 48
Old Bethel Church, 153–54, 156
Oliphant, Mary C. Simms, 253
O'Neill, Stephen, 268
Open doors policy of churches, 1–2, 354
The Ordeal of Mansart (Du Bois), 410n225
Orr, James L., 181
Ortiz, Jean, 15

Palmer, Benjamin Morgan, 98, 115, 124, 140
Palmer, Job, 105
Pan-Africanism, 226, 227
Parable of the Sower, 15, 18, 140

Parker, Thomas, 106, 107, 109, 112, 113, 115, 139
Parks, Rosa, 183
Paul, William, 102–3, 106, 385n102
"Paul Revere of American Methodism," 65
Payne, Daniel Alexander, 83, 377n64, 380n79
  AME conferences and, 94–95, 156–57, 383n94
  AME missionaries to South Carolina, 142–43, 148–49, 150–52, 153, 155, 167–68, 295n153
  basic facts about, 137, 138–40, 142
  on Morris Brown, 92
  Richard Harvey Cain and, 166–67, 202–3
  dedication of Emanuel by, 165
  on demise of African Church, 122
  on destruction in Charleston during Civil War, 156
  educational requirements for African Methodist clergy and, 140–41, 142
  on emancipation, 147
  on expulsion from South Carolina of Morris Brown and Henry Drayton, 123
  on mixing church and politics, 202–3
  on Northern Methodists, 157–58
  ordination of, 140
  ordination of women and, 145
  on persecution of leaders of African Church, 101
  return to Charleston of, 155
  on worship style of African Americans, 141, 171–72
Payne, London, 137–38
Penn Center, 258
Pennsylvania, 376n58
Perry, Benjamin Franklin, 184
Perry, Matthew J., Jr., 230, 251, 254–55
Philadelphia, 68–69, 74–76
Pickens, William, 243
Pinckney, Benjamin, 275
Pinckney, Charles Cotesworth, 94, 274
Pinckney, Clementa Carlos
  AME career of, 291–92
  basic facts about, 11, 13, 273–76, 283–84, 418n276
  complaints against, 11
  Emanuel's condition at arrival of, 6–7, 279–80
  killing of, 19
  memorial service for, 28–31, 317
  Barack Obama and, 282–83
  in politics, 11, 12, 183, 276, 280–82, 283–87, 291, 419n284, 420n286
  Quarterly Conference and, 8, 12–13
  recording by, at Dylann Roof trial, 308

458 INDEX

Pinckney, Clementa Carlos (*cont'd*):
 sermons by, 293–94
 welcome to Dylann Roof by, 18–19
Pinckney, Jennifer, 12, 22–23, 283, 292, 303, 343
Pinckney, John, 274, 306
Pinckney, Malana, 12, 22–23, 29, 303
Pinckney, Plenty, 274–75
Pinckney, Sallie, 274–75
Pinckney, Theopia, 274
Pittman, Helen, 282
The Pittsburgh Courier, 233–34
Plessy v. Ferguson (1896), 201
Plymouth Congregational Church, 278
Porter, A. Toomer, 209
The Post and Courier, 321, 333, 335
Poyas, Peter, 109
Price, James D., 156, 161, 175
Prioleau, John Cordes, 102
Prioleau, Peter, 102–3, 106, 385n102
Pritchard, "Gullah Jack," 109, 110, 112–13
Prosser, Gabriel, 45
Provost, Catherine, 174

Quakers, 58

Raboteau, Albert J., 55, 339–40
Rainey, Joseph H., 194
Randolph, A. Philip, 183
Randolph, Benjamin Franklin, 194–95
Ransier, Alonzo J., 187, 194
Read, Jacob, 59
Ready, Eliza, 176
Reconstruction
 AME bishops on, 405n202
 amnesty and, 183, 401n183
 Black men and politics during, 181, 182, 189, 194–98, 403n194
 Black suffrage, 184
 end of, 199–200
 public accommodations, 196–97, 403n196
 radical Republicans and, 186–87
 South Carolina during, 183–84, 186, 187–90, 198–99, 401n187
Reid, Frank Madison, Jr., 118
Reid, George, 98
Reid Chapel AME, 321, 426n321
Republican Party, 186–87, 201, 404n201
Reuther, Walter, 269
Revels, Hiram R., 183
Richardson, Julius Ness (Jay), 306
Richardson-Latham, Althea, 12–13, 319–20, 321
Riley, Charlotte S., 165
Riley, Joseph P., Jr., 29, 271–72, 277, 312

Riley, Stephney, 216–17, 409n217
Risher, Sharon, 306, 324, 331
Robinson, Marilynne, 31
Rogers, Charles, 384n99
Roof, Amber, 303
Roof, Amelia Cowles, 306
Roof, Carl Joseph (Joe), 299, 306
Roof, Dylann
 basic facts about, 18, 298, 300
 capture of, 303–4
 as characterized by Barack Obama, 30
 Confederate symbols after killings by, 314–16
 death penalty and, 305
 forgiven by families of victims and survivors, 26–28, 341–43, 349
 internet and, 300–301, 304–5
 luck of, 23, 371n23
 post-federal trial, 309
 selection of Emanuel by, 24
 white supremacy and, 24, 300–301, 424n309
Roof, Dylann, federal trial of
 appearance of Roof, 296, 307
 attendees, 306
 charges, 26, 304–5, 423n304
 competency assessments, 298
 defense, 296, 298–99, 306
 evidence presented, 296–97, 306–7
 presentations by relatives of victims and survivors, 307–9, 341–42
Roof, Dylann at Emanuel
 arrival of, 18
 Bible study, 7, 15–17, 19
 casing of, 23, 302
 date for killings and, 388n1046
 effect of killings in Charleston, 28, 329–32
 escape from, 23
 federal settlements with families of victims and survivors, 303
 killing by, 19, 20
 mutterings by, 22
 reasons for killings, 3, 21, 24, 295, 296, 301, 371n21, 424n309
 weapon used by, 19, 302–3
Roof, Franklin Bennett (Benn), 299, 300, 302, 306
Rush, Benjamin, 71, 74–75
Russel, Joseph F., 174, 175, 185, 401n185
Russel, Lydia, 174
Ryan, Thomas, 132

Salter, Moses B., 124, 198, 370n9
Sam (enslaved person), 382n88
Sanders, Doris Coaxum, 262, 319

Sanders, Felicia
  basic facts about, 16
  at Bible study, 16, 19, 20
  at Democratic National Convention
    (2016), 25
  Emanuel after killings and, 321–23, 325
  gun control and, 303
  Ka'mya Manigault and, 20
  move to new church by, 310–11
  Dylann Roof's reason for killings, 371n21
  at Dylann Roof's trial, 27, 306–7, 308–9,
    341–42
  Tywanza Sanders and, 21
Sanders, Tyrone, 16, 305, 306, 321–22
Sanders, Tywanza, 16, 19, 20, 21, 307
Saunders, William, 230, 268
Savage, Andrew J., III, 323
Savage, James, 384n99
Scott, Dot, 338
Scott, Hilda Blanche, "Mama Hilda," 238–40
Scott, Janet, 308
Scott, Robert K., 195
Scott, Tim, 29, 312
Scott, Walter, 284–85, 306
Seabrook, Whitemarsh B., 131
segregation
  backbone of, broken in Charleston, 266
  bomb shelters, 238
  church services, 134, 136, 157, 169
  schools, 245–46, 247, 252–55
Sellers, Cleveland, 230
Senter, Anthony, 85–86, 87–88, 89
Senter, Elizabeth, 380n85
Sernett, Milton C., 70
Shackelford, Roger, 380n85
Shealy, Mike, 286, 287
Sheheen, Vincent, 315–16
Sheppard, Polly
  basic facts about, 7
  Bible study and, 15–16
  at Democratic National Convention
    (2016), 25
  Emanuel after killings and, 310–11, 323, 325
  feelings about Dylann Roof, 305, 342–43
  gun control and, 303
  during killings, 20, 21–22
  move to new church by, 310–11
  Dylann Roof's reason for killings, 371n21
  at Dylann Roof's trial, 307
Sherman, William Tecumseh, 152, 153, 395n153
Shiloh AME Church, 278
Silver Bluff Church, 79
Simkins, Modjeska Monteith, 230
Simmons, Alana, 27, 342

Simmons, Dan, Jr., 308
Simmons, Daniel Lee, Sr., 7, 15, 19, 20, 352
Simpson, Peter, 86
Simpson, Smart, 86, 93, 95, 384n97, 384n99
Singleton, Camryn, 25–26
Singleton, Chris, 25–26, 323, 341
Singleton, Stephen, 10
Slager, Michael, 284–85, 305–6, 423n305
Slave Religion (Raboteau), 55
slaves/slavery. *See also* abolitionists/abolition;
    Christianity and slavery
  African rituals of, 55
  AME and, 84, 146–47
  beginning of, 32–33
  Morris Brown and freedom of, 88–89, 382n88
  in cities versus on plantations, 36–38
  in District of Columbia, 147
  freedom bought using church collections,
    87–88, 381n87
  free people of color as owners of, 41, 89, 175,
    382n89
  fugitive, 120
  Fundamental Constitutions and, 46
  insurrections by, 34, 36, 102–13, 115–16,
    129–31, 385nn102–3, 386nn103–4,
    386n108, 387n108
  laws concerning, 34–35, 45, 95, 100–101, 130,
    131, 139
  literacy and, 35, 38, 46, 374n49
  Magnolia Plantation & Gardens and, 13–14
  Methodism and, 48, 49, 51–52, 53–54, 57–58,
    61–62
  narratives of (Library of Congress), 375n51
  Native Americans as, 34
  as paternalistic, 61, 98, 106–7, 114, 125–26,
    129, 132
  population in South Carolina (1820), 100
  reinterpretation of, at tourist sites, 14
  split in Christian denominations over, 132
  stereotypes of, 34, 41
  Watch Night service in Black churches,
    352–53
  John Wesley on, 52
  George Whitefield and, 53
slave trade
  advertisements, 120
  federal importation prohibition, 33
  importance of Charleston in, 369n2
  Methodist stand on, 57–58
  transatlantic crossing, 33, 369n2
  John Wesley on, 52
Smalls, Robert, 150, 155
Smith, Tom, 86
Smith, William, 10

Society for the Propagation of the Gospel in Foreign Parts (SPG), 47, 374n49
The Souls of Black Folk (Du Bois), 225
the South
  AME missionaries after Civil War, 169
  Jim Crow laws, 184, 186, 196–97, 201, 215, 403n196
  Wesleys and spread of Methodism in, 47–49
South Carolina. *See also* Charleston; Charleston, pre–Civil War
  African American migration to North, 219–20, 232
  African Americans in government of, 280
  AME in, 158–59, 205
  AME missionaries to, 142–43, 148–49, 150–52, 153, 155, 167–68, 172, 295n153
  barrier island culture, 55
  Black population (2020), 34
  Confederate flag flown at Capitol, 25, 284, 308, 314–16
  definition and rights of Black persons, 186
  economics and race in, 241, 249–50
  hate crimes law and, 23, 316
  Jim Crow laws, 215–16
  lynchings in, 218
  NAACP in, 244, 245, 258–59
  population of (1865), 180–81
  Promised Land, 228, 232
  during Reconstruction, 183–84, 186, 187–90, 198–99, 401n187
  segregated schools in, 245–46, 247, 252–55
  Union occupation during Civil War, 145
South Carolina, pre–Civil War. *See also* free people of color
  Black population, 34, 372n32
  Christianity in charter for, 45–46
  economy of, 143
  law ending private manumission, 100–101
  laws about worship by Black persons, 45
  laws concerning slaves/slavery, 34–35, 45, 95, 100–101, 130, 131, 139
  Methodist churches in, 59–60, 87
  population of enslaved people in (1820), 100
  repression of African Americans, 126–31
  rice cultivation and, 33
  secession of, 144–45
  states' rights and, 143–44
South Carolina Association, 128
South Carolina Conferences (AME), 156–57, 158, 159, 165, 173
South Carolina Leader, 165, 185–86, 187
Southern Baptist Convention, 132
Southern Christian Leadership Conference, 230, 257, 258–59, 269

Southern Methodists. *See* Methodist Episcopal Church, South
Southern Patriot, 126–27
Southern Presbyterian Review, 134
Spencer, Marsha, 308
Spencer, Peter, 79, 380n79
Sprunt, Alexander, 223–24
St. George's Methodist Church, 68, 69–71, 77–78
St. Mark's Episcopal church, 170
St. Matthew Baptist Church, 279
St. Michael's Episcopal Church, 39
St. Philip's Episcopal Church, 39, 42, 49
Stansbury, Michael, 304
Sterrett, Norman Bascom, 205–8, 211–12, 406n204, 406n206
Stevenson, Levern, 273, 280
Steward, Theophilus G., 155, 158, 203
Stewart, Potter, 256
Stono Rebellion (1739), 36
Sturgis, Stokely, 64, 65
"Sugar House," 35, 69, 373n35
Susan (Denmark Vesey wife), 387n114
Svin'in, Pavel, 77

Tanner, Benjamin T., 141
Taylor, Alrutheus Ambush, 171
Taylor, Breonna, 333
Taylor, Elnora, 263
Tecklenburg, John, 335–36
Telemaque. *See* Vesey, Denmark
Thomas, John, III, 289
Thomas, William M., 170–71
Thompson, Anthony, 25, 27, 306, 307, 326, 342, 426n317
Thompson, Myra, 7, 15, 17, 19, 306
Thoughts Upon Slavery (John Wesley), 52
Thurman, Howard, 339
Thurmond, Paul, 315
Tillman, Benjamin, 201
Townsend, James M., 205–6
"The Tragedy," 6
Trapier, Paul, 135
Trenholm, Anna, 161
Trenholm, George Alfred, 160–61
Trinity Methodist Church, 58, 163
Trump, Donald, 317, 318
Turner, Henry McNeal, 133, 210
Turner, Nat, 45, 131
Turpin, London, 384n99
Tutu, Desmond, 345

"The Unity of the Races" (Delany), 157

Vanderhorst, Moses, 174
Vanderhorst, Richard H., 167

Veal, Frank, 401n182
Vesey, Denmark
  basic facts about, 45, 104, 105, 111, 113–14, 131, 387n114
  death of, 114–16
  insurrection by, 102–13, 114–17, 385nn102–3, 386nn103–4, 386n108, 387n108
  legacy of insurrection, 4, 117–19, 120–25, 126–31, 388n118
  religious beliefs of, 111–12
Vesey, Joseph, 113–14
Vesey, Robert, 155, 162
Vesey, Sandy, 111
Vincent, John, 287n108
violence against African Americans. *See also entries beginning with* Roof, Dylann
  beatings, 228, 233–36, 244, 412n234
  bombing of churches, 262
  during demonstrations, 263–64
  lynchings, 218, 231–32, 246
  murders, 216–19, 224, 332–33
  police abuse, 233–34, 284–85
  terrorism, 195–96, 200, 232, 246, 255, 280
Virginia, 46

Wade, Lisa Washington, 312, 351
Wagner, Theodore D., 161
Waring, J. Waties, 129, 245–48
Warnock, Raphael G., 182
War of 1812, 76
Washington, Booker T., 9, 56, 220, 221–23, 225
Washington, George, 71
Washington, Harold, 237, 340
Washington, Samuel, 209, 210
Watson, Theodora, 11, 13
Wayman, Alexander W., 147, 153–54, 208, 210, 396n153
Weaver, Elisha, 153–54, 396n153
Wedderburn, Nadine V., 338
"Welcome to the Ransomed" (Payne), 147
Wells-Barnett, Ida B., 219
Wesley, Charles, 47–49, 374n49
Wesley, John
  basic facts about, 48
  in Charleston, 49–50
  on cruelties of slavery, 52
  death of, 58
  departure from America of, 50
  lieutenants of, in America, 57
  Methodism and, 47–49, 50–51
Wesley, Samuel, 48
White, Dave, 130
White, Juanita, 276
White, Walter, 243
Whitefield, George, 52–53
white supremacists/white supremacy. *See also* Roof, Dylann
  Black churches and resistance to, 3, 261
  Christianity as threat to, 44
  eighty-eight in numerology of, 19
Wilberforce University, 142
Wilkerson, Isabel, 347
Wilkerson, William D., 174
Wilkins, Roy, 243, 259
Williams, Bruce H., 182
Williams, Charles N., 319
Williams, Jefferson, 181–82, 400n181
Williams, Nathan S., 306
Williams, Preston Warren, II, 290, 291, 292
Williams, Richard, 82
Williman, Christopher, 95
Wilson, George, 103, 106, 385n103
Wilson, John, 103
Witherspoon, Lavern, 10, 278, 293
Wolf, Jean K., 376n57
Wood, Betty, 55
Wood, Peter, H., 36
Woodard, Isaac, Jr., 244
Woodson, Carter G., 169
Woodward, Sidney, 215
World War II, 238, 249
Wright, Alonzo W., 230
Wright, Julia, 230
Wright, Vivian, 412n234
Wrighten, John H., III, 230
Wyoming, 316, 371n23

Young, Andrew, 258–59, 269

Zion-Olivet Presbyterian, 279
Zion Presbyterian Church, 134–35, 153, 156, 158, 159, 207

About the Author

Kevin Sack is a veteran journalist who has written about national affairs for more than four decades and has been part of three Pulitzer Prize–winning teams. A native of Jacksonville, Florida, and a graduate of Duke University, he spent thirty years on the staff of *The New York Times*, where he specialized in writing long-form narrative and investigative reports, often related to race. He has also written for the *Los Angeles Times* and *The Atlanta Journal-Constitution*, and his work has appeared in *The New York Times Magazine*. He was a 2019 Emerson Collective Fellow at New America. This is his first book.